INTERNATIONAL INSTITUTE OF HUMAN RIGHTS

N°41

ALESSANDRA LA VACCARA

WHEN THE CONFLICT ENDS, WHILE UNCERTAINTY CONTINUES: ACCOUNTING FOR MISSING PERSONS BETWEEN WAR AND PEACE IN INTERNATIONAL LAW

Foreword
Vincent CHETAIL

René Cassin Prize
2018

Published by
EDITIONS A. PEDONE AND HART PUBLISHING
PARIS – OXFORD
2019

This work is co-published by Editions Pedone in Paris, France and Hart Publishing Ltd in Oxford, United Kingdom. The series, under the editorship of Sébastien Touzé, publishes in English theses which have been awarded the Rene Cassin Prize by the International Institute of Human Rights in Strasbourg.

Published in France by Editions Pedone
13 rue Soufflot – 75005 – Paris
Telephone: +33 (0) 1 43 54 05 97
E-mail: editions-pedone@orange.fr
Website: http://www.pedone.info

Published in the United Kingdom by Hart Publishing Ltd
16C Worcester Place, Oxford, OX1 2JW UK
Telephone: +44 (0)1865 517530
E-mail: mail@hartpub.co.uk
Website: http://www.hartpub.co.uk

Published in North America (US and Canada) by
Hart Publishing
c/o International Specialized Book Services
920 NE 58th Avenue, Suite 300
Portland, OR 97213-3786 USA
Tel: +1 503 287 3093 or toll-free: (1) 800 944 6190
E-mail: orders@isbs.com
Website: http://www.isbs.com

British Library Cataloguing in Publication Data – Data Available
© HART Publishing – OXFORD –2019
I.S.B.N. 9781509931798
© Editions A. PEDONE – PARIS –2019
I.S.B.N. 978-2-233-00909-8

FOREWORD

This book represents an important contribution on a particularly complex and timely issue located at the cross-road of several fields of international law. Its key objective and added value are to assess the existing international legal framework on missing persons during and after an armed conflict. The book focuses on two distinctive albeit intertwined concerns: the need of families to know the fate of their missing relatives, as well as the correlative need for accountability for violations committed during the conflict. *Following this twofold approach, Alessandra La Vaccara unveils in a clear and coherent way the broad diversity of international rules on missing persons* in situations of armed conflicts and the byzantine complexity of their implementation during the challenging and precarious transition from war to peace.

While combining both theoretical and practical insights, the author explores the multifaceted and controversial linkages between humanitarian and accountability-driven efforts *vis-à-vis* post-conflict claims for information on missing persons. Her comprehensive and thorough approach takes into account the diverse roles and implications multiplicity of connotations and roles that information on missing persons may have in post-conflict settings. To highlight some of them, information on missing persons can be a bargaining tool in peace negotiation and dispute settlement; a societal and individual goal to be achieved in order to move forward after a conflict; a *medium* which gives access to certain legal rights at the domestic level; a tool to fight impunity and/or to promote reconciliation. The variety of implications and responses to address the issue of missing persons reflects the composite and contentious nature of any post-conflict environment, where the situation on the ground is neither one of war nor of peace. In such a volatile context, the duty to account for missing persons represents an integral component of any attempts to promote and establish sustainable peace in post-conflict situations.

Among many other interesting aspects of her work, the author convincingly substantiates the normative complementarity between international humanitarian law and international human rights law during the transition from conflict to peace. Both branches are indeed mutually reinforcing when their respective rules simultaneously apply to a given situation. Following this stance, Dr. La Vaccara thoroughly assesses the interplay between the two branches of international law by providing a critical account of the doctrines developed in this area. She identifies a set of three criteria to be used by lawyers, legal advisors and judges in resorting to the complementarity approach. These parameters include the nature of the rights at stake (absolute/relative; derogable/underogable), the principle of systemic integration, and the rule of the most favourable treatment. According to this cumulative and systemic articulation between international humanitarian law and international human rights law, the lacunae of one particular branch may be overcome by the most protective standard of the other one. The result is not only an increased level of protection for individuals. It also ensures a more coherent approach to the international legal framework governing post-conflict situations.

For these reasons and others, Dr. La Vaccara provides a groundbreaking contribution to the legal scholarship in order to better appraise the broad number of international rules that apply to missing persons in post-conflict situations and the ways to articulate and implement them in a comprehensive and coherent manner. This book offers scholars and practitioners of international law a solid and detailed understanding on a highly complicated and long neglected issue of our time.

Dr. Vincent CHETAIL
Professor of International Law
Head of the International Law Department
Director of the Global Migration Centre
Graduate Institute of International and Development Studies
November 2018

ACKNOWLEDGEMENTS

This book is based on a PhD thesis completed at the Graduate Institute of International and Development Studies in January 2018. While completing this book has often been a lonely journey, it has been made possible with the support of many who have crossed my path.

First, and foremost, I want to express my gratitude to my PhD supervisor, Professor Vincent Chetail, who has skillfully guided me in the exploration, development, and final drafting of my topic. I am also indebted to Professor Paola Gaeta, my second reader, whose comments and feedback have triggered new questions and challenged my initial assumptions. I want to thank Professor Manfred Nowak for being part of the jury and for sharing with me his hands-on experience in missing persons-related issues. Thanks also to Professor Patty Blum who identified constructive synergies between my project and her clinical work on missing persons at Cardozo Law School (NYC). Lastly, but not in terms of importance, I am immensely grateful to Professor Yves Sandoz for initiating me into the complexities of International Humanitarian Law and for making it clear that the issue of missing persons deserved a PhD: with his work as a *humanitarian* and renowned scholar, and his humanity and understanding, he is and always will be my role model.

I want to express my gratitude to the IHEID and to the Feris Foundation of America for awarding me their scholarships: their support allowed me to pursue this journey in Switzerland and abroad. During this journey, I had an opportunity to receive feedback from many individuals with whom I had the chance to work while at the IHEID and at Harvard Law School: their inputs, criticism and support have proven invaluable. Similarly, turning my doctoral work into a book would not have been possible without the International Human Rights Institute "René Cassin", which awarded me the 2018 René Cassin Thesis prize. It goes without saying that the views expressed in this book are mine and not those of the institutions mentioned thereof.

Moreover, it is only with the support of family and friends that I found the energy and strength to complete this endeavor. I am particularly thankful to Carolina and Tommaso: that this journey has reached a successful conclusion is due to the fact that they have always been there for me, no matter what. For their support, never-ending discussions, and mind-opening inputs, I am grateful to Antonio and Francesco. I am also grateful to Ariana, Morgane S., Morgane C., and Deborah, for being amazing inspirational supporters, and to the Harvard Italian gang for bringing the warmth of Italy to Cambridge. I am especially grateful to Marco for being the most intellectually stimulating companion and the firmest pillar of my life. Finally, *grazie* to my family: *a mia madre* for her unconditional support; to my brother for his humor, his midnight calls, and his chitchatting about tech – as if I were a geek; and to my father, for having taught me the importance of thinking outside the box, exploring the unknown, looking beyond appearances, and for everything he was. This work is dedicated to him.

Alessandra LA VACCARA

TABLE OF CONTENTS

CHAPTER III.
(RE)LOCATING THE RELATIONSHIP BETWEEN IHL AND IHRL
RULES ON MISSING PERSONS IN POST-CONFLICT SETTINGS 149

CHAPTER IV.
THE FAMILIES' CLAIM FOR INFORMATION
AND THE STATE'S REFUSAL/INABILITY TO RESPOND:
CONTEXTUALIZING TWO OPPOSITE CLAIMS IN POST-CONFLICT 187

CHAPTER V.
ACCOUNTING FOR MISSING PERSONS
IN PEACE PROCESSES: WHOSE DUTY?

CHAPTER VI.
THE FAMILIES' QUEST FOR INFORMATION
ON THEIR MISSING RELATIVES:
THE (POTENTIAL) CONTRIBUTION OF "JUSTICE IN TRANSITION"

ABBREVIATIONS

ACHR	American Convention on Human Rights
AfChHPR	African Charter on Human and Peoples' Rights
AfCommHPR	African Commission on Human and Peoples' Rights
AfCtHPR	African Court on Human and Peoples' Rights
AP I	Protocol Additional to the Geneva Conventions of 12 August 1949, and relating to the Protection of Victims of International Armed Conflicts
AP II	Protocol Additional to the Geneva Conventions of 12 August 1949, and relating to the Protection of Victims of Non-International Armed Conflicts
ArChHR	Arab charter on human rights
CAT	Convention against Torture and Other Cruel, Inhuman or Degrading Treatment or Punishment
CED	Committee on Enforced Disappearances
CIA	Central Intelligence Agency
CoE	Council of Europe
CPM	Committee on Missing Persons (Cyprus)
CRC	Convention on the Rights of the Child
CTA	Central Tracing Agency
DPKO	Department of Peacekeeping Operations
ECHR	Convention for the Protection of Human Rights and Fundamental Freedoms, better known as the European Convention on Human Rights
ECtHR	European Court of Human Rights
EU	European Union
EULEX Kosovo	European Union Rule of Law Mission in Kosovo
FEDEFAM	Federación Latinoamericana de Asociaciones de Familiares de Detenidos-Desaparecidos
GC I	Convention (I) for the Amelioration of the Condition of the Wounded and Sick in Armed Forces in the Field
GC II	Convention (II) for the Amelioration of the Condition of Wounded, Sick and Shipwrecked Members of Armed Forces at Sea
GC III	Convention (III) relative to the Treatment of Prisoners of War
GC IV	Convention (IV) relative to the Protection of Civilian Persons in Time of War

HRCee	Human Rights Committee
HRChBH	Human Rights Chamber for Bosnia Herzegovina
IAC	International Armed Conflict
IACommHR	Inter-American Commission on Human Rights
IACtHR	Inter-American Court of Human Rights
ICC	International Criminal Court
ICCPR	International Covenant on Civil and Political Rights
ICJ	International Court of Justice
ICJ	International Commission of Jurists
ICMP	International Commission on Missing Persons
ICPPED	International Convention for the Protection of All Persons from Enforced Disappearance
ICRC	International Committee of the Red Cross
ICTJ	International Center for Transitional Justice
ICTR	International Criminal Tribunal for Rwanda
ICTY	International Criminal Tribunal for the Former Yugoslavia
IDI	Institut de Droit International
IDPs	Internal displaced persons
IHL	International Humanitarian Law
ILA	International Law Association
ILC	International Law Commission
IMT	International Military Tribunal
IOM	International Organization for Migration
ITS	International Tracing Service
MoU	Memorandum of Understanding
NGOs	Non-governmental Organizations
NIAC	Non International Armed Conflict
NIB	National Information Bureaux
NKVD	Soviet People's Commissariat for Internal Affairs
NN	Nacht und Nebel
OAS	Organization of American States
OMPF	Office of Missing Persons and Forensics
OTP	Office of the Prosecutor
PCIJ	Permanent Court of International Justice
PHR	Physicians for Human Rights
PKK	Kurdistan Workers' Party
POW	Prisoner(s) of War

RoL	Rule of Law
SRSG	Special Representative of the Secretary-General
TJ	Transitional Justice
UDHR	Universal Declaration of Human Rights
UK	United Kingdom
UN	United Nations
UN OHCHR	United Nations Office of the High Commissioner for Human Rights
UNFICYP	United Nations Peacekeeping Force in Cyprus
UNGA	United Nations General Assembly
UNMIK	United Nations Mission in Kosovo
UNSC	United Nations Security Council
UNSG	United Nations Secretary-General
USA	United States of America
VCLT	Vienna Convention on the Law of Treaties
WGAD	Working Group on Arbitrary Detention
WGEID	UN Working Group on Enforced or Involuntary Disappearances
WWII	World War II

INTRODUCTION

In 1974, the United Nations General Assembly (UNGA) linked the humanitarian task of accounting for missing persons to efforts to promote international peace and security and considered the 'desire [of families] to know the fate of loved ones lost in armed conflicts [...] a basic human need'.[1] After four decades, in an Arria Formula meeting of the United Nations Security Council (UNSC) dedicated to the issue of missing persons, the UN High Commissioner for Human Rights (UN HCHR) made a similar connection, while reflecting upon the situations in Syria – where many thousands have been reported missing as a result of wrongdoings committed by all parties in the conflict – as well as in Nigeria, Cameroon, Chad.[2]

International concern over the issue of missing persons and related calls for action have not lost their intensity over the past four decades; what has changed, however, is the legal framework concerning the issue of missing persons and the claims of the families of the missing for information during and after an armed conflict. Indeed, the UN HCHR not only emphasized those humanitarian actions that must be undertaken when conflicts are ongoing (e.g. clarification of the fate of missing persons in a transparent, impartial, and effective way), but also repeated the centrality of the right to justice, and of the right to truth, as well as the significance of accountability where the issue of missing persons involves criminal accountability.[3]

* * *

As a result of prolonged uncertainty and lack of information regarding relatives reported missing in armed conflicts, families are emotionally and socially trapped. In the social science field, this limbo is called 'ambiguous loss', a form of grief that encompasses psychological and social aspects that are characterized by constant vacillation between hope and despair, which prevents families from moving forward.[4] Waiting for news on the fate of missing relatives also confronts communities with the consequences of this looming uncertainty:

---

[1] UNGA, 'Resolution on the Assistance and Cooperation in Accounting for Persons Who Are Missing or Dead in Armed' (1974) UN Doc A/RES/3220 (XXIX) Preamble.
[2] UN High Commissioner for Human Rights, 'Statement to the Security Council on Missing Persons' (Security Council open Arria formula meeting 'The Global Challenge of Accounting for Missing Persons from Conflict, Human Rights Abuses, Disasters, Organized Crime, Migration and other Involuntary Causes', 27 January 2016).
[3] ibid.
[4] Pauline Boss, 'Ambiguous Loss in Families of the Missing' (2002) 360 Medicine and Conflict - The Lancet Supplement 39; Pauline Boss, 'Ambiguous Loss: Working with Families of the Missing' (2002) 17 Family Process 14.

legal, administrative, social, and/or economic challenges characterize the life of many as a result of the disappearance of their loved ones.[5] Thus, the transition from an armed conflict to peace may never end for these families.

The practice shows that where uncertainty persists, the process of reconciliation between former parties to conflict can be severely affected despite the passage of time.[6] For instance, after more than a decade since the end of the armed conflict in Kosovo, tensions emerged between Serbia and Kosovo in relation to access to information on missing persons; the 2015 report of the UN Working Group on Enforced or Involuntary Disappearances (WGEID) noted that

> [s]ome requests to access information [on the fate and whereabouts of the missing] have been rejected by the competent authorities in Serbia'; despite the disclosure of the Ministry of interior's Archives, '[t]he archives of the Ministry of Defence are kept secret and are not fully available.[7]

In Cyprus, for over three decades following the inter-communal violence of 1963-1967, and the later Turkish invasion in 1974, the parties opted for 'a policy of silence' as part of their negotiated transition;[8] the humanitarian solution originated with the agreement of the parties in the 1980s – the Committee on Missing Persons (CMP) – became operative in 2004, when this body was finally able to carry out exhumations and ascertain the fate of the missing.[9]

In post-conflict situations, expected responses from State authorities may be delayed, should the rule of law (RoL) apparatus be in the process of being

---

[5] Since the status of 'missing person' might not exist at the domestic level, the legal status of the partner or progeny of the missing person will be pending, thereby having a negative impact in terms of property rights, custody of children, inheritance, remarriage, and right to social allowances of members of the family concerned. ICRC/IPU, *Missing Persons: A Handbook for Parliamentarians. No. 17* (Inter-Parliamentary Union; ICRC 2009) 11. See also WGEID, 'The Working Group on Enforced or Involuntary Disappearances Concludes Its Official Visit to Pakistan' (2012) <http://goo.gl/p3ZhBe> accessed 12 October 2015.

[6] Sassòli underlines that in the Srebrenica Case many families were left with the illusion that their relatives were still held in custody by Serb authorities; therefore, complete reconciliation was impossible. Marco Sassòli, 'Les disparus de guerre : Les règles du droit international et les besoins des familles entre espoir et incertitude' (2003) 15 Frontières 38, 39. Families of the missing find themselves in a legal limbo. For this reason, the UNGA has acknowledged the importance of addressing the needs of families of missing persons by calling upon UN members 'to take appropriate steps with regard to the legal situation of missing persons and the needs and accompaniment of their family members [...] in such fields as social welfare, psychological and psychosocial support, financial matters, family law and property rights'. Cf. UNGA, 'Resolution 69/184 - Missing Persons' (2015) UN Doc. A/RES/69/184 para 13. See also UNGA, 'Resolution 61/155 - Missing Persons' (2007) UN Doc. A/RES/61/155 para 10; UNGA, 'Resolution 63/183 - Missing Persons' (2009) UN Doc. A/RES/63/183 para 10; UNGA, 'Resolution 65/210 - Missing Persons' (2011) UN Doc. A/RES/65/210 para 11; UNGA, 'Resolution 67/177 - Missing Persons' (2013) UN Doc. A/RES/67/177 para 11.

[7] WGEID, 'Report of the Working Group on Enforced or Involuntary Disappearances - Mission to Serbia' (2015) UN Doc. A/HRC/30/38/add.1 para 37.

[8] Iosif Kovras, *Truth Recovery and Transitional Justice: Deferring Human Rights Issues* (Routledge 2014), 41, 45–46.

[9] See sub-section 2.1.2 in Chapter V.

restored;[10] only when the legal and institutional framework is fully operative, can the different procedures aimed at responding to families requests – planning, carrying out an investigation, identification measures – be properly activated.[11] Post-conflict reconciliation efforts can be affected by the continuing distress in which both families and communities live due to uncertainty.[12] Yet international post-conflict efforts and contributions aimed at helping the State affected to move towards a 'sustainable peace'[13] do not fully integrate the issue of missing persons and the claims for information of their families among their priorities. Multiple are the United Nations (UN) calls to include the issue of missing persons in the context of peacebuilding processes;[14] nevertheless, these calls fall short in terms of clarity, since they appeal to a mutual reinforcement between humanitarian efforts to account for the missing, and accountability-driven processes, without providing normative or operational guidelines on practice.[15]

This book addresses the international framework that regulates humanitarian and accountability-driven efforts to account for missing persons in the phase of transition from an armed conflict to peace; its legal application in this peculiar setting results in it being under-researched and, as the UNSC's Arria formula meeting shows, partially disregarded in practice. While the legal scholarship has mainly tackled the issue of enforced disappearances,[16] legal studies dedicated to the broader issue of missing persons – and notably to the case of those reported as missing in armed conflicts – are rare;[17] indeed, existing studies and publications pertain to other disciplines.[18]

---

[10] Human Rights Council, 'Report of the Special Rapporteur on the Promotion of Truth, Justice, Reparation and Guarantees of Non-Recurrence - Prosecutorial Prioritization Strategies in the Aftermath of Gross Human Rights Violations and Serious Violations of IHL' (2014) UN Doc A/HRC/27/56 para 33.

[11] ICRC/IPU (n 5) 50, 54–55.

[12] This problem has been addressed under several angles: from an anthropology perspective, see: Laura Huttunen, 'Liminality and Missing Persons: Encountering the Missing in Postwar Bosnia-Herzegovina' (2016) 2 Conflict and Society 201; Antonius Robben, *Political Violence and Trauma in Argentina* (University of Pennsylvania Press 2005) 318–340. From a humanitarian and rule of law perspective, see: ICRC, 'Living with Uncertainty. Needs of the Families of Missing Persons in Sri Lanka' (2016) iii, <https://www.icrc.org/en/document/sri-lanka-families-missing-persons> accessed 2 August 2016; ICMP, 'Conference Report', *The Missing: an Agenda for the Future (29 October – 1 November 2013), The Hague* 34.

[13] Chapter I and Chapter V will examine the issue of missing persons in the context of post-conflict peacebuilding; the conceptual and operational aspects of this concept that will be relevant to the subject matter will accordingly be taken into account.

[14] See sub-section 1.2 in Chapter V.

[15] UNSG, 'Report of the Secretary-General - Missing Persons' (2016) UN Doc A/71/299 para 73.

[16] See sub-sect 1.1 below (Key terminology).

[17] UNSG, 'Report of the Secretary-General' (n 15) para 73.

[18] For instance, Robins seeks both to understand the limitations of transitional justice processes in addressing the priorities of victims, and to provide the basis of an emancipatory victim-centred approach to transitional justice. See Simon Robins, *Families of the Missing. A Test for Contemporary Approaches to Transitional Justice* (Routledge 2013). Kovras investigates why some societies defer transitional justice issues – e.g., missing persons and enforced disappearances - after successful democratic consolidation, see Kovras (n 8). Edkins argues that contemporary political systems treat persons instrumentally, as objects to be administered rather than as singular beings; in contrast, relatives of the missing demand that authorities focus on a particular person. Therefore, she

Furthermore, dealing with the issue of missing persons across phases – i.e., *durante bello* and *post bellum* – entails a complex interplay of international norms. The *duo* International Human Rights Law (IHRL)/International Humanitarian Law (IHL) theoretically becomes a *solo* (i.e., IHRL) after the end of an armed conflict. This study intends to clarify that this is partly true, since, despite the termination of the conflict, some IHL rules remain applicable. However, there is no common understanding at the scholarly and practical level of how IHL/IHRL interact in the aftermath of an armed conflict and of how these branches of international law determine the conduct of the panoply of actors operating in post-conflict scenarios.

Two courses of action are detectable during and after an armed conflict: humanitarian-driven measures must be undertaken in order to ascertain the whereabouts of the missing and to address the emotional distress of families generated by lack of news on the fate of their loved ones. In the same scenarios, cases of missing persons may involve criminal accountability under international law, thereby triggering actions directed to answer questions like 'who is responsible?' and 'what are the circumstances of the crime?'. These courses of action, which intertwine with the overall transition process from an armed conflict to an enduring peace, respond to two different needs: i.e., the need of family members to receive information on their relatives' whereabouts and life conditions, and the societal and individual need for accountability.[19] Against this backdrop, the legal query at the core of this book is how the existing international legal framework meets these distinct but intertwined needs emerging during and after an armed conflict.

---

highlights stories from a range of circumstances that shed light on this critical tension. Jenny Edkins, *Missing: Persons and Politics* (Cornell University Press 2011). Diaz develops a guide focused on tracking humans (whether they are enemy combatants or lost children); he explains what it takes to be an expert tracker, from the physical stamina to the focus and perception necessary to do the job correctly, see David Diaz and VL McCann, *Tracking Humans: A Fundamental Approach to Finding Missing Persons, Insurgents, Guerrillas, and Fugitives from the Law* (Lyons Press 2013). The collection of contributions edited by Morewitz and Sturdy Colls surveys the science, forensics, politics, and ethics involved in responding to missing persons cases, see Stephen Morewitz and Caroline Sturdy Colls (eds), *Handbook of Missing Persons* (Springer 2016). The collection edited by Greene and Alys brings together ideas and expertise (e.g., human geography, migration studies, forensics) across this vast subject area into one interconnected publication and explores the subjects of missing children, missing adults, the investigative process of missing person cases, and the families of missing persons, see Karen Shalev Greene and Llian Alys (eds), *Missing Persons. A Handbook of Research* (Routledge 2017). Derek Congram's collection puts together twenty-two experts from academic, government, and civil sectors who study and help search for missing persons in Canada and internationally; the collection thus responds to growing public awareness of persons who have disappeared due to armed conflict, repressive regimes, criminal behavior, and racist and colonial policies towards Indigenous persons and minority populations, see Derek Congram (ed), *Missing Persons. Multidisciplinary Perspectives on the Disappeared* (Canadian Scholars' Press 2016).

[19] Recent studies have emphasized that the priority for the families is to know where their family members are and whether they are still alive. ICRC, 'Living with Uncertainty. Needs of the Families of Missing Persons in Sri Lanka' (n 12) 16; ICRC, 'Families of Missing Persons in Nepal: A Study of Their Needs' (ICRC 2009) 11.

By addressing such query, the book intends 1) to provide a comprehensive reading of the international rules on the issue of missing persons and 2) to conceive their implementation in a more effective manner in the transition phase from conflict to peace, i.e., when the former parties to the conflict must address the pending consequences of the armed conflict and return to normalcy. With regard to this last point, the present study will also reflect upon how to build linkages between humanitarian and accountability-driven efforts vis-à-vis the post-conflict claims for information on missing persons. Examples of situations where this question has emerged will help to cast light upon the reason why these efforts should be designed in a manner that reflects the distinct character of the aforementioned needs, but eventually results in mutually reinforcing – and not exclusive – courses of action.

Three directions will be followed, i.e., *i)* a review of the relevant legal framework and an examination of the principles subsumed under it will be conducted in order to find normative synergies implementable on the ground; *ii)* an explanation of the reason why the dialectic between IHL and IHRL matters in the aftermath of an armed conflict (even where the conflict ended 'too long ago') will be articulated;[20] lastly, the book will provide an understanding of the operationalization of the right of families to know the fate of their relatives and of the duty to account for missing persons within the remit of post-conflict peacebuilding processes.

1. TERMINOLOGY,
SCOPE OF THE STUDY, AND METHODOLOGICAL ASPECTS

1.1. Terminology

1.1.1. Missing persons

Although IHL treaties explicitly refer to 'missing persons', no international law treaty defines this expression. In light of the variety of definitions developed at the academic level[21] as well as at the operational level,[22] in this study the term

---

[20] The term 'too long ago' is borrowed from a seminal article of Higgins on 'Time and the Law", see Rosalyn Higgins, 'Time and the Law: International Perspectives on an Old Problem' (1997) 46 International and Comparative Law Quarterly 501, 501.

[21] In light of their transitional justice focus, La Rosa and Crettol provide a broader definition that goes beyond the case scenarios covered by IHL (i.e., 'the missing ...are all people unaccounted for as a result of an international or non-international armed conflict or internal violence'). Monique Crettol and Anne-Marie La Rosa, 'The Missing and Transitional Justice: The Right to Know and the Fight against Impunity' (2006) 88 International Review of the Red Cross 355, 355. According to Toman, 'the persons designated as missing were those whose assumed death could not be proven for lack of official records, which are required by national legislation, for example to regularize the family status of surviving spouses or children or to enable the surviving kin to inherit the estate of these persons.' In J Toman, 'Missing and Dead Persons' in Rudolf Bernhardt (ed), *Encyclopedia of Public International Law* (North-Holland Publishing Company 1997) 428, 429.

[22] The Advisory Committee of the UN Human Rights Council has construed the term 'missing persons' as 'those whose families are without news of them, as well as those who are reported, on the basis of reliable information, as unaccounted for as a result of an international or non-international

'missing persons' refers to those persons whose families remain without news and who, on the basis of reliable information, have been reported as missing as a result of events related to international or non-international armed conflicts.

Historically, 'missing in action' was an expression that referred to soldiers or combatants who disappeared during military operations.[23] More generally, one can infer from contemporary IHL treaties[24] that in an armed conflict, whether international or non-international, a person will be considered missing if his/her relatives or the power on which he/she depends have no information on his/her fate and whereabouts as a result of the armed conflict.[25] The terminology used in this study, e.g., 'persons unaccounted for' and 'the missing', refers to the same condition.

---

armed conflict'. UN Human Rights Council, 'Report of the Human Rights Council Advisory Committee on Best Practices on the Issue of Missing Persons' (2011) UN Doc A/HRC/16/70 para 11. See also ICRC, 'The Missing. ICRC Progress Report' (ICRC 2006) para 10 <goo.gl/og1Gf1> accessed 12 June 2016. The ICRC's definition reads as follows: 'a missing person is one "whose whereabouts are unknown to his/her relatives and/or who, on the basis of reliable information, has been reported missing in accordance with national legislation in connection with an international or non-international armed conflict, a situation of internal violence or disturbances, natural catastrophes or any other situation that may require the intervention of a competent State authority"'. ICRC - Advisory Service on IHL, 'Missing Persons and Their Families' (2015) <https://www.icrc.org/en/document/missing-persons-and-their-families-factsheet> accessed 10 February 2016. A slightly different definition is proposed by the International Commission on Missing Persons (ICMP): 'a missing person is anyone whose whereabouts are not known and who is being sought by another person or other persons'; thus, multiple scenarios are considered when addressing the problem of the missing and of their families (i.e., armed conflict, human rights abuses, natural or man-made disaster, organized crime, migration, trafficking). See ICMP, 'The Missing: Who Are the Missing?' <?" http://www.icmp.int/the-missing/who-are-the-missing/> accessed 12 October 2015.

[23] ICRC, 'Glossary of Restoring Family Links Terms' <http://goo.gl/eQiumM> accessed 20 September 2013.

[24] See Chapter II for more details on the legal framework. More generally, cf. Convention (I) for the Amelioration of the Condition of the Wounded and Sick in Armed Forces in the Field, Geneva, 75 UNTS 31 (12 August 1949) (hereinafter, GC I); Convention (II) for the Amelioration of the Condition of Wounded, Sick and Shipwrecked Members of Armed Forces at Sea, Geneva, 75 UNTS 85 (12 August 1949) (hereinafter, GC II); Convention (III) relative to the Treatment of Prisoners of War, Geneva, 75 UNTS 125 (12 August 1949) (hereinafter, GC III); Convention (IV) relative to the Protection of Civilian Persons in Time of War, Geneva, 75 UNTS 287 (12 August 1949) (hereinafter, GC IV); Protocol Additional to the Geneva Conventions of 12 August 1949, and relating to the Protection of Victims of International Armed Conflicts (Protocol I) 1125 UNTS 3 (8 June 1977) (hereinafter AP I); Protocol Additional to the Geneva Conventions of 12 August 1949, and relating to the Protection of Victims of Non-International Armed Conflicts (Protocol II), 1125 UNTS 609 (8 June 1977) (hereinafter AP II).

[25] During the *travaux préparatoires* (AP I), one of the delegations put forward the following definition: 'a missing person, whether military or civilian, was one who had not returned to his unit after a military operation or mission, or who had not returned to his home because of circumstances associated with the hostilities'. ICRC, 'Official Records of the Diplomatic Conference on the Reaffirmation and Development of International Humanitarian Law Applicable in Armed Conflicts, Vol XI' (1974) s CDDH/II/SR.20, paras 13, 192-193. The Working Group on this matter adopted the following working definition: 'the missing were those reported by another party as missing'. Ibid, CDDH/II/SR.34, paras 20, 353. The UNGA Resolution 3220 of 1974 used the expression 'missing in action' and, therefore, adopted a narrow approach with respect to the issue of missing persons. UNGA, 'Res 3220 (XXIX)' (n 1) para 2. See also Marco Sassòli, Antoine A Bouvier and Anne Quintin, *How Does Law Protect in War?: Cases, Documents, and Teaching Materials on Contemporary Practice in International Humanitarian Law. Vol. I - Outline of International Humanitarian Law. III (Online Version)* (ICRC 2011) 206; Robins (n 18) 4–5; Théo Boutruche, 'Missing and Dead Persons' in Rudiger Wolfrum (ed),

The term 'missing persons' can also be found in human rights-related documents. In the late 1970s, UN documents on the situation in Chile did not adopt a uniform terminology but used expressions such as 'missing and disappeared persons' (1979),[26] 'disappeared persons/persons who have disappeared' (1980)[27]. The French version of some of these documents reflected the same inhomogeneity: 'personnes portées manquantes ou disparues au Chili' (1979);[28] 'personnes disparues' (1980).[29]

At the regional level, both the Committee of Ministers and the Parliamentary Assembly of the Council of Europe (CoE) have tackled the issue of missing persons since the early 1970s.[30] Despite the initial terminological confusion in the usage of the expression missing person/forcibly disappeared person,[31] the CoE has adopted a working definition to address the private law-related problems raising when a person goes missing, i.e., when her 'existence has become uncertain, because he or she has disappeared without trace and there are no signs that he or she is alive.'[32] As clarified by the CoE's Committee of Ministers, this definition is to be read in the context of the Recommendation on Missing Persons and the Presumption of Death that also cover civilians and combatants that go missing in armed conflict from an exclusive civil law perspective.[33]

The Max Planck Encyclopedia of Public International Law - Ozone Layer, international protection, vol VII (Oxford University Press 2012) 288.

[26] Preamble, UNGA, 'Resolution on Protection of Human Rights in Chile' (1979) Res 34/179 (English version), UN Doc A/RES/34/179 at 193; see also UNSG, 'Report of the Experts on the Question of the Fate of Missing and Disappeared Persons in Chile, Note by the Secretary-General' (1979) UN Doc A/34/583/Add.1.

[27] UNGA, 'Resolution on Human Rights in Chile' (1980) Res 35/188, UN Doc A/RES/35/188 at 203, Preamble.

[28] UNGA, 'Res. 34/179' (n 26) (French version), Preamble.

[29] UNGA, 'Res 35/188' (n 27), Preamble. In the Spanish version, the same documents contained the following: 'personas desaparecidas o cuyo paradero se desconoce' (1979); 'personas desaparecidas/personas que han desaparecido' (1980). See UNSG, 'Report on the Question of the Fate of Missing' (n 26) (Spanish version); UNGA, 'Res. 34/179' (n 26), Preamble. See also UNGA, 'Res 35/188' (n 27) (Spanish version), Preamble.

[30] CoE – Committee of Ministers, 'Search for Missing Persons, Recommendation No R(79) 6' (1979), Preamble.

[31] The way in which the CoE initially dealt with the issue denoted a certain degree of confusion as to the issue of missing persons and of persons who have been forcibly disappeared. The Parliamentary Assembly invited the Committee to draw up recommendations with regard to, *inter alia*, the categories of missing persons for which searches should be made. CoE- Parliamentary Assembly, Recommendation no. 646 on 'Action to be Taken in Tracing Missing Persons' (1971), para. 7. The Committee included both 'persons who may have been victims of an accident' and 'persons disappearing in suspicious circumstances such as to cause apprehension for their physical and/or moral safety' (1971). The first category fell uniquely under domestic law (and where appropriate, private international law); on the other hand, the second category could potentially raise problems related to human rights terminology. CoE – Committee of Ministers, Recommendation no. R (79) (n 30), Appendix to Recommendation no. R (79) 6, para. 1.1.

[32] CoE – Committee of Ministers, 'Recommendation No. CM/Rec(2009)12 on "Principles Concerning Missing Persons and the Presumption of Death"' (2009), Part I – Definition (Appendix), 9.

[33] ibid (Appendix), para. 11. The Recommendation's Appendix stresses its complementary character to international law standards applicable in armed conflict situations (e.g., IHL and international criminal law), cf. ibid (Appendix), para. 12.

The terminological inhomogeneity at that time is easily explainable: first, Additional Protocol I (AP I), tackling the issue of 'the missing', had been recently adopted (1977); second, the enforced disappearance movement was starting to give shape to the UN debate towards the enhancement of a codification project revolving around the prohibition of enforced disappearances; third, at that time, enforced disappearances were not outlawed by any international binding or non-binding instrument. The two versions – English and French – of AP I referred to 'missing persons/personnes disparues'. In international law, the English expression 'missing person' is associated with an armed conflict situation, whereas the term 'enforced disappearance' or 'disappeared person' is not used solely in this scenario, for the practice of enforced disappearance can be perpetrated in situations of armed conflict, in situations of internal violence, and in situations of apparent peace. In line with the broad perspective adopted in this book on 'missing person', in armed conflicts every (forcibly) disappeared person is a missing person, but the contrary does not hold valid.[34] Being subjected to enforced disappearance means

> the arrest, detention, abduction or any other form of deprivation of liberty by agents of the State or by persons or groups of persons acting with the authorization, support or acquiescence of the State, followed by a refusal to acknowledge the deprivation of liberty or by concealment of the fate or whereabouts of the disappeared person, which place such a person outside the protection of the law.[35]

In armed conflicts a person can go missing due to an undefined number of reasons generated by the conflict itself, including – but not limited to – the difficulties of communication and contact, the voluntary/involuntary displacement of his/her family, the perpetration of human rights/IHL violations.[36] Thus, the 'status of missing' may not always be the result of a specific action/omission of the parties to the conflict and might/might not last for long. In the purview of this study, the term 'missing person' refers to those persons who are unaccounted for as a result of an armed conflict and who are being sought by their families or other persons; therefore, it is an umbrella term covering a multitude of situations: e.g.,[37]

---

[34] The ECtHR draws the distinction between the issue of missing persons in armed conflict (combatants and civilians reported as missing due to the conflict) and the 'much narrower concept' of enforced disappearance which is defined in light of Article 2 International Convention for the Protection of All Persons from Enforced Disappearance. Cf. ECtHR, *Palić v Bosnia and Herzegovina, Judgment* (2011) App no. 4704/04 [32–33].

[35] Cf. Article 2, International Convention for the Protection of All Persons from Enforced Disappearance, December 20, 2006, UNGA Res. 61/177, U.N. Doc. A/RES/61/177, 2716 UNTS 3 (hereinafter ICPPED).

[36] Hernan Salinas Burgos, 'The Application of International Humanitarian Law as Compared to Human Rights Law in Situations Qualified as Internal Armed Conflict, Internal Disturbances and Tensions, or Public Emergency, with Special Reference to War Crimes and Political Crimes' in Yves Sandoz and Frits Kalshoven (eds), *Implementation of International Humanitarian Law* (Martinus Nijhoff Publishers 1989) 14.

[37] Cf. UN Human Rights Council, 'Progress Report of the Human Rights Council Advisory Committee on Best Practices on the Issue of Missing Persons' (2010) UN Doc A/HRC/14/42 para 10.

- members of the armed forces whose families have not been informed of their death on the battlefield (i.e., missing in action);

- persons who have lost contact with their families in the course of an armed conflict due to motives connected to the conflict (e.g., displacement, communication obstacles);

- those who are unaccounted for in the context of a violation of IHL or IHRL;[38]

- those who are the victims of enforced or involuntary disappearances (which can occur in armed conflicts or in other situations).[39]

1.1.2. The family as the main information-seeker

In post-conflict settings, one of the main victims[40] is the family whose integrity is temporarily or permanently hampered[41] and needs to be restored; the family is also the first and most concerned information-seeker with regard to the fate and whereabouts of missing relatives. No international treaty provides a definition of the term 'family';[42] thus, the term needs to be understood against the societal practice and recognitions of each State composing the international community.[43]

The presence of the terms 'family' and 'relative(s)'[44] feature in several IHL-treaties' provisions without definitional details.[45] During the *travaux*

---

[38] For instance, the illegal bombing of civilian premises might cause several victims; should the bodies of the victims remain under the debris, their fate might remain unknown until a recovery operation is put into practice. Civilian death recording is not at the core of the GCs I-IV. As a Study carried out by the Oxford Research Group (ORG) points out, the universally ratified 1949 Geneva Conventions do not contain an actual obligation to record the identity of dead or missing civilians (*contra*: the ORG stresses that a rigorous process must be implemented with regard to the recording of combatants). See Susan C Breau and Rachel Joyce, *RCAC Legal Team Briefing: Obligations to Record Civilian Casualties* (ORG 2010) 1.

[39] This categorization is partly inspired by the one proposed by Marco Sassòli and Jean-François Rioux in a study carried out under the auspices of the ICRC. See Marco Sassòli and Jean-François Rioux, 'Study of Existing Mechanisms to Clarify the Fate of Missing Persons", in the Framework of 'The Missing: Action to Resolve the Problem of People Unaccounted for as a Result of Armed Conflict or Internal Violence and to Assist Their Families' (Hereinafter, "The Missing Project")' (ICRC 2003) 5.

[40] See ibid 11.

[41] Gerald i.a.d. Draper, 'La Réunion Des Familles En Période de Conflit Armé' (1977) 59 International Review of the Red Cross 65, 65. Šarčević, underscores that 'the prolonged absence of one or more family members sometimes results in a reversal of roles in war-affected families'. See Petar Šarčević, 'War and Disintegration of the Family' (1999) 1 Journal of Law and Family Studies 109, 115.

[42] Neither is the degree of relationship between family members specified.

[43] 'The term *family* and *relatives* must be understood in their broadest sense, including family members and close friends, and taking into account the cultural environment.' See ICRC, 'Report: The Missing and Their Families. Summary of the Conclusions Arising from Events Held prior to the International Conference of Governmental and Non –Governmental Experts (Geneva, February 19 - 21, 2003). The Missing Project' (ICRC 2003) Doc no TheMissing/Conf/01.2003/EN/10 Executive Summary, para 1.1.

[44] For instance, Article 34 (*Remains of Deceased*) of AP I contains the word 'relatives' (cf. para. 2 (a)), but it does not provide further details on that. Likewise, Article 74 (*Reunion of Dispersed Families*) of AP I utilizes the word 'family' without providing any definition. In the GCs, the word 'family' is widely used: cf. Article 25 GC IV focused on the exchange of 'family news'; Article 26

préparatoires of AP I, which dedicates Part II – Section III to 'Missing and Dead Persons', definitional aspects of the terms 'family' and 'relatives' were dropped, although the term 'family' was included in the provision laying down the general principle of the Section, i.e., the right of families to know the fate of their relatives.[46] The definition and, consequently, the scope of the terms, have been left to the Contracting Parties that will, therefore, be able to adapt such terms to their social and cultural environments.[47] By the same token, the ICRC model law on missing persons, which should serve as guidance in the drafting of any new legislation on the matter, stresses that the term "relative of the missing person" should be understood 'in accordance with provisions of the [Civil Code/Family Law]'[48] of the country concerned.

Under IHRL, '[t]he family is the natural and fundamental group unit of society and is entitled to protection by society and the state.'[49] The criteria that

---

GC IV centered on 'dispersed families'; Article 27 GC IV concerning the treatment of protected persons in the territory of the Party to the Conflict and in the Occupied territories *inter alia* deals with 'family rights'; the family needs of civilian internees are taken into account in Article 82 GC IV (Grouping of internees), Article 85 GC IV (Accommodation, Hygiene), Article 98 GC IV (Financial Resources), Article 106 GC IV (Internment Card); in case of transfer by the Occupying Power, the preservation of the family unit is tackled in Article 49 GC IV.

[45] However, the Commentary to Article 25 (*Family News*) of GC IV questionably affirms that '[t]he right to give family news ... applies to members of a family i.e., *to people who are related, or connected by marriage* (emphasis added)'Jean S Pictet (ed), *The Geneva Conventions of 12 August 1949: Commentary*, vol IV (ICRC 1958) 192.

[46] As for the word 'family', amendment CDDH/II/259 Add.1 - proposed by some delegations to the Committee II of the Diplomatic Conference - did not add any definitional aspects. As for the word 'relatives', the initial amendment, originally in French, employed the word *'proches'*, which was subsequently replaced by the word *'parents'* in a second amendment. This change is not evident in the English text that included the word 'relatives' in both amendments. See ICRC, 'Official Records of the Diplomatic Conference on the Reaffirmation and Development of International Humanitarian Law Applicable in Armed Conflicts' (1974), (CDDH/II/259 Add.1), at 102; (CDDH/II/354), 105. The USSR Representative expressed his doubts about the word 'relatives'. He pointed out that 'there were varying definitions of "family" and "relatives" throughout the world'. See ICRC. "Official Records of the Diplomatic Conference...." Vol. XI. Geneva, 1974-1977, (CDDH/II/SR.35), at 365.

[47] Yves Sandoz and others, *Commentary on the Additional Protocols: Of 8 June 1977 to the Geneva Conventions of 12 August 1949* (Martinus Nijhoff Publishers 1987) para 1215, 346. The ICRC Commentary to Article 74 (*Reunion of Dispersed Families*) of AP I adds that [i]n the narrow sense, the family covers persons related by blood and living together as one household. In a wider sense it covers all persons with the same ancestry. [...] In short, all those who consider themselves and are considered by each other, to be part of a family, and who wish to live together, are deemed to belong to that family'. See ibid para 2997, 859. Thus, the word 'family' covers 'relatives in a direct line - whether their relationship is legal or natural - spouses, brothers and sisters, uncles, aunts, nephews and nieces, but also less closely related relatives, or even unrelated persons, belonging to it because of a shared life or emotional ties (cohabitation, engaged couples etc.)'. See ibid.

[48] ICRC - Advisory Service on IHL, 'Guiding Principles: "Model Law on the Missing: Principles for Legislating the Situation of Persons Missing as a Result of Armed Conflict or Internal Violence. Measures to Prevent Persons from Going Missing and to Protect the Rights and Interests of the Missing and Their Families."' (2009), Article 2(2).

[49] Cf. Article 16 (3), Universal Declaration of Human Rights, Res. 217A (III), UN Doc. A/RES/217(III) A at 71 (December 10, 1948) (hereinafter UDHR); Article 23 (1), International Covenant on Civil and Political Rights, December 16, 1966, 999 UNTS 171 (hereinafter, ICCPR); Article 10 (1), International Covenant on Economic, Social, and Cultural Rights, December 16, 1966, 993 UNTS 3 (hereinafter ICESCR).

could contribute to defining a family might be blood relationship, statutory forms of establishing relations, economic ties, life together or other forms manifesting in an intensive, regular relationship.[50] The definition of who can be considered a family member will, in principle, be found in domestic law.[51] Since a review of all the domestic recognitions and legislations falls outside the scope of this study, the term will be used in accordance with the generic meaning that it has under international law; definitional details emerging from international case law with substantive impact on relevant obligations and entitlements will be taken into consideration.

1.2. Scope of the study

1.2.1. Contextualization of the issue in post-conflict

This book focuses on the post-conflict quest for information on persons who went missing in the context of an armed conflict. The interconnectedness of armed conflict/post-conflict requires further clarification on both settings and on the impossible task of depicting them as neatly separated settings. Paulus suggests that a definition of the term 'armed conflict' is important in order 'to ensure an effective extension of basic humanitarian guarantees to all types of armed conflicts;'[52] however, a single definition runs the risk of eliminating the conventional distinction between international armed conflicts (IAC) and non-international armed conflicts (NIAC), which triggers different regimes and, consequently, different rights and obligations for States parties.[53] According to the International Criminal Tribunal for the former Yugoslavia (ICTY), 'an armed conflict exists whenever there is a resort to armed force between States or protracted armed violence between governmental authorities and organized armed groups or between such groups within a State'.[54] Situations of internal

---

[50] Manfred Nowak, *U.N. Covenant on Civil and Political Rights: CCPR Commentary* (2nd rev ed, NP Engel 2005) 517.

[51] Before the 2009 reform of the Inter-American Court of Human Rights' Rules of Procedure, Article 2(15) of the Rules stated that 'the expression 'next of kin' refers to the immediate family, namely, direct ascendants, descendants, siblings, spouses or permanent companions, or those determined by the Court.' However, in 2009, the reference to next of kin was removed: this marked a broadening of the definition to reflect the interpretation in the jurisprudence up until that point (e.g., 'extended relatives' as well as children who may not have been recognized by their parents fall into the category 'next of kin'). See PILPG, 'Victim Recognition and Satisfaction of Reparations - Third Party Intervention in Janowiec and Others v. Russia' (2012) 4; see also Rules of Procedure of the Inter-American Court of Human Rights approved by the Court of its 49th Regular Session, 16-25 November 2000.

[52] Andreas Paulus, 'Non International Armed Conflict under Common Article 3 [Armed Conflicts and Parties to Armed Conflicts under IHL: Confronting Legal Categories to Contemporary Realities - 10th Bruges Colloquium 22-23 October 2009]' (2010) 40 Collegium 28, 30.

[53] A Clapham, 'The Concept of International Armed Conflict' in Andrew Clapham, Paola Gaeta and Marco Sassòli (eds), *The 1949 Geneva Conventions: A Commentary: A Commentary* (Oxford University Press 2015) 11.

[54] ICTY, *Prosecutor v Duško Tadić aka 'Dule', Decision on the Defence Motion for Interlocutory Appeal on Jurisdiction* (1995) Case no. IT-94-1-A, para. 70. A similar definition was adopted by the International Law Commission (ILC) in Article 2 of the Draft Articles on the Effects of Armed Conflicts on Treaties, 2011: '"armed conflict" means a situation in which there is resort to armed

disturbances and tensions, such as riots, isolated and sporadic acts of violence or other acts of a similar nature[55] do not fall within the scope of this factual

---

force between States or protracted resort to armed force between governmental authorities and organized armed groups'. See 'Titles an Texts of the Draft Articles on the Effects of Armed Conflicts on Treaties Adopted by the Drafting Committee on Second Reading' (2011) UN Doc. A/CN.4/L.777, para. 6 to Draft Article 2. In the commentary to the Draft Articles, the ILC emphasizes that the 'concluding words' (i.e., 'or between such groups within a State') of the *Tadić* decision's paragraph on armed conflicts are not reproduced in Article 2, 'since the present draft articles, under article 3, apply only to situations involving at least one State Party to the treaty'. See ILC, Report of the International Law Commission, Sixty-third session (26 April–3 June and 4 July–12 August 2011), UNGA OR Sixty-sixth session Supplement No. 10 (A/66/10), vol. II, Part Two, at 181. A partly different definition has been adopted by the Institute of International Law, Cf. Article 1, Institute of International Law, Resolution on 'The effects of Armed Conflicts on Treaties', adopted on 28 August 1985, Session of Helsinki. Controversially, a single definition for both IAC and NIAC has been proposed by the International Law Association (ILA)'s Committee on the Use of Force that has released a report on the meaning of armed conflict in international law; according to its findings, all armed conflicts have two features: (1) the existence of organized armed groups (2) engaged in fighting of some intensity. See ILA, 'Final Report on the Meaning of Armed Conflict in International Law - The Hague Conference' (2010) <http://www.ila-hq.org/en/committees/index.cfm/cid/1022> accessed 12 July 2016. *Contra:* Clapham (n 53) 16.

[55] Cf. Article 1 (2), AP II; Article 8 (2) (d), Rome Statute of the International Criminal Court, July 17, 1998, 2187 UNTS. With regard to NIAC, from the 1952 ICRC Commentary to Common Article 3 (GC I-IV) it can be inferred that 'a mere act of banditry or an unorganized and short-lived insurrection' does not trigger the application of the said Article; however, the Commentators clearly stated that 'the Article should be applied as widely as possible.' See Jean S Pictet (ed), *The Geneva Conventions of 12 August 1949: Commentary*, vol I (ICRC 1952) 50. The 2016 ICRC Commentary underlines that 'the qualification of "internal disturbances and tensions, such as riots, isolated and sporadic acts of violence and other acts of a similar nature" in Article 1 [AP II] as "not being armed conflicts" is also considered accurate for common Article 3'. ICRC, *Commentary on the First Geneva Convention: Convention (I) for the Amelioration of the Condition of the Wounded and Sick in Armed Forces in the Field* (2nd edn, 2016) <https://www.icrc.org/applic/ihl/ihl.nsf/Treaty.xsp?documentId=4825657B0C7E6BF0C12563CD002 D6B0B&action=openDocument> accessed 20 July 2016. Along the same lines, the ICTY specifies that the Tadić test, mentioned above 'serves to distinguish non-international armed conflict from banditry, riots, isolated acts of terrorism, or similar situations'. See ICTY, *Prosecutor v Haradinaj et al, Trial Judgment* (2008) Case no IT-04-84-T [38]. With regard to IAC, Partsch and others acknowledge that international violence similar to internal disturbances and tensions should not be encompassed by the concept of armed conflict (as it is used in Article 1, AP I). See Michael Bothe, Karl Josef Partsch and Waldemar A Solf, *New Rules for Victims of Armed Conflicts: Commentary on the Two 1977 Protocols Additional to the Geneva Conventions of 1949* (Martinus Nijhoff Publishers 1982) 46. Along the same lines, see CJ Greenwood, 'Scope of Application of Humanitarian Law' in Dieter Fleck and Michael Bothe (eds), *The Handbook of International Humanitarian Law* (Oxford University Press 2008) 42; Jelena Pejic, 'Terrorist Acts and Groups: A Role for International Law' (2004) 75 British Year Book of International Law 71, 73; Mary Ellen O'Connell, 'Saving Lives through a Definition of International Armed Conflict [Armed Conflicts and Parties to Armed Conflicts under IHL: Confronting Legal Categories to Contemporary Realities - 10th Bruges Colloquium 22-23 October 2009]' (2010) 40 Collegium 19, 27. *Contra:* Pictet's interpretation of IAC covers a broader range of situations: '[a]ny difference arising between two States and leading to the intervention of armed forces is an armed conflict within the meaning of Article 2 [GC I-IV], even if one of the Parties denies the existence of a state of war. It makes no difference how long the conflict lasts, or how much slaughter takes place.' Jean S Pictet (ed), *The Geneva Conventions of 12 August 1949: Commentary*, vol III (ICRC 1960) 23. Along the same lines, Clapham stresses that compared to NIAC, a lower threshold is required to trigger the application of the relevant IHL treaties. Clapham (n 53) 16.

definition.[56] Traditionally, IHL provides elements that serve to draw a line between the standards applicable in IAC and those applicable in 'armed conflicts not of an international character'.[57] As for the former, IHL applies

> to all cases of declared war or of any other armed conflict which may arise between two or more of the High Contracting Parties, even if the state of war is not recognized by one of them…";[58]

> 'to all cases of partial or total occupation of the territory of a High Contracting Party, even if the said occupation meets with no armed resistance[59] [and]

> to wars of national liberation', i.e., 'armed conflicts in which peoples are fighting against colonial domination and alien occupation and against racist regimes in the exercise of their right of self-determination […].[60]

As for the latter, IHL applies to conflicts covered by common Article 3 and conflicts covered by Additional Protocol II (AP II). While Common Article 3[61] does not provide any definitional detail on NIAC,[62] AP II specifies that its provisions are applicable to

> all armed conflicts which are not covered by Article 1 of [AP I] […] and which take place in the territory of a High Contracting Party between its armed forces and dissident armed forces or other organized armed groups which, under responsible command, exercise such control over a part of its territory as to enable them to carry out sustained and concerted military operations and to implement this Protocol.[63]

The quest for information on missing persons and efforts to trace their whereabouts take place during the contextual settings outlined above; however, at the close of hostilities, the path towards the restoration of peace requires

---

[56] Criteria to distinguish these situations from 'armed conflicts not of an international character' are the intensity of the conflict and the organization of the parties to the conflict. ICTY, *Prosecutor v Boškoski & Tarčulovski, Trial Judgment* (2008) Case no. IT-04-82-T [175–206].

[57] Cf. Common Article 3, GC I-IV.

[58] Cf. Common Article 2, para. 1, GCs I-IV

[59] Cf. Common Article 2, para. 1, GCs I-IV. Pursuant to Article 42 of 1907 Hague Regulations, 'Territory is considered occupied when it is actually placed under the authority of the hostile army. The occupation extends only to the territory where such authority has been established and can be exercised'. The definition is part of customary international law, cf. ICJ, *Legal Consequences of the Construction of a Wall in the Occupied Palestinian Territory, Advisory Opinion* ICJ Reports 2004, p.136 [78, 89]; ICJ, *Case concerning Armed Activities on the Territory of the Congo (Democratic Republic of the Congo v Uganda), Merits, Judgment* (2005) ICJ Reports 2005, p.168 [172]; ICTY, *Prosecutor v Kordić & Čerkez, Trial Judgment* (2001) Case no. IT-95-14/2-T [338–339].

[60] Cf. Article 1 (4), AP I.

[61] In this regard, Pictet states that 'it must be recognized that the conflicts referred to in common Article 3 are armed conflicts, with "armed forces" on either side engaged in "hostilities" - conflicts, in short, which are in many respects similar to an international war, but take place within the confines of a single country.' See Pictet, *Commentary Vol III (1960)* (n 55) 37.

[62] See ibid.

[63] Cf. Article 1 (1), AP II. This means that while Common Article 3 can also be applied to NIAC between non-state armed groups arising on the territory of a State Party to the Geneva Conventions of 1949 (without any State involvement), Additional Protocol II (AP II) cannot, as its scope of application is narrowly detailed. Sandoz and others (n 47) para 4461. This finds confirmation in the *Tadić Case*: in the sense of common Article 3, a NIAC exists 'whenever there is […] protracted armed violence between governmental authorities and organised armed groups or between such groups within a State'. See ICTY, *Prosecutor v. Duško Tadić, Decision on the Defence Motion … (n 54) [70].

further efforts and the willingness of all parties to continue searching for the missing. Temporal boundaries of an armed conflict are fluid; this study will briefly touch upon this aspect that is relevant to the continuing application/end of application of certain IHL rules regulating the conduct of the parties to the conflict in the handling of information on missing persons.

The term 'post-conflict' does not find any room in IHL treaties as well as in IHRL treaties, as it is a term that has been generated in the aftermath of the Cold War.[64] Indeed, it is not a legal term, but illustrates the phase of transition from an armed conflict to peace. In this respect, Kleffner highlights that armed conflict and peace are not static situations and, as dynamic processes, make it difficult to pinpoint when a transition from armed conflict to peace takes place and becomes definite.[65] Their dynamic character generates the risk of misconceiving both ends and means.[66] From a legal perspective, it would be simplistic to affirm that this study will put aside IHL due to the fact that in post-conflict situations IHL no longer applies, as the notion of "post-conflict" remains stranded in the middle of "war and peace". In this respect, Stahn points out that there are situations where 'there may not even be a proper "post" in the first place' (e.g., in cases of relapse of violence or transformation from an international to a non-international armed conflict).[67] In this sense, the term "post-" is fragile, as it seems to imply a fictional demarcation between 'conflict societies' and 'post-conflict societies'.[68]

The general issue concerning the definition of the temporal boundaries of the post-conflict phase goes beyond the limits of this study;[69] suffice to say that in the legal scholarship and at the practitioner level the attempts to draw such boundaries[70] are mainly related to the need to shed light upon the temporal

---

[64] It was the former UN Secretary General (UNSG), Boutros Boutros-Ghali, that used it for the first time in the 1992 *Agenda for peace;* this document was an ambitious call for engagement of the international community not only in prevention of conflicts, peace-making, and peace-keeping but also in *post-conflict* peacebuilding. See A Hozic, 'The Origins of "post-conflict"' in Keith Brown and Chip Gagnon (eds), *Post-conflict studies: an interdisciplinary approach* (Routledge 2014) 22.

[65] JK Kleffner, 'Introduction: From Here to There ... and the Law in the Middle' in Carsten Stahn and Jann K Kleffner (eds), *Jus Post Bellum: Towards a Law of Transition From Conflict to Peace* (Springer Verlag 2008) 2.

[66] ibid.

[67] C Stahn, 'Jus Post Bellum: Mapping the Discipline(s)' in Carsten Stahn and Jann K Kleffner (eds), *Jus Post Bellum: Towards a Law of Transition From Conflict to Peace* (Springer Verlag 2008) 233.

[68] ibid.

[69] Among the major collections of contributions, see Carsten Stahn and Jann K Kleffner (eds), *Jus Post Bellum: Towards a Law of Transition From Conflict to Peace* (Springer Verlag 2008); Carsten Stahn, Jennifer S Easterday and Jens Iverson (eds), *Jus Post Bellum: Mapping the Normative Foundations* (Oxford University Press 2014); V Chetail, 'Introduction: Post-Conflict Peacebuilding - Ambiguity and Identity' in Vincent Chetail (ed), *Post-conflict Peacebuilding: a Lexicon* (Oxford University Press 2009); Eric De Brabandere, *Post-Conflict Administrations in International Law: International Territorial Administration, Transitional Authority, and Foreign Occupation in Theory and Practice* (Martinus Nijhoff Publishers 2009).

[70] For instance, with regard to when the post-conflict phase might start, the end point of an armed conflict might be the reference point. In the words of the ICTY, the end of a conflict is sanctioned by the most traditional means, as IHL will apply 'until [...] a peaceful settlement is achieved'. ICTY. *Prosecutor v. Duško Tadić, Decision on the Defence Motion ...* (n 54) [70]. With regard to the end of the post-conflict phase, in his report on peacebuilding in the immediate aftermath of an armed

boundaries of the legal and policy framework applicable in this phase (see Chapter I, sec 3).

In this study I share the view of those who deem it purely artificial to define objectively what "post-" means.[71] As a matter of fact, the word "post-" is a temporal expression that indicates the period running from the end of an armed conflict towards the restoration of societal, economic, institutional, and legal normalcy.[72] Thus, the passage of time seems to be a meta-indicator of the transition from one phase (armed conflict) to another phase (peace) and, as such, should determine the sphere of law of reference. However, a neat shift from one phase to another is purely fictional and does not correspond to the reality on the ground. For instance, the UN approach focuses on operational and policy measures that are part of the so-called *post-conflict* peacebuilding, i.e.,

> identifying and supporting measures and structures which will solidify peace and build trust and interaction among former enemies, in order to avoid a relapse into conflict; often involves elections organized, supervised or conducted by the [UN], the rebuilding of civil physical infrastructures and institutions such as schools and hospitals, and economic reconstruction.[73]

These measures are peculiar to this phase of transition and are conducive to the establishment and consolidation of peace, which is not the immediate result of an armed conflict. From a legal point of view, this means that in the transition from an armed conflict to peace a variety of standards apply and interact with each other – probably – in a different way than they would interact during an armed conflict or in peacetime. In this sense, Chetail notes that the transition from armed conflict to peace is located at the intersection of various branches of law (international and domestic); in his view, the expression *jus post bellum* captures the extreme diversity of branches of law, which can be applied at the

---

conflict, the UNSG has provided a streamlined definition of 'immediate aftermath', i.e., 'the first two years after the main conflict in a country has ended'. UNSG, 'Report on Peacebuilding in the Immediate Aftermath of Conflict' (2009) UN Doc A/63/881–S/2009/304 para 2. Among the scholars, Wählisch suggests that 'the sum of a critical amount of post-conflict reform steps will indicate the outset of a state of normalcy'. M Wählisch, 'Conflict Termination from a Human Rights Perspective: State Transitions, Power-Sharing, and the Definition of the "Post"' in Carsten Stahn, Jennifer S Easterday and Jens Iverson (eds), *Jus Post Bellum: Mapping the normative Foundations* (Oxford University Press 2014) 34. By looking at the legal and policy framework applicable in this phase through the lenses of the *jus post bellum*, Kleffner underlines that 'the temporal scope of the applicability of *jus post bellum* needs to be approached with a degree of flexibility. The quest for a clear start and end date of the entire body of *jus post bellum* is ill-fitted to its function as a law that accompanies and regulates transitional processes from armed conflict to peace.' See JK Kleffner, 'Towards a Functional Conceptualization of the Temporal Scope of Jus Post Bellum' in Carsten Stahn, Jennifer S Easterday and Jens Iverson (eds), *Jus Post Bellum: Mapping the normative Foundations* (Oxford University Press 2014) 295.

[71] C Stahn, 'The Future of Jus Post Bellum' in Carsten Stahn and Jann K Kleffner (eds), *Jus Post Bellum: Towards a Law of Transition From Conflict to Peace* (Springer Verlag 2008) 233.

[72] Stahn considers that 'post' is a fragile concept; therefore, he highlights that what "in the aftermath of an armed conflict" means in an accurate way may need 'to be determined on a case-by-cases basis.' Stahn C, 'Jus Post Bellum and Transitional Justice' in Stahn (n 67) 106.

[73] Online glossary of the UN Department of Peacekeeping Operations (http://www.un.org/Depts/dpko/glossary/p.xhtml) in Chetail (n 69) XX.

close of an armed conflict.[74] Both Chetail and Stahn re-frame the Kantian interpretation of the law applicable in the period 'after the war' as follows: *jus post bellum*[75] is an instrument to enhance the sustainability of peace after conflict,[76] which paves the way for a contextualized application of existing norms in order to take into account 'the specificities which characterize the difficult transition from war to peace'.[77]

The components of the law − e.g., prosecution of individual perpetrators of international crimes, reparation measures, measures to account for missing persons − concerning these specificities 'have their individual temporal scopes and should apply as soon and for as long as the transitional process at hand calls for and allows for their implementation.'[78] This 'functional conceptualization of the temporal scope'[79] of the legal framework applicable in post-conflict situations requires constant monitoring of the situation on the ground; thus, such conceptualization entails that the facts on the ground would determine whether and to what extent that component of the law starts or ceases to apply.[80]

1.2.2. What this study does not cover

The peculiarities proper to the transition from war to peace briefly outlined above, and their implications for the subject matter, have led to narrow the focus of this book down to the families' quest for information and those efforts to account for missing persons in post-conflict settings. This choice does not imply that persons uniquely go missing in armed conflict, as other potential settings − natural disasters and internal violence − can generate uncertainty on the fate and whereabouts of persons. The ongoing debate on the right of families to know the fate of missing migrants[81] who die on maritime or terrestrial migration routes to Europe or other regions[82] will be left outside the scope of the present study;

---

[74] The law, which applies in the post-conflict phase, is scattered throughout a multitude of domains including IHL, IHRL, international criminal law, international refugee law, international development law, law of international relations relating to peaceful settlement of dispute, treaty law. See ibid 18.

[75] See section 3 in Chapter I for more details.

[76] Stahn (n 67) 112.

[77] Chetail (n 69) 17–18.

[78] Kleffner (n 70) 296.

[79] ibid.

[80] ibid.

[81] The term 'migrant' is considered by the UN a neutral term for a group of people who have in common a lack of citizenship attachment to their host country; OHCHR has defined an "international migrant" as 'any person who is outside a State of which he or she is a citizen or national, or, in the case of a stateless person, his or her State of birth or habitual residence'. UN OHCHR, 'Recommended Principles and Guidelines on Human Rights at International Borders' (2014) para 10 <www.ohchr.org/Documents/ Issues/ Migration/OHCHR_Recommended_Principles_Guidelines.pdf> accessed 12 July 2016; UN OHCHR, 'Opening Statement - Panel Discussion "Promoting Tolerance, Dispelling Myths, Protecting Rights: An Evidence-Based Conversation on Migration"' (2015) <www.ohchr.org/EN/NewsEvents/ Pages/DisplayNews. aspx?NewsID=16889&LangID=E> accessed 12 June 2016.

[82] For more details on this subject, see Stefanie Grant, '"Identity Unknown": Migrant Deaths at Sea' (2011) 38 Forced Migration Review 43; Stefanie Grant, 'Migration and Frontier Deaths: A Right to Identity' in Marie-Bénédicte Dembour and Tobias Kelly (eds), *Are human rights for migrants?: critical reflections on the status of irregular migrants in Europe and the United States* (Routledge 2011). Even though Fargues does not elaborate on the right to know, he uses the terminology of the

the complexity of the issue would require a dedicated research study in order to address it thoroughly. However, this choice does not entail that the findings of this book are irrelevant to those efforts aimed at delineating a pragmatic answer to the situation of missing migrants; indeed, these might be persons whose families are without news and/or, on the basis of reliable information, have been reported missing as a result of events related to IAC/NIAC.

Enforced disappearances have been central to the international agenda in recent years. Several dissertations, along with scholarly monographs and articles,[83] have already examined and critically commented on the substantive legal framework applicable: thus, the aim of this book is not to re-examine the legal framework that others have brilliantly studied. As explained previously, in armed conflicts every forcibly disappeared person is a missing person, but the contrary does not hold valid. This implies that the framework applicable to enforced disappearances will be observed through the prism of the perspective adopted by the present study vis-à-vis the issue of missing persons.

1.3. *Methodological aspects*

This book is based on the assumption that international law is a normative 'system, a process, rather than [just] rules or commands'.[84] This consideration

---

present study in connection with the phenomenon of irregular migrants. Philippe Fargues, 'Work, Refuge, Transit: An Emerging Pattern of Irregular Immigration South and East of the Mediterranean' (2009) 43 International Migration Review 544. In the case of irregular migrants in Mexico, Amnesty International considers a priority measure to '[e]stablish a database for disappeared migrants and related procedures, in consultation with civil society and international experts, in order that relatives can lodge information, including DNA, to assist in the identification of missing persons'. See Amnesty International., 'Irregular Migrants in Mexico: Ten Urgent Measures to Save Lives.' (2012).

[83] One of the first manuscripts on the subject in light of international human rights law is the work of Pérez Solla: María Fernanda Pérez Solla, *Enforced Disappearances in International Human Rights* (McFarland & Co, Publishers 2006). See also the seminal work of Prof Citroni and Scovazzi: Tullio Scovazzi and Gabriella Citroni, *The Struggle against Enforced Disappearance and the 2007 United Nations Convention* (Martinus Nijhoff Publishers 2007). Among the published PhD theses, see Lisa Ott, *Enforced Disappearance in International Law* (Intersentia 2011); Marthe Lot Vermeulen, *Enforced Disappearance: Determining State Responsibility under the International Convention for the Protection of All Persons from Enforced Disappearance* (Intersentia 2012). See also Nikolas Kyriakou, 'An Affront to the Conscience of Humanity: Enforced Disappearance in International Human Rights Law (PhD Thesis)' (European University Institute - Department of Law 2012). Among the many scholarly contributions, see: Kirsten Anderson, 'How Effective Is the International Convention for the Protection of All Persons from Enforced Disappearance Likely to Be in Holding Individuals Criminally Responsible for Acts of Enforced Disappearance?' (2006) 7 Melbourne Journal of International Law 245; S McCrory, 'The International Convention for the Protection of All Persons from Enforced Disappearance' (2007) 7 Human Rights Law Review 545; O De Frouville, 'La Convention Des NU Pour La Protection de Toutes Les Personnes Contre Les Disparitions Forcées: Les Enjeux Juridiques D'une Négociation Exemplaire. Première Partie : Les Dispositions Substantielles' (2006) 6 Droits fondamentaux 1; Gloria Gaggioli, 'The Prohibition of Enforced Disappearances: A Meaningful Example of a Partial Merger between Human Rights Law and International Humanitarian Law' in Gloria Gaggioli and Robert Kolb (eds), *Research Handbook on Human Rights and Humanitarian Law* (Edward Elgar Publishing 2013); CM Grossman, 'Disappearances' in Rudiger Wolfrum (ed), *The Max Planck Encyclopedia of Public International Law*, vol III (2013).

[84] Rosalyn Higgins, *Problems and Process: International Law and How We Use It* (Oxford University Press 1995) 10.

entails that methodologically the normative substance of treaty rules and the context in which such rules were adopted will be investigated; likewise, successive development and application of these rules will be considered.[85] However, since this book rejects the idea that international law can be boiled down to a mere 'impartial application of rules',[86] it intends to embed policy considerations which are 'an integral part of that decision making process which we call international law'.[87] Among these considerations are the humanitarian ones which have informed the development of IHL[88] and the accountability-driven ones: as for the former, humanitarian is the nature of the principle that shall prompt the activities undertaken in order to elucidate the fate and whereabouts of persons reported as missing in armed conflicts; humanitarian should also be the rationale that prompts the decisions of authorities to make information accessible to families concerned. As for the latter, whenever a person goes missing in the framework of IHRL/IHL violations, there is not just a need to elucidate where that person is, but a duty to carry out an investigation into alleged violations in order to find who is responsible arises.

In cases not covered by the law in force in situations of armed conflict, the protection of the 'principles of humanity and the dictates of the public conscience' remain in place.[89] Since the problem tackled in this study continues in the aftermath of a conflict, this book will address whether the principles embedded in the *Martens* formula and other principles play any role in the transition phase. Indeed, the person who views international law as a process cannot ignore that 'there are [...] tools for authoritative decision-making ...(e.g., by use of analogy, by reference to context, by analysis of the alternative consequences)' on a certain problem, notwithstanding the absence of a precise rule that must be applied.[90]

---

[85] The International Court of Justice (hereinafter ICJ) underlined that '[m]indful as it is of the primary necessity of interpreting an instrument in accordance with the intentions of the parties at the time of its conclusion, [...]the Court must take into consideration the changes which have occurred in the supervening half-century, and its interpretation cannot remain unaffected by the subsequent development of law [...]. Moreover, an international instrument has to be interpreted and applied within the framework of the entire legal system prevailing at the time of the interpretation.' See ICJ, *Legal Consequences for States of the Continued Presence of South Africa in Namibia (South West Africa) notwithstanding Security Council Resolution 276 (1970)*, Advisory Opinion, ICJ Reports 1971, p. 16, para. 53.

[86] R. Higgins, 'Policy Considerations and the International Judicial Process' (1968) 1 7 *ICLQ* 58 at 58–9 in Higgins, *Problems and Process* (n 84) 2.

[87] R. Higgins, 'Integrations of Authority and Control: Trends in the Literature of International Law and Relations', in B. Weston and M. Reisman (eds.), *Towards World Order and Human Dignity* (1976), at 85 in ibid 5.

[88] K Mujezinović Larsen, C Guldahl Cooper and G Nystuen, 'Introduction by the Editors: Is There a "Principle of Humanity" in International Humanitarian Law?' in Kjetil Mujezinović Larsen, Camilla Guldahl Cooper and Gro Nystuen (eds), *Searching for a 'Principle of Humanity' in International Humanitarian Law* (Cambridge University Press 2013) 9–11.

[89] Cf. Preamble, AP II; Article 1 (2), AP I.

[90] Higgins, *Problems and Process* (n 84) 10.

The adoption of the view of the law as a process entails that those who have to assess a situation in light of international law will not simply have the task of finding a rule and applying it. This is mainly due to two factors: the trend of past solutions and assessments or decisions taken vis-à-vis an issue cannot be applied oblivious to context; the determination of what is the relevant rule is part of the decision-makers' function.[91] For instance, international adjudicators[92] have made decisions in relation to the subject matter and have determined the relevant international rules applicable. And yet, it would be reductive to boil down their judicial function to making choices between fully justified claims and fully unjustified claims. [93] Therefore, the underlying assumption in the assessment of their judicial constructions is that judges make a choice 'between claims with varying degrees of legal merit'.[94]

International law as a system of normative conduct relates to organized groups and structures that see that conduct as obligatory.[95] In post-conflict settings, where multiple – national and international – organized groups and structures operate, the question of whether this variety of actors view the same normative conduct vis-à-vis the issue of missing persons as obligatory must be clarified. Nevertheless, this book does not intend to present specific case studies; the selection of examples illustrated in the chapters responds to the criteria of relevance and availability of legal and policy-related information germane to the subject matter. Based on the methodological premises above, this study will look at 'a variety of phenomena – claims and counterclaims, state practice, and decisions by authorized decision-makers',[96] e.g., governments, international organizations, and international adjudicators.[97]

---

[91] ibid 3.

[92] Specifically, the decisions and judgments of the following judicial bodies will be explored: the Human Rights Committee (HRCee), the European Court of Human Rights (ECtHR), the Inter-American Court of Human Rights (IACtHR), the African Commission on Human and Peoples' Rights (AfCommHPR) and the African Court of Human and Peoples' Rights (AfCtHPR), and the Human Rights Chamber for Bosnia and Herzegovina (HRChBH). This book will also look at the work of the Committee on Enforced Disappearances (i.e., the treaty body related to the ICPPED).

[93] See Hersch Lauterpacht, *The Development of International Law by the International Court* (Cambridge University Press 1982) 3.

[94] See ibid.

[95] Higgins, *Problems and Process* (n 84) 1.

[96] ibid 10.

[97] The making of decisions by persons without authority, who solely rely on their position of power, or by authorized persons on the basis of expediency or pragmatism is considered purely political decision-making. When decisions are made by authorized persons or organs, in appropriate forums 'within the framework of certain established practices and norms, then what occurs is legal decision-making'. In this sense, international law is a continuing process of authoritative decisions, which can be made by judges as well as international organizations and governments. Rosalyn Higgins, 'Policy Considerations and the International Judicial Process' (1968) 17 The International and Comparative Law Quarterly 58, 58–59, 75.

2. Structure

This book consists of six Chapters. Chapter I highlights the importance of the issue of missing persons in the history of warfare, starting from ancient times and up to the codification of contemporary IHL treaties. It also examines the post-World War II (WWII) practice of *ad hoc* post-conflict arrangements concerning the issue of missing persons. A reflection upon the value of information on the missing in the phase between war and peace is followed by the formulation of a normative approach to the international legal framework with a view to making it more coherent vis-à-vis the interrelation between the *durante bello* and *post bellum* phases of an armed conflict.

Chapter II defines to what – substantive and temporal – extent contemporary IHL regulates the handling of information on missing persons. The purpose is to identify the possible IHL rules that the (former) parties to the conflict must abide by when certain circumstances determined by the conflict itself continue in its aftermath. The Chapter also examines the protective framework of the right of family members to know the fate and whereabouts of their relatives under IHRL. Based on this analysis, the Chapter demonstrates that the duty to account for missing persons has a temporal crosscutting nature, since it requires actions before, during, and after an armed conflict.

The interconnectedness of the three aforementioned phases justifies the need to reformulate the reading of the relationship between IHL and IHRL. Chapter III addresses this need in two steps. First, it unpacks the basic principles of the *corpus juris* for the protection of all human beings, which includes IHRL and IHL. This step proves essential to explain the reasons why the recent IHRL advances concerning enforced disappearances – i.e., the adoption of the ICPPED – do not represent a merger of IHL rules on missing persons with the IHRL's: these sets of rules are distinct, but complementary. Second, a brief illustration of the debate on the classical understanding of the relationship between the two branches prepares the ground for studying the complementary character of the relationship of the relevant IHL and IHRL rules in post-conflict settings; the Chapter concludes with the delineation of fixed criteria to be considered when resorting to the complementarity approach in case of simultaneous application of rules belonging to IHL and IHRL.

Chapter IV assesses the legal merit of the families' claims for information on their relatives through the prism of international human rights case law. The Chapter intends to study the intertwined humanitarian and accountability-driven dimensions proper to IHRL in the context of missing persons as well as their pragmatic implications in post-conflict environments. This is conducive to an evaluation of whether it is legally admissible that post-conflict-related problems be an acceptable excuse presented by State authorities for not abiding by their international obligations. Moreover, in light of the conclusions reached in Chapter III on the relationship between IHL and IHRL in post-conflict situations, the Chapter examines the issue of whether under both branches there is room for lawful limitations of the right of families to know the fate of their relatives.

Chapter V takes stock of the foregoing in order to put forward the idea that, in post-conflict situations, temporary assistance or transitional exercise of the governance function can help address an enforcement gap generated by a weak State apparatus. Both options are reflective of a broader engagement in peace processes by the international community. Therefore, the Chapter sheds light on the extent to which the UN and other actors have provided and are still providing their contribution to resolving the issue of missing persons within the boundaries of the international legal framework surveyed in previous Chapters. The examination of specific examples unveils the role that international law plays in the international community's attempts to articulate humanitarian and accountability-driven post-conflict responses to the subject matter.

Chapter VI intends to examine the issue of missing persons through the prism of an essential component of peace processes, i.e., justice in transition. By building in the premises laid down in Chapter I, the Chapter investigates the mandate of selected examples of TJ bodies that have operated in post-conflict settings, how their *modus operandi* has addressed or disregarded the issue of missing persons, and what implications the foregoing has had on the quest of families for information. The temporary character of these bodies is one of the reasons why the Chapter broadens the investigation to international justice bodies, i.e., permanent judicial and quasi-judicial bodies whose work can impact on the transition process. The final aim is to understand whether the different facets of justice in transition constitute an integral part of a global system meant to address armed conflict-induced uncertainty on missing persons in post-conflict environments.

CHAPTER I.

THE EMERGENCE OF A DUTY TO ACCOUNT FOR MISSING PERSONS
AND THE COMPLEXITY OF THE LINK
BETWEEN CONFLICT AND POST-CONFLICT

Efforts to alleviate human suffering – including the anguish of families of missing in action – are as old as war itself;[1] however, the normative focus on the need of families to know the fate of their relatives who went missing in an armed conflict is relatively recent.[2] The civilian population and property remained legally unprotected from the impact of conflicts until the mid-twentieth century.[3] In this respect, Rousseau stated that in the past 'war was not a relation between man and man, but between State and State, and individuals were enemies only accidentally, not as men [...] but as soldiers'.[4] This chapter examines the relevance of the issue of missing persons in the history of warfare, starting from ancient times and up to the codification of contemporary IHL treaties. The analysis will shed light upon the interconnection between the *durante bello*-focused IHL codification efforts and the practice of post-conflict *ad hoc* arrangements aimed at addressing the issue of missing persons. Starting with some preliminary reflections on the legal, political, and societal value that information on the missing has in post-conflict scenarios, this chapter will inquire into what place the issue of the missing has in the law applicable post-conflict. The response to this query will be conducive to the formulation of a normative approach to the international legal framework with a view to providing a coherent legal appreciation of the issue of the missing in the transition from war to peace.

1. ACCOUNTING FOR MISSING PERSONS IN THE HISTORY OF WARFARE

The need of the State to locate and find its soldiers was the main driver that led to improve the system of identification of soldiers deployed in the battlefield. In the nineteenth century this need led to systematize the *durante bello* efforts

---

[1] Jean S Pictet, *Development and Principles of International Humanitarian Law: Course Given in July 1982 at the University of Strasbourg as Part of the Courses Organized by the International Institute of Human Rights* (Martinus Nijhoff Publishers 1985) 6.

[2] Cf. Article 32, AP I.

[3] *Contra:* in the Islamic law, verse 190 of the Surat Al-Baqarah makes an implicit distinction between combatants and non-combatants ("Fight in the way of Allah those who fight you but do not transgress ...") and, therefore, leaves aside the civilian population from the brutality of the conflict. See Mario Bettati, *Droit Humanitaire* (Dalloz 2012) 2.

[4] Jean-Jacques Rousseau, *Du contrat social ou principes du droit politique*, vol Livre I (Le Prieur, Libraire 1791) 15.

and to increase the awareness of the army about the impact that uncertainty had on the families of the fallen in war. With the two World Wars – and the Spanish civil war in the interwar period – it became clear that the civilian population needed to be protected under several respects, e.g., the family as the 'basic unit' of society required to be preserved from the harshness of the war. This section will examine the codification and policy milestones characterizing the development of the right of families to know the fate of their relatives as a general principle guiding the *durante bello* and *post bellum* efforts to account for the missing.

1.1. From ancient times to the 19th century

Ad hoc measures to account for those who fell in war date back to the ancient past. In his *History of the Peloponnesian War,* Thucydides narrates that

> Athenians gave a funeral at the public cost to those who had first fallen in [...] war. [...] In the funeral procession cypress coffins are borne in cars, one for each tribe. [...] Among these is carried one empty bier decked for the missing, that is, for those whose bodies could not be recovered.[5]

This acknowledgment was also backed by concrete efforts to account for those fallen in war and to track down the human loss in conflict. In this regard, the city of Athens inventoried and reported the names of hoplites – citizen-soldiers of Ancient Greek city-states – who died in conflict (uniquely after the end of hostilities); identification of the dead was undertaken throughout the memories of other hoplites who were still alive.[6] Similarly, during the Maurya Empire, Ashoka the Great (reign 272-232 BC) expressed in his Edict no XIII his regret for all those who fell as a result of the conquest of Kalinga and conveyed his compassion for the suffering of the family members of a fallen soldier.[7]

In the silence of the law, operational and policy-based solutions have been found in order to minimize the impact of uncertainty on the fate of fallen soldiers. During the American civil war, rather than being put in mass graves and ossuary, those who died on the battlefield had their own graves in military cemeteries.[8] Measures aimed at satisfying the need to know the fate of missing in action were already undertaken at the time of the Battle of Solferino in 1859.[9]

---

[5] See Chapter 34 of *'Pericles' Funeral Oration'* in Book II ch. 34-46 in Thucydide (translated by Steven Lattimore), *The Peloponnesian War* (Hackett Publishing 1998) 90.

[6] Véronique Harouel-Bureloup, *Traité de Droit Humanitaire* (Presses Universitaires de France - PUF 2005) 27.

[7] Bettati (n 3) 41.

[8] H Wayne Elliott, 'Identification' in Roy Gutman and David Rieff (eds), *Crimes of war: what the public should know* (W W Norton & Company 1999) 186. Nonetheless, most soldiers did not wear any sort of identification disk and, in case of death, were haphazardly identified; this fact explains the reason why almost half of the civil war graves in national cemeteries were marked 'unknown'. Ibid.

[9] In his *Un Souvenir de Solferino,* Henry Dunant emphasized the approach adopted by the French Army vis-à-vis the identification of the dead in the field: '[a] l'ordinaire ceux d'un même corps relèvent leurs compagnons d'armes; ils prennent le numéro de matricule, des effets de l'homme tué [...]. Les décorations, [...] les lettres et les papiers recueillis sur les officiers sont plus tard envoyés à leurs familles; mais avec une pareille masse de corps à ensevelir, il n'est pas toujours possible de remplir cette tâche'. Henry Dunant, *Un souvenir de Solferino* (anastatic reprint), Slatkine 1980) 38.

However, the American civil war helped pave the way for making individual identification of deceased persons[10] a common practice; moreover, the *Lieber Code*,[11] the first set of standing rules on humanity in warfare,[12] included a specific reference to the importance of family relations[13] and to the obligation to respect the civilian population and property.[14] The Code anticipated some of the basic humanitarian tenets, which were then enshrined in more recent documents and treaties.[15] In the following years, new rules on methods and means of warfare and humanitarian relief were conceived and imposed obligations upon parties to the conflict that directly benefitted the State itself.[16]

On the other side of the Atlantic, under Napoleon, the State was responsible for the mourning process of all soldiers who died on the battlefield.[17] National authorities were entrusted with recording the deceased: on the basis of the serial numbers of each military unit, the officer in charge of the vital records procedure had to count the dead and missing in action after each battle.[18] In the Franco-Prussian war, not only did the Prussian Army issue identification disks, but it also required each Prussian soldier to carry an identification card.[19] It is in this context[20] that the first tracing service[21] was established: indeed, those who provided direct care to soldiers found that most of them were in distress because of the state of uncertainty in which their families lived. Thus, the 1871 Treaty of

---

[10] Sophie Martin, 'The Missing' (2002) 84 International Review of the Red Cross 723, 723.

[11] Instructions for the Government of Armies of the United States in the Field (Lieber Code), April 24, 1863.

[12] Jan Egeland, 'Political "Disappearances" - a Challenge for Humanitarian Law' (1982) 51 Nordic Journal of International Law 189, 191. According to Paust, 'the Code undoubtedly lessened human suffering during the Civil War, and it formed an authoritative exposition of the laws of war for prosecution of soldiers and civilians then and for years to come'. See Jordan J Paust, 'Dr. Francis Lieber and the Lieber Code' (2001) 95 Proceedings of the Annual Meeting (American Society of International Law) 112, 114.

[13] The Lieber Code declares that '[t]he United States acknowledge and protect, in hostile countries occupied by them, ... *the sacredness of domestic relations* [emphasis added]'. Cf. Article 37, Lieber Code.

[14] Cf. Articles 22-34, Lieber Code.

[15] In this regard, Haimbaugh points out that 'the term humanitarian law is of relatively recent origin dating back only to the 1950s. However, Lieber captured the essence of the term in the word and spirit of his *Instructions*'. See George D Jr Haimbaugh, 'Introduction to Panel II: Humanitarian Law: The Lincoln-Lieber Initiative' (1983) 13 Georgia Journal of International and Comparative Law 245, 246.

[16] Kate Parlett, *The Individual in the International Legal System: Continuity and Change in International Law* (Cambridge University Press 2011) 179.

[17] Luc Capdevila and Danièle Voldman, 'Du Numéro Matricule Au Code Génétique: La Manipulation Du Corps Des Tués de La Guerre En Quête D'identité' (2002) 84 International Review of the Red Cross 751, 753.

[18] Ibid 754.

[19] Elliott (n 8) 186.

[20] See ICRC, *History of Central Tracing Agency*, July 2002, http://goo.gl/EFifiS accessed 12 August 2013.

[21] Nowadays, by 'tracing service' it is meant a unit within a number of National Societies that helps 'to restore or maintain contact between members of families separated as a consequence of armed conflict or other situations of violence, natural disasters or any other situations requiring a humanitarian response.' ICRC, *Glossary of Restoring Family Links Terms, https://backoffice.familylinks.icrc.org/ en/Pages/NewsAndResources/Glossary.aspx#89* accessed 12 June 2015.

Frankfurt, which sanctioned the end of the Franco-Prussian war, responded to the need to take care of those who fell on the battlefield, as it stated that '[l]e gouvernement français et allemand s'engagent à entretenir les tombes des militaires ensevelis sur leurs territoires respectifs'. [22] Yet in Europe identification attempts and regulation of the cemeteries were at their early stages; while the procedures for recording vital records on the battlefield were very strict, unidentified body remains of fallen soldiers were not preserved for successive identification, but put in collective graves or ossuary. [23]

1.2. The 'sacredness'[24] of family ties in the initial codification of IHL

The rules framed in the second half of the 19th century were consistent 'with the orthodox account of the framework of the international legal system as a system of rules between States and a system which did not confer rights or impose duties on individuals'. [25] The Hague Regulations[26] reflect this understanding[27] under several respects. [28] The main novelty of the 1899 Hague Regulations consisted in the obligation imposed on belligerents to establish a Bureau for Information in charge of answering 'all inquiries about prisoners of war'. [29] The *ratio legis* of such an obligation was two-fold: it embedded the need to protect and contributed to alleviating the anguish and distress of families of prisoners of war (POW) caused by uncertainty about the fate of their beloved

---

[22] Capdevila and Voldman (n 17) 755.

[23] ibid 756. The military graves were not sharply distinguished from civilian cemeteries. The fallen of the Franco-Prussian War had still been buried in the village churchyard (often in mass graves), nearest to the battle. No effort had been made to keep the graves separate from the village dead. See George L Mosse, *Fallen Soldiers: Reshaping the Memory of the World Wars* (Oxford University Press 1991) 91–92.

[24] The term is used in Article 37 of the Lieber Code.

[25] Parlett (n 16) 180.

[26] Convention (II) with Respect to the Laws and Customs of War on Land and its annex: Regulations concerning the Laws and Customs of War on Land. The Hague, July 29, 1899 (hereinafter, the 1899 Hague Regulations (II)) and Convention (IV) respecting the Laws and Customs of War on Land and its annex: Regulations concerning the Laws and Customs of War on Land. The Hague, October 18, 1907 (hereinafter, the 1907 Hague Regulations (IV)).

[27] For instance, Article 19 of the 1899 Hague Regulations (II) reflects such concerns. It affirms that 'the wills of prisoners of war are received or drawn up on the same conditions as for soldiers of the national army. The same rules shall be observed regarding death certificates, as well as for the burial of prisoners of war, due regard being paid to their grade and rank.'

[28] *Contra:* The Hague Regulations affirm that in the occupied territory of a hostile State, '[f]amily honour and rights, the lives of persons and property, as well as religious convictions and practices, must be respected'. Cf. Article 46, 1899 Hague Regulations (II) and 1907 Hague Regulations (IV). In addition to the Brussels Declaration and the Oxford Manual, the 'sacredness of domestic relations' and, consequently, the importance of family links, were the main aspects of the obligation to protect persons in occupied territories contained in Article 37 of the Lieber Code. Francis Lieber's most immediate concern was the conduct of soldiers during the U.S. Civil War; the Code's reference to occupied territories was necessarily aimed at regulating the Union's occupation of Confederate territories. Eyal Benvenisti, 'Part III. Governing Space in International Law. The Origin of the Concept of Belligerent Occupation' (2008) 26 Law and History Review 621, 640.

[29] Cf. Article 14, 1899 Hague Regulations (II).

ones.[30] The 1906 Geneva Convention[31] pointed to the importance of forwarding information on the fate and whereabouts of the wounded, sick, and dead in the Armies in the field.[32] Furthermore, the Convention imposed on belligerents the obligation 'to search for the wounded and to protect the wounded and dead from robbery and ill treatment'.[33] The 1907 Hague Regulations, which replaced the 1899's, espoused the same *ratio legis*, even though it provided more details with regard to the establishment of the Inquiry Office and its functions:[34] for instance the Office's main function was to 'reply to all inquiries about the prisoners' based on the information received; the Regulations did not specify whose (of the Government and/or of the family concerned) inquiries the Office should reply. Despite the *si omnes* clause,[35] the Hague Regulations triggered a gradual development of the laws of war towards a greater emphasis on their humanitarian nature.[36] This framework regulated the conduct of hostilities during WWI with meager results.

---

[30] Marco Sassòli, 'Le Bureau National de Renseignements En Faveur Des Victimes Des Conflits Armés' (1987) 69 International Review of the Red Cross 6, 6.

[31] Convention for the Amelioration of the Condition of the Wounded and Sick in Armies in the Field. Geneva, 6 July 1906 (hereinafter, 1906 Geneva Convention). This Convention is an updated version of the 1864 Geneva Convention for the Amelioration of the Condition of the Wounded in Armies in the Field, Geneva, August 22, 1864 (hereinafter, the 1864 Geneva Convention).

[32] Pursuant to Article 4 of 1906 Geneva Conventions, '[a]s soon as possible each belligerent shall forward to the authorities of their country or army the marks or military papers of identification found upon the bodies of the dead, together with a list of names of the sick and wounded taken in charge by him. Belligerents will keep each other mutually advised of internments and transfers, together with admissions to hospitals and deaths, which occur among the sick and wounded in their hands.'

[33] Cf. Article 3, 1906 Geneva Convention.

[34] Article 14 of the 1907 Hague Regulations (IV) stated that '[a]n inquiry office for prisoners of war is instituted on the commencement of hostilities in each of the belligerent States, and, when necessary, in neutral countries which have received belligerents in their territory. It is the function of this office to reply to all inquiries about the prisoners. It receives from the various services concerned full information respecting internments and transfers, releases on parole, exchanges, escapes, admissions into hospital, deaths, as well as other information necessary to enable it to make out and keep up to date an individual return for each prisoner of war. [...] The individual return shall be sent to the Government of the other belligerent after the conclusion of peace. [...].'

[35] The downside of both Hague Regulations consisted in the so-called *si omnes* clause, which provided that, if one party to a conflict was not a party to the treaty, the parties were not bound by the instrument. Cf. Article 2, 1899 Hague Regulations (II) and 1907 Hague Regulations (IV). As Provost suggests, the rejection of the *si omnes* clause 'can be construed as one illustration of this progression'. René Provost, *International Human Rights and Humanitarian Law* (Cambridge University Press 2004) 137. This clause was invoked as a defense during, and threatened the integrity of, the Nuremberg Prosecutions. It was only by considering The Hague Regulations as a mirror of customary law that the argument of the Nuremberg defendants could be answered. See Theodor Meron, *The Making of International Criminal Justice: A View from the Bench: Selected Speeches* (Oxford University Press 2011) 23.

[36] Cf. Article 16 of the Hague Convention (X) for the Adaptation to Maritime Warfare of the Principles of the Geneva Convention, The Hague, 18 October 1907: '[a]fter every engagement, the two belligerents, so far as military interests permit, shall take steps to look for the shipwrecked, sick, and wounded, and to protect them, as well as the dead, against pillage and ill-treatment. They shall see that the burial, whether by land or sea, or cremation of the dead shall be preceded by a careful examination of the corpse.' Cf. Article 17 of the same Convention: '[...] The belligerents shall keep each other informed as to internments and transfers as well as to the admissions into hospital and deaths which have occurred among the sick and wounded in their hands.'

As Capdevila and Voldmand underline, World War I (WWI) represents a turning point:

> les pouvoirs publics de tous les belligérants avaient accompli un immense effort pour permettre aux parents des tués du champ de bataille de pouvoir accomplir leur travail de deuil. Ils avaient construit et entretenu d'immenses cimetières militaires, et même – au moins pour la France et les États-Unis – restitué les corps aux familles qui en avaient exprimé le souhait.[37]

While the 'unknowns' were depicted either monumentally or with standard stones (i.e., countless identical crosses),[38] the name of soldiers who were identified started being inscribed on local war memorials.[39] Moreover, from 1914 to 1919, the large number of prisoners during WWI[40] emphasized gaps in the regulatory framework on the handling of information on POW: for instance, the Hague Regulations[41] were silent as to the question of transferring bodies for burial in their country of origin with the risk of leaving unattended family requests on their deceased relatives.[42] In light of the uncertainty and anxiety of an enormous number of families, the International Committee of the Red Cross (ICRC) established the Central Agency for POW;[43] based on the agreement reached with the belligerent nations and the national Red Cross Societies, the Agency's work consisted in obtaining 'information on individual prisoners and other victims covered by its remit' and in combining 'this information with the thousands of enquiries the ICRC received daily from families to be incorporated into a complex card-index system'.[44] In the post-conflict phase the repatriation of POW and thousands of civilians in the defeated countries entailed the continuation of the work of the Agency.[45]

The downside of the existing normative framework[46] and the operational advances put the ICRC at the forefront of the diplomatic endeavor towards the

---

[37] Capdevila and Voldman (n 17) 751.

[38] Laura Wittman, *The Tomb of the Unknown Soldier, Modern Mourning, and the Reinvention of the Mystical Body* (University of Toronto Press 2011) 56.

[39] At first, however, only officers or generals were named. ibid 99. As Mosse underlines, this changed by the 1860s, and in the aftermath of World War I when States sought to honor each one of the war dead through the inscription of the name at the burial place. Mosse (n 23) 91–92.

[40] According to the ICRC, eight million soldiers fighting on the front and two million civilians (e.g., those living abroad in enemy countries or areas under enemy occupation) were taken prisoner and interned in camps for several years. ICRC. 'The Archives of the International Prisoners-of-War Agency 1914-1919', http://grandeguerre.icrc.org accessed 12 July 2016.

[41] Cf. The 1899 Hague Regulations (II) and the 1907 Hague Regulations (IV).

[42] The Regulations limited themselves to declare that prisoners who died in captivity were to be buried on site under the same conditions as soldiers from the national army (cf. Article 19). ICRC, *Minutes from Meetings of the International Prisoner-of-War Agency, 21 August 1914 - 11 November 1918* (Daniel Palmieri ed, ICRC 2014) 7.

[43] Pictet (n 1) 36.

[44] ICRC, *Minutes from Meetings of the International POW Agency* (n 42) 6. At the end of the war the Agency held more than six million index cards including the names of POW and civilian internees, despite the silence of the law on the latter. Ibid.

[45] ICRC, *Minutes from Meetings of the International POW Agency* (n 42) 13.

[46] Cf. the 1899 Hague Regulations (II) and the 1907 Hague Regulations (IV); Kolb underlines that the humanitarian spirit characterizing some of their provisions was essentially directed to the military personnel. Kolb, R. "The Protection of the Individual in Times of War and Peace." In *The Oxford*

improvement of the existing normative framework. Mandated[47] by the 12th International Conference of Red Cross and Red Crescent (1925)[48] to carry out a 'study on measures to diminish the number of unaccounted for in time of war', the ICRC identified two strands of causes in relation to the phenomenon of missing in action: on the one hand ethic causes; on the other, administrative ones.[49] The former were related to the hatred for the enemy and were reflected in a range of ignominious acts which entailed the infliction of moral suffering to the population of the other party to the conflict (e.g., the refusal of transmitting the list of POW, the lack of identification of buried soldiers). The administrative causes stemmed from the lack of dedicated services within the Army (e.g., scant organization of the health service or services in charge of collecting dead bodies lying in the battlefield).[50] Therefore, the study emphasized the importance of identification tools,[51] as they could allow the identification of both the wounded and the dead.[52] The two 1929 Geneva Conventions reflected such consideration: both enhanced the system of transmission of information through the

---

Handbook of the History of International Law, edited by Bardo Fassbender and Anne Peters. Oxford: Oxford University Press, 2012, Chapter 13, at sects. 2.2.4 and 2.2.5. Among the non-binding documents, it is worth mentioning the Brussels Declaration which recognized the centrality of identification procedures: Article 34 introduced the requirement of identification tools – a certificate of identity - vis-à-vis those persons who might be made prisoners due to their proximity to the armies (i.e. correspondents, newspaper reporters, sutlers, contractors, etc.). Cf. Article 34, Project of an International Declaration concerning the Laws and Customs of War (hereinafter, Brussels Declaration), Brussels, August 27, 1874 (the Brussels Declaration never came into force). Moreover, the Declaration acknowledged the importance of the family links: pursuant to Article 38, '[f]amily honour and rights, and the lives and property of persons, as well as their religious convictions and their practice, must be respected [...]'. The mentioning of the family rights responded to the importance of preserving family life in time of war and of protecting it from, *inter alia*, the quartering or feeding of troops or the use of a house for military operations; these incidents shall be 'rendered as little irksome as possible'. See Percy Bordwell, *The Law of War Between Belligerents: A History and Commentary* (Callaghan & Company 1908) 310–311. Article 49 of the 1880 Oxford Manual is a *verbatim* reproduction of Article 38 of the Brussels Declaration; as for identification procedures, the Oxford Manual is more sensitive to humanitarian concerns, as it clearly states that '[t]he dead should never be buried until all articles on them which may serve to fix their identity [...] shall have been collected. The articles thus collected from the dead of the enemy are transmitted to its army or government.' Cf. Article 38 and Article 20, The Laws of War on Land, International Law Institute (the Oxford Manual), Oxford, September 9, 1880. Both documents were non-binding.

[47] Resolution VII, Measures to diminish the number of unaccounted for in time of war, 12th International Conference of the Red Cross and Red Crescent, Geneva, 1925.

[48] Robert Ruzé, 'Chronique des Faits Internationaux. La XIIe Conférence internationale de la Croix Rouge à Genève, 7-10 octobre 1925.' (1925) 7 Revue Générale de Droit International Public 471, 493.

[49] See 'Study on Measures to Diminish the Number of Unaccounted for in Time of War', 13th International Conference of the Red Cross and Red Crescent (1928), The Hague.

[50] Ibid.

[51] According to the ICRC study presented at the 13th International Conference (1928), among the measures that could enable a decrease in the number of missing persons were the establishment of an information service to be set up in peace times, a regular exchange of information on POW and on wounded, sick and dead soldiers, and the issuance by the Army of identification tags/disks for soldiers. Ibid.

[52] On the operational side, in the inter-war period the ICRC established the International Commission for the Standardization of medical material (1927) with the specific mandate of setting down the rules for a standard and common identification disk/tag. See, ibid.

establishment of Information Bureaux and improved the identification procedures.[53]

Thus, the Great War activated further legal advances with regard to the handling of information reflected in the 1929 Convention relative to the treatment of POW and in the 1929 Convention for the amelioration of the condition of the wounded and sick in Armies in the field. Both 1929 Geneva Conventions set forth obligations aimed at relieving the suffering of victims of war, including the families of those who were engaged in the battlefield. For instance, in the 1929 Convention on the wounded and sick, the need to know the fate of soldiers in the field was reflected in the setting up of an embryonic system aimed at handling information on different categories of persons: in particular, belligerents had to search for the wounded, sick and dead in the field,[54] to forward information conducive to their identification, to perform medical examinations on the dead before cremation, to mark the graves and organize a service aimed at facilitating exhumations as well as identification, and to exchange information on the location of the gravesites after the cessation of hostilities.[55] The 'grave registration service' should have been apt to operate even after the cessation of the hostilities, since this would have helped with the establishment of lists of graves; moreover, this service would have enabled families of the victims to mourn.[56]

Along the same lines, according to the 1929 Convention on POW, every prisoner 'shall be enabled to correspond personally with his family'[57] and 'to send a postcard to his family informing them of his capture and the state of his health'.[58] In addition to that, Article 77 of the Convention contained two fundamental aspects related to the elucidation of the fate of the missing: first of

---

[53] Cf. Article 4, Convention for the Amelioration of the Condition of the Wounded and Sick in Armies in the Field. Geneva, July 27, 1929, (hereinafter, 1929 Geneva Convention on WS); Article 77, Convention relative to the Treatment of Prisoners of War. Geneva, July 27, 1929 (hereinafter, 1929 Geneva Convention on POW).

[54] Article 3 of the 1929 Geneva Convention on WS states that [a]fter each engagement the occupant of the field of battle shall take measures to search for the wounded and dead, and to protect them against pillage and maltreatment. Whenever circumstances permit, a local armistice or a suspension of fire shall be arranged to permit the removal of the wounded remaining between the lines.'

[55] Pursuant to Article 4 of 1929 Geneva Convention on WS, '[b]elligerents shall communicate to each other reciprocally, as soon as possible, the names of the wounded, sick and dead, collected or discovered, together *with any indications which may assist in their identification.* They shall establish and *transmit to each other the certificates of death.* [...] They shall ensure that the burial or *cremation of the dead is preceded by a careful, and if possible medical, examination of the bodies, with a view to confirming death, establishing identity and enabling a report to be made.* They shall further ensure that the dead are honourably interred, that their graves are respected and *marked so that they may always be found.* To this end, at the commencement of hostilities, they shall organize officially a graves registration service, to render eventual exhumations possible, and *to ensure the identification of bodies whatever may be the subsequent site of the grave.* After the cessation of hostilities they *shall exchange the list of graves and of dead interred* in their cemeteries and elsewhere. [emphases added]'

[56] Paul Des Gouttes, *Commentaire de la Convention de Genève du 27 juillet 1929* (Comité International de la Croix-Rouge 1930) 35.

[57] Cf. Article 8, 1929 Geneva Convention on POW.

[58] Cf. Article 36, 1929 Geneva Convention on POW.

all, the temporal factor (the immediateness of the transmission of information); secondly, the necessity to transmit information on the POW both to the national authorities and to the family.[59] Despite the humanitarian emphasis of the provisions above, only specific categories benefited from such provisions: i.e., national authorities and families of POW. The 1929 Geneva Conventions constituted a humanitarian leap forward, for some of their provisions used a language suggestive of individual rights bestowed on POW.[60] Parlett points out that the 1929 Geneva Conventions were the first IHL treaties that provided for individuals rights.[61] Nevertheless, the pre-1949 Geneva Conventions treaties legally translated the steps required to diminish the risk for soldiers[62] of going missing and, therefore, to relieve the anxiety of their families.

1.3. The right to know as part of the obligation to respect 'family honour and rights' at Nuremberg

Earlier IHL treaties laid down the foundations of the contemporary system concerning the handling of information on specific categories of persons (see Chapter II). The duty to account for soldiers fallen in the battlefield that emerges from the Hague Regulations and the 1929 Geneva Conventions appears to be limited to the time-span of the armed conflict.

World War II (WWII) triggered further advances in regulating the identification procedures, the protection of family links, and the transmission of information to the party to the conflict and to the families concerned *durante bello*. Prior to the outbreak of the conflict, those attempts to adopt a new convention for the protection of civilians considered that an 'imperative necessity'[63] dominated 'the legal work of the [ICRC]';[64] in light of the exactions suffered by civilians during WWI, the organization set up a commission of experts in order to draw up a draft convention.[65] Presented and approved at the

---

[59] In this respect, pursuant to Article 77, 1929 Geneva Convention on POW, '[e]ach of the belligerent Powers *shall inform its Information Bureau as soon as possible of all captures of prisoners effected by its armed forces, furnishing them with all particulars of identity at its disposal to enable the families concerned to be quickly notified, and stating the official addresses to which families may write to the prisoners.* The Information Bureau *shall transmit all such information immediately to the Powers concerned,* on the one hand through the intermediary of the protecting Powers, and on the other through the Central Agency contemplated in Article 79. [...] [emphases added]'

[60] Pursuant to Article 8 of 1929 Geneva Convention on POW, '[POW] shall be enabled to correspond personally with his family'; cf. Article 36, 1929 Geneva Convention on POW.

[61] Parlett (n 16) 180.

[62] The Draft International Convention on the Condition and Protection of Civilians, presented and approved at the 15th International Conference of the Red Cross and Red Crescent, held in Tokyo in 1934, had the merit of considering the need to protect civilians of enemy nationality, but was not signed and ratified because of the outbreak of WWII. Draft International Convention on the Condition and Protection of Civilians of enemy nationality who are on the territory belonging to or occupied by a belligerent. Tokyo, 1934 (hereinafter, the Tokyo Draft Convention).

[63] JS Pictet, 'The New Geneva Conventions for the Protection of Victims of War' (1951) 45 American Journal of International Law 462, 473.

[64] Ibid.

[65] The Tokyo Draft Convention had the merit of considering the need to protect civilians of enemy nationality. It took into consideration both the importance of family links and the humanitarian

15th International Conference of the Red Cross and Red Crescent (Tokyo, 1934) the proposal was rejected by all sides of the upcoming WWII.[66] The absence of legal requirements concerning activities aimed at specifically tackling the issue of the missing would not justify the disappearance of persons as part of a military strategy or of a State policy. In this regard, Article 46 of the 1907 Hague Regulations (IV) – stating that '[f]amily honour and rights, the lives of persons, and private property, as well as religious convictions and practice, must be respected' – is key; this provision is considered to be part of international customary law since 1939.[67] During WWII, thousands of persons disappeared as a result of State-led policies (e.g., Hitler's Night and Fog Decree).[68] Moreover, at the end of the war almost forty million people were on the move, trying to reconnect with their families:[69] national authorities had to act in cooperation with humanitarian organizations[70] that sought to facilitate the restoration of family links.

---

necessity to transmit information on persons unaccounted for: Article 7 and Article 19 reflected both concerns. As for the former, it affirmed that 'enemy civilians shall have the possibility of giving news of a strictly private character to next of kin, and of receiving such news'. The latter, which focused on the conditions of enemy civilians in territories occupied by a belligerent, provided for the same possibility. Cf. Article 7 and 19, Tokyo Draft Convention.

[66] Lea Brilmayer and Geoffrey Chepiga, 'Ownership or Use? Civilian Property Interests in International Humanitarian Law' (2008) 49 Harvard International Law Review 413, 421.

[67] In the trials of the major war criminals, the Nuremberg International Military Tribunal (IMT), for the first time, acknowledged the customary character of the 1907 Regulations. The IMT held that the provisions of the Regulations had become part of customary international law by 1939; therefore, they are binding on all States. See International Military Tribunal at Nuremberg (IMT). *Trial of the Major War Criminals – Proceedings of the IMT* (1947) Vol 1 (14 November 1945-1 October 1946) 253–254. See also *Central Front-Eritrea's claims 2, 4, 6, 7, 8, and 22 between the State of Eritrea and the Federal Democratic Republic of Ethiopia* (2004) Partial Award [22]. According to the ICJ, the provisions of the Hague Regulations have become part of customary law. *Legal Consequences of the Construction of a Wall in the Occupied Palestinian Territory, Advisory Opinion* (2004) ICJ Reports 2004, p.136 [89]; *Case concerning Armed Activities on the Territory of the Congo (Democratic Republic of the Congo v Uganda), Merits, Judgment* (2005) ICJ Reports 2005, p.168 [217].

[68] Friends and families of the *Nacht und Nebel* (NN) persons arrested in occupied territories did not have access to any information on their fate and whereabouts. Thus, the practice of 'enforced disappearance' became a state-sponsored activity: the aim of this heinous practice was twofold: on the one hand, it removed individuals from the protection of the law; on the other, it carried out a form of deterrence through the intimidation and anxiety caused by the persistent uncertainty among the families of disappeared persons. Brian Finucane, 'Enforced Disappearance as a Crime Under International Law: A Neglected Origin in the Laws of War' (2010) 35 The Yale Journal of International Law 171, 176; Tullio Scovazzi and Gabriella Citroni, *The Struggle against Enforced Disappearance and the 2007 United Nations Convention* (Martinus Nijhoff Publishers 2007) 4–5. According to Christopher K. Hall, Stalin's reign of terror and use of secret arrests inspired Hitler. See Christopher K Hall, 'Enforced Disappearance of Persons' in Otto Triffterer and Kai Ambos (eds), *Commentary on the Rome Statute of the International Criminal Court: Observers' Notes, Article by Article* (C H Beck 2008) 221.

[69] In the aftermath of WWII, nearly forty million people, most of them civilians, were on the move across Europe in search of home or refuge. As Edkins analyses in her work on the politics of missing, 'many were walking from camp to camp, seeking news of relatives they had lost touch with in the turmoil; others were the uprooted and unwilling subjects of forced deportations from the East; yet others were escaping repatriation to the Russian zone.' See Jenny Edkins, *Missing: Persons and Politics* (Cornell University Press 2011) 38.

[70] The United Nations Relief and Rehabilitation Administration (an intergovernmental service agency) and the ICRC were among the major organizations operating in this sense. See ibid 42.

In reference to this provision and to the practice of enforced disappearances, the Nuremberg International Military Tribunal (IMT) emphasized two crucial aspects of the implementation of the so-called *Nacht und Nebel* (hereinafter, *NN*) program under the Nazi regime, i.e. the concealment of the fate of the *NN* prisoners to their families and communities; the disappearance of such prisoners.[71] Such conduct[72] was considered contrary *inter alia* to Article 46 of the 1907 Hague Regulations (IV) and to Article 6 (b)[73] of the Charter of the IMT.[74] In reaching such a conclusion, the Tribunal stressed the consequences of the implementation of the *NN* program, i.e., no word of the *NN* prisoners was allowed to reach their country of origin, nor their relatives; even in cases when they died awaiting trial, the families were not informed, the purpose being to create anxiety in the minds of the family of the arrested person.[75] Similarly, in the *Justice Case* the US National Military Tribunal[76] emphasized that

...many of the [NN] prisoners who were deported to Germany were not charged with serious offences [...]. But they were kept secretly and not permitted to communicate in any manner with their friends and relatives. This is inhumane treatment. It was meted out not only to the prisoners themselves, but also to their friends and relatives back home who were in constant distress of mind as to their whereabouts and fate. The families were deprived of the support of the husband, thus causing suffering and hunger. The purpose of the spiriting away of persons under the Night and Fog decree

---

[71] Specifically, civilians of occupied territories were subjected to the so-called 'protective arrests', without trial and without any other ordinary protection of the law; moreover, in concentration camps, the so-called *NN* prisoners were cut off from the outside world and deprived of any possibility of relation with the exterior: 'they disappeared without trace and no announcement of their fate was ever made by the German Authorities'. IMT. *Trial of the Major War Criminals – Proceedings of the IMT* (n 67).

[72] In the third count (i.e., war crimes) of the indictment filed against the Field-Marshall Wilhelm Keitel (hereinafter, Keitel) - Chief of the German Armed Forces High Command, the prosecutor considered the disappearance of those subjected to the *NN* program a war crime (under the Chapter Murder and Ill-treatment of civilian populations of or in occupied territory on the high seas). ibid.

[73] Pursuant to Article 6 (b) of the Charter of the International Military Tribunal 'war crimes', namely, violations of the laws or customs of war' are crimes coming within the jurisdiction of the Tribunal. Cf. Article 6 (b), Charter of the International Military Tribunal, London, 8 August 1945. Indeed, the IMT confirmed the indictment by adding that the acts listed in Article 6 (b) of the Charter were "already" recognized as war crimes under international law, for these were covered *inter alia* by Article 46 of the 1907 Hague Regulations (IV).

[74] In order to show the wickedness and the brutality of the *NN* program, the prosecution also presented the cover letter written five days after the enactment of the *NN* Decree, in which Keitel explained the rationale of the *NN* Program: i.e., 'efficient and enduring intimidation can only be achieved either by capital punishment or by measures by which the relatives of the criminals and the population do not know the fate of the criminal.' See Argument of Sir Hartley Shawcross, IMT. *Trial of the Major War Criminals – Proceedings of the IMT* (1948) Vol 19 (14 November 1945-1 October 1946) 478.

[75] IMT. *Trial of the Major War Criminals – Proceedings of the IMT* (1948) Vol 22 (14 November 1945-1 October 1946) 476.

[76] The events that occurred as a result of the *NN* Decree were also considered in the trials of the leading lawyers of the Third Reich for their roles in implementing the *NN* programme before national military tribunals under the aegis of the Allied Control Council governing the occupied German territory. The Allied Control Council assumed 'supreme authority in matters affecting Germany as a whole'. The Council acted as a superstructure of allied government, exercising control over military government in the four zones in which Germany was divided after the end of World War II. Carsten Stahn, *The Law and Practice of International Territorial Administration: Versailles to Iraq and Beyond* (Cambridge University Press 2008) 130.

was to deliberately create constant fear and anxiety amongst the families, friends, and relatives as to the fate of deportees. Thus, cruel punishment was meted out to the families and friends without any charges or claim that they actually did anything in violation of any occupation rule of the army, or any crimes against the Reich.[77]

Thus, the US Tribunal developed a legal assessment of the impact of the uncertainty on the families and society to which the *NN* disappeared persons belonged.[78] The most important inference is that the Nuremberg Tribunals implicitly recognized that keeping families unaware of the fate and whereabouts of their beloved ones was a violation of family rights (i.e., Article 46, 1907 Hague Regulations (IV)).

1.4. The issue of missing persons as part of post-WWII ad hoc arrangements

Although nothing specifically tackled the issue of the missing under earlier IHL treaties, at the end of WWII arrangements were concluded in order to facilitate the exchange of information in post-conflict. For instance,

> a Soviet-Italian communiqué, published on October 20, 1959 disclosed that the Italian Ambassador in Moscow had conducted talks with the Ministry for Foreign Affairs dealing with [...] Italians missing in the USSR since the [WWII]. [...] [T]he parties concurred that, in light of the protracted efforts of the Soviet Red Cross to ascertain the whereabouts of these people and the fact that 14 years had elapsed since the end of the war, the files on them should be closed and the status of their relatives finally regularized. Both countries agreed to maintain contacts in order to obtain information about particular individuals, which would help clarify the legal position of the surviving kin. For its part, the Italian Red Cross Society would co-operate with the Soviet Red Cross Society in providing it with intelligence on Soviet citizens missing as a result of the war who might have wound up in Italy. [Footnotes omitted][79]

---

[77] US Military Tribunals, *The United States of Americas vs Josef Altstötter, et al (the Justice Case), December 4, December 4 1947* (1951) Trials of War Criminals before the Nuremberg Military Tribunals under Control Council Law No. 10, Washington: United States Government Printing Office 1058.

[78] The most innovative aspect in the *Justice Case* lied in the fact that the *NN* program was not only considered a war crime, but also a crime against humanity. With regard to the latter, pursuant to Article 6 (c) of the Charter of the IMT, crimes against humanity include murder, extermination, enslavement, deportation, and other inhumane acts committed against any civilian population, before or during the war; or persecutions on political, racial or religious grounds in execution of or in connection with any crime within the jurisdiction of the Tribunal, whether or not in violation of the domestic law of the country where perpetrated. In this regard, the Tribunal held that '[t]he enforcement and administration of the NN directives resulted in the commission of war crimes and crimes against humanity in violation of the international law of war and international common law relating to recognized human rights. [...]'. The express purpose of the *NN* Decree was to inflict both mental and physical cruelty, for 'the NN victim was held incommunicado and the rest of the population only knew that a relative or citizen had disappeared in the night and fog; hence, the name of the decree. If relatives or friends inquired, they were given no information. If diplomats or lawyers inquired concerning the fate of an NN prisoner, they were told that the state of the record did not admit of any further inquiry or information. The population, relatives, or friends were not informed for what character of offense the victim had been arrested. Thus, they had no guide or standard by which to avoid committing the same offense as the unfortunate victims had committed which necessarily created in their minds terror and dread that a like fate awaited them'. ibid 1057–1058.

[79] George Ginsburgs, *Soviet Citizenship Law*, vol 1 (A W Sijthoff 1968) 256; George Ginsburgs and Robert Melville Slusser, *A Calendar of Soviet Treaties: 1958-1973* (Sijthoff & Noordhoff International Publishers BV 1981) 66.

Similar arrangements, however, were not the rule. For instance, Germany claimed back hundreds of thousands of POW in the USSR and 'pressed for the publication of the names of these people and their whereabouts, the identification of those who had perished and a search for the missing.'[80] However, these appeals remained fruitless.

Two main developments characterized the phase following WWII: a pragmatic normative response to the post-conflict crisis generated by the high number of missing persons at the end of WWII; and a *pro futuro* set of rules on operational efforts to be put in place during armed conflicts in order to trace missing persons (both combatants and civilians) and ensure a better *in bello* handling of information. The latter – the four 1949 Geneva Conventions (GCs I-IV) – intended to bridge the humanitarian *lacunae* characterizing the Spanish civil war[81] and WWII. Although GCs I-IV did not enshrine any specific provisions on missing persons, they, *inter alia,* set down a general framework that would reduce the risk of going missing both for protected persons and for the population of the States involved in the conflict.[82] As for the former, measures to tackle the legal status of persons missing as a result of the events of WWII or other disturbances of peace during the post-conflict years were discussed by States members of the – then newly established – UN.[83] Their efforts resulted in the Convention on the declaration of death of missing persons – an instrument of private international law – aimed at managing the pending legal situations of thousands of families who were waiting for answers as well as the pending status of those unaccounted for. However, the Convention was not meant to address similar consequences arising in future armed conflicts, as it specifically focused on people who went missing[84] between 1939-1945.[85] To date, this remains the sole international treaty that was adopted to address

---

[80] Ginsburgs (n 79) 244.

[81] With the development of new methods and means of warfare, the civilian population and property became a target of military attacks. Thus, from a humanitarian perspective, the Spanish Civil War (1936-1939) was 'a turning point in the international regulation of civil wars in many respects': the atrocities committed encouraged diplomats and military officers to conceptualize what would eventually become Common Article 3 GCs I-IV. La Haye, Eve. *War crimes in Internal Armed Conflicts.* Cambridge: Cambridge University Press, 2008, 38 in Gary D Solis, *The Law of Armed Conflict: International Humanitarian Law in War* (Cambridge University Press 2010) 79.

[82] See sub-section 1.2 in Chapter II.

[83] UNGA, 'Resolution 369 (IV) "Draft Convention on the Declaration of Death of Missing Persons"' (1949) UN Doc A/1251 paras 1, 3.

[84] The scope *ratione personae* of the Convention was defined in Article 1 of the Convention on the Declaration of Death of Missing Persons
1. The present Convention provides for declarations of death of persons whose last residence was in Europe, Asia or Africa who have disappeared in the years 1939-1945, under circumstances affording reasonable ground to infer that they have died in consequence of events of war or of racial, religious, political or national persecution. [...]
2. Contracting States may, by notification 10 the Secretary-General of the United Nations, extend its application to persons having disappeared subsequently to 1945 under similar circumstances. [...]

[85] The Convention was not intended to produce its effects for more than five years, since its adoption. For this reason, it was supposed to cease to have effect on 23 January 1957. However, its duration was extended as a result of the adoption of the Protocols of 16 January 1957 and 15 January 1967 and remained in force until 24 January 1972. See sub-section 1.1.3.1 in Chapter V.

pragmatic problems arising after the termination of an armed conflict where thousands of persons were reported missing.

Furthermore, in the years following the end of WWII, records and information on State-led policies as well as on persons on the move were gathered and preserved by the International Tracing Service (ITS), operating under the aegis of an International Commission and the ICRC.[86] The ITS' mandate was humanitarian driven, as the records contained therein were solely accessible to families of the victims who were pursuing deportation proceedings against ex-Nazis guilty of war crimes.[87] The Service had to trace missing persons and collect, classify, preserve the documents relating to persons "interned" in the National-Socialist concentration camps or displaced because of WWII;[88] accountability issues were not in the remit of the work of the ITS, as other bodies were expressly established to deal with them. Over the years, the ITS' mandate had to face operational constraints (e.g., information provided was limited; the families' requests were slowly processed) and political pressure that resulted into the eventual opening of the archives to the public in 2006.[89]

2. 1977 *ET L'OCCASION PERDUE:*
THE POLITICS OF MISSING PERSONS IN IHL CODIFICATION

Post-conflict responses to requests for information on the missing did not come from international legal texts even in successive conflicts.[90] In order to rectify violations of the obligation to report on the situation of POW and/or arrange for the joint search for missing victims and POW, States have concluded agreements, once conflicts were settled. For instance, the US-Vietnam Agreement of October 1992 on the opening of Vietnamese military archives facilitated access to government archives and unveiled the fate of some of the US

---

[86] As explained by Waltzer, 'in 1947, the International Relief Organization took over a Central Tracing Bureau that had operated at Supreme Headquarters Allied Expeditionary Force ("SHAEF") since 1944.' The International Relief Organization established the International Tracing Service which operated long after the end of the conflict under the aegis of the ICRC and of an international commission comprised of eleven member nations, including Belgium, Britain, France, Germany, Greece, Israel, Italy, Luxembourg, the Netherlands, Poland, and the United States. Kenneth Waltzer, 'Opening the Red Cross International Tracing Service Archive' (2008) 26 The John Marshall Journal of Information Technology and Privacy Law 161, 162–163.

[87] Neither historians nor foreign investigators could have access to the records. Such constraints were maintained until 2006, when the Bonn agreement that regulated the accessibility and the management of the ITS was amended with the unanimous consent of all the States members of the International Commission. Ibid 164.

[88] Ibid 162 (see n 2).

[89] Since the early 1990s the ITS had been put under pressure to open the archives to the wider public; such a request became a reality in 2006 with the amendment of the Bonn Agreement, i.e., the legal basis of the ITS. See ibid 165.

[90] Provisions concerning the collection and transmission of information on the Prisoners of War (POW) were severely violated during the Korean War, the border conflict between India and China in 1962, and the Vietnam War. Horst Fischer, 'Protection of Prisoners of War' in Dieter Fleck and Michael Bothe (eds), *The Handbook of International Humanitarian Law* (Oxford University Press 2008) 388.

missing soldiers in the Vietnam War.[91] This conflict, in particular, shed light on the downside of the then existing international normative framework;[92] indeed, according to the UK Manual of the Law of Armed Conflict, the right of families to know the fate of their relatives (cf. Article 32 API) 'was prompted by the difficulties experienced by the US in ascertaining the fate of missing American Personnel at the end of the Vietnam Conflict'.[93] The diplomatic efforts at the Red Cross[94] and UN[95] level contributed to codifying its recognition within an international treaty, although limited to the context of IAC.

---

[91] See, ibid.

[92] T. Meron argues that '[AP I] [...], in reaction to the Vietnam war, codified norms for recovering the missing and the dead and disposing of the remains of the dead'. See T Meron, 'Editorial Comment. The Time Has Come for the United States to Ratify Geneva Protocol I' (1994) 88 American Journal of International Law 678, 131 (see n 13).

[93] UK Ministry of Defence, *The Manual of the Law of Armed Conflict* (OUP Oxford 2005) 137 (see n 90).

[94] The 22nd International Conference of Red Cross and Red Crescent, held in Tehran in 1973, took the first step towards the legal acknowledgment of the issue of the missing by approving Resolution (V) on the missing and the dead in armed conflicts. The Conference urged the parties to a conflict to help locate the graves of the dead and to cooperate with the ICRC and with the National Societies in their work of accounting for the missing and the dead. See 22nd International Conference of Red Cross and Red Crescent (Tehran, 1973), Resolution (V) 'The Missing and the Dead in Armed Conflicts' in ICRC, *Handbook of the International Red Cross and Red Crescent Movement* (ICRC 2009) 1143. Resolution (V), instead, recognized that 'one of the tragic consequences of armed conflicts is a lack of information on persons missing, killed or deceased in captivity'. See ibid. By using the expression 'in captivity', the International Red Cross Conference adopted a perspective that was narrower than the one of the United Nations General Assembly (UNGA). This expression, in fact, refers to those who are detained in compliance with the rules of IHL, i.e., civilian internees or POW. As Sassòli, Bouvier and Quintin suggest, '[a] lawfully detained person can therefore not be missing for long, as the detaining authorities are also under an obligation to answer inquiries about protected persons'. See Marco Sassòli, Antoine A Bouvier and Anne Quintin, *How Does Law Protect in War?: Cases, Documents, and Teaching Materials on Contemporary Practice in International Humanitarian Law. Vol. I - Outline of International Humanitarian Law. III (Online Version)* (ICRC 2011) 207.

[95] In 1974 the UNGA Resolution 3220 on *Assistance and Cooperation in accounting for persons who are missing or dead in armed conflicts* reiterated the same recommendation of Resolution (V). In its preamble, Resolution 3220 recognized that 'one of the tragic results of armed conflicts [was] the lack of information on persons – civilians as well as combatants – who are missing or dead'. Thus, it underlined the crosscutting feature of the issue of missing persons: civilians and combatants alike could be affected. Two points of Resolution 3220 deserve particular consideration: first of all, the UNGA considered 'the desire to know the fate of loved ones lost in armed conflicts' as a 'basic human need which should be satisfied to the greatest extent possible';[95] secondly, in one of the operative paragraphs, the Assembly requested the Secretary-General to bring the aforesaid Resolution to the attention of the Diplomatic Conference on the Reaffirmation and Development of IHL applicable in Armed Conflicts (the Diplomatic Conference), which was working on the two Draft Additional Protocols to the four Geneva Conventions of 1949. UNGA, 'Resolution on the Assistance and Cooperation in Accounting for Persons Who Are Missing or Dead in Armed' (1974) UN Doc A/RES/3220 (XXIX) para 5. Among the States that voted for Resolution 3220 were Cyprus and Turkey, two countries that were facing the issue of missing persons as a consequence of the conflict in which they were involved at that time. Greek-Cypriot authorities complained of the occupation of Northern Cyprus carried out by the Turkish Government. The occupation, according to Greek-Cypriot authorities, caused 1600 Greek Cypriots to go missing and 200.000 Greek Cypriots to be displaced. Conversely, the Turkish Cypriots affirmed that the figure of 1600 described the number of persons who went missing during the 1974 Greek coup. Moreover, the Turkish Cypriots reported 800 missing persons as a consequence of the 1974 events. See Zaim M Necatigil, *The Cyprus Question and the Turkish Position in International Law* (Oxford University Press 1993) 136, 137.

While a full section of AP I is dedicated to missing persons and is based on the above-mentioned right of the families to know the fate of their relatives,[96] Additional Protocol II (AP II) – applicable to NIAC – provides for a minimal framework concerning aspects related to unaccompanied children, persons in captivity, and the dead.[97] At the codification level, this represented a setback: the initial draft of AP II provided for the obligation for the parties to the conflict to organize information bureaux to which they had to communicate 'all relevant information on the victims of the conflict who may be in their power'; the system of bureaux – explained in detail in Chapter II – was meant to ensure that the families would be informed, all enquiries concerning victims of the conflict would be replied, and, based on these enquiries, the necessary steps to search for them would be undertaken.[98] Shortly before the adoption of AP II, a considerable resistance to the Protocol became apparent; this may have hampered its adoption and its later ratification.[99] Two aspects appeared to be particularly problematic in order for the entire draft Protocol to be adopted: on the one hand, some delegations did not believe that this draft provided sufficient guarantees for the respect due to national sovereignty and for non-interference with internal affairs; on the other hand, some of the rules seemed to be too detailed to be realistic in situations of NIAC.[100] Although less sophisticated than the system under AP I, draft AP II would have filled a *lacuna* that is still partly present to date; despite advances under IHRL and the claim for the customary character of the duty to account for missing persons and to inform their families, the regulation of the handling of information in NIAC does not provide for the same protection to the families of those reported missing[101] as the one applicable in IAC. Moreover, the

---

The Resolution 3220 was sponsored in the Social, Humanitarian and Cultural Committee of the UN General Assembly (III Committee) by Austria, Bangladesh, Belgium, Costa Rica, Cyprus, Federal Republic of Germany, Honduras, Italy, Nepal, Pakistan, Philippines, Turkey, and the United States. The III Committee adopted the draft resolution with 72 votes to 0, and 27 abstentions. See United Nations, *Yearbook of the United Nations*, vol 28 (United Nations 1974) 644.United Nations.

[96] See Part II Wounded, Sick and Shipwrecked, Section III Missing Persons, AP I.

[97] There exists the possibility for the ICRC to offer its services pursuant to Common Article 3 GC (I-IV).

[98] Cf. Article 34 of the first draft of AP II on 'recording and information'. The provision also stated that 'the transmission of information or the search for the victims shall not be undertaken if they are liable to be prejudicial to the interests of the victims or of their relatives'. Cf. Article 34 (2) AP II. See ICRC, 'Official Records of the Diplomatic Conference on the Reaffirmation and Development of International Humanitarian Law Applicable in Armed Conflicts, Vol I' (1974) 43. The commentary to the Draft Additional Protocol I underscores that the above Article is based on Article 16 GC I, Article 19 GC II, Article 122 GC III and Articles 136, 137 and 138 GC IV. See ICRC, *Draft Additional Protocols to the Geneva Conventions of August 12, 1949. Commentary*. (ICRC 1973) 166.

[99] Sandesh Sivakumaran, *The Law of Non-International Armed Conflict* (Oxford University Press 2012) 208.

[100] Yves Sandoz and others, *Commentary on the Additional Protocols: Of 8 June 1977 to the Geneva Conventions of 12 August 1949* (Martinus Nijhoff Publishers 1987) paras 4412, 4414 at 1335. Before the plenary consultations, but after unofficial ones, the Pakistani delegation produced an abridged version of the initial draft of Protocol II, eventually reduced by half.

[101] See sub-sections 1.2.2 and 2.2.2 in Chapter II. Some delegations regretted the deletion of Article 34, for its adoption would have reminded the High Contracting Parties of the right of families to know the fate of their relatives. The Holy See's delegation, which introduced the amendment on the

arrangements mentioned above show that the parties to the conflict address the issue of missing persons in the aftermath of the conflict, be it NIAC or IAC. What is then the place of the missing and the efforts to account for them within the legal framework applicable post-conflict?

3. THE PLACE OF THE ISSUE OF MISSING PERSONS
IN THE LAW OF (POST-)ARMED CONFLICT

Access to information is paramount for families, the society, and State authorities (including those who operate in the judiciary, law enforcement sector, foreign affairs sector, or archival institutions). Among these three stakeholders, the most vulnerable is the family. Gathering information on fate and whereabouts of missing persons in the aftermath of an armed conflict (IAC or NIAC) is a challenging endeavor: those involved in this task – State authorities, humanitarian organizations, non-state actors – operate in order to address the requests forwarded by the families or associations acting on their behalf and/or by the State authorities of the enemy State. The practice shows that information on missing persons plays several roles in post-conflict and is, therefore, a multifaceted tool. For instance, information on the missing can be a bargaining tool in the peace talks that follow the conflict;[102] a bargaining tool in the hand of

---

right to know in the draft AP I, did not join in the consensus and expressed its hope that it will not be long before this right was reaffirmed in a text which might be worded as follows: '[i]t is the right of families to know the fate of their relatives that will prompt the parties to establish information bureaux in order to gather information and transmit it, if necessary through the intermediary of ICRC or some other impartial humanitarian organ.' See ICRC, 'Official Records of the Diplomatic Conference on the Reaffirmation and Development of International Humanitarian Law Applicable in Armed Conflicts, Vol VII' (1974) para (CDDH/SR.53), 158-159.

[102] For instance, the case of Nepal is significant: the peace process started in 2006 with the Nepal's Comprehensive Peace Agreement and was followed by subsequent agreements. These *inter alia* sought to establish a Truth and Reconciliation Commission and a separate Commission of Investigation on Enforced Disappeared Persons (2006-2015). These bodies are still struggling to become fully operational due to the lack of political will and resources, despite the fact that their mandate will soon expire; the main problem is that those in power fear prosecution should these two bodies be fully enabled to carry out their mandate. See ICTJ, 'Ten Years After Peace, Is Nepal Finally Serious About Finding Its Disappeared?' (29 August 2016) <https://www.ictj.org/news/nepal-disappeared-search> accessed 7 September 2016.ICRC, 'Nepal: Nine Years into the Peace Process, Relatives Still in the Dark about the Fate of Their Missing Members' (3 September 2015) <https://www.icrc.org/en/document/nepal-nine-years-peace-process-relatives-still-dark-about-fate-their-missing-members> accessed 7 September 2016; 'Shadows from the Past' (*The Kathmandu Post*, 3 August 2016) <http://kathmandupost.ekantipur.com/news/2016-08-03/shadows-from-the-past.html> accessed 7 September 2016. Colombia is another example: the recent peace process has tackled the issue of missing and disappeared as well as the possibility of an additional bonus in the form of special treatment before a court for those rebel and military members who would participate in activities aimed at accounting for missing persons, if they are found to have committed crimes during the conflict. See FARC-EP International, 'Joint Communiqué No 62 on Missing Persons' (*FARC-EP International*) <https://farc-epeace.org/index.php/communiques/joint-communiques/item/879-joint-communique-62-on-missing-persons> accessed 7 September 2016; Tihomir Gligorevic, 'Colombia: Government and FARC to Search Together for the Missing' [2015] *Inserbia Network Foundation* <http://inserbia.info/today/2015/10/colombia-government-and-farc-to-search-together-for-the-missing/#> accessed 7 September 2016.

opposite sides[103] with a view to elucidating the fate of their own missing; a tool conducive to the establishment of facts and responsibility whenever violations of IHRL and IHL have been committed and international crimes perpetrated;[104] a societal and individual goal to be achieved in order to move forward;[105] a *medium* that gives access to certain legal rights at the domestic level;[106] the prey of security measures enhanced in order to avoid new outbreaks of violence and/or to control the former enemy.[107]

---

[103] Israeli families seized the Supreme Court in order to prevent the ICRC from visiting Lebanese detainees unless Hezbollah would release information on the Israeli missing persons. See Marco Sassòli, 'Les disparus de guerre: Les règles du droit international et les besoins des familles entre espoir et incertitude' (2003) 15 Frontières 38, 40. The ICRC was initially prevented from having access to two Lebanese militants seized by the Israeli army to be used as bargaining chips in exchange for information about other Israeli soldiers and civilians held by the Hezbollah; access to them would have been possible under the condition of reciprocal visits to those held in captivity by the Hezbollah. Later in 2001, the Israeli Supreme Court ruled that the two Lebanese militants must be allowed to receive visits from ICRC; Chief Justice Aharon Barak stressed that 'the humanitarian considerations outweighed any security concerns'. BBC, 'Israel Court Orders Prisoner Access' (*BBC News*, 23 August 2001) <http://news.bbc.co.uk/2/hi/middle_east/1506129.stm> accessed 7 September 2016. In another case, however, the Supreme Court of Israel validated the continued administrative detention of ten Lebanese nationals held in Israeli prisons for the sole purpose of being used as "bargaining chips" for negotiations with Islamic militia groups believed to be holding, or having information about, Israel Defense Force soldiers missing in action in Lebanon, not for actions for which they are, or may be, held personally responsible. See Supreme Court of Israel, *Anonymous Persons v Minister of Defense* (1997) A.D.A. 10/94 (Supreme Court of Israel). For a critical reading of the case, see Orna Ben Naftali and Sean S Gleichgevitch, 'Missing in Legal Action: Lebanese Hostages in Israel' (2000) 41 Harvard International Law Journal 185.

[104] IACtHR, *Contreras et al v El Salvador, Judgment - Merits, Reparations and Costs* (2011) Series C no. 232 [170].

[105] For instance, the case of Lebanon demonstrates that although 15 years have elapsed since the termination of the armed conflict, governments have failed to open official inquiries into the fates of thousands of those who disappeared. Recently the ICRC has started collecting biological samples from the families of the missing, 'a step that will allow for the extraction of DNA and identification of human remains if and when a national commission is formed by the government.' The Associated Press, 'Red Cross Collecting Samples to ID Missing From Lebanon War' (*NYTimes.com*, 11 July 2016) <http://mobile.nytimes.com> accessed 18 July 2016.

[106] A recent ICRC report on the need of families of missing persons in Sri Lanka shows that 'the majority of the interviewed families reported that they face serious bureaucratic difficulties in the management of family assets registered under the name of the missing person. The fact that Sri Lankan law does not recognize the status of a person as 'Missing', obliges families to obtain a death certificate to carry out basic administrative tasks (e.g. access/close the bank account of the missing person, claim the monthly salary of the missing person deposited by the employer, or reclaim land owned by the missing person)'. See ICRC, 'Living with Uncertainty. Needs of the Families of Missing Persons in Sri Lanka' (2016) iv <https://www.icrc.org/en/document/sri-lanka-families-missing-persons> accessed 2 August 2016.

[107] After the cessation of hostilities between Chechens and Russia, Russia has enacted a legislation limiting the possibility for Chechen families to claim back the bodies of their beloved ones, should these be officially listed among terrorists in Russia; families have also been prevented from attending the funerals and from knowing the whereabouts of the graves. The main reason behind this legislation resides in the preservation of national security. See Sputnik International, 'Court Upholds Ban on Returning Terrorists' Bodies to Relatives -1' (28 June 2007) <https://sputniknews.com/russia/20070628/67977135.html> accessed 7 September 2016; cf. Russian Federation/State Duma, Federal Law on 'Amendments and additions to the Federal Law "on Burial and undertaking"', Draft no 256538-3 (2002), Article 1. Concerns over the possibility of the use of gravesites visits as cover for infiltration were expressed by the US Department of State (DoS) in parallel to the negotiations of

The variety of these connotations and responses to the issue of missing persons reflects the hybridity of the post-conflict phase: it is not war, but it is not peace either; all the former parties to the conflict have to operate together to address pending issues (including that of missing persons) regardless of the result of the conflict; national and international actors might deem it necessary to operate together. From a legal perspective, these situations entail the interplay of different legal orders (e.g., international and domestic) and, in relation to the international one, the relationship between rules belonging to different regimes. In order to address the hybridity of this phase, one of the main proposals is to look at the Law in a holistic manner,[108] i.e., as an 'objective, and partly independent framework for the articulation of rules of behavior regarding conflict termination and peace-making, including the process of transition itself',[109] capable of drawing on multiple spheres of law, including IHRL and IHL.[110] The following sub-sections will revolve around the general tenability of this proposal and its relevance within the purview of this book.

3.1. The post bellum dimension of the international legal framework

The recently revisited approach to *"jus post bellum"* decouples the concept of fair and just peace from 'the historical understanding, which associated fairness with the idea of justice in favor of the party which had fought a just and lawful war'.[111] In other words, 'considerations of fair and just peace must be deemed to apply equally to all parties to a conflict'.[112] This book follows this new approach and takes stock of the traditional one: indeed, the latter focused on the inter-state dimension of the armed conflict and its transition, which appears limited and anachronistic in light of today's increasing internal character of armed conflicts.[113] Its purely philosophical illustration of the tripartite dimension of the law of armed conflict (*ad bellum, in bello, post bellum*) has led many scholars to

---

the text of AP I with regard to the provisions on missing persons and the dead; in its internal correspondence (diplomatic cables) on the matter, the DoS suggested that internal measures might solve the problem of allowing families to know the whereabouts of the gravesites and visit them: e.g., requiring potential visitors to document relationship with deceased, limiting duration of visits, and restricting visits to actual cemeteries. However, in the same correspondence it was emphasized that communist regimes had barred *bona fide* visits by relatives. Cf. US Department of State, 'Law of War Conference: US Proposal for a New Article on Missing and Dead (Electronic Telegram Sent to Various US Embassies) - Declassified Document - Released by Wikileaks' (6 March 1974) para 4.

[108] C Stahn, 'Jus Post Bellum: Mapping the Discipline(s)' in Carsten Stahn and Jann K Kleffner (eds), *Jus Post Bellum: Towards a Law of Transition From Conflict to Peace* (Springer Verlag 2008) 105.

[109] C Stahn, 'The Future of Jus Post Bellum' in Carsten Stahn and Jann K Kleffner (eds), *Jus Post Bellum: Towards a Law of Transition From Conflict to Peace* (Springer Verlag 2008) 232.

[110] C Bell, 'Post-Conflict Accountability and the Reshaping of Human Rights and Humanitarian Law' in Orna Ben-Naftali (ed), *International Humanitarian Law and International Human Rights Law* (Oxford University Press 2011) 361.

[111] ibid 936.

[112] ibid 936.

[113] R Bartels, 'From Jus in Bello to Jus Post Bellum: When Do Non-International Armed Conflicts End?' in Carsten Stahn, Jennifer S Easterday and Jens Iverson (eds), *Jus Post Bellum: Mapping the normative Foundations* (Oxford University Press 2014) 297.

depict the *post bellum* dimension as a moral paradigm.[114] Pursuant to this understanding, a just and lawful war required a just peace.[115]

The most recent approach to *jus post bellum* is, therefore, about reframing the role of international law in post-conflict settings. This requires that *jus post bellum* be transformed from moral paradigm to legal framework beyond the traditional dualist conception of the armed conflict reflected in the division between *jus ad bellum* and *jus in bello*: this partition is narrowly focused on a specific period of time – i.e., from the outbreak of hostilities to conflict termination, neglects the connection of this period with what follows, and disregards the impact that international law has on the restoration of peace.[116]

In order to enhance this new approach, there is a need to get rid of the old understanding, which associated *jus post bellum* with moral considerations such as the righteousness of waging war.[117] The path towards the end-goal – a fair and sustainable peace – must embed objective rules and standards (including international ones) that regulate such path in the interest of those affected by the armed conflict. In this sense, the duo *jus ad bellum/jus in bello* is complemented by a third set of rules and principles that aim at balancing the interests of different stakeholders in the period of transition from conflict to peace.[118] The articulation of a similar framework would also 'identify the legal rules, which ought to be applied by [national] and international actors and clarify specific legal principles, which serve as guidance in making legal policy choices in situations of transition'.[119]

---

[114] Stahn underlines that *jus post bellum* was mostly theorized as a moral paradigm (by quoting 'Justice after war' by Orend and the definition of *jus post bellum* provided by the Stanford Encyclopaedia of Philosophy); he also points out to recent developments in the literature with regard to humanitarian interventions and the concept of moral responsibility to become engaged in the reconstruction (by quoting '"Post" as a justification: International Law and Democracy-building after Iraq' by Korhonen). Carsten Stahn, '"Jus Ad bellum", "Jus in bello"..."Jus Post Bellum"? Rethinking the Conception of the Law of Armed Forces' (2006) 17 European Journal of International Law 921, 931. A tripartite reading of the law of war dates back to Suarez (1621); for a detailed analysis of the historical origins of the tripartite reading (*jus ad bellum, jus in bello, jus post bellum*) of the law of war, see ibid 933–935. Chetail specifies that the notion "*jus post bellum*" was created by de Vittoria in the 16th century and developed by Suarez who emphasized the tripartite concept of *jus ad bellum/jus in bello/jus post bellum* (see *Disputaciones*, XIII, at 1621); Kant, in his *Metaphysics of Morals*, systematized the concept by identifying the right of going to war, the right during war and the right after war. V Chetail, 'Introduction: Post-Conflict Peacebuilding - Ambiguity and Identity' in Vincent Chetail (ed), *Post-conflict Peacebuilding: a Lexicon* (Oxford University Press 2009) 18. For a detailed examination of the foundations see L May, 'Jus Post Bellum, Grotius, and Meionexia' in Carsten Stahn, Jennifer S Easterday and Jens Iverson (eds), *Jus Post Bellum: Mapping the normative Foundations* (Oxford University Press 2014) 15–18; for a short but thought-through appraisal of the *jus post bellum* theories, see Eric De Brabandere, 'The Concept of Jus Post Bellum in International Law: A Normative Critique' in Carsten Stahn, Jennifer S Easterday and Jens Iverson (eds), *Jus Post Bellum: Mapping the normative Foundations* (Oxford University Press 2014).

[115] See, among the main recent philosophical reflections on the issue, Michael Walzer, *Just and Unjust Wars: A Moral Argument With Historical Illustrations* (3rd edn, Basic Books 2000).

[116] Stahn, '"Jus Ad bellum", "Jus in bello"..."Jus Post Bellum"?' (n 114) 926.

[117] ibid 936.

[118] ibid 936–937.

[119] ibid 942.

Based on this paradigm, the restoration of peace does not entail the restoration of the *status quo ante* but should aim to 'remove the causes of violence' and help achieve 'a higher level of human rights protection, accountability and good governance than in the period before the resort to armed force'.[120]

3.2. Jus post bellum: A limited interpretative device?

As noted by one of the detractors of *jus post bellum*, 'the "legal void" in the law regulating the "transition" from war to peace is overstated'.[121] This assertion, however, is not fully valid for the set of rules under international law concerning missing persons (see Chapter II). The legal *lacunae* are, for these scholars, at the level of implementation of international law on the one hand, and at the level of accountability on the other.[122] Therefore, if any legal void is found, certainly adding new rules or naming existing rules *jus post bellum* does not change the situation.[123]

The concept of *jus post bellum* emerges as a multidimensional one; as such it can be understood in a variety of ways. However, there seems to be convergence – at least among a few scholars[124] – with regard to the function that *jus post bellum* may play at this stage of its development, i.e., guiding the interpretation of international rules and policies relevant to the phase of transition from war to peace

---

[120]ibid 936; Bell (n 110) 362.

[121] De Brabandere (n 114) 133. Among others, see also, Antonia Chayes, 'Chapter VII½: Is Jus Post Bellum Possible?' (2013) 24 European Journal of International Law 291; Gregory Lewkowicz, 'Jus Post Bellum: Vieille Antienne Ou Nouvelle Branche Du Droit: Sur Le Mythe de l'Origine Venerable Du Just Post Bellum' (2011) 44 Revue Belge de Droit International / Belgian Review of International Law 11; Olivier Corten, 'Le Jus Post Bellum Remet-il en Cause Les Règles Traditionnelles du Jus Contra Bellum?' (2011) 44 Revue Belge de Droit International / Belgian Review of International Law 38; Eric De Brabandere, *Post-Conflict Administrations in International Law: International Territorial Administration, Transitional Authority, and Foreign Occupation in Theory and Practice* (Martinus Nijhoff Publishers 2009); SC Neff, 'Conflict Termination and Peace-Making in the Law of Nations: A Historical Perspective' in Carsten Stahn and Jann K Kleffner (eds), *Jus Post Bellum: Towards a Law of Transition From Conflict to Peace* (Springer Verlag 2008).

[122] De Brabandere (n 114) 136.

[123] See, for example, Corten (n 121) 68.

[124] See the constitutional perspective put forward by Easterday (arguing that *jus post bellum* is comprised of the laws and norms stemming from current settled bodies of international law as well as developing normative practices of non-state actors and organizations; also arguing that it offers an interpretive framework, a site of coordination, and a site of discourse that can help the transition to a sustainable peace). JS Easterday, 'Peace Agreements as a Framework for Jus Post Bellum' in Carsten Stahn, Jennifer S Easterday and Jens Iverson (eds), *Jus Post Bellum: Mapping the normative Foundations* (Oxford University Press 2014) 412. Gallen addresses the potential for *jus post bellum* to operate as an interpretive framework for international law as applied to societies in transition. J Gallen, 'Jus Post Bellum. An Interpretive Framework' in Carsten Stahn, Jennifer S Easterday and Jens Iverson (eds), *Jus Post Bellum: Mapping the normative Foundations* (Oxford University Press 2014) 59. De Brabandere sees the main relevance and importance of the concept in providing an interpretative framework for the conduct of post-conflict reconstruction. 'This idea of jus post bellum is considered to be important because of the need to interpret uniformly the various norms, rules, and practices applicable in post- conflict reconstruction.' De Brabandere (n 114) 133, 137 ff. See more generally the full work Carsten Stahn, Jennifer S Easterday and Jens Iverson (eds), *Jus Post Bellum: Mapping the Normative Foundations* (Oxford University Press 2014). See also Carsten Stahn, Jens Iverson and Jennifer Easterday, 'Special Issue: Jus Post Bellum and Foreign Investment' (2015) 16 The Journal of World Investment & Trade 583.

so as to foster coherence in addressing the diverse aspects peculiar to this phase. These aspects can be boiled down to three main areas, i.e., policy and legal regulation, the legal merit of the actions of international actors, and the interaction between international actors and the society in transition.[125] Under this perspective, the usefulness of *jus post bellum* as an interpretative framework would be to overcome the main challenge in post-conflict settings, i.e., to improve the effective implementation of international law applicable in such situation.[126]

Various scholars have identified overarching principles[127] that make part of this framework; among these are the principles of accountability, people-centered governance, and proportionality. Apart from the fact that some of these already existed under international law, there is a clear confusion in the approach to such principles: for instance, proportionality is depicted as a general principle of international law or as a means of assessment of the choices made in balancing competing interests in a variety of contingent areas, i.e., as a sort of policy instrument;[128] people-centered governance[129] is indicated at least in four

---

[125] For Gallen, these are the areas of complexity that can be evaluated under the broader framework of *jus post bellum* read through the prism of the Dworkin's conception of law as integrity; according to this conception, legal claims are interpretative judgments and, therefore, combine backward-looking and forward-looking elements. As such, they interpret contemporary legal practice seen as an unfolding political narrative. See Gallen (n 124) 70. Easterday focuses on *jus post bellum* as a site of coordination, which involves harmonization of multiple efforts in post-conflict, balancing the needs of the post-conflict State with the interests of foreign organizations that provide assistance/funding. Peace agreements are considered a valuable framework for this broad concept of *jus post bellum*, since these can set agendas for the future, mitigate tensions among parties to the conflict, create new institutions, bring international law into the domestic sphere, and offer a framework of coordination and discourse in the post-conflict society. Thus, peace agreements are the source of norms for *jus post bellum* intended as a framework. Easterday (n 124) 412-413.

[126] De Brabandere (n 114) 137.

[127] Stahn mentions the demise of the concept of punishment for aggression, fairness and inclusiveness of peace settlement, humanization of reparations and sanctions, the move towards an individualized notion of responsibility, a combined justice and reconciliation model, and people-centred governance. Stahn, '"Jus Ad bellum", "Jus in bello"..."Jus Post Bellum"?' (n 114) 938-941. Orend, who examines *jus post bellum* from a philosophical perspective, lists the following: just cause, right intention, public declaration and legitimate authority, discrimination, and proportionality. See Brian Orend, *War and International Justice: A Kantian Perspective* (Wilfrid Laurier Univ Press 2006) 232–233. De Brabandere lists the following: accountability, proportionality, and the principle that post-conflict reconstruction efforts should be for the benefit of the population. De Brabandere (n 114) 137–138. Gallen mentions accountability, stewardship, and proportionality. Gallen (n 124) 72-79. Gallen and De Brabandere, however, present a minimalist version of *jus post bellum* compared to Stahn's understanding.

[128] De Brabandere (n 114) 137-138; Gallen (n 124) 77-78.

[129] Stahn refers to people-centred governance in order to highlight the move of peacemaking towards the local sovereignty. Stahn, '"Jus Ad bellum", "Jus in bello"..."Jus Post Bellum"?' (n 114) 938–941. De Brabandere puts forward a periphrasis, i.e., 'the principle that post-conflict reconstruction efforts should be for the benefit of the population'; Gallen puts forward the notion of 'stewardship', i.e., the principle that responds to the need for a neutral account of the legal content and status of international assistance to *post bellum* States as well as to the need for international actors to respect local ownership. See De Brabandere (n 114) 138; Gallen (n 124) 75. Boon refers to 'trusteeship', i.e., a notion related to situations where persons or entities are incapable of functioning on their own (e.g., occupations, UN trusteeship mandates system). Kristen Boon, 'Legislative Reform in Post-Conflict Zones: Jus Post Bellum and the Contemporary Occupant's Law-Making Powers' (2005) 50 McGill Law Journal/Revue de Droit de McGill 285, 294.

different ways with slightly different meanings. It is therefore hard to consider *jus post bellum* as a holistic normative framework that would guide the interpretation of rules in this phase. Indeed, the scholars who have initiated this new reading of *jus post bellum* identify the lack of consensus on its tenets among the key weaknesses of their proposal.[130]

3.3. The place of 'jus post bellum' in this study

As professor Stahn points out in his reflections upon the relevance of *jus post bellum*

> there is a considerable degree of uncertainty about the applicable law, the interplay of different structural frameworks as well as the possible space for interaction between different legal orders and bodies of law (international law v. domestic law, human rights law v. law of occupation etc.) in a post-conflict environment.[131]

Thus, the criticism against *jus post bellum* does not address or propose solutions vis-à-vis what Stahn emphasizes; the legal uncertainty highlighted by Stahn is not just an academic problem, but also a pragmatic reality with tangible consequences on the ground. The reason that leads to stress the relevance of the terminology '*jus post bellum*' is both descriptive and normative and is related to the motives behind this book. First, the use of the term *jus post bellum* can facilitate a contextualized interpretation and application of existing norms so that the specificities proper to the transition from conflict to peace are taken into consideration;[132] this might ultimately confirm the important impact that international law can have on the efforts for the establishment of an enduring peace. Second, the term *jus post bellum* is powerful enough to enable us to illustrate international law and policies applicable in post-conflict in a uniform and coherent fashion. Third, this illustration is meaningful if connected to a clear-cut purpose, i.e., the clarification of how international law in post-conflict meets the needs of different constituencies (in our case, the families of persons reported missing and their communities at large).

The understanding of *jus post bellum* outlined above explains the motivations behind the choice of not considering Transitional Justice (TJ) as the framework that guides this book's approach to international law in post-conflict.[133] Teitel

---

[130] J Iverson, JS Easterday and C Stahn, 'Epilogue: Jus Post Bellum - Strategic Analysis and Future Directions' in Carsten Stahn, Jennifer S Easterday and Jens Iverson (eds), *Jus Post Bellum: Mapping the normative Foundations* (Oxford University Press 2014) 546 ff.

[131] Stahn, '"Jus Ad bellum", "Jus in bello"..."Jus Post Bellum"?' (n 114) 941.

[132] Chetail (n 114) 18.

[133] The aim here is not to restate what scholars and practitioners have stated about TJ, but to set down the contours of the framework within which law and policy factors operate against the subject matter. For a detailed analysis of TJ, the evolution of the concept, and TJ in practice I refer to their work. For instance Ruti Teitel, *Transitional Justice* (Oxford University Press 2002); Ruti Teitel, 'Transitional Justice Genealogy' (2003) 16 Harvard Human Rights Journal 69; Mark Freeman and Drazan Djukić, 'Jus Post Bellum and Transitional Justice' in Carsten Stahn and Jann K Kleffner (eds), *Jus Post Bellum: Towards a Law of Transition From Conflict to Peace* (Springer Verlag 2008); AM La Rosa and X Philippe, 'Transitional Justice' in Vincent Chetail (ed), *Post-conflict Peacebuilding: a Lexicon* (Oxford University Press 2009); Pablo de Greiff, 'Theorizing Transitional Justice' (2012) 51 Nomos 31. For an historical account, see Paige Arthur, 'How "Transitions" Reshaped Human Rights: A Conceptual

stresses that the expression *"post bellum"* is 'too limited or inappropriate today because of the unstable or undetermined boundaries between conflict and post-conflict situations'; in this sense, TJ seems to be 'more capacious because it allows for purposes beyond those associated with a war's beginning, such as transformation, namely purposes going beyond retributive or restorative justice.'[134] TJ, traditionally understood as a 'conception of justice associated with periods of political change, characterized by legal responses to confront the wrongdoings of repressive predecessor regimes',[135] can coexist with *jus post bellum* or be successive to it according to some scholars.[136] As noted by others, the set of principles behind *jus post bellum* and TJ differ and, at some point, overlap.[137] For those authors who look at *jus post bellum*/TJ from a teleological perspective, the main difference consists in their relationship with the duo war/peace: pursuant to the traditional understanding of TJ, a violent past and major political changes in the transitional phase are key factors in order for TJ to be relevant.[138] Thus, while *jus post bellum* looks at peace as the main end-goal, TJ proponents have considered military intervention as an option for the achievement of a more democratic order.[139]

History of Transitional Justice' (2009) 31 Human Rights Quarterly 321; Pierre Hazan, *Judging War, Judging History. Behind Truth and Reconciliation* (Stanford University Press 2010) 13-62.

[134] Ruti Teitel, 'Rethinking Jus Post Bellum in an Age of Global Transitional Justice' [2013] European Journal of International Law 335, 339.

[135] Teitel, 'Transitional Justice Genealogy' (n 133) 69; Teitel, *Transitional Justice* (n 133) 3. A diverse range of definitions exists; without the pretention of being comprehensive, this study adopts the one that depicts TJ as a discipline with a defined focus. See, among others, the definition proposed by the ICTJ, 'What Is Transitional Justice? | ICTJ' (*International Center for Transitional Justice*, 2011) <https://www.ictj.org/about/transitional-justice> accessed 11 September 2016; UNSG, 'Report on the Rule of Law and Transitional Justice in Conflict and Post-Conflict Societies' (2004) UN Doc S/2004/616 para 8.

[136] MU Walker, 'Post-Conflict Truth Telling' in Larry May and Andrew Forcehimes (eds), *Morality, Jus Post Bellum, and International Law* (Cambridge University Press 2012) 11–12. More generally, see the collective book dedicated to the *jus post bellum* and TJ: Larry May and Elizabeth Edenberg (eds), *Jus Post Bellum and Transitional Justice* (Cambridge University Press 2013).

[137] Jus post bellum's key principles are retribution, reconciliation, rebuilding, restitution, reparations, and proportionality; the TJ's key principles are the rule of law, democracy, truth, forgiveness, and punishment. L May and E Edenberg, 'Introduction' in Larry May and Elizabeth Edenberg (eds), *Jus Post Bellum and Transitional Justice* (Cambridge University Press 2013) 2–12.

[138] La Rosa and Philippe (n 133) 370. The UN Special Rapporteur on the promotion of truth, justice, reparation and guarantees of non-recurrence (hereinafter UN Special Rapporteur on the promotion of truth) affirms that 'even a cursory review of the development of the paradigm of [TJ] over the past 30 years suggests that it emerged from the experiences of a set of countries – in the Southern Cone of Latin America, to a lesser extent from those in Central and Eastern Europe, and then in South Africa – that shared many characteristics. [...] The human rights violations committed in these States were the result of the brutal exercise of State power [...]. These States were emerging from authoritarianism. Their conflicts were not civil wars, conventional or unconventional [...]. The violations were the result of the abusive exercise of a tremendously asymmetric State power.' According to him, these States shared 'a type of transition that may be characterized as "regime failure"'. UN Human Rights Council, 'Report of the Special Rapporteur on the Promotion of Truth, Justice, Reparation and Guarantees of Non-Recurrence (Advanced Edited Version)' (2017) UN Doc A/HRC/36/50 paras 34, 37-38.

[139] For instance, Teitel argues that TJ should enshrine the idea of humanitarian war rather than the achievement of peace at any cost. See Teitel's remarks at a conference on *jus post bellum* sponsored by the *Grotius Center* in the Hague, 1 June 2012 in May and Edenberg (n 137) 14.

I. The Emergence of a Duty to Account for Missing Persons

From the practitioners' standpoint, TJ refers to 'the set of judicial and non-judicial measures that have been implemented by different countries in order to redress the legacies of massive human rights abuses'.[140] In practice, TJ is a toolbox that incorporates four instruments, i.e., criminal prosecutions, reparations, institutional reform, and truth commissions.[141] Two are its driving principles, i.e., accountability[142] and redress; in this respect its emphasis is on responding to human rights violations in order to achieve justice in times of transition from conflict/past regime[143] as well as on unveiling the truth about past violations. TJ's[144] overall objective revolves around the notion of accountability within the narrative of the fight against impunity.[145] However, accountability for past crimes cannot be framed as a component of a compulsory and previously established framework or as a blueprint to be applied in different context in a similar manner.[146] In other words, the fight against impunity for past crimes is a void slogan, if it is disconnected from the individuals and communities directly affected. Expectations in the contexts affected by the conflict – e.g., accountability for past crimes committed – are best addressed if local culture and legal tradition are taken into account.[147]

---

[140] ICTJ (n 135).

[141] See ICTJ, 'The Elements of a comprehensive TJ policy' in ibid. La Rosa and Philippe consider that these are not the instruments, but the main goals of TJ. La Rosa and Philippe (n 133) 371. Freeman argues that case of *Velásquez Rodríguez* (IACtHR) enshrines the core of this toolbox: pursuant to the IACtHR's pronouncements, States have four obligations, i.e., take reasonable steps to prevent human rights violations; conduct a serious investigation of violations when they occur; impose an appropriate punishment on those responsible for the violations; ensure reparations for the victims of the violations. *Velásquez-Rodríguez v Honduras, Judgment - Merits* (1988) Series C No. 4 (IACtHR) in Freeman and Djukić (n 133) 218.

[142] According to legal theorists, the principle of accountability in *jus post bellum* terms is connected to a retributive notion of punishment, i.e., bringing to account those who committed wrongs by, for instance, waging war unjustly; under a TJ paradigm, the same principle is associated with a distributive understanding of punishment, i.e., distribute the guilt among all those who played a role in it. See May and Edenberg (n 137) 3, 10, 12.

[143] Jens Iverson, 'Transitional Justice, Jus Post Bellum and International Criminal Law: Differentiating the Usages, History and Dynamics' (2013) 7 International Journal of Transitional Justice 413, 422; J Iverson, 'Contrasting the Normative and Historical Foundations of Transitional Justice and Jus Post Bellum' in Carsten Stahn, Jennifer S Easterday and Jens Iverson (eds), *Jus Post Bellum: Mapping the normative Foundations* (Oxford University Press 2014) 85; Freeman and Djukić (n 133) 227; ICTJ (n 135).

[144] Turgis states that 'the risk of broadening the meaning of the concept is to dilute it and turning it into something meaningless.' Noémie Turgis, 'What Is Transitional Justice?' (2010) 1 International Journal of Law, Transitional Justice and Human Rights 9, 14.

[145] Truth-finding, truth-telling, reparations, reconciliation can also be part of the transitional process. De Brabandere (n 114) 135.

[146] Stahn emphasizes that among the factors to be taken into account for each context are the nature of 'the underlying conflict, the commitment of parties to the peace process, the need and degree of protection for particular groups (minorities, displaced persons, abducted children), the potential for public and victim consultation, and the condition of the country's legal and political system, in general'. Carsten Stahn, 'The Geometry of Transitional Justice: Choices of Institutional Design' (2005) 18 Leiden Journal of International Law 425, 426–427. The UN Special Rapporteur on the promotion of truth stresses that TJ is not 'a "universal policy tool" that works equally well in all contexts. [...] The early successes of [TJ] depended on the close fit between problem and remedy, between context and solution, something that is less apparent in some more recent [TJ] efforts.' UN Human Rights Council (n 138) para 33.

[147] De Brabandere (n 114) 135.

TJ has never really aspired to become the framework of reference which covers all the aspects that might arise in the transition from an armed conflict to peace. It is here that resides the main motive for considering *jus post bellum* more apt to capture the diversity of these aspects that include areas of international law and policy relevant to furthering the efforts towards peace.[148] These aspects are all beyond the core of TJ.[149] Thus, unveiling the truth about past violations and achieving justice are objectives that must be read within – and not in contrast to – the broader spectrum of *jus post bellum*.[150]

CONCLUSIONS

In the history of warfare, the measures aimed at accounting for certain categories of persons during and in the aftermath of an armed conflict responded to two main needs, i.e., the need to ensure the transmission of information among the parties to the conflict and the need of the State's army to track down its missing in action. These needs shaped post-conflict efforts to address the issue of missing persons. With the Nuremberg trials, it became clear that keeping families unaware of the fate and whereabouts of their beloved ones was a violation of the customary duty to respect family rights under the 1907 Hague Conventions; the human need of families to know could no longer be disregarded or deemed secondary. At the same time, where State authorities had to deal with the pressing issue of missing in action and/or other missing persons as a result of the events occurred in WWII, *ad hoc* arrangements were made years after the termination of the conflict. Despite the advances concerning the civilian population and its protection under GC IV, the missed opportunity of 1977 with the deletion of the issue of missing persons in the draft AP II sheds light upon the level of politicization of the issue. It also highlights the need to assess the alternative manners found by the parties to the conflict and other actors to solve the issue of the missing during and in the aftermath of a NIAC.[151] Chapter II will show that, although the "post-" is vaguely addressed under contemporary IHL treaties, this branch of international law is residually applicable in post-conflict settings; it will also examine whether the vagueness of the treaties leaves a broad leeway to the (former) parties to the conflict in the handling of information on missing persons in the phase comprised between conflict and peace.

---

[148] In one of his recent reports, the UN Special Rapporteur on the promotion of truth has questioned whether 'the same model of [TJ] forged in post-authoritarian transitions can be applied to post-conflict transitions without modification'; indeed, in the latter, there exists 'a scandalous gap in redress for violations of rights'. See UN Human Rights Council (n 138) para 29.

[149] Gallen (n 124) 59.

[150] Walker stresses that a truth recovery process can importantly contribute to the establishment and stability of long-term peace insofar as truth commissions can help create societal conditions conducive to respecting human rights; as such truth recovery and public truth telling are seen as part of the efforts to seek justice post-conflict. See Urban Walker (n 136) 11–13; M Urban Walker, 'Nunca Más: Truth Commissions, Prevention, and Human Rights Culture' in Larry May and Elizabeth Edenberg (eds), *Jus Post Bellum and Transitional Justice* (Cambridge University Press 2013) 262–284.

[151] See sub-section 1.2.2 in Chapter II.

The hybridity[152] of this phase is determined by the situation on the ground as well as by multiple regimes (e.g., IHL and IHRL) and legal orders (e.g., international and domestic) that interact. Thus, there is a need to address effectively this hybridity in order to (re-)conceive the role that international law can play in this phase in a more coherent and uniform fashion. Such a re-conceptualization will facilitate a contextualized interpretation and application of existing norms so that the specificities peculiar to the transition phase are taken into consideration, specifically when they impact on the issue of missing persons.[153] It will also facilitate the examination of international law and policies applicable in post-conflict in a uniform and coherent manner; and ultimately, it will help clarify how international law in post-conflict meets the needs of different constituencies (in our case, the families of persons reported missing and their communities at large).

The issue of missing persons makes part of the pending consequences to be addressed in the context of peace processes; however, it is not systematically included in the design, establishment, and implementation of such processes.[154] The common aim of these processes (see section 1 in Chapter V), which are a mix of legal and policy measures, is to establish an enduring peace. The term 'post-conflict peacebuilding' is used to indicate the 'range of measures targeted to reduce the risk of lapsing or relapsing into conflict by strengthening national capacities at all levels for conflict management, and to lay the foundations for sustainable peace and development'.[155] In order to lay such foundations, it is, therefore, paramount to capture the diversity of the relevant international rules, organize their relationship[156] in case of sequential or simultaneous application, and define their interplay with policy tools that emerge in this phase.[157]

---

[152] Hybridity is not a legal term, but perfectly describes what are the difficulties in the immediate aftermath of a conflict: the situation on the ground is stuck between war and peace; former parties to the conflict need to operate together to address pending issues, including the issue of missing persons; national and international actors might find necessary to operate together.

[153] Chetail (n 114) 18.

[154] UNGA, 'Resolution 63/183 - Missing Persons' (2009) UN Doc. A/RES/63/183 para 11 (stressing 'the need for addressing the issue of missing persons as a part of peacebuilding processes'); similarly, see UNSG, 'Report of the Secretary General - Missing Persons' (2009) UN Doc A/HRC/10/28 para 41. See also ICMP, 'A Cornerstone of Peacebuilding – Addressing the Issue of Missing and Disappeared Persons' (28 January 2016) <http://www.icmp.int/?story=a-cornerstone-of-peacebuilding-addressing-the-issue-of-missing-and-disappeared-persons;> accessed 10 June 2016.

[155] See section 1 in Chapter V for an examination of the conceptual origins and of its operationalization. See also UN Peacebuilding Support Office, 'UN Peacebuilding: An Orientation' (2010) 6 <http://www.un.org/en/peacebuilding/pbso/pdf/peacebuilding_orientation.pdf> accessed 12 July 2016. The literature proposes various approaches to peacebuilding: e.g., maximalist (a range of measures addressing the root causes of armed conflict); minimalist (measures that help avoid a renewed armed conflict); middle ground (measures that seek to avoid a renewed armed conflict and, at the same time, intend to enhance a decent governance). For a review of the plethora of definitions and approaches to peacebuilding, see Chetail (n 114) 4–7.

[156] Stahn, 'The Future of Jus Post Bellum' (n 109) 234; Chetail (n 114) 17 ff.

[157] Stahn, 'The Future of Jus Post Bellum' (n 109) 234.

CHAPTER II.

BEFORE, DURING, AND AFTER THE CONFLICT:
THE CROSSCUTTING NATURE OF THE DUTY TO ACCOUNT
FOR MISSING PERSONS UNDER INTERNATIONAL LAW

The legal framework regulating the handling of information (i.e., collection and record of/transmission of/and access to information) on specific categories of persons is the result of a *labor limae* that started with the negotiation of the first Geneva Convention in the 19th century. This progressive cognizance of the importance to avoid that people go missing in armed conflicts has led to broaden the scope of the categories of persons covered by the system regulating the handling of information under IHL; it has also resulted into the integration of humanitarian considerations vis-à-vis "the family",[1] i.e., the most basic social unit, in contemporary[2] IHL treaties.[3] In order for this legal framework to be effective, preliminary steps undertaken in peacetime can reduce the likelihood that people go missing during the conflict. Similarly, measures that follow the termination of an armed conflict can contribute to elucidating the whereabouts and the fate of those persons who are reported missing. This Chapter intends to explore whether the interrelation among the three phases − before, during, and after − of an armed conflict is indicative of temporal and substantive extended boundaries of IHL rules on the missing. To this end, the Chapter will proceed in two steps: first, it will define to what − substantive and temporal − extent IHL regulates the handling of information on missing persons (sections 1 and 2); this examination will highlight the implications of the continuing application of a set of IHL rules for the post-conflict conduct of (former) parties to the conflict. Second, it will examine the protective framework of the right of family members to know the fate and whereabouts of their missing relatives under IHRL (sections 3), including the viability of limitations of the access of families to information on their relatives (section 4).

---

[1] As Đurović observes, in the GCs I-IV, the general principle of the right to know was not as explicit as it is in AP I. Gradimir Đurović, 'L'Agence centrale de recherches du Comité international de la Croix-rouge: activité du CICR en vue du soulagement des souffrances morales des victimes de guerre' (University of Geneva - Institut Henry Dunant 1981) 272.

[2] In this book the term 'contemporary' IHL refers to post-1949 IHL treaties.

[3] In this book the term 'IHL' indicates those 'international rules, established by treaties or custom, which are specifically intended to solve humanitarian problems directly arising from international or non-international armed conflicts and which, for humanitarian reasons, limit the right of Parties to a conflict to use the methods and means of warfare of their choice or protect persons and property that are, or may be, affected by conflict.' See Yves Sandoz and others, *Commentary on the Additional Protocols: Of 8 June 1977 to the Geneva Conventions of 12 August 1949* (Martinus Nijhoff Publishers 1987) xxvii.

1. MISSING PERSONS AND THE RIGHT OF FAMILIES TO KNOW UNDER IHL

While it is traditionally accepted that IHRL enshrines both rights and obligations, IHL is perceived as the branch of international law that is meant to reduce the effects of armed conflicts. In light of the focus of this book, these assertions need to be re-considered, as it is an IHL treaty that, for the first time in the history of international law, has set down the right of families to know the fate of their relatives (sub-section 1.1). The exploration of the legal framework concerning preventive and reactive measures to be undertaken vis-à-vis the issue of missing persons will follow these theoretical considerations (sub-section 1.2).

1.1. Obligations and entitlements under IHL: Theoretical clarifications

In the literature, IHL has been depicted as the branch of international law that 'indicates how a party to a conflict is to behave in relation to people at its mercy, whereas IHRL concentrates on the rights of the recipients of a certain treatment'.[4] By the same token, others have stressed that IHL is about obligations, while IHRL is about individual entitlements;[5] this dichotomy has often been used as an argument to refute the complementarity between the two branches.[6] These assumptions are legally untenable for a series of reasons: first, the fact that under IHL there is no international procedure enabling individuals to enforce their claims as well as no obligation providing individuals with procedures to enforce these guarantees at the domestic level[7] does not imply that IHL does not bestow upon individuals legal entitlements;[8] second, IHRL embeds both entitlements and obligations;[9] third, the formula according to which IHL is about obligations of the parties to an armed conflict, whereas IHRL is about individual rights is simplistic and does not reflect the complexity of both regimes;[10] fourth, the history of IHL is

---

[4] Louise Doswald-Beck and Sylvain Vité, 'International Humanitarian Law and Human Rights Law' (1993) 33 International Review of the Red Cross (1961 - 1997) 94, 101.

[5] René Provost, *International Human Rights and Humanitarian Law* (Cambridge University Press 2004) 13. Meyrowitz stressed that the main difference between the law of war and IHRL laid in the fact that while the former is driven by what is considered the essence of the war, i.e., the clash between two States, the latter tackled the relationship between the citizens and their own State. Apart from his appraisal of the relationship between IHL and IHRL ("antinomie intrinsèque"), he emphasized that the GCs I-IV provided for two categories of rights, i.e., human rights and the rights of the enemy citizen. See H Meyrowitz, 'Droit de Guerre et Droits de L'homme' [1972] Revue du Droit Public et de la Science Politique en France et à l'étranger 1059, 1100.

[6] Dominic McGoldrick, 'Human Rights and Humanitarian Law in the UK Courts' (2007) 40 Israel Law Review 527, 533. Both authors are quoted in Gerd Oberleitner, *Human Rights in Armed Conflict: Law, Practice, Policy* (Cambridge University Press 2015) n 2, 176.

[7] Walter Kälin and Jörg Künzli, *The Law of International Human Rights Protection* (Oxford University Press 2009) 164; Provost (n 5) 16.

[8] Cf. Articles 6/6/6/7 and 7/7/7/8 GCs I-IV which are aimed at preventing the renunciation of individual rights of protected persons; respect for family rights must be guaranteed under Article 27 GC IV; pursuant to Article 32 of AP I, families have the right to know the fate of their relatives.

[9] Frédéric Mégret, 'Nature of Obligations' in Sangeeta Shah and others (eds), *International Human Rights Law* (Oxford University Press 2010) 127 ff.

[10] Oberleitner (n 6) 177.

also about broadening the scope of protected persons and providing more specific protection to the most vulnerable ones.[11]

From a mere wording perspective, 'a plethora of IHL treaty provisions employ terms explicitly recognizing individual persons' rights, such as "rights", "entitlement" or "benefit"'.[12] From a substantive standpoint, the thrust of both the GCs of 1949 and the APs is 'to go beyond the interstate level and to reach for the level of the real (or ultimate) beneficiaries of humanitarian protection, i.e. individuals and groups of individuals'.[13] This is confirmed by the fact that the inspiration of some provisions of AP I can be traced back to IHRL.[14] The co-presence of two normative paradigms within certain IHL provisions seems to be confirmed by the fact that

> [...] the laws of war, like the laws of peace, also prescribe rights and duties assumed directly by individual human beings. In all the branches of the laws or warfare [...] the account is on State rights and duties. But in all branches of the laws of warfare, without distinction there is a segment, which creates human rights and human duties.[15]

That the rules of IHL do not confer rights on private individuals or private actors, but simply regulate the conduct of belligerents is therefore no longer acceptable: this construct could have been propounded in the past, at a time when individuals had no status at all in international law.[16] Individuals are no longer 'objects' of rights accruing only to States, but are also considered to enjoy rights themselves vis-à-vis States under international law. As a corollary, it would be legally untenable to affirm that in situations of armed conflict, when individuals are more vulnerable than ever, the position of individuals as rights-holder dissolves.[17]

---

[11] ibid 184.

[12] Yutaka Arai, *The Law of Occupation: Continuity and Change of International Humanitarian Law, and Its Interaction With International Human Rights Law* (Martinus Nijhoff Publishers 2009) 263. The author, for instance, gives the following examples: Article 4, AP II; Article 78, GC III; Article 30, GC IV. See ibid.

[13] Georges Abi-Saab, 'The Specificities of Humanitarian Law' in Christophe Swinarski (ed), *Studies and Essays on International Humanitarian Law and Red Cross Principles in Honour of Jean Pictet* (Martinus Nijhoff Publishers 1984) 269.

[14] For instance, the paragraphs providing for the due process guarantees in Article 75 of AP I are drawn from Article 14 of the International Covenant on Civil and Political Rights. Provost (n 5) 32.

[15] Yoram Dinstein, 'The International Law of Inter-State Wars and Human Rights' (1977) 7 Israel Yearbook of Human Rights 392–393. Meron observes that the concern for human rights was nonetheless in the air at the time of the adoption of the four GCs, as it is evidenced by a French proposal for a preamble to the draft convention at the Red Cross International Conference in 1948: *[t]he High Contracting Parties, conscious of their obligation to come to an agreement in order to protect civilian populations from the horrors of War, undertake to respect the principles of human rights which constitute the safeguard of civilization...* [emphasis added]. In Jean S Pictet (ed), *The Geneva Conventions of 12 August 1949: Commentary*, vol I (ICRC 1952) 12, reproduced in Theodor Meron, 'The Humanization of Humanitarian Law' (2000) 94 American Journal of International Law 239, 245.

[16] P Gaeta, 'Are Victims of Serious Violations of International Humanitarian Law Entitled to Compensation?' in Orna Ben-Naftali (ed), *International Humanitarian Law and International Human Rights Law* (Oxford University Press 2011) 318–319.

[17] ibid 319. Gaeta also emphasizes that at the domestic level, national courts have not found it difficult to state that individuals possess rights under IHL; what they have found difficult is to recognize that individuals have a 'right to present a claim towards the State responsible for the violations

In terms of obligations, under 'traditional international law' the manner in which an obligation is supposed to be discharged is not specified and, consequently, States enjoy a certain leeway vis-à-vis the choice of means by which they do what they commit themselves to do.[18] This debatable viewpoint is not practicable under IHRL: States are to 'respect and ensure rights to all individuals' (cf. Article 2 ICCPR).

The charting of obligations and entitlements concerning the handling of information starts from the premise above. Although the rationale behind each branch of international law is different,[19] IHL and IHRL share a common concern over the protection of persons from those in power.

1.2. The handling of information on missing persons in armed conflict

Contemporary IHL treaties applicable in IAC provide for measures that, if put into practice before or during the conflict, will reduce the likelihood of being reported missing; they also set down measures that require parties to the conflict to react and account for persons reported missing during and in the aftermath of an armed conflict (sub-section 1.2.1).[20] The same structured system does not seem to emerge from contemporary IHL rules applicable in NIAC (sub-section 1.2.2).

---

of these rules'. ibid 320 (mentioning the following Case law: Federal Constitutional Court of Germany, in the Italian Military Internee Case, Joint Constitutional Complaint, 28 June 2004 para. 38 a; Decision by the German federal High Court of Justice in the so-called Bridge of Varvarin case (35 Citizens of the former Federal Republic of Yugoslavia v. Germany), 2 November 2006 para. 10 a).

[18] Mégret (n 9) 130.

[19] While IHL aims to attenuate the unnecessary harshness of war by protecting people who do not or are no longer taking part in hostilities, IHRL protects physical integrity and human dignity in all circumstances. See Jean S Pictet, *Development and Principles of International Humanitarian Law: Course Given in July 1982 at the University of Strasbourg as Part of the Courses Organized by the International Institute of Human Rights* (Martinus Nijhoff Publishers 1985) 61; Meron (n 15) 240.

[20] Contemporary IHL sets down measures that help prevent disappearances, including – but not limited to – the issuance and registration of identification cards and tags to military and associated personnel [cf. Article 4 (POW), GC III; Article 17 (Questioning of prisoners), GC III; Article 16 (Recording and forwarding of information), GC I; Article 19 (Recording and forwarding of information) GC II] and to civilian medical and religious personnel [Article 20 (Hospital Staff), GC IV; Article 40 (Identification of medical and religious personnel), GC I; Article 41 (Identification of auxiliary personnel), GC I; Article 42 (Identification of medical and religious personnel), GC II; Article 2 (Identify Card for permanent civilian medical and religious personnel) and Article 3 (Identify Card for temporary civilian medical and religious personnel) Annex I, AP I]; the marking and respect of graves [Cf. Article 17 (Prescriptions regarding the Dead), GC I; Article 130 (Burial and cremation), GC IV; Article 34 (Remains of deceased), AP I]; the recording of any particulars conducive to the identification of the wounded and sick [Cf. Article 16 (Recording and forwarding of information), GC I]; the recording and transmission of information on the dead [Cf. Article 16 (Recording and forwarding of information), GC I; Article 130 (Burial and cremation), GC IV; Article 33 (Missing Persons), AP I]; the exchange of information concerning protected persons kept in custody [Cf. Article 136 (National Bureaux), GC IV]; the possibility for POW [Cf. Article 71 (Correspondence), GC III] and civilian internees [Cf. Article 107 (Correspondence), GC IV] to be in contact with their families; the registration of vulnerable individuals, e.g., children [in case of evacuation of children, with a view of facilitating their return, the authorities of the receiving countries must establish for each children a card with photographs to be sent to the Central Tracing Agency (CTA), cf. Article 78 (Evacuation of children), AP I].

Recently, the ICRC has played a key role in detecting IHL rules that have become part of customary international law, including those governing the transmission of information to families of missing persons. Pursuant to Rules 105 and 117 of the ICRC Study on Customary IHL, in IAC and in NIAC

[f]amily life must be respected as far as possible.[21]

Each party to the conflict must take all feasible measures *to account for* persons reported missing as a result of armed conflict and must *provide their family members with any information* it has on their fate.[22](emphases added)

Despite the fact that the ICRC affirms the customary character of rules originally codified in treaties applicable in IAC, this is not sufficient *per se* to extend the scope of application of these rules to NIAC.[23] However, there is an increasing practice of embedding the core of the abovementioned rules in post-conflict settlements between State authorities and non-state armed groups. The connection of these rules with other customary rules under international law (for instance, the prohibition of inhuman treatment) and other rules in various bodies of law (for instance the duty to investigate IHL/IHRL violations and to inform the family members) signals the fact that, if these rules are not customary, are on their way to becoming customary.[24]

1.2.1. Legal standards under contemporary IHL treaties applicable in IAC

Commentaries and explanatory notes[25] on the legal standards concerning the missing in situations of armed conflict as well as a thorough study sponsored by

---

[21] Cf. Rule 105 'Respect for family life' in Jean-Marie Henckaerts and Louise Doswald-Beck, *Customary International Humanitarian Law: Volume 1, Rules* (Cambridge University Press 2005) 379 ff.

[22] Cf. Rule 117 'Accounting for Missing Persons' in ibid 421 ff.

[23] Jean d'Aspremont and Jérôme de Hemptinne, *Droit International Humanitaire: Thèmes Choisis* (Pedone 2012) 39; V Chetail, 'Droit International Général et Droit International Humanitaire: Retour Aux Sources' in Vincent Chetail (ed), *Permanence et mutations du droit des conflits armés* (Bruylant 2013) 38. In the Tadić Case, the Appeals Chamber of the ICTY in a more cautious way held that '[t]he emergence of the aforementioned general rules on internal armed conflicts does not imply that internal strife is regulated by general international law in all its aspects. Two particular limitations may be noted: (i) only a number of rules and principles governing international armed conflicts have gradually been extended to apply to internal conflicts; and (ii) this extension has not taken place in the form of a full and mechanical transplant of those rules to internal conflicts; rather, the general essence of those rules, and not the detailed regulation they may contain, has become applicable to internal conflicts'. ICTY. *Prosecutor v Duško Tadić aka 'Dule', Decision on the Defence Motion for Interlocutory Appeal on Jurisdiction* (1995) Case no. IT-94-1-A [126]. Moreover, the Study overlooks the fact that States engaged in NIAC will always oppose anything that could confer upon rebels the status of belligerent. See George H Aldrich, 'Customary International Humanitarian Law — An Interpretation on Behalf of the International Committee of the Red Cross' (2006) 76 British Yearbook of International Law 503, 507.

[24] Sandesh Sivakumaran, *The Law of Non-International Armed Conflict* (Oxford University Press 2012) 285.

[25] Sandoz and others (n 3) paras 1183-1362, 339-379. See also Michael Bothe, Karl Josef Partsch and Waldemar A Solf, *New Rules for Victims of Armed Conflicts: Commentary on the Two 1977 Protocols Additional to the Geneva Conventions of 1949* (Martinus Nijhoff Publishers 1982) 168–181. A Petrig, 'Search for Missing Persons' in Andrew Clapham, Paola Gaeta and Marco Sassòli (eds), *The 1949 Geneva Conventions: A Commentary: A Commentary* (Oxford University Press 2015); D Gavshon, 'The Dead' in Andrew Clapham, Paola Gaeta and Marco Sassòli (eds), *The 1949 Geneva Conventions: A Commentary: A Commentary* (Oxford University Press 2015). The International Review of the Red Cross dedicated a special issue on missing persons in which scholars

the ICRC on the legal and operational facets of the issue[26] have been developed since the adoption of the two APs. For a comprehensive and detailed review of each standard set out in the contemporary IHL treaties this book redirects to these previous works. The purpose of the present section is to cast light upon the interlinked application of IHL rules related to the handling of information on missing persons in three phases, i.e., prior to an armed conflict (sub-section 1.2.1.1 *(a)*), during an armed conflict, and in post-conflict settings (sub-sections 1.2.1.1 *(b)* and 1.2.1.2 respectively).

1.2.1.1. *Preventive measures before and during the conflict*

a) *Preventing uncertainty in peacetime*

Efforts that envisage the prevention of cases of missing persons should be performed at the outbreak of the hostilities: for instance, these include the issuance of identity cards[27] or other identifications tools (e.g., identity discs)[28] to all those categories of persons mentioned in Article 4 of GC III;[29] to this end, States parties 'must take the necessary measures in *good time*' (emphasis added).[30] This also implies that such measures are undertaken 'even before the

---

and experts examined different facets relating to the restoration of family links, collection and management of personal data, and mechanisms for handling cases of missing persons. Cf. International Review of the Red Cross, *Missing Persons*, no. 848 (2002).

[26] ICRC, 'Report: The Missing and Their Families. Summary of the Conclusions Arising from Events Held prior to the International Conference of Governmental and Non–Governmental Experts (Geneva, February 19 -21, 2003). The Missing Project' (ICRC 2003) Doc no TheMissing/Conf/01.2003/EN/10.

[27] Cf. Article 17 (3) GC III. The Commentary to Article 16 (1) (f) GC I and Article 19 (1) (f) GC II specifies that 'the identity cards referred to [in these sub-paragraphs] are those provided for in the Third Convention (in Article 17 (3), in the case of combatant members of the armed forces and in Article 4, A (4), in the case of persons who accompany the armed forces without actually being members thereof)'. See Jean S Pictet (ed), *The Geneva Conventions of 12 August 1949: Commentary*, vol II (ICRC 1960) 139. Pictet, *Commentary Vol I (1952)* (n 15) 163.

[28] ICRC, 'Member of Armed Forces and Armed Groups: Identification, Family News, Killed in Action, Prevention – Final Report and Outcome, in the Framework of "The Missing: Action to Resolve the Problem of People Unaccounted for as a Result of Armed Conflict or Internal Violence and to Assist Their Families" (Hereinafter, The Missing Project)' (ICRC 2002) 7. Moreover, cf. Article 34, Project of an International Declaration concerning the Laws and Customs of War. Brussels, August 27, 1874; Article 20, Oxford Manual, see The Laws of War on Land, International Law Institute, Oxford, September 9, 1880; Resolution I 'Wearing of identity discs', 24th International Conference of the Red Cross and Red Crescent (Manila, 1981).

[29] Article 4 GC III enumerates the following categories: members of the armed forces of a party to the conflict; members of other militias and members of other volunteer corps, including resistance movements belonging to a Party, provided that these groups fulfill certain conditions enumerated in Article 4; members of regular armed forces who profess allegiance to a government or an authority not recognized by the detaining power; persons who accompany the armed forces without actually being members thereof (e.g., civilian members of military aircraft crews, war correspondents, supply contractors, ...); members of crews, including masters, pilots and apprentices, of the merchant marine and the crews of civil aircraft of the parties to the conflict, who do not benefit by more favorable treatment under any other provisions of international law; inhabitants of a non-occupied territory, who on the approach of the enemy spontaneously take up arms to resist the invading forces, without having had time to form themselves into regular armed units, provided they carry arms openly and respect the laws and customs of war. Cf. Article 4, GC III.

[30] Jean S Pictet (ed), *The Geneva Conventions of 12 August 1949: Commentary*, vol III (ICRC 1960) 161.

commencement of hostilities, in order to ensure that the competent authorities are in a position to perform their duties'.[31] A forward-looking approach can contribute to diminishing the number of persons reported missing, including the so-called *missing in action*. To this end, in time of peace, the enactment of legislative provisions aimed at defining identification methods and requirements and setting up the institutional framework for the collation and recording of information is ideal.[32]

In this respect, recording the information following the examination of corpses and their interment is part of the preventive efforts: to this end, the parties to the conflict shall organize 'at the commencement of hostilities' an 'Official Graves Registration Service, to allow subsequent exhumations and to ensure the identification of bodies [...]'.[33] Such a Service cannot be established after the conflict or during the heat of the battle, but should be part of the preventive framework that a State puts in place at the commencement of hostilities at the latest.[34] The Service should remain operational beyond the conclusion of hostilities, as exhumations and repatriation of the bodies can take place more frequently after the conflict.[35]

Furthermore, GCs I-IV require the parties to the conflict to establish an official National Information Bureau (NIB)[36] 'upon the outbreak of a conflict and in all cases of occupation'.[37] Accordingly, delay in the organization of the NIB is not admissible: its establishment should occur well before requests for information reach parties to the conflict on enemy civilians in their territory or before POW are taken.[38] Ideally, the establishment of the NIB should be conceived in peacetime: if planned and outlined in advance, its setting and

---

[31] Commentary on Article 16 GC I. See Pictet, *Commentary Vol I (1952)* (n 15) 161.

[32] In this respect, the US have enacted an Instruction which sets forth the requirements for the form, issuance and use of identity cards required by the GCs I-IV. Cf. United States - Department of Defense. Instruction, No. 1000.1, 16 April 2012, Incorporating Change 1, 9 June 2014 at http://www.dtic.mil/whs/directives/corres/pdf/100001p.pdf accessed on 10 September 2015. See also ICRC, 'Member of Armed Forces and Armed Groups..., The Missing Project' (n 28) 39.

[33] Cf. Article 17 (2), GC I. Article 120 (6) GC III states '[i]n order that graves may always be found, all particulars of burials and graves shall be recorded with a Graves Registration Service established by the Detaining Power.' The GC III is not referring to another service; it is simply outlining one of the tasks this service has to perform, in addition to those listed in GC I. See, in this regard, Pictet, *Commentary Vol I (1952)* (n 15) 182.

[34] The purpose of this Service is not only to maintain the graves and keep record of the examinations of corpses and their interment, but also to enable them to be found. The Services of the opposing Parties are required to exchange 'as soon as possible, and at the latest at the end of hostilities' all information relating to the dead: preventing a dead body from going missing is the paramount objective of the full provision. ibid 181.

[35] ICRC, *Commentary on the First Geneva Convention: Convention (I) for the Amelioration of the Condition of the Wounded and Sick in Armed Forces in the Field* (2nd edn, 2016) para 1702 <https://www.icrc.org/applic/ihl/ihl.nsf/Treaty.xsp?documentId=4825657B0C7E6BF0C12563CD002 D6B0B&action=openDocument> accessed 20 July 2016.

[36] No specification on the setting of the NIB is provided in the Conventions; the only reference to its structure is provided for in Article 50 (4) GC IV: "A special section of the Bureau [...] shall be responsible for taking all necessary steps to identify children whose identity is in doubt".

[37] Cf. Article 122 (1), GC III; Article 136 (1), GC IV.

[38] Jean S Pictet (ed), *The Geneva Conventions of 12 August 1949: Commentary*, vol IV (ICRC 1958) 524.

establishment can be easily foreseen in case of conflict[39] thereby contributing to the prevention of disappearances related to armed conflicts.[40]

As next-sub-section will show, promptness and accuracy in recording information are essential to reduce the risk for the wounded/sick/and dead of going missing.[41] Prior to the conflict preparatory measures can help fulfill these requirements: for instance, these measures include identification of the form that records should take, the training of personnel who should undertake recording activities, and the establishment of prompt identification/processing procedures.[42]

Yet in some countries these forward-looking steps might be unviable; manual methods of record keeping, poor communications, undeveloped economic infrastructure, lack of access to education or modern technology combined to a reduced capacity for satisfactory identification procedures have characterized the way some countries have approached the need for identification tools and institutions.[43]

b) Preventing uncertainty and ensuring the right of families to know during the conflict and in situations of belligerent occupation

The obligation to search for the wounded and sick, and the dead covers all the persons affected by an armed conflict, including the civilian population of the party to the conflict concerned:[44] GCs I,[45] II[46], III and IV[47] set down a detailed

---

[39] This is the case for the UK NIB, which is only activated during times of war; it will run whilst an occupying power is present and may continue when the situation becomes one of support to another government when British Service personnel have a responsibility for detaining security internees (cf. the situation in Iraq). See ICRC/IPU, *Missing Persons: A Handbook for Parliamentarians. No. 17* (Inter-Parliamentary Union; ICRC 2009) 18. In Argentina the Legal Department of the Ministry of Foreign Affairs, International and Worship will act as National Information Bureau upon the outbreak of an armed conflict in conformity with Article 122 GC III, Cf. Article 1, Decreto 1430/2004 del 19 de octubre de 2004 sobre la creación de la Oficina Nacional de Información, https://www.boletinoficial.gob.ar/#!Portada/Primera/all/20041021 accessed on 20 May 2015. See also 'Circulaire n°126/DEF/EMA/ESMG/JUROPS du 2 février 2010 relative au bureau national de renseignements sur les prisonniers de guerre' which regulates the establishment of the French NIB in period of armed conflict in ICRC, 'IHL National Implementation Database' <goo.gl/hr5j2C> accessed 10 June 2015.

[40] Marco Sassòli and Jean-François Rioux, 'Study of Existing Mechanisms to Clarify the Fate of Missing Persons", in the Framework of "The Missing: Action to Resolve the Problem of People Unaccounted for as a Result of Armed Conflict or Internal Violence and to Assist Their Families (Hereinafter, "The Missing Project")"' (ICRC 2003) 17. See also Marco Sassòli, 'Le Bureau National de Renseignements En Faveur Des Victimes Des Conflits Armés' (1987) 69 International Review of the Red Cross 6, 14–15.

[41] ICRC, *Commentary on the First Geneva Convention (2016)* (n 35) paras 1541, 1554.

[42] ibid 1542.

[43] See ICRC, 'Member of Armed Forces and Armed Groups..., The Missing Project' (n 28) 39.

[44] Pursuant to Article 16 (2) GC IV 'each Party to the conflict shall facilitate the steps taken to search for the killed and wounded, to assist the shipwrecked and other persons exposed to grave danger, and to protect them against pillage and ill-treatment.' This provision is among those that ensure the general protection of the civilian population of the Party to the conflict; moreover, the expression 'other persons exposed to grave danger' refer to 'any civilians who while not being either wounded or shipwrecked are exposed to some grave danger as a result of military operations'. See Pictet, *Commentary Vol IV (1958)* (n 38) 136.

framework concerning the tracing activities. Pursuant to this framework, '[a]t all *times, and particularly after an engagement* Parties to the conflict shall, *without delay*, take all possible measures to search for and collect the wounded and sick [and the shipwrecked, in case of naval war]' (emphases added); [48] with the same promptness, they have 'to protect them against pillage and ill-treatment, to ensure their adequate care, and to search for the dead and prevent their being despoiled'.[49] The obligation to search for the dead therefore helps to prevent people from going missing. The obligation to mark the graves[50] is nested within the preventive system which is aimed at avoiding that people go missing during the conflict, as it is a prerequisite to guarantee access to burial places.[51] Its scope *ratione temporis* does not end with the termination of an armed conflict:[52] considered as an obligation that applies at all times, it has practical implications for those States that are responsible for the maintenance of burial sites during the conflict as well as long after the conflict.[53]

---

[45] Article 13 GC I enumerates the categories of persons who fall under the scope of the Convention ("Protected Persons"), including members of the armed forces of a party to the conflict as well as persons who accompany the armed forces without actually being members thereof. The enumeration does not serve the same purpose as Article 4 GC III (concerning the status of 'POW'). As Pictet underlines in the commentary, 'in virtue of a humanitarian principle, universally recognized in international law, of which the Geneva Conventions are merely the practical expression, any wounded or sick person whatever... is entitled to respect and humane treatment and the care which his condition requires. [...] At most, Article 13 will serve to determine under what Convention the wounded man is to be respected and cared for.' See Pictet, *Commentary Vol I (1952)* (n 15) 145.

[46] Article 13 GC II enumerates the categories of persons who fall under the scope of the Convention ("Protected Persons"). As for the purpose of this Article, Pictet puts forward considerations similar to those on Article 13 GC I. See Pictet, *Commentary Vol II (1960)* (n 27) 96.

[47] Pursuant to Article 13 GC IV, the obligation to search and care for the wounded applies to the "whole population of the countries in conflict"; in the case of naval warfare, this obligation will apply to civilian casualties resulting from naval action. See Pictet, *Commentary Vol IV (1958)* (n 38) 136.

[48] Cf. Article 15, GC I. See also Article 18, GC II. As for the latter, the terms 'at all times' are not reproduced in the Convention: the provision, which refers to 'naval engagement', reproduces the old wording used in the 1907 Hague Regulation and is phrased differently from GC I, as the terms '"after each engagement"' were better suited to the special conditions prevailing at sea'. See Pictet, *Commentary Vol II (1960)* (n 27) 131.

[49] Cf. Article 15, GC I; Article 18, GC II. See also Article 16, GC IV. Article 15 is a *verbatim* reproduction of the provision of the Draft Convention for the Relief of the Wounded and Sick in Armed Forces in the Field, approved by the 17th International Red Cross Conference (1948). This Article reiterates the provisions of Article 3 of the 1929 Geneva Convention on WS. However, as remarked in the comments of the Committee I in charge of the Draft Convention on the wounded and sick, Article 15 defined the provisions more extensively: the imperative duty is no longer confined to the search for the wounded, as these must also be collected. The same Draft Convention provided for the obligation to identify the sick, wounded, and dead. During the negotiations, the amendments to this provision focused *inter alia* on the level of specificity of the information to be collected. See ICRC. "Final Record of the Diplomatic Conference of Geneva of 1949." Vol. II A. Bern: Federal Political Department. 1950-1951, at 191- 192.

[50] Cf. Article 17 (3), GC I; Article 120(4), GC III; Article 130(1), GC IV; Article 34(1), AP I.

[51] Petrig, Anna. "The War Dead and Their Gravesites." *International Review of the Red Cross* 874, no. 91 (2009), at 358.

[52] For a detailed list of obligations applicable at all times, see Sandoz and others (n 3) para 149, 67.

[53] This obligation under AP I applies to those categories of persons who do not fall under the protective umbrella of GCs I-IV or other provisions of AP I: viz., 'persons who have died for reasons related to occupation', persons who have died 'in detention resulting from occupation or hostilities'

The promptness of reaction, particularly with regard to the wounded and sick, entails that parties to the conflict react 'every time that there is reason to believe that there are wounded and sick people in the area and as soon as circumstances permit'.[54] Although temporally strict ('without delay'), the obligation to carry out tracing activities is a continuous (*at all times, i.e.,* even during an engagement) obligation of conduct, i.e., parties to the conflict are not required to go beyond 'what is possible'.[55] The collation and recording of information during an armed conflict is connected and dependent on the preliminary steps outlined above and is essential for preventing people from going missing. In line with the immediate character proper to the search operations, information collected and any particulars[56] on the wounded and sick, and the dead must be recorded 'as soon as possible' so as to assist in the identification efforts.[57] Humanitarian considerations drive this obligation: 'it is essential that [families of the missing], whose anxiety increases hourly, should be relieved of their painful uncertainty as soon as this is physically possible'.[58] Furthermore, promptness and accuracy in recording are key to minimize the risk for wounded/sick/and dead persons of going missing;[59] nevertheless, humanitarian (urgent medical treatment) or military (urgent evacuation) circumstances might affect the recording capacity of the parties. Such circumstances can defer the obligation to record information but cannot supersede it.[60]

When it comes to the civilians, the obligation to search for and collect 'killed and wounded' civilians can only been conducted as far as military conditions allow (the obligation to search for and collect the dead under GC I does not apply to dead

---

and 'persons not nationals of the country in which they have died as a result of hostilities' unless their remains or gravesites receive 'more favourable consideration under the [Geneva] Conventions' or any other provision of AP I. Cf. Article 34 (1), AP I. Read *a contrario,* the provision excludes combatants who have died in battle and who are covered by Articles 15-17 GC I, and by Articles 18-20 GC II; POW who have died during a period of detention and who are covered by Articles 120 and 121 GC III; protected civilians who have died during internment and who are covered by Articles 129-131 GC IV. In any case, it does not apply to the nationals of the Party to the conflict. See ibid para 1297, 366.

[54] See ICJ, *Application of the Genocide Convention case, Merits, Judgment* (2007) ICJ Reports 2007 [431] in ICRC, *Commentary on the First Geneva Convention: Convention (I) for the Amelioration of the Condition of the Wounded and Sick in Armed Forces in the Field* (2nd edn, 2016) para 1488. <https://www.icrc.org/applic/ihl/ihl.nsf/Treaty.xsp?documentId=4825657B0C7E6BF0C12563CD002 D6B0B&action=openDocument> accessed 20 July 2016.

[55] ICRC, *Commentary on the First Geneva Convention (2016)* (n 35) paras 1488, 1508–1509.

[56] Even though this is not clearly stated in the Article above, the Commentary helps construe the provision and confirms the importance of identifying the dead bodies and of collecting the belongings of the wounded, for 'such objects may *inter alia* be of assistance in establishing their identity'. Pictet, *Commentary Vol I (1952)* (n 15) 151–152.

[57] Cf. Article 16 (1), GC I; Article 19 (1), GC II.

[58] Pictet, *Commentary Vol I (1952)* (n 15) 161–162.

[59] ICRC, *Commentary on the First Geneva Convention (2016)* (n 35) paras 1541, 1554.

[60] For instance, the UK operates 'a multi-stage system: a truncated documentation, involving the recording of basic details at the point of capture, and a more detailed documentation as soon as reasonably practical thereafter'. United Kingdom, *Joint Doctrine Captured Persons,* 2015 in ibid 1556. See also Rule 123 ('the personal details of persons deprived of their liberty must be recorded') in Henckaerts and Doswald-Beck (n 21) 439 ff.

civilians).[61] Thus, GC IV provides for a nuanced version of the obligation laid out in GC I and II, as the immediacy factor ('without delay') related to the carrying out of tracing operations is completely absent; a collaborative approach to these operations shall be adopted.[62] In practice, 'the military and civilian bodies will usually carry out a joint relief operation covering all war casualties'.[63]

The collation of information is an essential part of the treatment of POW: the first and foremost duty of the detaining Power is to collect the information which helps establish the rank and the status of the persons 'in its hands'.[64] Similarly to what denoted above, this duty has to be performed 'immediately following the

---

[61] Cf. Article 16, GC IV. Pictet's commentary clarifies that 'saving civilians is the responsibility of the civilian authorities rather than of the military. That is why the wording of Article 16 ('each Party to the conflict shall facilitate the steps'...)' is different from GC I's ('Parties to the conflict shall, without delay [...] take all possible measures [...]'). Pictet, *Commentary Vol IV (1958)* (n 38) 135–136.

[62] Article 16 (2) GC IV (Wounded and Sick: General Protection) states that 'as far as military considerations allow, each Party to the conflict shall facilitate the steps taken to search for the killed and wounded, to assist the shipwrecked and other persons exposed to grave danger, and to protect them against pillage and ill-treatment'. Article 16 GC IV also differs from Article 15 GC I and Article 19 GC II, as it includes a reservation concerning the obligation to search (i.e., 'As far as military considerations allow,...'): this reservation seems to be related to the relief operations and to the authorities tasked with search-related activities under GC IV. In this case, civilian authorities will perform these activities and, therefore, military requirements will be taken in due account by these authorities before sending the relief teams in the battlefield. See ibid 136. A collaborative approach should also be adopted by the parties to the conflict in their relations vis-à-vis the search for the dead throughout the medium of arrangements for the establishment of teams tasked with searches for, identification and recovery of the dead from the battlefield. Cf. Article 34 (4), AP I. Making such arrangements is, of course, a step forward with regard to the activities that the parties to the conflict should carry out to recover dead bodies on the battlefield. Nonetheless, the pragmatic viability of this provision remains unclear. Despite the inclusion of the term 'shall', the wording used in the first sentence of Article 34 (4) ('shall endeavour to agree') makes the entire paragraph not 'strictly obligatory'. Bothe, Partsch and Solf (n 25) 175. Furthermore, the second sentence of the excerpt of Article 34 (4) above presupposes cooperation between the parties to the conflict in recovering the dead from the battlefield, should the recovery of the dead of a Party take place in the territory controlled by the adverse Party. The agreement of the latter is necessary, but appears to be difficult to obtain whenever the tension between parties to the conflict is still vivid and ongoing. Sandoz and others (n 3) para 1286, 362. The manner in which the identification of the bodily remains should be carried out is not specified in the Article.

[63] Pictet, *Commentary Vol IV (1958)* (n 38) 136. In this regard, see, for instance, Rule 7 of the Canada's Code of Conduct: 'Following an engagement in which you were involved, you have an obligation, without delay, to take all possible measures to search for and collect the wounded and sick from all sides, opposing forces or not, as well as civilians.' Canada's Code of Conduct for Canadian Forces Personnel (2005), Office of the Judge Advocate General, Rule 7 (3); Basic Rule 5 of the Côte d'Ivoire Teaching Manual: 'Collect, protect and care for the wounded, shipwrecked and sick, whether they be friends, enemies or civilians.' Côte d'Ivoire. *Droit de la guerre, Manuel d'Instruction – Livre I: Instructions de base*, Ministère de la Défense, Forces Armées Nationales, 2007, at pp-21-25; Hellenic Navy's International Law Manual: '...the duty to provide care is combined with the duty to search and rescue, in cases when during an armed conflict the sinking of an enemy vessel occurs. ... If the shipwrecked are civilians, ...the aforementioned protection shall be afforded.' Greece, *International Law Manual*, Hellenic Navy General Staff, Directorate A2, Division IV, 1995, at Chapter 7, Part I, para.6. In ICRC. "Customary IHL" Updated Database, Rule 109 – Practice, https://www.icrc.org/customary-ihl/eng/docs/v2_rul_rule109 accessed 20 August 2015.

[64] Pictet, *Commentary Vol III (1960)* (n 30) 156. However, this is not tantamount to asking any information, as the POW 'is bound to give only his surname, first names and rank, date of birth, and army, regimental, personal or serial number, or failing this, equivalent information'. Cf. Article 17 (1), GC III.

capture',[65] as the establishment of the rank and status under the Convention will allow the detaining Power to ensure the treatment to which these persons are entitled.

GCs I-IV also require parties to the conflict to establish an official NIB. This body is part of a system driven by the humanitarian principle of reducing the suffering of families due to uncertainty; at the same time, it should serve the concrete purposes of ensuring the centralization of information and data and transmitting them to the parties to the conflict concerned.[66] This is also the reason why the timeliness in forwarding information and data to the NIB is a central aspect in order for the system to be efficient towards the achievement of its purpose. *As soon as possible*, therefore, the parties to the conflict shall forward the information[67] on the wounded, sick, shipwrecked and the dead as well as on POW and on protected persons kept in custody to their NIB.[68] In the case of POW and of 'protected persons[69] who are kept in custody for more than two weeks, who are subjected to assigned residence, or who are interned', GCs III and IV do not leave any doubt: the forwarding of the information must be performed 'within the shortest possible period'.[70] Furthermore, the NIB shall 'immediately' forward the information 'by the most rapid means' to the Power concerned, through the intermediary of Protecting Powers[71] or through the Central Tracing Agency (CTA),[72] the aim being that of quickly advising the next of kin concerned.[73]

---

[65] ibid 157.

[66] In the context of POW, Article 122 GC III casts light on the actual purpose of the information system - i.e., inform families of POW – that is 'established primarily in the interest of the next of kin, although also useful to the State'. ibid 576.

[67] The information referred to both in Article 16 (1) GC I and in Article 19 (1) GC II is the following: (a) designation of the Power on which he depends; (b) army, regimental, personal or serial number; (c) surname; (d) first name or names; (e) date of birth;(f) any other particulars shown on his identity card or disc; (g) date and place of capture or death; (h) particulars concerning wounds or illness, or cause of death. Article 122 (3) GC III also adds the following: place of birth, first name of the father, and maiden name of the mother, name and address of the person to be informed, and the address to which correspondence for the prisoner may be sent. Article 138 (1) GC IV also includes 'the date, place, and nature of the action taken with regard to the individual'.

[68] Cf. Article 16 (2), GC I; Article 19 (2), GC II; Article 122 (2), GC III; Article 136 (2), GC IV.

[69] Article 4 GC IV defines the 'protected persons' as those 'who, at a given moment in any manner whatsoever, find themselves, in case of a conflict or occupation, in the hands of a Party to the conflict or Occupying Power of which they are not nationals'. Article 5 GC IV specifies that '[w]here, in the territory of a Party to the conflict, the latter is satisfied that an individual protected person is definitely suspected of or engaged in activities hostile to the security of the State, such individual person shall not be entitled to claim such rights and privileges under the present Convention as would, if exercised in the favour of such individual person, be prejudicial to the security of such State.[...].'

[70] Cf. Article 122 (2), GC III; Article 136 (2), GC IV.

[71] Although these two intermediaries are mentioned both in GCs I-IV and in AP I, the system of Protecting Powers mainly persists as 'law on the books'. See Frits Kalshoven and Liesbeth Zegveld, *Constraints on the Waging of War: An Introduction to International Humanitarian Law* (Cambridge University Press 2011) 69–70. The Protecting Powers system was put in place during the Franco-Prussian war. Eric David, *Principes de droit des conflits armés* (IV, Bruylant 2008) 572–573.

[72] Cf. Article 16 (2), GC I; Article 19 (2), GC II; Article 122 (3), GC III; Article 137 (1), GC IV.

[73] Cf. Article 122 (4), GC III; Article 138 (1), GC IV.

The CTA[74] is specifically tasked with forwarding the data received to the Power concerned, but its chief tasks are 'to keep [the] families informed,[75] [...] to form a permanent link between them and their captured relatives',[76] and to answer enquiries of the families on persons fallen into the power of parties to the conflict.[77] Its activities are concerned more with human relations than with administrative aspects:[78] in the case of POW, after receiving the information, the CTA has 'to transmit it *as rapidly as possible* to the country of origin of the [POW] or to the Power on which they depend' (emphasis added).[79] As for protected persons *ex* GC IV, the CTA is tasked with the same function (to be performed within the same timing of immediacy, i.e., '*as rapidly as possible*').[80]

The CTA will rely on the NIB in order to obtain the necessary information on the person in captivity: in this respect, the NIB is directly responsible for 'replying to all enquiries sent to it [on POW], including those who have died in captivity'.[81] No specification of who can be the applicant is provided in GC III, which implies that the intention of the drafters was to leave open the possibility for private individuals to apply to the NIB 'for information concerning [POW] whose fate was of interest to them.'[82] With regard to civilian internees, the impact of the information on the persons concerned or their relatives is taken into

---

[74] The CTA is named 'Central Prisoners of War Information Agency' under Article 123 (1) GC III and 'Central Information Agency' for protected persons under Article 140 (1) GC IV. In 1960, the ICRC changed the Agency's name in CTA, due to the fact that by 1960, the former denomination no longer corresponded to the new activities the ICRC had been conducting during the conflicts of the Cold War period (e.g., the uprising in Hungary in 1956), or during conflicts connected with decolonization (e.g. the Algerian War or the Mau-Mau rebellion in Kenya). See ICRC, 'ICRC Central Tracing Agency: Half a Century of Restoring Family Links' (7 April 2010) <goo.gl/o9wVTw> accessed 3 June 2016. Article 123 of the GC III confirms both the structure and the legal basis. It was the 1929 Geneva Convention on POW that laid down the legal basis of the Agency. This was the result of the experience gained in earlier conflicts. Indeed, it was in 1914, that the establishment of an international POW Agency faced the ICRC with all the complexities of the vast problem of collecting and forwarding information concerning wounded, sick or deceased prisoners as well as civilians. Article 79 of the 1929 Geneva Convention on POW, therefore, gave the legal basis to the ICRC, which enabled it to open the Central POW Agency in Geneva in 1939. See ICRC, 'Final Record of the Diplomatic Conference of Geneva of 1949. Vol. II A' (Federal Political Department 1950-1951) 581–582. See also Philippe Mathez, 'L'Agence internationale des prisonniers de guerre (1914 - 1923): un patrimoine exceptionnel' in Sylvie Caucanas and others (eds), *Les prisonniers de guerre dans l'histoire: contacts entre peuples et cultures* (Éditions Privat 2003).
[75] In this regard, the CTA might be of help to ensure the family correspondence, should the circumstances make it difficult or impossible. Cf. Article 25 (2), GC IV.
[76] Pictet, *Commentary Vol I (1952)* (n 15) 168.
[77] Đurović highlights that 'pendant plusieurs années qui ont suivi la Seconde Guerre mondiale et jusqu'en 1970 environ, cette tâche, bien qu'elle n'eût pas été prévue par les Conventions de Genève de 1929 et de 1949, occupa même une place prépondérante parmi les activités de l'Agence, qui a continué à répondre aux demandes de recherche pour des raisons d'ordre strictement humanitaire [...]'. Đurović (n 1) 237.
[78] ibid.
[79] Cf. Article 123 (2), GC III.
[80] Cf. Article 140 (2), GC IV.
[81] Cf. 122 (7), GC III.
[82] Pictet, *Commentary Vol III (1960)* (n 30) 579.

account:[83] should this be detrimental to them, the NIB has to warn the CTA,[84] which will take due precautions.[85]

Although sophisticated, the regulation of the handling of information is specifically envisaged for ensuring that those persons caught in the territory of the enemy as well as the links with their families are protected. Not all the persons (e.g., civilian nationals of the Contracting Powers) who are affected by the effects of an armed conflict fall under the category of 'protected persons' and are direct or indirect beneficiaries of the information system. This does not imply that they do not have access to any means allowing the transmission of information: in this respect, all persons in the territory of a party to the conflict, or in a territory occupied by it, 'shall be *enabled to give news of a strictly personal nature to members of their families, wherever they may be, and to receive news from them. This correspondence shall be forwarded speedily and without undue delay* [...]' (emphases added).[86] Should the circumstances make family correspondence impossible or difficult, the parties to the conflict can rely on a neutral intermediary – for instance the CTA – to discharge their obligations. The degree and type of support that the CTA can give is to be decided in relation to the circumstances existing at the time.[87] Thus, GC IV recognizes the existence of a right to send/receive family news,[88] i.e., all 'particulars, news, questions, information etc.

---

[83] This reservation was also considered with regard to POW. During the Diplomatic Conference, Mr. Gardner, the UK delegate, pointed out that 'there was a fundamental difference between the position of civilian internees and that of [POW]. Civilians might already be on foreign territory at the outbreak of hostilities and might have reason for not wishing to give news of themselves to their country of origin, whereas [POW] were then in the service of their country, who already knew all essential particulars concerning them. He, therefore, considered that there was no reason to insert the reservation in question in the [POW] Convention.' See ICRC, 'Official Records of the Diplomatic Conference..., Vol II A' (n 74) 407.

[84] Cf. article 137 (2), GC IV.

[85] Cf. Article 140 (2), GC IV. For instance, the CTA might consider viable options with the persons concerned. See Pictet, *Commentary Vol IV (1958)* (n 38) 546.

[86] Cf. Article 25 (2), GC IV.

[87] Pictet, *Commentary Vol IV (1958)* (n 38) 193.

[88] The Diplomatic Conference did not immediately accept the current wording of Article 25 GC IV: even though Article 25 reflected the draft proposal adopted at the 17th International Red Cross Conference in 1948, delegations presented several amendments that were eventually dropped. The Draft Convention for the Protection of Civilian Persons in Time of War, adopted in 1948, provided that '[a]ll persons in the territory of a Party to the conflict, or in a territory occupied by it, shall be enabled to give news of a strictly personal nature to members of their families, wherever they may be, and to receive news from them. This correspondence shall be forwarded as rapidly as possible [...]' (Article 22). ICRC, 'Final Record of the Diplomatic Conference of Geneva of 1949. Vol. I' (Federal Political Department 1950) 117. The Committee in charge of the text of the Draft Convention on civilians considered the possibility of including the provision above under Part III (Status and Treatment of Protected Persons). ICRC, 'Official Records of the Diplomatic Conference..., Vol II A' (n 74) 710. However, this was not 'a merely drafting change': the ICRC representative underlined that such a change would have also had the effect of reducing the significance of the Article. It would have meant that 'the right to exchange family news would be limited to protected persons. The right to receive family news must be recognized as an indefeasible right'. Consequently, limiting its scope would have been tantamount to a 'retrograde step'. The ICRC Representative, Mr. Pilloud also added that, in case of rejection of the amendment, it would have been necessary to go back to the Stockholm wording (i.e., 'All persons in the territory of a Party to a

concerning the personal and family life of a person'.[89] Providing access to news and information on family members is part of those measures preventing people from going missing; in light of the advances in communication tools, today this right should no longer be connected solely to access to and functioning of postal communication services.

The right to information and news along with the possibility of forwarding them to the family members at any time during the conflict has been considered one of 'the inalienable rights of man [...] [which] must be respected fully and without reservations'.[90] The reality, however, proves different, as national authorities abusively limit the possibility of exchanging family news.[91] In case of inability of the party to the conflict to fulfill the obligation to enable families to exchange news, the ICRC — directly through its staff on the field and/or the CTA — can help realize the right to family news.[92] Parties to the conflict have also a duty to facilitate enquiries[93] made by 'members of families dispersed owing to the war',[94] the purpose being twofold, i.e., safeguarding the family unit[95] and preventing people from going missing.

---

conflict...'). The ICRC's view obtained the support of the USSR representative. See declaration of Mr. Pilloud in ibid 711.

[89] Pictet, *Commentary Vol IV (1958)* (n 38) 192.

[90] ibid.

[91] ICRC, 'The Missing. ICRC Progress Report' (ICRC 2006) 9 <goo.gl/og1Gf1> accessed 12 June 2016. As explained in the Progress Report, by means of the worldwide Red Cross and Red Crescent Family Links Network, the ICRC helps to maintain and restore contact between family members. See ibid.

[92] ICRC, *The Need to Know: Restoring Links between Dispersed Family Members* (ICRC 2010) 4. ICRC.

[93] To this end, each party to the conflict, 'shall encourage.... the work of organizations engaged on this task provided they are acceptable to it and conform to its security regulations' (cf. Article 26, GC IV). The inclusion of such a condition resulted from a UK amendment: 'it was essential that organizations responsible for the reunion of dispersed families should be prevented from playing a political role outside their humanitarian functions'. ICRC, 'Official Records of the Diplomatic Conference..., Vol II A' (n 74) 639.

[94] Cf. Article 26, GC IV. However, as some highlight, the provision (Each Party to the conflict shall facilitate enquiries made by members of families...) does not contain 'a very strong obligation', as it resembles an 'exhortation'. Sandoz and others (n 3) para 2994, 859; Gerald i.a.d. Draper, 'La Réunion Des Familles En Période de Conflit Armé' (1977) 59 International Review of the Red Cross 65, 67. Article 78 (Evacuation of children) of AP I contributes to responding to need for the preservation of family unity in armed conflicts. Paragraph 3 states that '[w]ith a view to facilitating the return to their families and country of children evacuated ..., the authorities of the Party arranging for the evacuation and, as appropriate, the authorities of the receiving country shall establish for each child a card with photographs, which they shall send to the CTA of the [ICRC]'. During the diplomatic conference, the obligation under Article 75 of AP I was restricted on the initiative of Hungary, as 'the obligation to accommodate, as family units, families held in the same place of internment could not always be fulfilled by countries in armed conflict'. See ICRC, 'Official Records of the Diplomatic Conference on the Reaffirmation and Development of International Humanitarian Law Applicable in Armed Conflicts, Vol XV' (1974) CDDH/III/SR.44, para 35; CDDH/III/SR. 43 paras 52-54 (Australia, expressing its support for the proposal) and SR.44 para 9 (Sudan, referring to the need to adopt the amendment as 'families scattered during armed conflicts should be reunited').

[95] This purpose is pursued by other provisions under GC IV: Article 49 GC IV imposes upon the occupying power, which undertakes transfers or evacuations of the population, the obligation to ensure that members of the same family are not separated; pursuant to Article 82 (2) and (3) GC IV, in case of internment, separation of family members must be avoided and, wherever possible, housed

Further to the adoption of AP I, the duty holders are the parties to the conflict as well as the High Contracting Parties not involved in the conflict, as it often happens that nationals of a country involved in an armed conflict seek refuge or are taken to neutral countries.[96]An exceptional case in which the right to family news might be restrained is that of a protected person who is detained as a spy/saboteur or is under definite suspicion of activity hostile to the security of the occupying power.[97] Such person is regarded as having forfeited her/his rights of communication,[98] the pre-condition being the presence of absolute military security reasons. Nonetheless, the detaining power is not released from its obligation to notify the arrest to its official NIB for transmission of information on this person to the official NIB of the country of nationality of the person concerned.[99] The information system should be preserved and not affected in its functioning by security reasons arising during the conflict.

The information system that results from the GCs I-IV should reduce to zero the likelihood of going missing during an IAC and situations of occupation. In principle, it should be impossible for a POW or a civilian internee to be reported as unaccounted for, since the parties to the conflict have a clear obligation to inform each other on their respective POW and civilian internees. The civilian population as such is among the incidental beneficiaries of the good functioning of communication channels ensured throughout the intermediary of the CTA. The *hic et nunc* dimension of the duty to forward information and relevant particulars to the NIB (and then to the CTA) makes it clear that no excuse is tenable: families need to be informed during an armed conflict of what is happening to their beloved ones as rapidly as possible.

---

in the same premises; health or employment reasons can, however, justify separation of a temporary nature. Article 74 of AP I (Reunion of dispersed families) develops Article 26 GC IV: the novelty consists in the fact that the obligation to facilitate the reunion of family members is binding upon the Parties to the conflict and the High Contracting Parties - States that ratified AP I - which are not involved in the conflict. This aspect is paramount: it is not rare that, during an armed conflict, nationals of a country involved in a conflict seek refuge in countries not involved in that conflict. Sandoz and others (n 3) para 2998, 859. Surprisingly, the provision was not embedded in the 1973 Draft of AP I; the ICRC and the League of Red Cross and Red Crescent Societies, with the support of the UN High Commission or for Refugees, agreed on a text and succeeded in persuading several governments to submit it as a new article in a later stage of the negotiations. The text was proposed under the co-sponsorship of twenty-six delegations led by Jordan; it emerged from the Working Group unchanged and was adopted by consensus without further comment. See ibid para 2995, 859; see also ICRC, 'Official Records of the Diplomatic Conference..., Vol XV' (n 94) CDDH/III/SR. 42, para 71; CDDH/III/SR.49, para 11. The obligation laid down in Article 74 AP I responds to the above-mentioned need: as Draper underlines, although the preservation of the family unity should be recognized as a social and humanitarian value, it has been and continues to be one of the main victims of armed conflicts. See Draper (n 94) 66.
[96] Sandoz and others (n 3) para 2998, 859.
[97] Cf. Article 5 (2), GC IV; Article 45 (3) AP I.
[98] Cf. Article 5 (2), GC IV. Pursuant to Article 45 (3) AP I, this restriction is limited to spies operating in an occupied territory.
[99] Pictet, *Commentary Vol IV (1958)* (n 38) 57–58.

1.2.1.2 Accounting for missing persons during and after the end of the conflict

The GCs I-IV are forward-looking in considering the possibility of a gap in the information collected and recorded with regard to POW: pursuant to Article 122 (7) of GC III, it is under the NIB responsibility to 'make any enquiries necessary to obtain the information which is asked for, if this is not in its possession'. The fact that no urgency-related wording is used in this provision substantiates that what is missing is an important piece of information (e.g., is the POW dead or alive? Is he in good health or not?). It is at the cessation of active hostilities[100] or the end of the occupation[101] that the disorganization engendered by operations run at the final stage of an armed conflict might affect the record-keeping capacity of the parties to the conflict; thus, complete lists of POW or civilian internees might be unavailable or poorly maintained. Should this be the case, 'by agreement between the Parties of the conflict' specific entities shall be established for the purpose of searching for 'dispersed internees' as well as 'dispersed [POW]'; these tracing operations, starting after the close of the hostilities, may continue after the termination of the conflict.[102] The positive result of these operations would be conducive to the achievement of their repatriation with 'the least possible delay'.[103]

Nevertheless, violations of the obligations to collect, record, and forward information on POW occurred, for instance, during the Korean War, the conflict between India and China in 1962, and the Vietnam War.[104] The Vietnam War, in particular,[105] is considered to be the triggering event that led States to explicitly recognize the right of families to know the fate of their relatives. The IHL treaty that explicitly tackles and regulates the tracing activities (i.e., the activities aimed

---

[100] Cf. Article 118 (1), GC III. Article 133 (3), GC IV uses the terms 'after the close of hostilities'.

[101] Cf. Article 133 (3), GC IV.

[102] Cf. Article 119 (7), GC III; Article 133 (3), GC IV.

[103] Although this specification is included in Article 119 (7) GC III, the same purpose is not overtly stated in Article 133 (3) GC IV. However, Article 134 GC IV specifies that the '[t]he High Contracting Parties shall endeavor, upon the close of hostilities or occupation, to ensure the return of all internees to their last place of residence, or to facilitate their repatriation.' Clearly, locating and finding the dispersed internees will contribute to fulfilling this obligation. The practice concerning these committee/commissions is inexistent.

[104] Horst Fischer, 'Protection of Prisoners of War' in Dieter Fleck and Michael Bothe (eds), *The Handbook of International Humanitarian Law* (Oxford University Press 2008) 388. In order to rectify violations of the obligation to report, States have concluded agreements, once conflicts are settled, to arrange for the joint search for missing victims and POW. For instance, the US-Vietnam Agreement of October 1992 on the opening of Vietnamese military archives has facilitated some access to government archives and has unveiled the fate of some of the US missing soldiers. See ibid.

[105] T. Meron argues that '[AP I] [...], in reaction to the Vietnam war, codified norms for recovering the missing and the dead and disposing of the remains of the dead'. See T Meron, 'Editorial Comment. The Time Has Come for the United States to Ratify Geneva Protocol I' (1994) 88 American Journal of International Law 678, 679. See also GH Aldrich, 'Why the United States of America Should Ratify Additional Protocol I' in Astrid JM Delissen and Gerard J Tanja (eds), *Humanitarian Law of armed conflict. Challenges ahead. Essays in honour of Frits Kalshoven* (Martinus Nijhoff Publishers 1991) in n 13, 131. Moreover, according to the UK Manual of the Law of Armed Conflict, the right provided for in Article 32 of AP I 'was prompted by the difficulties experienced by the US in ascertaining the fate of missing American Personnel at the end of the Vietnam Conflict'. In UK Ministry of Defence, *The Manual of the Law of Armed Conflict* (OUP Oxford 2004) in n 90, 137.

at clarifying the fate of persons reported missing in armed conflicts) is AP I, solely applicable in times of IAC.[106] Section III (Part II) of AP I, fully dedicated to the missing and the dead,[107] is introduced by a 'general principle' which shall inform the tracing operations and any identification effort[108] related to the missing and the dead.[109] Pursuant to Article 32 AP I,

> [i]n the implementation of [the Section on the Missing and Dead Persons], the activities of the High Contracting Parties, of the Parties to the conflict and of the international humanitarian organizations mentioned in the Conventions and in this

---

[106] Cf. Article 2 (1), GCs I-IV read in conjunction with Article 1 AP I.

[107] Cf. Article 32, AP I.

[108] Article 32 of AP I states that the activities of the following actors should be prompted by this general principle: i.e., High Contracting Parties, parties to the conflict and international humanitarian organizations mentioned in GCs I-IV and in AP I. High Contracting Parties are the States that have ratified AP I; any other entity or actor is excluded: in this regard, some authors observe that concluding a treaty is both attribute and exercise of State sovereignty. See Patrick Daillier, Alain Pellet and Nguyen Quoc Dinh, *Droit International Public* (7e éd, LGDJ 2009) para 60, 139. High Contracting Parties that are also parties to the conflict shall be bound by AP I in relation to each of the Parties which are not bound by it, if the latter accepts and applies the provisions thereof. Cf. Article 96 (2), AP I. In this regard, the ICRC Commentary underlines that '[a]cceptance is however, limited to the current conflict and the Party making the declaration of acceptance retains total freedom as regards its formal participation in the Protocol'. See Sandoz and others (n 3) para 3756, 1087. 'Parties to the conflict' does not necessarily coincide with 'High Contracting Parties': some parties to the conflict may not be Contracting Parties and yet be bound by the Protocol. ibid para 1206, 344. As for 'international humanitarian organizations', neither the GCs I-IV nor AP I provides for a comprehensive list of these organizations. The first draft of Section III included a vague expression, i.e., 'international organizations'. ICRC, 'Official Records of the Diplomatic Conference on the Reaffirmation and Development of International Humanitarian Law Applicable in Armed Conflicts, Vol XI' (1974) (CDDH/II/SR.35), para 13, 365. The ICRC commentary clarifies that the provision is not limited to inter-governmental organizations (the ICRC and its CTA are therefore included). See Sandoz and others (n 3) para 1209, 345. Article 9 (2) (c) of AP I (Field of Application of Part II) refers to the 'permanent and medical units and transports' which are made available to a Party to the conflict by, *inter alia*, 'an impartial international humanitarian organization'. Impartiality is one of the fundamental aspects of the humanitarian assistance and, as a corollary, one of the main features of an international humanitarian organization. In the view of the International Court of Justice (hereinafter the ICJ), '[a]n essential feature of truly humanitarian aid is that it is given "without discrimination" of any kind.' This means that in order for humanitarian assistance to be considered as such and not as an intervention in the internal affairs of a State, 'not only must it be limited to the purposes hallowed in the practice of the Red Cross, namely "to prevent and alleviate human suffering" and "to protect life and health and to ensure respect for the human being"; it must also, and above all, be given without discrimination to all in need [...]'. See ICJ, *Case concerning Military and Paramilitary Activities in and against Nicaragua (Nicaragua v United States of America), Merits, Judgment* (1986) ICJ Reports 1986, p.14 para 243, 125. The organization's activities, in the context of the armed conflict, 'must retain a purely humanitarian character' and cannot have a political or commercial character. Sandoz and others (n 3) para 440, 143. In order to cast light on the terminology of Article 32 of AP I, Article 125 (*Relief societies and other organizations*) GC III is a helpful tool: specifically, it mentions 'religious organizations, relief societies, [and] any other organization assisting prisoners of war'. National Red Cross and Red Crescent Societies are part of 'relief societies'. The innovative element in the Convention is the reference to 'religious organizations': the spiritual assistance is part of the relief activities. Moreover, the open-ended character of the expression 'any other organizations...' aims to address the activities of those bodies whose main purpose is not the assistance to POW but which during a conflict could include such assistance among their task. The humanitarian character of this type of bodies could be temporary. See Pictet, *Commentary Vol III (1960)* (n 30) 595.

[109] Cf. Articles 33 (*Missing Persons*) and 34 (*Remains of Deceased*), AP I.

Protocol shall be prompted mainly by *the right of families to know the fate of their relatives* (emphasis added).

During the *travaux préparatoires,* some States' representatives rejected the reference to this right;[110] moreover, in the literature, scholars have questioned its legal character.[111] As Zegveld points out, 'the recognition of rights is one thing and the right to claim those rights is another';[112] however, it is undeniable that the general principle at issue informs the implementation of the provisions laid down in this Section of AP I ('Missing and dead persons'). To a certain extent, it plays the role of interpretive guidance not only for the measures detailed in the above-mentioned Section, but also for measures concerning the tracing of protected persons as well as the handling of information under GCs I-IV.[113]

Pursuant to Article 33 (1) AP I, parties to the conflict bears a general obligation to search for persons reported missing[114] by an 'Adverse Party';[115] the latter must transmit the necessary information to conduct tracing operations. The tracing activities uniquely concern those 'persons who have been reported missing', including those 'who would not receive more favourable consideration under the Conventions and [the] Protocol'.[116]

---

[110] According to the UK's representative, the activities of the parties to the conflict 'were certainly not mainly prompted by the fundamental right of families to know what had happened to their relatives but by the desire to win the war'. Cf. Declaration on amendment CDDH/II/259 Add.1 made by the UK Representative, Mr. Pugh. In ICRC, 'Official Records of the Diplomatic Conference..., Vol XI' (n 108) CDDH/II/SR.35, para 49, 371; for the Canada's and New Zealand's representatives, the inclusion of this right 'added little to what was essentially a legal document and there was nothing like it elsewhere in the Protocol or in the Conventions.' Cf. Declaration on amendment CDDH/II/259 Add.1 made by the Canada's Representative, Mr. Green in ibid CDDH/II/SR.35, para 50, 371; Declaration on amendment CDDH/II/259 Add.1 made by the New Zealand's Representative in ibid CDDH/II/SR.35, para 61, 373.

[111] According to Bothe, Partsch, and Solf, AP I does not create a legal right of families to get information from parties to the conflict. The same authors argue that Article 32 AP I entitles families of missing persons to a right without specifying whether it has a legal/moral character and without establishing an enforcement procedure. They also add that it is a quite unusual legal technique to introduce a small portion of a treaty with 'a special preamble' within a treaty. See Bothe, Partsch and Solf (n 25) 170–171. Conversely, Đurović observes that the right enshrined in Article 32 AP I represents the confirmation of a principle of customary international law and makes a right impliedly embedded in the GC I-IV explicit. Đurović (n 1) 272. See also Isaac Paenson, *Manual of the Terminology of the Law of Armed Conflicts and of International Humanitarian Organizations* (Bruylant and Martinus Nijhoff Publishers 1989) 654.

[112] Liesbeth Zegveld, 'Remedies for Victims of Violations of International Humanitarian Law' (2003) 85 International Review of the Red Cross 497, 497.

[113] As specified in its Article 1 (3), AP I 'supplements the Geneva Conventions of 12 August 1949 for the protection of war victims'.

[114] Bothe, Partsch, and Solf argue that the obligation to search for missing persons 'applies to any victim', but 'there must be some link between the Party requesting the search and the victim'. Bothe, Partsch and Solf (n 25) 172. The term 'victim' is not, however, mentioned in the entire Section on Missing and Dead. Neither is such expression mentioned in the transcripts of the *travaux préparatoires*. Moreover, this interpretation could narrow down the scope of the provision and have misleading consequences: a missing person might not always be a victim of some unspecified violation of IHL rules.

[115] Cf. Article 33 (1), AP I. An adverse Party can report missing its own nationals, persons upon whom it conferred the refugee status, its soldiers (including alleged deserters), and all those persons in whom there is a 'genuine interest based on the general principle of Article 32'. Sandoz and others (n 3) para 1225, 350.

[116] Cf. Article 33 (2), AP I.

The Protocol does not reiterate obligations that are mentioned in other IHL instruments, but sets down new duties on the parties to the conflict for the benefit of 'persons who were previously inadequately covered or not covered at all'.[117] Indeed, the four GCs do not cover and protect all those who are affected by IAC.[118] Although it might seem logical that nationals of the Party to the conflict are among those persons 'inadequately covered', the specific paragraph which mentioned this aspect in the draft version of Section III was eventually deleted, for it was self-evident that the obligation did not apply to a Party's own nationals.[119] These persons are not, however, left without any legal protection, as IHRL is applicable in armed conflicts; however, under AP I, the obligations of parties to the conflict solely impact on 'enemy nationals' (e.g., mercenaries[120] and spies[121]).[122] Such a legalistic and strict reading of the obligation to search for the missing, however, is contradictory to the wording of the above-mentioned 'general principle'[123] and to the object and purpose of the Protocol itself, i.e.,

---

[117] In other words, POW and civilian internees cannot be included among persons 'who would not receive more favourable consideration under the Conventions or the Protocol', for IHL contains rules designed to ensure that they do not go missing (e.g., Cf. Article 119 and Article 122, GC III; Article 137 and Article 133, GC IV). Sandoz and others (n 3) para 1247, 355.

[118] For a detailed list of persons who are not included among those considered as 'protected' under GC IV, see Pictet, *Commentary Vol IV (1958)* (n 38) 46. See Sandoz and others (n 3) para 1255, 357. For instance, Article 4 (Definition of Protected Persons) of GC IV defines the categories of persons that shall be considered as 'protected persons'. Read *a contrario,* the Article presupposes the existence of non-protected persons, i.e., nationals of a State not Party to the Convention; nationals of a neutral or co-belligerent State, so long as the State in question has normal diplomatic representation in the State in whose territory they are; nationals of a co-belligerent State in occupied territories, so long as the State in question has normal diplomatic representation in the occupying State.

[119] ICRC, 'Official Records of the Diplomatic Conference..., Vol XI' (n 108) (CDDH/II/SR.34), para 18, 365. Indeed, in a situation of IAC in which two or more States are involved, the obligations laid down in Article 33 (2) will impact on the enemy nationals and not on the State's own nationals who were held in captivity or who died for reasons related to the hostilities.

[120] These are individuals who meet the conditions listed in Article 47 of AP I and, as a result, are not entitled to the POW status and treatment provided for in GC III. Pursuant to Article 47(2) of AP I, '[a] mercenary is any person who: (a) is specially recruited locally or abroad in order to fight in an armed conflict; (b) does, in fact, take a direct part in the hostilities; (c) is motivated to take part in the hostilities essentially by the desire for private gain and, in fact, is promised, by or on behalf of a Party to the conflict, material compensation substantially in excess of that promised or paid to combatants of similar ranks and functions in the armed forces of that Party; (d) is neither a national of a Party to the conflict nor a resident of territory controlled by a Party to the conflict; (e) is not a member of the armed forces of a Party to the conflict; and (f) has not been sent by a State which is not a Party to the conflict on official duty as a member of its armed forces'.

[121] Articles 33 (2) of AP I applies to them in the case in which they do not benefit from the POW status. Cf. Article 46, AP I.

[122] Not falling under the category of POW, spies and mercenaries are civilians who could be covered by Article 5 GC IV (Derogations), for they are 'suspected of or engaged in activities hostile to the security of the State'. Cf. Article 5(1), GC IV. Consequently, they are no longer able to claim rights and privileges flowing from the status of 'protected person' under such Convention, should these rights be prejudicial to the security of the State: the right to correspond is, for instance, one of the rights to which the Article refers and is normally granted to protected persons under detention. See Pictet, *Commentary Vol IV (1958)* (n 38) 56. This is not tantamount to accepting that these individuals could be submitted to inhuman treatment or deprived of the fundamental guarantees.

[123] At the time of the Diplomatic Conference, the wording of the above-mentioned general principle enshrined in Article 32 of AP I was highly debated, for, as one delegation underlined, it involved not

reaffirm and develop the provisions protecting the victims of armed conflicts.[124] In the words of one of the sponsors of the general principle, such a principle concerned 'one of the natural and fundamental rights of families'.[125] In this regard, Draper observes that in an armed conflict the very first victim is the family whose integrity is temporarily or permanently hampered.[126]

Under AP I, the obligation to search for the persons reported missing by an adverse Party[127] is unique in its genre,[128] as it sets down the parameters to pursue a real investigation,[129] during and after an armed conflict ('as soon as circumstances permit, and at the latest from the end of active hostilities').

With respect to 'persons who would not receive more favourable consideration under the Conventions and [the] Protocol', each Party to the conflict shall record information regarding persons who have been detained for more than two weeks and persons *who died during any period of detention'* (emphasis added);[130] it shall also 'facilitate and, if need be,[131] carry out the search for' persons who died in other

---

only points of style, but also points of substance. See the Declaration on the amendment (CDDH/II/259 Add.1) made by the UK representative, Mr. Pugh. ICRC, 'Official Records of the Diplomatic Conference..., Vol XI' (n 108) (CDDH/II/SR.35) para 49, 371.

[124] Preamble, third recital, AP I.

[125] See the Declaration on amendment CDDH/II/259 Add.1 made by the Greek Representative, Mrs. Mantzoulinos. In ICRC, 'Official Records of the Diplomatic Conference..., Vol XI' (n 108) (CDDH/II/SR.35) para 10, 364. The amendment aimed to remedy 'an omission, namely the absence of any reference to families, and to call the attention of all representatives... and their States to the suffering caused to families as a result of armed conflicts.' See Declaration on amendment CDDH/II/259 Add.1 presented by the Representative of the Holy See, Mr. Kein. In ibid (CDDH/II/SR.35) para.2, at 363. The delegations accepted that the right of families to know the fate of their relatives constituted a separate article and, at the same time, rejected the proposal of its deletion. See, for instance, the declaration made by the Brazil's Representative, Mr. Carnauba, and by the Democratic Republic of Germany's Representative, Mr. Felber. In ICRC, 'Official Records of the Diplomatic Conference on the Reaffirmation and Development of International Humanitarian Law Applicable in Armed Conflicts, Vol XII' (1974) (CDDH/II/SR.76) para 35, 233 and para 43, 235.

[126] Draper (n 94) 65. Šarčević underscores that 'the prolonged absence of one or more family members sometimes results in a reversal of roles in war-affected families'. See Petar Šarčević, 'War and Disintegration of the Family' (1999) 1 Journal of Law and Family Studies 109, 115.

[127] Cf. Article 33 (1), AP I.

[128] In this regard, during the *travaux préparatoires* of AP I, the ICRC representative, Mrs. Bujard, observed that '[t]he Conventions were silent on one important matter: they did not oblige the Parties to a conflict to search at all times for soldiers of the opposing side whose names did not appear on the lists of captured or deceased persons. Nor were they obliged to carry out such searches in the case of civilians.' ICRC, 'Official Records of the Diplomatic Conference..., Vol XI' (n 108) CDDH/II/SR.19, para 86, 184.

[129] AP I does not spell out the specific measures to be undertaken in order to trace missing persons. The ICRC Commentary pinpoints a series of steps to be taken so as to comply with the obligation of Article 33 (1): first, check the last known place of residence of the person concerned or inspect registers of detention centers and, second, search for family members who could give information or question neighbors and colleagues. The obligation may not be considered fulfilled whether the first step has not been taken. However, the Protocol is silent on the extent of the obligation. See Sandoz and others (n 3) para 1224, 350 and paras 1232-1234, 352.

[130] Cf. Article 33 (2) (a), AP I.

[131] The reason behind the inclusion of the expression 'if need be' was that in occupied territory 'the search for and recording of information concerning the persons referred to in paragraphs 2 (a) and (b) would normally be left to the local municipal authorities and the Occupying Power would not exercise

circumstances as a result of hostilities or occupation.[132] AP I partly fills a *lacuna* under GC IV: under the Convention, no obligation to record information on persons kept in detention for less than two weeks is imposed on the parties to the conflict.[133] The temporal factor is a crucial aspect: whereas Article 33 (2) AP I contains the same *lacuna* with regard to persons kept in detention, the provision imposes an obligation to record information on persons who have died during any period of detention, thereby eliminating the time-limit of two weeks. The information gathered and recorded is to be transmitted 'directly or through the Protecting Power or the [CTA][134] of the [ICRC]' or national Red Cross/Red Crescent Societies.[135] Indeed, the transmission of information requires a mechanism that puts the Parties to the conflict – the requesting Party and the requested Party – into contact.[136]

Whether elucidating the fate of the missing implies a right of families to receive human remains of their deceased relatives is questionable; in practice though, the need of families is not met with a mere transmission of information on the life conditions, as families want to receive the human remains of their relatives.[137] AP I[138] reflects these multiple needs:

---

direct and immediate responsibility.' Cf. Declaration of the UK representative, Mr. Pugh, ICRC, 'Official Records of the Diplomatic Conference..., Vol XV' (n 94) CDDH/II/SR.35, para 46, 370.

[132] Cf. Article 33 (2) (b), AP I.

[133] The recording and exchange of information is carried out in relation to persons who are kept in custody for more than two weeks, who are subjected to assigned residence, and who are interned. Bothe, Partsch and Solf (n 25) 173. With regard to GC III, the same authors observe that a potential *lacuna* could have flown from the reservation of Socialist States to Article 85 (*Offences committed before capture*): viz. war criminals are not entitled to POW status, even before being convicted as such by a competent tribunal. See ibid. A note sent by the Ministry of Foreign Affairs of the USSR to the Swiss Government clarified this reservation. According to this note, POW accused of war crimes or crimes against humanity will continue to enjoy the benefits of the Convention until such time as the penalty to which they have been sentenced becomes enforceable, that is to say until all courses of appeal have been exhausted. See Pictet, *Commentary Vol III (1960)* (n 30) 425. Without such note, Article 33 (2) of AP I would apply to them.

[134] As Đurović observes, this transmission should be avoided during hostilities, for the information gathered could be used for purposes that clash with the humanitarian spirit of the provision. See Đurović (n 1) 273.

[135] Cf. Article 33 (3) AP I.

[136] Whereas under the GCs I-IV the ICRC 'shall, if it deems necessary, propose to the Powers concerned the organization of the [CTA]', AP I makes the CTA a permanent and mandatory mechanism. Cf. Article 33 (3), AP I. The parties to the conflict cannot refuse the assistance of the ICRC in organizing the Agency services. See also Article 123, GC III and Article 140, GC IV. The ICRC, through the intermediary of the CTA or by itself, has played and continues to play a paramount role in assisting with the transmission of this information. Article 33 of AP I also mentions the Protecting Powers. The system was put in place during the Franco-Prussian war. See Eric David, *Principes de droit des conflits armés* (III, Bruylant 2002) 572–573; Đurović (n 1) 273–274. In the event of severance of diplomatic relations between States A and B, A could ask C to act as protector of its interests and those of its nationals in respect of and with the agreement of State B. Although last applied during World War II – WWII (with the neutral States - Sweden and Switzerland - acting as protecting powers), 'the system persists mainly as 'law on the books'. See Kalshoven and Zegveld (n 71) 69–70. Their role in the transmission of information is barely reported, for this activity has been carried out by the CTA.

[137] Marco Sassòli, 'Les disparus de guerre: Les règles du droit international et les besoins des familles entre espoir et incertitude' (2003) 15 Frontières 38, 41.

'[the] High Contracting Parties in whose territories graves and [...] other locations of the remains of persons who have died as a result of hostilities or during occupation or in detention are situated, shall conclude agreements in order: a) to facilitate access to the gravesites by relatives of the deceased [...]; b) to protect and maintain such gravesites *permanently*; c) *to facilitate the return of the remains of the deceased [...] to the home country upon its request or, unless that country objects, upon the request of the next of kin.*'[139] (emphases added)

The conclusion of the agreements mentioned above will occur 'as soon as the circumstances and the relations between the adverse Parties permit': the flexibility in the implementation timing is due to the fact that the conclusion of agreements concerning the disposal of human remains entirely depends upon the relations between the parties.[140]

The maintenance of the gravesites is a long-term engagement that goes beyond the end of the conflict; as such, it should be the subject of these agreements, as it can be overburdening for the State responsible of the physical maintenance of the graves. In the absence of any agreement, *i)* respect for the remains and the interest of families should be maintained; *ii)* if the home country or the family intends to meet the costs of the maintenance, the Contracting Party in whose territory the gravesites are situated is obliged to ensure permanent maintenance.[141]

Although the need of families to receive the remains of their relatives is taken into due account, this can be hardly considered as a legal entitlement of the families:[142] the 'next of kin'[143] can request the return of the remains of the deceased and personal effects, but the 'home country' can exercise a right of veto[144] ('unless that country objects'). Since the provision does not mention the reason why the right of veto can be exercised, the next of kin might have his or her request rejected for unspecified reasons. Nevertheless, the driver of the conduct of States vis-à-vis the dead is the right of families to know the fate of their relatives: the general principle is not mentioning the missing relatives or the deceased ones; it is mentioning 'the relatives' *per se*. In order for this principle to

---

[138] Part II Section III of AP I *inter alia* supplements the provisions on the tracing of missing and dead persons contained in the GCs I–IV. See Kalshoven and Zegveld (n 71) 135.

[139] Cf. Article 34 (2) (c), AP I.

[140] Sandoz and others (n 3) para 1319, 371.

[141] Frits Kalshoven and Liesbeth Zegveld, *Constraints on the Waging of War: An Introduction to International Humanitarian Law* (Cambridge University Press 2011) 69–70. Cf. Article 34 (3), AP I.

[142] Robben points out that the first time the right to mourning appeared in IHL, albeit obliquely, was in AP I. Antonius Robben, 'The Human Right to Mourning. Social Trauma and Transitional Justice in Post-Conflict Argentina' in Ineke Boerefijn and Ronald Janse (eds), *Human Rights and Conflict: Essays in Honour of Bas De Gaay Fortman* (Intersentia 2012) 494–495.

[143] An additional aspect to be underlined is the use of the expression 'next of kin': this term designates only the closest living relatives, and is, therefore, more restrictive than the term 'relatives' used *inter alia* in Article 32. Conversely, the French text uses a broader expression, i.e., *famille*, that the ICRC Commentary deems more appropriate. Sandoz and others (n 3) para 1344, 375. The interpretation of this Article should consider that the general principle laid down in Article 32 is the *fil rouge* of all the activities relating to the missing and dead.

[144] ibid para 1345, 376.

be meaningful, the veto power should be reduced at a minimum.[145] The rationale of allowing the home country to decline the request for the return of the remains might be uniquely related to temporal and practical considerations.[146]

1.2.2. Legal standards under contemporary IHL treaties applicable in NIAC

Substantively, the legal framework applicable in NIAC and concerning preventive actions (sub-section 1.2.2.1) as well as reactive measures (sub-section 1.2.2.2) vis-à-vis the issue of the missing is not as structured as the one applicable in IAC. Common Article 3 GC I-IV and AP II do not provide for the general principle set down under AP I; neither do they provide for measures aimed at elucidating the fate of missing persons. In this respect, the ICRC Commentary argues that it would not have been 'realistic' to lay down rules that were as detailed as those on the missing and the dead contained in AP I, given the specific circumstances of NIAC. [147] Contradictorily, however, it also underlines the importance for families to know the fate of their relatives in 'an internal fratricidal conflict'.[148]

The humanitarian gap is evident, in particular, when families of the missing are concerned: the gathering and recording of information and the transmission of such information to families hinge on the willingness of the parties to the conflict. Essential, in this regard, can be the contribution of the ICRC that 'may offer its services to the Parties to the conflict';[149] however, the parties to the conflict are allowed to decline this offer.[150]

1.2.2.1. Preventing uncertainty during the conflict

The regulation of the handling of information on specific categories of persons and the tracing of missing persons is almost inexistent in NIAC. Although addressed in the initial draft[151] of AP II,[152] the issue of missing persons was eventually deleted along with half of other provisions.[153]

---

[145] Article 34 (3) of AP I specifies that '[i]n the absence of the agreements [...] and if the home country of such deceased is not willing to arrange at its expense for the maintenance of such gravesites, the High Contracting Party in whose territory the gravesites are situated may offer to facilitate the return of the remains of the deceased to the home country.

[146] In this respect, repatriation, exhumation, and transfer of remains from well-established past gravesites such as those dating back to WWI or WWII should be carried out with the consent of the home country: this would facilitate the maintenance of war cemeteries in foreign countries. This was the concern expressed during the Diplomatic Conference, particularly with regard to the burial sites of WWI; the same reasoning can be extended to the gravesites of WWII. ICRC, 'Official Records of the Diplomatic Conference..., Vol XI' (n 108) CDDH/II/SR.20, para 4, 189; CDDH/II/SR.34, para 25, 353. Should exhumation and repatriation be a matter of the individual request of the family, these cemeteries could not be maintained in a decent manner. See Bothe, Partsch and Solf (n 25) 179.

[147] Sandoz and others (n 3) para 4657, 1415.

[148] ibid.

[149] Cf. Common Article 3, GCs I-IV.

[150] Pictet, *Commentary Vol IV (1958)* (n 38) 41.

[151] The UNGA Resolution 3220, which informed the discussion on missing persons during the negotiations for the adoption of the two Protocols, referred to all types of armed conflict and did not limit itself to IAC.

[152] See Section 2 in Chapter I.

[153] Some delegations regretted the deletion of Article 34 first Draft AP II, for its adoption would have reminded the High Contracting Parties of the right of families to know the fate of their relatives. The

The final text contains a few measures aimed at preventing people from going missing: although temporally less stringent, Common Article 3 and AP II provide for the obligation to search for the wounded, sick, shipwrecked, and the dead.[154] In addition to that, all appropriate steps to facilitate the reunion of families temporarily separated shall also be taken, with a specific focus on unaccompanied children;[155] such an obligation can continue to have effects after the termination of the conflict.[156]

Although a text as detailed as that of AP I would have been far from the reality on the ground,[157] the importance for families to know the fate of their relatives in 'an internal fratricidal conflict'[158] remains as realistic as it is in IAC. Therefore, the ICRC[159] can offer its services based on its right of initiative,[160]

Holy See's delegation, which introduced the amendment on the right to know in the draft protocol I, did not join the consensus and expressed its hope that it will not be long before this right was reaffirmed in a text which might be worded as follows: 'It is the right of families to know the fate of their relatives that will prompt the parties to establish information bureaux in order to gather information and transmit it, if necessary through the intermediary of ICRC or some other impartial humanitarian organ.' See ICRC, 'Official Records of the Diplomatic Conference on the Reaffirmation and Development of International Humanitarian Law Applicable in Armed Conflicts, Vol VII' (1974) (CDDH/SR.53), 158-159.

[154] Cf. Article 8, AP II. The temporal reference ('whenever circumstances permit') appears to be less stringent and more flexible than the ones mentioned in the GCs I-IV with regard to the same obligation. The temporal element is the main difference between this Article and the corresponding provisions in GCs I, II and IV as to the search for the wounded and sick. In fact, Article 8 does not apply 'at all times' (as in GC I), or only 'after each engagement' (as in GC II), but 'whenever circumstances permit...'. See Bothe, Partsch and Solf (n 25) 659. No temporal reference is contained in Common Article 3 (2) GCs I-IV ('The wounded and sick shall be collected and cared for.').

[155] Article 4(3) APII reads as follows, 'children shall be provided with the care and aid they require, and in particular: [...] all appropriate steps shall be taken to facilitate the reunion of families temporarily separated'. The provision echoes what is provided for in Article 26 GC IV and entails that the parties to the conflict must do their best to enable the families to make inquiries with the aim of finding their dispersed members, including children.

[156] The IACtHR case law has addressed the continuity of certain IHL obligations after the end of the armed conflict and the inextricable link between these obligations and the ones under IHRL. The point of conjunction between these two sets of obligations is the family and the impact that an armed conflict can have on it, even when it ends, should its consequences persist. The Court has underlined that in NIAC the reference standard is laid down in Article 4(3) AP II. Cf. IACtHR, *Rochac Hernández and others v El Salvador, Judgment - Merits, Reparations and Costs* (2014) Series C No. 285 [110].

[157] Sandoz and others (n 3) para 4657, 1415.

[158] ibid.

[159] Pursuant to common article 3 GC I-IV, the ICRC 'may offer its services to the Parties to the conflict'.

[160] Yet, in 1921, during the X International Conference of the Red Cross, the Conference adopted Resolution XIV conferring upon the ICRC the mandate of intervening in cases of 'civil war'; the ICRC interpreted this mandate in broad terms thereby covering activities such as the organization of information bureau in such contexts. This pioneering approach corresponded to the main priority of this organization, i.e., ensuring humanitarian protection and assistance for victims of armed conflict. Đurović (n 1) 85. Its approach to the issue has been improved in the 2000s, particularly with regard to methods of preventing disappearances, to processing cases of missing persons and to assisting their families, and to fostering an agreement on common practices in this area in order to move the issue further up the international agenda. See ICRC, 'The Missing. ICRC Progress Report' (n 91) 1.

which constitutes the legal basis for the CTA's activities[161] in NIAC.[162] In this regard, as a 'humanitarian organization specialized in the field of bringing about the reunion of dispersed families',[163] the CTA has found itself involved in a variety of situations, including in NIAC,[164] in line with its duty to act based upon the principle of humanity.[165]

The implementation of a system that aims at preventing uncertainty and ensuring the transmission of information to the party concerned as well as to families seems to rely on the willingness of the parties to the conflict. The same is valid for all those measures that envisage elucidating the fate of those who are reported as unaccounted for in the context of a NIAC.

1.2.2.2 Accounting for missing persons during and after the end of the conflict

Under contemporary IHL treaties, the duty to account for the missing is not contemplated. Neither do IHL treaties contemplate a right of families to know the fate of their relatives in relation to NIAC. Some scholars argue that the relevance of distinguishing NIAC/IAC is being diminishing due to the approximation of rules applying in both situations.[166] In light of this standpoint, the above-mentioned *lacuna* might be overcome. The reality shows that the elimination of this distinction is often purely theoretical;[167] for instance, the

---

[161] In this respect, after WWII, the CTA has delivered its services in NIAC in light of the humanitarian principles stemming from common Article 3 GC [I-IV] of 1949. Đurović (n 1) 243. The Agency delivered its services in other NIAC occurred before WWII (e.g., the Spanish Civil War). See ibid.

[162] In not so recent conflict, one of the services accepted by the parties to the conflict has been the transmission of news and information to families. Đurović (n 1) 244.

[163] The [CTA] is often 'called upon in situations of international or internal conflicts'; its main function 'consists of keeping families together or bringing them together'. Sandoz and others (n 3) para 4553, 1379.

[164] Most of the conflicts in which the Agency has worked in the past have been of a non-international character. Đurović mentions the Spanish Civil war of 1935-39, the Algerian Conflict of 1955, and the Chadian civil war of 1965. Đurović (n 1) 94, 243, 248–253. During the Spanish Civil War, neither of the rival governments would accept the ICRC's offer to set up information bureaux to exchange details on prisoners; the Agency obtained its information from indirect sources (prison directors, camp commanders, military and civilian administrations, the prisoners themselves). However, it was the first time that ICRC delegates carried out tracing work and ensured mailing services for combatants and civilians in the field, despite the fact that the ICRC had no legal basis to do so. ICRC, 'History of the Central Tracing Agency of the ICRC - ICRC' (2002) <https://www.icrc.org/eng/resources/documents/misc/57jqrj.htm#1> accessed 12 September 2016.

[165] Georges Willemin, Roger Heacock and Jacques Freymond (eds), *The International Committee of the Red Cross* (M Nijhoff 1984) 100.

[166] See among others M Bothe, 'The Law of Neutrality' in Dieter Fleck and Michael Bothe (eds), *The Handbook of International Humanitarian Law* (Oxford University Press 2008) 597–601. See also the ICRC Study on Customary IHL, which offers a list of customary rules applicable in both types of conflict. Henckaerts and Doswald-Beck (n 21) xxix; Lindsay Moir, 'Towards the Unification of International Humanitarian Law?' in Richard Burchill, Nigel D White and Justin Morris (eds), *International Conflict and Security Law* (Cambridge University Press 2005) 108–128; Dapo Akande, 'Classification of Armed Conflicts: Relevant Legal Concepts' in Elizabeth Wilmshurst (ed), *International Law and the Classification of Conflicts* (Oxford University Press 2012) 35, 37.

[167] Pivotal differences are in place: for instance, the combatant status is not recognized in NIAC; this status is however a pre-condition of the status of POW. Similarly, the system addressing the status of civilian internee does not exist either. See JK Kleffner, 'Human Rights and International

status of combatant and, as a consequence, the full system addressing the status of POW does not exist in NIAC. The ICTY has taken this position a step further by arguing that

> in the area of armed conflict the distinction between interstate wars and civil wars is losing its value as far as human beings are concerned. Why protect civilians from belligerent violence, or ban rape, torture or the wanton destruction of hospitals, churches, museums or private property, as well as proscribe weapons causing unnecessary suffering when two sovereign States are engaged in war, and yet refrain from enacting the same bans or providing the same protection when armed violence has erupted "only" within the territory of a sovereign State?[168]

The ICTY's words corroborate the view on the contemporary purpose of international law that is adopted in this book: while duly safeguarding the legitimate interests of States, international law 'must gradually turn to the protection of human beings'[169] (see Chapter III).

Legally speaking, IHL as whole might be applicable in NIAC after a recognition of belligerency[170] by the government vis-à-vis the insurgents or after the conclusion of special agreements between the parties (the latter being an option outlined in Common Article 3).[171]

Humanitarian Law: General Issues' in Terry D Gill and Dieter Fleck (eds), *The Handbook of the International Law of Military Operations* (Oxford University Press 2011) 56–57.

[168] ICTY, *Prosecutor v. Duško Tadić, Decision on the Defence Motion ...* (n 23) [97].

[169] ibid.

[170] Recognition of belligerency by the government of a State in which civil war is raging, which has the effect of making the laws and customs of war applicable between that government and its adversaries (apart from the law of occupation), must not be confused with recognition of belligerency by the government of another State, which has the effect of making the law of neutrality applicable between that State and the parties involved in the civil war. Bougnion offers a historical account of the foundations of the doctrine of the recognition of belligerency, starting from Vattel, as well as an account of the practice: with regard to the latter, Bougnion underlines that the only known example of recourse to the mechanism of recognition of belligerency in the twentieth century is the civil war in Nigeria (1967). See François Bugnion, 'Jus Ad Bellum, Jus in Bello and Non-International Armed Conflicts' (2003) 6 Yearbook of International Humanitarian Law 167, 171–181. The practice of recognition of belligerency appears to have declined since the creation of the concept 'NIAC'. Although it seems that no instance of recognition of belligerency has been reported since the Boer War (1899-1902), there have been instances of third States recognizing belligerency of insurgency operating in other countries: e.g., recognition of the belligerency of the Nicaraguan Sandinistas by the Andean Group in 1979; recognition in 1981 by France and Mexico of El Salvadoran rebels, and recognition by Venezuela of the FARC group in Colombia in January 2008. See Akande (n 166) 50. Scholars have pointed out that recognition of belligerency is the most effective way of limiting violence in the event of civil war, since it brings into force the major part of the laws and customs of war: Erik Castrén, *Civil War* (Suomalainen tiedeakatemia 1966) 152; Paul Guggenheim and Denise Bindschedler-Robert, *Traité de Droit International Public: Avec Mention de La Pratique Internationale et Suisse*, vol 1 (Librairie Georg & Cie 1953) 207; N Mugerva, 'Subjects of International Law' in Max Sørensen (ed), *Manual of Public International Law* (MacMillan 1968) 287; Charles Zorgbibe, *La Guerre Civile* (Presses univ de France 1975) 47–56; Georg- Schwarzenberger, *International Law: As Applied by International Courts and Tribunals /. Vol. 2, The Law of Armed Conflict* (Stevens 1968) 691; Lassa Francis Lawrence-Oppenheim, *International Law: A Treatise /Vol 2, Disputes, War and Neutrality* (Hersch Lauterpacht ed, 7th ed, [5th impr], Longmans Green 1963) 211–212, 371.

[171] cf. Common Article 3 (3), GC I-IV. As the practice shows, this possibility is not mere 'law on the books'. For instance, in 1992, at the invitation of the ICRC, the various parties to the conflict within the Republic of Bosnia and Herzegovina concluded a special agreement in which the parties stated their

Furthermore, specific measures aimed at handling information on persons reported as missing during a NIAC are part of *ad hoc* commitments[172] – different from the ones referred to under Common Article 3 – concluded between the parties during and, most often, at the termination of the conflict. For instance, these commitments have set down the terms for the search for, identification and return of the remains in a dignified manner of those still missing as well as the establishment of special units whose tasks are the search for the whereabouts of individuals reported missing and the collation of relevant information;[173]

---

commitment to respect and to ensure respect for the provisions of common Article 3 and agreed to bring into force additional provisions concerning the protection of the wounded, sick and shipwrecked, of hospitals and other medical units, of the civilian population; among other examples of special agreements are a 1962 agreement in Yemen and a 1967 agreement in Nigeria, both negotiated by the ICRC and both containing commitments to abide by the GCs I-IV. See ICRC, *Increasing Respect for International Humanitarian Law in Non-International Armed Conflicts* (ICRC 2008) 17-18 <https://www.icrc.org/en/publication/0923-increasing-respect-international-humanitarian-law-non-international-armed-conflicts> accessed 12 September 2016. Another well-known special agreement was concluded between the parties to the conflict in Croatia (1991-5): the Memorandum of Understanding of 27 November 1991 relating to the conflict in Croatia provided *inter alia* that 'the Parties agree to set up a Joint Commission to trace missing persons; the Joint Commission will be made up of representatives of the parties concerned, all Red Cross organizations concerned and in particular the Yugoslav Red Cross, the Croatian Red Cross and the Serbian Red Cross with ICRC participation'. Reproduced in Sivakumaran (n 24) 125.

[172] The nature of these commitments – as non-traditional sources of international law - is examined by Sivakumaran who investigates about the purpose of these commitments (e.g., propaganda, interpretative tool), their normative status, and their implications on the implementation of IHL by non-state armed groups. See Sivakumaran (n 24) 107–113.

[173] This should be part of the measures to be implemented as part of the Agreement between the Fuerzas Armadas Revolucionarias de Colombia (FARC) and the Government of Colombia; the ICRC will be central in developing the action points conducive to the accomplishment of these measures. See Point I and II, FARC-EP International, 'Joint Communiqué No 62 on Missing Persons' (*FARC-EP International*) <https://farc-epeace.org/index.php/communiques/joint-communiques/item/879-joint-communique-62-on-missing-persons> accessed 7 September 2016. See also BBC Mundo, 'El Gobierno de Colombia Y Las FARC Llegaron a Un Acuerdo Para Buscar a Los Desaparecidos' (*BBC Mundo*, 18 Octubre 2015) <http://www.bbc.com/mundo/noticias/2015/10/151017_colombia_farc_ desaparecidos_acuerdo_ilm> accessed 12 September 2016. After being announced on August 24, a final peace accord was not agreed upon in a recent referendum. See Oficina del alto Comisionado para la paz, 'Comunicado Conjunto | Gobierno Y FARC-EP Anunciamos Que Hemos Llegado a Un Acuerdo Final, Integral Y Definitivo' (24 August 2016) <http://www.altocomisionadoparalapaz.gov.co/procesos-y-conversaciones/documentos-y-comunicados-conjuntos/Paginas/Comunicado-Conjunto-No-93-24-de-agosto-de-2016.aspx> accessed 31 August 2016. Nevertheless, the Colombian government and the FARC signed a revised peace deal on 24 November; this was directly sent to Congress for ratification: both houses of Congress ratified the revised peace accord on 29-30 November, 2016, thus marking an end to the conflict. See Joshua Partlow and Nick Miroff, 'Colombia's Congress Approves Historic Peace Deal with FARC Rebels' *The Washington Post* (30 November 2016) <https://www.washingtonpost.com/world/the_americas/colombian-congress-approves-historic-peace-deal/2016/11/30/9b2fda92-b5a7-11e6-939c-91749443c5e5_story.html> accessed 26 April 2017. A similar commitment is embedded in Article IV (4), Government of the Republic of Philippines (GRP)/Moro Islamic Liberation Front (MILF), 'Implementing Guidelines on the Humanitarian, Rehabilitation, and Development Aspects of the GRP-MILF Tripoli Agreement on Peace of 2001' (2002) <http://www.c-r.org/downloads/06s_3Key%20texts_2003_ENG.pdf> accessed 12 July 2016. It is interesting to note that similar commitments are also included in Articles 1 and 5, Russian Federation/Chechen Republic of Ichkeriya, 'Protocol of the Meeting of the Working Groups, Formed

the undertaking of every possible measure to search for missing persons and the dead;[174] the transmission of information, through the tracing mechanism of the ICRC, to the families of all persons who are unaccounted for;[175] the 'immediate' publication of the whereabouts of people reported missing during the conflict.[176] These measures are essentially driven by the willingness of the parties to collaborate, since the elucidation of the fate of those reported missing is key towards the achievement of reconciliation.[177] The capability of the parties to the conflict to carry out these measures is another essential aspect.[178] As Chapters III and IV will show, these commitments consolidate the standpoint that in post-conflict the (former) parties to the conflict bear an obligation to cooperate in their efforts to account for the missing. This obligation derives from a complementary understanding of the simultaneous application of IHL and IHRL rules on missing persons.

Willingness and operational capability can be volatile factors: although at the termination of a NIAC these commitments can be concluded, the constant presence of tensions – not reaching the threshold of NIAC – could change the approach of the State towards the missing or could slow it down.[179] Legislations can be enacted in order to prevent the handing over of any information and data

---

under the Negotiations Commissions, to Locate Missing Persons and to Free Forcibly Detained Persons' (1996) <http://peacemaker.un.org/russia-agreementmissingpeople96> accessed 12 July 2016.

[174] cf. Article 4 (9), Part IV, GRP/National Democratic Front of the Philippines, Comprehensive Agreement on Respect for Human Rights and International Humanitarian Law between the GRP and the National Democratic Front of the Philippines (1998) <http://peacemaker.un.org/philippines-agreement-human-rights98> accessed 17 October 2015.

[175] Cf. Article IV (4) (on the 'Respect for Human Rights and observance of international humanitarian laws'), GRP/ MILF, Implementing Guidelines - GRP-MILF Tripoli Agreement (n. 173).

[176] Cf. Article 17, Government of Nepal/CPN-Maoist, 'Ceasefire Code of Conduct Agreed between the Government of Nepal and the CPN-Maoist - (Unofficial Translation)' (Uppsala University website 2006) <http://www.ucdp.uu.se/downloads/fullpeace/Nep%2020060525.pdf> accessed 12 July 2016.

[177] On this point, see Monique Crettol and Anne-Marie La Rosa, 'The Missing and Transitional Justice: The Right to Know and the Fight against Impunity' (2006) 88 International Review of the Red Cross 355, 355–362.

[178] Sivakumaran (n 24) 285.

[179] For instance, this is the case of Sri Lanka, where only after six years since the termination of the NIAC the Government has enacted a bill dedicated to the establishment of the Office of Missing Persons – OMP (to be established at the time of writing). The mandate includes most of the provisions applicable in NIAC and IAC, e.g., the undertaking of search and tracing operations (directly or by means of identified mechanisms), the protection of the rights of missing persons as well as those of their families, and the collation of data previously collected by other bodies in order to centralize the information on missing persons. It would also have investigative powers, e.g., to initiate an inquiry and/or investigation into the whereabouts and/or circumstances of disappearance of a missing person pursuant to a complaint made to the OMP or on the basis of information received from previously established Commissions. The scope *ratione personae* of the work of the OMP is limited to 'missing persons' that corresponds to the following definition: 'person whose fate or whereabouts are reasonably believed to be unknown and which person is reasonably believed to be unaccounted for and missing: i) in the course of, consequent to, or in connection with the conflict which took place in the Northern and Eastern Provinces or its aftermath, or is a member of the armed forces or police who is identified as "missing in action"'. Cf. Article 10 (1) (a, c, e), Article 12 (b), Article 27 (i), Sri Lanka/Parliament. Office on Missing Persons (Establishment, Administration and Discharge of Functions) Act No 14, 23 August 2016.

on the burial sites as well as the human remains of adverse party's members, turned into 'terrorist group's members'.[180]

1.2.3. Conclusive observations

The analysis above unveils five main features proper to the system concerning the handling of information on missing persons in the context of an armed conflict. First, since AP I qualifies 'the right to know' as a general principle, it is arguable that the explicit recognition of this right is a confirmation of a legal tenet that has emerged all along the codification of IHL treaties. Although at the time of negotiations the right to know was not considered a legal right, the regulation of the handling of information under IHL treaties applicable in IAC concurs to the realization of this right. Second, the lack of universal ratification of AP I and the absence of a similar provision under the framework applicable in NIAC[181] partly affect the breadth of protection of the system concerning the handling of information. Although it has been advanced that there exists a customary rule[182] applicable in NIAC and IAC[183] concerning the duty of

---

[180] This has been the case of the Russian Federation and Chechnya: the adoption of the Protocol on the establishment of Working Groups aimed at locating Missing Persons seems to be part of the past (1996); with military operations still ongoing, in 2002 the Russian Federation enacted a federal law forbidding authorities to return the bodies of persons qualified as terrorists (or allegedly thought to be terrorists) to their families and to inform the relatives about the place of burial. On 28 October 2007, the Russian Federation's Constitutional Court upheld this ban, saying that this provision was necessary and justified: in the Court's words 'the burial of those who have taken part in a terrorist act, in close proximity to the graves of the victims of their acts, and the observance of rites of burial and remembrance with the paying of respects, as a symbolic act of worship, serve as a means of propaganda for terrorist ideas and also cause offence to relatives of the victims of the acts in question, creating the preconditions for increasing inter-ethnic and religious tension. [...] In such circumstances, the federal legislature may introduce special arrangements governing the burial of individuals whose death occurred as a result of the interception of a terrorist act in which they were taking part.' See ECtHR, *Arkhestov and others v Russia, Judgment* (2014) App no 22089/07 [39].

[181] In a progressive manner, the Commentary to AP I edited in 1987 emphasized that the recognition of a right to know in IAC would have had 'further repercussions, particularly with regard to the families of missing persons in [NIAC] and in the framework of human rights, even during internal disturbances'. Sandoz and others (n 3) para 1211, 346 (footnote 19).

[182] On the existence of a specific customary IHL, Chetail underlines that '[l]'expression même de "droit international humanitaire coutumier" est [...] discutable, en ce qu'elle procède à une confusion des genres entre deux registres distincts. Il existe certes un droit international coutumier qui reflète diverses règles de droit international humanitaire. Néanmoins une norme est coutumière indépendamment de son rattachement à une discipline spécifique et l'appartenance à une branche du droit international public ne présume pas de sa nature coutumière'. Chetail, 'Droit International Général et Droit International Humanitaire: Retour Aux Sources' (n 23) 43.

[183] Rule 117 which states that each Party to the conflict bears the above-mentioned duties poses other problematic issues: in a NIAC the expression 'each Party to the conflict' is clearly referring to both the governmental side and the non-state armed group(s); the ICRC CTA could help perform the activities concerning the gathering of information and its transmission to the families (the consent of the State being necessary); yet the extent of this provision is to be weighed against the capabilities of Parties. On this last aspect, see Sivakumaran (n 24) 285. Secondly, the norm under Article 32 AP I, which focuses on the right to know, is couched in obligation-based terms: the Rule no longer provides for a right of families to know the fate of their relatives, but an obligation of each party to the conflict to provide families with any information it has on missing persons' fate. The attempt to simplify the provisions contained in AP I has led to a downgrade of the right to know in the commentary note to Rule 117. On the simplification aspect, see Aldrich (n 23) 507. The Study

each party to the conflict to account for missing persons and to provide family members with any information on their fate,[184] there are still a gaps concerning the regulation of access to information on missing persons in both settings.[185] Moreover, the customary nature of this rule in NIAC cannot uniquely depend on the fact that the same rule exists in IAC.[186] From an operational perspective, the existence of customary rule applicable in NIAC does not clarify whether the non-state armed group(s) would be allowed to exchange information and data on an equal footing[187] at the end of the conflict.[188] Likewise, problematic and uncertain

---

underlines that, although the commentary note may contain useful clarifications, 'only the black letter rules are identified as part of customary international law, and not the commentaries to the rules'. Henckaerts and Doswald-Beck (n 21) lvii.

[184] Cf. Rule 117 'Accounting for Missing Persons' in Henckaerts and Doswald-Beck (n 21) 421 ff. Several critical comments have been put forward in the literature on the overall methodology of the ICRC Study on Customary IHL, mainly in relation to the use of other branches of international law (e.g., IHRL) to support, to strengthen, and to clarify the content of some rules, including Rule 117. In the words of the editors of the ICRC Study, the Study does not provide an assessment of customary IHRL, but practice under IHRL has been included because IHRL continues to apply during armed conflicts. See ibid xxxvi–xxxvii. *Contra*: Hampson states that the Study repurposes IHRL 'as evidence adding weight to other evidence'; Chetail observes that it draws from IHRL the existence of customary IHL rules. See Françoise Hampson, 'Other Areas of Customary Law in Relation to the Study' in Elizabeth Wilmshurst and Susan Breau (eds), *Perspectives on the ICRC study on customary international humanitarian law* (Cambridge University Press 2007) 72; Chetail, 'Droit International Général et Droit International Humanitaire: Retour Aux Sources' (n 23) 43.

[185] Scattered traces are present in the Conventions solely with regard to the possibility of making enquiries for the relatives of those who are in captivity and for members of dispersed families. Cf. Article 122 (7), GC III: 'The Information Bureau shall also be responsible for replying to all enquiries sent to it concerning POW, including those who have died in captivity; it will make any enquiries necessary to obtain the information which is asked for, if this is not in its possession'. Cf. Article 26, GC IV. Oddly enough, the Commentary specifies that 'Article 26 is concerned only with the re-establishing of family ties and therefore applies solely to members of dispersed families, not to all "displaced persons"'. See Pictet, *Commentary Vol IV (1958)* (n 38) 196.

[186] d'Aspremont and de Hemptinne (n 23) 39; Chetail, 'Droit International Général et Droit International Humanitaire: Retour Aux Sources' (n 23) 38. More generally, with regard to customary rules, the Appeals Chamber of the ICTY in the *Tadić Case* cautiously held that '[t]he emergence of the aforementioned general rules on [IAC] does not imply that internal strife is regulated by general international law in all its aspects. Two particular limitations may be noted: (i) only a number of rules and principles governing [IAC] have gradually been extended to apply to [NIAC]; and (ii) this extension has not taken place in the form of a full and mechanical transplant of those rules to internal conflicts; rather, the general essence of those rules, and not the detailed regulation they may contain, has become applicable to [NIAC]'. ICTY. *Prosecutor v. Duško Tadić, Decision on the Defence Motion ...* (n 23) [126]. With regard to the ICRC Study on Customary IHL, Aldrich underlines that it overlooks the fact that States engaged in NIAC will always oppose anything that could confer upon rebels the status of belligerent. Aldrich (n 23) 507.

[187] Interestingly, the commentary note to Rule 117 does not add many details as to the implementation of such a rule in NIAC; but it simply underlines that 'the obligation to account for missing persons is recognized in numerous agreements between parties to both international and non-international armed conflicts'. See Henckaerts and Doswald-Beck (n 21) 422. The same section on the dual-applicability of this rule refers to the Sudan People's Liberation Movement/Army's practice vis-à-vis the search for missing persons.' ibid 423. Two complications arise from this reference: first of all, the approach adopted by the ICRC to the custom formation, specifically with regard to the practice of non-state actors; secondly, the reference to one single example. In the introductory note of the Study, the ICRC apparently adopts a traditional approach: 'it is generally agreed that the existence of a rule of customary international law requires the presence of two elements, namely State practice (*usus*) and a behalf that such practice is required, prohibited or allowed, depending on

is the definition of the temporal scope of the duty to account for those who went missing in armed conflict.[189] For instance, after a certain amount of time since the termination of the conflict or since the termination of a specific military operation, nothing under IHL prevents a State from declaring dead persons reported missing.[190] Nevertheless, IHL must be read in light of 'any relevant rules of international law applicable in the relations between the parties',[191] which include IHRL (see sub-section 2.3.2.2, Chapter III).

---

the nature of the rule [...].' Accordingly, it clarifies that '[t]he practice of armed opposition groups, such as codes of conduct, commitments made to observe certain rules of [IHL] and other statements, does not constitute State practice as such. While such practice may contain evidence of the acceptance of certain rules in [NIAC], its legal significance is unclear and it has [...] been listed under "Other Practice"'. See ibid xxxvii ff.; xxxvii-xxxviii; xlii. The reason why the practice of armed groups is not set aside in a separate paragraph is ambiguous. See Ian Scobbie, 'The Approach to Customary International Law in the Study' in Elizabeth Wilmshurst and Susan Breau (eds), *Perspectives on the ICRC study on customary international humanitarian law* (Cambridge University Press 2007) 45–47. Assuming *arguendo* that the practice of non-state actors is to be considered in the customary formation process, one would expect more relevant examples in the commentary note, which should serve as an interpreting guidance. The digest of practice mentions one more example, i.e., the practice of the Hezb-i-Islami faction in Afghanistan with regard to the tracing of missing persons. Jean-Marie Henckaerts and Louise Doswald-Beck, *Customary International Humanitarian Law: Practice*, vol II (Cambridge University Press 2005) 2765. In addition to that, a series of bilateral treaties between State and non-state actors are considered. See ibid 2743, 2751, 2757–2758 and 2774. Certainly, the disclaimer in the introductory note of the Study helped the ICRC to avoid two orders of issues: first, the weight to attribute to an armed group in order for its practice to be counted as relevant; second, the weight to be given to the contrary practice of armed groups vis-à-vis a customary rule. See Scobbie 47.

[188] In some cases, the role of the ICRC in guiding the parties towards the adoption of a humanitarian approach to the issue of missing persons has contributed to facilitating the direct involvement of the non-state armed groups in the tracing activities. The role of the ICRC is essential with regard to the missing and their families. The traditional activities of the ICRC focused on the issue of missing persons are the visit to detained persons (with regard to IAC, cf. Articles 124 and 126, GC III; Articles 76, 142, and 143, GC IV; with regard to NIAC, cf. common Article 3, GCs I-IV), the protection of civilians affected by the conflict (Cf. Articles 10, 14, 59, 109, GC IV), the restoration of family links and the processing of tracing requests ('Restoration of family links' is a general expression that is implicitly embedded in several IHL Provisions, cf. Article 140, GC IV; Article 123, GC III; Article 78 (3) and Article 81, AP I). On this last point, see ICRC, *Restoring Family Links Strategy - Including Legal References* (ICRC 2009) 15 <https://www.icrc.org/eng/assets/files/other/icrc_002_0967.pdf> accessed 12 June 2015. In addition to the above, the ICRC' statute affirms that 'the role of the ICRC shall be *in particular...* to ensure the operation of the [CTA] as provided in the Geneva Conventions'. Cf. Article 4, para 1 (e), ICRC Statutes (1973). For a general overview of the ICRC's activities in relation to the missing, see Marco Sassòli and Marie-Louise Tougas, 'The ICRC and the Missing' (2002) 84 International Review of the Red Cross 727, 733–736.

[189] No temporal specification was added at the time of the negotiation of AP I, as the issue of the missing might remain pending for long after the termination of the conflict.

[190] For instance, pursuant to Article 21 (2) Egypt's Law no. 2 amending some provisions of Act no. 25 of 1929 concerning certain personal status provisions (2006), 'a missing person shall be presumed dead after fifteen days at least from the date his/her disappearance, in case evidence proved he/she was on board of a sinking ship, or a crashing plane, and after one year if he/she was a member of the armed forces and was reported missing during military operations'. ICRC, 'IHL National Implementation Database' (n 39).

[191] Article 31 (3) (c), Vienna Convention on the Law of Treaties, 1155 UNTS 331 (23 May 1969) (hereinafter VCLT).

Third, the examination above has also unveiled that although the terms 'enforced disappearance' are not enshrined in the IHL texts, the prohibition of enforced disappearance is directly connected with the system of handling of information.[192] Enforced disappearance is *per se* based on the idea of withholding information on the fate and whereabouts of persons; thus, it is in strong contrast with the rationale behind the rules examined in this Chapter.[193] Moreover, *durante bello,* while the GCs are silent with regard to a proactive obligation to investigate and uncover IHL violations which may represent the cause of the disappearance, the AP I requires the commanders to suppress and report to the competent authorities breaches of the GCs – including common Article 3 – and AP I.[194]

Fourth, at the operational level, some aspects of the regulation of the handling of information have proved unviable: as Sassòli and Rioux underline in their 2002 study[195] on the mechanisms aimed at elucidating the fate of the missing, 'in modern State practice, the parties to [IAC] generally do not meet their obligation to set up a [NIB], although the authorities do sometimes collect and transmit the information required. [...]. Often, it is the ICRC's delegates who have to perform the NIB's tasks.'[196] Although record-keeping is mentioned under GC I-IV and AP I, a broad leeway is left to the parties to the conflict with regard to the management of these records in the post-conflict phase and to the definition of the access policies.

2. THE TEMPORAL DIMENSIONS – *PRE, DURANTE, POST –*
OF THE HANDLING OF INFORMATION ON MISSING PERSONS UNDER IHL

After the examination of the incidence of the time factor in international law (sub-section 2.1), this section intends to delve deep into the interrelation among the temporal dimensions – *pre/durante/post* – of IHL rules concerning the handling of information and the overall question of the application *ratione temporis* of IHL (sub-section 2.2). This analysis will be conducive to the formulation of an

---

[192] Indeed, the ICRC Study on Customary IHL lists, among the rules, the prohibition of enforced disappearance. Cf. Rule 98, Henckaerts and Doswald-Beck (n 21) 340.

[193] For instance, in IAC the obligations to record certain pieces of information on those held in captivity, to collect particulars and objects belonging to the deceased, to ensure external communication in case of captivity, to exchange information or to facilitate the exchange of information on persons in vulnerable conditions (deprivation of liberty, wounded and sick, separated families) clearly aim at preventing that a person goes missing or 'is disappeared'. At the same time, in NIAC the fact that specific guarantees, including the communication with the external world, are ensured vis-à-vis people deprived of their liberty during and after the conflict and that efforts are put in place to trace the missing through the intermediary of alternative means (*ad hoc* commitments) confirms that the prohibition of enforced disappearance is embedded in the system itself.

[194] Cf. Article 87 (1) AP I.

[195] At the time of writing the practice does not seem to have changed compared to the findings of Sassòli and Rioux in Sassòli and Rioux (n 40).

[196] Clear difficulties in the setting up of the NIB have been emphasized during the studies and workshops related to the International Conference on the Missing organized by the ICRC. ibid 17.

understanding of the "post-" dimension[197] of the IHL rules on missing persons (sub-section 2.3).

2.1. General remarks on the effect of the time factor on international law

The time factor is inherent to the situation of persons who went missing in armed conflict under several respects: first, during the conflict, the handling of information on persons finding themselves at the hand of the enemy cannot be postponed at the end of the conflict; second, a fictional time limit cannot be put on the obligations concerning the tracing of those dispersed or reported as missing due to an armed conflict; third, although – optimistically – temporary, uncertainty about the fate of missing persons might last for decades. On the other hand, as soon as families realize that their relatives are missing, they would start searching for information. A never-ending quest for information might be generated by poor record keeping, temporary security issues blocking access to information, dispersion and fragmentation in the holding of data and information, and diversity of access policies of the institutions holding relevant information with temporal or other kinds of limit. What is then the outcome of the relationship between the passage of time and the legal framework applicable to the matters above?

What time is and how the impact of the passage of time can be evaluated has been tackled in different areas; yet Saint Augustine in his Book XI of *Confessions* humbly answers 'if no one asks me, I know what it is. If I wish to explain it to him who asks me, I do not know'.[198] Interrogating himself on the past and the future, he concludes that the present of past things is memory, the present of present things is attention, and the present of future things is expectation.[199] Although part of a complex autobiographical work focusing, *inter alia,* on his conversion to Christianity, this cameo of St. Augustine's thought sums up the three dimensions that characterize the 'present' of persons reported missing in armed conflict and that of their families. The effects of the passage of time on the present time of families that live in complete uncertainty can be termed according to St. Augustine's triad, i.e., memory, attention which the mind devotes to present things, expectations.

The examination of the incidence of the temporal dimension in law has not been sufficiently developed in contemporary (international) legal scholarship.[200]

---

[197] In the *Tadić case*, the Appeal Chamber has stressed that '[…] the temporal and geographical scope of both internal and international armed conflicts extends beyond the exact time and place of hostilities. With respect to the temporal frame of reference of international armed conflicts, each of the GCs I-IV contains language intimating that their application may extend beyond the cessation of fighting.' ICTY. *Prosecutor v. Duško Tadić, Decision on the Defence Motion ...* (n 23) [67].

[198] Saint Augustine/Outler, *Confessions and Enchiridion* (Albert Cook ed, Albert Cook tr, SCM Press 1955) ch Chapter XIV, para 17.

[199] Ibid, para 26.

[200] Antônio Augusto Cançado Trindade, *Judge Antônio A. Cançado Trindade. The Construction of a Humanized International Law: A Collection of Individual Opinions (1991-2013)* (Brill-Nijhoff 2014) 369. Nonetheless, *ad hoc* conferences have been organized on the matter: for instance, the 34th colloquium of the *Société française de Droit International* was solely dedicated to the topic "*Droit international et le temps*", see Société française pour le droit international. Colloque. *Le droit*

The passage of time is not a legal notion; undeniably, international law is related to it, but this relationship is a consequence of the fact that international law *se meut dans l'universe du temps.*[201] However, it is by observing the passage of time that how the law regulates events occurring at a certain point in time can be understood. The law operates in the present time with the generation of effects that are visible and manifest in the very moment in which they are generated:[202] thus, it is not definite that the law always succeeds in mastering the future.

At the international law level, the relation between law and time has been tackled in thematic contexts that are different from the one under analysis: questions have been posed with regard to how international law regulates the passage of time or what effect the passage of time has on international law.[203] No clear-cut answer has been found and, as a consequence, it has been submitted that the absence of rules concerning the setting of fixed deadlines reflects the flexibility of international law to adapt itself to concrete circumstances.[204] In light of this flexibility, a State may be able to choose from a range of policies, all of which will – optimistically – be legal.[205]

What is the choice – if any – that States can make vis-à-vis uncertainty generated by an armed conflict? Prevention of uncertainty is key to pave the way towards normalcy; therefore, pursuant to IHL, the parties to the conflict must ensure that information on the fate and whereabouts of specific categories of persons is shared with the families and the State of nationality. IHL is 'a permanent

---

international et le temps : Colloque de Paris. Paris: A. Pedone, 2001; similarly, in 2015, the Graduate Institute of International and Development Studies held a conference on "International Law and Time", see more details at http://goo.gl/lMvhd0 accessed 15 October 2015.

[201] J Combacau, 'L'écoulement du temps' in Société française pour le droit international. Colloque (dir.), *Le droit international et le temps : Colloque de Paris* (A. Pedone 2001) 77.

[202] Ibid 105.

[203] Martin Dawidowicz, 'The Effect of the Passage of Time on the Interpretation of Treaties: Some Reflections on Costa Rica v. Nicaragua' (2011) 24 Leiden Journal of International Law 201, 201–222; Antônio Augusto Cançado Trindade, 'The Time Factor in the Application of the Rule of Exhaustion of Local Remedies in International Law' (1978) 61 Rivista di Diritto Internazionale 61 232, 232–257; Rosalyn Higgins, 'Time and the Law: International Perspectives on an Old Problem' (1997) 46 International and Comparative Law Quarterly 501, 501.Dawidowicz, Martin. "The Effect of the Passage of Time on the Interpretation of Treaties: Some Reflections on Costa Rica v. Nicaragua." *Leiden Journal of International Law* 24, no. 01 (March 2011), at 201–222;

[204] Paul Reuter (Professor), 'Oral Argument, Counsel of the Government of Cambodia, Case Concerning the Temple of Preah Vihear (Cambodia v. Thailand), ICJ Reports, Pleadings, Oral Arguments (in French)' (1962) Documents, II 203. Professor Reuter also pointed out that three elements should be considered in order to specify the concrete circumstances that must be taken into account in the assessment of deadlines and/or periods of time: the subject matter under analysis; the time's density, as what makes the density of the human time as regarded at the juridical level, is the density, i.e., the multitude of the juridical acts that have occurred or that could have occurred; and the situation between the Parties. See Ibid. A similar stance has been argued by Ambrus and Wessel; in their words, 'international legal rules may ...function as tools to deal with non-permanent or constantly changing issues, and rather than stable, international law may have to be flexible or adaptive'. Mónika Ambrus and Ramses A Wessel, 'Between Pragmatism and Predictability: Temporariness in International Law' (2014) 45 Netherlands Yearbook of International Law 1, 4.

[205] On the flexible nature of international law, see Martin Dixon, *Textbook on International Law* (Oxford University Press 2013) 12.

reminder that armed conflict [...] is a temporary, exceptional situation';[206] this also implies that IHL is not crafted in order to be applied permanently. Nevertheless, when people go missing in an armed conflict, the obligation to account for them continues for as long as their fate remains unknown.

2.2. The temporal dimensions of the rules on the issue of missing persons

Traditionally, the definition of the beginning[207] and end of IHL application is not an easy task[208] in relation to IAC[209] and is even more complex with regard to NIAC. With regard to the beginning, a fact-based assessment of the situation on the ground requires to take into account whether 'there is a resort to armed force between States or protracted armed violence between governmental authorities and organized armed groups or between such groups within a State. [IHL] applies from the initiation of such armed conflicts'.[210] With regard to the end,[211]

---

[206] Michel Veuthey, 'From Solferino to Kosovo: The Contribution of International Humanitarian Law to International Security' in John Carey, William V Dunlap and R John Pritchard (eds), *International Humanitarian Law: Origins, Challenges, Prospects (3 Vols)* (Transnational Publishers 2005) 207.

[207] Cf. Article 5, GC I; Article 5, GC III; Article 6, GC IV; Article 3, AP I; Article 2 (2), AP II.

[208] Marko Milanović, 'The End of Application of International Humanitarian Law' (2014) 96 International Review of the Red Cross 163, 164; Julia Grignon, 'The Beginning of Application of International Humanitarian Law: A Discussion of a Few Challenges' (2014) 96 International Review of the Red Cross 139, 140.

[209] For instance, in the case of an IAC, the starting point might be as soon as the first protected person is affected by the conflict, the first segment of territory occupied, the first attack launched; or, in case of a NIAC, as soon as the necessary level of violence and of organization is reached. See Marco Sassòli, Antoine A Bouvier and Anne Quintin, *How Does Law Protect in War?: Cases, Documents, and Teaching Materials on Contemporary Practice in International Humanitarian Law. Vol. I - Outline of International Humanitarian Law. III (Online Version)* (ICRC 2011) Part I, Ch 2, 34.

[210] ICTY, *Prosecutor v. Duško Tadić, Decision on the Defence Motion ...* (n 23) [70].

[211] The end of application of IHL may be connected to the end of an armed conflict; however, this section proves that this is not the case for all the IHL rules. The terminology used under IHL treaties with regard to the termination of an armed conflict is fact-driven. In IAC, the wording used is the following: 'general close of military operations' in Article 6 (2), GC IV and Article 3 (b), AP I; 'one year after the general close of military operations' or 'the termination of the occupation' in Article 3 (b), AP I. In NIAC: 'end of the armed conflict' in Article 2 (2), AP II. In the words of the ICTY, the end of an armed conflict is sanctioned by the most traditional means, as IHL will apply 'until [...] a peaceful settlement is achieved'. ICTY. *ibid.* Although the stance put forward in the *Tadić case* might look like a revival of traditional formalism concerning peace treaties, the ICTY's view 'holds true as a matter of law to the extent that the "peaceful settlement" is also an accurate description of the factual situation on the ground.' JK Kleffner, 'Towards a Functional Conceptualization of the Temporal Scope of Jus Post Bellum' in Carsten Stahn, Jennifer S Easterday and Jens Iverson (eds), *Jus Post Bellum: Mapping the normative Foundations* (Oxford University Press 2014) 290–291. With regard to NIAC, scholars are quite divided: some consider NIACs in the same way as IACs and identify the end of a NIAC accordingly (i.e., 'so long as some hostilities continue, so would a NIAC' or 'the general close of military operations' will mark the general termination), see Sivakumaran (n 24) 252–254; Julia Grignon, *L'applicabilité Temporelle Du Droit International Humanitaire* (Schulthess éd romandes 2014) 275. Others underline that the only legally relevant question is whether the intensity threshold, spelled out in AP II and implicitly contained in Common Article 3, continues to be satisfied. See Milanović (n 208); ILA, 'Final Report on the Meaning of Armed Conflict in International Law - The Hague Conference' (2010) 30–31 <http://www.ila-hq.org/en/committees/index.cfm/cid/1022> accessed 12 July 2016; R Bartels, 'From Jus in Bello to Jus Post Bellum: When Do Non-International Armed Conflicts End?' in Carsten Stahn, Jennifer S Easterday and Jens Iverson (eds), *Jus Post Bellum: Mapping the normative Foundations* (Oxford

IHL does not cease to apply as a whole at the same time, but it will be phased out gradually and functionally.[212] Therefore, the continuing character of certain situations, such as uncertainty about the fate of missing persons,[213] entails a continuing application of a set of IHL rules in the aftermath of an armed conflict. In addition to a factual appraisal of the situation on the ground, the interpretation of the scope *ratione temporis* of IHL is strongly related to how within a certain professional setting (government, military, academia, humanitarian organizations) a number of competing policy considerations are weighted.[214] Despite the foregoing, the literature on this topic remains scant.[215] Thus, this sub-section aims at providing an understanding of the temporal dimensions of the rules on missing persons applicable in IAC/belligerent occupation (sub-section 2.2.1) and NIAC (sub-section 2.2.2) situations.

University Press 2014) 297-414. The standpoint that might tip the scale is that put forward by the ICTY: once the necessary level of violence and of organization of the Parties is such that the IHL of NIACs is applicable, that law continues to apply until the end of the conflict, even when those levels are no longer met. The foregoing reasoning was framed by the ICTY by referring to the *Tadić Test*, see ICTY. *Prosecutor v Haradinaj et al. Trial Judgment* (2008) Case no IT-04-84-T [100]. The issue was addressed before the ICTY by an accused who proposed that an intensity and organization threshold should apply to the case against him; the Trial Chamber, however, held that the relevant situation amounted to an IAC and, consequently, did not consider the proposed determination. See ICTY. *Prosecutor v Ante Gotovina, Trial Judgment* (2011) Case no. IT-06-90-T [1694].

[212] Robert Kolb, *Ius in bello: le droit international des conflits armés; précis* (II, Helbing & Lichtenhahn 2009) 221.

[213] Still unknown is the fate of tens of thousands after the Iran/Iraq Conflict of 1980-1988, see ICRC, 'Iran-Iraq: Still Missing since the 1980-1988 War' (10 October 2014) <https://www.icrc.org/en/document/iran-iraq-still-missing-1980-1988-war> accessed 2 June 2015; 300.000 are still missing due to thirty years of fighting before 1975, see ICMP, 'Where Are the Missing? - Vietnam' <http://www.ic-mp.org/the-missing/where-are-the-missing/vietnam/> accessed 2 July 2015; about 1700 remain unaccounted for in Kosovo after the 1999 conflict, see ICMP, 'Where Are the Missing? – Kosovo' <http://www.ic-mp.org/the-missing/where-are-the-missing/kosovo/> accessed 2 July 2015. The countries where the issue is still pending are numerous; these include Afghanistan, Colombia (ongoing conflict), Cyprus, DRC, India/Pakistan (Kashmir and Jammu), Kuwait. A comprehensive list is provided in the ICMP's website, available at the following link http://www.ic-mp.org/the-missing/where-are-the-missing/, accessed on 23 July 2015.

[214] On top of this factor, Milanovic considers the lack of coherency within this body of law, which has been tailored by different lawyers in different times, as well as the fragmented factual and objective thresholds of modern IHL. See Milanović (n 208) 164.

[215] See, for instance, Grignon (n 211); Derek Jinks, 'The Temporal Scope of Application of International Humanitarian Law in Contemporary Conflicts' [2003] HPCR Background Paper; Milanović (n 208); Grignon (n 208). For a general overview see Marco Sassòli, Antoine A Bouvier and Anne Quintin, *How Does Law Protect in War?: Cases, Documents, and Teaching Materials on Contemporary Practice in International Humanitarian Law*, vol I-Outline of International Humanitarian Law (III, ICRC 2011) 134–135. Some aspects on the issue are touched on by Y Dinstein, 'The Initiation, Suspension and Termination of War' in Michael N Schmitt (ed), *International Law Across the Spectrum of Conflict: essays in honour of Professor L.C. Green on the occasion of his eightieth birthday*, vol 75 (Naval War College 2000); Vaios Koutroulis, *Le Début et La Fin de L'application Du Droit de L'occupation* (Pedone 2010); Collège d'Europe, 'Le Champ D'application Du Droit International Humanitaire', *Actes du Colloque de Bruges, 13th Bruges Colloquium, 19-19 October 2012* <https://www.icrc.org/fre/resources/documents/news-release/2012/belgium-news-2012-10-18.htm> accessed 12 June 2015.

2.2.1. Considerations on the temporal dimensions of the rules on missing persons applicable in IAC/belligerent occupation

Both in GCs I-IV and in the Protocols, temporal indications on the activation of the implementation of some IHL provisions are introduced with the use of diverse expressions (e.g., 'from the end of active hostilities',[216] the 'cessation of active hostilities',[217] and 'at latest at the end of hostilities'[218]). The expression 'at the end/close of hostilities' is also used to set down the temporal limit within which the implementation of the obligations needs to be carried out (e.g., the obligation to exchange the records related to the location and marking of the graves).[219]

Of a different nature is the expression 'as soon as the circumstances permit': if it is possible, the parties to the conflict must put these obligations into practice during the conflict (e.g., the exchange of records on the marking of graves and their locations); as a corollary, the notion of immediacy is implicitly embedded.[220] A similar wording is used in AP I: pursuant to Article 33, the obligation to search for the missing cannot be carried out during the heat of battle, but 'as soon as the circumstances permit' and 'at latest from the end of active hostilities'. In other words, nothing prevents a party to the conflict from starting the tracing operations during the hostilities.[221] However, the end of active hostilities is considered the temporal limit to start fulfilling the obligation.[222] The use of the expression 'active hostilities' can bring about an extension of the temporal applicability of the provision concerned; this implies that the provision would remain applicable well beyond the 'general close of military operations'.[223]

The end/close of (active) hostilities does not correspond to 'the general close of military operations': the latter seems to refer to the end of application of IHL.[224] The meaning of 'active hostilities' − a terminology which is used in the

---

[216] Cf. Article 33(1) AP I.

[217] Cf. Article 118 GC III; Article 45 GC IV.

[218] Cf. Article 17 GC I.

[219] Pursuant to Article 17 (4) GC I, '[a]s soon as circumstances permit, and at latest at the end of hostilities, these [Official Graves Registration] Services shall exchange, through the Information Bureau mentioned in the second paragraph of Article 16 lists showing the exact location and markings of the graves together with particulars of the dead interred therein' (emphasis added). Pursuant to Article 130 (3) GC IV of 1949, '[a]s soon as circumstances permit, and not later than the close of hostilities, the Detaining Power shall forward lists of graves of deceased internees to the Powers on whom the deceased internees depended, through the Information Bureaux provided for in Article 136. [...]'

[220] The Commentary to Article 17 underlines that 'the Diplomatic Conference adopted the proposal of the Government Experts of 1947, who had pointed out that in the WWII such exchanges had actually taken place during hostilities. The practice was a desirable one and deserved to be officially recognized'. See Pictet, *Commentary Vol I (1952)* (n 15) 182.

[221] Đurović (n 1) 273.

[222] The provision on the dead does not refer to the end of (active) hostilities; the expression used, (i.e., 'As soon as circumstances and the relations between the adverse Parties permit') has a direct connection with the key aspect of the conflict, i.e., the relations among the parties. A certain leeway is left to the Parties vis-à-vis the final appraisal of their relations. See Sandoz and others (n 3) para 149, 371.

[223] Grignon (n 211) 326–327.

[224] This expression is used in Article 6 GC IV, which regulates the scope of application *ratione temporis* of the Convention. Its wording is not straightforward and leaves room to various interpretations. Pursuant to this provision '[t]he present Convention shall apply from the outset of any conflict or

provisions concerning missing persons – is not clear-cut: it might refer to the end of 'armed hostilities'[225] or, as suggested by some authors, might be tantamount to saying that the latest time when a party to the conflict should start searching for missing persons is the time when POW have to be repatriated.[226] Indeed, such expression 'is also used in GC III: Article 118 (1) on the repatriation of POW refers to the 'cessation of active hostilities', i.e., when the time of fighting is over.[227] Furthermore, after the end of armed hostilities, parties to the conflict might still adopt a hostile conduct and run military operations without the use of armed force. Therefore, these considerations confirm that 'end of active hostilities' cannot be equated to 'general close of military operations'.[228] Since no time-limit is set down with regard to how long the tracing operations should last, these should continue until the persons reported missing are no longer listed as missing, regardless of 'the final end of all fighting between all those concerned'.[229] This interpretation finds a confirmation in the fact that, during the Diplomatic Conference for the adoption of the Protocols, nobody expressed a contrary standpoint with regard to the unlimited duration of these operations.[230]

GCs I-IV provide for duration-related provisions:[231] while some scholars interpret these as provisions that set down the temporal application of the Conventions,[232] others[233] point out that those under GC I and GC III[234] exclusively

---

occupation mentioned in Article 2. In the territory of Parties to the conflict, the application of the present Convention *shall cease on the general close of military operations*. In the case of occupied territory, the application of the present Convention *shall cease one year after the general close of military operations*; [...] Protected persons whose release, repatriation or re-establishment may take place *after such dates* shall meanwhile continue to benefit by the present Convention. [Emphases added]'. According to Pictet, 'in most cases the general close of military operations will be the final end of all fighting between all those concerned'. Pictet, *Commentary Vol IV (1958)* (n 38) 62.

[225] Sandoz and others (n 3) para 1238, 352.

[226] Bothe, Partsch and Solf (n 25) 172.

[227] Pictet, *Commentary Vol III (1960)* (n 30) 547.

[228] With regard to the latter, difficult is to determine the exact moment of the general close of military operations: contemporary armed conflicts result in unstable cease-fires, continue at a lower intensity, or are frozen by an armed intervention by outside forces or by the international community. Sassòli, Bouvier and Quintin (n 215) 134. Greenwood states that 'since armed conflict is not a technical, legal concept but a recognition of the fact of hostilities, the cessation of active hostilities should be enough to terminate the conflict'. See CJ Greenwood, 'Scope of Application of Humanitarian Law' in Dieter Fleck and Michael Bothe (eds), *The Handbook of International Humanitarian Law* (Oxford University Press 2008) 72.

[229] Pictet, *Commentary Vol IV (1958)* (n 38) 62.

[230] Sandoz and others (n 3) para 149, 353. During the Diplomatic Conference, the Rapporteur of the Working Group remarked that '[t]he representative of the [CTA] of the ICRC had in fact suggested adding a provision to the effect that the search should continue without any limit of duration, but the members of the Working Group had considered that such a provision was implicit in the paragraph.' ICRC, 'Official Records of the Diplomatic Conference..., Vol XII' (n 125) (CDDH/II/SR.76) para 28, 232.

[231] Article 5 GC I focuses on the duration of the application; similarly, Article 5 GC III and Article 6 GC IV tackle the beginning and end of application. By contrast, GC II does not contain a provision on the duration of application; its Article 4 uniquely regards the field of application *ratione materiae* of the Convention itself.

[232] Sassòli, Bouvier and Quintin (n 215) 134; Anna Petrig, 'The War Dead and Their Gravesites' (2009) 874 International Review of the Red Cross 341, 363 (Footnote n 180).

[233] Grignon (n 211) 245.

concern the temporal duration of the status of specific categories of persons (i.e., the wounded and sick and the POW). The two remarks are intertwined:[235] for instance, Article 5 of GC III underlines that the Convention 'shall apply' to the persons covered by the Convention – POW – 'from the time they fall into the power of the enemy and until their final release and repatriation'. POW will be repatriated for health reasons[236] during the conflict or 'without delay at the cessation of active hostilities';[237] no exact temporal detail is provided with regard to when active hostilities may be considered as ceased.[238] The case of GC IV is peculiar, as it sets down an explicit temporal limit in case of occupation, i.e., the application of GC IV 'shall cease one year after the general close of military operations' except for some provisions that will continue to bind the Occupying Power.[239]

AP I fills some of the *lacunae* under GCs I-IV. For instance, it covers those persons who will not receive a more favorable treatment under the Conventions or under the Protocol itself. This implies that the obligation to search for the missing and to transmit the relevant information to the adverse party is not related to a specific status at all and does not depend on the termination of such status. As long as the fate of persons reported missing remains unknown, the parties to the conflict have a duty to account for them and to provide the families with any piece of information that is relevant to clarify the fate of their relatives. Indeed, Articles 33 (*the missing*) and 34 (*the dead*) enshrine provisions 'applicable at all times',[240] i.e., their application may continue beyond the end of armed conflict.[241] The same consideration holds valid for the obligation to

---

[234] Cf. Article 5 GC I and GC III.

[235] For instance, this is inferable from what the Pictet's Commentary to Article 5 GC I puts forward: 'it is clear [....] that the Convention will cease to apply to the wounded and sick from the moment they are cured. This does not result from the actual Article under review, but from the general structure of the Convention. [...] Once they have regained their health, only the Third Convention, relative to the treatment of [POW], applies'. See Pictet, *Commentary Vol I (1952)* (n 15) 65.

[236] Cf. Annexes I and II GC III.

[237] Cf. Articles 118-119 GC III.

[238] However, in the French version of the Commentary, i.e., the original one, the following indication is added after 'cessation of active hostilities': 'c'est-à-dire après le cessez-le-feu'. The lack of this reference in the English text shows that the editors of the commentary tried to avoid connecting the activation of the obligation to any formal step (e.g., adoption of an agreement, cease-fire *etc*...), as the Commentary to the Protocol emphasizes with regard to the expression 'active hostilities' in Article 34. The appraisal of the amount of days constituting a delay in the repatriation of POW after the 'cessation of active hostilities' has been developed by the Eritrea-Ethiopia Claims Commission. The Commission held that 'Ethiopia violated its obligations under Article 118 of [GC] III by failing to repatriate 1,287 POWs by September 13, 2002, and that it is responsible to Eritrea for the resulting delay of seventy-seven days.' Eritrea Ethiopia Claims Commission. *Prisoners of War - Eritrea's Claim 17, between the State of Eritrea and the Federal Democratic Republic of Ethiopia* (2003) Partial Award para 163, 38. The appraisal has been subjected to critical analyses in the literature. See Grignon (n 211) 344-349.

[239] These include, for instance, provisions that aim at ensuring guarantees to protected persons. Cf. Article 6, GC IV of 1949.

[240] The expression is mentioned under Article 3 (b) of AP I.

[241] Sandoz and others (n 3) para 149, 66-67. Article 32 AP I is implicitly included in these provisions, for it is the 'general principle' that shall prompt the activities that are carried out under Part II, Section III of AP I. The ICRC commentary observes that the provisions applicable at all times can be divided into various degrees or groups: viz., 'a) the Final Provisions [...], some of which necessarily apply even before the Protocol enters into force; b) provisions which apply as soon as the Protocol enters into force

'facilitate enquiries made by members of families dispersed owing to the war' and to 'encourage […] the work of organizations engaged on this task'.[242] As for the temporal limit in case of occupation, AP I has adopted a different approach which reflects the draft version of GC IV (rejected in 1949): 'the application of the Conventions and of [the] Protocol shall cease […] in the case of occupied territories, on the termination of the occupation, except […] for those persons whose final release, repatriation or re-establishment takes place thereafter'.[243] This holds valid 'without prejudice to the provisions which are applicable at all times', including those on missing persons.[244]

In light of the humanitarian character of the Conventions, of the existence of successive treaties – e.g., AP I – and of the subsequent practice,[245] among the measures to be taken during and after the conflict/occupation[246] are the following ones: search operations, collation and transmission of information on missing persons and specific categories of persons, and the restoration of family links by

---

[…]; c) provisions which may apply from the entry into force of the Protocol […]; d) articles whose application in relation to a conflict may continue beyond the termination of this conflict, such as Articles 33 (*Missing Persons*) [and] 34 (*Remains of deceased*) …[emphasis added]'. See ibid para 149, 67.

[242] As a matter of fact, this obligation covers the civilian population of the party to the conflict. Cf. Article 26 GC IV.

[243] Cf. Article 3 (b), AP I; Sandoz and others (n 3) para 154 ff, 68.

[244] Cf. Article 3 *chapeau*, AP I; ibid para 149, 66-67.

[245] States have often decided to handle these requests of information concerning dispersed family members with the creation of *ad hoc* bodies. For instance, mechanisms whose objectives include clarifying the fate of missing persons and support for their families have been created in East Timor (Commission for Reception, Truth and Reconciliation in East Timor), Bosnia and Herzegovina (Missing Persons Institute) and Iraq (the department for missing persons, POW, and human remains of the Ministry of Human Rights). See ICRC, 'The Missing. ICRC Progress Report' (n 91) 13. A recent example is Sri Lanka. See Interview of Dominic Stillhart, Director of Operations: ICRC, 'Sri Lanka: Clarifying the Fate of Missing Persons Requires Sustained Commitment' (*International Committee of the Red Cross*, 26 March 2015) <https://www.icrc.org/en/document/clarifying-fate-missing-persons-sri-lanka-requires-sustained-commitment> accessed 12 September 2016. Another example is Angola where, after the 2002 ceasefire, the ICRC, working in cooperation with the Angola Red Cross, has set up a major tracing program and has opened tracing offices that allow Angolan people to restore and maintain family links interrupted during the war; open tracing requests to find family members whose fate or location is unknown; find families of separated children; ad trace children based on parents' requests. ICRC, 'The Missing. ICRC Progress Report' (n 91) 10. For an appraisal of the work of some of these bodies in post-conflict peacebuilding, see Chapter V.

[246] Article 26 GC IV is implicitly connected to Article 27 GC IV on the treatment of protected persons. The latter is one of those provisions that remain applicable after the clear-cut limit fixing the ceasing of application of IHL in case of occupation: it might occur that, after the close of military operations, the occupation is prolonged beyond the one-year limit (e.g., the Occupying Power is victorious); in this respect, the Diplomatic Conference drew up a list of Articles that 'the Occupying Power must observe after the period of one year has elapsed, so long as the occupation lasts, in so far as that Power exercises governmental functions'. Among these is Article 27 GC IV, which *inter alia* provides for the respect of family rights (e.g., family ties must be maintained; these ties must also be restored, should they have been broken as a result of wartime events as provided for in Articles 25 and 26 GC IV). In addition, Article 27 (4) sets forth a safety valve for protected persons who could not have been able to resume a normal existence when the Convention - taken as a whole - ceases to apply both in the territory of the Parties to the conflict and in occupied territory: accordingly, the persons concerned will continue to enjoy all their rights under the Convention. See Pictet, *Commentary Vol IV (1958)* (n 38) 63-64, 202-203.

enabling families to reconnect with their dispersed members.[247] The absence of a fixed timeframe for such activities is in line with the humanitarian character of the duty to relieve the suffering of the next of kin of missing persons; this is the rationale behind Part II, Section III on *Missing and Dead Persons* in AP I. The ICRC study on customary rules confirms this reading (cf. Rule 117 and Rule 105 highlighted above): the only limit that can restrain the efforts to account for missing persons is related to the capacity of the parties to the conflicts (these are required to take 'all feasible' measures) not to the duration of this obligation.[248]

2.2.2. Considerations on the temporal dimensions of the rules on missing persons applicable in NIAC

In the context of NIAC, temporal indications on the termination/continuation of specific measures are embedded into AP II: the protection deriving from rules relating to internment/detention[249] and to judicial guarantees[250] goes beyond the duration of the conflict in situations of deprivation or restriction of liberty for reasons related to the conflict. This holds valid in all situations in which the deprivation/restriction of liberty occurs after the conflict for the same reasons (the limit being the termination of deprivation/restriction of liberty). In other words, these rules apply at all times and without any restriction in time.[251] The handling of information concerning persons deprived of their liberty or whose liberty has been restricted is barely tackled;[252] in this regard, the protective framework outlined in AP II is minimal:[253] Parties to the conflict bears the obligation to respect a 'legal right'[254] bestowed upon persons deprived of their liberty for reasons relating to the conflict, i.e., the right to send and receive letters (subjected to restrictions if necessary).[255]

---

[247] The practice shows that this has been the case in those post-conflict contexts where the issue of missing persons was among the consequences of the armed conflict; in such contexts the commitment of the former parties to the conflict to account for the missing has been integrated in the peace agreements. Cf. Chapter III of the 1973 Agreement on Ending the War and Restoring Peace in Vietnam signed on behalf of the USA, the Republic of Vietnam, and the Provisional Revolutionary Government of South Vietnam, Paris, 27 January 1973. Article 5 of Annex 7 of the Dayton Agreements states: 'The Parties shall also cooperate fully with the ICRC in its efforts to determine the identities, whereabouts and fate of the unaccounted for'. See Annex 7 - Agreement on Refugees and Displaced Persons of the General Framework Agreement for Peace in Bosnia and Herzegovina, signed by the Republic of Bosnia and Herzegovina, the Federation of Bosnia and Herzegovina, and the Republic Srpska, Dayton 22 November 1995 in Henckaerts and Doswald-Beck (n 187) 2757.

[248] Henckaerts and Doswald-Beck (n 21) 426.

[249] Cf. Article 5 of AP II.

[250] Cf. Article 6 of AP II concerns Penal Prosecutions.

[251] Sandoz and others (n 3) para 4495, 1360.

[252] Article 5 of AP II covers persons whose liberty has been restricted.

[253] Pursuant to the *chapeau* of Article 5 of AP II, the provisions concerning detention and internment as well as other form of deprivation/restriction of liberty are additional to the fundamental guarantees listed in Article 4 of APII. As a matter of logic, since detention-related guarantees are already 'the minimum' to be respected vis-à-vis persons deprived of their liberty and this minimum is 'additional' to the fundamental guarantees, the latter would not cease to apply until the end of the deprivation of liberty.

[254] Sandoz and others (n 3) para 4585, 1390.

[255] Cf. Article 5 (2) (b), AP II.

'Persons under house arrest or who live under surveillance in any other way'[256] for reasons related to the armed conflict might not fall under the scope of application *ratione personae* of detention/internment-related rules under the Protocol:[257] these persons 'shall be treated humanely in accordance with Article 4 and with paragraphs 1 (a), (c) and (d), and 2 (b)' of Article 5 AP II. Thus, should this situation of captivity go beyond the end of armed conflict, these persons must enjoy the possibility of receiving and sending letters and, at same time, must benefit from measures aimed at facilitating the reunion of families who are temporarily separated due to the conflict[258] (i.e., measures clearly aimed at preventing their disappearance).

As the practice shows, the commitment of all the former parties to the conflict to account for missing persons is part of post-conflict peace settlements. [259] Moreover, in the post-conflict phase, national authorities have enacted legislations concerning the search for those who went missing as a result of an armed conflict.[260] Despite the absence of direct reference to the international framework, these *ad hoc* legislations show a concrete engagement in the clarification of the fate of missing persons in this phase.[261]

---

[256] Sandoz and others (n 3) para 4495, 1393.

[257] Cf. Article 5 (3) of AP II. Article 5 (1), AP II specifies that 'the following provisions shall be respected as a minimum with regard to persons deprived of their liberty for reasons related to the armed conflict'.

[258] Cf. Article 4 (3) (b), AP II.

[259] The reference to the engagement of the Parties to search for the missing and/or account for them in peace agreements is a further confirmation of this finding: as for NIAC, Cf. Article 4 (i): 'the contracting Parties, [h]aving signed the Principal Agreement by which the parties committed themselves to implementing accountability and reconciliation with respect to the conflict; [...] [decided that [t]he Government shall by law establish a body to be conferred with all the necessary powers and immunities [to inquire into the past and related matters], whose functions shall include: [...] (i) to gather and analyze information on those who have disappeared during the conflict.' Annexure to the Agreement on Accountability and Reconciliation signed between the Government of the Republic of Uganda and the Lord's Resistance Army/Movement in 2007, Juba, signed on 19 February 2008, see *Practice Relating to Rule 117. Accounting for Missing Persons* in ICRC, 'Customary IHL - Online Database' <https://www. icrc.org/customary-ihl/eng> accessed 1 July 2016. See also Articles 1 and 5 of the Protocol of the Meeting of the Working Groups, Formed under the Negotiations Commissions, to locate Missing Persons and to Free Forcibly Detained Persons between the Russian Federation and Chechnya, Nazran, 10 June 1996 available at the UN Peacekeeper http://goo.gl/CDL9W0 accessed 20 October 2015.

[260] See, for instance, El Salvador (Decreto núm. 45: créase la Comisión Interinstitucional de Búsqueda de Niños y Niñas Desaparecidos a Consecuencia del Conflicto Armado en El Salvador - Decree No 45 creating the Inter-institutional Commission of search for missing children as a consequence of the armed conflict, October 6, 2004, http://goo.gl/S7vSb4 Accessed 20 May 2013); Guatemala (Presidential Decree No. 264 on the Creation of a Permanent Commission on Missing Persons, May 25, 2006), Kosovo (Law No. 04/L–023 on missing persons, Official Gazette of the Republic of Kosova/No. 16, September 14, 2011, Pristina), Bosnia and Herzegovina (Law on Missing Persons, PS BiH No 109/04, October 21, 2004, Sarajevo). After the termination of the internal conflict in Sri Lanka in 2009, there has been a positive reaction of the government authorities in Colombo vis-à-vis the establishment of an independent process aimed at clarifying the fate of the missing. See the Interview of Dominic Stillhart, Director of Operations at the ICRC, *Sri Lanka: Clarifying the fate of missing persons requires sustained commitment*, available at https://www.icrc.org/en/document/clarifying-fate-missing-persons-sri-lanka-requires-sustained-commitment, accessed 15 July 2015.

[261] In certain cases, the (tardy) enactment of specific legislations has been part of a reconciliatory strategy (Guatemala, El Salvador) or of a reparation scheme (in Spain, Ley 52/2007, de 26 de

2.3. Framing the "post-" dimension of the IHL rules on missing persons

The foregoing shows that the duration of the conflict does not impact on the timeframe of some of the obligations and entitlements outlined above, as these relate to situations (e.g., deprivation of liberty, internment, separation of families, POW, disappearance as a result of the conflict) that arose out of the conflict itself and might continue after it.[262] While some of these situations – the status of internee or POW in IAC – are inherently temporary and will come to an end at a certain point in time, others might persist for an indeterminate period of time (e.g., in NIAC the deprivation of liberty for reasons related to the conflict).

Three interconnected temporal dimensions can be identified in the handling of information concerning various categories of persons under contemporary IHL treaties: i.e., in peacetime State authorities shall delineate the legislative and domestic framework apt to handle information in possible situations of armed conflict; during the conflict, each party to the conflict must collect and transmit information and data as well as carry out efforts to account for the missing, should persons be reported as missing; at the close of military operations, each party to the conflict shall continue to perform activities aimed at accounting for the missing and inform both the adverse party and the families concerned on the findings. Thus, a duty to implement a systematic procedure aimed at accounting for the missing emerges from the IHL framework applicable in IAC. Although minimal, a set of measures intended for preventing that persons go missing and addressing the lack of information on the fate and whereabouts of persons emerge from the framework applicable in NIAC; the core of these measures continue to have effect after the end of the armed conflict.

---

diciembre, por la que se reconocen y amplían derechos y se establecen medidas en favor de quienes padecieron persecución o violencia durante la guerra civil y la dictadura establishes rights and measures for victims of the Civil War and Dictatorship instructs the relevant public authorities to facilitate the location and identification of persons unaccounted for as a result of the Civil War and the dictatorship, as well as the recovery and reburial of human remains by the families. The main purpose of the law is to recognize and implement the right to rehabilitation, individual recognition and reparations for persons who suffered persecution or violence on political, religious or ideological grounds during the Spanish Civil War and the military dictatorship).

[262] The ICTY has clearly stated that 'the temporal scope of the applicable rules clearly reaches beyond the actual hostilities'. ICTY. *Prosecutor v. Duško Tadić, Decision on the Defence Motion ...* (n 23). See also Akande (n 166) 43. Similar is the situation for other provisions; as Eric Davis underlines, the cessation of armed hostilities and the consequential termination of the conflict does not have an impact on Articles 14 (Hospital and Safety zones and localities) and 144 (dissemination of the Convention) of GC IV or on Articles 49/50/129/146 (on Penal sanctions) of GCs I-IV. See David (n 136) 234. Chetail also adds the rules relating the control of weapons (e.g., Article 9, 1996 Protocol on Prohibitions or Restrictions on the Use of Mines, Booby-Traps and other devices) as well as the rules governing military occupation. See V Chetail, 'Introduction: Post-Conflict Peacebuilding - Ambiguity and Identity' in Vincent Chetail (ed), *Post-conflict Peacebuilding: a Lexicon* (Oxford University Press 2009) 19-20.

Table 1 – Temporal dimensions of IHL rules		
Prior to an armed conflict	**During an IAC**	**In the aftermath**
Ideally: • Enactment of legislative provisions aimed at defining identification methods • Issuance of ID Card/Disc • Organization of an official gravesite registration service • Definition of legal and institutional bases for the establishment of a NIB • Identification of the form that the records should take • Training of the personnel that would undertake recording activities • Establishment of speedy and accurate identification procedures to be followed during and in the aftermath of the conflict	Compulsory: • Obligation to search for wounded, sick & shipwrecked, and the dead (W/S&S/D) • Obligation to facilitate the steps taken to search for killed and wounded civilians • Obligation to timely collect and record information on the W/S&S/D and on those held in captivity (POW and Civilian Internees - CI) • Obligation to record information on those detained for more than 2 weeks and who could not receive a more favorable consideration under the GCs I-IV and the AP I or who died at any time during their detention • Obligation to forward information on W/S&S/D, on POW, and Protected Persons held in custody to the NIB • Obligation to facilitate enquiries made by members of dispersed families • **Activities concerning missing persons shall be prompted by the right of families to know the fate of their relatives** • **Obligation to search for those reported missing by the adverse party** • **Obligation to establish commissions tasked with searching for dispersed POW and dispersed internees** • **Obligation to enable all persons to give/receive news to/from members of their families** • **Obligation to facilitate the return of remains to the home country upon its request/the request of the family** • **Obligation to permanently respect (and maintain) the gravesites**	
	During a NIAC	**In the aftermath**
	• Obligation to search for W/S&S/D • The services of the CTA can be extended to NIAC • **Activities concerning missing persons shall be prompted by the right of families to know the fate of their relatives** • **Obligation to search for those reported missing by the Adverse Party** • **Obligation to undertake appropriate steps to facilitate the reunion of families temporarily separated (focus on: unaccompanied children)**	

111

3. MISSING PERSONS AND THEIR FAMILIES' RIGHT TO KNOW UNDER IHRL

IHRL is not a time-bound regime, as it applies during the conflict, in post-conflict settings, and in peacetime. Although the existing human rights treaties can be acceded only by States, non-state actors are to abide by human rights obligations as well; it is important to bear in mind that non-state armed groups are not the sole non-state actor who might be playing an important role with regard to the missing in the transition phase. Thus, it is essential to cast light upon the duty-holders under IHRL while taking into account the peculiarity proper to the post-conflict phase (sub-section 3.1). An examination of the duty to account for missing persons and the right of families to know under IHRL will follow (sub-section 3.2). Indeed, no human rights treaty is exclusively dedicated to the issue of missing persons and the preservation of the family unity through the guarantee of access to information on the fate and whereabouts of the relatives.

3.1 The complex profile of duty-bearers in post-conflict settings

An important factor that should be taken into account when considering the rules applicable in the post-conflict phase is that under IHL non-state armed groups[263] are bound by treaty provisions[264] and customary provisions[265] applicable in NIAC. As shown in sub-section 2.3 of the present Chapter, the application of IHL in post-conflict settings is residual; within the remit of this book, those provisions that continue to apply in post-NIAC entail that all the former parties to the conflict must take part to the efforts aimed at accounting for missing persons. Although the existing human rights treaties can be acceded only by States, non-state armed groups cannot be considered freed from abiding by human rights obligations. Therefore, the assertion according to which IHRL

---

[263] There is no definition of non-state armed group internationally accepted; with this expression, I refer to armed groups other than those of a State and not operating under the control of the State(s) in which they are militarily active; private military companies and groups whose objectives are purely lucrative are excluded. See Annyssa Bellal, Gilles Giacca and Stuart Casey-Maslen, 'International Law and Armed Non-State Actors in Afghanistan' (2011) 93 International Review of the Red Cross 47, 48.

[264] Certain IHL instruments are specifically intended to bind both States and non-state armed groups and provide that 'each party to the conflict shall be bound to apply' certain rules (e.g., Common Article 3, GCs I-IV; Article 19, Hague Convention on Cultural Property; Article 1 (3), Amended Convention on Certain Conventional Weapons; Article 1 (3), Amended Protocol II to the Convention on Certain Conventional Weapons). At a first glance, a similar provision is not enshrined in AP II; nonetheless, as underlined by the ICRC commentary and by other scholars, a similar provision was enshrined in the initial draft of the AP II and then deleted during the Diplomatic Conference. States were concerned over affording recognition and status to non-state armed groups. See Sandoz and others (n 3) para 4442, 1345; Sivakumaran (n 24) 240. In addition to that, the ICRC Commentary emphasizes that 'the commitment made by a State not only applies to the government but also to any established authorities and private individuals within the national territory of that State and certain obligations are therefore imposed upon them.' See Sandoz and others (n 3) para 4444, 1345. Pictet, *Commentary Vol I (1952)* (n 15) 51–52. Thus, when a State ratifies a treaty, it does so not only on behalf of the State, but also on behalf of all individuals within its jurisdiction. See Sivakumaran (n 24) 240 (and notes therein).

[265] It is today accepted that customary IHL is binding upon States and non-state armed groups. Cf. ICJ, *Nicaragua v. United States of America (1986)* (n 108) [217–219]. See also Sivakumaran (n 24) 236.

obligations only bind State authorities is no longer legally tenable.[266] This is not the place to develop a detailed examination of the doctrinal debate on the obligations of non-state actors under IHRL; suffice it here to put forwards three main points.

First of all, the respect for IHRL reflects the legitimate expectation of the international community, particularly when the non-state armed group is in control of the territory or part of it;[267] the adoption of a conduct that is consistent with what the international legal order requires contributes to maintaining and restoring international peace and security. In this regard, in its Berlin session, the *Institut de Droit International* stressed that '[r]espect for [IHL] and fundamental human rights constitutes an integral part of international order for the maintenance and reestablishment of peace and security, in particular in armed conflicts in which non-state entities are parties'.[268] The legitimacy of the expectation is directly related to the final aim to be achieved, i.e., the protection of individuals, [269] and does not affect the legitimacy of the actors to whom human rights obligations are addressed. Non-state armed groups respond to such expectations by means of overt commitments to abide by IHL and IHRL during armed conflicts and in the context of the peace process.[270]

Second, IHL rules present *lacunae,* including in relation to the subject matter[271] and do not cover all the actions of non-state armed groups; thus,

---

[266] Andrew Clapham, *Human Rights Obligations of Non-State Actors* (Oxford University Press 2006) 280.

[267] Jean-Marie Henckaerts and Cornelius Wiesener, 'Human Rights Obligations of Non-State Armed Groups: A Possible Contribution from Customary International Law?' in Robert Kolb and Gloria Gaggioli (eds), *Research Handbook on Human Rights and Humanitarian Law* (Edward Elgar Publishing 2013) 161.

[268] Institut de Droit International (IDI), 'The Application of International Humanitarian Law and Fundamental Human Rights, in Armed Conflicts in Which Non-State Entities Are Parties' (1999) Berlin Session para III.

[269] In this respect, after one of his country visits in Sri Lanka, the Special Rapporteur on extra-judicial executions pointed out that '[...] [t]he [Liberation Tigers of Tamil Eelam - LTTE] does not have legal obligations under ICCPR, but it remains subject to the demand of the international community, first expressed in the Universal Declaration of Human Rights, that every organ of society respect and promote human rights. [...] It is increasingly understood, however, that the human rights expectations of the international community operate to protect people, while not thereby affecting the legitimacy of the actors to whom they are addressed.' Human Rights Council, 'Report of the Special Rapporteur on Extra-Judicial, Summary or Arbitrary Executions Concerning the Mission to Sri-Lanka' (2006) UN Doc E/CN.4/2006/53/Add.5 paras 25–27. In another instance, the SRSG on business and human rights has stressed that '[t]he responsibility to respect human rights is a global standard of expected conduct for all business enterprises wherever they operate. It exists independently of States' abilities and/or willingness to fulfill their own human rights obligations, and does not diminish those obligations.' See Human Rights Council, 'Report of the Special Representative of the Secretary- General on the Issue of Human Rights and Transnational Corporations and Other Business Enterprises, John Ruggie. Guiding Principles on Business and Human Rights: Implementing the United Nations "Protect, Respect and Remedy" Framework' (2011) UN Doc A/HRC/17/31 13.

[270] See sub-section 1.2.2 in the present Chapter and footnotes thereto; see also sub-section 1.1.3 in Chapter V.

[271] AP I's provisions on the missing do not cover a party to the conflict's own nationals; neither these cover situations arising in NIACs. Although the ICRC has deemed customary the obligation of the parties to the conflict 'to account for persons reported missing as a result of armed conflict' and to

'individuals remain under the protection of international law guaranteeing fundamental human rights'[272] even when the actions of non-state armed groups do not reach the threshold for the application of IHL, but tensions are ongoing in the territory.[273] Third, in any case, under IHRL, States have an obligation of due diligence which directly derives from the positive obligations to ensure the protection of human rights at all times.[274] Positive obligations also require State

---

'provide their family members with any information it has on their fate' (IAC/NIAC), the practice quoted by the pioneering ICRC study on customary IHL is questionable when it comes to NIAC. For instance, the 2004 UK Manual quoted in the ICRC Study specifies that it 'deals with the law relating to [IAC] except where otherwise specified': Chapter 7 of the same Manual, which addresses the issue of the missing, does not refer to NIAC; the excerpt on the missing shows that the Manual exclusively refers to IHL treaties applicable in IAC. Cf. UK Ministry of Defence (n 105) paras 1.9, 7.38, 7.38.1. The Canadian Manual stresses that it 'is an account of the law applicable to traditional State on State international armed conflicts (Chapters 1-16) and to non-international armed conflicts (Chapter 17)'; the part on the tracing of missing persons' requests is under Chapter 9. Cf. Canada National Defence, *Law of Armed Conflict at the Operational and Tactical Level (Canada Joint Doctrine Manual)* (Office of the Judge Advocate General 2001) i and paras 924-925. In the Mexican Manual, the reference to the actions to be undertaken by the Parties to the conflict vis-à-vis those unaccounted for are mentioned under the section summarizing provisions relating to the POW under GC (III) of 1949, cf. México, *Manual de Derecho Internacional Humanitario Para el Ejercito y la Fuerza Aérea Mexicanos* (Ministry of National Defence 2009) 204. Among the Manuals, it is also quoted a Belgian document explaining the structure of the POW Information Bureaux, which will not be set up in NIAC. Cf. Belgium, *Structure et Fonctionnement Du Bureau de Renseignements Sur Les Prisonniers de Guerre, Procédure Spécifique* (Ministère de la Défense 2007). The US Annotated Supplement to the US Naval Handbook mentions Article 32 AP I in a footnote in the realm of naval warfare: cf. Oceans Law and Policy Department (US), *Annotated Supplement to the Commander's Handbook on the Law of Naval Operations* (Center for Naval Warfare Studies, Naval War College 1997) 408 [para 8.2.1 (n 35)]; apart from the fact that the US has not ratified AP I, one should not ignore the successive positioning of the US vis-à-vis the right of families to know (e.g., cf. the Declaration of the US representative during the negotiation for the ICPPED: see *infra* sub-section 3.2.2.2 and sub-section 2.3.2 in Chapter IV). Although the practice of non-state armed groups falls outside the scope of the practice to be considered in the assessment of whether a norm has become customary, the conduct of non-state armed groups vis-à-vis the families' request for information on their relatives is barely mentioned. For the full overview of the practice in the ICRC study on Customary IHL, see Henckaerts and Doswald-Beck (n 187) 2742–2774.

[272] International Law Institute, Resolution on 'The Application of International Humanitarian Law and Fundamental Human Rights, in Armed Conflicts in which Non-State Entities are Parties', Berlin Session – 1999, para X. The Guatemalan Historical Clarification Commission noted that 'the [non-state armed group] that participated in the internal armed confrontation had an obligation to respect the minimum standards of [IHL] that apply to armed conflicts, as well as the general principles common to [IHRL].' Guatemala Commission for Historical Clarification, 'Memory of Silence. Report of the Commission for Historical Clarification: Conclusions and Recommendations' (1998) para 127.

[273] For instance, in its early reports the UN Independent International Commission of Inquiry on the Syrian Arab Republic (Commission of Inquiry on Syria) did not consider IHL applicable due to the lack of information on the Free Syrian Army (FSA)'s level of organization at the time. However, it reviewed the operations and activities of FSA groups under IHRL and noted that, 'at a minimum, human rights obligations constituting peremptory international law (*ius cogens*) bind States, individuals and non-state collective entities, including armed groups. Acts violating *ius cogens* – for instance, torture or enforced disappearances – can never be justified.' Cf. Human Rights Council, '2nd Report of the Independent International Commission of Inquiry on the Syrian Arab Republic' (2012) UN Doc A/HRC/19/69 para 106.

[274] HRCee, 'General Comment No. 31: The Nature of the General Legal Obligation Imposed on State Parties to the Covenant' (2004) UN Doc. CCPR/C/21/Rev.1/Add.13 para 8. See also Section 2, Chapter IV.

authorities to protect human rights 'against acts committed by private persons or entities that would impair the enjoyment' of such rights.[275] As Chapter IV will show 'the very notion of due diligence can have a consequential effect on the addressees of the international rules for which the violation has to be prevented or redressed'.[276] When the responsibility of the State is triggered under the obligation of due diligence,

> one may assume that the violation in question has been – or at least will be – committed by private actors which are thus the holder of the relevant international obligation. [...] As violations are not directly imputable to the state itself, private actor must be considered the direct bearer of the violated rule.[277]

Such horizontal application[278] of human rights is in line with the call for interpretation and application of existing human rights standards in a practical and effective manner.[279] In post-conflict contexts, this contribute to strengthening the idea that respect for and protection of human rights from all the – former – parties to the conflict can be conducive to the maintenance and re-establishment of peace and security.

In post-NIAC, two scenarios are likely: *i)* the non-state armed group is successful and becomes the new government/creates a new State; *ii)* the State is successful. In the former case, the connection between the *durante bello* conduct and the post-conflict's is sanctioned by the following rule: the conduct of an insurrectional movement, which succeeds in becoming the new government/establishing a new State in part of the territory of the pre-existing State, shall be considered an act of that State/of the new State under international law.[280] In the latter case, the members of the non-state armed groups who have committed international crimes can be held individually responsible. However, can anyone say that the unsuccessful non-state armed group is freed from any international law obligation in the post-conflict phase? In light of the considerations put forward in this Chapter, in Chapter III, and Chapter IV, I argue that there exists an IHRL-based duty to cooperate between the former parties to the conflict in the post-conflict phase as far as the efforts to account for

---

[275] ibid.

[276] Vincent Chetail, 'The Legal Personality of Multinational Corporations, State Responsibility and Due Diligence: The Way Forward' in Vincent Chetail and others (eds), *Unité et diversité du droit international/Unity and Diversity of International Law. Essays in Honour of Prof. Pierre-Marie Dupuy* (Brill | Nijhoff 2014) 127.

[277] ibid.

[278] This approach emerges from the assessment developed by the Panel of Experts tasked by the UNSC to provide information on the sanctions regime in Sudan; in the words of the Panel, 'all parties to the conflict in Darfur have a responsibility to safeguard and protect human rights, while the Government of the Sudan has an added responsibility under the relevant human rights treaties'. See UNSC, 'Report of the Panel of Experts Established pursuant to Resolution 1591 (2005) Concerning the Sudan Prepared in Accordance with Paragraph 2 of Resolution 1713 (2006)' (2007) S/2007/584 para 325.

[279] See section 2.2 in Chapter IV.

[280] Cf. Article 10 (1-2), UNGA, 'ILC's Articles on the Responsibility of States for Internationally Wrongful Acts. Annex to Resolution 56/83 Responsibility of States for Internationally Wrongful Acts.' (2001) UN Doc A/RES/56/83.

the missing are concerned; this makes the protective framework concerning the right to humane treatment effective and practical (see sub-section 2.3.2.3, Chapter III; sub-section 2.2 of Chapter IV).

Post-IAC/NIAC situations are characterized by the presence of other non-state actors, e.g., inter-governmental organizations.[281] This book focuses on the UN (see Chapter V) and the role that this organization has played and continues to play in armed conflict/post-conflict scenarios in relation to the missing and the claims for information of their families. Chapter V will argue that in those situations where the UN – or other international organizations – administers the territory, the organization is not *legibus solutus* under IHRL.

3.2. The duty to account for missing persons and the right of families to know in the human rights legal framework

Since IHRL does not explicitly focus on missing persons, the examination will revolve around three key themes proper to the issue of missing persons in armed conflicts: information, the importance of family ties, and disappearances. Through these drivers it will be possible to detect the areas of interaction/overlap of IHRL with IHL during and in the aftermath of an armed conflict.[282] After the identification of those instruments that IHRL treaties set down in order to contrast uncertainty immediately after a person is reported missing (sub-section 3.2.1), this sub-section will examine the human right legal framework at the international (sub-section 3.2.2) and regional level (sub-section 3.2.3).

3.2.1. Contrasting uncertainty in the immediate aftermath of a disappearance

In the immediate aftermath of a disappearance the main thought is that the person could be executed or arbitrarily detained. A reaction – *proprio motu* or upon request – of human rights adjudicators consists in ordering provisional measures of protection[283] ('interim measures' and 'precautionary measures' are

---

[281] This characterization is boldly stated in the seminal work of Professor Clapham. See Clapham (n 266) 20 and Chapter 4 of his book.

[282] This analysis is, therefore, a necessary premise to the formulation of this book's approach to the interplay of such branches in post-conflict (see Chapter III).

[283] For a thorough overview of the functioning of provisional measures in human rights adjudication, see Eva R Rieter, *Preventing Irreparable Harm: Provisional Measures in International Human Rights Adjudication* (Intersentia 2010); Eva Rieter, 'Provisional Measures: Binding and Persuasive? Enabling Human Rights Adjudicators to Follow up on State Disrespect' (2012) 59 Netherlands International Law Review 165; Pasqualucci, Jo M., 'Interim Measures in International Human Rights: Evolution and Harmonization' (2005) 38 Vanderbilt Journal of Transnational Law 1. For a comparative (ECtHR/HRCee and AfCommHPR/IACommHR) examination of these measures, see Helen Keller and Cedric Marti, 'Interim Relief Compared: Use of Interim Measures by the UN Human Rights Committee and the European Court of Human Rights' (2013) 73 Heidelberg Journal of International Law 325; C Burbano-Herrera, F Viljoen and Y Haeck, 'Preventing Human Rights Violations: Recommendations for Enhancing the Effectiveness of Interim Measures Before the Inter-American and African Human Rights Commissions' in Clara Burbano Herrera and others (eds), *The Realisation of Human Rights: When Theory meets Practice - Studies in Honour of Leo Zwaak* (Intersentia 2013). For a detailed analysis of these measures in the IACtHR framework, see Clara Burbano Herrera, *Provisional Measures in the Case Law of the Inter-American Court of Human Rights* (Intersentia ; Portland, OR 2010); C Burbano-Herrera, 'The Inter-American Court of Human

other expressions used by various bodies).[284] These are granted with the aim of preventing irreparable damage[285] to persons. Uncertainty about the whereabouts

Rights and Its Role in Preventing Violations of Human Rights through Provisional Measures' in Yves Haeck, Oswaldo Ruiz-Chiriboga and Clara Burbano-Herrera (eds), *The Inter-American Court of Human Rights: Theory and Practice, Present and Future* (Intersentia 2015). On the IACommHR's precautionary measures, see Diego Rodríguez-Pinzón, 'Precautionary Measures of the Inter-American Commission on Human Rights: Legal Status and Importance' (2013) 20 The Human Rights Brief 13. For an overview of the ECtHR's interim measures, see William A Schabas, *The European Convention on Human Rights: A Commentary* (Oxford University Press 2015) 731–752; Y Haeck and C Burbano-Herrera, 'The Use of Interim Measures Issued by the European Court of Human Rights in Times of War or Internal Conflict' in Antoine Buyse (ed), *Margins of Conflict: The ECHR and Transitions to and from Armed Conflict* (Intersentia 2011). On the functioning of the provisional measures in the African system, see Gino J Naldi, 'Interim Measures of Protection in the African System for the Protection of Human and Peoples' Rights' (2002) 2 African Human Rights Law Journal 1; F Bostedt, 'The African Court on Human and Peoples' Rights and the Use of Provisional Measures for the Protection of the Civilian Population in Armed Conflict Situations' in Philipp Ambach and others (eds), *The protection of non-combatants during armed conflict and safeguarding the rights of victims in post-conflict society: essays in honour of the life and work of Joakim Dungel* (Martinus Nijhoff Publishers 2015). For an analysis of the HRCee's interim measures, see Gino J Naldi, 'Interim Measures in the UN Human Rights Committee' (2004) 53 International & Comparative Law Quarterly 445; Sandy Ghandhi, 'The Human Rights Committee and Interim Measures of Relief' (2007) 13 The Canterbury law Review 203. For an insight into the urgent actions procedure before the CED, see Gabriella Citroni and Maria Giovanna Bianchi, 'The Committee on Enforced Disappearances: Challenges Ahead' (2012) 6 Diritti umani e diritto internazionale 127, 146–154.

[284] Article 25 (Precautionary measures), Rules of Procedure, cf. IACommHR. 'Rules of procedures of the IACommHR', approved by the Commission at its 137th regular period of sessions, held from 28 October-13 November 2009 and modified on 2 September 2011 and during the 147th Regular Period of Sessions, held from 8-22 March 2013, for entry into force on 1 August 2013; Rule 39 (interim measures), Rules of Court, Cf. ECtHR (Registry of the Court). 'Rules of Court', Strasbourg (2016), http://www.echr.coe.int/Documents/Rules_Court_ENG.pdf, accessed 12 April 2016; Article 63 (3), ACHR (provisional measures); Rule 27 (provisional measures), Rules of procedure of the IACtHR, cf. IACtHR. 'Rules of procedure of the IACtHR', approved by the Court of its LXXXV Regular Period of Sessions, 16-28 November 2009; Rule 92 (interim measures), Rules of procedure of the HRCee, cf. HRCee. 'Rules of procedure of the Human Rights Committee', UN Doc. CCPR/C/3/Rev.10 (2012); Rule 98 (provisional measures) Rules of Procedures, cf. AfCommHPR. 'Rules of Procedures of the AfCommHPR', approved by the AfCommHPR during its 47th ordinary session held in Banjul (Gambia) from May 12 to 26, 2010; Rule 51 (interim measures), cf. AfCtHPR. 'Rules of Court', replacing the Interim Rules of Procedure of 20 June 2008, following the harmonization of the Interim Rules of the Court and the Commission, July 2009 Arusha, October 2009 Dakar, April 2010 Arusha; Article 27 (2) (provisional measures), Protocol to the African Charter on the Establishment of the African Court on Human and Peoples' Rights (Protocol on the establishment of the AfCtHPR), OAU Doc. OAU/LEG/AFCHPR/PROT (III), entered into force January 25, 2004; Article 35 (provisional measures), Protocol on the Statute of the African Court of Justice and Human Rights (Protocol on the Statute of the AfCtHPR), adopted on 1 July 2008.

[285] The concept of 'irreparable damage' is common to most of the bodies mentioned in this subsection; it is mentioned in the Conventions [cf. Article 63 (2) American Convention on Human Rights, 1144 UNTS 143 (21 November 21, 1969) (hereinafter ACHR); Article 27 (2), Protocol to the African Charter on the Establishment of the AfCtHPR; Article 35 (1), Protocol on the Statute of the AfCtHPR]; the Rules of procedures (cf. Article 25, Rules of procedures of the IACommHR; Rule 27, Rules of Procedure of the IACtHR; Rule 92, Rules of procedure of the HRCee; Rule 98, Rules of procedure of the AfCommHPR), and in the case law. The ECtHR explicitly acknowledged that 'in practice the Court applies Rule 39 only if there is an imminent risk of irreparable damage', cf. ECtHR, *Mamatkulov and Askarov v Turkey, Judgment (GC)* (2005) App nos. 46827/99 46951/99 [104]. The sole document providing a definition is the Rules of procedure of the IACommHR that

of a person following life-threatening circumstances provides room for the action of adjudicators, as the person concerned might face a situation with irreversible consequences. The inherent gravity of an armed conflict is a factor that is part of the assessment of the requirements for ordering provisional measures.

Despite the different functioning of these measures under general human rights treaties, the main common point to human rights adjudicators is to act because of the urgency of the situation in order to protect the life and limb of persons who might be victims of human rights violation.[286] The feature that should be key is the promptness to assess the requests or a *proprio motu* decision, which is essential in most of the cases brought to their attention.[287]

In the inter-American system, in cases of persons gone missing during military operations,[288] the IACommHR[289] has indicated precautionary measures

---

affirms that 'irreparable harm refers to injury to rights which, due to their nature, would not be susceptible to reparation, restoration or adequate compensation.' Cf. Article 25 (2) (c), Rules of procedure of the IACommHR.

[286] The most common scenarios in which the HRCee, the ECtHR, the IACtHR, the IACommHR, the AfCommHPR and the AfCtHPR have requested the States to implement these measures are: i) to halt the execution of petitioners who are sentenced to death until the adjudicator has been able to examine their complaints; ii) to halt the expulsion, extradition or deportation of petitioners until the adjudicator has been able to examine their complaints involving non-refoulement; iii) to intervene in a timely manner in detention situations involving risks to health and dignity; iv) to order a State to provide protection to witnesses, human rights defenders and others against threats to their lives and physical integrity. The urgency of the measures is therefore due to the irreparable harm that might be caused due to a violation of the right to life and the prohibition of torture and inhuman and degrading treatment of the individuals in most of these scenarios. See Rieter, 'Provisional Measures' (n 283) 177; ECtHR, *Mamatkulov and Askarov v. Turkey, Judgment (GC)* (n 285) [104] (stating that 'requests for [interim measures] application usually concern the right to life [...], the right not to be subjected to torture or inhuman treatment [...]'). Although the African Charter makes some social and economic rights justiciable, the case law on interim measures shows that these measures are most often adopted to protect traditional civil and political rights. See Burbano-Herrera, Viljoen and Haeck (n 283) 231. However, other scenarios have also been the focus of provisional measures, e.g., the ECtHR has ordered *interim* measures in cases where the right to respect for private and family life was concerned; the IACommHR, the IACtHR and the HRCee have requested the State to adopt provisional measures to protect indigenous cultural and religious rights. For the ECtHR, see Keller and Marti (n 283) 340 and footnotes thereof. See also ECtHR, *Mamatkulov and Askarov v. Turkey, Judgment (GC)* (n 285) [104] (specifying that requests for interim measures 'exceptionally' concern 'the right to respect for private and family life [...] or other rights guaranteed by the Convention'). For the Inter-American system and the HRCee see Rieter, *Preventing Irreparable Harm* (n 283) 451–500.

[287] From existing studies on this matter, the responsiveness of these bodies in answering the requests has changed and improved, by becoming a matter of days (or even of hours). Rieter, *Preventing Irreparable Harm* (n 283) 106-115-156-177; Keller and Marti (n 283) 335; Ghandhi (n 283) 205–206; Pasqualucci, Jo M. (n 283) 36.

[288] Rieter notes that 'in the 1970s and 1980s the [IACommHR] intervened informally on behalf of disappeared persons'. Rieter, *Preventing Irreparable Harm* (n 283) xxxi; 319-321. The Commission has also made use of the precautionary measures vis-à-vis the situation generated in Colombia as a result of the disappearance of individuals allegedly detained/abducted by armed groups (e.g., the United-self Defence Forces of Colombia - *Autodefensas Unidas de Colombia* - an active party to the NIAC until 2006). The Commission has requested the Colombian government to take 'the necessary actions to ascertain the whereabouts of allegedly disappeared persons' and 'to launch a prompt and effective investigation using the urgent search mechanism' established under its domestic law (Law 589/2000). Cf. IACommHR. 'Precautionary Measures 1999', point (f) 'Colombia' para. 23 (precautionary measures granted on 29 November 1999 and concerning the disappearance of Edgar

aimed at clarifying their whereabouts. For instance, during the NIAC in Peru,[290] the Commission took precautionary measures in order to protect the inmates held in the 'Miguel Castro-Castro Prison' in Lima, where the army launched an attack (6-9 May 1992).[291] Neither the Commission exercising its good offices nor the ICRC could access the prison during the initial stage of the operation. Four days after the termination of the operation, the Chairman of the Commission[292] addressed a letter to the Minister of Foreign Affairs of Peru asking for the re-establishment of family visits as well as complete lists of the following categories: inmates before the outbreak of the attack, individuals who were killed, wounded, or had been missing since the starting of the attack, and survivors and their whereabouts.[293] The lack of response from Peru triggered the order of precautionary measures on August 14, 1992, including,

> [t]hat the Government of Peru forward to the [IACommHR] the official list of persons who died and disappeared as a result of the events that occurred at the Miguel Castro Castro penal institution, as well as a list of the wounded and the whereabouts of those transferred.'[294]

Quiroga and Gildardo Fuentes) http://www.cidh.org/medidas/1999.eng.htm accessed 12 July 2015. See also IACommHR. 'Precautionary Measures 2000', point (f) 'Colombia' para. 21 (precautionary measures granted on 21 June 2000 and concerning the disappearance of Roberth Cañarte Montealegre allegedly detained by *Autodefensas) http://www.cidh.org/medidas/2000.eng.htm* accessed 12 July 2015; 'Precautionary Measures 2001', point (c) 'Colombia' para. 26 (precautionary measures granted on 18 December 2001 concerning the disappearance of Robinson Ríos Uribe and José Gregorio Villada, allegedly abducted by a paramilitary group), http://www.cidh.org/medidas/2001.eng.htm accessed 23 June 2015.

[289] Whereas the IACtHR deals only with States that have accepted its jurisdiction under the ACHR, the Commission has a broader competence, which extends to all members of the Organization of American States (OAS), including those that have not ratified the ACHR. Rieter observes that official information on the Commission's early practice in the context of disappearances is lacking due to an institutional choice made by its president in the 1970s. Apparently, a direct bilateral contact with the State was preferred, if the Commission felt a person was at risk; it is in these earlier years of its work that the IACommHR developed a practice of urgent intervention in the context of disappearances. Ibid 159. See also the webpage dedicated to Precautionary Measures of the IACommHR, which lists the measures indicated in the course of the years, including those lifted. IACommHR. "Precautionary Measures" http://www.oas.org/en/iachr/decisions/precautionary.asp accessed on 15 April 2016.

[290] The NIAC started in the early 1980s and determined a continuative State of emergency as well as military operations carried out by the army and the police forces in order to suppress the activities of the armed groups thereof. The main groups were the Peruvian Communist Party known as *Sendero Luminoso* and the Tupac Amaru Revolutionary Movement. The IACtHR has noted that between the 1980s and 2000 'Peru lived a conflict between armed groups and agents of the police force and the military. This conflict got worse in the midst of a systematic practice of violations to human rights, among them extrajudicial killings and forced disappearances of people suspected of belonging to armed groups that existed on the fringe of the law'. Cf. IACtHR, *Miguel Castro-Castro Prison v Peru, Judgment – Merits, Reparations and Costs* (2006) Series C n. 160 [198].

[291] IACommHR, 'Report on the Situation of Human Rights in Peru' (1993) OEA/Ser.L/V/II.3, Doc. 31 paras 8, 95.

[292] Ibid, para. 95.

[293] Ibid 97.

[294] Ibid 100.

Almost five months after the events, the Commission was eventually granted access to the prison concerned.[295]

The need to use this mechanism arises 'from a reasonable presumption of extreme and urgent risk of irreparable damage to persons.'[296] The humanitarian character of the Commission's duties[297] is exemplified in the Peruvian case. In armed conflicts, uncertainty can be the consequence of intentional/ unintentional disregard of recording practices in detention centers which, in certain cases, is accompanied by abusive practices against the inmates. In this respect, precautionary measures can make a difference.

Similarly, uncertainty about the whereabouts of an individual into the custody of 'enemy' State authorities is another triggering factor for the use of provisional measures. For instance, in the context of the NIAC in Libya,[298] the National Transitional Council detained Saif Al-Islam Gaddafi (the second son of the former Libyan President Muammar Gaddafi) in isolation, i.e., without access to family, friends, or any lawyer. The African Court on Human and Peoples' Rights (AfCtHPR) deemed his life at risk and ordered provisional measures *suo motu* to preserve the physical integrity of the detainee and to protect his right to access legal representation and family.[299] Since Saif's whereabouts were unknown, the Court proactively reacted to the passivity of authorities in providing any information; it is also noteworthy to stress the Court's focus on the family ties and the importance of restoring them as a matter of urgency.

Until very recently, the ECtHR[300] has received very few requests of *interim* measures with the aim of clarifying the whereabouts of allegedly disappeared

---

[295] Ibid 101.

[296] The Commission tries to solve - to a certain extent – the problematic situation that arises when it can adopt precautionary measures pursuant to its own rules or request that the Court adopt provisional measures when the requirements for admissibility of a petition have not been met pursuant to Article 63 (2) ACHR. The Commission, in fact, has stressed that the aforementioned risk absolves the Commission itself from the necessity of defining the admissibility pursuant to the ACHR. IACommHR. Request for provisional Measures in Case 10.548, IACtHR 25, 27, OAE/ser.G/CP, doc. 2146 (1991) (with regard to the precautionary measures it can adopt; the reasoning applies to the provisional measures requested to the Court as well), in Pasqualucci, Jo M. "Provisional Measures in the Inter-American Human Rights System: An Innovative Development in International Law." *Vanderbilt Journal of Transnational Law* 26 (1993), at 828.

[297] Aguilar A., 'Procedimiento Que Debe Aplicar La Comisión Interamericana de Derechos Humanos En El Examen de Las Peticiones O Comunicaciones Individuales Sobre Presuntas Violaciones de Derechos Humanos' in Carlos Alberto Dunshee de Abranches and Inter-American Commission on Human Rights (eds), *Derechos humanos en las Américas: homenaje a la memoria de Carlos A. Dunshee de Abranches* (Organización de los Estados Americanos, 1984) 204.

[298] Saif Al-Islam Gaddafi was arrested in November 2011 when the conflict in Libya had already turned to be a NIAC again after a brief phase of internationalization. On the transformation of the nature of the conflict during 2011, see Katie A Johnston, 'Transformations of Conflict Status in Libya' (2012) 17 Journal of Conflict and Security Law 81.

[299] After a first attempt of AfCommHPR the lack of response from the authorities led the Court to act. Cf. AfCtHPR, *AfCommHPR v Libya, Order of Provisional Measures* (2013) App no 002/2013 [15-16, 18].

[300] ECtHR's interim measures are applied only in a limited number of areas and most of them concern expulsion and extradition. They usually consist in a suspension of the applicant's expulsion or extradition for as long as the application is being examined. ECtHR (Press Unit), 'Factsheet –

persons.[301] The measures indicated by the Court are not different from the ones ordered by the IACommHR:[302] the State is requested to submit any available information concerning the whereabouts of the person allegedly disappeared as well as copies of any relevant documents concerning the search for the person concerned.[303] However, after the outbreak of the Ukrainian conflict, [304] following 165 individual applications lodged by persons affected by the consequences of conflict, the Court indicated *interim* measures and invited the respective Government/s – Russia and Ukraine – to ensure respect for the ECHR's rights of persons deprived of liberty as well as those whose whereabouts are unknown.[305] These new developments are particularly relevant, since 'a failure by a Contracting State to comply with interim measures is to be regarded [...] as a violation of Article 34 [Right to individual application, ECHR]'.[306] The breadth of these measures along with their binding character[307] are two aspects attributable to the Court's increasingly proactive approach towards fostering *in bello* protection of human rights.

Interim Measures' (2016) 2. Citroni underlines that the Court has often dealt with 'sequence of disappearances' (cf. the worrisome situation in Chechnya; however, this tool has not been used by the applicants and by their representatives to protect the life and personal integrity of those whose whereabouts are unknown. Tullio Scovazzi and Gabriella Citroni, *The Struggle against Enforced Disappearance and the 2007 United Nations Convention* (Martinus Nijhoff Publishers 2007) 222–223.

[301] Differently from other bodies, the ECtHR does not publish its decisions on the request of interim measures; it refers to them in the decisions on the merits and in inadmissibility decisions.

[302] The difference lies in the fact that, although the request for interim measures may be presented even before the submission of an application (during the proceedings or simultaneously with the application's submission), such a request should be followed by the submission of a formal application before the ECtHR. If this is not the case, the interim measure will be lifted. Haeck and Burbano-Herrera (n 283) 80–81. For the IACommHR, precautionary measures can be disconnected from a formal petition. Cf. Article 25 (1), Rules of Procedures of the IACommHR.

[303] In a case concerning an alleged disappearance in the context of the Chechnya conflict, the Court indicated, upon the request of the wife of the alleged victim, an interim measure where the Russian Government was requested: to inform whether the applicant's husband - Mr. Magomadov - had been detained by a State authority in Grozny, and to submit any available information concerning his whereabouts as well as copies of any relevant documents concerning the search for him. The applicant - Mrs. Shabazova - lodged an application with the ECtHR alleging violations of Articles 3, 5, 8 ECHR on account of her husband's abduction and disappearance. The Government timely replied to the request of information by explaining that investigative steps had been conducted by the Prosecutor of the Chechen Republic who concluded that Mr. Magomadov had not been apprehended by State authorities. After reconsidering the application, the Court lifted the measure, as the applicant's representative confirmed that the applicant had lost interest in pursuing the case. ECtHR, *Elbika Shabazova v Russia, Decision* [2009] App No 402305. Procedure. On the adoption of interim measures in armed conflicts by the ECtHR, see Haeck and Burbano-Herrera (n 283).

[304] The scarcity of details is due to the fact that this information is not accessible online, but an on-site visit in Strasbourg is required.

[305] In 45 of those cases, the respective interim measures have been subsequently lifted, most frequently following the information that the person concerned had been released. Cf. ECtHR, 'European Court of Human Rights Extends Time Allowed for Russia's Observations on Admissibility of Cases Concerning Crimea and Eastern Ukraine (Press Release)' (2015) Doc. ECHR 122.

[306] Cf. ECtHR, *Mamatkulov and Askarov v. Turkey, Judgment (GC)* (n 285) [126].

[307] Cf. ECtHR, *Mamatkulov and Askarov v. Turkey, Judgment (GC)* (n 285); ECtHR (President of the Court), 'Practice Directions – Rules of Court' (2016) <http://www.echr.coe.int/Documents/PD_interim_measures_ENG.pdf> accessed 2 March 2016.

Human rights adjudicators[308] have also ordered provisional measures with the aim of protecting the civilian population[309] caught in an armed conflict; the adjudicators have asked for the respect of the provisions of human rights treaties and abstention from actions [310] that might result in irreparable harm to the civilians (e.g., abusive actions or omissions that might generate uncertainty about the whereabouts of civilians such as arbitrary detentions and *incommunicado* detentions).

In different circumstances, [311] the HRCee has made use of an alternative tool – i.e., the rule on transmission to State/request for information – to ascertain the health conditions of persons allegedly detained and whose whereabouts were unknown to the family. Considered by scholars 'informal provisional measures',[312] this tool can contribute to reaching the same purpose as the measures used by other bodies, although their rationale differs.[313]

---

[308] The African Court issued provisional measures *proprio motu* in the context of the armed conflict in Libya in 2011. The Court had the power to resort to this kind of measures without having been seized by the parties: the Court ordered that Libya had to refrain from any action that would result in a loss of life or violation of physical integrity of persons, which could be a breach of the provisions of the Charter or of other international human rights instruments to which it is a party. Cf. AfCtHPR *AfCommHPR v Great Socialist People's Libyan Arab Jamahiriya, Order of Provisional Measures* (2011) App no 004/2011 [25]. The ECtHR has ordered interim measures in the interstate case *Georgia v. Russia* where the Court decided to call upon 'both the High Contracting Parties concerned to honour their commitments under the Convention, particularly in respect of Articles 2 and 3 of the Convention'. Cf. ECtHR, *Georgia v Russia (II)*, Decision (2011) App no. 38263/08 [5]. In the case of *Georgia v. Russia,* the interim measures were extended several times in light of the unsatisfying answers received by the Parties. Cf. ibid [7].

[309] The focus on the protection of the civilian population has been reiterated in another interstate case before the ECtHR - *Ukraine v. Russia* - where, pursuant to Rule 39, the President of the ECtHR has called upon both Contracting Parties concerned to 'refrain from taking any measures [...] which might entail breaches of the Convention rights of the civilian population'. ECtHR, 'Interim Measure Granted in Inter-State Case Brought by Ukraine against Russia'(Press Release)' (2014) Doc. ECHR 073.

[310] The AfCommHPR has indicated these measures in the context of the armed conflict in Djibouti where the government was asked not to undertake any action that might have resulted in an irreparable situation for the victims - the Afar ethnic group - of the alleged violations (rapes, arbitrary detentions, torture) committed by the State armed forces. Cf. AfCommHPR, *Association pour la défense des droits de l'Homme et des libertés v Djibouti* (2000) Communication no. 133/94 [2 and 5]. See also Bostedt (n 283) 340–341.

[311] In post-dictatorship settings - a series of cases concerning Algeria - the Committee has upheld the decision of the Rapporteur on New Communications and interim measures to require the State not to invoke the provisions of an amnesty law against individuals who have submitted or may submit communications to the HRCee. This legislative text rejected 'all allegations aiming at rendering the State responsible for deliberate disappearances'; it also affirmed that the Algerian people 'consider that reprehensible acts on the part of State agents, which have been punished by law each time they have been proved, cannot be used as a pretext to discredit the whole of the security forces who were doing their duty for their country and received public backing'. Cf. HRCee, *Boucherf v Algeria, Comm No 1196/2003* (2006) UN Doc. CCPR/C/86/D/1196/2003 [1.2 and 11]; *Messaouda Grioua née Atamna and Mohamed Grioua v Algeria, Comm no 1327/2004* (2007) UN Doc. CCPR/C/90/D/1327/2004 [1.2 and 9]; *Kimouche et al v Algeria, Comm no 1328/2004* (2007) UN Doc. CCPR/C/90/D/1328/2004 [1.3 and 9]. In all these three cases, the Committee did not invoke Rule 92 of the Rules of procedure (interim measures).

[312] Cf. Rule 91, Rules of Procedure of the HRCee. The formal ones are those outlined under Rule 92 (former Rule 86) of the Rules of Procedure of the HRCee, see Rieter, *Preventing Irreparable Harm*

The urge to avoid an irreparable damage to the individual is inherent in Article 30 ICPPED (urgent action):[314] the relatives of a disappeared person or their legal representatives, their counsel or any other person authorized by them/having a legitimate interest can submit to the Committee on Enforced Disappearances (CED) – the ICPPED's treaty body – a request that a disappeared person should be sought and found.[315] The provision contained in Article 30 enshrines the twofold nature of the functions of the CED, i.e., a combination of "humanitarian" procedures with more conventional legal procedures.[316]

After having verified the validity of such request, the CED shall 'request the State Party concerned to provide it with information on the situation of the persons sought, within a time limit set by the Committee'.[317] The CED

(n 283) xxxi. Keller and Marti underline that the Committee has used provisional measures without naming them as such. See Keller and Marti (n 283) 361.

[313] See Rieter, *Preventing Irreparable Harm* (n 283) 311. Cf. HRCee, *Raul Noel Martinez Machado v Uruguay, Communication No 83/1981* (1984) UN Doc. Supp. No. 40 (A/39/40) [2 and 8] (where, pursuant to Rule 91 and in order to gather information relevant to the admissibility of the Communication, the Committee transmitted the case and requested information on the petitioner's brother who disappeared from a prison in Uruguay. Following the request of the Committee, the victim was located after five months during which he was held *incommunicado*); cf. *El Megreisi v The Libyan Arab Jamahiriya, Comm No 440/1990* (1994) UN Doc CCPR/C/50/D/440/1990 [5.2] (where the Rapporteur requested information under Rule 91 on the whereabouts of the petitioner's brother and his state of health).

[314] No treaty-body has been entrusted with such a competence so far. However, the CED's competence concerning the 'urgent actions' recalls the 'humanitarian mandate' of the WGEID. Citroni and Bianchi (n 283) 146. During the negotiation process, some delegations underlined the risk of overlap between the functions of the CED and those of the WGEID, particularly with regard to the consideration of urgent appeals examined by the WGEID. To avoid such a potential overlap, Article 30 (2) (e) ICPPED states that the same matter must not be examined under another procedure of international investigation or settlement of the same nature. The *ratio legis* is to avoid that the same urgent request is submitted simultaneously to the WGEID and to the CED. UN Commission on Human Rights, 'Draft Report of the Inter-Sessional Open-Ended Working Group to Elaborate a Draft Legally Binding Normative Instrument for the Protection of All Persons from Enforced Disappearances (Document Subject to Restricted Distribution)' (2005) UN Doc. E/CN.4/2005/WG.22/CRP.9 para 148. In order to face this and other similar problems, the ICPPED imposes on the CED a duty to cooperate with 'all relevant organs, offices and specialized agencies and funds of the UN, with the treaty bodies instituted by international instruments, with the special procedures of the UN and with the relevant regional intergovernmental organizations or bodies as well as all relevant State institutions, agencies or offices working towards the protection of all persons against enforced disappearance'. Cf. Article 28 (1) ICPPED. However, whether this technical difference is as neat as it seems for those most concerned, i.e., the relatives of an alleged disappeared person, is doubtful: in the perspective of a relative, it could make more sense to exploit both procedures rather than just one of them. Moreover, the relatives might not know that the State concerned ratified the ICPPED. See Citroni and Bianchi (n 283) 148–150.

[315] Cf. Article 30 (1) ICPPED.

[316] UN Commission on Human Rights, 'Draft Report of the Inter-Sessional Open-Ended Working Group, UN Doc. E/CN.4/2005/WG.22/CRP.9' (n 314) para 160.

[317] Pursuant to Article 30 (2) of the ICPPED, the Committee will consider that the request (a) is not manifestly unfounded; (b) does not constitute an abuse of the right of submission of such requests; (c) has already been duly presented to the competent bodies of the State Party concerned, such as those authorized to undertake investigations, where such a possibility exists; (d) is not incompatible

contributes to uncovering the truth about the fate of the disappeared persons by informing 'the person submitting the urgent action request of its recommendations [to the State Party concerned[318]] and of the information provided to it by the State as it becomes available'.[319] The Committee may not only transmit recommendations to the State Party, but also request that the State Party takes the necessary measures, including interim measures, to locate and protect the person concerned.[320] Differently[321] from other procedures, under the ICPPED the interim measures cannot be ordered by the CED *proprio motu,* as the urgent procedure must always be initiated by external actors.[322]

More generally, the efficacy of provisional measures does not appear to be related to their binding/non-binding nature;[323] crucial is the focus of such

---

with the provisions of this Convention; and (e) that the same matter is not being examined under another procedure of international investigation or settlement of the same nature.

[318] Furthermore, the CED's efforts to work with the State Party concerned 'shall continue for as long as the fate of the person sought remains unresolved' and, as a corollary, the persons submitting the request must be kept informed. Cf. Article 30 (4) ICPPED.

[319] Cf. Article 30 (3) ICPPED.

[320] Ibid.

[321] Compared to other treaty bodies within the UN 'treaty body system', the CED's competence to order interim measures is independent of the CED's power to deal with the individual complaint procedure. Such a procedure is optional for the State in question, as it is the case with regard to other UN treaty bodies. In this sense, the interim measures function represents a preventive measure against the negative consequences that could affect not only the allegedly disappeared person, but also the person submitting the request. NS Rodley, 'The Role and Impact of Treaty Bodies' in Dinah Shelton (ed), *The Oxford Handbook of International Human Rights Law* (Oxford University Press 2013) 637.

[322] Pursuant to Article 30 (1) ICPPED these are the 'relatives of the disappeared person or their legal representatives, their counsel or any person authorized by them, as well as by any other person having a legitimate interest'.

[323] With regard to the ECtHR's interim measures and their binding character, cf. ECtHR, *Mamatkulov and Askarov v. Turkey, Judgment (GC)* (n 285). The IACommHR held that 'OAS member States, by creating the Commission and mandating it through the OAS Charter and the Commission's Statute to promote the observance and protection of human rights of the American peoples, have implicitly undertaken to implement measures of this nature where they are essential to preserving the Commission's mandate.' Cf. IACommHR, *Garza v United States, Case 12243* (2001) Report No.52/01, OEA/ser.L/V/ II.111, Doc. 20 [117]. With regard to the binding character of the AfCommHPR's provisional measures, some authors argue that it directly derives from the fact that if the State concerned does not implement the precautionary measures requested and the beneficiary suffers an irreparable damage, then it would be possible to submit a complaint before the regional human rights organs for non-compliance of precautionary measures; in order for this to be possible, the conditions outlined under Article 56 AfChHPR must be met. See Burbano-Herrera, Viljoen and Haeck (n 283) 226. The African Court has plainly affirmed that 'an Order of Provisional Measures issued by the Court is as binding as any judgment of the Court'. Cf. AfCtHPR, 'Interim Report of the African Court on Human and Peoples' Rights Notifying the Executive Council of Non-Compliance by a State, in Accordance with Article 31 of the Protocol' with Regard to Non-Compliance with the Measures Indicated in Relation to Application No. 002/2013 (on Gaddafi's Son)' para 8 <http://goo.gl/kblUfT>. As for the HRCee, in *Piandiong et al. v the Philippines* the Committee clarified the binding character of these measures by saying that 'interim measures [...], are essential to the Committee's role under the [Optional] Protocol. Flouting of the Rule, especially by irreversible measures such as the execution of the alleged victim or his/her deportation from the country, undermines the protection of Covenant rights through the Optional Protocol. [...] The Committee reiterates its conclusion that the State committed a grave breach of its obligations under the Protocol

measures, i.e., the urgency of avoiding irreparable harm to a person or, in other words, the need to avoid that violations of fundamental rights are committed (e.g., the right to life, the prohibition of torture/inhuman and degrading treatment, the right to personal integrity; the prohibition of enforced disappearance).[324]

3.2.2. Information, family ties, and disappearances in international human rights treaties

The recognition of the impact that uncertainty about the fate and whereabouts of a person can have on others' human rights is the result of the dynamic interpretation of IHRL treaties by judicial and quasi-judicial bodies (see Chapter IV). Before addressing how general human rights treaties have been interpreted and applied, it is important to explore protective standards that are set down under general (sub-section 3.2.2.1) and thematic (sub-section 3.2.2.2) human rights treaties in relation to three main drivers, i.e., the search for/transmission of information, the preservation of the family as the basic unit of society, and the disappearance of persons.

3.2.2.1. Information and family ties: Two (dis-)connected subjects in the general human rights treaties

IHRL provides for the right to seek, impart, and receive information[325] whose broad meaning and scope have been further specified by human rights-related documents under different angles (including in relation to the right to *habeas corpus* or to other guarantees that a person deprived of her liberty has).[326]

---

by putting the alleged victims to death before the Committee had concluded its consideration of the communication.' HRCee, *Piandiong et al v the Philippines, Comm no 869/1999,* (2000) UN Doc. CCPR/C/70/D/869/1999 [5.4 and 8]; see also Naldi, 'Interim Measures in the UN Human Rights Committee' (n 283) 453-454.

[324] For a discussion of various reasons forwarded by States for not complying with provisional measures, see Rieter, *Preventing Irreparable Harm* (n 283) 943–1019.

[325] At the global level, cf. Article 19 (2), ICCPR; Article 19, Universal Declaration of Human Rights, Res. 217A (III), UN Doc. A/RES/217(III) A at 71 (10 December 1948). Although religion-driven, two other documents are noteworthy: the Universal Islamic Declaration of Human Rights states that '[p]ursuit of knowledge and search after truth is not only a right but a duty of every Muslim' and that '[t]here shall be no bar on the dissemination of information provided it does not endanger the security of the society or the State and is confined within the limits imposed by the Law'. Cf. Article XII (b) and (d), Universal Islamic Declaration of Human Rights, adopted by the Islamic Council in Paris on 19 September 1981. The Cairo Declaration on Human Rights in Islam affirms that '[i]nformation is a vital necessity to society. It may not be exploited or misused in such a way as may violate sanctities and the dignity of Prophets, undermine moral and ethical Values or disintegrate, corrupt or harm society or weaken its faith.' Cf. Article 22 (c), Cairo Declaration on Human Rights in Islam, adopted on 5 August 1990 by the Nineteenth Islamic Conference of Foreign Ministers of the Organization of Islamic Cooperation, Annex to Resolution no. 49/19-P.

[326] Several non-binding documents address this right under different angles: cf. section A of principle 10 (disclosure of information on violations of human rights and humanitarian law) and section B of Principle 10 (safeguards for the right to liberty; to life; etc., including in armed conflict) of the Tshwane Principles: '[i]n no circumstances may information be withheld on national security grounds that would result in the secret detention of a person, or the establishment and operation of secret places of detention, or secret executions. Nor are there any circumstances in which the fate or whereabouts of anyone deprived of liberty by, or with the authorization, support, or acquiescence of,

However, this right has been rarely[327] taken into account vis-à-vis the issue of missing persons in the context of armed conflicts. This might be due to the fact that the right at issue can be limited in specific circumstances and under certain conditions and can also be derogated from[328] under a number of IHRL treaties. The UN Special Rapporteur on Freedom of Expression affirms that the obligations of States to disclose information[329] regarding violations of IHRL and IHL and to take proactive measures to ensure the preservation and dissemination of information of this kind are generally acknowledged. He also affirms that 'limitations to these obligations, especially in situations of [TJ], can be invoked only under very specific circumstances.'[330] Indeed,

> the right to access information on human rights violations, as enshrined by the right to freedom of expression, should be considered to be part of the right to truth in all

---

the State may be concealed from, or otherwise denied to, the person's family members or others with a legitimate interest in the person's welfare.' Global Principles on National Security and the Right to Information (known as the Tshwane Principles)", Tshwane, South Africa (12 June 2013) published by the Open Society Justice Initiative https://goo.gl/l9aCpy accessed 13 June 2015. Guideline 13 (Disclosure of information) of the UN Basic Principles on the right to bring proceedings before a court affirms that '[t]he detaining authority shall provide all relevant information to the judge, the detainee and/or his or her lawyer. Disclosure must include exculpatory information, which includes not only information that establishes an accused person's innocence [...].' UN Working Group on Arbitrary Detention, 'UN Basic Principles and Guidelines on the Right of Anyone Deprived of Their Liberty to Bring Proceedings before a Court' (2015) UN Doc WGAD/CRP.1/2015 para 97. Among the recommendations put forward in the Joint Study on global practices in relation to secret detention in the context of countering terrorism is the following: '[...] domestic legislative frameworks should not allow for any exceptions from *habeas corpus*, operating independently from the detaining authority and from the place and form of deprivation of liberty. The study has shown that judicial bodies play a crucial role in protecting people against secret detention. The law should foresee penalties for officials who refuse to disclose relevant information during *habeas corpus* proceedings.' UN Human Rights Council, 'Joint Study on Global Practices in Relation to Secret Detention in the Context of Countering Terrorism' (2010) UN Doc A/HRC/13/42 para 292 (b).

[327] In the IACtHR's case law, violations of the right to know the truth in an enforced disappearance case can be the result of a breach of the right to access information set forth in article 13 of the ACHR. Cf. IACtHR, *Gomes-Lund et al (Guerrilha do Araguaia) v Brazil, Judgment - Preliminary Objections, Merits, Reparations, and Costs* (2010) Series C No. 219 [225]. Both the IACommHR and its Special Rapporteur for freedom of expression have advanced the thesis that 'under any circumstances, but especially in processes of transition to democracy, victims and their relatives have the right to know with regard to information on serious violations of human rights in the archives of the State.' See IACommHR, 'Annual Report of the [IACommHR] 2010: Report of the Office of the Special Rapporteur for Freedom of Expression Dr. Catalina Botero' (2011) Doc No OEA/Ser.L/V/II Doc. 5 283. At the national level, an interesting example is Lebanon: in early 2014 the Shura Council ruled that the families of people who disappeared during the civil war (1975–1990) should have full access to official documents, including confessions by former militants related to cases of missing Lebanese, giving important impetus to disclosure. Jana El Hassan, 'Families of Disappeared Remain Skeptical' (*The Daily Star (Lebanon)*, 2014) <http://www.dailystar.com.lb/News/Lebanon-News/2014/Mar-14/250203-families-of-disappeared-remain-skeptical.ashx>; Christalla Yakinthou, 'Living with the Shadows of the Past. The Impact of Disappearance on Wives of the Missing in Lebanon' (ICTJ 2015) 9.

[328] Not all IHRL Treaties provide for a derogation clause; the ICCPR is among those enshrining a clause (cf. Article 4).

[329] Another aspect of the right to access information is that of 'access by persons to personal data being held by public authorities.' See UNGA, 'Report of the Special Rapporteur on the Promotion and Protection of the Right to Freedom of Opinion and Expression' (2013) UN Doc A/68/362 para 39.

[330] ibid para 37.

circumstances – whether it relates to past or present situations, is claimed by victims, their relatives or by anyone in the name of public interest, in situations of political transition or not, and irrespective of the existence of legal proceedings, including when judicial action has expired.'[331]

In this specific passage the lack of reference to IHL violations is problematic. Moreover, the reference to proactive measures does not take into due consideration that such measures may clash with the witnesses' own interests or ongoing prosecutorial investigations; thus, a similar stance leaves room for asking whether the foregoing is still *de lege ferenda*, as the *lex lata* provides for a right which has a narrower scope.

IHL and IHRL similarly provide for the protection of family unit;[332] indeed, the protection of the family as the basic unit of the society is provided for under the ICCPR, which reproduces the formulation of the UDHR (i.e., 'the family is the natural and fundamental group of society and is entitled to protection by society and the State'[333]).[334] The ICCPR also enshrines the right of every individual to the protection of the law against arbitrary or unlawful interferences with his privacy, family, home or correspondence.[335] It is important to stress that, while the provisions on the protection of the family as the natural and fundamental group revolve around the family as an institution under private law, the provision on the right to the protection from any arbitrary interference is centered on 'the protection of the privacy of individual family members, as expressed in family life'[336] against such interference. In this respect, the right to be protected from arbitrary/unlawful interference implicitly admits lawful restrictions of the same right, which is not an absolute entitlement. Admissible interferences with this right include, *inter alia*, the deprivation of the personal liberty:[337] detention of individuals during the conflict and continuing in its aftermath must take into consideration the impact that captivity has on the person concerned and on her family members, particularly when restrictive measures are taken in relation to the communication rights of the inmate. As Section 4 of the present Chapter and Section 4 of Chapter IV will demonstrate, the disregard of the parameters that make similar interferences lawful can be indicative of violations of the rights of inmates as well as of a situation of emotional distress for the family members.

---

[331] ibid para 92.
[332] Louise Doswald-Beck, *Human Rights in Times of Conflict and Terrorism* (Oxford University Press 2011) 122.
[333] Cf. Article 16 (3), UDHR.
[334] Cf. Article 23(1), UDHR.
[335] Cf. Article 17 (1-2), ICCPR; this provision reproduces Article 12, UDHR.
[336] Manfred Nowak, *U.N. Covenant on Civil and Political Rights: CCPR Commentary* (2nd rev ed, NP Engel 2005) 299.
[337] ibid 301. See also section 4 in Chapter IV.

3.2.2.2. Theme-focused human rights treaties

a. Enforced disappearances and the right of each victim to know the truth

The ICPPED is the only[338] global treaty that provides for specific provisions aimed at elucidating what happens whenever a person is subjected to the practice of enforced disappearance. The Preamble recognizes 'the right of any victim to know the truth about the circumstances of an enforced disappearance and the fate of the disappeared person, and the right to freedom to seek, receive and impart information to this end'.[339] Arguably unclear, the connection between these two rights intends to highlight that access to information is paramount for the realization of the right to know the truth. Such connection is not reiterated in the text of the treaty; while the right to truth is articulated as an absolute right under Article 24 (2), the right to information is spelled out as a restrictable right under Articles 18 and 20. The Convention imposes on each State party[340] an obligation

---

[338] The other universal document, which is not binding, is the 1992 Declaration on the protection of all persons from enforced disappearances adopted by the UNGA. The Declaration does not provide for a right to know the truth. Cf. UNGA, 'Resolution Adopting the Declaration on the Protection of All Persons from Enforced Disappearances, Res 47/133' (1992) UN Doc A/RES/47/133. However, According to Pérez Solla, Article 9 (1), providing for the right to 'a prompt and effective judicial remedy', enshrines the content of the right to know: i.e., 'determining the whereabouts or state of health of persons deprived of their liberty and/or identifying the authority ordering or carrying out the deprivation of liberty'. María Fernanda Pérez Solla, *Enforced Disappearances in International Human Rights* (McFarland & Co, Publishers 2006) 92. Similarly, the WGEID, in the General Comment on the Right to Truth in relation to Enforced Disappearance, argues that the 1992 Declaration 'enumerates a number of obligations that flow from this right'. See Preamble of General Comment on the Right to the Truth in Relation to Enforced Disappearances in WGEID, 'Compilation of General Comments on the Declaration on the Protection of All Persons from Enforced Disappearance' <http://goo.gl/6P0Izl> accessed 12 May 2015. At the international level uncertainty is also tackled by means of reference to an overly vague right to truth: for instance, the UN High Commissioner for Human Rights has concluded that '[t]he right to the truth as a stand-alone right is a fundamental right of the individual and therefore should not be subject to limitations. [...] Amnesties or similar measures and restrictions to the right to seek information must never be used to limit, deny or impair the right to the truth.' Cf. UN OHCHR, 'Study on the Right to the Truth' (2006) UN Doc E/CN.4/2006/91 paras 58-60.

[339] This unclear way of couching the last paragraph of the Preamble is the result of a compromise, which appeared to be necessary in order to adopt the Convention. In fact, in 2005, when the text of the Convention was adopted by the Open-ended Working Group, the US delegation declared its reservation both to the Preamble and to Article 24 (2): the notion of the right to know the truth was therefore to be understood 'in the context of the freedom of information, which is enshrined in article 19 of the International Covenant on Civil and Political Rights'. UN Commission on Human Rights, 'Report of the Inter-Sessional Open-Ended Working Group to Elaborate a Draft Legally Binding Normative Instrument for the Protection of All Persons from Enforced Disappearances' (2006) UN Doc. E/CN.4/2006/57, Annex 2, 48. This restrictive attitude is in contrast to the one held during the negotiations of the AP I, where the US representative objected to the deletion of the right of families to know the fate of their relatives; such a deletion might have led to misinterpret the entire section and to consider it as 'referring to the right of Governments...to know what had happened to certain missing persons.' See Declaration of the US Representative on amendment CDDH/II/259 Add.1, in ICRC, 'Official Records of the Diplomatic Conference...', Vol XII' (n 125) CDDH/II/SR.76, para 28, 231. The United States (hereinafter, US) signed but did not ratify the AP I.

[340] Cf. Article 18, ICPPED. Corresponding provisions can be found in Article 10 of the UNGA Declaration on Enforced Disappearances.

to guarantee to any person[341] with a legitimate interest in this information access to a minimum of information on the person deprived of liberty.[342] In light of the sensitivity of the situation in which persons deprived of their liberty are, Article 20 sets down the conditions for limiting[343] the right to information.[344] Restrictions on this right shall not result in conducts amounting to an enforced disappearance or secret detention.[345] Moreover, should information on a person deprived of liberty be denied or restricted, a judicial remedy is granted.[346]

These rights have to be read in conjunction with Article 2[347] which defines what enforced disappearance means under the ICPPED: the narrow definition embodied in Article 2 differs from the general broader understanding of "missing person" (see "Terminology" in Introduction) under two respects, i.e., the presence of an action (arrest, detention, abduction or any other form of deprivation of liberty)/omission (withholding information and denying the disappearance thereby failing to inform) and the State element (action/omission perpetrated by State agents or by persons/groups of persons acting with the authorization/support/acquiescence of the State).

---

[341] This expression covers the relatives of the person deprived of liberty; their representative, or their counsel.

[342] The information that can be accessed is in particular related to the whereabouts of the person deprived of liberty; elements relating to the state of health of this person; the authority responsible for the deprivation of liberty; in the event of death during the deprivation of liberty, the circumstances and the cause of death as well as the destination of the remains. The use of personal information – including medical and genetic data- is under the conditions laid down in Article 19 of the ICPPED: i.e., collection and/or transmission of the information within the framework of the search for a disappeared person shall not be used or made available for purposes other than the search for the disappeared person; the collection/processing/use and storage of personal information shall not infringe the human rights, fundamental freedoms or human dignity of an individual. Cf. Article 19, paras. 1-2, ICPPED. The recognition of such an extensive right to information to all persons with a legitimate interest is coupled with an obligation to protect these persons from intimidation. Cf. Article 18 (2), ICPPED.

[343] Some delegations were concerned that these restrictions might have impacted on the ICPPED's purpose as well as on the realization of the right to know the truth. UN Commission on Human Rights, 'Draft Report of the Inter-Sessional Open-Ended Working Group, UN Doc. E/CN.4/2005/WG.22/CRP.9' (n 314) paras 6, 12. On this point, in its conclusive statement on the final draft, Italy pointed out that it would have preferred specific provisions binding the State to grant all the information listed in article 18. UN Commission on Human Rights, 'Report of the Inter-Sessional Open-Ended Working Group' (n 339) General Statements, 50.

[344] The right provided for in Article 18 (1) can be restricted only where a person is under the protection of the law and the deprivation of liberty is subject to judicial control. The restriction must be necessary and provided for by law. Cf. Article 20 (1), ICPPED.

[345] Cf. Articles 20 (1), Article 17 and Article 2, ICPPED.

[346] On this aspect, Article 20 states that '[w]ithout prejudice to consideration of the lawfulness of the deprivation of a person's liberty, States Parties shall guarantee to the persons referred to in article 18, paragraph 1, the right to a prompt and effective judicial remedy as a means of obtaining without delay the information referred to in article 18, paragraph 1. This right to a remedy may not be suspended or restricted in any circumstances.' On this point, Argentina pointed out that the article could, under no circumstances, be interpreted as meaning that it was permissible to deny or conceal information relating to the crime of enforced disappearance. See UN Commission on Human Rights, 'Report of the Inter-Sessional Open-Ended Working Group' (n 339) para 136.

[347] See 'Introduction' of this book.

The right to know the truth has been recognized as the cornerstone of the combat against impunity in the realm of gross human rights violations; it denotes a paradigmatic shift from a model of conventional criminal justice toward a model of victim-oriented justice.[348] The broad definition of "missing person" outlined in the introduction of this book entails that IHL and/or IHRL violations can be the trigger of uncertainty about the fate and whereabouts of human beings. International law addresses the needs nested within the fight against impunity,[349] including the need to know what happened to victims of IHL/IHRL violations.

As reflected in the Orentlicher's principles, uncertainty about IHRL/IHL violations is contrary to the tenets of a fight-against-impunity strategy: the principles affirm that 'every people has the inalienable right to know the truth about past events concerning perpetration of heinous crimes'; embedded in this collective right is the imprescriptible victims' and their families' right to know truth.[350] Both are essentially expressed in a way that over-emphasizes the collective dimension, but overshadows the individual one. Its respect and protection are inherently aimed at preserving collective memory from extinction.[351] As such, the right to truth exclusively makes part of the "post-" narrative. The principles also enshrine the right of the family of the direct victim 'to be informed of the fate and/or whereabouts of the disappeared person', which is part of the right to reparation.[352] The fact that the right of families to know is framed as remedial in nature does not correctly reflect its substantive nature: the latter is not only deductible from the case law of various supervisory bodies, but also from the *jus scriptum*.[353]

Multiple problems arise from the foregoing: where the case of enforced disappearance is attributable to a non-state armed group which operates without the authorization/support/acquiescence of the State,[354] the State is obliged to take

---

[348] Ruti Teitel, 'Symposium - Human Rights on the Eve of the next Century: Beyond Vienna & Beijing. Human Rights Theory: Human Rights Genealogy.' (1997) 66 Fordham Law Review 301, 315.

[349] "Impunity" means the impossibility, *de jure* or *de facto*, of bringing perpetrators of violations to account - whether in criminal, civil, administrative or disciplinary proceedings - since they are not subject to any inquiry that might lead to their being accused, arrested, tried and, if found guilty, sentenced to appropriate penalties, and to making reparations to their victims. Cf. Definitions (a), UN Commission on Human Rights, 'Promotion and Protection of Human Rights: Impunity. Add.1 "Updated Set of Principles for the Protection and Promotion of Human Rights through Action to Combat Impunity (Orentlicher Principles)"' (2005) UN Doc E/CN.4/2005/102/Add.1.

[350] Cf. Principles 2 and Principle 4, ibid.

[351] Cf. Principles 3-4, ibid.

[352] Cf. Principle 34, ibid.

[353] UN Commission on Human Rights, 'Report of the Independent Expert to Update the Set of Principles to Combat Impunity, Diane Orentlicher' (2005) UN Doc E/CN.4/2005/102 para 63.

[354] Some delegations thought it would be worth examining the responsibility of those commonly called 'non-state actors'. The majority of delegations recognized that States bore the prime responsibility for preventing and punishing enforced disappearances, including those perpetrated by non-state actors, and for ensuring compensation. See UN Commission on Human Rights, 'Report of the Inter-Sessional Open-Ended Working Group to Elaborate a Draft Legally Binding Normative Instrument for the Protection of All Persons from Enforced Disappearances' (2003) UN Doc. E/CN.4/2003/71 para 35. As a result of this view, Article 3 was eventually included in the final text. Pursuant to this Article, '[e]ach State Party shall take appropriate measures to investigate acts defined

appropriate measures to investigate these acts and to bring those responsible to justice.[355] The other provisions concerning the right to truth and access to information are related to "enforced disappearance" as defined under Article 2 and, therefore, do not apply. In this respect, it is meaningful that during the negotiations for the adoption of the ICPPED the question of whether the convention should include a right to truth in the case of enforced disappearance perpetrated by non-state armed actors was raised, [356] but remained unanswered.

Although the general prohibition of enforced disappearance seems to have attained the status of customary law[357] and, as such, is binding upon States and

---

in Article 2 committed by persons or groups of persons acting without the authorization, support or acquiescence of the State and to bring those responsible to justice'.

[355] Cf. Article 3, ICPPED. The provision enshrined in Article 3 is also relevant for another aspect: it provides for State responsibility over acts of enforced disappearance perpetrated by non-state actors but does not extend international responsibility to acts of enforced disappearances by non-state actors. Non-state actors will be held individually criminally responsible in international law only for acts of enforced disappearance that reach the level of a crime against humanity, and not for acts of enforced disappearance *per se*. K Anderson, 'How Effective Is the International Convention for the Protection of All Persons from Enforced Disappearance Likely to Be in Holding Individuals Criminally Responsible for Acts of Enforced Disappearance' (2006) 7 Melbourne Journal of International Law 1, 274. See also on this aspect, UN Commission on Human Rights, 'Report of the Inter-Sessional Open-Ended Working Group to Elaborate a Draft Legally Binding Normative Instrument for the Protection of All Persons from Enforced Disappearances' (2004) UN Doc E/CN.4/2004/59, Annex 2, paras 30-32. On State responsibility, several delegations pointed out that the instrument must take account of the situation on the ground and of the fact that States were no longer the sole subjects of international law. However, it was underlined that a reference in the instrument to acts by non-state actors ought not, under any circumstances, to exonerate the State from responsibility, and that establishing direct responsibility for non-state actors under the future instrument was not an option. UN Commission on Human Rights, 'Report of the Inter-Sessional Open-Ended Working Group to Elaborate a Draft Legally Binding Normative Instrument for the Protection of All Persons from Enforced Disappearances' (2005) UN Doc. E/CN.4/2005/66 paras 30-31.

[356] UN Commission on Human Rights, 'Report of the Inter-Sessional Open-Ended Working Group' (n 355) para 14. The question whether non-state actors should be mentioned in the definition of the offence was particularly relevant, for Article 7 (2) (i) of the 1998 ICC Statute defines the crime of enforced disappearance of persons as 'the arrest, detention or abduction of persons by, or with the authorization, support or acquiescence of, a State or *a political organization*...[emphasis added]'.

[357] The HRCee has clearly stated that 'the prohibitions against taking of hostages, abductions or unacknowledged detention are not subject to derogation. The absolute nature of these prohibitions, even in times of emergency, is justified by their status as norms of general international law. Cf. HRCee, 'General Comment No 29: States of Emergency (Article 4)' (2001) UN Doc CCPR/C/21/Rev.1/Add.11 para 13 (b). The prohibition of enforced disappearance is among the customary IHL rules applicable both in NIAC and in IAC. Cf. Rule 98, Henckaerts and Doswald-Beck (n 21) 340. According to Cassese, '[i]t may be noted that with respect to this crime the ICC Statute has not codified existing customary law but contributed to the crystallization of a nascent rule, evolved primarily out of treaty law (that is, the numerous treaties on human rights prohibiting various acts falling under this heading), as well as the case law of the Inter-American Commission and Court of Human Rights, in addition to a number of UN General Assembly Resolutions. These various strands have been instrumental in the gradual formation of a customary rule prohibiting enforced disappearance of persons.' Antonio Cassese, *International Criminal Law* (2nd edn, Oxford University Press 2008) 113. See also UN Department of Peacekeeping Operations (Criminal Law and Judicial Advisory Service), *Handbook for Judicial Affairs Officers in UN Peacekeeping Operations*, (2013) 59 <http://www.un.org/en/peacekeeping/publications> accessed 13 October 2015. Moreover, the IACtHR has affirmed that 'the prohibition of the forced disappearance of persons and the corresponding obligations to investigate and punish those responsible has attained the status of *jus*

non-state actors,[358] it is questionable to assert the same with regard to the right of each victim to know the truth. In any case, should this right be customary, it would be highly debatable to assert that all families of persons reported as missing – regardless of the enforced disappearance definition – as result of an armed conflict enjoy the rights provided for under the ICPPED by analogy. Thus, during[359] and in the aftermath of an armed conflict, only a portion of cases might fall under the coverage of this treaty; the slow pace of ratifications (at the time of writing, the Convention has 58 States Parties) significantly impacts this coverage.

b. The importance of family ties in the IDPs and child protection frameworks

Under today's global human rights framework, considerations on how to address uncertainty about the fate of persons in the context of an armed conflict are solely embedded in a soft law instrument,[360] i.e., the Guiding Principles on Internal Displacement. This document provides for the right of internally displaced persons (IDPs) to know the fate of their relatives.[361]

To a certain extent, these considerations are also present in the Convention on the Rights of the Child: should a child be separated from his parents because of an action[362] initiated by a State Party, the State Party shall, upon request, provide the parents/child/another member of the family 'with the essential information concerning the whereabouts of the absent member(s) of the family unless the provision of the information would be detrimental to the well-being of the child'.[363] While other human rights treaties do not enshrine a similar provision, IHL treaties provide for measures that guarantee the preservation of family unit and the transmission of information to this end.[364]

---

cogens', cf. IACtHR, *Goiburú et al v Paraguay, Judgment - Merits, Reparations and Costs* (2006) Series C No. 153 [84]. Along the same lines, IACtHR, *Rochac Hernández and others v. El Salvador (Merits...)* (n 156) [92].

[358] See, in this regard, Human Rights Council, '2nd Report of the Independent International Commission of Inquiry on the Syrian Arab Republic' (n 273) para 106.

[359] The ICPPED clearly states that '[n]o exceptional circumstances whatsoever, whether a state of war or a threat of war, internal political instability or any other public emergency, may be invoked as a justification for enforced disappearance'. Cf. Article 1 (2) ICPPED.

[360] The Guiding Principles derive their authoritative character from the fact of reflecting or restating guarantees contained in IHRL and IHL. For a thorough compilation and analysis of legal norms that constitute the foundations of the Guiding Principles, see Walter Kälin, *Guiding Principles on Internal Displacement. Annotations* (The American Society of International Law 2008).

[361] Cf. Principle 16 (1); Principle 17 (3) protects family integrity and provides for an obligation to expedite the reunion of family which are separated by displacement. See 'Report of the Representative of the Secretary-General, Mr. Francis M. Deng, Submitted pursuant to Commission Resolution 1997/39. Addendum: Guiding Principles on Internal Displacement' (UN Commission on Human Rights 1998) UN Doc E/CN.4/1998/53/Add.2.

[362] A likely situation might be detention, imprisonment, exile, deportation or death - even when the death occurs in the custody of the State - of one or both parents or of the child.

[363] Cf. Article 9 (4), Convention on the Rights of the Child (CRC), 2 September 1990, 1577 UNTS 3. NB: for ensuring the enjoyment of this guarantee, Article 9 specifies that 'States Parties shall further ensure that the submission of such a request shall of itself entail no adverse consequences for the person(s) concerned'.

[364] See *supra* sub-section 1.2. Moreover, a similar standard is also outlined in a soft law document, the Beijing Rules on juvenile justice, which under Rule 10.1 states that '[...] upon the apprehension of a

3.2.3. The issue of missing persons in regional human rights treaties

The search for/transmission of information on the fate and whereabouts of persons, the preservation of the family as the basic unit of society (sub-section 3.2.3.1), and the disappearance of persons (sub-section 3.2.3.2) are three separate issues under the regional human rights framework. Only does one human rights treaty address the first two issues as intertwined (see below sub-section 3.2.3.1). However, in the human rights case law, which will be explored in Chapter IV, the human rights adjudicators – especially the ECtHR and the IACtHR – have examined these issues by addressing them jointly under specific human rights provisions.

3.2.3.1 Information on the fate of a family member and the protection of the family unit

Considerations on how to address uncertainty about the fate and whereabouts of persons in the context of an armed conflict are solely embedded in the African Charter on the rights and welfare of the child: this instrument stresses that where separation is caused by internal and external displacement arising from armed conflicts or natural disasters, States Parties to the Charter shall undertake all the necessary measures to trace and re-unite children with parents or relatives. [365]

The right of families to search for and to access information can be inferred from the right to seek, receive, and impart information, which is provided for by most of the regional treaties;[366] the majority of these treaties[367] offers States the

---

juvenile, his or her parents or guardian shall be immediately notified of such apprehension, and, where such immediate notification is not possible, the parents or guardian shall be notified within the shortest possible time thereafter'. Cf. 1985 UN Standard Minimum Rules for the Administration of Juvenile Justice ("The Beijing Rules"), UN Doc. A/RES/40/33, 29 November 1985. Although not specifically focused on children, similar provisions are also enshrined in the 1955 Standard Minimum Rules for the Treatment of Prisoners (cf. Rules 37 to 39 on 'Contact with the outside world' and Rule 44 on 'Notification of death, illness…'), *First UN Congress on the Prevention of Crime and the Treatment of Offences*, Annex 1(a), UN Doc. A/CONF.6/1 (1956). See also Sharon Detrick, *A Commentary on the United Nations Convention on the Rights of the Child* (Martinus Nijhoff Publishers 1999) 179.

[365] The African Charter on the rights and welfare of the child states that if families are separated as a result of State action, the State must provide the children with essential information concerning the whereabouts of their family members; where separation is caused by internal and external displacement arising from armed conflicts or natural disasters, States Parties to the Charter shall undertake all the necessary measures to trace and re-unite children with parents or relatives. Cf. Article 19 (3) and Article 25 (2), African Charter on the Rights and Welfare of the Child, July 1990 (entered into force November 29, 1999) OAU Doc. CAB/LEG/24.9/49 (1990). At the moment of writing, 41 African States have signed and ratified the Charter: http://www.achpr.org/instruments/child/ratification/ accessed on 12 January 2016.

[366] Article 10 ECHR is narrower than Article 19 ICCPR, as it provides for the 'freedom to receive and impart information'; Article 13 (1) ACHR proposes a formula similar to the ICCPR, i.e., freedom to seek, receive, and impart information and ideas of all kinds; Article 32 (1) of the ArChHR provides for the right to information and the right to seek, impart, and receive information, Arab Charter on Human Rights (ArChHR), adopted by the League of Arab States (23 May 2004). Although not binding, particularly interesting is the ASEAN Declaration of Human Rights which includes the right to seek, receive and impart information without interference (Article 23), Cf. Article 23, ASEAN Human Rights Declaration, adopted on 18 November 2012, 21st ASEAN Summit and Special Meeting of the ASEAN Intergovernmental Commission on Human Rights.

[367] Cf. Article 15, ECHR; Article 27, ACHR; Article 4, ArChHR.

possibility of derogating from this right in exceptional circumstances[368] and of limiting its scope lawfully.[369]

The "right to information" has emerged as a legal entitlement in those situations entailing State-held information and public access to it.[370] As shown in Sections 1 and 2 of this Chapter, under IHL the possibility of seeking, imparting, and receiving information is instrumental to the restoration and maintenance of family ties. Nevertheless, such link does not neatly emerge from the regional human rights case law concerning the right to seek, impart, and receive information. This right has been construed as having a collective scope; the IACtHR is the sole judicial body that has recognized its private dimension with regard to the next of kin of victims of human rights violations.[371]

While the protection of the family as the natural unit of the society[372] is solely enshrined in the AfChHPR and in the ArChHR – which reproduce *verbatim* the UDHR, the right of every individual to be protected from unlawful/arbitrary interference with his family life is provided for by the ECHR, the ACHR, and the

---

[368] Article 9 AfChHPR provides for the right to receive information, which is not only underogable, but also absolute. Cf. Article 9 AfChHPR, African [Banjul] Charter on Human and Peoples' Rights, June 27, 1981, OAU Doc. CAB/LEG/67/3 rev. 5, 21 I.L.M. 58 (1982) (AfChHPR). With regard to State-held information, the AfCommHPR has adopted a non-binding Declaration spelling out the principles on Freedom of Expression in Africa. Pursuant to its Article IV (1), '[p]ublic bodies hold information not for themselves but as custodians of the public good and everyone has a right to access this information, subject only to clearly defined rules established by law.' Cf. Article IV (1), AfCommHPR. Declaration of Principles on Freedom of Expression in Africa, adopted during its 32nd session, on October 17-23, 2002 (Banjul).

[369] Article 10 ECHR includes the basis for possible restrictions that the State can apply to this right. Cf. Article 10 Convention for the Protection of Human Rights and Fundamental Freedoms (ECHR), 213 UNTS 222 (4 November 1950). The broad reach of the admissible restriction *ex* Article 10 (2) is mainly due to the proposal put forward by the UK at the time of the negotiation of the ECHR. Cf. Council of Europe (CoE) - European Commission of Human Rights, 'Preparatory Work on Article 10 ECHR' (1956) Doc no DH (56) 15 paras 12-13, 10-11.

[370] The IACtHR has gone so far as to state that 'the right to freedom of thought and expression includes the protection of the right of access to State-held information'. The Court's pronouncement relates to a case about the conduct of the forestry company Trillium and the Río Condor Project in the implementation of a deforestation project that could be prejudicial to the environment and to the sustainable development of Chile). IACtHR, *Claude-Reyes et al v Chile, Judgment - Merits, reparations and costs* (2006) Series C No. 151 [77]. Moreover, the OAS has adopted the Declaration of Principles on Freedom of Expression - a non-binding document - that affirms what follows: 'access to information held by the State is a fundamental right of every individual' and 'States have the obligation to guarantee the full exercise of this right'. Cf. Principle 4, OAS. Declaration of Principles on Freedom of Expression, adopted on October 19, 2000, http://www.oas.org/en/iachr/expression/showarticle.asp?artID=26 accessed 10 January 2015.

[371] The IACtHR has recognized that the State has the obligation to search for such information by all possible means. In this regard, the Inter-American Court has affirmed that 'every person, including the next of kin of the victims of grave violations of human rights, has the right to the truth. Therefore, the next of kin of the victims [or the victims themselves] and society as a whole must be informed of everything that has happened in connection with said violations.' See IACtHR, *Myrna Mack Chang v Guatemala - Judgment - Merits, Reparations and Costs* (2003) Series C No 101 [274].

[372] Cf. Article 18(1), AfChHPR; Article 33 (1), ArChHR.

ArChHR.[373] Similarly to the international framework, in the regional framework, it is rare to find missing persons-related issues addressed under both provisions.

The ECHR is the only treaty that provides for a different provision, declaring that 'everyone has the right to respect for his private and family life, his home and his correspondence'.[374] The 'respect for family life' revolves around the protection of the family as the fundamental unit of society and conceives the protection of the integrity of the family as the main focus of the protection system.[375] The similarity with the protective standards concerning the family under IHL is only apparent, as Article 8 ECHR is centred on the ontological aspect of the protection of the family, i.e., whether or not a family exists (e.g., the marriage is not a required feature for being considered a family, since key is the existence of close family ties).[376]

This provision is formulated in a manner that would presume a mere abstention from interference, as the notion of respect – rarely present in the ECHR – is not clear-cut and remains relatively imprecise.[377] However, 'at the heart of the word "respect" sit both positive and negative dimensions.[378] Thus, Article 8 requires that protective measures be fully implemented by State authorities; specifically, positive obligations can arise under two respects, i.e., the State must undertake some action to ensure respect for the right to family life (i.e., the State must do something more than the simply refraining from interfering with the right) or the State must protect an individual from interference by other individuals' action.[379] A balance between the interests of the individual and of the community as a whole must be struck; in doing so, the State has a margin of appreciation.[380] In any case,

> whether the question is analysed in terms of a positive duty on the State to take reasonable and appropriate measures to secure the applicant's rights under paragraph 1 of Article 8 or in terms of an "interference by a public authority" to be justified in accordance with paragraph 2, the applicable principles are broadly similar.[381]

For instance, the national legal order must enshrine rules that protect the essential features of Article 8(1),[382] including the family life of every individual.

---

[373] Cf. Article 8 (1-2) ECHR; Article 11(2) ACHR; Article 21 (1), ArChHR.

[374] Cf. Article 8 (1) ECHR.

[375] Ovey 4th ed, 247

[376] ECtHR, *K and T v Finland, Judgment (GC)* (2001) App no 25702/94 [150]. See also Clare Ovey and Robin White, *Jacobs and White: The European Convention on Human Rights* (4 edition, Oxford University Press 2006) 247.

[377] William A Schabas, *The European Convention on Human Rights: A Commentary* (Oxford University Press 2015) 367; Ovey and White (n 376) para 242.

[378] Schabas (n 377) 368; Ovey and White (n 376) 242–245.

[379] Ovey and White (n 376) 242–245.

[380] See among others ECtHR, *Aksu v Turkey, Judgment (GC)* (2012) App nos 4149/04 and 41029/04 [59]; *Gurgenidze v Georgia, Judgment* (2006) App no 71678/01 [38].

[381] ECtHR, *Di Sarno and others v Italy, Judgment (Merits and Just Satisfaction)* (2012) App no 30765/08 [105].

[382] In the context of Article 8 ECHR, the Court has insisted on the need to develop a proper legislative framework with regard, *inter alia*, to the collection and protection of information and data of a personal nature. See ECtHR, *MM v The UK, Judgment* (2012) App no 24029/07 [198]; *S and*

By taking the considerations above a step further, I argue that the respect for family life in its ontological meaning requires the State to put in place measures that enable family members to preserve the integrity of family ties[383] during and in the aftermath of situations that put at risk such integrity, e.g., armed conflicts. Thus, among the actions to be undertaken in peacetime might be the development and enactment of a legislative framework for addressing, preventing, and resolving situations where the fate and whereabouts of persons are unknown due, *inter alia,* to armed conflicts.[384] In other words, the respect for family life requires 'to the degree possible, the maintenance of family unity'; in order to put it in practice, the contacts between family members and the provision of information on the whereabouts of family members must be guaranteed.[385] A regulatory framework would, therefore, enable the State to put in place an effective protective framework for the family integrity at all times. Indeed, 'the importance of a regulatory framework is imposed both by the notion of the rule of law [...]' and by the requirement that any restrictions on private and family life be 'in accordance with the law', as provided for under Article 8 (2) ECHR. Although Article 8 ECHR is among the most open-ended provisions[386] within the ECHR and, in recent years, has proven to be one of the richest areas of legal developments by the ECtHR,[387] the issue of missing persons and of their families[388] is not among the recurring issues[389] that are addressed by the Court under this provision.[390] Based on the characteristics underlined above,

---

Marper v the UK, Judgment (GC) (2008) App nos 30562/04 and 30566/04 [103]. Similarly, the Court has set down the obligation for State authorities to set in place 'regulations geared to the special features' of dangerous activities, particularly with regard to the level of risk potentially involved for the citizens living in the areas affected. See among others ECtHR, *Di Sarno and others v Italy, Judgment (Merits and Just Satisfaction)* (n 381) [106].

[383] The integrity of family ties is directly connected to the possibility, for instance, of a mutual enjoyment by parent and child of each other's company; in the case law of the Court, this is a fundamental aspect of "family life". Cf. ECtHR, *B v The UK, Judgment* (1987) App no 9849/82 [60].

[384] The ICRC has set down a set of guiding principles aimed at helping State authorities to design the legislation that should address the situation of missing persons or to complete the existing framework; as the ICRC underlines in its model law, 'it is important for all States to act with determination to prevent disappearances, not perpetrating abductions or other enforced disappearances, to clarify the fate of missing persons and to lend assistance to families who are without news of their relatives.' ICRC - Advisory Service on IHL, 'Guiding Principles: "Model Law on the Missing: Principles for Legislating the Situation of Persons Missing as a Result of Armed Conflict or Internal Violence. Measures to Prevent Persons from Going Missing and to Protect the Rights and Interests of the Missing and Their Families."' (2009), 3.

[385] These considerations are inferred from the commentary note to Rule 105 of the ICRC Study on Customary IHL which declares that '[f]amily life must be respected as far as possible'. See Henckaerts and Doswald-Beck (n 21) 379–380.

[386] Ovey and White (n 376) 241.

[387] Schabas (n 377) 366.

[388] See sub-section 1.3 in Chapter IV.

[389] These include *inter alia* the right to marry and found a family, the equality between spouses, adoption, inheritance rights, immigration issues, sexual orientation, prisoners (notably, prisoners' correspondence, the family life of prisoners). See Ovey and White (n 376) 245–297.

[390] Nevertheless, the issue of the missing and the families' quest for information have been addressed under Article 8 ECHR by the HRChBH, which was a temporary internationalized domestic judicial body. For more details on this body and on the relevant case law, see sub-section 1.1.3.1 in Chapter VI.

I cannot exclude that similar interpretations will be viable in future case law; these might have a pervasive effect and impact on the whole international system of protection of human rights, in light of the judicial cross-referencing that characterizes the human rights case law.

3.2.3.2. Enforced disappearances and the right to truth

The Inter-American Convention on Forced Disappearance of Persons makes it clear that exceptional circumstances, including war, can never be invoked to justify the forced disappearance of persons. 'States Parties shall establish and maintain official up-to-date registries of their detainees and, in accordance with their domestic law, shall make them available to relatives, judges, attorneys, any other person having a legitimate interest, and other authorities'.[391] Similar guarantees are enshrined in the Principles and Guidelines on the Right to a Fair Trial and Legal Assistance in Africa, a non-binding document.[392] Non-binding is also the declaration adopted by the MERCOSUR in which the States Parties affirmed the right to truth of the victims of human rights violations.[393] Similarly, the General Assembly of the Organization of the American States has recognized 'the importance of respecting and ensuring the right to truth to help end impunity and to promote and protect human rights'.[394]

3.3. Conclusive observations

This section has shed light upon the human rights facet of the subject matter. It emerges that in post-conflict settings a range of "duty-holders", including non-state actors, must have a conduct which is consistent with IHRL, at least as long as customary law and *jus cogens* norms are concerned. Moreover, the analysis has also brought to light what kind of preventive tools IHRL offers in order to avoid the occurrence of any harm to individuals who are reported as missing. Human rights adjudicators and treaty bodies can react to uncertainty about the

---

[391] Cf. Articles X (1) and XI (2), Inter-American Convention on Forced Disappearance of Persons, June 9, 1994, 33 I.L.M. 1429 (1994).

[392] Section S (m), Principles A(4) and A(5) of the Principles on the Right to a Fair Trial in Africa affirm: 'entrusts judicial bodies to, at all times, hear and act upon petitions for habeas corpus, *amparo* or similar procedures, and states that no circumstances whatever must be invoked as a justification for denying the right to habeas corpus, *amparo* or similar procedures. These are defined as "a legal procedure brought before a judicial body *to compel the detaining authorities to provide accurate and detailed information regarding the whereabouts and conditions of detention of a person* or to produce a detainee before the judicial body".' AfCommHPR, Principles and Guidelines on the Right to a Fair Trial and Legal Assistance in Africa, Doc. No. DOC/OS(XXX)247 (29 May 2003). Moreover, the ArChHR provides for further guarantees concerning persons in detention and their family ties: i.e., Article 14 (3) declares that 'anyone who is arrested [...] shall be entitled to contact his family members'; Article 16 states that '[e]veryone charged with a criminal offence [...] shall enjoy the following minimum guarantees: [...] 2. [t]he right to [...] be allowed to communicate with his family'.

[393] Cf. Comunicado conjunto de los Presidentes de los Estados Partes del MERCOSUR y de los Estados asociados, XXVIII Summit of Heads of State held in *Asunción*, Paraguay, 20 June 2005, para. 5.

[394] Cf. OAS – General Assembly. 'Resolutions on the Right to the Truth' adopted between 2006-2014 [AG/RES. 2175 (XXXVI-O/06); AG/RES. 2267 (XXXVII-O/07); AG/RES. 2406 (XXXVIII-O/08); AG/RES. 2509 (XXXIX-O/09); AG/RES. 2595 (XL-O/10); AG/RES. 2662 (XLI-O/11); AG/RES. 2725 (XLII-O/12); AG/RES. 2800 (XLIII-O/12); AG/RES. 2822 (XLIV-O/14)], para. 1.

fate and whereabouts of persons: in this respect, provisional measures are a potentially powerful humanitarian tool that enable human rights adjudicators to prevent abusive conduct/omission of State authorities from resulting in irreparable harm for any individual. Enshrined in the ICPPED, the urgent action procedure undertaken by the CED is an essentially humanitarian tool that the family members themselves can trigger in order to request that a disappeared person should be sought and found as a matter of urgency. These tools however can solely concern and impact on the conduct of the States parties to the relevant treaties.

In terms of obligations and entitlements, the existing IHRL treaties do not address the issue of missing persons as broadly defined in the introduction of this book; thus, the examination of the normative framework has been carried out by looking at how the IHRL framework tackles three key themes strictly related to the issue of missing persons in the context of an armed conflict, i.e., information, family ties, and disappearances.

The link between the importance of information on the fate and whereabouts of relatives and the protection of the family as the basic unit of the society does not emerge from general human rights treaties. Both the international and regional treaties provide for the right of every individual to be protected from any unlawful/arbitrary interference with his family life; this right is not absolute and can be subjected to restrictions. The formulation of this right under the ECHR provides room for affirming that among the positive obligations that State authorities have under Article 8 ECHR is the duty to set up a regulatory framework that addresses, prevents, and finds a solution when people are reported as missing, including as a result of an armed conflict. The compliance with this duty would enable the State to protect one of the features of Article 8(1) ECHR, i.e., the family life and unity, from situations that would put it at risk. Although still missing in the case law of the ECtHR, such development might be viable in light of the open-ended formulation of this provision and the current advances under IHRL in relation to disappearances and the right of families to know[395]

Should access to information be perceived as the *conditio sine qua non* for the realization of the right to truth, problematic is to outline what fits into "the truth" and to clarify whether an overall truth satisfies the individual request for information. Three main elements are detected in the examination of thematic human rights treaties: first, the preservation of the family ties and the duty to keep the family members up-to-date on State-driven actions affecting them emerges from the framework on child's rights; second, the notification of the detention of an individual to, *inter alios*, the family members is among the guarantees to which a person deprived of his/her liberty is entitled[396] coupled

---

[395] At the domestic level this link has been drawn by the HRChBH. Cf. HRChBH, *Ferida Selimović et al v The Republika Srpska ('Srebrenica Cases'), Decision on Admissibility and Merits* (2003) Case nos. CH/01/8365 et al. [175]. For a detailed analysis of the HRChBH's contribution to the clarification of the legal framework concerning the subject matter, see sub-section 1.1.3.1 in Chapter VI.

[396] Apart from the treaty provisions mentioned above, cf. Principle 16 (1), UNGA, 'Body of Principles for the Protection of All Persons under Any Form of Detention or Imprisonment' (1988) UN Doc A/RES/43/173. Among the safeguards that are essential for the prevention of torture and for

with the possibility of communicating with the outside world.[397] Third, the prohibition of enforced disappearance is the core of the ICPPED: from its provisions, it can be inferred that concealment of information is the pre-condition of forced disappearance of persons; nevertheless, pursuant to this treaty, access to information on persons deprived of their liberty can be limited for the family members, provided that the persons deprived of their liberty are under the protection of the law.

The premise of this book is that international law is not just rules, but is a decision-making process; therefore, this section has shed light upon the rules that are relevant to framing the boundaries for the conduct of multiple actors vis-à-vis the issue of missing persons and the quest of their families for information. As such it is preliminary to our next step, i.e., casting light upon the decision-making process that has enshrined, interpreted, and applied such rules. Accordingly, next chapters will aim at understanding what principles and values are behind these rules in order to find normative linkages among them, at testing the legal merit of the families' claims for information on their relatives, and at reflecting upon the operationalization of this legal framework within peace processes. This last step will be conducive to the exploration of venues for synergies between the *modus operandi* of the various actors who are directly or indirectly involved in addressing the issue of the missing in post-conflict environments.

---

the protection of persons in any form of detention, the HRCee's General Comment no. 35 mentions the existence of a centralized official register with the names and places of detention, and times of arrival and departure, as well as of the names of persons responsible for their detention; the information contained in this register should be made readily available and accessible to those concerned, including relatives. The Comment also underlines that 'in conflict situations, access by the [ICRC] to all places of detention becomes an essential additional safeguard for the rights to liberty and security of person.' The ICRC's visits help the families of detainees to maintain the contact with their relatives who find themselves into custody. Cf. HRCee, 'General Comment No 35: Article 9 (Liberty and Security of Person)' (2014) UN Doc CCPR/C/GC/35 paras 58 and 64.

[397] While there is no prohibition under international law of *incommunicado* detention (i.e., solitary confinement characterized by the denial of access to the family, an attorney, or an independent physician) *per se*, UN human rights bodies agree on the fact that such practice may entail serious human rights violations and should thus be prohibited. For instance, in the General Comment No. 20 (Article 7, ICCPR), the HRCee recommends that provisions be taken against *incommunicado* detention. Cf. HRCee, 'General Comment No 20: Article 7 (Prohibition of Torture or Cruel, Inhuman or Degrading Treatment or Punishment)' (1992) UN Doc HRI/GEN/1/Rev.9 (Vol.1) at 182 para 11; similarly, the former UN Commission on Human Rights stressed that 'prolonged incommunicado detention may facilitate the perpetration of torture and can in itself constitute a form of cruel, inhuman or degrading treatment or even torture.' Cf. UN Commission on Human Rights, 'Resolution on Torture and Other Cruel, Inhuman or Degrading Treatment or Punishment, Human Rights Resolution 2003/32' (2003) UN Doc E/CN.4/RES/2003/32 para 14. The UN Special Rapporteur on the question of torture has pointed out that torture 'is most frequently practiced during incommunicado detention', and he has therefore proposed that such detention 'be made illegal and persons held incommunicado ... be released without delay.' UN Commission on Human Rights, 'Report of the Special Rapporteur on the Question of Torture' (1995) UN Doc E/CN.4/1995/34 para 926 (d).

4. IMPLICATIONS OF TREATY-BASED RESTRICTIONS
FOR THE FAMILIES' QUEST FOR INFORMATION

International law does not disregard the impact that the transmission/ withholding of information can have on multiple stakeholders, including the families, the State authorities, and the persons who find themselves in circumstances that present a high degree of vulnerability (e.g., detention). During an armed conflict, although IHL takes this impact into account, it provides for the possibility of restricting the transmission of information to the families in peculiar circumstances: for instance, the possibility for persons held in captivity (POW, civilian internees in IAC; persons detained for reasons related to the conflict in NIAC) to correspond with their families can be restricted (in terms of frequency of the correspondence as well as of the content of the messages sent).[398] Restrictions can be implemented when the information is deemed detrimental to the family members who are in their country of origin and/or to their beloved one who, after fleeing from that country, finds him/herself in enemy hands (IAC situation).[399] Peculiar is also the situation of saboteurs and spies who operate in armed conflict and who, if caught, are supposed to have forfeited their rights of communication, including those with their families (IAC situation).[400]

Diversified can be the purpose behind each of these measures (e.g., the protection of civilians from the arbitrary conduct of their governments during an armed conflict, the presence of military security reasons). In any case, the restrictions cannot waive the obligation to transmit the information to the NIB and the CTA[401] (the end of armed conflict and the continuation of captivity of individuals in the post-conflict phase does not waive this obligation, see *supra* sub-section 2.3). Furthermore, the ICRC should be allowed to carry out its visits in order to keep track of the conditions of persons held in captivity. Broadly speaking, under IHL there exists a right of persons held in captivity (POW, civilian internees in IAC and persons in detention in NIAC) to correspond with

---

[398] Cf. Article 71 (1) GC III (POW); Article 107 (1) GC IV (civilian internees); Article 5 (2) (b) AP II to be read in conjunction with Article 5 (3) AP II (prisoners for reasons related/unrelated to the armed conflict).

[399] Should the information be detrimental to them, the NIB has the duty to warn the CTA, from which the information cannot be withheld. Cf. Article 137 (2) GC IV. Negotiators of the GCs I-IV had in mind the experience of WWII, when many fled their country of origin for persecution and did not want that country to have any news on their fate and whereabouts; at the same time, any piece of information on their situation might have been detrimental to their family members at home. The negotiators recognized the need to protect civilians from the arbitrary conduct of governments. See Pictet, *Commentary Vol IV (1958)* (n 38) 531.

[400] Pursuant to Article 5 (2) GC IV, the right to family news can be restrained when the protected person is detained as a spy/saboteur or is under definite suspicion of activity hostile to the security of the occupying power. The detaining power, nonetheless, is not released from its obligation to notify the arrest to its official NIB for transmission of information on this person to the official NIB of the country of nationality of the person concerned. ibid 57–58.

[401] As specified by the Pictet's Commentary, 'it is not ...the rights and privileges accorded to the protected person by [GC IV] which are forfeited, but only his rights of communication'. See Ibid 57.

the family. The treaty-based restrictions mentioned above are not very detailed and their contours are not as circumscribed as the contours of human rights-based restrictions; should the captivity of a person apprehended in armed conflict continue after the end of such conflict, it would be appropriate 'to take human rights law into account in evaluating the actual need and extent of restrictions'.[402]

Family's access to information on a relative who is reported as missing in the context of an armed conflict and as a result of an IHL/IHRL violation cannot be restricted. Nevertheless, there are situations where a person is not technically considered 'missing', since it is evident that this person died in specific circumstances – e.g., military operations: in these situations, the family might not be entitled to receive the human remains, might be prevented from knowing where the body is kept, and/or might be prohibited from participating in the burial procedure and knowing where the burial site is (see Chapter IV). Thus, restricting the access of family members to information on their beloved ones interferes with the enjoyment of their human rights.

Broadly speaking, under general human rights treaties, State authorities can lawfully restrict a set of rights under specific conditions. Human rights treaties incorporate limitation clauses – in general terms (e.g., ACHR and AfChHPR)[403] or in relation to specific rights (e.g., ICCPR, ECHR, ACHR, ArChHR).[404]

---

[402] Doswald-beck proposes the same in relation to persons held in captivity during an armed conflict. See Doswald-Beck (n 332) 448–449. For a thorough examination of the simultaneous application of IHL and IHRL restrictions regime, see sub-section 2.3.2.2 in Chapter III; see also section 4 in Chapter IV.

[403] The American Convention on Human Rights (ACHR) and the AfChHPR contain a general provision on limitations, which, in principle, may impact all rights included in these treaties: i.e., pursuant to the ACHR, '[t]he rights of each person are limited by the rights of others, by the security of the general welfare, in a democratic society.' Cf. Article 32 (2), ACHR; pursuant to the AfChHPR, '[t]he rights and freedoms of each individual shall be exercised with due regard to the rights of others, collective security, morality and common interest', cf. Article 27 (2), AfChHPR. Nonetheless, the AfCommHPR has stated that '[t]he only legitimate reasons for limitations to the rights and freedoms of the African Charter are found in Article 27(2) [...]. The reasons for possible limitations must be founded in a legitimate State interest and the evils of limitations of rights must be strictly proportionate with and absolutely necessary for the advantages which are to be obtained. Even more important, a limitation may never have as a consequence that the right itself becomes illusory.' Cf. AfCommHPR, *Media Rights Agenda and Constitutional Rights Project v Nigeria* (1998) Comm nos 105/93, 128/94, 130/94, 152/96 [68–70]. Murray underlines that in terms of limitation of rights, 'the African Commission has not satisfied the concerns of those who believed that the Charter focused on the community at the expense of the individual'. See Rachel Murray, *The African Commission on Human and People's Rights and International Law* (Hart Publishing 2000) 127. The IACtHR has stated that the impositions of limitations should always be employed strictly under Article 32 (2) ACHR: this provision 'contains a general statement that is designed for those cases in particular in which the [ACHR], in proclaiming a right, makes no special reference to possible legitimate restrictions'. Therefore, it does not apply to the Articles of the Convention which embed a clawback clause (for instance, Article 13 - Freedom of expression). See IACtHR, *Advisory Opinion requested by the Government of Costa Rica, Compulsory Membership in an Association prescribed by law for the practice of Journalism (Arts 13 and 29 ACHR)* (1985) OC-5/85 [65]; *Advisory Opinion, the Word 'Laws' in Article 30 of the ACHR* (1986) OC-6/86, Series A N. 6 [17]. In addition to general clauses in human rights treaties, the UDHR provides for a similar clause under Article 29 (2).

[404] The ICCPR's clawback clauses are incorporated in the following provisions: Articles 13 (Expulsion of Aliens), 17 and 23 (Private and Family Life); 18 (Freedom of Religion and belief), 19-20 (Freedom of

Common to these treaties is that the limitation measures must *i)* be provided by law; *ii)* aim at protecting one or more of the collective needs that are listed in the limitation clause; and *iii)* be necessary in order to protect such need(s).[405] The parameters to assess the lawfulness of the interference under each of these requirements are detailed in the human rights case law (see Table 2 below).[406]

Restrictions of a similar genre are enshrined under Article 20 ICPPED; pursuant to this provision, family members of persons deprived of their liberty have a right to information concerning their beloved ones.[407] By using a similar language to that of human rights claw-back clauses, (*'on an exceptional basis, where strictly necessary and where provided for by law...'*), Article 20 (1) ICPPED allows State authorities to limit this right

> where a person is under the protection of the law and the deprivation of liberty is subject to judicial control, and if the transmission of the information would adversely affect the privacy or safety of the person, hinder a criminal investigation, or for other equivalent reasons in accordance with the law, and in conformity with applicable international law and with the objectives of this Convention.[408]

Expression), 21-22 (Freedom of Assembly and Association). In addition to the general clause, the ACHR also contains provisions that allow for permissible restrictions to specific rights (e.g., Article 13 (2)'s limitations relating to the right to freedom of expression). The ECHR provides for clawback clauses in the following provisions: Articles 8 (Private and Family Life), 9 (Freedom of Religion and Belief), 10 (Freedom of Expression), 11 (Freedom of Assembly and Association). The ArChHR contains a clawback clause applicable in relation to political rights, cf. Article 24 (7), ArChHR.

[405] The human rights treaties provide for variations relating to these clauses: for instance, all the ECHR clawback clauses make it clear that limitation measures must be 'necessary in a democratic society'; a similar variation is *inter alia* present in Article 16 (2) ACHR (Freedom of Association), Article 15 ACHR (Right to Assembly), Article 21 ICCPR (Right to Assembly) as well as in the ArChHR's clause concerning political rights. Doswald-Beck stresses that 'it cannot be inferred that those without these additions are to be interpreted more restrictively.' See Doswald-Beck (n 332) 71.

[406] It is beyond the scope of this book to analyze the regime of limitations in general terms. For a general understanding of the topic see, for instance, ibid 68–105 (on the regime of limitations and derogations in relation to armed conflicts and terrorism); Bernadette Rainey, Elizabeth Wicks and Clare Ovey, *The European Convention on Human Rights* (6 edition, Oxford University Press 2014) 307–333 (on the limitations common to Articles 8-11 ECHR); Alex Conte, 'Limitations to and Derogations from Covenant Rights' in Alex Conte and Richard Burchill (eds), *Defining Civil and Political Rights: The Jurisprudence of the United Nations Human Rights Committee* (Routledge 2016); Oscar M Garibaldi, 'The General Limitations on Human Rights: The Principle of Legality United Nations' (1976) 17 Harvard International Law Journal 503; Gino J Naldi, 'Limitation of Rights under the African Charter on Human and Peoples' Rights: The Contribution of the African Commission on Human and Peoples' Rights Notes and Comments' (2001) 17 South African Journal on Human Rights 109; Els Elisabeth Debuf, *Captured in War: Lawful Internment in Armed Conflict* (A Pedone 2013) 35–87(thorough analysis of the requirements for a lawful deprivation of liberty); Kevin Iles, 'Limiting Socio-Economic Rights: Beyond the Internal Limitations Clauses' (2004) 20 South African Journal on Human Rights 448.

[407] Pursuant to Article 18 ICPPED, this information should, at least, include the authority that ordered the deprivation of liberty; the date, time and place where the person was deprived of liberty and admitted to the place of deprivation of liberty; the authority responsible for supervising the deprivation of liberty; the whereabouts of the person deprived of liberty; the date, time and place of release; elements relating to the state of health of this person; in the event of death during the deprivation of liberty, the circumstances and cause of death and the destination of the remains.

[408] Conversely, pursuant to Article XI of the Inter-American Convention on the Forced Disappearance of Persons, '[t]he States Parties shall establish and maintain official up-to-date

IHL-based restrictions of transmission of information to the families may be construed in light of Article 20 ICPPED; yet in IAC as well as in NIAC the Parties to the conflict must inform the families about the fate of their missing relatives.[409] Furthermore, in the post-conflict phase, the right of families to know the fate of their relatives continues to prompt efforts that ae undertaken in order to account for the missing. A scenario where the family can be left in total uncertainty in light of the application of Article 20 ICPPED[410] is, therefore, untenable.

Although the ICPPED excludes the possibility that the restriction be used for abusive purposes,[411] criticism has been expressed[412] against the motives that can lead the authorities to prevent family members and/or the legal counsel of the person concerned from receiving the above-mentioned information. Indeed, the protection of the privacy of the person – mindful of the willingness of the person held in captivity to communicate or not news about his/her status – is not the driver of these motives. For instance, national security is not mentioned among the viable grounds to justify a restriction of the right to information, but the open-ended wording of the provision – 'other equivalent reasons' – does not exclude it; it should be borne in mind that, in some cases, enforced disappearances have been perpetrated under the 'national security' banner.[413] Chapter IV will build in these preliminary considerations in order to understand the degree of the impact of the above-mentioned restrictions on the quest of families for information on the fate and whereabouts of their relatives.

---

registries of their detainees and, in accordance with their domestic law, shall make them available to relatives, judges, attorneys, any other person having a legitimate interest, and other authorities'. No limitation is mentioned.

[409] Cf. Rule 117, Henckaerts and Doswald-Beck (n 21) 421 ff.

[410] Section 4 in Chapter IV will examine whether, in case of detention, the family can lawfully be left without information.

[411] The ICPPED makes it clear that the restriction is not aimed at providing room for violating Article 2 (prohibition of enforced disappearances) and Article 17 (1) (prohibition of secret detention); in addition to that, pursuant to Article 20 (2), the right to judicial remedy cannot be restricted or suspended at any time.

[412] Some delegations were concerned that these restrictions might have impacted on the ICPPED's purpose as well as on the realization of the right to know the truth. UN Commission on Human Rights, 'Draft Report of the Inter-Sessional Open-Ended Working Group, UN Doc. E/CN.4/2005/WG.22/CRP.9' (n 314) paras 6, 12. See among others T Scovazzi, 'Il lato oscuro dei diritti umani: aspetti di diritto internazionale' in Massimo Meccarelli, Carlo Sotis and Paolo Palchetti (eds), *Il lato oscuro dei diritti umani: esigenze emancipatorie e logiche di dominio nella tutela giuridica dell'individuo* (Editorial Dykinson, SL 2014) 130; Scovazzi and Citroni (n 300) 337–339.

[413] For a detailed analysis of the different positions held by States during the negotiations, see Scovazzi and Citroni (n 300) 339–341.

Table 2 – Requirements for a lawful interference with a limited set of human rights			
Provided by the Law			
i. The interference must have a legal basis		ii. The legal basis/law must have some specific qualities	
ICCPR	**ECHR**	**IACHR**	**AfChHPR**
Qualities of the law[414] – consistent with ICCPR's provisions, aims and objectives – cannot be a traditional/religious/or other such customary law – must specify the precise circumstances in which such interferences may be permitted	Qualities of the law[415] – accessible to the person concerned = it must provide an indication of what the legal rules applicable in a certain case are – foreseeable as to its effects for the person concerned = it must set forth with sufficient precision the conditions in which a measure may be applied – the word "law" is to be interpreted as covering written law/unwritten law	Qualities of the law[416] – contextualized in the legal system to which it belongs – passed by the Legislature in accordance with the Constitution – formally proclaimed	Qualities of the law[417] – cannot have precedent over the international law of the Charter – if contradictory with IHRL, the latter prevails

---

[414] See HRCee, 'General Comment No. 16: Article 17 (Right to Privacy)' (1988) UN Doc HRI/GEN/1/Rev.1 at 21 (1994) paras 3 and 8; HRCee, 'General Comment No. 34: Article 19 (Freedoms of Opinion and Expression)' (2011) UN Doc CCPR/C/GC/34 para 24. See also UN ECOSOC, 'Siracusa Principles on the Limitation and Derogation Provisions in the ICCPR' (1985) UN Doc E/CN.4/1985/4, Annex paras 15–18. Such parameters must be considered when assessing limitations of, for instance, Article 17 ICCPR (private and family life). Although the ICJ's consideration on Article 17 ICCPR portrays it as an absolute right, from the HRCee's General Comment and, more generally, the HRCee's case law, it is submitted that it is not the case. Cf. ICJ, *Legal Consequences of the Construction of a Wall in the Occupied Palestinian Territory, Advisory Opinion* (2004) ICJ Reports 2004, p.136 [136 in fine].

[415] Cf. among many others ECtHR, *Malone v The UK, Judgment* (1984) App no 8691/79 [66]; *Amann v Switzerland, Judgment (GC)* (2000) App no 27798/95 [56]; *Sabanchiyeva and others v Russia, Judgment* (2013) App no 38450/05 [124].

[416] Pursuant to Article 30 ACHR, ACHR-based restrictions may be applied 'in accordance with laws enacted for reasons of general interest and in accordance with the purpose for which such restrictions have been established' (emphasis added). See IACtHR, *Advisory Opinion, the Word 'Laws' in Article 30 of the ACHR* (n 403) [20–22, 24].

[417] AfCommHPR, *Media Rights Agenda et al v Nigeria* (n 403) [64–68].

Legitimate Purpose[418]			
Prevention of disorder/crime Protection of others' rights		National security/Security of all Public safety of the country	
Necessary			
ICCPR	ECHR	ACHR	AfChHPR
An interference is necessary[419] if it responds to a pressing public or social need it pursues a legitimate aim, and is based on one of the grounds justifying limitations recognized by the relevant article of ICCPR it is proportionate to that aim (i.e., in applying a limitation, no more restrictive means than are required shall be used for the achievement of its purpose)	An interference will be considered "necessary[420] in a democratic society" for a legitimate aim, if it answers a "pressing social need" the reasons adduced to justify it are "relevant and sufficient" iii. it is proportionate to the legitimate aim pursued. In addition, - No mechanical application of restrictions - There must be the possibility of recourse to an alternative measure - States enjoys a margin of apprecia-tion (narrower where the right at stake is crucial to the individual's key/intimate rights).	Necessity[421] of a measure depends upon showing that i. the restrictions are required by a 'compelling governmental interest' ii. such an interest 'clearly outweigh the social need for the full enjoyment' of the right at stake. The measure must be - proportional - closely tailored to the legitimate governmental objective - the reasonableness and proportiona-lity of a measure can only be ascertained through the examination of a specific case.	The justification of limitations[422] must be strictly proportionate with and absolutely necessary for the advantages which follow. 'A limitation may not erode a right such that the right itself becomes illusory.'

[418] This list is not exhaustive, as it contains those purposes that can be relevant in post-conflict, in light of a situation of transition from armed conflict to peace. Cf. Article 8(2) ECHR; under this provision, legitimate can also be the economic wellbeing of the country, the protection of health or morals. Article 17 ICCPR does not draw up a list of viable legitimate purposes. Similar is the case of Article 11 ACHR (right to privacy); nonetheless, Article 32(2) ACHR states that 'the rights of each person are limited by the rights of others, by the security of all, and by the just demands of the general welfare in a democratic society.' When invoked as a ground for limiting human rights, these purposes must be subjected to an interpretation that is strictly limited to 'the "just demands" of "a democratic society", which takes account of the need to balance the competing interests involved and the need to preserve the object and purpose of the Convention.' IACtHR, *Advisory Opinion - Arts 13 and 29 ACHR (1985)* (n 403) [67].

[419] A thorough analysis of the parameters is provided for in the Siracusa Principles. See UN ECOSOC (n 414) paras 10–14.

[420] On the concept of pressing social need, see ECtHR, *Handyside v The UK, Judgment* (1976) App no 5493/72 [48]. The Court has pointed out that the breadth of the *margin of appreciation* 'varies and depends on a number of factors, including the nature of the [ECHR] right in issue, its importance for

CONCLUSIONS

This admittedly rather lengthy Chapter demonstrates that the parties to an armed conflict have an obligation to account for missing persons which has a cross-cutting nature, as it requires them to implement measures before, during, and in the aftermath of the conflict (IAC/NIAC). The implementation of preventive and reactive measures should lead to the establishment of a structured system aimed at efficiently handling information and facilitating the efforts to account for specific categories of persons during and after an armed conflict. States' practice indicates that impracticalities of the system emerging from contemporary IHL treaties are surmountable through the intermediary of alternative means.[423]

The Chapter also shows that the exact definition of the scope of application *ratione temporis* of IHL does not affect the duration of such obligation. The duty to account for missing persons is directly connected with the duty to inform the families of those reported as missing; both directly respond to the rights of families to seek and receive information on their relatives as well as to have access to it. A mere temporal perspective on the issue would contradict the foundation that underpins the system, i.e., relieving the suffering of those who do not have news about their beloved ones.

However, the Chapter reveals that the framework is partially complete. IHL treaties applicable in IAC indirectly embed post-conflict considerations on situations that might have arisen during the armed conflict;[424] for instance, while during an IAC there exists a duty to keep records on deceased persons[425] and on

---

the individual, the nature of the interference and the object pursued by the interference.' Cf. among others, ECtHR, *Sabanchiyeva and others v Russia* (n 415) [134]. For more details on the margin of appreciation, see ECtHR, *Connors v The UK, Judgment* (2004) App no 66746/01 [82–84] (and references therein); *Handyside v The UK* [48] ('by reason of their direct and continuous contact with vital forces of their countries, State authorities are in principle in a better position than the international judge to give an opinion on the exact content of these requirements as well as on the "necessity" of a "restriction" or "penalty" intended to meet them'.)

[421] The IACtHR's approach to limitations can be boiled down to the following: in order to be compatible with the Convention, restrictions must be justified by collective objectives that are so important that they clearly outweigh the social need to guarantee the full exercise of rights guaranteed in the Convention and are not more limiting than strictly necessary. IACommHR. *Ms X v Argentina, Case 10506* (1996) Report No. 38/96, Doc no OEA/Ser.L/V/II.95 Doc. 7 rev. at 50 [58, 70-72]. The parameters concerning such requirement are inferred from the ECtHR's *Handyside Case*. Cf. IACtHR, *Advisory Opinion - Arts 13 and 29 ACHR (1985)* (n 403) [46, 67].

[422] AfCommHPR, *Constitutional Rights Project, Civil Liberties Organization, and Media Rights Agenda v Nigeria* (1999) Comm nos 140/94, 141/94, 145/95 [42].

[423] For instance, section 2 illustrates that instead of establishing a NIB, the help of the ICRC delegates has been accepted; the lack of specific provisions in NIAC has been overcome with *ad hoc* commitments.

[424] The counter-argument might be that IHL applies only in times of armed conflict. See, in this regard, Ingrid Detter Delupis, *The Law of War* (Cambridge University Press 2000) 161; UNSG, *Women, Peace and Security: Study Submitted by the Secretary-General Pursuant to Security Council Resolution 1325 (2000)* (United Nations Publications 2002) 36.

[425] Pursuant to Article 19, GC II 'The Parties to the conflict shall record as soon as possible, in respect of each […] dead person of the adverse Party falling into their hands, any particulars which

146

persons deprived of their liberty,[426] nothing is said about the management of such records after the termination of the conflict (these pieces of information might prove essential to account for the missing in the post-conflict phase). Regulation of access to information is tackled in passing, even though in post-conflict situations information and data can be used in ways that may be detrimental to the persons concerned (both the families and the missing in this case).[427] Gray areas exist in the system, as the duty to record information and data with regard to 'persons who have been detained, imprisoned or otherwise held in captivity' who do not fall under the category 'protected persons' solely refers to cases of deprivation of liberty that last 'for more than two weeks as a result of hostilities or occupation'.[428] In NIAC, the scenario is much more complex: under contemporary IHL treaties, the framework concerning the handling of information is meager; nevertheless, the duty of all parties to the conflict to account for the missing is customary and applicable in NIAC and IAC according to the ICRC study on customary IHL. Despite the criticism against the methodology of the ICRC study, it is undoubted that, more and more frequently, arrangements concerning the accounting for those reported missing during a NIAC have been concluded at the end of the conflict.[429] Chapter V will elaborate on the legal merit of these arrangements.

The relationship between time and law runs throughout the whole legal framework applicable in armed conflict. The passage of time is a meta-indicator of the transition from a phase (armed conflict) to another phase (post-conflict) and, as such, should determine the sphere of law of reference. Nevertheless, duration of *ad hoc* situations entails an extension of obligations and entitlements peculiar to a specific phase; such an extension requires understanding how these entitlements and obligations intersect with those of the next phase. IHRL is not time-bound and, therefore, always applicable. Based on the foregoing considerations, its relationship with IHL rules on missing persons must be assessed during and after the end of an armed conflict (see Chapter III). Information, the preservation of family as the basic unit of the society, and disappearances are three themes that are not necessarily connected under the

---

may assist in his identification'; according to Article 120, GC III 'Death certificates [...] of all persons who die as [POW] shall be forwarded as rapidly as possible to the [POW] Information Bureau established in accordance with Article 122. [...] The burial or cremation of a [POW] shall be preceded by a medical examination of the body with a view to confirming death and enabling a report to be made.' Pursuant to Article 129, GC IV 'Deaths of internees shall be certified in every case by a doctor, and a death certificate shall be made out, showing the causes of death and the conditions under which it occurred. [...] An official record of the death, duly registered, shall be drawn up in accordance with the procedure relating thereto in force in the territory where the place of internment is situated, and a duly certified copy of such record shall be transmitted without delay to the Protecting Power as well as to the [CTA] referred to in Article 140'.

[426] Cf. Articles 122 and 123, GC III on the establishment of an official Information Bureau for POW as well as of a CTA; cf. Articles 136, 137, and 140, GC IV on the establishment of similar institutions for collecting information and particulars on civilian internees.

[427] Scant reference to the impact of information on the persons concerned is made with regard to a specific category of protected person (i.e., civilian internees). See *supra* sub-section 1.2.1.2.

[428] Cf. Article 33, AP I.

[429] See *supra* sub-section 1.2.2.2.

IHRL framework; the ICPPED enshrines all of them in relation to enforced disappearances. More generally, the legal framework under IHRL is not as detailed and matter-focused as the provisions under IHL with regard to the handling of information on missing persons; conversely, IHRL is considered the framework of reference when certain guarantees – e.g., family visits in detention – are restrained both in conflict and post-conflict settings.[430] A harmonized interpretation and application of the relevant rules requires identifying the tenets that are mutually shared by IHL and IHRL; these will be the foundation for building normative linkages that will increase the effectiveness of the protective system concerning the missing and their families.

---

[430] This aspect will be further developed in Chapter IV (section 4).

CHAPTER III.

(RE)LOCATING THE RELATIONSHIP
BETWEEN IHL AND IHRL RULES ON MISSING PERSONS
IN POST-CONFLICT SETTINGS

From the examination developed in Chapter II, it emerges that the phase preceding the conflict, the *durante bello* phase, and the post-conflict one are interconnected in terms of measures and actions that must be undertaken in order to prevent and/or to react to the situation of missing persons. The interconnectedness of these phases requires re-locating the interplay between IHL and IHRL − traditionally conceived within the boundaries of an armed conflict − in post-conflict. Against this backdrop, this Chapter will demonstrate that in post-conflict settings IHL and IHRL rules on missing persons are complementary and mutually reinforce each other in case of simultaneous application. To this end, the principles that lie at the basis of the *corpus juris* for the protection of all human beings will be examined. In this manner it will be possible to identify the principled considerations behind each set of rules and to detect synergies and discrepancies that justify the assertion according to which IHRL rules on enforced disappearances are complementary to, but distinct from IHL rules on missing persons (section 1).[1] Second, the main positions of the debate concerning the interplay between IHL and IHRL *durante bello* will be analyzed in order to show the relevance of the complementarity approach during and after the conflict (section 2). This examination will be followed by the proposal of criteria aimed at making complementarity a workable concept for the variety of actors dealing with the claims of families for information on their missing relatives *durante bello* and in post-conflict.

---

[1] Gloria Gaggioli, 'The Prohibition of Enforced Disappearances: A Meaningful Example of a Partial Merger between Human Rights Law and International Humanitarian Law' in Gloria Gaggioli and Robert Kolb (eds), *Research Handbook on Human Rights and Humanitarian Law* (Edward Elgar Publishing 2013) 331.

1. THE ISSUE OF MISSING PERSONS UNDER INTERNATIONAL LAW: AT THE CROSSROAD BETWEEN ACCOUNTABILITY-DRIVEN AND HUMANITARIAN CONSIDERATIONS

1.1. Towards a principled understanding of the international legal framework: Preliminary considerations

The principles of humanity and accountability lie at the basis of the *corpus juris* concerning the protection of the human being, which include IHL and IHRL. While humanity is a general principle of international law,[2] accountability is, *inter alia,* one of the core goals[3] of measures adopted in the transition from war to peace. Both influence the whole legal system concerning the protection of human beings, but while the former[4] has *per se* a normative dimension, the latter's normative dimension[5] emerges only when it is incorporated in specific rules concerning, for instance, individual criminal responsibility for international crimes or responsibility of States and international organizations for international wrongdoings.

In international law, the term 'principles' is commonly associated with the formula used in Article 38 (1) (c) of the International Court of Justice (ICJ) Statute (i.e., 'general principles of law recognized by civilized nations'). The scholarly debate on the general principles as a source of international law is still vivid, mainly with regard to their identification, ranking (if any) among the sources, enforceability and applicability.[6] Without entering into the debate on

---

[2] The ICTY states that when interpreting and applying loose international rules, the principle of humanity as framed by the ICJ in its case law - 'elementary considerations of humanity' - should be fully used on the basis that it is 'illustrative of a general principle of international law'. See ICTY, *Prosecutor v Kupreškić et al, Trial Judgment* (2000) Case no IT-95-16-T [524]. However the Tribunal has not been consistent in framing the function of the principle: while in *Kupreškić et al* case the principle was not 'elevated to the rank of independent sources of international law, in the *Martić* case, the Tribunal affirmed that the norms concerning the prohibition against attacking the civilian population as such, as well as individuals, and the general principle limiting the means and methods of warfare emanated from, *inter alia,* the elementary considerations of humanity. Thus, it recognized the normative character of the principle of humanity. Cf. ICTY, ibid 525; *Prosecutor v Martić, Decision* (1996) Case no IT-95-11-I [13]. For an examination of the ICJ's standpoint, see *infra* sub-section 1.2.1.

[3] C Bell, 'Of Jus Post Bellum and Lex Pacificatoria What's in a Name?' in Carsten Stahn, Jennifer S Easterday and Jens Iverson (eds), *Jus Post Bellum: Mapping the normative Foundations* (Oxford University Press 2014) 182; E De Brabandere, 'The Concept of Jus Post Bellum in International Law: A Normative Critique' in Carsten Stahn, Jennifer S Easterday and Jens Iverson (eds), *Jus Post Bellum: Mapping the normative Foundations* (Oxford University Press 2014) 139.

[4] Both Doswald-Beck and Meron argue that the principle of humanity is among the factors that restrain the freedom of States to do what is not expressly prohibited by treaty or custom. See Theodor Meron, *The Humanization of International Law,* vol 3 (Martinus Nijhoff Publishers 2006) 28; Louise Doswald-Beck, 'International Humanitarian Law and the Advisory Opinion of the International Court of Justice on the Legality of the Threat or Use of Nuclear Weapons' (1997) 316 International Review of the Red Cross 35, 49.

[5] De Brabandere (n 3) 139.

[6] For a detailed summary of the main scholarship, see M Cherif Bassiouni, 'A Functional Approach to General Principles of International Law' (1990) 11 Michigan Journal of International Law 816.

each single aspect, clarifications on what this book means by 'principles' are needed. The ICJ and Permanent Court of International Justice (PCIJ) Statutes are not helpful in explaining what general principles of international law are; the *travaux préparatoires* of the former do not offer an explanation of the inclusion of Article 38 formula, as it is a *verbatim* reproduction of the PCIJ Statute's one. At the time of the drafting of the latter, the formula 'general principles...' was the result of a compromise[7] among the diverging positions of the Advisory Committee of Jurists on whether the principles had to be considered part of international law.[8]

Scholars still diverge on the generating source of the principles:[9] on the one hand, general principles are such when they are common to and derive from the

---

[7] In Bassiouni's view, the framers of the Statute may have accepted 'the notion that natural law may be separate from the naturalists' understanding of that term, and that it may arise from concrete applications and common practices existing in and among "civilized nations". Such a composite conception may be viewed as a compromise between positivism and naturalism, if that is at all possible, and as a blending of Common Law pragmatism and the more conceptual approach of the Romanist Civilist system.' ibid 774.

[8] The Advisory Committee of Jurists in charge of the drafting did not immediately agree on the wording of Article 38 (1) (3) of the Statute of the PCIJ: for instance, Baron Descamps, the chairman, proposed to include among the rules that the PCIJ would apply 'the rules of international law as recognized by the legal conscience of civilized nations'. PCIJ - Advisory Committee of Jurists, 'Procès-Verbaux of the Proceedings of the Committee, with Annexes' (1920) 306. For Mr. Root, the US member and proponent of the final text, this reference would have empowered the PCIJ to 'apply principles, differently understood in different countries', ibid 308. Lord Phillimore, the UK member, emphasized that 'all the principles of common law are applicable to international affairs. They are in fact part of international law', ibid 316. Based on the proposal by Mr. Root reflecting the current text, Mr. Fernandes, Brazilian member, suggested that the PCIJ should apply 'those principles of international law which, before the dispute, were not rejected by the legal traditions of one of the States concerned with the dispute', ibid 346. Mr. de Lapradelle, the French member, 'admitted that the principles which formed the bases of national law, were also sources of international law' (Sources of International Law), but he 'thought it preferable to keep to a simple phrase: such, for example, as "the general principles of law".' Ibid 335–336.

[9] Cassese makes a distinction between general principles of international law and general principles of law recognized by the community of nations: the former are 'sweeping and loose standards of conduct that can be deduced from treaty and customary rules by extracting and generalizing some of their most significant common points'; the latter are subsidiary sources – i.e., norm-setting processes – that generate 'rules to which recourse may only be had if and when no rule produced by a primary or secondary sources'. Antonio Cassese, *International Law* (Oxford University Press 2005) 188. *Contra:* Bassiouni considers that general principles of law are co-equal primary source, standing with conventions and customs', see Bassiouni, 'A Functional Approach to General Principles of International Law' (n 6) 785. With regard to general principles of international law, Cassese specifies that two series of principles can be relied upon: on the one hand, the general principles of international law, i.e., those principles that can be inferred or extracted by way of induction and generalization from conventional and customary rules of international law; on the other, principles peculiar to a particular branch of international law and that are general legal standards overarching the whole body of law governing a specific area. There can also be the case of the former turning into principles that are common to the whole body of international law, as it is the case for the principle of respect for human dignity. See Cassese 189. General principles of international law are abstractions or generalizations from the products of one or several law-creating processes (i.e., treaty, custom, general principles of law). See Georg Schwarzenberger, *The Fundamental Principles of International Law*, vol 87– Collected Courses of the Hague Academy of International Law (Brill | Nijhoff 1955) 201–202.

national legal systems;[10] on the other, general principles derive from international law.[11] However, incongruous is to think that the drafters of the ICJ Statute intended to exclude those principles that emerged from the customary practice of States or from international treaties from the formulation of Article 38. [12] In this respect, in his examination of the practice of the ICJ, Judge Gaja, writing extra-judicially, concludes that the Court asserted 'the existence of principles in international law irrespective of their correspondence to principles pertaining to municipal laws'. [13] Indeed, Gaja explains that '[w]hen a given principle is only part of international law, recognition of that principle would reflect the attitude that is taken in its regard by the international community, and thus essentially by States.'[14] Thus, general principles of international law disclose the basic values that inspire the whole international legal order.[15]

In order to define what impact the general principles of international law have within the scope of this book, it is important to identify the function(s)[16]

---

[10] Bassiouni strongly asserts that 'there is a well established consensus that "General Principles" are to be derived from national legal systems'; his proposed empirical methodology to identify the principles (inductive approach: identifying the principles in the world's major legal systems) does not suggests an explanation on the existence of principles that are not embodied in the so-called 'major legal systems'. Bassiouni, 'A Functional Approach to General Principles of International Law' (n 6) 809-811.

[11] Giorgio Gaja, 'General Principles of Law' in Rudiger Wolfrum (ed), *The Max Planck Encyclopedia of Public International Law*, vol III (Oxford University Press 2007) paras 17 ff. Schwarzenberger suggests that 'the general principles of law recognized by civilized nations may be principles which international and municipal law have in common'; however, this feature makes them relevant solely to the comparative lawyers. He stresses that 'whether any such general principle must be regarded as a fundamental principle of international law, depends on the importance of the individual principle in this category'. Thus, a sort of hierarchy among principles exists in international law: fundamental will be a principle that is significant for international law, that stands out from others by covering a relatively wide range of rules of international law, and that is either 'so typical of international law that it is an essential part of any known system of international law or so characteristic of existing international law that if it were ignored, we would be in danger of losing sight of an essential feature of modern international law'. See Schwarzenberger (n 9) 204–205.

[12] Judge Cançado Trindade deems this attitude 'a static outlook of the "formal sources" of international law, in respect of the formulation in 1920 of Article 38 of the PCIJ Statute, regarded as immutable and sacrosanct. [...] Attempts to identify general principles of law only within given national systems (or in each of them individually), besides being a static exercise, makes abstraction of the time dimension, and renders it impossible to advance towards a universal international law'. ICJ, *Separate Opinion of Judge Cançado Trindade, Pulp Mills on the River Uruguay (Argentina v Uruguay), judgment* (2010) ICJ Reports 2010, p 14 [207–208]. Although Bassiouni assertively affirms that 'there is a well established consensus that "General Principles" are to be derived from national legal systems', he also admits that 'it seems that principles deemed basic to international law can emerge in the international legal context without having a specific counterpart in national legal systems because of the differences that characterize these two legal systems'. Bassiouni, 'A Functional Approach to General Principles of International Law' (n 6) 770, 817. Along the same lines, see Gaja (n 11) paras 7–8.

[13] Gaja (n 11) para 19.

[14] ibid.

[15] Judge Cançado Trindade adds that these principles reveal those values that constitute the foundations of this legal order. See ICJ, *Separate Opinion of Judge Cançado Trindade, Pulp Mills Case* (n 12) [209].

[16] One of the main proponents of the functional approach - Bin Cheng - suggests that the general principles of law serve three functions, i.e., i) 'they constitute the source of various rules of law,

that these play in international law: based on the case law and on the abundant scholarship on the issue, general principles can be considered gap-fillers,[17] conflict mediators of diverging interpretation of a treaty or customary rules,[18] norm-creators[19]. In legal theory the principles-related terminology is connected, *inter alios*, with Dworkin. It is beyond the scope of this study to embark on a thorough analysis of Dworkin's theories or, more generally, on the exploration of the debate about the concept of law.[20] However, Dworkin's reflections upon the substantive contours of policies/principles/rules are relevant to the extent that

---

which are merely the expression of these principles'; ii) 'they form the guiding principles of the juridical order according to which the interpretation and application of the rules of law are oriented'; iii) they apply directly to the facts of the case wherever there is no formulated rule governing the matter'. Bin Cheng, *General Principles of Law as Applied by International Courts and Tribunals* (Cambridge University Press 1994) 390. Bassiouni - who suggests a fourth function, i.e., principles as modifier of conventional and customary law - stresses that the second function is the one that has been mostly recognized in the legal scholarship. "General Principles" have been primarily used to clarify and interpret international law: e.g., 'as Schlesinger notes, "General Principles" must be considered in determining the meaning of treaty terms; Lauterpacht points out that recourse by the ICJ to "General Principles" has constituted "no more than interpretation of existing conventional and customary law by reference to common sense and the canons of good faith." This interpretive function is [...] [therefore] in contrast to the use of "General Principles" as a method to supplant or remedy deficiencies in conventional and customary international law.' (footnotes omitted) See Bassiouni, 'A Functional Approach to General Principles of International Law' (n 6) 776, 779–781.

[17] For instance, the ICTY, after finding no homogeneity in the national legislation of States, had recourse to a general principle of international law – 'the general principle of respect for human dignity' - in order to solve the issue of whether forced oral penetration amounted to rape as a crime against humanity or war crime; in accordance with this principle considered 'the very *raison d'être of* [IHL] and [IHRL]...of such a paramount importance as to permeate the whole body of international law', the tribunal concluded that 'such an extremely serious sexual outrage as forced oral penetration should be classified as rape'. ICTY, *Prosecutor v Anto Furundžija, Trial Judgment* (1998) Case no. IT-95-17/1-T [183].

[18] In the Right of Passage case, Judge Wellington Koo used "General Principles" to determine if Portugal had a right of access to the Dadra enclaves. Two conflicting rights existed: Portugal had a sovereign claim over the enclaves while India claimed the right to passage. Based on the elementary principle of justice founded on logic and reason which is evidenced in international customary law, Judge Koo concluded that a principle dictates that States, as a necessity, have a right of passage in surrounding territories and suggested Portuguese sovereignty over the enclaves is subject to the control and regulation by India. Similarly, in the *Asylum case*, Judge Castilla's dissenting opinion referred to principles of international law in order to determine if the doctrine of asylum as evidenced in various conventions enabled Colombia to unilaterally qualify an offense for the purpose of granting asylum to a Peruvian citizen charged with organizing a military rebellion in Peru. Cf. ICJ, *Right of Passage Over Indian Territory (Portugal v India)*, 1960 ICJ 66-68; ICJ, *Asylum Case (Colombia v Peru)*, 1950 I.C.J. 359, both quoted in Bassiouni, 'A Functional Approach to General Principles of International Law' (n 6) 799.

[19] In the *Martić* case, the ICTY affirmed that the norms concerning the prohibition against attacking the civilian population as such, as well as individuals, and the general principle limiting the means and methods of warfare emanated from, *inter alia*, the elementary considerations of humanity. Thus, it recognized the normative character of the principle of humanity. Cf. ICTY, *Martić (Decision, 1996)* (n 2) [13].

[20] Ronald Dworkin, 'The Model of Rules' (1967) 35 University of Chicago Law Review 14; HLA Hart, *The Concept of Law* (2nd with a new Postscript, Oxford University Press 1994); Scott Shapiro, 'The "Hart-Dworkin" Debate: A Short Guide for the Perplexed' (2007) Working Paper no.77 University of Michigan Law School Public and Legal Theory Working Paper Series <http://www.law.yale.edu/documents/pdf/Faculty/Shapiro_Hart_Dworkin_Debate.pdf> accessed 4 April 2016.

these contribute to shedding light on the role of principles in relation to the subject matter of this book (see *infra* sub-sect. 1.2.).

Dworkin refers to policy to illustrate 'a standard that sets out a goal to be reached, generally an improvement in some economic, political, or social feature of the community'; the term 'principle', instead, refers to 'a standard that is to be observed, not because it will advance or secure an economic, political, or social situation [...], but because it is a requirement of justice or fairness or some other dimension of morality'.[21] For Dworkin, principles and rules are both legal norms;[22] while rules are '"all or nothing" standards'[23] that provide conclusive reasons for action and, as such, cannot conflict, principles provide justificatory support to various courses of actions, but they are not necessarily conclusive.[24] Principles can 'intersect' (i.e., can conflict); however, each principle has a peculiar weight or importance (i.e., the dimension of weight/importance). Thus, when they intersect, an assessment of their 'weight' will solve the conflict by putting aside the principle less weighty/important in the specific circumstances of the case.[25] The following sections will show that the principled-considerations that derive from the principles of humanity and accountability can "intersect" in relation to the subject matter. By taking the considerations above a step further, I argue that, although these considerations have an equal weight, they mutually reinforce each other when both are simultaneously at stake; disregarding a set of considerations can be detrimental to the beneficiaries of the courses of action justified by such considerations.

1.2. The principles of humanity and accountability

The rules on missing persons are reflective of principled considerations that are inferred from the principles of humanity (i.e., humanitarian considerations, see sub-section 1.2.1) and accountability (i.e., accountability-based considerations, see sub-section 1.2.2). For instance, during the negotiations of the IHL rules on missing persons, humanitarian considerations motivated the amendment of the initial draft of AP I; indeed, the integration in the draft of the right to know provided for in Article 32 AP I remedied 'an omission, namely the absence of any reference to families, and [called] the attention of all representatives... and their States to the suffering caused to families as a result of armed conflicts.'[26] Article

---

[21] Dworkin (n 20) 23.

[22] Shapiro (n 20) 9.

[23] Dworkin (n 20) 25.

[24] Shapiro (n 20) 9.

[25] Dworkin (n 20) 27.

[26] Declaration on amendment CDDH/II/259 Add.1 presented by the Representative of the Holy See, Mr. Kein. ICRC, 'Official Records of the Diplomatic Conference on the Reaffirmation and Development of International Humanitarian Law Applicable in Armed Conflicts, Vol XI' (1974) (CDDH/II/SR.35), para 2, 363. *Contra:* some delegations declared that the activities of the parties to the conflict 'were certainly not mainly prompted by the fundamental right of families to know what had happened to their relatives but by the desire to win the war'. See Declaration on amendment CDDH/II/259 Add.1 made by the UK Representative, Mr. Pugh, ibid (CDDH/II/SR.35), para 49, 371. For others, the aforesaid amendment 'added little to what was essentially a legal document and there was nothing like it else-where in the Protocol or in the Conventions.' Declaration on

32 AP I takes the form of preamble to Part II Section III of AP I[27] and, as such, sheds light upon the "object and purpose" of the other provisions thereof.[28] Thus, where the text of the Protocol in relation to missing persons leaves open several possible venues for interpretation,[29] the one that takes into account the right of families to know and the humanitarian considerations thereof is the correct one. Accountability-based considerations are instead the drivers of the object and purpose of the ICPPED: pursuant to the Convention's preamble, the States parties express their determination 'to prevent enforced disappearances and to combat impunity for the crime of enforced disappearance' and affirm 'the right of victims to justice and reparation' as well as 'the right of any victim to know the truth'.[30] The core of these two sets of rules is similar: both intend to ensure the respect for human dignity.

1.2.1. Humanity as a general principle of international law

A group of scholars has recently sought to assess whether humanity[31] exists as a principle of IHL; they have found that 'if by principle one means a legal norm, legally binding as such, it seems safe to conclude that such a principle of humanity does not exist, and there are limited grounds for even arguing that such a principle is emerging'.[32] However, the question of whether humanity exists as a

---

amendment CDDH/II/259 Add.1 made by the Canada's Representative, Mr. Green, ibid para 50, at 371. The New Zealand's Representative shared the viewpoint of the Canada and the UK Representatives on amendment CDDH/II/259 Add.1. ibid para 61, at 373.

[27] Michael Bothe and others, *New Rules for Victims of Armed Conflicts: Commentary on the Two 1977 Protocols Additional to the Geneva Conventions of 1949* (Second Edition, Martinus Nijhoff Publishers 2013) 196; Michael Bothe, Karl Josef Partsch and Waldemar A. Solf, *New Rules for Victims of Armed Conflicts: Commentary on the Two 1977 Protocols Additional to the Geneva Conventions of 1949* (Martinus Nijhoff Publishers 1982) 171.

[28] Cf. Articles 33 and 34, AP I. The fact of considering Article 32 AP I as a sort of preamble leads us to proceed by analogy with the preamble of a treaty; indeed, the preamble might serve as an interpretative tool and help identify the intention of the parties and the context of the treaty. Cf. Article 31 (2) VCLT.

[29] Bothe and others (n 27) 196; Bothe, Partsch and Solf (n 27) 171.

[30] Cf. Preamble, ICPPED. The preamble of a treaty can serve the purpose of providing elements for interpreting the treaty and sheds light upon its object and purpose. Makane Moïse Mbengue, 'Preamble', *Max Planck Encyclopedia of Public International Law (Online)* (2006) <http://opil.ouplaw.com/view/10.1093/law:epil/9780199231690/law-9780199231690-e1709> accessed 25 January 2017.

[31] The term "humanity" possesses multiple connotations: it derives from the Latin word *humanitas*. At the time of Romans the term included 'an intense concern for the welfare of mankind as a whole as well as for the proper ordering of the individual's inner life'. Oscar E Nybakken, 'Humanitas Romana' (1939) 70 Transactions and Proceedings of the American Philological Association 396, 410. Grounded on the Greek sophists' belief that the use of reason was mankind's peculiar feature, the term *humanitas* was adopted by, *inter alios*, Cicero to contrast humanity with inhumanity (*homo romanus* with *homo humanus*). Jean-Luc Blondel, 'The Meaning of the Word "humanitarian" in Relation to the Fundamental Principles of the Red Cross and Red Crescent' (1989) 29 International Review of the Red Cross (1961 - 1997) 507. In recent times, the term humanity is *inter alia* associated to the following definition: 'the quality of or state of being humane' i.e., 'marked by compassion, sympathy, or consideration for humans'. Humane [Def. 1]. (n.d.). *Merriam-Webster Online* <http://www.merriam-webster.com/dictionary/humane> accessed 2 July 2016.

[32] K Mujezinović Larsen and C Guldahl Cooper, 'Conclusions: Is There a "Principle of Humanity" in International Humanitarian Law?' in Kjetil Mujezinović Larsen, Camilla Guldahl Cooper and Gro

principle of IHL is misplaced here, as this book considers humanity a general principle of international law (not simply of IHL).

The principle of humanity permeates the whole international *corpus juris* concerning the protection of human beings, i.e., IHL, IHRL, and Refugee law.[33] IHL and IHRL treaties show that ensuring a minimum of guarantees and humanity to all human beings is part of the international law's mission.[34] Both IHRL's and IHL's essence revolves around the 'respect for human values and the

---

Nystuen (eds), *Searching for a 'Principle of Humanity' in International Humanitarian Law* (Cambridge University Press 2013) 355. Dinstein strongly affirms that there is no principle of humanity but 'what we actually encounter are humanitarian considerations, which pave the road to the creation of legal norms and thus explain the evolution of IHL. While impacting on the law, these considerations do not by themselves amount to law: they are meta-juridical in nature.' Y Dinstein, 'The Principle of Proportionality' in Kjetil Mujezinović Larsen, Camilla Guldahl Cooper and Gro Nystuen (eds), *Searching for a 'Principle of Humanity' in International Humanitarian Law* (Cambridge University Press 2013) 73.

[33] See AA Cançado Trindade, 'Quelques reflexions sur l'humanité comme sujet du droit international' in Denis Alland and others (eds), *Unité et diversité du droit international/Unity and Diversity of International Law: Ecrits en l'honneur du Professeur Pierre-Marie Dupuy/Essays in Honour of Professor Pierre-Marie Dupuy* (Martinus Nijhoff Publishers 2014) 163; AA Cançado Trindade, 'Some Reflections on the Principle of Humanity in Its Wide Dimension' in Gloria Gaggioli and Robert Kolb (eds), *Research Handbook on Human Rights and Humanitarian Law* (Edward Elgar Publishing 2013) 194–195. See also, ICJ, *Separate Opinion of Judge Cançado Trindade, Pulp Mills Case* (n 12) [210]. From a constitutionalist perspective, Peters argues that there is a shift from domestic to global constitutionalism, where the two poles of power vs liberty of natural persons are embedded into the idea of State sovereignty vs humanity. In this sense, one of the main claims of global constitutionalism is that sovereignty of States should be based on and derived from the principle of humanity. Thus, Peters argues that a principle of humanity underlies the whole international system of human rights protection, which prevents the State from doing what it wants to its own citizens. See A Peters, 'Are We Moving towards Constitutionalization of the World Community?' in Antonio Cassese (ed), *Realizing Utopia : the Future of International Law* (Oxford University Press 2012) 120. In his seminal work Meron looks at the process of humanization of public international law brought about by the reforming effect that both IHRL and IHL have had on other branches of international law; although he does not reflect on the semantics of humanization of the law *per se*, Meron suggests that the principle of humanity can be considered the common denominator of both systems. Meron, *The Humanization of International Law* (n 4) 6. Janmyr highlights that the common denominator to both IHL and refugee law appears to be the principle of humanity; while under IHL humanity revolves around the idea that 'humankind should be treated humanely in all circumstances', under refugee law it focuses on the idea that the provision of asylum is a 'peaceful and humanitarian act'. See M Janmyr, 'Revisiting the Civilian and Humanitarian Character of Refugee Camps' in Jean-François Durieux and David Cantor (eds), *Refuge from Inhumanity: war refugees and international humanitarian law* (Martinus Nijhoff Publishers 2014) 241–242. Along the same lines, Giuffrida, who examines the system of the subsidiary protection for humanitarian reasons under the EU legislation, reiterates the Cançado Trindade's argument, i.e., the principle of humanity permeates the whole *corpus juris* of the international protection of human beings encompassing IHL, IHRL, and refugee law. See R Giuffrida, 'Subsidiarity Protection in International and European Law' in Pia Acconci and others (eds), *International Law and the Protection of Humanity. Essays in honor of Flavia Lattanzi*, vol 3 (Brill | Nijhoff 2016) 130.

[34] Jean Pictet, *Les principes du droit international humanitaire* (Comité international de la Croix-Rouge 1966) 28. Coupland affirms that '[h]umanity is the lowest common denominator of most, if not all, international law and thus continues to influence a much wider spectrum of international law than is traditionally thought'. However, he concludes that the ambiguity of the term makes it perceived as little more than a source of international law with tenuous links to natural law. Robin Coupland, 'Humanity: What Is It and How Does It Influence International Law?' (2001) 83 International Review of the Red Cross 969, 987–988.

dignity of the human person; both bodies of law take as their starting point the concern for human dignity, which forms the basis of a list of fundamental minimum standards of humanity'.[35]

The *Martens* Clause, which embodies the principle(s)/laws of humanity confirms this understanding of the principle. The most recent version of the Clause[36] states that

[i]n cases not covered by [AP I] or by other international agreements, civilians and combatants remain under the protection and authority of the *principles of international law derived from* established custom, from the principles of humanity and from the dictates of public conscience. (emphasis added)

Abundantly commented in the literature and the case law,[37] this clause has been interpreted as serving the purpose of clarifying that, in the context of IHL and situations covered by this branch of law, 'general principles of law recognized by civilized nations' can arise 'from established custom, from the principles of humanity and from the dictates of public conscience'.[38] Therefore,

---

[35] ICTY, *Prosecutor v Mucić et al, Trial Judgment* (1998) Case no IT-96-21-T (ICTY) [149]. The UDHR affirms that 'recognition of the inherent dignity and of the equal and inalienable rights of all members of the human family is the foundation of freedom, justice and peace in the world'. Cf. Preamble, UDHR. This has been reproduced in the preamble of the main international human rights treaties (e.g., the ICCPR, the CAT, the ICESCR). The Preambles of the ICCPR and of the CAT also add that the States Parties recognize 'that these rights derive from the inherent dignity of the human person'. Apart from the Martens clause, Common Article 3 GCs I-IV, which lays down a set of fundamental rights that each Party to the conflict must respect in NIAC (and, that, in IAC, constitute a 'minimum yardstick' in the words of the ICJ), reflects 'elementary considerations of humanity'. ICJ, *Case concerning Military and Paramilitary Activities in and against Nicaragua (Nicaragua v United States of America), Merits, Judgment* (1986) ICJ Reports 1986, p.14 [218]. Although not within the scope of this book, important is to note that humanitarian considerations are not exogenous within refugee law; the Convention on the Status of Refugees' Preamble recognizes the 'social and humanitarian nature of the problem of refugees' who, as human beings, shall enjoy fundamental rights and freedoms without discrimination. Cf. Preamble, Convention relating to the Status of Refugees, Geneva, 28 July 1951, 189 UNTS 137. In Zimmermann's commentary, Alleweldt explains that in the context of the 1951 Convention, receiving refugees is seen as a humanitarian act, not as a political measure; as such, it is an act for the benefit of an individual persons. See R Alleweldt, 'Preamble to the 1951 Convention' in Andreas Zimmermann, Jonas Dörschner and Felix Machts (eds), *The 1951 Convention Relating to the Status of Refugees and Its 1967 Protocol: A Commentary* (Oxford University Press 2011) 238.

[36] Article 1 (2) AP I; see also Article 63 GC I; Article 62 GC II; Article 142 GC III; Article 158 GC IV (in all four GCs the wording used is 'laws of humanity'). The clause was included in the St Petersburg Declaration of 1868 and in the Preamble to The Hague Convention (II) of 1899 and (IV) of 1907 concerning the Laws and Customs of War on land. A vast literature exists on the clause: e.g., Theodor Meron, 'The Martens Clause, Principles of Humanity, and Dictates of Public Conscience' (2000) 94 American Journal of International Law; Daniel Thürer, *International Humanitarian Law: Theory, Practice, Context* (Martinus Nijhoff Publishers 2011) 398–402; Antonio Cassese, 'The Martens Clause: Half a Loaf or Simply Pie in the Sky?' (2000) 11 European Journal of International Law 187.

[37] For a detailed analysis of the practice as well as of the recent and past judicial and scholarly pronouncements on the clause, see ICRC, *Commentary on the First Geneva Convention: Convention (I) for the Amelioration of the Condition of the Wounded and Sick in Armed Forces in the Field* (2nd edn, 2016) paras 3284–3301 <https://www.icrc.org/applic/ihl/ihl.nsf/Treaty.xsp?documentId=4825657B0C7E6BF0C12563CD002D6B0B&action=openDocument> accessed 20 July 2016.

[38] ibid para 3295. In his dissenting opinion in the ICJ's Advisory Opinion on *Nuclear Weapons* (1996), Judge Shahabuddeen affirmed that 'the Martens Clause provided authority for treating the principles of humanity and the dictates of public conscience as principles of international law,

'principles of international law' resulting from these elements would consequently be read as similar to the 'general principles of [international] law'.[39] In the words of the ICJ, 'a great many rules' of IHL are today so 'fundamental to the respect of the human person and "elementary considerations of humanity"' that States must respect them, as these constitute 'intransgressible principles of international customary law'[40] and 'incorporate obligations which are essentially of an *erga omnes* character'.[41]

States cannot overlook the impact that the disregard of their international obligations concerning the use of force can have on human beings[42] (whether in armed conflict or otherwise).[43] These obligations are based 'on certain general and well-recognized principles', which include '*elementary considerations of humanity*, even more exacting in peace than in war'.[44] The concept of 'elementary considerations of humanity' is enshrined in concepts like 'human dignity, respect for human life, and universal principles of justice recognized by all civilized nations, aimed at ensuring friendly relations among States'.[45] Both in armed conflict and in peacetime these are 'the norms of behavior based

---

leaving the precise content of the standard implied by these principles of international law to be ascertained in the light of changing conditions, inclusive of changes in the means and methods of warfare and the outlook and tolerance levels of the international community'. ICJ, *Dissenting Opinion of Judge Shahabuddeen - Legality of the Threat or Use of Nuclear Weapon, Advisory Opinion* (1996) ICJ Reports 1996, p.226, 406.

[39] ICRC 2016 Commentary, para 3295 (quoted therein: Bothe, Michael, Partsch, Karl Josef and Solf, Waldemar A., New Rules for Victims of Armed Conflicts: Commentary on the Two 1977 Protocols Additional to the Geneva Conventions of 1949, Martinus Nijhoff Publishers, The Hague, 1982, 44, commenting on Article 1(2) of AP I; Meyrowitz, Henry, 'Réflexions sur le fondement du droit de la guerre', in Christophe Swinarski (ed.), *Etudes et essais sur le droit international humanitaire et sur les principes de la Croix-Rouge en l'honneur de Jean Pictet*, ICRC/Martinus Nijhoff Publishers, Geneva/The Hague, 1984, 424-425; and Thürer, Daniel, *International Humanitarian Law: Theory, Practice, Context*, Pocketbooks of the Hague Academy of International Law, 2011, 399, 402–406.)

[40] ICJ, *Legality of the Threat or Use of Nuclear Weapon, Advisory Opinion* (1996) ICJ Reports 1996, p.226 [79].

[41] ICJ, *Legal Consequences of the Construction of a Wall in the Occupied Palestinian Territory, Advisory Opinion* (2004) ICJ Reports 2004, p.136 157.

[42] Zyberi stresses that the damage to life and limb of British Navy personnel due to the lack of notification of the minefield in the territorial sea of Albania, albeit not the only consideration, was an important consideration for the Court in reaching the conclusion that Albania was internationally responsible and, therefore, had to make reparations. See Gentian Zyberi, *The Humanitarian Face of the International Court of Justice: Its Contribution to Interpreting and Developing International Human Rights and Humanitarian Law Rules and Principles* (Intersentia 2008) 94. More narrowly focused are the pronouncements of the ICJ in the *Nicaragua* case where the Court used 'the fundamental general principles of *humanitarian law* (emphasis added)' to assess the conduct of the USA. Cf. ICJ, *Nicaragua v. United States of America (1986)* (n 35) [218]. Cf. also ICJ, *Dissenting Opinion of Judge Tanaka, Case of South West Africa (Liberia v South Africa), Second Phase, Judgment* (1966) ICJ Reports 1966, p 6 [78].

[43] Dale Stephens, 'Human Rights and Armed Conflict - The Advisory Opinion of the International Court of Justice in the Nuclear Weapons Case' (2001) 4 Yale Human Rights & Development Law Journal 1, 16.

[44] ICJ, *Corfu Channel Case, Merits, Judgment* (1949) ICJ Reports 1949, p.4 22.

[45] Zyberi (n 42) 94.

on common sense which aim to prevent unnecessary harm being inflicted upon other human beings or State interests'.[46]

As Chapter IV will show, the suffering generated by uncertainty about the fate and whereabouts of individuals might amount to an inhuman treatment at the detriment of family members.[47] Therefore, in post-conflict, the 'provision of information on those who are missing or who have died in armed conflicts should not be delayed merely because other issues remain pending'.[48] The withholding of information or the sub-standard conduct of State authorities against requests for information forwarded by the families of missing persons in post-conflict must be appraised against the considerations above.[49]

Against this backdrop, humanity as a general principle of international law legally entitles 'any relevant international subject to claim compliance by any other international subject, whether or not non-compliance has damaged the former subject'.[50] This entails that the principle of humanity is intimately related to the principle of accountability. Demanding compliance with IHL and IHRL as an entitlement of the whole international community[51] inevitably generates two

---

[46] ibid. *Contra:* the ICJ put forward a different reasoning in the *South West Africa Cases* (Second Phase), where it stated that '[h]umanitarian considerations may constitute the inspirational basis for rules of law, just as, for instance, the preambular parts of the [UN] Charter constitute the moral and political basis for the specific legal provisions thereafter set out. Such considerations do not, however, in themselves amount to rules of law.' ICJ, *South West Africa Cases (Ethiopia v South Africa; Liberia v South Africa), Second Phase, Merits, Judgment* (1966) ICJ Reports 1966, p 6 [50]. Higgins criticizes this approach undertaken by the Court in light of the fact that the role of the judge in "making a choice" and in "finding the correct rule" entails to have consideration for the humanitarian, moral, and social purposes of the law. Assuming *arguendo* that these are policy considerations, in any case they make part of that 'decision-making process which we call international law'. See Rosalyn Higgins, 'Policy Considerations and the International Judicial Process' (1968) 17 The International and Comparative Law Quarterly 58, 61–62.

[47] Inhuman treatment is 'a serious attack on human dignity' and, as such, is 'intentional treatment which does not conform with the fundamental principle of humanity'; acts inconsistent with the principle of humanity constitute 'examples of actions that can be characterized as inhuman treatment'. ICTY, *Mucić et al (1998)* (n 35) [543]. Chapter IV will investigate this matter.

[48] ICRC, 'Official Records of the Diplomatic Conference..., Vol XI' (n 26) (CDDH/II/SR.19) para 68, at 184.

[49] Indeed, 'the desire to know the fate of loved ones lost in armed conflicts is a basic human need which should be satisfied to the greatest extent possible'. UNGA, 'Resolution on the Assistance and Cooperation in Accounting for Persons Who Are Missing or Dead in Armed' (1974) UN Doc A/RES/3220 (XXIX) Preamble. In accordance with what the UNGA Resolution 3220 on *Assistance and Cooperation in accounting for persons who are missing or dead in armed conflicts*, the UN Secretary General (UNSG) presented the content of the Resolution to the Diplomatic Conference for the adoption of the two APs by emphasizing the humanitarian nature of the Resolution and the importance of acknowledging the human need of families to know. See ICRC, 'Official Records of the Diplomatic Conference..., Vol XI' (n 26) CDDH/II/SR.19) paras 67-69, at 184.

[50] Cassese (n 9) 64–65. Cassese identifies 'respect for human rights' as a principle of international law that requires States to 'refrain from seriously and repeatedly infringing a basic right [...], and from trampling upon a whole series of rights'. In these terms, the principle of respect for human rights derives 'its most solid guarantee from the UN system'. ibid 59.

[51] Bassiouni emphasizes that as a result of the demands for compliance at the international level (see, for instance, the establishment of the *ad hoc* tribunals), accountability and justice emerge 'as internationally recognized values that are necessary for the maintenance of world order and for the restoration and maintenance of peace.' See MC Bassiouni, 'Accountability for Violations of

courses of action in the purview of this book, i.e., action vis-à-vis the request of families for information and reaction vis-à-vis infringements of IHL and IHRL as the cause of uncertainty about missing persons.

1.2.2. The principle of accountability: Between law and policy

The term "accountability" does not have a definition under any international law treaty;[52] as such, it emerges as a multifaceted[53] concept that can take different forms (e.g., legal, political, administrative, or financial accountability).[54] When applied to State action, the principle of accountability is paramount for the realization of respect for human dignity in a democratic setting; indeed, under international law,[55] interference with individual liberties and rights requires State authorities to provide a legally tenable justification.[56] As a principle of public governance, accountability is commonly associated with 'the process of being called "to account" to some authority for one's actions', which, therefore, entails a form of social interaction and implies rights on the side of those who call for the account.[57]

In conflict and post-conflict settings, accountability is depicted as one of the 'international legal principles' that constitute the foundation of the fight against impunity for gross violations of IHRL and IHL.[58] Therefore, accountability is *per se* 'an indispensable component of peace and eventual reconciliation';[59] indeed, it shapes the measures adopted for ascertaining the political, legal, and moral responsibility of individuals and institutions for past violations of human dignity. In this respect, the concept of accountability 'includes, but goes beyond the investigation and prosecution of serious crimes'.[60]

International Humanitarian Law and Other Serious Violations of Human Rights', in MC Bassiouni (ed), *Post Conflict Justice* (Transnational Publishers 2002) 384.

[52] The International Law Association (ILA), in its work on the accountability of international organizations, considers accountability a concept linked to 'the authority and power of an [international organization] or treaty-based organ'; in this context, accountability is the duty to account for the exercise of power. ILA, 'Final Report: Accountability of International Organizations (Berlin Conference)' (2004) 5.

[53] At the terminological level, the ILA emphasizes that there is no exact equivalent of the English word 'accountability' in other languages; for instance, Italian, Spanish and French 'need to borrow the English word if they wish to indicate "la responsabilité des gouvernants devant le peuple, au double sens de lui rendre compte et de tenir compte de lui". See ibid.

[54] ibid.

[55] Marianne FH Hirsch Ballin, *Anticipative Criminal Investigation: Theory and Counterterrorism Practice in the Netherlands and the United States* (Springer Science & Business Media 2012) 555.

[56] See section 4 in Chapter II.

[57] Mulgan develops this definition by building in the various positions in the context of the existing studies on public administration; his main point is that at the moment the notion of accountability is being extended leading to a relentless ramification. This might result in an unnecessary academic complication of the concept. Richard Mulgan, '"Accountability": An Ever-Expanding Concept?' (2000) 78 Public Administration 555, 555–557.

[58] UN Commission on Human Rights, 'Basic Principles and Guidelines on the Right to a Remedy and Reparation for Victims of Gross Violations of IHRL and Serious Violations of IHL - Human Rights Resolution 2005/35' (2005) UN Doc E/CN.4/RES/2005/35.

[59] M Cherif Bassiouni, 'Searching for Peace and Achieving Justice: The Need for Accountability' (1996) 59 Law and Contemporary Problems 9, 18–19.

[60] UNSG, 'Report of the Secretary-General's Panel of Experts on Accountability in Sri Lanka' (2011) para 429.

From a post-conflict policy perspective, the principle of accountability must embody the following considerations:

(1) the cessation of the conflict and thereby the ending of the process of victimization;

(2) prevention of conflicts in the future;

(3) deterrence of conflicts in the future [...];

(4) rehabilitation of the society as a whole and of the victims as a group; and

(5) reconciliation between the different peoples and groups within the society.[61]

Measures that enshrine this principle range from the prosecution of all potential violators to the establishment of the truth.[62]

Moreover, both studies on missing persons[63] and scholarly works on post-conflict settings[64] consider accountability a goal to be achieved.[65] These characteristics feature in the UN Secretary-General (UNSG)'s report on RoL and TJ in conflict and post-conflict societies. Specifically, the principle of accountability is embedded in the notions of justice, RoL[66] and TJ: 'justice' is defined as 'an ideal of accountability and fairness in the protection and vindication of rights and the prevention and punishment of wrongs'; furthermore, accountability is both one of the end-goals of TJ (together with justice and reconciliation) and one of the benchmark principles for the measures aimed to (re)-establish the RoL.[67]

---

[61] Bassiouni, 'Searching for Peace and Achieving Justice' (n 59) 23–24.

[62] ibid 19.

[63] ICRC, 'The Missing: Action to Resolve the Problem of People Unaccounted for as a Result of Armed Conflict or Internal Violence and to Assist Their Families. Conference Acts' (ICRC 2003) TheMissing/Conf/03.2003/EN/90.

[64] Bell argues that accountability is the main objective of political demands for transition that consolidates the idea of a merged regime in post-conflict. See C Bell, 'Post-Conflict Accountability and the Reshaping of Human Rights and Humanitarian Law' in Orna Ben-Naftali (ed), *International Humanitarian Law and International Human Rights Law* (Oxford University Press 2011) 334. See also De Brabandere (n 3) 139.

[65] Stahn states that a modern view of *jus post bellum* is focused on the establishment of sustainable peace, which requires peace settlement to achieve, *inter alia*, a higher level of human rights protection and accountability. C Stahn, 'Jus Post Bellum: Mapping the Discipline(s)' in Carsten Stahn and Jann K Kleffner (eds), *Jus Post Bellum: Towards a Law of Transition From Conflict to Peace* (Springer Verlag 2008) 107.

[66] In post-conflict societies, RoL 'refers to a principle of governance in which all persons, institutions and entities, public and private, including the State itself, are accountable to laws that are publicly promulgated, equally enforced and independently adjudicated, and which are consistent with international human rights norms and standards. It requires, as well, measures to ensure adherence to the principles of supremacy of law, equality before the law, accountability to the law, fairness in the application of the law, separation of powers, participation in decision-making, legal certainty, avoidance of arbitrariness and procedural and legal transparency.' UNSG, 'Report on the Rule of Law and Transitional Justice in Conflict and Post-Conflict Societies' (2004) UN Doc S/2004/616 para 6.

[67] The others are supremacy of law, equality before the law, fairness in the application of the law, separation of powers, participation in decision-making, legal certainty, avoidance of arbitrariness, and procedural and legal transparency. Cf. ibid 6–8.

In addressing the issue of missing persons, the motto 'justice for all' remains a difficult goal to be achieved; 'States may want to find certain missing persons over other missing persons [...],'[68] since the efforts to gather information on all those reported as missing might unveil evidence of crimes. Thus, if one operationalizes the concept of accountability in post-conflict contexts, 'prosecuting and judging all of those responsible at the outset of a transition might be simply impossible'; the process of being called to account for a wrongdoing would be hindered by 'the credibility, capability and resource constraints faced almost inevitably by judiciaries in the aftermath of [...] conflict, particularly in weakly institutionalized contexts'.[69] The question, then, is not 'whether to pursue justice and accountability, but rather when and how'.[70]

1.3. Humanitarian and accountability-driven considerations in post-conflict settings

Humanitarian considerations and accountability-driven considerations underpin decisions and courses of action intended to account for persons reported as missing as a result of abusive/non-abusive conduct held by the parties during the conflict. It is in this phase that peace settlements try to address the issue of missing persons from a humanitarian and/or accountability-driven perspective.[71] Thus, it is not rare to read that, in post-conflict contexts, the phenomenon of "missing persons" is not just a humanitarian issue;[72] that humanitarian needs of the families clash with the legal and accountability-based needs of judicial authorities (domestic/international);[73] that there is a need to adopt a unified humanitarian/accountability-led approach to the issue of the missing;[74] that the issue has to be addressed 'from, *inter alia,* a humanitarian and [RoL] perspective'.[75] In principle, accountability considerations cannot be the

---

[68] Julia Crawford, '"Missing Persons Are More Than A Humanitarian Issue"' (*Justiceinfo.net*, 6 July 2016) <http://www.justiceinfo.net/en/component/k2/28188.html> accessed 7 September 2016.

[69] Human Rights Council, 'Report of the Special Rapporteur on the Promotion of Truth, Justice, Reparation and Guarantees of Non-Recurrence - Prosecutorial Prioritization Strategies in the Aftermath of Gross Human Rights Violations and Serious Violations of IHL' (2014) UN Doc A/HRC/27/56 para 33.

[70] UNSG (n 66) para 21.

[71] See the examination of peace settlements in section 1, Chapter V.

[72] Crawford (n 68).

[73] See in this regard Eric Stover and Rachel Shigekane, 'The Missing in the Aftermath of War: When Do the Needs of Victims' Families and International War Crimes Tribunals Clash?' (2002) 84 International Review of the Red Cross 845; Stover, Eric and Shigekane, Rachel, 'Exhumation of Mass Graves: Balancing Legal and Humanitarian Needs' in Stover, Eric and Weinstein, Harvey M. (eds), *My neighbor, my enemy. Justice and Community in the aftermath of mass atrocity* (Cambridge University Press 2004) <http://www.cambridge.org/us/knowledge/isbn/item1151345/?site_locale=en_US>; L Milner, 'The ICTY Legacy in Finding Missing Persons' in Richard H Steinberg (ed), *Assessing the Legacy of the ICTY* (Martinus Nijhoff Publishers 2011).

[74] See, for instance, Isabelle Lassée, '"Criminal" and "Humanitarian" Approaches to Investigations into the Fate of Missing Persons: A False Dichotomy (Position Paper)' (South Asian Centre for Legal Studies 2016).

[75] UNGA, 'Resolution 69/184 - Missing Persons' (2015) UN Doc. A/RES/69/184 para 7th (Preamble).

sole driver of the actions vis-à-vis the issue of missing persons; as noted above (sub-section 1.2.1), they intermingle with the humanitarian considerations that are subsumed under the legal framework concerning the missing.

From a policy perspective, the setting of a road map intended for addressing the situation of missing persons and their families in conflict/post-conflict scenarios can enshrine both series of considerations. An example of this merger is included in the 2015 Resolution on Missing Persons where the UN General Assembly (UNGA)

> *[called] upon* States that are parties to an armed conflict to take all appropriate measures to prevent persons from going missing in connection with the armed conflict, to account for persons reported missing as a result of such a situation and, in cases of the missing persons, to take such measures, as appropriate, to ensure thorough, prompt, impartial and effective investigations and the prosecution of offences linked to missing persons, consistent with their obligations under international law, with a view to full accountability;[76] [...]

> *[urged]* States that are parties to an armed conflict to cooperate, consistent with their international obligations, in order to effectively solve cases of missing persons, including by providing mutual assistance in terms of information-sharing, victim assistance, location and identification of missing persons and recovery, identification and return of human remains and, if possible, by identifying, mapping and preserving burial sites; [...]

> *[urged]* States, and encourages intergovernmental and non-governmental organizations, to take all necessary measures at the national, regional and international levels to address the problem of persons reported missing in connection with armed conflict and to provide appropriate assistance, as requested by the concerned States, and welcomes in this regard the establishment and efforts of commissions and working groups on missing persons; [...]

> *[stressed]* the need to address the issue of missing persons as a part of peace and peacebuilding processes, with reference to all justice and rule-of-law mechanisms, including the judiciary, parliamentary commissions and truth-finding mechanisms, on the basis of transparency, accountability and public involvement and participation.[77]

Nevertheless, in practice, the situation on the ground does not facilitate the perfect mix of humanitarian and accountability-driven courses of action. In post-conflict settings, demands for justice[78] are 'at or near its apex' while the

---

[76] The Advisory Committee of the UN Human Rights Council explains that such measures 'must preferably be adopted in peacetime' (referring to the identical paragraph enshrined in Res 61/155); moreover, it also adds that mechanisms ensuring coordination and an information-sharing process between the parties 'are usually set up in the period following the end of the conflict and might be included in documents aiming at settling the situation, such as ceasefire and peace agreements'. Cf. UN Human Rights Council, 'Report of the Human Rights Council Advisory Committee on Best Practices on the Issue of Missing Persons' (2011) UN Doc A/HRC/16/70 paras 25, 37.

[77] UNGA, 'Resolution 69/184 - Missing Persons' (n 75) paras 2, 10, 12, 16.

[78] In post-conflict demands for accountability can therefore take different forms; Bell identifies two series of demands for accountability in post-conflict, i.e., i) that those responsible for IHRL and IHL violations during the conflict are held accountable (post-conflict transitional justice); ii) that third parties with post settlement responsibility are held accountable (third party accountability). The author also argues that both areas are connected in the way they have resulted in a revisited application of IHRL and IHL in post-conflict. Bell (n 64) 328, 333.

possibility of delivering justice is 'at or near its nadir'.[79] Should both sets of the above-mentioned considerations be taken into account separately or in opposition, the post-conflict process towards the restoration of normalcy might be hindered by a variety of challenges: e.g., information on missing persons might be used to support 'intransigent positions, such as that one conflict party would not want to start the investigation of cases until the other side acknowledges guilt and responsibility';[80] the evidentiary needs embedded in the prosecutorial strategy of international or internationalized judicial bodies might prevail upon the humanitarian needs of the family members.[81]

2. IHL/IHRL IN THE POST-CONFLICT LEGAL FRAMEWORK: A TENABLE DUO?

The peculiarity of the post-conflict environment consists in a systemic hybridity determined by a series of factors, including the war/peace hybridity (i.e., there is not a neat and immediate shift), the presence of a mix of State/non-state actors, the political and legal landscape characterized by the presence of domestic and international actors.[82] Both IHL and IHRL are the sources of the rules to be considered in the definition of the boundaries to the quest for information on missing persons in post-conflict settings. This means that in the phase following the armed conflict there is still scope for interaction among these rules; yet, in this phase, the application of IHL rules is residual.

The criteria to define the interaction among the rules applicable in post-conflict settings have not been set down by the main proponents of *jus post bellum*, despite the purported objective of their normative project, i.e., to organize the interplay between different bodies of law. Similarly, the literature on the relationship between IHL and IHRL has paid very little attention to the continuation of the effects of IHL in post-conflict settings and of its interplay with IHRL.[83] Yet, these issues deserve further consideration.[84] To this end, after

---

[79] Mark Freeman and Drazan Djukić, 'Jus Post Bellum and Transitional Justice' in Carsten Stahn and Jann K Kleffner (eds), *Jus Post Bellum: Towards a Law of Transition From Conflict to Peace* (Springer Verlag 2008) 215. Freeman and Djukic underline that demands for accountability can have both judicial and non-judicial responses, i.e., truth-commissions, victim reparation programs, and institutional reform strategies. ibid 216–217.

[80] UN Human Rights Council, 'Progress Report of the Human Rights Council Advisory Committee on Best Practices on the Issue of Missing Persons' (2010) UN Doc A/HRC/14/42 para 52.

[81] Stover and Shigekane (n 73) 847, 858.

[82] Bell (n 64) 330–331.

[83] Bell has concluded that in post-conflict IHL and IHRL share a common denominator, which is shaped by the politics of transition, i.e., the prohibition of broad amnesties. See ibid 335. While most of the scholars addressing *jus post bellum* agree on the application of IHRL in post-conflict, Wilde challenges this assertion by posing the question of whether and to what extent *jus post bellum* has an IHRL component, mainly in the context of extraterritorial *post bellum* situations (foreign occupation/administration), see R Wilde, 'Are Human Rights Norms Part of the Jus Post Bellum, and Should They Be?' in Carsten Stahn and Jann K Kleffner (eds), *Jus Post Bellum: Towards a Law of Transition From Conflict to Peace* (Springer Verlag 2008). By analyzing the points of convergence/divergence of *jus post bellum* and TJ, Freeman and Djukić point out that the typology of

an illustration of the nuts and bolts of the debate on the issue of the interplay between the two branches *durante bello* (sub-section 2.1), the focus will be put on the common denominator(s) of these two branches (sub-section 2.2). The terms of the relationship between IHL and IHRL rules on missing persons applicable in post-conflict contexts will be formulated by means of the delineation of criteria that make their simultaneous application a source of increased protection (sub-section 2.3).

2.1. The debate on the IHL/IHRL relationship and its relevance in post-conflict settings

As Modirzadeh wisely warns '[a]ny argument that attempts to take on a topic on which there has been so much scholarship runs the risk of becoming mired in a literature review or a rehashing of existing material'.[85] However, the literature and the case law become scant when today's question "how does IHRL apply in situations of armed conflict?"[86] is transformed in "how does IHL apply in post-conflict situations?". In order to address the latter, it is necessary to review pivotal doctrinal positions characterizing the traditional debate, as these can be geared towards a better understanding and a more complete answer to this question.

States are *aficionados* of the old maxim *lex specialis derogat legi generali*, which has been recalled in recent negotiations concerning the ICPPED (see *infra* sub-section 2.3); this attitude unveils the attempts to limit the applicability of IHRL or, at least, most part of IHRL standards, in situations of armed conflicts.[87]

---

relationship between IHL and IHRL can affect TJ's foundations: for instance, TJ treats 'the investigation of past violations as one of the state's fundamental obligations in the area of human rights; depending on the prevailing *lex specialis* argument a state's obligations with regard to lawful acts of war (e.g., use of lethal force) could be altered considerably'. Freeman and Djukić (n 79) 223. On the continuation of the application of some IHL provisions see, in particular, V Chetail, 'Introduction: Post-Conflict Peacebuilding - Ambiguity and Identity' in Vincent Chetail (ed), *Post-conflict Peacebuilding: a Lexicon* (Oxford University Press 2009) 19–20. Conversely, an abundant literature has been produced on the *in bello* IHL/IHRL interplay.

[84] C Stahn, 'The Future of Jus Post Bellum' in Carsten Stahn and Jann K Kleffner (eds), *Jus Post Bellum: Towards a Law of Transition From Conflict to Peace* (Springer Verlag 2008) 234, 236. The issue of interaction is among those issues 'which might drive future research'. See J Iverson, JS Easterday and C Stahn, 'Epilogue: Jus Post Bellum - Strategic Analysis and Future Directions' in Carsten Stahn, Jennifer S Easterday and Jens Iverson (eds), *Jus Post Bellum: Mapping the normative Foundations* (Oxford University Press 2014) 553.

[85] Naz Modirzadeh, 'The Dark Sides of Convergence: A Pro-Civilian Critique of the Extraterritorial Application of Human Rights Law in Armed Conflict' (2010) Vol. 86 U.S. Naval War College International Law Studies 349, 401. Thus, it is important to develop considerations on how IHL/IHRL provisions tackling it interact *post bellum*. Although the effort might sound purely theoretical, the pragmatic implications of the findings are intended to impact on real-life contexts.

[86] S Sivakumaran, 'International Humanitarian Law' in Sangeeta Shah and others (eds), *International Human Rights Law* (2nd edn, Oxford University Press 2010) 538.

[87] Apart from the declarations of the USA and of the UK during the negotiations of the ICPPED (see *infra* sub-section 2.3.2), see also USA, 'Observations of the United States of America on the HRCee's Draft General Comment 35: Article 9' (2014) paras 20–22 (affirming that the draft did not accord 'sufficient weight to the well-established principle that [IHL], as the *lex specialis* of armed conflict, is the controlling body of law with regard to the conduct of hostilities and the protection of war victims'); USA, 'Observations of the United States of America on the HRCee's General

The States' attitude is coupled with an 'abiding notion' that the IHL/IHRL relationship should be seen through an application of the *lex specialis* maxim that leads to consider IHL the *lex specialis* in situation of armed conflict.[88] However, the conventional understanding of this maxim applies to a conflict of norms,[89] i.e., whenever the overlapping application of the two norms leads to two opposite results or diverging standards.[90]

Moreover, the maxim has been vested with an interpretative function, i.e., a rule can be *lex specialis* in regard to 'another rule [...] as a supplement [and] a provider of instructions on what a general rule requires in some particular case'.[91] Nevertheless, the extension of its possible practical applications does not clarify the usefulness of the maxim for those who undertake the pragmatic endeavor to understand how the simultaneous application of two norms works.

In its Advisory Opinion on *Nuclear Weapons,* the ICJ has sought to outline a *lex specialis*-based model intended for explaining the application of IHL and IHRL norms in relation to the right not arbitrarily to be deprived of one's life: pursuant to the Court's reasoning, i) the protection of the ICCPR does not cease in armed conflict, except in the case of treaty-based derogations; ii) in principle, the right not arbitrarily to be deprived of one's life applies also in hostilities;

Comment 31 (Nature of the General Legal Obligation Imposed on States Parties to the Covenant)' (2007) para 25 (stating that the HRCee's assertion 'that the Covenant invariably applies in situations of armed conflict to which the rules of [IHL] are applicable sweeps too broadly'; also affirming that 'during armed conflict, [IHL] will often serve as the *lex specialis,* thus being the relevant legal standard that would apply to a particular activity'); Government of Canada, 'Comments by the Government of Canada - HRCee, Draft General Comment No 35 (Article 9)' (2014) para 11 (stating that '[IHL] is the *lex specialis* in factual situations of armed conflict and therefore the controlling body of law in armed conflict').

[88] A Clapham, 'The Complex Relationship between the Geneva Conventions and International Human Rights Law' in Andrew Clapham, Paola Gaeta and Marco Sassòli (eds), *The 1949 Geneva Conventions: A Commentary: A Commentary* (Oxford University Press 2015) 729. Vettel illustrated the maxim as follows: '*[o]f two laws or two conventions, we ought (all other circumstances being equal) to prefer the one which is less general, and which approaches nearer to the point in question:* because special matter admits of fewer exceptions than that which is general; it is enjoined with greater precision, and appears to have been more pointedly intended. [...]' Emer de Vattel, *The Law of Nations: Or, Principles of the Law of Nature Applied to the Conduct and Affairs of Nations and Sovereigns* (GG and J Robinson 1797) book II, ch XVII, para 316.

[89] Milanović emphasizes that '[a] further distinction must be made between apparent and genuine norm conflicts, and consequently between conflict avoidance on the one hand, and conflict resolution on the other. An apparent conflict is one where the content of the two norms is at first glance contradictory, yet the conflict can be avoided, most often by interpretative means. In instances in which all techniques of conflict avoidance fail, a genuine, as opposed to an apparent, conflict will emerge.' (fn omitted). M Milanović, 'Norm Conflicts, International Humanitarian Law, and Human Rights Law' in Orna Ben-Naftali (ed), *International Humanitarian Law and International Human Rights Law - Pas de deux* (Oxford University Press 2011) 102.

[90] d'Aspremont, J and E Tranchez, 'The Quest for a Non-Conflictual Coexistence of International Human Rights Law and Humanitarian Law: Which Role for the Lex Specialis Principle?' in Gloria Gaggioli and Robert Kolb (eds), *Research Handbook on Human Rights and Humanitarian Law* (Edwar Elgar Publishing 2013) 225.

[91] Martti Koskenniemi, 'Report of the Study Group of the International Law Commission on Fragmentation of International Law: Difficulties Arising from the Diversification and Expansion of International Law' (2006) UN Doc. A/CN.4/L.682 para 98.

however iii) what is arbitrary deprivation cannot be established in light of the ICCPR, but 'can only be decided by reference to the law applicable in armed conflict', i.e., the *lex specialis,* which is 'designed to regulate the conduct of hostilities'.[92] The pronouncement[93] of the Court has generated a panoply of interpretations concerning the interplay between IHL and IHRL through the prism of the *lex specialis* maxim, ranging from "IHL is the *lex specialis*" (i.e., total supremacy of IHL over IHRL) to "IHL and IHRL could be both either the *lex specialis* or *lex generalis*" depending on the circumstances of the case.[94] To these it must be added the interpretation of those who have pointed out that by accepting the continuing applicability of the ICCPR in time of armed conflict – at least for that part of the Covenant that is non-derogable – the Court acknowledged the complementarity of IHL and IHRL: accordingly, the use of the maxim cannot mean the displacement of IHRL by IHL; since the maxim is considered a 'discretionary aid in interpreting conflicting but potentially applicable treaty rules', its use appears to be not relevant in determining the complementary nature of treaty rules.[95] Indeed, the Court used the maxim not to solve a conflict of norms, but 'to determine which rules of IHL or [IHRL] would constitute the primary interpretative standard of reference'.[96]

The traditional meaning of *lex specialis derogat legi generali* is unfitting to answer the question posed in the introduction to this book; although the present study does not aim at articulating a thorough review of the different positions that scholars have developed against it, three considerations will be put forward to justify the unfitting character of the maxim within the remit of this book. First, this maxim presupposes a conflict of norms, which does not exist in the context of the rules on missing persons. Second, the maxim is silent on how the category *specialis* should be interpreted and, consequently, requires a subjective appreciation, which can trigger an inundation of further interpretations/comments

---

[92] ICJ, *Legality of the Threat or Use of Nuclear Weapon, Advisory Opinion* (n 40) [25].

[93] Criticism against this pronouncement revolves around the fact that its scope is very narrow, as the Court's reasoning was limited to the specific case of the right to life. William A Schabas, 'Lex Specialis - Belt and Suspenders - The Parallel Operation of Human Rights Law and the Law of Armed Conflict, and the Conundrum of Jus Ad Bellum' (2007) 40 Israel Law Review 592, 596.

[94] Prud'homme offers a full review of the different interpretations of ICJ's pronouncements, see Nancie Prud'homme, 'Lex Specialis: Oversimplifying a More Complex and Multifaceted Relationship' (2007) 40 Israel Law Review 356, 370–378. With regard to the interpretation that endorses a total supremacy of IHL over IHRL, see Michael J Dennis, 'Application of Human Rights Treaties Extra-Territorially in Times of Armed Conflict and Military Occupation - Agora: ICJ Advisory Opinion on Construction of a Wall in the Occupied Palestinian Territory' (2005) 99 American Journal of International Law 119, 139, 141 quoted in Prud'homme 372. With regard to the latter, see d'Aspremont, J and Tranchez (n 90) 240.

[95] Vera Gowlland-Debbas, 'The Relevance of Paragraph 25 of the ICJ's Advisory Opinion on Nuclear Weapons' (2004) 98 Proceedings of the Annual Meeting (American Society of International Law) 358, 359.

[96] Giacca underlines that 'the scope of the right was determined by reference to IHL, which was elected as the special law by the ICJ, stemming from its application in armed conflict situations with the specific purpose to govern the means of warfare. In other words, the [ICCPR] does not create an absolute right to life; it only proscribes the 'arbitrary' deprivation thereof. The question of what constitutes arbitrariness in a situation of armed conflict is a matter of IHL'. Gilles Giacca, *Economic, Social, and Cultural Rights in Armed Conflict* (Oxford University Press 2014) 183.

as the ICJ's advisory opinion shows.[97] Third, the malleability of the maxim,[98] its multiple functions, and the scholarly transposition of this maxim to the relationship between two legal regimes as a whole[99] make it impractical for clarifying the interplay of IHL/IHRL rules[100] on missing persons in post-conflict contexts where hybridity and complexity are inherently present. The ICJ almost abandoned it in its successive advisory opinion on *The Wall* and did not mention it in *Congo v Uganda*;[101] in the latter, the relationship IHL/IHRL is framed in complementary terms.

Pursuant to the ICJ's new approach, there are three possible situations that illustrate the difficulties arising in relation to identification and application of the relevant rule: i) 'some rights may be exclusively matters of [IHL]'; ii) 'others may be exclusively matters of [IHRL]'; iii) 'yet, others may be matters of both these branches of international law.' [102] The Court regrettably does not offer examples or further details on which rule falls in which category. Although tailored to armed conflict scenarios, this classification can be further specified and made valuable by means of the identification of these typologies of norms in post-conflict settings. For instance, until the repatriation of POW is not concluded, guarantees related to the status of POW and the status of POW *per se* continue to apply (situation − mainly, but not solely − covered by IHL);[103] freedom of expression or the right to vote remain aspects mostly addressed by IHRL; the issue of missing persons (including enforced disappearances) can be deemed a matter of both branches of international law. Despite this classification, nothing tells us how the rules on missing persons should simultaneously apply.

---

[97] The vagueness of the tentative model proposed by the Court is demonstrated by the multiple and opposite interpretations that have mushroomed over the years. See Anja Lindroos, 'Addressing Norm Conflicts in a Fragmented Legal System: The Doctrine of Lex Specialis' (2005) 74 Nordic Journal of International Law 27, 44 (the author also specifies that the maxim does not help when two special rules belonging to two different branches of the law are at stake); Chetail points out that 'there are now as many possible criteria for determining the special or general nature of a particular norm as the number of authors undertaking such an exercise'. V Chetail, 'Armed Conflict and Forced Migration: A Systemic Approach to International Humanitarian Law, Refugee Law and Human Rights Law' in Paola Gaeta and Andrew Clapham (eds) (Oxford University Press 2014) 702.

[98] Prud'homme (n 94) 384.

[99] Giacca (n 96) 183.

[100] For instance, d'Aspremont and Tranchez understand the relation between IHL and IHRL in terms of competition (a broader conception of conflict of norms which permits to embrace situations of contradictions of norms, situation of potential conflict between permissive and prescriptive norms, situations of norms pointing in different directions without conflicting) and not in terms of conflict. Based on this assumption, they seek to evaluate the use of the maxim to calibrate 'the systemic integration of international law'. Nevertheless, such an unorthodox use of the maxim 'does little to alleviate the uncertainty inherent in the competitive character of the relationship between IHL and IHRL'. d'Aspremont, J and Tranchez (n 90) 233, 242.

[101] ICJ, *Case concerning Armed Activities on the Territory of the Congo (Democratic Republic of the Congo v Uganda), Merits, Judgment* (2005) ICJ Reports 2005, p.168; *Legal Consequences of the Construction of a Wall in the Occupied Palestinian Territory, Advisory Opinion* (n 41).

[102] ICJ, *DRC v Uganda (2005)* (n 101) [216].

[103] The same is true for those arrested, detained and interned for reasons related to the armed conflict. Cf. Article 75 (6) AP I.

IHL and IHRL have a common denominator – i.e., humanity – and a shared objective, i.e., protect the individual from abuses of those in power (see *infra* sub-section 2.2).[104] Their distinct features[105] have not prevented scholars[106] and international adjudicators and bodies[107] from considering the two branches

---

[104] Rosemary Abi-Saab considers that 'if [IHL and IHRL] have as a common and identical objective, the protection of the individual from all possible attempts on his personal integrity, in armed conflicts or in peacetime, it is no surprise that these two branches of international law should find complementarity'. See R Abi-Saab, 'Human Rights and Humanitarian Law in Internal Conflicts' in Daniel Warner (ed), *Human Rights and Humanitarian Law. The quest for Universality*, vol 29 (Martinus Nijhoff Publishers 1997) 122–123. Along similar lines, see T Meron, 'Convergence of International Humanitarian Law and Human Rights Law' in Daniel Warner (ed), *Human Rights and Humanitarian Law. The quest for Universality*, vol 29 (Martinus Nijhoff Publishers 1997) 100.

[105] The main peculiar feature peculiar to IHL is that its triggering point of application must be an armed conflict; another feature peculiar to IHL is the narrow attention paid to the protection required from the belligerent party vis-à-vis its own nationals.

[106] Partsch admits that 'as far as the instruments of both categories are applicable, a reciprocal application is not excluded by either of them. [...] [T]he antagonism, which formerly existed between the two concepts, has faded away. This does not justify the merging of both concepts into one, the result of which might be a rather low level of protection and a loss of the merits which they each separately possess.' KJ Partsch, 'Human Rights and Humanitarian Law' in Rudolf Bernhardt (ed), *Encyclopedia of Public International Law* (North-Holland Publishing Company 1985) 292 912. El Kouhene points out that 'les droits de l'homme et le droit humanitaire atteignent toujours un haut degré de complémentarité et de compatibilité tout en étant deux systèmes juridiques distincts'. Mohamed El Kouhene, *Les Garanties Fondamentales de la Personne en Droit Humanitaire et Droits de l'Homme* (Martinus Nijhoff Publishers 1986) 12. Gasser underscores that '[o]nly an approach which emphasizes the complementarity character of the two bodies of international law leads to reasonable answers to the issues raised by armed conflict. In short, [IHRL] and [IHL] have distinct but related roles to play in the fight for better protection of basic human rights. Hans-Peter Gasser, 'International Humanitarian Law and Human Rights Law in Non-International Armed Conflict: Joint Venture or Mutual Exclusion' (2002) 45 German Yearbook of International Law 149, 162. Prud'homme stresses that '[t]he necessity to clarify this "unexploited potential of complementarity" is clear. It is time to develop a thorough approach capable of circumventing manipulation of the law and setting stage for a harmonious and optimal co-existence of [IHRL] and [IHL]' (fn omitted). Prud'homme (n 94) 395. Kolb underlines that 'au vu de la pratique internationale la doctrine des "complémentaristes" paraît la plus fondée, à condition toutefois de maintenir la distinction conceptuelle entre le droit des conflits armés et les droits de l'homme. [...] Il n'y a aucune raison valable de refuser cette synergie et ces apports complémentaires, d'autant moins si l'on tient compte du but protecteur du droit humanitaire, tel qu'énoncé entre autres dans la Clause Martens'. In Robert Kolb, *Ius in bello: le droit international des conflits armés; précis* (II, Helbing & Lichtenhahn 2009) 143. Along the same lines see also Eric David, *Principes de droit des conflits armés* (IV, Bruylant 2008) 98. Calogeropoulos-Stratis observes that 'la "thèse complémentariste"[...] ne voit ni "intégration" ni "contradiction", mais une "complémentarité" entre le droit humanitaire et les droits de l'homme. [...] La complémentarité des deux droits [...] est plus favorable à la protection de la personne humaine en période de conflit armé'. A. Calogeropoulos-Stratis, *Droit Humanitaire et Droits de L'homme – La Protection de La Personne En Période de Conflit Armé* (UHEI, Sijthoff 1980) 237–238.

[107] See for instance, ICJ, *Dissenting Opinion, South West Africa Case* (n 42); *DRC v Uganda (2005)* (n 101); *Legal Consequences of the Construction of a Wall in the Occupied Palestinian Territory, Advisory Opinion* (n 41). HRCee, 'General Comment No. 31: The Nature of the General Legal Obligation Imposed on State Parties to the Covenant' (2004) UN Doc. CCPR/C/21/Rev.1/Add.13 para 31; IACommHR, 'Decision on Request for Precautionary Measures (Detainees at Guantanamo Bay)' (2002) PM 259/02 para 4 (affirming that 'in situations of armed conflict, the protections under international [IHL/IHRL] may complement and reinforce one another, sharing as they do a common nucleus of non-derogable rights and a common purpose of promoting human life and dignity.');

complementary. For instance, the HRCee has framed the interplay of the two branches as follows: '[w]hile, in respect of certain Covenant rights, more specific rules of [IHL] may be specially relevant for the purposes of the interpretation of Covenant rights, both spheres of law are complementary, not mutually exclusive'.[108] The problem that emerges from this excerpt is the focus on the complementarity of the two branches as a whole and not on the rules and circumstances in which these rules apply.

Despite its policy-related nature,[109] the concept of complementarity can have a legal understanding, as the international case law shows. The simultaneous application of IHL and IHRL during an armed conflict and in its aftermath entails that these branches can reinforce each other mutually[110] 'in as much as they complete and perfect each other'.[111] In light of the triadic approach of the ICJ in *Congo v Uganda,* mutual reinforcement manifests itself in multiple manners that depend on whether a certain conduct/situation is regulated by rules belonging to IHL/IHRL/both.[112] Against this backdrop, the "complementarity approach" is to be deemed relevant to the 'co-application'/[113] 'cumulative

---

IACtHR, *Serrano-Cruz Sisters v El Salvador, Judgment - Preliminary Objections* (2004) Series C no 118 [112]. See also 'Tehran Conference, General Resolution XXIII, "Respect for Human Rights in Armed Conflicts"' (1968) UN Doc A/Conf.32/41; UNGA, 'Resolution for Human Rights in Armed Conflicts' (1968) Res 2444 (XXIII); UNGA, 'Resolution for Human Rights in Armed Conflicts' (1970) Res 2674 (XXV); UNSC, 'Resolution 237' (1967) UN Doc S/RES/237 preamble (*'considering* that essential and inalienable human rights should be respected even during the vicissitudes of war'); UNSC, 'Resolution 1882' (2009) UN Doc S/RES/1882 preamble and para 15 (referring to the application of the human rights of the child in armed conflicts).

[108] HRCee (n 107) para 11. The relevance of more specific rules of IHL for the interpretation of human rights provisions has been spelled out by the ECtHR with regard to the human right to personal liberty. The ECtHR has stated that '[b]y reason of the coexistence of the safeguards provided by [IHL] and by the [ECHR] in time of armed conflict, the grounds of permitted deprivation of liberty set out [under the Convention] should be accommodated, as far as possible, with the taking of [POW] and the detention of civilians who pose a risk to security under [GC III and IV].' Cf. ECtHR, *Hassan v The UK, Judgment (GC)* (2014) App no 29750/09 [102, 104].

[109] Cordula Droege, 'The Interplay between International Humanitarian Law and International Human Rights Law in Situations of Armed Conflict' (2007) 40 Israel Law Review 310, 337. Interpretative maxims as *lex specialis, lex posterior,* and *lex superior* are techniques that form part of legal reasoning. Cf. Koskenniemi (n 91) para 119 ff.

[110] Droege (n 109) 340. Fleck and Bothe affirm that in cases of simultaneous application, the relationship between the two branches is referred to as complementary; 'the two fields are thus regarded to be mutually reinforcing in as much as they complete and perfect each other'. JK Kleffner, 'Scope of Application of International Humanitarian Law' in Dieter Fleck and Michael Bothe (eds), *The Handbook of International Humanitarian Law* (Oxford University Press 2008) 73. See also UN Commission on Human Rights, 'Resolution on "Protection of the Human Rights of Civilians in Armed Conflicts"' (2005) UN Doc E/CN.4/RES/2005/63 Preamble (the Commission also added that 'all human rights require protection equally and that the protection provided by human rights law continues in armed conflict situations, taking into account when [IHL] applies as *lex specialis').*

[111] JK Kleffner, 'Human Rights and International Humanitarian Law: General Issues' in Terry D Gill and Dieter Fleck (eds), *The Handbook of the International Law of Military Operations* (Oxford University Press 2011) 58.

[112] ibid.

[113] Orna Ben-Naftali and Yuval Shany, 'Living in Denial: The Application of Human Rights in the Occupied Territories' (2003) 37 Israel Law Review 17, 56.

application'/[114] 'parallel application'/[115] 'concurrent application'[116] of specific rules belonging to both branches that maintain their independence and distinct features. Moreover, the "complementarity approach" better fits this book's understanding of international law as a dynamic process that, for the purpose of ensuring effective protection, does not reject overlapping and connections among its branches.[117]

2.2. *Defining the common denominator(s) to the rules on missing persons*

Humanity is the main point of contact between IHL and IHRL. Pictet initially depicted 'humanitarian law' as an umbrella term covering 'that considerable portion of international law which owes its inspiration to a feeling for humanity and which is centered on the protection of the individual.' [...].[118] In this wide sense, humanitarian law included 'all the international legal provisions, whether written or customary, ensuring respect for the individual and his well-being', and, therefore, consisted of two branches of law, i.e., 'the law of war and human rights.'[119] These considerations do not entail, as some have suggested, that IHL is IHRL.[120] 'Biological taxonomies' that depict IHL as a specialized branch of IHRL and IHRL as a 'modern humanitarian code' blur the different historical origins of the two branches[121] and obscure even more their interplay[122] *durante*

---

[114] Chetail, 'Armed Conflict and Forced Migration' (n 97) 703.

[115] Prud'homme (n 94) 360.

[116] Droege (n 109) 335.

[117] In this respect, Chetail underlines that the branches of international law are doctrinal reconstructions that show an ongoing trend towards the specialization of public international law; yet the specialization is *per se* part of the current development of public international law. See V Chetail, 'Droit International Général et Droit International Humanitaire: Retour Aux Sources' in Vincent Chetail (ed), *Permanence et mutations du droit des conflits armés* (Bruylant 2013) 43. Along similar lines, in referring to specific areas of customary law (customary IHL, customary law of the sea, etc...), Hampson stresses that the label is simply a tool of convenience and a descriptive label, which does not indicate legally distinct areas of customary law. See Françoise Hampson, 'Other Areas of Customary Law in Relation to the Study' in Elizabeth Wilmshurst and Susan Breau (eds), *Perspectives on the ICRC study on customary international humanitarian law* (Cambridge University Press 2007) 56.

[118] Jean S Pictet, 'The Principles of International Humanitarian Law' (1966) 6 International Review of the Red Cross 455, 455–456.

[119] ibid.

[120] Richard Baxter, 'Humanitarian Law or Humanitarian Politics? The 1974 Diplomatic Conference on Humanitarian Law' in Theodor Meron and others (eds), *Humanizing the Laws of War: Selected Writings of Richard Baxter* (Oxford University Press 2013) 307. Smith underlines that '[IHL] "fills the gap" providing a minimum standard of treatment for all during hostilities. As such, it is human rights law for application in the most extreme situations', Rhona KM Smith, *Textbook on International Human Rights* (OUP Oxford 2012) 14. *Contra:* among others, Meron states that IHL and IHRL 'are different and will remain different' and that 'it makes no sense to pretend that [IHL and IHRL] are one and the same'. Meron, 'Convergence of International Humanitarian Law and Human Rights Law' (n 104) 100.

[121] On this point see, Gerd Oberleitner, *Human Rights in Armed Conflict: Law, Practice, Policy* (Cambridge University Press 2015) 124; Droege (n 109) 312–317. Among those participating in the debate on a common/distinct origins are Charles E Rousseau, *Le Droit des conflits armés* (Editions A. Pedone 1983) 22 (observing that 'il y a désaccord en doctrine quant à la nature respective de la théorie des droits de l'homme et du droit humanitaire de la guerre'); Dietrich Schindler, 'Le Comité

bello and *post bellum*. As Pictet himself explained years later, he intended to show 'the connection between the law of armed conflicts and human rights' and 'to find what connected the two [...] instead of what separated them'; thus, he was 'merely looking for a term which might cover two undoubtedly connected, yet independent disciplines on an equal footing'.[123]

From a teleological perspective, while IHL aims at regulating the conduct of parties to the conflict and addressing situations arising *in bello*, IHRL intends to protect the individual from the abuse of power at all times.[124] In both cases, the protection of individuals from suffering and death is the central concern of the law[125] and is directly connected to the basic consideration of the respect for human dignity, i.e., 'the basic underpinning and indeed the very *raison d'être* of [IHL] and [IHRL]'.[126] Therefore, during an armed conflict, in its aftermath, and in peace times, humanity permeates the *corpus juris* on the protection of human beings; in this sense, it provides 'l'une des illustrations des [...] convergences entre ses branches distinctes et complémentaires'.[127]

It is, however, impossible to disregard the fact that accountability is also part of the considerations outlined above: where the conduct of State or non-state actors is in violation of human rights and/or IHL, States authorities have the duty

---

International de La Croix-Rouge et Les Droits de L'homme' (1979) 61 International Review of the Red Cross 3 (stating that '[l]es droits de l'homme et le droit de la guerre se sont développés de manières différentes et totalement distinctes, bien que leurs racines spirituelles soient partiellement les mêmes et que, à partir du XIXe siècle, on puisse observer un certain parallélisme dans l'évolution de ces deux branches du droit'); Louise Doswald-Beck and Sylvain Vité, 'International Humanitarian Law and Human Rights Law' (1993) 33 International Review of the Red Cross (1961 - 1997) 94, 94 (noting that 'as human rights law and humanitarian law have totally different historical origins, the codification of these laws has until very recently followed entirely different lines').

[122] Oberleitner (n 121) 123–124.

[123] Jean S Pictet, *Humanitarian Law and the Protection of War Victims* (Henry Dunant Institute 1975) 14.

[124] Droege (n 109) 310. Both IHL and IHRL, however, share the common 'need to protect the individual against those who would crush him'. Pictet, *Humanitarian Law and the Protection of War Victims* (n 123) 15.

[125] Baxter (n 120) 307. See also Partsch (n 106) 912; Droege (n 109) 341.

[126] ICTY. *Prosecutor v. Anto Furundžija, Trial Judgment* (n 17) [183]. Meron asserts that IHL and IHRL have both 'the same and different jurisprudential roots: human rights law is based on the principle of humanity, which also underlies [IHL], as in the famous Martens clause. [IHL] grew out of additional roots as well, especially the tension between the principles of humanity and military necessity. [...] modern [IHL], like human rights law, is based less on reciprocity than on the objective, normative value of the protection of the human person and human dignity'. See Meron, 'Convergence of International Humanitarian Law and Human Rights Law' (n 104) 100.

[127] On this point see Cançado Trindade, 'Quelques reflexions sur l'humanité comme sujet du droit international' (n 33) 164. Similarly, Zyberi argues that 'elementary considerations of humanity are a fundamental legal concept both in international human rights and humanitarian law because of their intrinsic link with the principle of humanity, as a thread which permeates these two branches of international law in their entirety'. Zyberi (n 42) 95 (footnotes omitted). In this regard, the interpretation provided by the ICRC commentary on the rules concerning the missing in armed conflict under API as a series of rules applicable at all times is based on humanitarian considerations. Yves Sandoz and others, *Commentary on the Additional Protocols: Of 8 June 1977 to the Geneva Conventions of 12 August 1949* (Martinus Nijhoff Publishers 1987) para 149, 67 and para 160, 69. Cf. Article 75 (1) and (6) AP I and related commentary (ibid para 3125, 885).

to put an end to impunity and prosecute those responsible in order to promote accountability,[128] respect for the law, and justice for the victims.[129] This duty, emerging from IHL and IHRL texts,[130] is deeply interrelated to the duty to respect and secure respect for human dignity and, ultimately, for the human rights of all individuals.[131] *Durante bello* and in a post-conflict situation, cases of 'missing persons involve conduct that may constitute criminal offences':[132] 'as a general principle, there should be no recourse to pardon, amnesty or similar political measures to terminate the criminal prosecution or punishment of crimes linked to missing persons.'[133] In these terms, accountability makes the duty to respect and secure respect for human dignity effective.[134]

2.3. The terms of the relationship between IHL/IHRL rules on missing persons in post-conflict settings

The examination of the relationship between IHL and IHRL as one between regimes requires a too much higher level of abstraction[135] and does not suit the interest of those operating on the ground. Furthermore, as remarked in Chapter II, the IHL regime is not entirely applicable in post-conflict settings (e.g., the norms on the conduct of hostilities cease to be applicable at the general close of hostilities); consequently, the focus on the interaction between regimes would be

---

[128] *Contra:* some authors have questioned the incorporation of IHL in post-conflict when TJ mechanisms have been set up. See, on this point, Salmon E, 'Reflections on International Humanitarian Law and Transitional Justice: Lessons to Be Learnt from the Latin American Experience' (2006) 88 International Review of the Red Cross 327; HRW, 'Selling Justice Short. Why Accountability Matters for Peace' (2009) Doc no 1-56432-508-3; Pablo Kalmanovitz, 'Ius Post Bellum and the Imperative to Supersede IHL - Symposium on the Colombian Peace Talks and International Law' (2016) 110 AJIL Unbound 193, 194 (arguing that 'superseding IHL [...] must be one of the central goals of the political project of transitioning from war to peace'; the contrary would allow invocations of military necessity and proportionality - and ultimately - of national security, thereby providing the justifications for the use of force in post-conflict).

[129] Cf. UN Commission on Human Rights, 'Resolution on Impunity, Res 2004/72' (2004) UN Doc E/CN.4/RES/2004/72 Preamble; UN Commission on Human Rights, 'Promotion and Protection of Human Rights: Impunity. Add.1 "Updated Set of Principles for the Protection and Promotion of Human Rights through Action to Combat Impunity (Orentlicher Principles)"' (2005) UN Doc E/CN.4/2005/102/Add.1 Principle 1.

[130] Cf. among others: Article 49 GC I; Article 50, GC II; Article 129, GC III; Article 146, GC IV; cf. also Rule 158, Jean-Marie Henckaerts and Louise Doswald-Beck, *Customary International Humanitarian Law: Volume 1, Rules* (Cambridge University Press 2005) 607. For IHRL, cf. Preamble, Articles 3-7, 9, 11 ICPPED; Article 7 Convention against Torture and Other Cruel, Inhuman or Degrading Treatment or Punishment, December 10, 1984, 1465 UNTS 85 (hereinafter CAT).

[131] UN Commission on Human Rights, 'Orentlicher Principles' (n 129) Preamble.

[132] UNGA, 'Resolution 69/184 - Missing Persons' (n 75) preamble (Preamble, UNGA Resolution 2014). The pursuit of accountability can impinge upon the efforts to obtain information, since information holders might fear prosecution. UN Human Rights Council, 'Report of the Human Rights Council Advisory Committee on Best Practices on the Issue of Missing Persons' (n 76) para 68.

[133] UN Human Rights Council, 'Report of the Human Rights Council Advisory Committee on Best Practices on the Issue of Missing Persons' (n 76) para 67.

[134] In the process towards peace, accountability is one of the fundamental tenets of the fight against impunity and of the efforts to restore the RoL. V Gowlland-Debbas and V Pergantis, 'Rule of Law' in Vincent Chetail (ed), *Post-conflict Peacebuilding: a Lexicon* (Oxford University Press 2009) 320.

[135] Milanović (n 89) 98–99.

ambiguous. The examination of the relationship between norms[136] is indeed the most logical and plausible.

The mutual reinforcement derived from the complementary nature of IHL/IHRL rules can be detectable in terms of development of international law as a direct result of the reciprocal influence between the two branches (sub-section 2.3.1). It can also be discernible at the operational level, i.e., when two rules simultaneously apply to the same conduct/situation in a post-conflict situation. In order to expound on the simultaneous application of two rules belonging to two different regimes in practice, this sub-section will identify and appraise a set of criteria aimed at making complementarity an operational and workable concept on the ground (sub-section 2.3.2). Indeed, the lack of analysis of or proposals for such criteria is the core of the critique against the proponents of the complementarity approach. [137]

2.3.1. Normative reinforcement

Mutual reinforcement between IHL and IHRL rules on missing persons is discernable in terms of development of international law as a result of the reciprocal influence between these branches. Usually, it is argued that IHRL has influenced IHL, by referring, for instance, to Article 75 AP I drafted on the basis of standards already included in the ICCPR.[138] Nonetheless, the reverse is also true,[139] especially in the context of missing persons. IHL and IHRL rules on missing persons have not been written at the same time: IHL treaties have paved the way for regulating information access and communication rights in relation

---

[136] ICJ, *Dissenting Opinion, South West Africa Case* (n 42) [25]; *Legal Consequences of the Construction of a Wall in the Occupied Palestinian Territory, Advisory Opinion* (n 41) [106]. However, the ICJ adopted a different approach in Congo/Uganda, as it framed the question as one concerning the relationship between regimes. Cf. ICJ, *DRC v Uganda (2005)* (n 101) [216]. The same vagueness is detectable in the HRCee's General Comment no. 31, cf. HRCee (n 107) para 11. In addition to that, the norm/norm approach needs to be framed within the broad spectrum of systemic integration embodied in Article 31 (3) (c), VCLT.

[137] Milanović (n 89) 100; John Tobin, 'Seeking Clarity in Relation to the Principle of Complementarity: Reflections on the Recent Contributions of Some International Bodies' 8 Melbourne Journal of International Law 356, 366. Hampson and Salama highlight that 'the relationship between IHL and [IHRL] is paradoxal in the sense that there is an increasing awareness on the part of the international community of the convergence between those two sets of norms, while there is also an unexploited potential of complementarity.' See Ibrahim Salama and Françoise Hampson, 'Working Paper on the Relationship between Human Rights Law and International Humanitarian Law' (UN Commission on Human Rights 2005) UN Doc E/CN.4/Sub.2/2005/14 para 5.

[138] Article 75 (4) was drafted in light of Article 14 ICCPR (right to a fair trial). Sandoz and others (n 127) para 3092, 879. Similarly, at the time of the drafting of the GCs I-IV, the UDHR was taken into consideration; Article 99(1) GC III (*nullum crimen sine lege*) is a clear example of the influence that article 11(2) of the UDHR had on the text. Another example is Article 27 GC IV concerning *inter alia* the protection of family rights of protected persons, clearly inspired by Article 16(3) of the UDHR. See, in this respect, Jean S Pictet (ed), *The Geneva Conventions of 12 August 1949: Commentary*, vol III (ICRC 1960) 470; Jean S Pictet (ed), *The Geneva Conventions of 12 August 1949: Commentary*, vol IV (ICRC 1958) 202.

[139] For instance, non-derogable provisions of ICCPR closely resemble the guarantees incorporated under Common Article 3 GCs I-IV. On this point see Gasser (n 106) 157; Sandesh Sivakumaran, *The Law of Non-International Armed Conflict* (Oxford University Press 2012) 87.

to dispersed families, missing persons' families, and unaccompanied children in armed conflict. The most recent treaty-based advance in this field – i.e., the recognition of the right of families to know the fate of their relatives – derives from the intertwined efforts undertaken by the UN and the ICRC with regard to the inclusion of this issue in the APs of 1977. Indeed, after the illustration of the UNGA Resolution 3220 on *Missing Persons* by the UNSG to the framers of the Protocols, the right of families to know the fate of their relatives was incorporated in an advanced draft of AP I. Thus, the joint effort of the UN/ICRC resulted in a full section dedicated to missing and dead persons.

Today's global set of rules concerning enforced disappearances, embodied in the ICPPED, has partly integrated[140] the core of IHL's rules on missing persons, i.e., the right of families to know the fate of their relatives[141] as well as communication and family rights enshrined in GC IV.[142] However, normative influence does not imply a merger of the rules concerning missing persons and enforced disappearances;[143] while the specificity of the latter resides in the focus on persons subjected to enforced disappearance, i.e., a human rights violation and an international crime, the former were designed for the mitigation of the suffering of the families of missing persons in armed conflicts and not for the protection of missing persons *per se*.[144] This distinction is today maintained: pursuant to the ICRC Study on Customary IHL, the prohibition of enforced disappearance is the core of a separate rule from that on the obligation of parties

---

[140] Cf. Article 24(2) and Article 18, ICPPED.

[141] Cf., Article 32, AP I; Droege affirms that the right to know under Article 32 AP I has influenced not only the *jus scriptum* (cf. Article 24 (2) ICPPED on the right to truth) but, prior to that, the human rights bodies' case law. See Droege (n 109) 343. Boutruche considers that the right to truth, 'as an individual right under [IHRL], finds its origins in the provision of [IHL] related to missing persons', including Article 32 AP I. See Théo Boutruche, 'Seeking the Truth About Serious International Human Rights and Humanitarian Law Violations: The Various Facets of a Cardinal Notion of Transitional Justice' in Mariëlle Matthee, Brigit Toebes and Marcel Brus (eds), *Armed Conflict and International Law: In Search of the Human Face* (T M C Asser Press 2013) 310. Similarly, Tullio Scovazzi and Gabriella Citroni, *The Struggle against Enforced Disappearance and the 2007 United Nations Convention* (Martinus Nijhoff Publishers 2007) 347. Bérangère Taxil, 'À La Confluence Des Droits: La Convention Internationale Pour La Protection de Toutes Les Personnes Contre Les Disparitions Forcées' (2007) 53 Annuaire français de droit international 129, 139. More generally, the right to know is considered at the origins of 'the right to truth' in the framework of the fight against impunity and the promotion and protection of human rights. Cf. UN Human Rights Council, 'Resolution 9/11 - Right to the Truth' (2005) UN Doc A/HRC/RES/9/11 Preamble and para 1; UN Human Rights Council, 'Resolution 12/12 - Right to the Truth' (2009) UN Doc A/HRC/RES/12/12 Preamble and para 1. See also UN OHCHR, 'Study on the Right to the Truth' (2006) UN Doc E/CN.4/2006/91 para 5.

[142] On this point, see Droege (n 109) 343; Ruona Iguyovwe, 'The Inter-Play between International Humanitarian Law and International Human Rights Law' in Aldo Zammit Borda (ed), *International Humanitarian Law and the International Red Cross and Red Crescent Movement* (Routledge 2013) 43.

[143] *Contra*: Gaggioli (n 1) 331.

[144] Declaration on amendment CDDH/II/259 Add.1 presented by the Representative of the Holy See, Mr. Kein. ICRC, 'Official Records of the Diplomatic Conference...', Vol XI' (n 26) (CDDH/II/SR.35) para 2, 363. Théo Boutruche, 'Missing and Dead Persons' in Rudiger Wolfrum (ed), *The Max Planck Encyclopedia of Public International Law - Ozone Layer, international protection*, vol VII (Oxford University Press 2012) para 6.

to the conflict to account for missing persons and to provide the families with any information on their fate (cf. Rule 98 and Rule 117 respectively).

2.3.2. Translating simultaneous application into practice

Although contested,[145] in post-conflict settings the coexistence between IHL and IHRL should be plausible. Indeed, the *a priori* rejection of the continuing effects of IHL rules in post-conflict contexts is impracticable, due to the continuation in such contexts of some of the situations emerged during the conflict. Such a rejection might have a series of consequences: first, should a traditional vertical perspective on IHRL obligations prevail, the range of actors obliged to undertake efforts to account for missing persons would be narrower, as this perspective would exclude non-state armed groups from the category 'duty-bearers' (both *durante bello* and in post-conflict situations);[146] second, and most important, the disregard of the continuing effects of IHL rules in post-conflict settings might result in neglecting the humanitarian facet of the right of families to know under international law.

Two human rights treaties focused on enforced disappearances define the terms of the relationship with IHL treaties *durante bello*;[147] these are the Inter-American Convention on Forced Disappearance of Persons and the ICPPED. The former states that '[t]his Convention shall not apply to the [IAC] governed by the 1949 [GCs] and its Protocol concerning protection of wounded, sick, and shipwrecked members of the armed forces; and [POW] and civilians in time of war.'[148] Pursuant to this clause, i) the Inter-American Convention is applicable in NIAC[149] and in post-NIAC cases that arose during the conflict;[150] ii) in IAC, IHL treaties fill the gap created by this clause both during and after the conflict; iii) in post-IAC, the Convention is applicable to those cases arising in this phase.

As for the ICPPED, Article 43 affirms that

[t]his Convention is without prejudice to the provisions of [IHL] including the obligations of the High Contracting Parties to the four [1949 GCs] and the two [APs] thereto, or to the opportunity available to any State Party to authorize the [ICRC] to visit places of detention in situations not covered by [IHL].[151]

---

[145] Milanović emphasizes the continuing effects of a set of IHL rules after the end of an armed conflict; however, he also points out that the application of IHL rules in post-conflict might generate concern over the legitimizing effect that such rules would have against non-state armed group. See Marko Milanović, 'The End of Application of International Humanitarian Law' (2014) 96 International Review of the Red Cross 163, 181.

[146] *Contra:* see sub-section 3.1 in Chapter II.

[147] Clapham (n 88) 706 ff.

[148] Cf. Article XV, Inter-American Convention on Forced Disappearance of Persons.

[149] See, for instance, IACommHR, *Gudiel Álvarez et al ('Diario Militar') v Guatemala, Judgment - Admissibility and Merits (363)* (2010) Report no 116/10-Case 12.590 [7].

[150] Cf. Article III ('the offense shall be deemed continuous or permanent as long as the fate or whereabouts of the victim has not been determined'), Inter-American Convention on Forced Disappearance of Persons.

[151] Cf. Article 43, ICPPED.

This means that the ICPPED is applicable in times of armed conflict (NIAC and IAC) and, as a consequence, to those situations that arise during an armed conflict and continue beyond its termination (for those States that have ratified/acceded to the treaty).[152] Yet the critical aspects of this provision derive from the position of some delegations against it during the negotiations: pursuant to the UK's understanding, Article 43 should operate 'as a "savings clause" in order to ensure that the relevant provisions of [IHL] took precedence over any other provisions contained in the Convention;'[153] in the US' understanding, Article 43 aims to confirm that 'the provisions of the law of armed conflict [...] remain the *lex specialis* in situations of armed conflict and in other situations to which [IHL] applies.'[154] Both understandings are lamentable and distort Article 43, as this provision offers an indication that the ICPPED should be interpreted 'in harmony with IHL provisions'.[155] In other words, 'specific rules applying to certain forms of deprivation of liberty [...] [e.g.,] the rules relating to the protection of [POW], are not modified' by the Convention; acts of enforced disappearance against POW or civilian population are in conflict with the existing IHL rules and might fall under the scope of the ICPPED.[156] The indications of these two treaties leave unaddressed the question of how the relationship should be conceived in practical terms, when the analysis is narrowed down to the rule/rule relationship.

More generally, the 'rhetoric of complementarity'[157] about the fact that IHL and IHRL 'complete and perfect each other'[158] does not help find practical solutions to actual cases.[159] Moreover, such a theoretical assertion leaves a wide margin of appreciation to those who have to figure out the functioning of the co-application of rules belonging to different regimes; this might be detrimental to legal certainty. Thus, next-sub-sections (2.3.2.1, 2.3.2.2, and 2.3.2.3) will expound on the criteria to be used when resorting to the complementarity approach in case of simultaneous application of rules belonging to IHL and IHRL. These criteria are not mutually exclusive but are intertwined with each other. The focus will be on those rules that are relevant to the subject matter; yet this does not mean that such criteria are merely applicable to these rules, since they can be a helpful guidance in other comparable scenarios of normative simultaneousness.

---

[152] Article 24 (6), ICPPED provides for the obligation to continue the investigation until the fate of the disappeared person has been clarified.

[153] UNGA, 'Third Committee Approves Draft Resolution Concerning Convention on Enforced Disappearances' (2006) UN Doc GA/SHC/3872.

[154] 'Note Verbale Dated 20 June 2006 from the Permanent Mission of the United States of America to the UN Office at Geneva Addressed to the Secretariat of the Human Rights Council (Geneva)' (2006) UN Doc A/HRC/1/G/1, 4. See also Taxil (n 141) 132.

[155] Gaggioli (n 1) 330.

[156] Scovazzi and Citroni (n 141) 266.

[157] Tobin (n 137).

[158] Kleffner (n 110) 73.

[159] Milanović (n 89) 100.

2.3.2.1 The typology of the right at stake

From an application standpoint, the first of these criteria is the typology of right at stake, i.e., derogable/non-derogable; absolute/relative. *In bello* and in its aftermath, the protection offered by IHRL does not cease except for the effects of derogations admitted under a limited number of IHRL treaties;[160] however, the derogation regime seems to be irrelevant in post-conflict scenarios, as it is acknowledged that the end of armed conflict would signal 'the resumption of the normal IHRL regime (to the extent that IHL was actually capable of displacing it).'[161] An assessment of the notifications of derogations from the ICCPR and the ECHR shows that States derogating from these instruments have terminated the effects of the derogations at the end of the conflicts where they were involved.[162] The practice, therefore, confirms that the derogation regime is not of much importance in the framework of this book for the following reasons: i) should the conditions necessary to derogate from the treaty provisions be present in a post-conflict scenario, most of the IHRL provisions under which families can claim to

---

[160] For instance, Article 4, ICCPR; Article 15, ECHR; Article 27, ACHR; Article 4, ArCHR.

[161] Milanović (n 145) 181.

[162] Sri Lanka is the sole country that extended the derogations from the ICCPR until 2011, i.e., for two years after the official termination of the NIAC in 2009; in its notification, the State initially referred to 'the existence of an extraordinary security situation' or 'the progressive escalation of violence' and not to an armed conflict. The practice shows that where States have derogated from the ICCPR in concomitance with an armed conflict, the measures have been time-bounded and limited to the duration of the situation on the ground: for instance, Azerbaijan (IAC with Armenia; the measures were taken 'as a result of the escalating aggression by the armed forces of Armenia threatening the very existence of the Azerbaijani State'): state of emergency for a period of 60 days as from 3 April 1993 until 3 June 1993; extended until 2 August 1993; lifted on 22 September 1993); El Salvador (NIAC - the State referred to other reasons motivating the State of emergency, e.g., 'the use of terror and violence by the *Frente Farabundo Marti* to obtain the political authority': different derogation measures have been notified; the last one dates back to 13 November 1989 and lasted 30 days. The conflict lasted twelve years and ended in 1992 with a peace agreement signed under the aegis of the UN); Nepal (NIAC - the State referred to other reasons motivating the State of emergency, e.g., 'terrorist attacks perpetrated by the Maoists in various districts': several derogation measures have been notified between 2002-2005; in may 2005 Nepal notified the termination of the State of emergency. After ten years, the conflict ended in 2006 with the signature of the Comprehensive Peace Agreement); Russia (NIAC, conflict in the Prigorodnyi region of North Ossetia, 1992-1994: the State notified a series of state of emergency declarations including derogatory measures from the ICCPR as of late 1992 until 1994, when this was partly lifted). Ukraine has derogated from the ICCPR and the ECHR due to the outbreak of an armed conflict in its territory (IAC turned into a NIAC); at the time of writing the derogation measures have been adjusted and limited *ratione loci* to the areas where the hostilities are still intense (e.g., territory of certain areas of Donetsk and Luhansk oblasts of Ukraine). This assessment is based on the analysis of two online databases: i.e., the Council of Europe (CoE) database on Reservations and Declarations for the ECHR (<http://www.coe.indt/en/web/conventions/full-list/-/conventions/treaty/005>, accessed 5 July 2016); and the UN Treaty Collection – Section 'Human Rights' - ICCPR (<https://treaties.un.org/Pages/ViewDetails.aspx?src=TREATY&mtdsg_no=IV-4&chapter=4&clang=_en> accessed 2 October 2016). The assessment does not include the Inter-American context, as there is no database available that gathers the list of notifications (despite the existence of a link in the website of the IACommHR). In general, States have not derogated from IHRL provisions because of an armed conflict; this is even more evident in extraterritorial situations. See Milanović (n 89) 104. For an exhaustive review of examples of conflicts where derogations have not been used, see Els Elisabeth Debuf, *Captured in War: Lawful Internment in Armed Conflict* (A Pedone 2013) 164.

have access to information on their missing relatives are non-derogable;[163] ii) those IHL provisions, which are relevant to the subject matter and continue to apply in the aftermath of an armed conflict, are non-derogable.[164]

Different is the case of restrictions that may be applied to certain IHRL provisions at any time. Limitations of the correspondence and communication rights of persons held in captivity are admissible under IHL;[165] the continuation of these situations of deprivation of liberty in the aftermath of an armed conflict cannot exclude the continuation of the application of IHL-based restrictions. Nevertheless, 'the limits to such restrictions are not as carefully circumscribed as in [IHRL]'.[166] Thus, this leads us to the second criterion to be considered when resorting to the complementarity approach vis-à-vis a similar situation.

2.3.2.2. The systemic integration principle

Complementarity often finds its legitimacy within the broad spectrum of the principle of systemic integration enshrined in Article 31 (3) (c) of the VCLT;[167] pursuant to such provision, in the interpretation of a treaty 'any relevant rules of international law applicable in the relations between the parties' shall be taken into account. Such a principle is 'a guideline according to which treaties' should be construed against 'all rules and principles of international law – in other words, international law *understood as a system*'.[168] Against this backdrop, affirming that IHL and IHRL are complementary means that the provisions belonging to one of these branches should be read and interpreted by taking into account other relevant rules belonging to the other.[169]

---

[163] For instance, this is the case of the prohibition of inhuman treatment or the right of each victim of enforced disappearance to know the truth.

[164] Meron highlights that the non-derogability principle of IHL is balanced by 'a certain inherent weakness: the possibility to argue, as governments frequently do, that a particular [IHL] instrument is inapplicable to a given conflict situation'. Meron, 'Convergence of International Humanitarian Law and Human Rights Law' (n 104) 101–102.

[165] See section 4, Chapter II; section 4, Chapter IV.

[166] Louise Doswald-Beck, *Human Rights in Times of Conflict and Terrorism* (Oxford University Press 2011) 448–449.

[167] For instance, Droege underlines that the concept of complementarity is of a policy rather than of a legal nature. In her view, complementarity can mean that 'human rights law and humanitarian law do not contradict each other but, being based on the same principles and values can influence and reinforce each other mutually. In this sense, complementarity' directly reflects the principle of systemic integration which is enshrined in Article 31 (3) (c) VCLT. See Droege (n 109) 337.

[168] ILC, 'Report of the International Law Commission, Fifty-Seventh Session, Chapter XI "Fragmentation of International Law: Difficulties Arising From Diversification and Expansion of International Law"' (2005) UN Doc A/60/10 para 467; Campbell McLachlan, 'The Principle of Systemic Integration and Article 31(3)(C) of the Vienna Convention' (2005) 54 The International and Comparative Law Quarterly 279, 280.

[169] Various international judicial bodies have referred to this principle. These include, for instance, the ICJ and the WTO Appellate Body. For a review of the international and regional case law where this principle has been used, see d'Aspremont, J and Tranchez (n 90) 235–238; McLachlan (n 168). With regard to its use in relation to the interplay between IHL and IHRL rules, cf. ECtHR, *Hassan v The UK (GC)* (n 108) [102]. See also IACommHR, *Inter-State Petition IP-02 Admissibility, Franklin Guillermo Aisalla Molina, Ecuador - Colombia* (2010) Report No 112/10 [121] and AfCommHPR, 'General Comment No. 3 on the African Charter on Human And Peoples' Rights: The Right to Life (Article 4)' (2015) para 13.

In this sense, the principle of systemic integration has been considered a criterion reflective of the need to interpret a set of provisions in harmony with other rules of international law of which both form part.[170]

Chapter II emphasized that the restriction regime under IHRL is much more developed in terms of parameters that must be met by State authorities in order to lawfully interfere with a human right. As briefly mentioned in the previous sub-section, limitations of the correspondence and communication rights of persons held in captivity are admissible under IHL. The continuation of deprivation of liberty in the aftermath of an armed conflict cannot exclude the continuation of IHL-based restrictions. In light of the considerations above in relation to the principle of systemic integration, the limited scope of the regulatory regime of IHL-based restrictions should be interpreted in light of the restriction regime under IHRL.[171] Since the latter fills the gaps present under IHL, it should be considered the reference framework for regulating any form of IHL-based restriction that might still be applicable in post-conflict settings.[172]

While during the conflict the application of any restriction under IHL requires to strike a balance between humanity and military necessity (see, for instance, the situation of spies), in post-conflict settings this exercise is not tenable in light of the absence of any military necessity-based justification. Yet restrictions of certain guarantees might still be necessary for the preservation of, *inter alia,* national security, State order, or protection of others' rights; thus, the balance to be struck is between individual rights and society's needs, as required by IHRL (see Section 4 of Chapter IV).

2.3.2.3. The most favourable rule

Where the provision at stake concerns an absolute − i.e., not limitable − right or guarantee, which is present under both branches with different degrees of protection, the principle of the most-favorable/protective-rule for the individual applies. Enshrined in the main universal and regional human rights treaties as well as in the IHL ones,[173] this clause aims at safeguarding the rights recognized or existing under domestic or international law independently of the instrument where these rights are recognized to a lesser extent/are not recognized. Its rationale is inferable from the general function of contemporary international law,[174] i.e.,

---

[170] Cf. ECtHR, *Hassan v The UK (GC)* (n 108) [102].

[171] The interpretation of IHL in light of IHRL is not unusual. Cf. ICTY, *Prosecutor v. Anto Furundžija, Trial Judgment* (n 17) [143]; IACommHR, *Inter-State Petition IP-02 Admissibility, Franklin Guillermo Aisalla Molina, Ecuador - Colombia* (n 169) [121].

[172] Doswald-Beck (n 166) 449.

[173] Cf. Article 5(2) ICCPR, Article 53 ECHR, Article 29(b) ACHR, Article 41 CRC, Article 1 CAT. As for IHL, cf. Article 75(8) AP I.

[174] As underlined by the ICTY '[a] State-sovereignty-oriented approach [to international law] has been gradually supplanted by a human-being-oriented approach. Gradually the maxim of Roman law *hominum causa omne jus constitutum est* […] has gained a firm foothold in the international community as well.' ICTY, *Prosecutor v Duško Tadić aka 'Dule', Decision on the Defence Motion for Interlocutory Appeal on Jurisdiction* (1995) Case no. IT-94-1-A [97].

to safeguard international peace, security and justice in relations between States, and human rights as well as the [RoL] domestically inside States for the benefit of human beings, who, in substance, are the ultimate addressees of international law.[175]

The principle of the most-favorable/protective-rule is part of the framework addressing the issue of missing persons: specifically, Article 37 ICPPED states that

[n]othing in this Convention shall affect any provisions which are more conducive to the protection of all persons from enforced disappearance and which may be contained in:

(*a*) The law of a State Party;

(*b*) International law in force for that State.

The exogenous effects of this clause consist in the regulation of the relationship of the ICPPED with external domestic/international standards: those that are more conducive to the protection of the individuals should prevail.

Under IHL, the most-favorable/protective-rule clause generates two kinds of effects, i.e., exogenous and endogenous. The former are germane to the scope of this argumentation; for instance, these effects derive from the reading of the Preambles of AP I and AP II which put an emphasis on the purpose of both instruments, i.e., to reaffirm and develop the provisions protecting the victims of armed conflicts and to supplement measures intended to reinforce their application' (AP I); to 'ensure a better protection for the victims of ... armed conflicts' (AP II). In both cases it is clear that the standard ensuring better protection for the victims of the conflict should be the one that prevails. The endogenous effects, i.e., relationship of an IHL rule with other IHL rules, are those generated by Article 33(2) AP I (*missing persons*): this provision serves the purpose of filling possible gaps within the IHL system, since it lays down the obligations of the Parties to the conflict 'with respect to persons who would not receive more favorable consideration under the Conventions and [AP I]', i.e., 'persons who were previously inadequately covered or not covered at all'.[176]

The clause of the most-favorable/protective-rule is mentioned among the conflict-solving tools when a conflict of norms arises;[177] nevertheless, it can also be conceived as a compatibility clause regulating the relationship of concurring – not conflicting – standards.[178] In other words, where IHL and IHRL rules regulate the same conduct or provide for the same guarantee with different

---

[175] Christian Tomuschat, *International Law: Ensuring the Survival of Mankind on the Eve of a New Century: General Course on Public International Law*, vol 281 (1999) (Brill, Nijhoff 2001) 23.

[176] Sandoz and others (n 127) para 1247, 355.

[177] See Ali Sadat-Akhavi, *Methods of Resolving Conflicts Between Treaties* (Martinus Nijhoff Publishers 2003) 213 ff; AL Graf-Brugère, 'A Lex Favorabilis? Resolving Norm Conflicts between Human Rights Law and Humanitarian Law' in Gloria Gaggioli and Robert Kolb (eds), *Research Handbook on Human Rights and Humanitarian Law* (Edward Elgar Publishing 2013).

[178] Sadat-Akhavi (n 177) 217.

degree of protection for the same person, this clause clarifies and helps understand how the cumulative application of these rules works.[179]

For instance, although, at the scholarly level, the IHL-based right of families to know the fate of their relatives is considered the embryonic version of the more articulated IHRL-based right to know the truth regarding the enforced disappearance of persons (cf. Art. 24 ICPPED),[180] the former remains preliminary to the latter. Indeed, the former is disconnected from any form of criminal conduct and, consequently, its realization is not immediately associated with an enforced disappearance nor with a criminal investigation. While access to information is implicit in the former,[181] it cannot be taken for granted in the latter (see Chapter IV); indeed, access to information might be delimited in the framework of a criminal investigation, which is not primarily meant to inform the family members.[182] Based on these considerations, the IHL-based right of families to know the fate of their relatives should be the protective baseline against which to consider the requests for information of families of persons reported as missing. The IHRL-based right to know the truth regarding the enforced disappearance of persons is triggered by the co-presence of a set of factors[183] and would be added as a further layer of protection to the former when these factors are present.

Simultaneous application of similar rules belonging to different branches of international law can generate interpretative discrepancies; from the sub-sections above, such discrepancies result from the foundational tenets enshrined in the measures aimed at handling uncertainty. For instance, the IHL-based duty to account for persons reported as missing in an armed conflict and the IHRL-based duty to carry out an investigation into an alleged human rights violation are not interchangeable; both are not set forth in the *jus scriptum* but have been inferred from existing provisions under IHL[184] and IHRL.[185] The investigative character of the measures aimed at implementing the obligation to account for missing persons entails two possible scenarios: on the one hand, efforts to account for missing persons respond to a human need of family members to know the fate

---

[179] In this sense, see ibid. Moreover, by recalling the above-mentioned clause, the OHCHR has stressed that 'the individual should be entitled to the most protective provisions of applicable international, national, or local laws. Accordingly, if humanitarian law affords better rights protections than human rights law, humanitarian law should be applied - and vice versa.' See OHCHR, 'Training Manual on Human Rights Monitoring' (United Nations 2001) UN Doc HR/P/PT/7, 38; OHCHR, 'Manual on Human Rights Monitoring' (United Nations 2011) UN Doc HR/P/PT/7/Rev.1, Chapter 5, 15.

[180] See, for instance, Droege (n 109) 343.

[181] ECtHR, *Janowiec and others v Russia, Judgment* (2012) App nos. 55508/08 and others (ECtHR) [163]; *Varnava and Others v Turkey, Judgment (GC)* (2009) App nos. 16064/90 and others [161].

[182] See, for instance, ECtHR, *Cakicisoy et al v Cyprus, Decision* (2014) App no. 5523/12 [45]; contra: ECtHR, *Imakayeva v Russia, Judgment* (2007) App no. 7615/02 [165].

[183] For instance, a case of enforced disappearance, which falls under the ICPPED, can trigger this further protective layer. For an examination of the judicial assessment of the legal implications of armed-conflict-generated uncertainty, see Chapter IV.

[184] In this sense, see Jean-Marie Henckaerts and Louise Doswald-Beck, *Customary International Humanitarian Law: Practice*, vol II (Cambridge University Press 2005) 2757.

[185] See Chapter IV on the role of the judiciary in extrapolating these obligations.

and whereabouts of their relatives and, therefore, exclusively aim at informing the family; on the other, in case of serious human rights violations, the duty to account for missing persons can intermingle with the duty to carry out a prompt, impartial, thorough, and independent official investigation aimed at identifying those responsible and prosecuting them. Chapter IV will explore the intertwined relation of these obligations in light of the human rights case law. Suffice it here to state that these two obligations are not mutually exclusive but seem to overlap; yet the duty to account for a missing person is not mandatorily triggered by an alleged violation of IHL or IHRL. Moreover, under IHL the duty of parties to the conflict to account for missing persons entails investigative activities aimed at responding to the families' requests for information on their missing relatives. Human rights judicial bodies have inferred this obligation from human rights treaty provisions and have framed it in humanitarian terms, i.e., its purpose is to address the requests for information of the family members. Different is the case of the apparently similar duty to carry out an investigation into alleged violations of human rights law: its purpose is to shed light upon the circumstances of the violations and to find those responsible. In this sense, the duty to account for missing persons is a humanitarian-driven protective baseline to which further layers of protection can be added depending on the circumstances of the case.

In sum, the immediate implication that the clause of the most-favorable/protective-rule has on State authorities is that of serving as a reminder of their obligations under other treaties, if these are more favorable for the protection of the individual concerned.[186] Pragmatically, when thousands of people are missing in the aftermath of an armed conflict, it is immediately impossible to discern who is missing because of a violation and who is missing due to other reasons connected to the conflict (e.g., missing in action).[187] In such situation, the State not only might lack the capacity of carrying out measures making such discernment conceivable, but also might lack the political, judicial, and economic resources that would make a full implementation of the dual facets of the duty to account for missing persons achievable.[188] The need for external support offered by international actors becomes key; in this respect, their conduct must be consistent with the legal standards concerning missing persons and their families; a reality-check will confirm/refute that this is the case in practice.[189]

The families of missing persons live in constant anxiety; uncertainty does not enable them to move on to reconciliation and rehabilitation despite the end of the conflict. Enabling them to have access to information on the whereabouts and on

---

[186] Sadat-Akhavi (n 177) 231.

[187] Nonetheless, this distinction can emerge in the assessment of the needs of the families. See ICRC, 'Living with Uncertainty. Needs of the Families of Missing Persons in Sri Lanka' (2016) 12 <https://www.icrc.org/en/document/sri-lanka-families-missing-persons> accessed 2 August 2016.

[188] For instance, the ECtHR has detected similar difficulties in the first ten year following the war in Bosnia and Herzegovina. Cf. ECtHR, *Palić v Bosnia and Herzegovina, Judgment* (2011) App no. 4704/04 (ECtHR) [70].

[189] Chapter V will revolve around the duty to account for missing persons in peace processes.

the life conditions of their relatives[190] is an essentially humanitarian act. At the same time, need of families for accountability of those who are involved in the disappearance of their beloved ones is not secondary. Thus, the tenets[191] that underpin the international legal framework must be part of the assessment of which rule is more favorable/protective vis-à-vis the range of needs of families of missing persons in post-conflict settings.

CONCLUSIONS

This Chapter argues that while the contemporary legal framework applicable in armed conflict mainly focuses on addressing the suffering of the families, IHRL tackles the criminal conduct behind the disappearances. The examination of the legal responses to the post-conflict uncertainty about the fate and whereabouts of persons under international law requires an untraditional approach to these branches with a view to understanding how they interrelate in the transition process from an armed conflict to peace. It also requires recognizing that, in post-conflict settings, State authorities might not have a full-fledged capacity to abide by the basic obligation of the framework on missing persons, i.e., the duty to account for the missing and to inform their families.[192]

The Chapter has identified the underlying principles of the international legal framework intended for the protection of human beings at all times. First, humanity is a general principle of international law that is at the foundation of both IHL and IHRL; second, accountability is one of the end-goals[193] of the measures adopted to address past crimes and violations. The two principles constitute the barebones of the legal framework and of the institutional design concerning the protection of all human beings. Both influence the whole legal system in post-conflict settings; however, while the former has a normative dimension and can be source of rights and obligations, this is not the case for the latter.[194] Indeed, humanitarian and accountability-driven courses of actions make part of the broader project that international and national entities undertake in this phase. These must be examined in order to assess whether the operationalization on the ground of the principles identified above is consistent with the international legal framework on the missing (see Chapter V). From a policy perspective, the theoretical accounts illustrated in the present Chapter will be conducive to the clarification of the tenets of a (coordinated) humanitarian/accountability-driven strategy that fully integrates the issue of missing persons in post-conflict peacebuilding processes.

---

[190] See among others Petar Šarčević, 'War and Disintegration of the Family' (1999) 1 Journal of Law and Family Studies 109; ICRC, 'Living with Uncertainty. Needs of the Families of Missing Persons in Sri Lanka' (n 187); ICRC, 'Families of Missing Persons in Nepal: A Study of Their Needs' (ICRC 2009).

[191] See *supra* sub-sections 1.2 and 2.2 of the present Chapter.

[192] See sub-section 3.1.2 in Chapter IV.

[193] Bell (n 3) 182; De Brabandere (n 3) 139.

[194] De Brabandere argues that the principle of accountability can have a normative dimension when incorporated in specific rules. De Brabandere (n 3) 139.

Chapter II reached the conclusion that in post-conflict settings, although residual, IHL still applies; in the same contextual setting, while fully applicable, IHRL is challenged by the obstacles on the ground that State authorities face in implementing their obligations. This general picture is looked at through the prism of *jus post bellum,* understood as a normative guidance in the evaluation of action, application, interpretation, and interplay of norms.[195] In these terms, post-conflict settings feature a complementary relationship between IHL and IHRL rules on missing persons.

In light of the wide margin of appreciation left to those who have to figure out the functioning of the co-application of rules belonging to different regimes, this Chapter has identified the criteria to be used in resorting to the complementarity approach. The definition of the set of criteria expounded on in sub-section 2.3.2 shows the possibility of overcoming existing *lacunae* that are present under IHL in relation to the protection of human beings. It also shows that there is the need to conceive the implementation of the whole *corpus juris* for the protection of human beings in a more effective manner by, for instance, identifying the most protective standard when two rules simultaneously apply. The result is not only an increased level of protection, but also a contribution to the post-conflict efforts towards reconciliation.

Such an understanding of the relationship between IHL and IHRL rules furthers the *jus post bellum* project of restoring peace, which is not tantamount to restoring the *status quo ante,* i.e., the situation that led to the conflict. Indeed, this reading of the interplay is conducive to the detection of a duty to cooperate between the (former) parties to the conflict. Since the IHL-based duty to account for missing persons requires a certain degree of cooperation between parties to the conflict *durante bello,* the continuation of the application of such duty cannot be disconnected from the obligation of former parties to the conflict to cooperate in post-conflict contexts.[196] The failure to do so might directly impact on the

---

[195] See the constitutional perspective put forward by Easterday (arguing that *jus post bellum* is comprised of the laws and norms stemming from current settled bodies of international law as well as developing normative practices of non-state actors and organizations; also arguing that it offers an interpretive framework, a site of coordination, and a site of discourse that can help the transition to a sustainable peace). JS Easterday, 'Peace Agreements as a Framework for Jus Post Bellum' in Carsten Stahn, Jennifer S Easterday and Jens Iverson (eds), *Jus Post Bellum: Mapping the normative Foundations* (Oxford University Press 2014) 412. See, more generally, the full anthology: Carsten Stahn, Jennifer S Easterday and Jens Iverson (eds), *Jus Post Bellum: Mapping the Normative Foundations* (Oxford University Press 2014). See also Carsten Stahn, Jens Iverson and Jennifer Easterday, 'Special Issue: Jus Post Bellum and Foreign Investment' (2015) 16 The Journal of World Investment & Trade 583.

[196] The post-conflict duty to cooperate between State and non-state armed actors has been detected by the ICJ in *Congo v Uganda* case. The Court affirmed that 'while it has pronounced on the violations of [IHRL] and [IHL] committed by Ugandan military forces on the territory of the DRC, it nonetheless observes that the actions of the various parties in the complex conflict in the DRC have contributed to the immense suffering faced by the Congolese population. *The Court is painfully aware that many atrocities have been committed in the course of the conflict. It is incumbent on all those involved in the conflict to support the peace process in the DRC and other peace processes in the Great Lakes area, in order to ensure respect for human rights in the region.*' (emphasis added). ICJ, *DRC v Uganda (2005)* (n 101) [221]. Peace and reconciliation processes can be fragile when the

human rights of those who live with uncertainty and might result into a violation of the State's obligation of due diligence under IHRL. Chapter IV will, *inter alia,* elaborate on the legal nuances of this final point.

issue of missing persons is not effectively addressed; cooperation is therefore essential even at a more advanced phase of the reconciliation process. For instance, this has been the case in the Former Yugoslavia, where Bosnia and Herzegovina, Croatia, Serbia, and Montenegro signed the Declaration on the Role of the State in Addressing the issue of the Missing in 2014. Among other things, these States asserted their conviction that 'cooperation between governments is necessary and that the exchange of information is encouraged and is often a necessary condition for establishing efficient, reliable, and transparent processes of locating and identifying the missing [...]'. They also expressed their commitment to addressing the issue of persons missing as result of armed conflicts and human rights abuses 'as a responsibility of the State to ensure a lasting peace [...]'. See 'Declaration on The Role Of The State In Addressing The Issue Of Persons Missing As A Consequence Of Armed Conflict And Human Rights Abuses', Mostar, 29 August 2014, paras 1, 4 https://www.icmp.int/wp-content/uploads/2014/08/signed-declaration-2.pdf accessed 12 January 2017.

CHAPTER IV.

THE FAMILIES' CLAIM FOR INFORMATION AND THE STATE'S REFUSAL/INABILITY TO RESPOND: CONTEXTUALIZING TWO OPPOSITE CLAIMS IN POST-CONFLICT

Families of those reported missing in the context of IHRL/IHL violations committed during an armed conflict have not only the right to know where their relatives are and whether they are still alive, but also the right to know who is responsible for the violations and why their loved ones were targeted.[1] In other words, they have the right to be informed.[2] Ideally, one would expect State authorities to carry out information-seeking measures aimed at informing the families (humanitarian measures) and shedding light upon human rights and IHL violations (accountability-driven measures). What if, however, State authorities are overwhelmed by the circumstances on the ground and the domestic legal system is incapable of dealing effectively with human rights and IHL violations committed during the conflict? Far from being merely theoretical, this question has arisen in specific contexts.[3] Can post-conflict circumstances justify any form of restriction on the efforts of families to have access to information on their relatives?[4]

As pointed out in the introduction to this book, the role of the judge entails to carry out an assessment of claims with varying degrees of legal merit:[5] through the prism of the case law of human rights adjudicators, the legal merit of two claims must be assessed, i.e., the claim of families for information on their relatives and the claim of State authorities for refusing/delaying to uphold the families' requests. This Chapter will, therefore, look at these claims in light of the case law of human rights bodies (judicial and quasi-judicial).[6] This analysis

---

[1] Cf. Principles 2 and Principle 4, UN Commission on Human Rights, 'Promotion and Protection of Human Rights: Impunity. Add.1 "Updated Set of Principles for the Protection and Promotion of Human Rights through Action to Combat Impunity (Orentlicher Principles)"' (2005) UN Doc E/CN.4/2005/102/Add.1. See also Jeffrey Davis, *Seeking Human Rights Justice in Latin America. Truth, Extra-Territorial Courts, and the Process of Justice* (Cambridge University Press 2015) 111–112.

[2] Davis affirms that the right to truth entitles the families to have access to 'documents, testimony, images, and other forms of recorded evidence'. Davis (n 1) 111–112.

[3] Cf. ECtHR, *Palić v Bosnia and Herzegovina, Judgment* (2011) App no. 4704/04 (ECtHR) [70]; *Sejdić and Finci v Bosnia and Herzegovina, Judgment (GC)* (2009) Apps no 27996/06 and 34836/06 [47].

[4] See *infra* section 4 of this Chapter.

[5] See Hersch Lauterpacht, *The Development of International Law by the International Court* (Cambridge University Press 1982) 3.

[6] These include the IACtHR, the ECtHR, and the AfCtHPR. As far as quasi-judicial bodies are concerned, the assessments of the HRCee, the IACommHR, and the AfCommHPR will be the focus of the examination. The CAT's assessments will also be part of the examination, where these are relevant to the subject matter. Although the contribution of the CED to this discourse might be

will lead to identify the legal implications of uncertainty for the rights of family members (section 1) and to unfold the interplay of the humanitarian and accountability dimensions (sections 2 and 3) peculiar to the issue of missing persons through the prism of IHRL. This Chapter will also build in the considerations which have been articulated in Chapter III on the relationship between IHL and IHRL in post-conflict settings so as to unravel the issue of whether under international law there is room for lawful restrictions on the right of families to know the fate of their relatives (section 4).

1. THE INHUMANITY OF UNCERTAINTY
ABOUT THE FATE AND WHEREABOUTS OF MISSING RELATIVES

The complacency of State authorities towards mental suffering generated by uncertainty about the fate of a relative is one of the forms in which human dignity can severely be affected. The anguish and distress endured over a prolonged period of time makes the general principle of respect for human dignity void. As a matter of fact, families of missing persons endure the same experiences as the rest of the population affected by an armed conflict, but are also afflicted by additional problems relating to the disappearance (including constant fear that death will be confirmed; no official acknowledgement of the status of "missing person"). [7] Uncertainty can be the source of a 'direct injury'[8] at the detriment of those who are most in need to know, [9] i.e., family members of

---

valuable, at the time of writing (April 2016), the CED has issued only one View on an individual communication against Argentina (under Article 31 ICPPED, the CED may receive and consider individual communications, also called complaints; according to the working methods of the CED, the decisions on the merits of the communications are of a quasi-judicial character. CED, 'Working Methods' para 43 <http://www.ohchr.org/EN/HRBodies/CED/Pages/WorkingMethods.aspx> accessed 12 March 2015.) More generally, judicial and quasi-judicial bodies assessments fall within the realm of 'subsidiary means for the determination of rules of law'. Cf. Article 38 (1) (d), Statute of the International Court of Justice, 59 Stat. 1055, 33 UNTS 993 (26 June 1945) (hereinafter ICJ Statute).

[7] ICRC, 'The Missing. ICRC Progress Report' (ICRC 2006) <goo.gl/og1Gf1> accessed 12 June 2016.

[8] See Tamar Feldman, 'Indirect Victims, Direct Injury: Recognising Relatives as Victims under the European Human Rights System' [2009] European Human Rights Law Review 50.

[9] The inhumanity of disappearance of a person and the distress caused by the uncertainty to the family members have led the HRCee to broaden the scope *ratione materiae* and *personae* of Article 7 ICCPR (protection from torture). The ECtHR adopts a dynamic approach to the interpretation of the ECHR, particularly, but not limited to, the context of Article 3 ECHR (prohibition of torture and of inhuman or degrading treatment), which 'enshrines one of the fundamental values of the democratic societies'. Soudre talks about 'dynamisme interprétatif' in order to explain the interpretative process used by the ECtHR; with this expression he refers to the 'ensemble des techniques d'interprétation utilisées par le juge européen pour conférer aux droits consacrés par la Convention leur pleine effectivité'. Frédéric Sudre, 'L'économie Générale de L'article 3 CEDH' in Catherine-Amélie Chassin (ed), *La portée de l'article 3 de la Convention européenne des droits de l'homme* (Bruylant 2006) 8. On the fundamental values, see ECtHR, *Soering v The UK, Judgment* (1989) App no. 14038/88 [88]. The dynamic interpretation developed by the ECtHR is less present in the case law of the IACtHR, since Article 5 ACHR (right to human treatment) is much more structured and detailed than Article 3 ECHR: the general idea that lays at the basis of the Article is the preservation of the integrity – physical, mental and moral – of every person (cf. Article 5(1) ACHR). When the issue has been tackled by the AfCommHPR, the main provision at stake has been Article 5 AfChHPR (Prohibition of Torture and Cruel, Inhuman and Degrading Treatment).

missing persons, and of their human rights.[10] In cases of disappearance occurred during an armed conflict or in another setting, international and regional human rights bodies have unveiled the humanitarian spirit[11] of specific human rights provisions. Uncertainty about the fate and whereabouts of individuals not only can infringe upon the human rights of family members of the missing, but also can mean that the State has not done enough to prevent and/or address this situation.

The contextual setting – armed conflict/post-conflict – impacts on the capacity of State authorities to uphold the requests of family members for information. Context-related factors, which directly/indirectly have prevented State authorities from abiding by their IHRL obligations, can be of relevance in the judicial assessment of the conduct of State authorities and of the impact of such conduct on the human rights of family members (sub-section 1). The inter-American system deeply differs from other human rights systems, as the context is meaningless when there are allegations of enforced disappearance (sub-section 1.2). Discrepancies in the judicial assessment seem to emerge vis-à-vis the legal merit of the claim that uncertainty infringes upon the human rights standards aimed at preserving the right to respect for family life (sub-section 1.3).[12]

1.1. The importance of factors connected to the post-conflict situation on the ground

In considering whether a family member is a victim of a human rights violation due to the disappearance of the next of kin,[13] the HRCee[14] has adopted

---

[10] Jenny Edkins, *Missing: Persons and Politics* (Cornell University Press 2011) viii.

[11] 'Humanitarian treaties' is a *formula* that has been embedded in Article 60 (5) of the VCLT, mentioning the 'provisions relating to the protection of the human person contained in treaties of humanitarian character'. As the VCLT's commentary states though, Article 60 (5) mainly refers to 'multilateral conventions such as the 1949 Geneva Conventions and the 1977 Additional Protocols'; however, the question is highly debated of whether para. 5 plays also a role at the contractual level, where it addresses the so-called non-reciprocal treaties which create rights in favour of individuals. See Mark Eugen Villiger, *Commentary on the 1969 Vienna Convention on the Law of Treaties* (Martinus Nijhoff Publishers 2009) 747.

[12] Cf. Article 8 ECHR (right to respect for private and family life), Article 17 ACHR (rights of the family), Article 11(2) (right to privacy) ACHR.

[13] Only in one occasion - *Quinteros v Uruguay* - the HRCee has explicitly recognized that the relatives are victims of the same violations of the disappeared victim and have a right to know the fate of their beloved ones. Indeed, as early as 1983, in *Quinteros v Uruguay*, the Committee found a violation of Article 7 ICCPR at the detriment of the mother of the victim of disappearance due to the anguish and stress caused to her by the disappearance of her daughter and by the continuing uncertainty concerning her fate and whereabouts; thus, the mother of the disappeared was considered a victim of a violation under the Covenant. HRCee, *María del Carmen Almeida de Quinteros et al v Uruguay, Comm No 107/1981* (1983) UN Doc. CCPR/C/OP/2 at 138 [14]. In *Sarma v Sri Lanka* the Committee recalled *Quinteros v Uruguay* with regard to the relatives' right under Article 7 and, in the footnote no. 24, clarified that in *Quinteros* the Committee considered the family members of the disappeared persons victims of the same violations perpetrated against the disappeared, i.e., violation of the right to liberty and security (Article 9, ICCPR), and violation of the right of all persons in custody to be treated humanely (Article 10 (1), ICCPR). HRCee, *Sarma v Sri Lanka, Comm No 950/2000* [2003] UN Doc CCPRC78D9502000 [9.5].

[14] The Committee itself recognizes that its function is limited to considering individual communications; as such, it is not 'that of a judicial body'. Nonetheless, 'the views issued by the Committee under the

an approach that is sensitive to the suffering of family members, be they parents, children, siblings, spouses, aunts and uncles, grandchildren or cousins of the missing person.[15] There is no criterion that is expressly intended for the assessment of the proximity of family links (*contra:* ECtHR), for the main focus is on the suffering generated by uncertainty.

A set of factors that generate uncertainty and/or show an evident disregard by the authorities of the impact of uncertainty on family members of missing persons have been inferred from the case law related to disappearances in the context of armed conflicts (e.g., Nepal, Bosnia-Herzegovina): notably,

– the disappearance as such;[16]

– the conduct of State authorities (i.e., no explanation to the family members with regard to the fate of their beloved one;[17] no investigation to elucidate the fate of the missing person and, in case of death, to return his human remains to the family;[18] delay in providing information and failure of making the progress of the investigation promptly accessible[19]);

Optional Protocol exhibit some important characteristics of a judicial decision. They are arrived at in a judicial spirit, including the impartiality and independence of Committee members, the considered interpretation of the language of the Covenant, and the determinative character of the decisions.' Cf. HRCee, 'General Comment No. 33: The Obligations of States Parties under the Optional Protocol to the International Covenant on Civil and Political Rights' (2008) UN Doc. CCPR/C/GC/33, para 11. This book, therefore, deems it appropriate to address the Views of the Committee as 'case law'. On the quasi-judicial role of the HRCee, see T Buergenthal, 'The U.N. Human Rights Committee' in Armin von Bogdandy, Rüdiger Wolfrum and Christiane E Philipp (eds), *Max Planck Yearbook of United Nations Law Online*, vol 5 (Martinus Nijhoff Publishers 2001) 364, 395–396.

[15] As for parents: cf. HRCee, *El Abani v The Libyan Arab Jamahiriya, Comm no 1640/2007* (2010) UN Doc. CCPR/C/99/D/1640/2007; *Boucherf v Algeria, Comm No 1196/2003* (2006) UN Doc. CCPR/C/86/D/1196/2003 [9.7]. As for children: cf. HRCee, *Zarzi v Algeria, Comm No 1780/2008* (2011) UN Doc. CCPR/C/101/D/1780/2008 [8]. As for siblings: HRCee, *El Abani v The Libyan Arab Jamahiriya* [7.5]. As for spouses: HRCee, *Bousroual v Algeria, Comm No 1085/2002* [2006] UN Doc CCPRC86D10852002 [9.8]; *Zarzi v Algeria* [8]; *Abubakar Amirov v Russia Federation, Comm no 1447/2006* (2009) UN Doc. CCPR/C/95/D/1447/2006 [11.7]. As for aunts and uncles: HRCee, *Benaziza v Algeria, Comm No 1588/2007* (2010) UN Doc CCPR/C/99/D/1588/2007 [10]. As for grandchildren: ibid. As for cousins: HRCee, *Salem Saad Ali Bashasha v The Libyan Arab Jamahiriya, Comm No 1776/2008* (2010) UN Doc. CCPR/C/100/D/1776/2008 [7.5]. All quoted in Helen Keller and Olga Chernishova, 'Disappearance Cases before the European Court of Human Rights and the UN Human Rights Committee: Convergence and Divergences' (2012) 32 Human Rights Law Journal 237, 242.

[16] Keller and Chernishova (n 15) 242.

[17] In the context of the NIAC in Nepal (1996-2006) more than 1,500 persons have been claimed missing; several cases have been brought before the UN HRCee. The context *per se* - the armed conflict - does not appear to be decisive in order for the Committee to find a violation of the rights of the family members of the disappeared person; moreover, the disappearance *per se* is not the sole cause impacting on the family members. As noted in *Sharmila v Nepal*, the violation of Article 7 ICCPR with regard to the wife and the minor daughter of the disappeared person is the result of a set of elements (i.e., the disappearance, the fact that no explanation was given from the authorities to the family members with regard to the fate of their beloved one, the fact that no investigation has been carried out to elucidate his fate and, in case of death, to return his human remains to the family). Cf. HRCee, *Sharmila Tripathi v Nepal, Comm no 2111/2011* (2008) UN Doc. CCPR/C/112/D/2111/2011 [7.5].

[18] ibid.

[19] 'To oblige families of disappeared persons to have the family member declared dead, in order to be eligible for compensation, while the investigation is ongoing, makes the availability of compensation

– the familial dynamics generated by the disappearance (e.g., the fact that one of the family members needs to play the role of breadwinner in order to minimize the impact of the absence of the missing person – the actual breadwinner – on the family);[20]

– post-conflict institutional/legislative constraints on the family in order to get social allowances/state's support (e.g., the case where the family is forced to declare dead the missing person in order to have access to pensions/social allowances).[21]

---

dependent on a harmful process and constitutes inhuman and degrading treatment in violation of article 7, read alone and in conjunction with article [2 (3) ICCPR] with respect to the authors'. Cf. HRCee, *Tija Hero, Ermina Hero, Armin Hero v Bosnia and Herzegovina, Comm no 1966/2010* (2014) UN Doc. CCPR/C/112/D/1966/2010 [9.7]; *Fatima Rizvanović and Ruvejda Rizvanović v Bosnia and Herzegovina, Comm no 1997/2010* (2014) UN Doc. CCPR/C/110/D/1997/2010 [9.6]; *Zilkija Selimović et al v Bosnia and Herzegovina, Comm no 2003/2010*, (2014) UN Doc. CCPR/C/111/D/2003/2010 [12.7]; *Nevzeta Durić and Nedzad Durić v Bosnia and Herzegovina, Comm No 1956/2010* (2014) UN Doc. CCPR/C/111/D/1956/2010 [9.8].

[20] Specifically, the Committee observed that due to the disappearance of his cousin in the context of the conflict in Nepal, 'Top Bahadur Basnet took over the responsibility as head of the Basnet family and provided for his cousin's four sisters and father, and that both authors have not only a formal family link, but a very close relationship since they grew up living in the same house as one family. It also [observed] that Top Bahadur Basnet submitted a request for investigation to the [Nepal Human Rights Commission] and addressed himself to several authorities and private institutions in order to establish his cousin's whereabouts; and that he received contradicting information as to his cousin's fate and whereabouts by the authorities'. Cf. HRCee, *Jit Man Basnet and Top Bahadur Basnet v Nepal, Comm no 2051/2011* (2014) UN Doc. CCPR/C/112/D/2051/2011 [8.4]. The Committee found a violation of Article 7 read alone; a violation of the right to remedy – Article 2(3) ICCPR - read in conjunction with Article 7 was also found. Cf. Ibid [8.8]. The HRCee demanded Nepal to adopt measures aimed, *inter alia*, at providing information about the missing person pursuant to the obligation to provide the authors with an effective remedy (cf. Article 2 (3) ICCPR): cf. ibid [10 (e.g., conducting a thorough and effective investigation into the facts surrounding the detention of Jit Man Basnet and the treatment suffered at the Bhairavnath barracks; providing the authors with detailed information about the results of this investigation)]. See also HRCee, *Ram Kumar Bhandari v Nepal, Comm no 2031/2011* (2014) UN Doc CCPR/C/112/D/2031/2011 [8.6 and 10]; *Sharmila Tripathi v. Nepal* (n 17) [7.5 and 9]. David affirms that the right to know the facts surrounding an enforced disappearance, including the fate and whereabouts, is part of the right to remedy. See Valeska David, 'The Expanding Right to an Effective Remedy: Common Developments at the Human Rights Committee and the Inter-American Court' (2014) 3 British Journal of American Legal Studies 259, 269.

[21] The Committee does not specify what aspect of Article 7 is violated (torture, inhuman or degrading treatment); in relation to the last factor listed above, the Committee underlines that such a conduct 'constitutes inhuman and degrading treatment in violation of article 7, read alone and in conjunction with article 2, paragraph 3, of the Covenant with respect to the authors.' HRCee, *Tija Hero, Ermina Hero, Armin Hero v. Bosnia and Herzegovina* (n 19) [9.7]; *Fatima Rizvanović and Ruvejda Rizvanović v. Bosnia and Herzegovina* (n 19) [9.6]; *Zilkija Selimović et al. v. Bosnia and Herzegovina* (n 19) [12.7]; *Nevzeta Durić and Nedzad Durić v. Bosnia and Herzegovina* (n 19) [9.8]. Similarly, the Committee Against Torture (CAT) has noted that requiring the families of missing persons to certify the death of the family member in order to receive compensation could constitute a form of inhuman and degrading treatment for such persons by laying them open to additional victimization; the CAT, therefore, has strongly recommended that 'the State party should abolish the rule obliging families to certify the death of the missing person in order to receive compensation'. Cf. CAT, 'Considerations of Reports Submitted by States Parties under Article 19 of the Convention - Algeria. Concluding Observations of the Committee against Torture.' (2008) UN Doc. CAT/C/DZA/CO/3 paras 12–13. In its first case on the disappearances occurred in Bosnia and Herzegovina during the 1992-1995 conflict, the HRCee faced the same issue and found a violation of

The factors above do not need to be cumulatively present. And yet each single factor may generate a situation in which the rights of family members under Article 7 ICCPR (prohibition of torture)[22] – read alone or/and in conjunction with Article 2 (3) ICCPR (right to a remedy) – are infringed.[23]

The reactions and attitudes of the authorities vis-à-vis the anguish of family members generated by the disappearance of the next of kin is one of the central factors for the ECtHR in its assessment of the alleged violation of Article 3 ECHR[24] at the detriment of the family members. Thus, the essence of the violation 'does not much lie in the fact of "the disappearance"'.[25] Sudre considers that this interpretation and the shaping of the conceptual definition of Article 3 ECHR (prohibition of torture) constitute a normative progress based on the qualitative development of human rights 'par l'œuvre de la Cour'.[26] In the leading case *Kurt v Turkey*,[27] the ECtHR has found that the anguish generated by the unacknowledged detention of a son in the context of the counter-terrorism

---

Article 2 (3) read in conjunction with Articles 6, 7, and 9 ICCPR with regard to the authors and their missing relatives. The Committee stated that 'the social allowance provided to the authors depends upon their acceptance to recognize their missing relatives as dead. [...] [F]or a State which is investigating disappearances conducted on its territory to oblige families of disappeared persons to have the family member declared dead in order to be eligible for compensation, while the investigation is ongoing, is a breach of [Article 2 (3)], read in conjunction with [Arts.] 6, 7 and 9 in that it makes the availability of compensation dependent on the family's willingness to have the family member declared dead.' Cf. HRCee, *Fatima Prutina and others v Bosnia and Herzegovina, Comm nos 1917/2009 and others* (2013) UN Doc. CCPR/C/107/D/1917,1918,1925/2009&1953/2010 [9.6]. In his individual opinion to the View, Mr. Salvioli made a forward-looking remark by saying that 'the Committee should have stated that the requirement by the State that the relative of a disappeared person must apply for a death certificate in order to obtain a benefit or compensation constitutes inhuman and cruel treatment'. Cf. HRCee, Individual opinion of Committee member Fabián Salvioli (partly dissenting) in *Fatima Prutina and others v Bosnia and Herzegovina* (2013) UN Doc. CCPR/C/107/D/1917,1918,1925/2009&1953/2010 [15 (Appendix)]. This pronouncement of the HRCee has also been strongly criticized by Citroni who considered it difficult 'to see how the obligation to declare the disappeared person dead violates the right to life and the right to liberty and security of the person.' Gabriella Citroni, 'The Pitfalls of Regulating the Legal Status of Disappeared Persons Through Declaration of Death' (2014) 12 Journal of International Criminal Justice 787, 799.

[22] Article 7 ICCPR reads as follows 'No one shall be subjected to torture or to cruel, inhuman or degrading treatment or punishment. In particular, no one shall be subjected without his free consent to medical or scientific experimentation.'

[23] The Committee has reiterated the General Comment no. 20's formula, i.e., 'Article 7 should be read in conjunction with Article [2 (3) ICCPR]'. Cf. HRCee, *Yubraj Giri v Nepal, Comm no 1761/2008* (2011) UN Doc CCPR/c/101/D/1761/2008 [7.7]; *Dev Bahadur Maharjan v Nepal, Comm No 1863/2009* (2012) UN Doc CCPRC105D18632009 [8.5].

[24] Article 3 ECHR reads as follows: '[n]o one shall be subjected to torture or to inhuman or degrading treatment or punishment.'

[25] ECtHR, *Çakici v Turkey,* Judgment (GC) (1999) App no. 23657/94 [98].

[26] Sudre (n 9) 8.

[27] This case law is clearly inspired by the HRCee's leading case - *Quinteros v Uruguay.* In *Quinteros v Uruguay,* the Committee emphasized the factors that led to consider the relatives of disappeared persons victims of a violation under Article 7 of the ICCPR, i.e., 1) the anguish and stress caused to the relative by the disappearance of the beloved one and by the continuing uncertainty concerning her fate and whereabouts; 2) the right to know what happened to the disappeared person. Because of the disregard of the national authorities of both factor 1) and factor 2) the Committee held that the mother of the disappeared person was 'a victim of the violations of the [ICCPR] suffered by her daughter and, in particular, of article 7'. HRCee, *Quinteros et al. v. Uruguay* (n 13) [14].

operations run in south-eastern Turkey against the Kurdistan Workers' Party (PKK),[28] the complacency of authorities against the anguish of a mother, and the complete absence of official information engendered a treatment in violation of Article 3 ECHR.[29] Nevertheless, no general principle that a family member of a missing person in the same circumstances is automatically a victim of treatment contrary to Article 3 ECHR has been established.

The scope of the *Kurt* decision has been restrained in favor of more formalism[30] in the successive case law,[31] where the ECtHR has identified a series of 'special factors'[32] for the assessment of the victim status of the relatives of the disappeared under Article 3 ECHR, i.e.,

1 – the proximity of the family tie,

2 – the particular circumstances of the relationship,

3 – the extent to which the family member witnessed the events in question,

4 – the involvement of the family member in the attempts to obtain information about the disappeared person and the way in which the authorities responded to those enquiries.[33]

---

[28] The existence of a conflict is disputed in the case of the operations run against the Kurdistan Workers' Party (PKK) in the Turkish territory. Turkey has been reluctant to acknowledge that an armed conflict has been taking place either within its border (NIAC) or in the cross-border operations into Kurdistan, Iraq (IAC). The reasons for this reluctance have been multiple; Yildiz and Breau mention i) the fact that the recognition places obligations on the State party to ensure adherence to IHL; ii) the fact that the recognition of armed conflict may be felt to confer undue legitimacy to the non-state party. They consider that these factors have contributed to influencing the disparity between 'the State and the non-state party in recognizing the conflict in the Kurdish conflict. To date, the PKK has been much keener to recognize the situation as an armed conflict [...].' Kerim Yildiz and Susan Breau, *The Kurdish Conflict: International Humanitarian Law and Post-Conflict Mechanisms* (Routledge 2010) 228–229.

[29] The Court reached such a conclusion, after noting that 'ill-treatment must attain a minimum level of severity if it is to fall' under Article 3'. ECtHR, *Kurt v Turkey, Judgment* (1998) App no. 24276/94 [133–134].

[30] Ott and Feldman have expressed criticism against this formalistic approach. See Lisa Ott, *Enforced Disappearance in International Law* (Intersentia 2011) 98; Tamar Feldman, 'Indirect Victims, Direct Injury: Recognising Relatives as Victims under the European Human Rights System' [2009] European Human Rights Law Review 50, 61–62.

[31] ECtHR, *Çakici v. Turkey (GC)* (n 25) [98]. *Çakici v Turkey* departed from the findings of the first case – *Kurt v Turkey*. The Court emphasized that the *Kurt* Case did not establish 'any general principle that a family member of a "disappeared person" is thereby a victim of treatment contrary to Article 3'; thus, it listed a series of factors. Cf. ibid. Neither in *Kurt v Turkey* nor in *Çakici v Turkey* the Court specified which element of the provision enshrined in Article 3 ECHR was infringed. The application of the factors above has produced questionable results in both the *Çakici* Case and the subsequent case law concerning enforced disappearances. In the *Çakici* Case 'the applicant was the brother of the disappeared person. Unlike the applicant in the *Kurt* case, he was not present when the security forces took his brother [...]. It appears also that, while the applicant was involved in making various petitions and enquiries to the authorities, he did not bear the brunt of this task, his father Tevfik Çakıcı taking the initiative in presenting the petition of 22 December 1993 to the Diyarbakır National Security Court. [...]' Consequently, the Court perceives no special features existing in this case, which would justify finding an additional violation of Article 3 of the Convention in relation to the applicant himself.

[32] Cf. ECtHR, *Çakici v. Turkey (GC)* (n 25) [98].

[33] Cf. ibid.

The presence of these factors 'give the suffering[34] of the person concerned a dimension and character distinct from the emotional distress which may be regarded as inevitably caused to relatives of a victim of a serious human-rights violation'.[35] Humanitarian considerations are overlooked in light of an excessive automaticity in the application of special factors (see examples in the table 3 below).

ECtHR's factors for the status of victim of MP's relatives under Article 3 ECHR – Examples			
Factor 1	**Factor 2 and 3**	**Factor 3 and 4**	**Factor 4**
Çakici v Turkey **Applicant**=victim's brother **Assessment** *Factor 1: absent[36] Factor 2: - Factor 3: the applicant did not witness the arrest. Factor 4: absent, as the applicant did not bear the brunt of presenting inquiries to the authorities, but was solely involved in the formulation of the petitions. **Finding**: the applicant is not considered a victim of violation of Article 3.	*Orhan v Turkey:* **Applicant**=father of one of the victims and brother of the other two **Assessment** Factor 1: present *Factor 2: – (no explanation) but read in light of the 3rd factor. *Factor 3: the applicant witnessed the disappearrance and 'bore the weight of the pursuit of the numerous enquiries and petitions'. Factor 4: present, as he has never received any information or explanation from the authorities as to what has become of the Orhans […]'.[37] **Finding**: the applicant is a victim of a violation of Article 3.	*Akdeniz et al. v Turkey* **Applicant**=fathers, brothers, sons and uncle of victims **Assessment** Factor 1: present Factor 2: - *Factor 3: absent. Only one applicant witnessed the arrest and successive detention of the victim. *Factor 4: partly present, for some applicants were more active than other in addressing the authorities.[38] **Finding**: the applicants are not considered victims of a violation of Article 3.	*İpek v Turkey* **Applicant**=father of the victims **Assessment** Factor 1: present Factor 2: - Factor 3: present *Factor 4: present, for the authorities' reaction limited to denials that İpek brothers had ever been detained by the security forces. **Finding**: the applicant is a victim of a violation of Article 3.[39]
*Decisive factor to reach a positive/negative conclusion			**Table 3**

[34] In the ECtHR case law the intensity of the suffering has helped the Court to differentiate the scope *ratione materiae* of torture, inhuman treatment, and degrading treatment. Sudre (n 9) 8. In *Ireland v UK,* the Court stated that 'ill-treatment must attain a minimum level of severity if it is to fall within the scope of Article 3 […]. The assessment of this minimum is, in the nature of things, relative'. Cf. ECtHR, *Ireland v The UK, Judgment* (1978) App no. 5310/71 [162]. A shift in the case law took place in *Tomasi v France* (where a presumption of severity has been admitted vis-à-vis the use of physical force against a detained person). Cf. ECtHR, *Tomasi v France, Judgment* (1992) App no. 12850/87 [115]. In *Selmouni v France*, the Court underlined the dynamic character of the Convention, by confirming that international law is a process and not just rules ('the Convention is a "living instrument which must be interpreted in the light of present-day conditions" […] the Court considers that certain acts which were classified in the past as "inhuman and degrading treatment" as opposed to "torture" could be classified differently in future […].'), cf. ECtHR, *Selmouni v France, Judgment* (1999) App no. 25803/94 [101].
[35] ECtHR, *Çakici v. Turkey (GC)* (n 25) [98].
[36] ibid [99].
[37] ECtHR, *Orhan v Turkey, Judgment* [2002] App No 2565694 [359–360]. Along the same lines, see ECtHR, *Çiçek v Turkey, Judgment* (2001) App no. 25704/94 [173–174] (finding a violation of Article 3 in regard to the authorities' refusal to disclose to the mother of the victims their whereabouts, after having been taken into custody by gendarmes).
[38] ECtHR, *Akdeniz and others v Turkey, Judgment* (2001) App no. 23954/94 [102]. The case related to the disappearance of eleven people following a massive operation led by the Turkish Security Forces in Alaca village (south-eastern Turkey); the applicants were fathers (Sabri Avar and Kemal Taş), brothers (Mehmet Emin Akdeniz, Sabri Avar, Keleş Şimşek, Seyithan Atala, Aydın Demir, Süleyman Yamuk and Ramazan Yerlikaya), son (Sabri Tutuş) and uncle (Mehmet Emin Akdeniz) of the disappeared persons. ibid [17].

Scholars have expressed their criticism[40] vis-à-vis the inconsistency in applying these factors and the different weight given to each of them; indeed, the suffering of the family becomes secondary. In successive case law, the Court has identified another factor to be added to the above-mentioned 'special factors', i.e., a long period of uncertainty which follows the disappearance and which lasts until the body of the missing person is discovered.[41] Should the duration of uncertainty be relatively too short, the Court would adopt a restrictive approach;[42] 'a long period of alternating hope and despair *may justify* finding a separate violation of Article 3 on account of the particularly callous attitude of the domestic authorities to [the family's] quest for information (emphasis added)'.[43] However, a case-by-case assessment is needed, as this consideration is not automatic in the assessment of the Court.

---

[39] ECtHR, *İpek v Turkey, Judgment* (2004) App no. 25760/94 [182]; *Tekdag v Turkey, Judgment* (2004) App no. 27699/95 [86].

[40] Fedelman highlights that the '*a priori* presumption that a parent suffers more than others close to the victim due to the violation should be questioned. [...] The concept of family is far from being universally defined. The proximity of family ties depends on many factors, including family structure, social circumstances [...], the division of care-taking responsibilities, and actual emotional association. Therefore, the actual proximity of a relationship cannot be determined on the basis of objective clear-cut categories.' Feldman (n 30) 61–62. As remarked by one of the dissenting judges in *Çakici v Turkey*, weighing the aforesaid special factors against the pain of a family member caused by the uncertainty about the fate of his/her loved one is problematic: by recalling the *Kurt* Case, Judge Thomassen considered 'obvious that the pain of a mother who sees her son arrested and then has to live in uncertainty about his fate because of the acts and negligence of the authorities must be unbearable. However, a brother [the applicant in *Çakici v Turkey*] can also suffer deeply in face of the uncertainty of the fate of a sibling'. ECtHR, Partly dissenting opinion of Mrs. Thomassen joined by Mr Jungwiert and Mr Fischbach annexed to *Çakici v Turkey (GC)* App no. 23657/94. Nonetheless, that in the Court's view the suffering of a mother or a father is more serious than the suffering of a brother was confirmed in *Timurtaş v Turkey*. This Case did not differ in the facts from the *Çakıcı* Case: it related to the abduction by governmental security forces of the applicant's son suspected of being one of the local leaders of the PKK. The conclusion of the Court is not surprising, but raises issues of consistency vis-à-vis the case law of the Court itself: the applicant was the father of the disappeared and the fact that he did not witness his son's disappearance 'by no means precluded him from feeling grave concern upon receipt of the news of his son's apprehension'. ECtHR, *Timurtas v Turkey, Judgment* (2000) App no. 23531/94 [96]; Jérôme Benzimra-Hazan, 'En Marge de L'arrêt Timurtas c. La Turquie (13 Juin 2000): Vers L'homogénéisation des Approches du Phénomène des Disparitions Forcées de Personnes' (2001) 12 Revue trimestrielle des droits de l'homme 983, 983–997; Tullio Scovazzi and Gabriella Citroni, *The Struggle against Enforced Disappearance and the 2007 United Nations Convention* (Martinus Nijhoff Publishers 2007) 198.

[41] ibid [178]. In *Varnava v Turkey*, the Court stresses that '[t]he length of time over which the ordeal of the relatives has been dragged out and the attitude of official indifference in face of their acute anxiety to know the fate of their close family members discloses a situation attaining the requisite level of severity.' Whether or not this created a new factor to be added to the list of special factors may be answered in the affirmative in light of *Janowiec and others v Russia* (GC). Cf. ECtHR, *Varnava and Others v Turkey, Judgment (GC)* (2009) App nos. 16064/90 and others [202].

[42] The Court emphasized that it has adopted 'a restrictive approach in situations where the person was taken into custody but later found dead following a relatively short period of uncertainty as to his fate'; the case law quoted by the Court - *Tanlı v Turkey* (2001) and *Bitiyeva and Others v Russia* (2009), although related to detention cases, did not provide any explanatory element concerning the length of uncertainty. ECtHR, *Lejla Fazlić and others v Bosnia and Herzegovina, Decision* (2014) App no 66758/09 [179].

[43] ECtHR, *Janowiec and others v. Russia (GC)* (n 41) [186].

The strictness in applying such factors diminishes when the Court is confronted with situations of armed conflict; in these settings, the dismissive conduct of State authorities is pivotal to assess their responsibility for the suffering of family members. For instance, in the context of the IAC in Cyprus, although the relatives might not have made any attempt to obtain information (factor 4) from the authorities of the respondent State (i.e., Turkey) or may not have witnessed the alleged events (factor 3),[44] their status of victims under Article 3 ECHR was not questioned due to the circumstances on the ground.[45] The existence of an armed conflict represented a key factor in the Court's assessment of the State conduct against the quest of families for information. In this respect, the Court observed that

> [t]he fact that a very substantial number of Greek Cypriots had to seek refuge in the south coupled with the continuing division of Cyprus must be considered to constitute very serious obstacles to their quest for information. The provision of such information is the responsibility of the authorities of the respondent State. This responsibility has not been discharged [...] The silence of the authorities of the respondent State in the face of the real concerns of the relatives of the missing persons attains a level of severity which can only be categorised as inhuman treatment (emphasis added).[46]

The obstacles that a State encounters in the phase following the conflict have led the Court to put on hold specific human rights standards in the assessment of the conduct of State authorities vis-à-vis families of missing persons (see *contra*: HRCee above). For instance, in *Palić v Bosnia and Herzegovina*,[47] the ECtHR has emphasized that

---

[44] In *Varnava and others v Turkey*, focused on the same context as the inter-state case *Cyprus v Turkey*, the Court confirmed the approach undertaken in *Cyprus v Turkey*, i.e., the secondary character of the special factors. The Court lists the 'special factors' as an additional element, but not the principal ('Other relevant factors include [...]'); while in *Çakici v Turkey*, the Court considered pivotal the fulfillment of the 'special factors,' in *Varnava*, the conduct – attitudes and reactions – of the authorities come first. Ibid [200].

[45] The Court noted that 'the military operation resulted in a considerable loss of life, large-scale arrests and detentions and enforced separation of families. The overall context must still be vivid in the minds of the relatives of persons whose fate has never been accounted for by the authorities. They endure the agony of not knowing whether family members were killed in the conflict or are still in detention or, if detained, have since died.' The applicant State - Cyprus - claimed that about 1,491 Greek Cypriots were still missing twenty years after the cessation of the hostilities. ECtHR, *Cyprus v Turkey, Judgment (GC)* (2001) App no. 25781/94 [157].

[46] ibid.

[47] ECtHR, *Palić v. Bosnia and Herzegovina* (n 3) [75]. The case was also handled by the HRChBH a few years before the presentation of the case before the ECtHR. See also sub-section 1.1.3.1 in Chapter VI. Ms. Esma Palić complained that 'she and her children [suffered] severely under the uncertainty of the whereabouts of Colonel Palić and [asserted] a violation of "the right to know about the fate of one's husband and father"'. On the merits, the Chamber recalled the ECtHR's view (i.e., the *Kurt* Case) according to which 'the essence of a violation Article 3 [ECHR] in relation to a family member does not so much lie in the fact of the disappearance of the family member but rather concerns the authorities' reactions and attitudes to the situation'. The Chamber particularly focused on the agony suffered by both Ms. Palić and her children for more than five years as a result of two factors: 1) the lack of any investigation into Col. Palić fate and, 2) the absence of official information as to his fate after the Agreement came into force. Thus, since Ms. Palić was herself 'the victim of the authorities' complacency in the face of her anguish and distress' (exemplified by factor 1 and 2),

[s]ome weight must [...] be attached to the fact that the mortal remains of Mr. Palić were eventually identified and that an independent and effective criminal investigation was eventually carried out, although with some delays. Therefore, while there is no doubt that the applicant suffered and continues to suffer because of this case, the Court finds that the authorities' reactions cannot be categorized as inhuman and degrading treatment.[48]

An effective and independent criminal investigation was performed after 2005 (ten years after the termination of the conflict during which Mr Palić disappeared), i.e., when, according to the Court, the domestic legal system regained the full capability of dealing effectively with disappearances and other serious violations of IHL.[49] Such a conclusion derived from a thorough examination of the post-conflict setting in the country and took into account the advances that Bosnia-Herzegovina had experienced since the end of the conflict.

Yet in *Lejla Fazlić and others v Bosnia and Herzegovina* the relatives of the applicants[50] expressed their disapproval vis-à-vis

the fact that relatives of missing persons had been required since June 2004 (with regard to missing combatants) and since September 2006 (with regard to missing civilians) to obtain declarations of presumed death with respect to their missing relatives in order to maintain some social benefits.[51]

The "peacetime" conduct, although impact-less on the applicants, might have hampered other families' entitlements; nevertheless,

[a]ll of the applicants obtained declarations of presumed death with respect to their next-of-kin prior to the entry into force of the impugned legislation [War Veterans and their Families Act 2004, the 2006 amendment to the Social Care Act 1999]. In view of that, even assuming that it could raise an issue under Article 3 [ECHR], their argument that relatives of missing persons might have felt pressured by that legislation to declare their missing relatives dead does not concern the present applicants.[52]

The excerpt above shows that, despite the dismissal of this part of the claim, the Court does not exclude the eventuality that a similar post-conflict domestic legislation could be in violation of Article 3 ECHR.

---

the Chamber found that the respondent Party was in breach of Article 3 in respect of Ms. Palić. Cf. HRChBH, *Avdo and Esma Palić v The Republika Srpska, Decision on Admissibility and Merits* (2001) Case no. CH/99/3196 [36, 78–80]. For a detailed examination of the work of the HRChBH vis-à-vis the missing, see Tilman Blumenstock, 'Legal Protection of the Missing and Their Relatives: The Example of Bosnia and Herzegovina' (2006) 19 Leiden Journal of International Law 773, 782. See also sub-section 1.1.3.1, Chapter VI.

[48] HRChBH, *Palić* (2001) (n 47).
[49] ECtHR, *Palić v Bosnia and Herzegovina* (n 3) [70].
[50] The relatives of the missing brought a complaint on their behalf to a treatment contrary to Article 3, since they suffered from 'insomnia, depression and post-traumatic stress disorder because of the authorities' indifference towards their concerns and anguish'. ECtHR, *Lejla Fazlić and others v. Bosnia and Herzegovina* (n 42) [44].
[51] ibid.
[52] ibid [47].

The conduct of State authorities vis-à-vis the quest for information of missing persons is one of the central factors in the assessment developed by the AfCommHPR.[53] Specifically, inhuman treatment[54] against both family members and missing persons can be the result of *i)* the detention of an individual without permitting him or her to have any contact with his or her family and *ii)* the refusal of providing information to the family on whether and where the individual is detained.[55]

1.2. The centrality of the disappearance regardless of other contextual factors in the Inter-American system

In the case law of the IACtHR, the settings in which people have been subjected to enforced disappearances vary from dictatorial regimes to countries involved in NIAC. Almost contemporarily to the *Kurt* case, the IACtHR addressed the disappearance of Efraín Bámaca-Velásquez, the leader of a guerrillas group – Luis Ixmata Front – whose fate and whereabouts remained

---

[53] The AfCommHPR has received a number of applications concerning, *inter alia,* the disappearance of persons in the context of an armed conflict, internal turmoil or totalitarian government. With regard to armed conflict, see AfCommHPR, *Commission nationale des droits de l'Homme et des libertés v Chad* (1995) Comm no. 74/92 [4, 22] ('Noting the accounts of killings, disappearances and torture as a result of the civil war between the security services and other groups, the Commission acknowledged that Chad had failed to provide security and stability in the country, thereby allowing serious and massive violations of human rights'). In relation to internal turmoil, see AfCommHPR, *Mouvement burkinabé des droits de l'Homme et des peuples v Burkina Faso* (2001) Comm no. 204/97 [44] (the case concerned human rights violations reported to have been committed in Burkina Faso from the days of the revolutionary government, i.e., 1983, until 1991. The Commission affirmed that '[t]he disappearance of persons suspected or accused of plotting against the instituted authorities [...] constitutes a violation of the above-cited texts and principles [i.e., Articles 5 and 6 AfChHPR; Article 1 (2) Declaration on the Protection of all Persons against Forced Disappearances]'). As for totalitarian government, see AfCommHPR, *Liesbeth Zegveld and Mussie Ephrem v Eritrea* (2003) Comm no. 250/02 [55] (stating that 'incommunicado detention is a gross human rights violation that can lead to other violations such as torture or ill-treatment or interrogation without due process safeguards. Of itself, prolonged incommunicado detention and/or solitary confinement could be held to be a form of cruel, inhuman or degrading punishment and treatment'; affirming that 'there should be no secret detentions and States must disclose the fact that someone is being detained as well as the place of detention').

[54] Cf. Article 5 AfChHPR.

[55] Cf. AfCommHPR, *Amnesty International et al v Sudan* (1999) Comm nos. 48/90-50/91-52/91-89/93 [54]. Accordingly, the Commission has emphasized the relevance of the family links and the importance of external relations of inmates to avoid a violation of the rights in the AfChHPR. *Malawi African Association et al. v Mauritania* is an interesting case in this regard. It concerned the human rights violations (arbitrary detentions of Black Mauritanians), committed by the Mauritanian State authorities, following the events that triggered the conflict with Senegal in 1989 - i.e., the expulsion of 50,000 Mauritanian citizens allegedly considered Senegalese. In its decision on the merits, the Commission stressed that '[h]olding people in solitary confinement both before and during the trial, and during such detention, which is, on top of it all, arbitrary [...] [and] depriving them of their right to a family life constitutes a violation of article 18.1 [AfChHPR]'. Clearly the Commission put its focus on the direct victims – the inmates – and on the effects of such isolation on their entitlements. Cf. AfCommHPR, *Malawi African Association et al v Mauritania* (2000) Comm nos. 54/91 et al. [123]. Deprivation of both reveals the inhumanity of abusive detention practices and a violation of the prohibition of inhuman treatment in relation both to the victim and her family. AfCommHPR, *Amnesty International et al. v Sudan* [54].

unknown after a gunfight between the army and the guerrillas in 1992. The approach of the Court to the case has been driven by the considerations embedded in IHL in light of the ongoing NIAC at the time of the alleged violations.[56] In relation to the relatives of Efraín,[57] the Court has followed a similar path to the one of the ECtHR and has identified the actions/omissions that resulted in an inhuman treatment[58] at the detriment of the relatives of the victims: i.e.,

– the continued obstruction of the efforts of the victim's wife to learn the truth about the facts;

– the concealment of the corpse of the victim;

– the obstacles to the attempted exhumation procedures;

the official refusal to provide relevant information.[59]

The suffering of the wife generated by the elements above constituted cruel, inhuman or degrading treatment in violation of Article 5 (1) and 5 (2) ACHR. The fact that other relatives – the victim's father and the victim's sisters – of the direct victim endured the same suffering and anguish led the Court to consider them victims of the violation of the same provision.[60]

This is not the general approach undertaken by the Court. As the subsequent case law shows,[61] the violation of the right to mental and moral integrity of the next of kin of the victim 'is, precisely, a direct consequence' of the disappearance (*contra:* ECtHR), 'which causes them severe suffering'. Thus, the conduct of State authorities vis-à-vis the family is an aggravating factor – but not the principal one – which exacerbates the status of the mental integrity of the

---

[56] The Court has assessed some of the violations against the direct victim in light of a joint reading of Article 1 (1) ACHR – obligation to respect the rights under the Convention – and Common Article 3 GCs (I-IV). Cf. IACtHR, *Bámaca-Velásquez v Guatemala, Judgment - Merits* (2000) Series C No. 70 [203 ff].

[57] Burgorgue-Larsen has underlined that the Court reiteratively affirms that, when it has to assess alleged violations of Article 5, this assessment will take into account a double perspective: that of the direct victim and that of the next of kin. The multiplicity of the victims derives from a methodology based on the double perspective doctrine. See, Laurence Burgorgue-Larsen, 'La Prohibition de La Torture et Ses Équivalents Dans Le Système Interaméricain Des Droits de L'homme' in Catherine-Amélie Chassin (dir.), *La portée de l'article 3 de la Convention européenne des droits de l'homme* (Bruylant 2006) 40.

[58] Such a treatment is in violation of Article 5 (1) and (2) (right to humane treatment) ACHR.

[59] IACtHR, *Bámaca-Velásquez v. Guatemala (Merits)* (n 56).

[60] ibid [165].

[61] IACtHR, *Goiburú et al v Paraguay, Judgment - Merits, Reparations and Costs* (2006) Series C No. 153; *Ticona-Estrada et al v Bolivia, Judgment - Merits, Reparations and Costs* (2008) Series C No. 191; *Tiu Tojín v Guatemala, Judgment – Merits, Reparations and Costs* (2008) Series C No. 190; *Anzualdo-Castro v Peru, Judgment - Preliminary Objection, Merits, Reparations and Costs* (2009) Series C No. 202; *Heliodoro Portugal v Panama, Judgment - Preliminary Objections, Merits, Reparations, and Costs* (2008) Series C No.186; *Radilla Pacheco v Mexico, Judgment - Preliminary Objections, Merits, Reparations and Costs* (2009) Series C No. 209. All quoted in Laurence Burgorgue-Larsen and Amaya Úbeda de Torres, *The Inter-American Court of Human Rights. Case Law and Commentary* (Oxford University Press 2011) 381–382.

next of kin.[62] Moreover, in contrast to the ECtHR's assessment, the proximity of the family tie is not a pivotal factor:

> a violation of the right to mental and moral integrity of the direct next of kin of victims of certain human rights violations can be declared, applying a presumption *iuris tantum* with regard to mothers and father, daughters and sons, husbands and wives, permanent companions (hereinafter "direct next of kin"), provided this responds to the specific circumstances of a case, as has happened, for example, in the cases of [...] forced disappearance of persons [...]. With regard to these direct next of kin, it is for the State to disprove their claim.[63] [...] In relation to those persons regarding whom the Court does not presume that the right to personal integrity has been harmed, because they are not direct next of kin, the Court must assess, for example, whether there is a particularly close tie between them and the victims in the case that would allow the Court to declare a violation of their right to personal integrity.[64]

Suffering goes beyond a mere automaticity of the application of a fictional criterion of familial proximity. A broad interpretation of 'direct next of kin' and the fact of keeping the list open-ended implies that the IACtHR does not introduce a fictional distinction concerning the intensity of suffering that may be felt by a person whose familial proximity with the victim is not that close.[65] In this context, the Court has taken into consideration the negative role that multiple obstacles to the access to information can play vis-à-vis the enforcement of the rights of next of kin, considered individually and as a group. Similarly, the Court has recognized the importance of the impact that uncertainty could have had on those, among the relatives, that did not bring the case before the Court.[66]

The context – NIAC/post-NIAC – is addressed in the judicial assessment, but is not a factor that impacts on the foregoing; indeed, the Court turns to IHL in order to consolidate its standpoint on the right of families to know the fate and whereabouts of the missing beloved ones and the inhumane treatment that flows

---

[62] IACtHR, *La Cantuta v Peru, Judgment - Merits, Reparations and Costs* (2006) Series C no 162 [123]; *Gómez-Palomino v Peru, Judgment - Merits, Reparations and Costs* (2005) Series C No. 136 [60].

[63] IACtHR, *Valle-Jaramillo et al v Colombia, Judgment - Merits, Reparations and Costs* (2008) Series C No. 192 [119].

[64] ibid.

[65] See on this point, Burgorgue-Larsen and Torres (n 61) 382; Scovazzi and Citroni (n 40) 344.

[66] In *Mapiripán Massacre v Colombia*, the Court acknowledged that 'the fact that the very circumstances of the case have not allowed the national authorities, as well as this Court, to have more information on other next of kin of the victims, makes it reasonable to presume that all of these, whether identified or not, suffered the extreme circumstances of the massacre or its consequences. Thus, the Court deems that the next of kin of the victims individually identified in this proceeding [...], as well as those who have not been identified, must also be considered victims of the abridgment of the right to humane treatment, embodied in Article 5(1) and 5(2) of the Convention, in combination with Article 1(1) of said treaty. Cf. IACtHR, *Mapiripán Massacre v Colombia, Judgment - Merits, Reparations, and Costs* (2005) Series C No 134 [146]. See also IACtHR, *Pueblo Bello Massacre v Colombia, Judgment - Merits, Reparations and Costs* (2006) Series C No. 140 [160, 162]; *Ituango Massacres v Colombia, Judgment - Preliminary Objections, Merits, Reparations and Costs* (2006) Series C no. 148 [258–259, 263, 265]. On the disputed difference between extra-judiciary executions and enforced disappearances when the mortal remains of the executed person are not located and identified, see Scovazzi and Citroni (n 40) 171.

from the concealment of information.[67] For instance, in *Diario Militar* (Guatemala),[68] the Court has recognized that the alleged disappearances in the case took place in the context of the NIAC in Guatemala. These circumstances gave 'particular relevance' to 'the elucidation of the truth of what happened', especially in the consolidation of the reconciliation and peace process of the country.[69] Concealment of information was not only typical of the conduct of the authorities during the conflict, but also of their conduct after the signature of the Peace Accords; indeed, this conduct directly affected the work of the Historical Clarification Commission. Against this backdrop, the Court has underlined that the right to know the truth of family members of victims is *inter alia*

> supported by [IHL], according to which family members have the right to know the truth about the fate of the disappeared victims, including the victims of forced disappearance, and this is applicable to both international and non-international armed conflicts. [footnotes omitted][70]

As some suggest, the aim of this reference to IHL is to strengthen the argument on the applicability of the right to the truth in the context of an armed

---

[67] Elizabeth Salmon, 'Institutional Approach between IHL and IHRL: Current Trends in the Jurisprudence of the Inter-American Court of Human Rights' (2014) 5 Journal of International Humanitarian Legal Studies 152, 184.

[68] The NIAC in Guatemala lasted for more than 30 years (1962-1996). In 1999, a leaked Guatemalan government death squad diary revealed details about 183 political opponents of the former military regime (e.g., names, photos, alleged affiliations, and the facts of their executions between 1983 and 1985). In light of the inactivity of the government vis-à-vis their enforced disappearance and execution over the past 30 years, the IACtHR found Guatemala responsible for the disappearances and the failure to investigate them, thereby violating the rights of the victims and their families, as well as the right to truth. Cf. IACtHR, *Gudiel Álvarez et al ('Diario Militar') v Guatemala, Judgment - Merits, Reparations, and Costs* (2012) Series C no. 253 [54–62].

[69] ibid [298–299].

[70] ibid [299]. Interestingly, the Court based this assertion on Rule 117 of the ICRC Study on Customary IHL and on a couple of UN Documents, i.e., the Resolution of the Commission on Human Rights 2002/60 on Missing Persons and UNGA Resolution 3220 (XXIX). Concealment of information or denial of the truth about what happened results in 'a form of cruel and inhuman treatment for the closest family members and therefore the violation of the right to personal integrity can be linked to a violation of their right to know the truth [footnotes omitted]'. The Court not only found violation of Article 5 (1) (moral and mental integrity), but also of Article 5 (2) (cruel, inhuman, or degrading punishment or treatment). Cf. ibid [301]. Cf. also IACtHR, *Velásquez-Rodríguez v Honduras, Judgment - Merits* (1988) Series C No. 4 (IACtHR) [181]; *Gelman v Uruguay, Judgment - Merits and Reparations,* (2011) Series C no. 221 [243]; *Trujillo-Oroza v Bolivia, Judgment - Merits* (2000) Series C no. 64 [114]; *Anzualdo-Castro v. Peru (P.O., Merits, ...)* (n 61) [113]. In *Bámaca Velásquez* case, based on the circumstances of the case (i.e., the continued obstruction of Jennifer Harbury's efforts to learn the truth of the facts, the concealment of the corpse of Bámaca Velásquez, the obstacles to the attempted exhumation procedures that various public authorities created and the official refusal to provide relevant information), the Court '[considered] that the suffering to which Jennifer Harbury was subjected clearly constitutes cruel, inhuman or degrading treatment, violating Article 5(1) and 5(2) of the Convention. The Court also [considered] that ignorance of the whereabouts of Bámaca Velásquez caused his next of kin the profound anguish mentioned by the [HRCee] and, therefore, considers that they, too, are victims of the violation of the said Article.' In order to reach this conclusion, the Court referred to its own jurisprudence (i.e. *Blake v Guatemala*), to the case law of the ECtHR (i.e., *Kurt v Turkey*), and to the HRCee's Views (i.e., *Quinteros v Uruguay*). Cf. IACtHR, *Bámaca-Velásquez v. Guatemala (Merits)* (n 56) [160, 162, 164, 165].

conflict;[71] it is also possible that the Court intended to emphasize the continuity of the applicability of this right between the moment of the conflict and the post-conflict phase.

Similar considerations have been outlined against the disappearance of children, which has been used as a military strategy in the context of the NIAC in El Salvador.[72] In relation to this context,[73] the Court has also defined the lack of information as a source of deep sorrow and anguish. As a corollary, it has directly linked uncertainty-induced suffering to the violation of the right of families to know the truth.[74] Thus, considerations on the psychosocial impact of the concealment of information on the next of kin acquire a significant weight in the Court's analysis. [75]

---

[71] Salmon (n 67) 184.

[72] From 1980 to 1991, El Salvador was engaged in an internal armed conflict that ultimately ended with the signing of a UN-facilitated peace agreement on 16 January 1992. The peace agreement called for the establishment of a national truth commission tasked with accounting for individual acts and overall patterns of violence inflicted by both State agents and members of the Farabundo Martí National Liberation Front (FMLN) guerrilla group. Within the context of the armed conflict, there was a marked pattern of forced disappearances of children, who were taken and illegally detained by members of the armed forces. As of April 2014, there were 926 registered cases of missing children, with 239 being reunited with their families, 96 pending reunion, 54 determined having died, and 537 remaining missing. IACtHR, *Rochac Hernández and others v El Salvador, Judgment - Merits, Reparations and Costs* (2014) Series C No. 285 [46–47, 49].

[73] The Court reiterated the approach outlined in this sub-section. Specifically, it pinpointed the factors generating a violation of the mental and moral integrity of the family members, i.e., (i) a personal, physical and emotional impact of the disappearance *per se*; (ii) an irreversible alteration of the family unit and life; (iii) direct involvement in various actions such as seeking justice or information on the whereabouts of the victims; (iv) the fact that the uncertainty on the victims' whereabouts has an impact on the possibility of mourning thereby prolonging the psychological effects of the disappearance on the family, and (v) the lack of collaboration of the State in determining the whereabouts of the victims and those responsible for the disappearances as an aggravating factor. It also considered the conduct of the authorities - the constant refusal of State authorities to provide information on the whereabouts of the victims or to initiate an effective investigation to clarify what happened - an aggravating factor of the suffering of the next of kin. ibid [121, 123].

[74] ibid [123].

[75] In the context of the Colombian conflict between the Government and the guerilla group M-19 (the *Disappeared from the Palace of Justice* case), the Court observed that testimonial statements, and also the reports on the psychosocial impact on the next of kin of the disappeared victims, reveal that the personal integrity of all of them was affected by one or several of the following circumstances: '(i) "the uncertainty caused [...] by not knowing the whereabouts of their loved ones and [...] the unsatisfactory response of the State"; (ii) personal, physical and emotional consequences; (iii) "the stigmatization [...] that isolated them from friends and neighbours"; (iv) the changes in their family and personal life projects; (v) the threats they reported having received as a result of their search activities; (vi) the alteration of their social relations, the breakdown of the family dynamics, as well as changes in role assignment within the family; (vii) the impunity of the facts, as well as (viii) the hope to find their family members, or (ix) the impossibility of burying them decently in accordance with their beliefs, altering their mourning process and perpetuating the suffering and uncertainty. [Footnotes omitted]'. IACtHR, *Rodríguez Vera et al (the Disappeared from the Palace of Justice) v Colombia, Judgment - Preliminary Objections, Merits, Reparations and Costs* (2014) Series C no. 287 [534].

1.3. Uncertainty about the fate and whereabouts of a relative and its impact on the right to respect for family life

As Chapter II has shown, rare are complaints brought before human rights judicial bodies focusing on uncertainty as the cause of infringement of the right to respect for family life. Yet, uncertainty on a relative's fate is detrimental to the family's existence.

In some of the cases brought before the ECtHR, Article 8 ECHR (right to respect for private and family life) has been invoked by the applicants as one of the provisions allegedly violated by State authorities.[76] These complaints usually focused on the treatment to which 'the relatives of the missing persons were subjected in their attempts to ascertain the latter's fate'.[77] In light of the conclusions reached under Article 3 ECHR, the Court has found it unnecessary to examine them separately, for these conclusions addressed the effect of the lack of information on the families of missing persons.[78] Where the fate of the relatives − who were missing at a certain point in time − is known, while the location of their human remains is unknown, the Court has assessed the merits of the complaint of family members under Article 8 ECHR.

For instance, the Court has been confronted with a case of uncertainty about the whereabouts of human remains of the applicants' relatives – Greek soldiers sent to Cyprus – who died in a plane crash due to friendly fire during the 1974 IAC in Cyprus (*Tzilivaki et al. v Cyprus*).[79] The legal issue to be tackled under Article 8 ECHR was 'whether the authorities have shown a lack of respect for the family life of the applicants due to alleged failures in exhuming their relatives' bodies or in providing information on this matter'.[80] As stressed under sub-section 3.2.3 in Chapter II, under Article 8 ECHR State authorities have to protect the individual and his/her family life from State's interference and to

---

[76] ECtHR, *Cyprus v. Turkey (GC)* (n 45) [159–161]; *Luluyev and others v Russia, Judgment* (2006) App no. 69480/01 [130–133]; *Osmanoğlu v Turkey, Judgment* (2008) App no. 48804/99 [105–107].

[77] ECtHR, *Cyprus v. Turkey (GC)* (n 45) [160].

[78] ibid [161].

[79] The case is about the plane crash of a military aircraft carrying the 1st commando battalion of Chania sent from Greece which, on 22 July 1974, was shot down by friendly fire in Tymvos; 31 commandos and crew died. Among the victims were the first applicant's brother, and the son and brother of the second and third applicant. At the time of the accident, the authorities decided to convert the crash site into a memorial for all the Greek soldiers who fell; some unidentified remains were buried in a mass grave at the Memorial site, while most of the bodies were buried separately in Lakatamia cemetery; only in 1979 the army authorities exhumed and returned the bodies of some of the Greek soldiers buried in graves close to the crash site. It was in 1999 that Physicians for Human Rights, in agreement with the authorities, conducted exhumations in Lakatamia and other cemeteries and found that burials in 1974 were run in a confusing way generating confusion in the identification verification of the remains, mistaken attributions of identities and mixes of skeletons' bones. ECtHR, *Tzilivaki v Cyprus, Decision* (2014) App no. 23082/07 [3, 6].

[80] ibid [32]. In light of the circumstances, the Court stated that the fate of the applicants' relatives was not unknown, the core of the complaint being the uncertainty of the location of the bodies: thus, although the applicants complained under Articles 2 and 8 ECHR about the failure of authorities to provide information on the excavations and exhumations, the Court decided to examine the issue under Article 8. Cf. Ibid [22-23, 27].

secure respect for family life through the adoption of specific measures (i.e., positive obligations).[81] The ways to ensure the rights under Article 8 are multiple and depend on the aspect of family life at issue;[82] nevertheless, the applicable principles are broadly similar.[83] Since no definition of 'family life' exists in the ECHR, guidance on the definition of private and family life *per se* and on the ways to ensure its respect must be found in the Court's case law and depends on the Court's interpretation of the provision.

Despite the vagueness of the concept 'private and family life' and the flexibility in defining what kind of measures ensures the respect for it, in *Tzilivaki et al. v Cyprus* the Court found that no case law existed 'indicating that in any general sense Article 8 requires Contracting States to ensure identification, exhumation or burial of remains on request of family members'.[84] Thus, for the Court, it was not appropriate to attempt to define the responsibilities in this respect. The inappropriateness of this attempt remains unclear in the context of Article 8. Even in the absence of previous case law on the issue, the Court might have looked at the context and read Article 8 in conjunction with IHL rules on dead persons. As a matter of fact, in previous case law concerning article 8, the Court has admittedly recognized that 'the concepts of private and family life are broad terms not susceptible to exhaustive definition'.[85] Indeed, both the European Commission on Human Rights (ECommHR) and the Court have considered the following issues falling under the scope of the provision:

− the wish to have one's ashes scattered on one's own land (covered by the first concept);[86]

− whether a mother had the right to change the family name on the tombstone of her stillborn child (covered by the first concept);[87]

− the excessive delay in returning the body of the applicants' child following an autopsy (considered as interference with the private and family life of the applicants);[88]

− the refusal to authorize the transfer of the urn containing the applicant's husband's ashes (the Court considered it a matter within the scope of Article 8,

---

[81] See sub-section 3.2.3 of Chapter II.

[82] ECtHR, *Tzilivaki v. Cyprus* (n 79) [33].

[83] ECtHR, *Di Sarno and others v Italy, Judgment (Merits and Just Satisfaction)* (2012) App no 30765/08 [105]. See sub-section 3.2.3 in Chapter II.

[84] ECtHR, *Tzilivaki v. Cyprus* (n 79) [34].

[85] Cf. ECtHR, *Hadri-Vionnet v Switzerland, Judgment* (2008) App no. 55525/00 [51] (where the Court was faced with a situation where the applicant was unable to attend the funeral of her stillborn baby.) Schabas underlines that no neat dividing line exists between private and family life, and certain problems, including matters concerning the dead, may be examined under both rubrics. See William A Schabas, *The European Convention on Human Rights: A Commentary* (Oxford University Press 2015) 366-367.

[86] Cf. ECommHR, *X v Germany, Decision* (1981) App no. 8741/79 [137].

[87] Cf. ECtHR, *Znamenskaya v Russia, Judgment* (2005) App no. 77785/01 [27].

[88] Cf. ECtHR, *Pannullo and Forte v France, Judgment* (2001) App no. 37794/97 [36].

without stating whether the interference found related to the concept of private life or family life);[89]

– whether the applicant was entitled to attend the burial of her stillborn child and to have the child's remains transported in an appropriate vehicle (the Court considered it a matter within the scope of Article 8, without stating whether the interference found related to the concept of private life or family life).[90]

The plethora of circumstances covered by Article 8 makes it difficult to understand the reason why ensuring identification, exhumation, and burial of remains upon request of family members should not fall under Article 8. One reason might be the fact that exhumations *per se* and the management of post-war cemeteries are a sensitive issue, featuring political, social, economic aspects. The fact that exhumations would have entailed 'to disturb the Memorial' of fallen in war as well as existing gravesites might be another factor that has led the Court to avoid opening the *Pandora* box in relation to the management of war cemeteries.[91] Nevertheless, as the Court has noted elsewhere, the adoption of 'a "politically-sensitive" approach to the missing persons problem [...] can have no bearing on the application of the provisions of the [ECHR]'.[92]

Despite the rejection of the complaint, the Court ambiguously noted that, even assuming that the case fell under Article 8, Cyprus undertook a set of actions with regard to the exhumation/identification issue. Without any reason relevant to the assessment, the Court illustrated the list of actions undertaken by the Cypriot authorities. This resembles a description of what would be required from State authorities to abide by the obligation to secure the right to respect for private and family life, should missing persons-related issues, e.g., exhumations and identification, fall under Article 8 ECHR. Furthermore, there is a clear connection with those actions that are required under IHL rules on the dead and the treatment of human remains: e.g.,

– as soon as the misidentification problem came to light, steps have been taken by, and under the auspices of, the authorities, to identify correctly the remains;

– DNA samples were obtained from relatives, including the applicants' families;

– families were invited to return remains for DNA analysis;

---

[89] Cf. ECtHR, *Elli Poluhas Dödsbo v Sweden, Judgment* (2006) App no. 61564/00 [24].

[90] Cf. ECtHR, *Hadri-Vionnet v. Switzerland* (n 85) [52].

[91] Edkins notes that, after World War I, families reclaimed back the bodies of soldiers fallen in the battlefield and buried far from the home country. While France initially did not back the efforts of the families to repatriate the bodies, the right to reclaim the bodies was supported as of 1922; UK, Germany, and the USA ruled these requests out. She also refers to the contemporary instance of the US' politics of bringing home the fallen soldiers (e.g., the case of Vietnam where the return of missing bodies has become an obsession for the government). Jenny Edkins, *Trauma and the Memory of Politics* (Cambridge University Press 2003) 96.

[92] ECtHR, *Varnava and Others v. Turkey (GC)* (n 41) [193].

– steps were taken to locate remains in known graves at the site and elsewhere;

– reports were issued giving progress and recommendations;

– the applicants' families have been informed of any identification results for their own relatives.[93]

The protection of the "family life" is the pivotal issue examined by the IACtHR in a series of cases concerning the disappearance of children in armed conflict. The disappearance of children in Latin America would require a separate study; [94] without disregarding the gravity of this practice, this book limits itself to the implications of the withholding of information on the family members and its legal consequences. The context of El Salvador is relevant, as State authorities were involved in the practice of the enforced disappearance of children with the purpose of countering alleged opposition members. These authorities acted outside the boundaries of the law by interfering in the family life of the children subjected to such practice as well as in the family life of their relatives.[95] In this respect, the Court found a violation of Article 11 (2) (including the right to family life), and Article 17 (family rights) read in conjunction with Article 1 (1) ACHR against the family members of the missing children. Moreover, the protection of the family unit as such appeared to be the point of conjunction between IHL and IHRL provisions. [96]

The case law of the African Commission provides room for considerations on the intertwined link between the entitlements of the individual and of his/her family members: in cases of *incommunicado* detention the Commission has noted that depriving detainees of entering into contact with their families is an inhuman treatment which 'does not guarantee neither the protection of the family, nor its physical and moral health.'[97] The premise of this considerations is to be found in Article 18 (1) AfChHPR which affirms that 'the family shall be

---

[93] Cf. ECtHR, *Tzilivaki v. Cyprus* (n 79) [35].

[94] Among the scholarly works that have tackled it, see Avery, Lisa, 'The Right to Identity and the Right to Identify Argentina's Living Disappeared' (2004) 27 Harvard Women's Law Journal 235; Elizabeth B Ludwin King, 'A Conflict of Interests: Privacy, Truth, and Compulsory DNA Testing for Argentina's Children of the Disappeared' (2011) 44 Cornell International Law Journal 535; Celia Petty, 'Family Tracing and Reunification - Safeguarding Rights and Implementing the Law' (1996) 4 International Journal of Children's Rights 165.

[95] *In casu*, the families were torn apart due to the disappearance of the children. Cf. IACtHR, *Rochac Hernández and others v. El Salvador (Merits...)* (n 72) [113, 115].

[96] The disappeared children in the case were Emelinda Lorena Hernández, José Adrián Rochac Hernández, Santos Ernesto Salinas, Manuel Antonio Bonilla and Ricardo Abarca Ayala. Among the victims the Court also included their family members. Cf. ibid [34, 52–87]. The case also sheds light upon the continuity of certain IHL obligations after the end of the armed conflict and the inextricable link between these obligations and the ones under IHRL. Cf. ibid [110]. See sub-section 2.2 in Chapter II.

[97] AfCommHPR, *Interights, ASADHO and Madam O Disu v Democratic Republic of Congo (DRC)* (2014) Comm nos. 274/03 and 282/03 [82] (concerning a series of human rights violations committed following the assassination of the President of DRC in 2001, e.g., mass arrests without judicial warrants, torture and inhuman treatments, secret interrogations, trial of civilians before a military court); *Malawi African Association et al. v. Mauritania* (n 55) [123].

the natural unit and basis of society. It shall be protected by the State, which shall take care of its physical and moral health'.[98] In the Commission's words, 'the spirit underlying this provision of the Charter is that persons in detention must as a matter of course enjoy material and psychological support of their close relations'.[99]

1.4. Concluding observations

The ECtHR, the IACtHR, and the HRCee – the most active judicial bodies against the subject matter[100] – have provided an assessment of the impact of uncertainty on family members, notably by focusing on factors that make family members victims themselves of a human right violation. The judicial bodies' interpretative techniques have played a pivotal role in unveiling the humanitarian nature of specific provisions: a *pro homine* principle guides the human rights adjudicators in assessing the inhumanity of the withholding of information at the detriment of the family members.[101] An evolutive method of interpretation

---

[98] Cf. Article 18, AfChHPR.

[99] AfCommHPR, *Interights, ASADHO and Madam O. Disu v. DRC* (n 97) [80]. In the context of enforced disappearance, the Commission has explicitly admitted that the act *per se* – enforced disappearance – constitutes a violation of, *inter alia*, the right to a family life. Cf. AfCommHPR, *JE Zitha and PJL Zitha (represented by Prof Dr Liesbeth Zegveld) v Mozambique* (2011) Comm no. 361/08 [81].

[100] The case law of the AfCtHPR is in its infancy. Nonetheless the AfCommHPR has touched on the issue in the *Amnesty International et al. v Sudan* Case. The case addressed a series of human rights violations (e.g., arbitrary arrests, detention in secret detention centers known as 'ghost houses', widespread torture and ill-treatment of detainees in such detention centers, extra-judicial executions) to the detriment of opposition members, lawyers and human rights activists that took place following the 1989 Sudan coup. In the analysis of the allegations of violation of Article 5 of the African Charter (Prohibition of torture and of cruel, inhuman and degrading treatment), the Commission recognized that 'holding an individual without permitting him or her to have any contact with his or her family, and refusing to inform the family whether the individual is being held and his whereabouts is inhuman treatment of both the detainee and the family concerned.' AfCommHPR, *Amnesty International et al. v. Sudan* (n 55) [154].

[101] On the HRCee: in their dissenting opinion in *Cifuentes Elgueta v Chile*, Keller and Salvioli underlined that the HRCee is not prevented 'from employing an evolutive interpretation of the [ICCPR] and enriching it by drawing upon elements of the contemporary *corpus juris* of international human rights law in order to accomplish its object and purpose more fully and arrive at an effective interpretation. This interpretive task, which is an intrinsic function of a body belonging to a comprehensive international system for the promotion and protection of the inherent rights of each and every woman and man, should be performed on the basis of the pro-*persona* principle and in line with that postulate's implications.' They also underline that the view according to which 'it is the Committee's obligation to "apply the Covenant, the whole Covenant and nothing but the Covenant"' has been put forward in the dissenting minority opinion in the case *Norma Yurich v Chile* (appendix). Cf. HRCee, *Individual opinion of Committee members Ms Helen Keller and Mr Fabián Salvioli (dissenting) in Cifuentes Elgueta v Chile*, (2009) UN Doc CCPR/C/96/D/1536/2006 [10–11]. On the ECtHR: the *pro-homine* approach is inferable from the Court *dictum* in, *inter alia*, *Varnava v Turkey (GC)* where the Court specifies that 'it is of crucial importance that [the ECHR] is interpreted and applied in a manner that renders [human rights] practical and effective, not theoretical and illusory'. Cf. ECtHR, *Varnava and Others v. Turkey (GC)* (n 41) [160]. In this respect, criticism has been expressed by the Baroness Hale of Richmond – Justice of the Supreme Court of the UK, who has stated that many will consider this approach 'a humane understanding of the peculiar anguish caused by not knowing whether, how and why a loved one has disappeared. From the point of view of a

distinguishes the way the adjudicators frame States obligations in this context (see *infra* section 2).[102]

On the substantive facet of the impact of uncertainty on the rights of family members, the IACtHR and the ECtHR stand out for their different approaches. From their case law, two strands of arguments can be identified: for the former, inhumanity is inherent in any enforced disappearance, since this violation always entails the withholding of information on the fate and whereabouts of a human being; as to the latter, State authorities' reaction and attitudes *might* inhumanely impact on family members depending on the co-presence of a set of factors and based on the circumstances on the ground. More generally, uncertainty about the fate and whereabouts of a human being and unresponsiveness vis-à-vis the quest of the family for information are the sources of an increased level of suffering for family members compared to other violations of human rights.

2. THE HUMANITARIAN DUTY TO PROVIDE FAMILY MEMBERS WITH INFORMATION ON THE FATE OF THEIR MISSING RELATIVES UNDER IHRL

The obligation to account for missing persons and to inform their families emerges from the complex set of IHL rules examined in Chapter II; the temporal open-ended formulation of this duty involves that State authorities 'shall' (and not should)[103] account for missing persons, i.e., elucidate their fate and whereabouts and inform their families, both in armed conflicts and in post-

---

national court [...] this is a development which will cause us real difficulty.' CoE - ECtHR, *Dialogue between Judges 2011: 'What Are The Limits to the Evolutive Interpretation of the Convention?'* (CoE 2011) 15. On the IACtHR: Burgorgue Larsen states that the protection of the victims is the *desideratum* of the inter-American system and the *raison d'être* of the IACtHR; in this perspective the IACtHR has adopted an extensive notion of victim, so that the family members can also be included in the judicial assessment. Overall, by assessing alleged violations of Article 5 ACHR (right to humane treatment) the IACtHR adopts a *pro homine* approach. Burgorgue-Larsen (n 57) 39,44,46. See also M De Pauw, 'The Inter-American Court of Human Rights and the Interpretative Method of External Referencing: Regional Consensus v Universality' in Yves Haeck, Oswaldo Ruiz-Chiriboga and Clara Burbano-Herrera (eds), *The Inter-American Court of Human Rights: Theory and Practice, Present and Future* (Intersentia 2015) 8–9.

[102] The IACtHR underlines that IHRL 'has moved forward substantially by means of an evolutive interpretation of the international protection instruments'. Cf. IACtHR, *Gómez-Paquiyauri Brothers v Peru, Judgment – Merits, Reparations, and Costs* (2004) Series C No. 110 [165]. *Contra:* Murphy argues that both the IACtHR and the HRCee do not engage in evolutive interpretation, contrary to what the ECtHR does; he explains that when a tribunal does this, 'it is consciously departing from an inquiry solely into the meaning of the treaty at the time of its adoption and is engaging in a subjective assessment of the meaning of the practice of States over time [...]'. SD Murphy, 'The Relevance of Subsequent Agreement and Subsequent Practice for the Interpretation of Treaties' in Georg Nolte (ed), *Treaties and Subsequent Practice* (Oxford University Press 2013) 87. In more general terms relating to evolutive interpretation, see Pierre-Marie Dupuy, 'Evolutionary Interpretation of Treaties: Between Memory and Prophecy' in Enzo Cannizzaro (ed), *The Law of Treaties Beyond the Vienna Convention* (Oxford University Press 2011).

[103] In the context of Article 6 ICCPR, the HRCee affirms that 'States parties should take specific and effective measures to prevent the disappearance of individuals and establish facilities and procedures to investigate thoroughly [...] cases of missing and disappeared persons [...]'. Cf. HRCee, *Elcida Arévalo Perez et al v Colombia, Comm No 181/1984* (1989) UN Doc. CCPR/C/37/D/181/1984 [10].

conflict scenarios. Under IHRL, the implementation of actions and measures to account for missing persons contributes to making effective the prohibition of inhuman treatment, particularly with regard to those who live with uncertainty, i.e., the family members (sub-section 2.1). The obligation of the former parties to the conflict to cooperate in their efforts to trace the missing emerges from the simultaneous application of IHL and IHRL rules in post-conflict contexts (sub-section 2.2). Indeed, 'it is incumbent on all those involved in the conflict to support the peace process […], in order to ensure respect for human rights […]'[104]. More generally, ongoing transitional efforts aimed at restoring peace cannot justify an unlawful departure from residually applicable IHL provisions and fully applicable human rights[105] obligations.

2.1. A conditio sine qua non for the effective implementation of the prohibition of inhuman treatment

It is commonly accepted that under IHRL the negative obligation to abstain from infringing the human rights of any individual is accompanied by a set of positive obligations aimed at ensuring the protection of such rights.[106] For instance, the HRCee stresses that, under the ICCPR, 'States are reminded of the interrelationship between the positive obligations imposed under article 2 and the need to provide effective remedies in the event of breach under article 2, paragraph 3.'[107] In this respect, HRCee's General Comment no. 20 (Article 7)

---

[104] ICJ, *Case concerning Armed Activities on the Territory of the Congo (Democratic Republic of the Congo v Uganda), Merits, Judgment* (2005) ICJ Reports 2005, p.168 [221].

[105] For instance, see the ECtHR approach *vis-à-vis* the inter-communal talks that took place in Cyprus as of 1974. Cf. ECtHR, *Cyprus v. Turkey (GC)* (n 45) [174].

[106] For instance, under the ICCPR the negative obligation to abstain from infringing the rights recognized thereof is accompanied by a positive obligation to ensure the same rights. Cf. Article 2 (1) ICCPR. See HRCee, 'General Comment No. 31: The Nature of the General Legal Obligation Imposed on State Parties to the Covenant' (2004) UN Doc. CCPR/C/21/Rev.1/Add.13 paras 6–8. D Shelton and A Gould, 'Positive and Negative Obligations' in Dinah Shelton (ed), *The Oxford Handbook of International Human Rights Law* (Oxford University Press 2013) 576. The landmark case in this regard is *The Social and Economic Rights Action Center and the Center for Economic and Social Rights v Nigeria*: the Commission stressed that '[i]nternationally accepted ideas of the various obligations engendered by human rights indicate that all rights […] generate at least four levels of duties for a State that undertakes to adhere to a rights regime, namely the duty to respect, protect, promote, and fulfill these rights. These obligations universally apply to all rights and entail a combination of negative and positive duties. As a human rights instrument, the African Charter is not alien to these concepts […] At a primary level, the obligation to respect entails that the State should refrain from interfering in the enjoyment of all fundamental rights'. Cf. AfCommHPR, *The Social and Economic Rights Action Center and the Center for Economic and Social Rights v Nigeria* (2001) Comm No. 155/96 [44–45].

[107] The General Comment no. 31 specifies that on top of the negative obligation, States are required to 'adopt legislative, judicial, administrative, educative and other appropriate measures in order to fulfill their legal obligations'. It also underlines that 'the positive obligations on States Parties to ensure Covenant rights will only be fully discharged if individuals are protected by the State, not just against violations of Covenant rights by its agents, but also against acts committed by private persons or entities'. The Comment also recognizes that 'there may be circumstances in which a failure to ensure Covenant rights as required by article 2 would give rise to violations by States Parties of those rights, as a result of States Parties' permitting or failing to take appropriate measures or to exercise

specifies that Article 7 ICCPR has to be read in conjunction with Article 2(3) ICCPR: this entails that in each State Party the legal system must effectively guarantee the immediate termination of all the acts prohibited by article 7 as well as appropriate redress; it also involves that '[c]omplaints must be investigated promptly and impartially by competent authorities so as to make the remedy effective.'[108]

The joint reading of these two provisions reflects the dual nature proper to Article 2(3) ICCPR, i.e., procedural and substantive, applied in the framework of Article 7 ICCPR.[109] The HRCee's reading of the substantive provisions in conjunction with Article 2 (3) ICCPR makes the latter the source of all positive obligations under the Covenant.[110] Where the author of the complaint is a next of kin of the victim, the Committee takes into account the dual nature of Article 2 (3). Keller and Chernishova note that the HRCee expounds on the substantive conditions subsumed under the duty to carry out an effective investigation into disappearance cases by referring to the positive obligations under the procedural limb of Article 7 ICCPR.[111] The procedural duty to investigate under Article 2 (3) ICCPR directly impacts on the next of kin and, if fulfilled, contributes to avoiding a long-lasting uncertainty, which the Committee qualifies as inhuman or degrading treatment against the next of kin of missing person(s).[112]

In the context of an armed conflict the State cannot use the declaration of the State of emergency to explain delays in informing the families of persons who have been arrested. In this respect, the Nepalese context is significant:[113] in *Giri v Nepal* the Committee has underlined that Article 7 allows 'no limitation, even in situations of public emergency'.[114]

---

due diligence to prevent, punish, investigate or redress the harm caused by such acts by private persons or entities.' Cf. HRCee, 'General Comment No. 31' (n 106) paras 6–8.

[108] HRCee, 'General Comment No 20: Article 7 (Prohibition of Torture or Cruel, Inhuman or Degrading Treatment or Punishment)' (1992) UN Doc HRI/GEN/1/Rev.9 (Vol.1) at 182 para 14.

[109] Procedurally, the right to remedy under Article 2 (3) corresponds to the duty to ensure individual's access to independent and competent authorities that are capable of deciding in a fair way upon a claim of a violation of their rights. In this sense, the case *Kazantzis v Cyprus* (972/01) is considered a watershed for the justiciability of Article 2(3). See Sarah Joseph and Melissa Castan, *International Covenant on Civil and Political Rights: Cases, Materials, and Commentary* (3rd ed, Oxford University Press 2013) 869–871, 882. Substantively, the right to a remedy is tantamount to the relief or redress afforded to a person who has been found to be a victim of a violation. David (n 20) 263.

[110] Yet, Article 2 (1) ICCPR has a minimal impact in the examination of individual communications, including those concerning the disappearance of persons. In this respect, David observes that almost every breach of a positive obligation in relation to a substantive right is decided 'by declaring the violation of that right in conjunction with article 2(3) ICCPR'. David (n 20) 284–285; see also Dinah Shelton, *Remedies in International Human Rights Law* (Oxford University Press 2015) 7.

[111] Keller and Chernishova (n 15) 247.

[112] ibid.

[113] In *Giri v Nepal* case, Nepal observed that the armed conflict prevailing in the country prompted the declaration of the State of Emergency; consequently, 'informing families of the arrest of individuals a long time after arrest was dictated by a state of necessity, to ensure the security of detainees and their families, as well as the security of places of detention.' Cf. HRCee, *Yubraj Giri v. Nepal* (n 23) [4.3].

[114] Cf. HRCee, General Comment no. 20 para 3 quoted in ibid [7.6]. Thus, the disregard of the next of kin's request for information on their beloved one held in *incommunicado* detention – source of

The post-conflict conduct of State authorities is not immune from the Committee's scrutiny, in light of the difficulties for families in obtaining answers despite the end of the conflict. For instance, the Committee has taken note of 'the particular difficulties that a State party may face in investigating crimes [such as enforced disappearances] [...] committed on its territory by the hostile forces of a foreign State'[115] in the Bosnia and Herzegovina context. In light of these circumstances and the peculiar characteristic of the obligation to investigate enforced disappearances and to bring the culprits to justice – i.e., an obligation of means and not of result – the Committee has not found a violation of Article 2 (3) ICCPR, read alone. However, apart from the difficulties of the State in elucidating the fate and whereabouts of disappeared persons, the Committee has considered other aspects, i.e.,

– the passage of time since the disappearance occurred and since domestic adjudicators found that State authorities failed to take investigative measures in this respect;[116]

– the possibility of pursuing investigations by other means (since the duty to investigate must be interpreted in a way which does not impose an impossible or disproportionate burden on the authorities);

– whether the State proactively provided the family with information;

– whether the information was provided to the family members at their own request or after very long delays;

– the psychosocial situation of family members due to continuing uncertainty resulting from the disappearance of their relative.[117]

In light of the foregoing, the Committee has recognized the multiple facets of the State obligation to provide families of persons reported missing with information on their fate (e.g., the obligation to undertake steps aimed at elucidating the fate and whereabouts of the missing even after years since the termination of the conflict). A disregard of any of these facets[118] has led the

---

distress and anguish – amounts to a violation of Article 7, read in conjunction with Article 2 (3) ICCPR, with regard to the author's wife and his two children. ibid [7.7]. Cf. HRCee, *El Alwani v The Libyan Arab Jamahiriya, Comm No 1295/2004* (2007) UN Doc. CCPR/C/90/D/1295/2004 [4]; *El Abani v. The Libyan Arab Jamahiriya* (n 15) [7.5]; *Quinteros et al. v. Uruguay* (n 13) [14]; *Sarma v. Sri Lanka* (n 13) [9.5].

[115] Cf. HRCee, *Emina Kožljak and Sinan Kožljak v Bosnia and Herzgovina, Comm no 1970/2010*, (2014) UN Doc. CCPR/C/112/D/1970/2010 [9.5].

[116] 18 years passed since the authors' missing husband and father was last seen, in an area where enforced disappearances are known to have occurred in a systematic manner; more than three years passed since the Bosnian Constitutional Court held that the State authorities had violated the rights of the authors by failing to take effective measures to investigate the fate and whereabouts of their relatives - February 2006 - and that those authorities had failed to enforce its February decision - November 2006. Cf. ibid [9.6].

[117] ibid. On the duty to investigate as an obligation of means, cf. HRCee, *Fatima Rizvanović and Ruvejda Rizvanović v. Bosnia and Herzegovina* (n 19) [9.5]; *Fatima Prutina and others v. Bosnia and Herzegovina* (n 21) [9.5].

[118] In the HRCee's case law cited in the previous footnotes of the present study, this was tantamount to prolonged uncertainty, lack of availability of alternative means of investigation, passivity of State

Committee to find a violation of Article 7 read in conjunction with Article 2 (3) ICCPR at the detriment of family members of missing persons.

The duty to account for missing persons and to inform their families about their fate has been judicially developed by the ECtHR in the examination of the dual nature – substantive/procedural – of the ECHR's provisions. The reasoning of the Court is more sophisticated than the HRCee's and, as noted in section 1 of the present Chapter, takes into account the context on the ground. In an armed conflict, 'from a humanitarian point of view', the lack of record keeping on persons who are held in custody and on the locations where they are held cannot be excused 'with reference either to the fighting ... or to the overall confused and tense state of affairs.'[119] This consideration makes part of the framework regulating the duty to account for missing persons; specifically, in the leading case *Cyprus v Turkey*, the Court noted that

> the absence of such information has made it impossible to allay the concerns of the relatives of the missing persons about the latter's fate. Notwithstanding the impossibility of naming those who were taken into custody, the respondent State should have made other inquiries with a view to accounting for the disappearances. [...].[120]

In this case, the Court delineated the contours of the duty to inform the family member(s) under the procedural limb of Article 5 ECHR (right to liberty and security).

Humanitarian measures cannot, *per se,* satisfy the requirements enshrined in the obligation to carry out an investigation enshrined, *inter alia,* in Article 5 ECHR.[121] *Ad hoc* bodies might be mandated with investigatory tasks resembling the duty to conduct an investigation into alleged disappearance of persons who found themselves under the authorities' custody. For instance, this was the case

---

authorities vis-à-vis requests for information, scant information received by the family after several attempts to obtain it.

[119] This *dictum* concerns the IAC occurred in Cyprus in the 1970s where thousands went missing; their fate and whereabouts were unknown due to the lack of any record keeping on their detention. In the leading case on the matter - *Cyprus v Turkey* - the Court deemed 'irrefutable' the evidence that Greek Cypriots were held by Turkish or Turkish-Cypriot forces. ECtHR, *Cyprus v. Turkey (GC)* (n 45) [148].

[120] Following this reasoning, the Court found that 'there has been a continuing violation of Article 5 [right to liberty and security, ECHR] by virtue of the failure of the authorities of the respondent State to conduct an effective investigation into the whereabouts and fate of missing Greek-Cypriot persons in respect of whom there is an arguable claim that they were in custody at the time they disappeared'. ibid [149–150]. Already at the time of the leading case *Kurt v Turkey,* the Court acknowledged that the State has an obligation to account for a person in its detention pursuant to Article 5 ECHR. Cf. ECtHR, *Kurt v. Turkey* (n 29) [124]. Under this obligation are subsumed the duty to keep records of the person detained as well as the duty to carry out an investigation into alleged detention. Cf. ibid [125] (referring to the lack of any record about the date, time, location of detention, the name of the detainee, the reasons for detention, and the name of the person effecting it). On the obligation to keep records, see also ECtHR, *Anguelova v Bulgaria, Judgment* (2002) App no. 38361/97 [157].

[121] The Court stated the foregoing by referring to the procedural obligation subsumed under Article 5 (right to liberty and security of person), i.e., the duty to conduct a prompt and effective investigation into an arguable claim that a person has been taken into custody and has not been seen since then. See ECtHR, *Kurt v. Turkey* (n 29) [124].

of the humanitarian body created in Cyprus under the auspices of the UN – the Committee on Missing Persons (CMP):[122] the purpose of its investigative mandate was to determine whether or not any of the missing persons on its list were dead or alive. In this respect,

> the Court has underlined that the respondent State [Turkey]'s procedural obligation at issue cannot be discharged through its contribution to the investigatory work of the CMP. [...] Although the CMP's procedures are undoubtedly useful for the humanitarian purpose for which they were established, they are not of themselves sufficient to meet the standard of an effective investigation [...]. [123]

Thus, the *Cyprus v Turkey's* perspective on the duty to carry out an investigation represents an important clarification of the extent of the duty to account for missing persons and of its implications under IHRL.[124]

The ECtHR has recognized that in armed conflict scenarios practical solutions on the ground can be the only viable ones vis-à-vis the issue of missing persons: it might be possible that the parties to the conflict would prefer 'a "politically-sensitive" approach to the missing persons problem' and that, therefore, a humanitarian mechanism with a limited mandate would be the only solution which could be agreed upon by the parties to the conflict. However, in the words of the Court, this 'can have no bearing on the application of the provisions of the [ECHR]'.[125] Thus, the circumstances of the armed conflict, where normal investigative procedures might not be available, [126] do not create a waiver for disregarding the obligations under the Convention. In this context, the Court outlined the terms of implementation of the 'obligation to account for the whereabouts and fate of a missing person'[127] under Article 3 ECHR. Terminologically and substantively, such obligation coincides with the IHL-based duty to account for missing persons. Article 3 ECHR[128] imposes 'a

---

[122] In 1981 the talks between the Turkish Cypriot and Greek Cypriot leaders held under the auspices of the UN led to an agreement to set up the CMP in Cyprus, mandated to 'draw up comprehensive lists of missing persons of both communities, specifying as appropriate whether they are alive or dead, and in the latter case approximately time of the deaths' (cf. Article 13, CMP Terms of Reference, 1981, http://www.cmp-cyprus.org/about-the-cmp/terms-of-reference-and-mandate/ accessed 12 February 2016). The Committee is not mandated to establish the cause of death or attribute responsibility for the death of missing persons (Cf. Article 11, CMP Terms of Reference, 1981). See also sub-section 2.1.2 in Chapter V.

[123] ECtHR, *Cyprus v. Turkey (GC)* (n 45) [27, 135, 149].

[124] Alastair R Mowbray, *Cases, Materials, and Commentary on the European Convention on Human Rights* (3rd ed, Oxford University Press 2012) 257.

[125] ECtHR, *Varnava and Others v. Turkey (GC)* (n 41) [193].

[126] In assessing the compliance of the applicants with the six-month rule, the Court considered that 'the applicants, who were among a large group of persons affected by the disappearances, could, in the exceptional situation of international conflict where no normal investigative procedures were available, reasonably await the outcome of the initiatives taken by their government and the United Nations.' Ibid [170].

[127] The Court released its Grand Chamber judgment in 2009, i.e., four years after the publication of the ICRC Study on Customary IHL that spells out the 'obligation to account for the missing persons' in explicit terms in its Rule 117. Although the Court did not rely on this document, it is certain that it made use of a similar wording that is not proper to IHRL.

[128] Sudre points out that the Court 're-writes' Article 3 ECHR, by adding the obligation to act in a certain way to the prohibition to act in a certain way. He underlines that the strengthening of the

primarily negative obligation' on State authorities 'to refrain from inflicting serious harm',[129] i.e., the prohibition of torture and of inhuman and degrading treatment. However, in the successive case law – *Varnava and others v Turkey* – focused on the same context of the inter-state case *Cyprus v Turkey*, the Court detects[130] a positive substantive obligation[131] to account for missing persons.[132]

The *Varnava's* obligation to account for the missing must be differentiated from the procedural obligation[133] to carry out an investigation under Article 3 ECHR. As Xenos underlines, in the context of disappearances the State is under a positive obligation 'to take operational steps (an investigation) to trace missing persons […], that is the substantive positive obligation in *ex ante* circumstances,'

---

protection of the individual operated under Article 3 ECHR lies in the redefinition of State's obligations made by the ECtHR. Sudre (n 9) 12.

[129] Schabas (n 85) 191.

[130] Some commentators underline that the Court has made use of the doctrine of positive obligations without explicitly declaring it (e.g., Brand v The Netherlands, 2004; Doğan and Others v Turkey, 2004). Frédéric Sudre and others, *Les grands arrêts de la Cour européenne des droits de l'homme* (Presses universitaires de France 2003) 22–23.

[131] Mowbray notes that the Court has not provided an authoritative definition of positive obligations; he also observes that 'their key characteristic is the duty upon States to undertake specific affirmative tasks'. Alastair R Mowbray, *The Development of Positive Obligations under the European Convention on Human Rights by the European Court of Human Rights* (Hart Publishing 2004) 1–2. In his dissenting opinion in *Gül v Switzerland*, Judge Martens specified that '[n]egative obligations require member States to refrain from action, positive to take action'. Cf. ECtHR, *Dissenting Opinion of Judge Martens - Gül v Switzerland, Judgment* (1996) App no. 23218/94. Akandji-Kombe underlines that positive obligations require national authorities to take the necessary measures to safeguard a right and to adopt reasonable and suitable measures to protect the rights of the individual. See Jean-François Akandji-Kombe, *Positive Obligations under the European Convention on Human Rights. A Guide to the Implementation of the European Convention on Human Rights* (Council of Europe 2007) 8. For a review of the doctrine of positive obligations and of the different scholarly positions on the issue see Sandra Krähenmann, *Positive Obligations in Human Rights Treaties (PhD Dissertation No. 949)* (Graduate Institute of International and Development Studies 2012) 39–91; Hugues Dumont and Isabelle Hachez, 'Les Obligations Positives Déduites Du Droit International Des Droits de L'homme : Dans Quelles Limites?' in Yves Cartuyvels and et al. (eds), *Les droits de l'homme, bouclier ou épée du droit pénal?* (Facultés Universitaires Saint-Louis 2007) 45–73; Silvia Borelli, 'Positive Obligations of States and the Protection of Human Rights' (2006) 15 Interights Bulletin 101, 101–104; S Krähenmann, 'Positive Obligations in Human Rights Law during Armed Conflicts' in Gloria Gaggioli and Robert Kolb (eds) (Edward Elgar Publishing 2013). For an overview of the doctrine in the context of human rights case law, see, for instance, Dimitris Xenos, *The Positive Obligations of the State under the European Convention of Human Rights* (Routledge 2012); Frédéric Sudre, 'Les "obligations Positives" dans La Jurisprudence Européenne Des Droits de L'homme' (1995) 6 Revue trimestrielle des droits de l'homme 363; Alain Didier Olinga, 'The African Charter on Human and Peoples' Rights and Positive Obligations' (2006) 15 Interights Bulletin 117; TJ Melish and A Aliverti, 'Positive Obligations in the Inter-American Human Rights System' (2006) 15 Interights Bulletin 120; MN Montoya Céspedes, 'The Inter-American Court of Human Rights' Positive Obligations Doctrine: Between Unidirectional Influence and Judicial Dialogue' in Yves Haeck, Oswaldo Ruiz-Chiriboga and Clara Burbano-Herrera (eds), *The Inter-American Court of Human Rights: Theory and Practice, Present and Future* (Intersentia 2015).

[132] Cf. ECtHR, *Varnava and Others v. Turkey (GC)* (n 41) [200]. See also ECtHR, *Zorica Jovanović v Serbia, Judgment* (2013) App no. 21794/08 [70]; *Palić v Bosnia and Herzegovina* (n 3) [74].

[133] Sudre observes that 'à l'obligation positive substantielle s'ajoute […] l'obligation procédurale de procéder à une enquête officielle, approfondie et effective en vue de l'identification et de la punition des responsables en cas d'allégation défendable de traitements contraires à l'article 3 commis par des agents de l'Etat [footnotes omitted]'. Sudre (n 9) 14.

i.e., before harm is sustained.[134] Nevertheless, accounting for the missing entails investigative activities; therefore, where does the difference lie? The nature of the obligation to investigate under Article 3, which includes the duty to account for the missing, is two-fold: substantive and procedural. Akandji-Kombe stresses that the difference between the substantive character of the obligation and its procedural character lies in the fact that

> le défaut d'investigation effective s'analyse en un mauvais traitement au sens de l'article 3. Il ne sera alors pris en compte par le juge qu'en tant qu'il constitue la cause d'une souffrance qui atteint le seuil de gravité déterminant l'applicabilité de cette disposition. La problématique est [...] réservée à un cas-type tout à fait particulier: celui où des proches [...] d'une personne disparue revendiquent pour eux-mêmes la qualité de victime d'une violation de l'article 3. [...] La Cour ne retiendra la violation de l'article 3 que si elle est convaincue que la carence ou l'inertie des autorités a généré chez le requérant – le proche – une souffrance ou une douleur particulières, lesquelles seront appréciées en fonction d'un certain nombre de critères. [...] Dans cette perspective, l'absence d'enquête effective peut donc s'analyser théoriquement en un traitement inhumain [...]. [emphasis added].[135]

Thus, the first factor that allows us to make the distinction lies in the substance of the action: while a substantive obligation consists in undertaking those measures needed for full enjoyment of rights, a procedural obligation consists in organizing domestic procedures to ensure better human rights protection and in setting up sufficient remedies in cases of violation.[136] The second factor resides in the principled-considerations behind these two dimensions: the substantive obligation to account for the missing is inherently humanitarian, since it is meant to respond to the need of families to know the fate and whereabouts of their missing relatives and is directly connected to the duty of all parties to the conflict to account for missing persons under IHL;[137]

---

[134] In Xenos' words 'there should be [domestic] access to enforce the standards of law before harm is sustained', as it stems from Article 35(1) ECHR (exhaustion of domestic remedies) read in conjunction with Article 13 ECHR (right to a remedy). He argues that 'such access should be available against the private parties who have failed to comply with the regulated standards that condition the operation of their activities (i.e., the substantive content of positive obligations)'. He also stresses that 'substance of positive obligations regards the active protection of human rights. The content of the active protection is ultimately determined against the aim of the actual prevention of human rights violations'. Xenos (n 131) 187–188, 189.

[135] See Jean-François Akandji-Kombe, 'L'obligation Positive D'enquête Sur Le Terrain de L'article 3 CEDH' in Catherine-Amélie Chassin (ed), *La portée de l'article 3 de la Convention européenne des droits de l'homme* (Bruylant 2006) 128–129.

[136] Akandji-Kombe (n 131) 16. In addition to that, the two dimensions have different legal bases (i.e., in the context of Article 3: Article 3 for the substantive obligation; articles 3 and 1 ECHR for the procedural).

[137] In this sense, the obligation under Article 3 is of '*a more general humanitarian nature*, for it enjoins the authorities to react to the plight of the relatives of the dead or disappeared individual in a humane and compassionate way.' Cf. ECtHR, *Janowiec and others v Russia, Judgment* (2012) App nos. 55508/08 and others [152]. Mowbray underlines that 'the effective investigation obligation under article 3 is less well developed and more uncertain in its application at Strasbourg that the corresponding obligation created via Article 2.' This is the result of an inconsistent pattern in reaching decisions on complaints relating to allegations of breaches of both the substantive prohibitions and effective investigation duties enshrined in Article 3. Mowbray, *The Development of*

the procedural obligation to carry out an investigation under Article 3 read in conjunction with Article 1 ECHR has to be (see *infra*, section 3) capable of leading to the identification and punishment of those responsible.[138] Under the ECHR, the duty to account for a missing person[139] will, therefore, be fulfilled when the requests of the relatives of the missing are taken into consideration by the authorities and are answered accordingly; passivity and 'silence of the authorities [...] in the face of the real concerns of the relatives of the missing persons' may attain that level of severity that triggers a violation of the prohibition of inhuman treatment.[140]

Despite the existence of the phenomenon of persons unaccounted for as result of *in bello* IHL/IHRL violations in many of the African countries,[141] the case law on the issue is not abundant.[142] In general terms, the AfCommHPR has made it clear that in the context of an armed conflict the State 'must take all possible measures to ensure that [civilians] are treated in accordance with [IHL]',[143] which includes the obligation to prevent cases of missing persons and to account for them. While the African Court has not delivered a judgment on the issue of missing persons yet, the Commission has assessed the conduct of States, in

---

Positive Obligations under the European Convention on Human Rights by the European Court of Human Rights (n 131) 64.

[138] *Assenov and others v Bulgaria* is the first case in which the Court recognized the procedural limb of Article 3 ECHR and acknowledged the above accountability-driven considerations embedded in the obligation to carry out an investigation. Cf. ECtHR, *Assenov and others v Bulgaria, Judgment* (1998) App no. 24760/94 [102].

[139] The Court has considered it an obligation of means and not of result under both its dimensions. Cf. ECtHR, *Janowiec and others v. Russia* (n 137) [152] (on the substantive dimension); ECtHR, *Paul and Audrey Edwards v The UK, Judgment* (2002) App no. 46477/99 [71] (on the procedural dimension).

[140] ECtHR, *Cyprus v. Turkey (GC)* (n 45) [157].

[141] The ICMP dedicates a page on 'where are the missing'; among the countries featuring this problem are, for instance, Algeria (due to civil insurgency); Libya (due to the 2011 conflict); Burundi (due to the genocide and to the conflict); DRC (due to the 1998 conflict); Guinea (due to waves of political violence); Chad (due to the civil war). See ICMP. "Where are the missing", http://www.icmp.int/the-missing/where-are-the-missing/ accessed 12 June 2018.

[142] Confronted with a case of enforced disappearance, the Commission has stated that regardless of when the disappearance occurred, the fact of not fulfilling the obligation to account for the missing person triggers a continuing violation of the Charter and the competence of the Commission. The obligation to investigate cases of alleged forced disappearances has been identified in *J.E. Zitha and P.J.L. Zitha v Mozambique* where the Commission has developed its own view of the concepts 'continuing act/instantaneous act' in order to decide on its competence *ratione temporis*: the Commission has noted that the fact that the State has not proved the whereabouts of the victim and neither has it demonstrated efforts made to investigate the whereabouts makes the forced disappearance a continuing violation. AfCommHPR, *J.E. Zitha and P.J.L. Zitha v Mozambique* (n 99) [94]. The Commission did not decide on the merits of the case, as the requirement of the exhaustion of the local remedies – cf. Article 56 AfChHPR – had not been fulfilled by the applicant; thus, the Commission found the communication inadmissible. Cf. ibid [95–115].

[143] AfCommHPR, *Amnesty International et al. v. Sudan* (n 55) [50]. In this respect, the ECtHR has noted that the obligation to account for missing persons arises where a person's fate and whereabouts are unknown because of the situation on the ground; 'in a zone of international conflict Contracting States are under obligation to protect the lives of those not, or no longer, engaged in hostilities'. Cf. ECtHR, *Varnava and Others v. Turkey (GC)* (n 41) [185]. See also Louise Doswald-Beck, *Human Rights in Times of Conflict and Terrorism* (Oxford University Press 2011) 239.

particular, with regard to the State obligations arising in cases of *incommunicado* detention and enforced disappearances. Based on the Commission's assessment, the State has an obligation to adopt 'preventive measures such as halting of *incommunicado* detention, effective remedies under a transparent, independent and efficient legal system, and ongoing investigations into allegations of torture'.[144] This obligation is directly connected to the prohibition of depriving a detainee of any relation with the family and of refusing to inform his family on his fate and whereabouts. Such a conduct amounts to an 'inhuman treatment of both the detainee and the family concerned.'[145]

The IACtHR's emphasis is on the State's duty to conduct an investigation into 'every situation involving a violation of the rights protected by the Convention.'[146] Accordingly, the States parties to the ACHR would fail to comply with their duty to ensure the free and full enjoyment of the Convention rights to the persons within their jurisdiction when they act 'in such a way that the violation goes unpunished and the victim's full enjoyment of such rights is not restored as soon as possible'.[147] Since its first case on disappearances – *Velásquez Rodríguez v Honduras* – the IACtHR has implicitly adopted the positive obligations doctrine as an interpretative tool[148] of the ACHR. Grounded on Article 1(1) of the ACHR – obligation to respect the rights and to ensure their free and full exercise,[149] this doctrine characterizes the approach of the Court to the obligations of State authorities vis-à-vis the next of kin of the victim, including in the context of enforced disappearances.

For instance, Article 1 (1) is an 'endogenous vector'[150] within the Convention that is used by the Court in order to pinpoint the procedural facet of some of the Convention's provisions, including Article 5 ACHR (right to humane treatment).

---

[144] AfCommHPR, *Amnesty International et al. v. Sudan* (n 55) [56].

[145] ibid [54].

[146] IACtHR, *Velásquez-Rodríguez v. Honduras (Merits)* (n 70) [176]. The Court has changed the approach in the successive case law: only those of particular gravity must be investigated and punished. See Burgorgue-Larsen and Torres (n 61) 305.

[147] Burgorgue-Larsen and Torres (n 61) 305. In the *Goiburú* case, the Court has reached the conclusion that this obligation is to be considered part of the *jus cogens*. Cf. IACtHR, *Goiburú et al. v. Paraguay (Merits ...)* (n 61) [84].

[148] Montoya underlines that the ACHR explicitly provides for positive obligations (e.g., Article 2 obliging the State to adapt the national legislation to the Convention or Article 19 ordering States to provide for protection measures for children). Montoya Céspedes (n 131) 768.

[149] The obligation to respect the rights under the Convention means that the 'exercise of public authority has certain limits which derive from the fact that human rights are inherent attributes of human dignity and are, therefore, superior to the power of the State.' The obligation to ensure the free and full exercise of the rights 'implies the duty of the States Parties to organize the governmental apparatus and, in general, all the structures through which public power is exercised, so that they are capable of juridically ensuring the free and full enjoyment of human rights. As a consequence of this obligation, the States must prevent, investigate and punish any violation of the rights recognized by the Convention and, moreover, if possible attempt to restore the right violated'. Cf. IACtHR, *Velásquez-Rodríguez v. Honduras (Merits)* (n 70) [165–166].

[150] Some authors consider that the Court makes recourse to two techniques, i.e., exogenous vectors (external sources to the ACHR but that are part of the Inter-American system) and endogenous vectors (internal sources to the ACHR) in order to develop the procedural aspects of Article 5 ACHR. Burgorgue-Larsen and Torres (n 61) 383.

In this respect, the non-compliance of State authorities with the duty to investigate a violation of the ACHR, such as an enforced disappearance, infringes upon the rights of the family members of the victim of such violation, including their right to humane treatment[151] and/or their right to moral and mental integrity.[152]

The interpretation of the Court makes the negative and positive obligations[153] under Article 5 ACHR almost inseparable, where it admits that the disappearance

---

[151] For instance, in the context of the NIAC in El Salvador, two girls - *Ernestina and Erlinda Serrano Cruz* - disappeared; presumably they had been abducted by the Salvadorian armed forces during a military operation. Although the Court did not assess the disappearance of the two sisters due to the lack of jurisdiction to do so, it was able to find a violation of article 5 read in conjunction with Article 1 (1) ACHR at the detriment of the next of kin of Ernestina and Erlinda. The Court underlined that '[f]or years, the next of kin of Ernestina and Erlinda have lived with feelings of family disintegration, insecurity, frustration, anguish and impotence owing to the failure of the judicial authorities to investigate the reported facts diligently and within a reasonable time and to adopt any other measure to determine the whereabouts of Ernestina and Erlinda. [...] This failure to investigate what happened to Ernestina and Erlinda and their whereabouts has been and continues to be a source of suffering for their next of kin, who are still hoping to find them alive and achieve family reunification. [...]' In light of the foregoing, the Court declared that the State violated the right to humane treatment embodied in Article 5 [ACHR], in relation to Article 1(1) thereof, to the detriment of the next of kin of Ernestina and Erlinda Serrano Cruz. Cf. IACtHR, *Serrano-Cruz Sisters v El Salvador, Judgment - Merits, Reparations and Costs* (2005) Series C No. 120 [112–115]. From some of the testimonies listed in the case, the continuity of uncertainty between these two phases - conflict →post-conflict - emerges. For instance, the Director of the *Asociación Pro-Búsqueda*, the main NGO that tried to look for children abducted during the conflict, affirmed that during the armed conflict it was almost impossible to report a disappearance, because the families of those who disappeared did not have documents, there were roadblocks, and they had no money. The expert witness, Ana Deutsch, stated that 'the uncertainty of the next of kin who do not know where Ernestina and Erlinda are "was aggravated when, once the war had ended [,] the family renewed the search with the help of institutions [...] and did not succeed in discovering their whereabouts. With the passing of the years, the traumatic impact became more severe.' From the arguments of the representatives of the alleged victims and their next of kin, it is clear that the State did not act with due diligence to give the Serrano Cruz children and their family the possibility of a reunion during or after the conflict. Cf. ibid [113, 120].

[152] *Serrano Cruz sisters* is an atypical case, as the Court finds a violation of the right to humane treatment *per se* in connection with Article 1 (1). Oftentimes, the IACtHR has read Article 5 (1) - right to moral and mental integrity - in conjunction with Article 1 (1) in order to examine the attitude of the State authorities thereby condemning both the inertia and/or the obstacles put in place to hamper the search for information run by the next of kin. For instance, in *Blake* - the same context as *Bamaca* -, although the IACommHR did not invoke a violation of the right against the relatives, the Court considered such an allegation on the merits of the case by virtue of the principle *iura novit curia*. The violation of Article 5 to the detriment of the relatives of the disappeared person in relation to Article 1 (1) of the Convention resulted from the co-presence of three elements: i) the mental and physical impairment of the relatives generated by the enforced disappearance of Mr. Blake; ii) the sense of frustration, insecurity and impotence as a result of the public authorities' failure to investigate; iii) and the disregard for the cultural values in burning Mr. Blake's remains. Cf. IACtHR, *Blake v Guatemala, Judgment - Merits, Series C No 36* (1998) Series C No. 36 [113–115]. Together with the IACommHR, the Court is the body that has made the most extensive use of the principle *iura novit curia* in the human rights field in order to reframe petition and include rights not invoked by the petitioners (e.g., in *Blake v Guatemala*). Dinah Shelton, 'Jura Novit Curia in International Human Rights Tribunals' in Nerina Boschiero and others (eds), *International Courts and the Development of International Law* (T M C Asser Press 2013) 199.

[153] The negative obligations under the ACHR can be boiled down to the duty to abstain from infringing the rights recognized under the ACHR. Montoya Céspedes (n 131) 766.

per se causes the suffering of the next of kin and, therefore, amounts to a violation of Article 5.[154]

2.2. The duty of the (former) parties to the conflict to cooperate in accounting for the missing: IHRL implications

The case law shows that the duty to inform the families about the fate of their missing relatives is directly connected to an effective implementation of the prohibition of inhuman treatment. This entails that the circumstances on the ground cannot legitimate any form of lawful departure from this obligation.

The foregoing leads to build in the considerations put forward in Chapter II, particularly in relation to the NIAC settings where most of the normative gaps are present. Under IHRL, State authorities bear the above-mentioned duty in IAC/NIAC and post-IAC/NIAC settings; in addition to that, non-state armed groups are not freed from abiding by human rights obligations during the conflict and in post-conflict settings (being these groups successful or unsuccessful).

Under IHRL,[155] State authorities must exercise due diligence and prevent the harm that could be caused by the conduct of private persons/entities, which include non-state armed groups.[156] As emphasized in sub-section 3.1 of Chapter II, 'for justifying the duty of the State to act in due diligence to prevent, investigate or redress violations' the non-state actor concerned must be considered the holder of the duty that has been disregarded.[157] Although this horizontal interpretation of IHRL does not emerge from the pronouncements of the human rights judicial bodies, their call for application and interpretation of human rights in a manner that renders them practical and effective[158] should take

---

[154] The conduct of the authorities (e.g., failure to conduct an investigation into the disappearance, lack of support) is an aggravating factor that determines the violation of Article 5 read in conjunction with Article 1 (1) ACHR. For instance, in the *Mapiripán Massacre* Case – a case concerning the campaign of massive extra-judiciary executions and enforced disappearances run by a paramilitary group in Colombia – the Court has recognized that the next of kin of the victims suffered damage due to the latter's disappearance and execution, the lack of support by State authorities in the search for those missing, the fear to begin or continue the search for their next of kin in face of possible threats, the impossibility of honoring their deceased beloved ones. Cf. IACtHR, *Mapiripán Massacre v. Colombia (Merits ...)* (n 66) [144].

[155] Cf. Article 3, ICPPED; HRCee, 'General Comment No. 31' (n 106) paras 6–8. A violation of Article 3 ECHR at the detriment of the family members is not limited to cases where State authorities have been found responsible for the disappearance, but also arises in the case of disappearances perpetrated by non-state armed groups. Cf. ECtHR, *Açış v Turkey, Judgment* (2011) App no. 7050/05 [36, 51–54].

[156] HRCee, 'General Comment No. 31' (n 106) para 8; *Velásquez-Rodríguez v. Honduras (Merits)* (n 70) [172 and 174].

[157] Vincent Chetail, 'The Legal Personality of Multinational Corporations, State Responsibility and Due Diligence: The Way Forward' in Vincent Chetail and others (eds), *Unité et diversité du droit international/Unity and Diversity of International Law. Essays in Honour of Prof. Pierre-Marie Dupuy* (Brill | Nijhoff 2014) 127.

[158] Cf. ECtHR, *Maskhadova and others v Russia, Judgment* (2013) App no 18071/05 [222]; *Sabanchiyeva and others v Russia, Judgment* (2013) App no 38450/05 [132]; *Kushtova and others v Russia, Judgment* (2014) App no 21885/07 [38]; *Abdulayeva v Russia, Judgment* (2014) App no 38552/05 [33]; *Zalov and Khakulova v Russia, Judgment* (2014) App no 7988/09 [81]; *Arkhestov and*

stock of these considerations. These are particularly relevant in contexts of transition from an armed conflict to peace where the former parties to the conflict should cooperate in order to address the pending consequences of the conflict itself.

The prohibition of inhuman treatment is embedded in common Article 3 GC I-IV under the form of an obligation of humane treatment to be implemented by both State and non-state parties to NIAC vis-à-vis all the persons not or no longer participating in the hostilities. In light of the interconnectedness between conflict/post-conflict phases, this obligation of humane treatment does not stop providing its effects abruptly at the termination of the NIAC; indeed, '[p]ersons protected under common Article 3 must never be treated as less than fellow human beings and their inherent human dignity must be upheld and protected.'[159] In addition to that, the customary duty of the parties to the conflict to account for the missing also continues to be applicable in the post-conflict phase; consequently, this duty requires a direct involvement of the non-state armed group in the efforts to account for the missing. The simultaneous application of IHL and IHRL rules concerning investigative activities in relation to the missing entails that the duty to account for missing persons is a protective baseline (see sub-section 2.3.2.3 of Chapter III) that should be guaranteed regardless of the circumstances on the ground.

What the right to humane treatment entails in terms of protection is spelled out under IHRL; the sub-sections above have illustrated this protective framework vis-à-vis the specific situation of missing persons and their families. Thus, all former parties to the conflict must cooperate to account for missing persons and, consequently, respect and protect the right to humane treatment of the family members. Despite the current skeptical[160] approach of the judicial

---

others v Russia, Judgment (2014) App no 22089/07 [87]. Chetail points out that '[s]uch a conclusion is not only implicit in the notion of due diligence as inferred from the regime of State responsibility. It is further required by [IHRL] for ensuring effective respect of human rights.' See Chetail (n 157) 127.

[159] ICRC, Commentary on the First Geneva Convention: Convention (I) for the Amelioration of the Condition of the Wounded and Sick in Armed Forces in the Field (2nd edn, 2016) para 557 <https://www.icrc.org/applic/ihl/ihl.nsf/Treaty.xsp?documentId=4825657B0C7E6BF0C12563CD002D6B0B0B&action=openDocument> accessed 20 July 2018.

[160] The HRCee highlights that 'obligations are binding on States [Parties] and do not, as such, have direct horizontal effect as a matter of international law'. Cf. HRCee, 'General Comment No 35: Article 9 (Liberty and Security of Person)' (2014) UN Doc CCPR/C/GC/35 para 8. Although such an approach can be justified in light of the treaty for which it has a monitoring and quasi-judicial function, its stance does not reflect the current developments under international law (see, in this respect, sub-section 3.1 of Chapter II). Reporting and inquiry bodies are taking a different approach: for instance, the Panel of Experts tasked by the UNSC to provide information on the sanctions regime in Sudan has taken the approach according to which 'all parties to the conflict in Darfur have a responsibility to safeguard and protect human rights, while the Government of the Sudan has an added responsibility under the relevant human rights treaties.' Accordingly, the Panel has concluded that the Sudan Liberation Army/Minni Minawi faction 'failed to effectively investigate the case involving the disappearance and subsequent killing of persons previously detained by the group'; in other words, the non-state armed group concerned failed to undertake those actions that ensure the protection and safeguard of human rights. See UNSC, 'Report of the Panel of Experts Established pursuant to Resolution 1591 (2005) Concerning the Sudan Prepared in Accordance with Paragraph 2 of Resolution 1713 (2006)' (2007) S/2007/584 paras 325, 341. Along the same lines, the Commission

bodies to the horizontal application of human rights, it is submitted that the lack of cooperation between State authorities/non-state armed group might be considered as a failure of both 'to respond to the quest for information by the relatives or the obstacles placed in their way, leaving them to bear the brunt of the efforts to uncover any facts'.[161] Similar remarks hold valid in the contextual setting of IACs: the former parties to the conflict must collaborate in order to account for the missing. An un-collaborative conduct would result in the disregard of the obligation to account for the whereabouts and fate of missing persons and in a failure to ensure the family members' right to humane treatment.

3. The Accountability Dimension of the Measures to Ascertain the Fate and Whereabouts of Missing Persons

Ex officio investigations[162] – i.e., investigations run regardless of any explicit request for information/allegation of violation – are mandatory depending on the human rights violation concerned (e.g., extrajudicial executions, forced disappearances).[163] Sivakumaran points out that an investigation tries to avoid

---

of Inquiry on Syria broadened the spectrum of the legal analysis, as at the beginning of its work it did not have enough elements to consider applicable IHL: after having recognized that non-state actors could not formally become parties to IHRL treaties, the Commission firmly stated that 'they must nevertheless respect the fundamental human rights of persons forming customary international law […], in areas where such actors exercise *de facto* control'. See Human Rights Council, '7th Report of the Independent International Commission of Inquiry on the Syrian Arab Republic' (2012) UN Doc A/HRC/21/50 Annex II, para 10. See also UNSG, 'Report of the Secretary-General's Panel of Experts on Accountability in Sri Lanka' (2011) para 188.

[161] ECtHR, *Varnava and Others v. Turkey (GC)* (n 41) [200].

[162] The ICPPED explicitly provides for an obligation to investigate 'acts defined in article 2 committed by persons or groups of persons acting without the authorization, support or acquiescence of the State and to bring those responsible to justice', i.e., enforced disappearances perpetrated by non-state actors. Cf. Article 3, ICPPED. The CAT provides for a duty to ensure that State's competent authorities proceed to a prompt and impartial investigation, wherever there is a reasonable ground to believe that an act of torture has been committed in any territory under the State's jurisdiction. Cf. Article 12, CAT. The ECtHR has noted that '[i]t falls to the authorities to uncover, as far as may be practicable and reasonable in the circumstances, the facts surrounding the death and the identities of any persons involved in unlawful acts in that regard with a view to holding them to account.' ECtHR, *Charalambous and others v Turkey and other applications, Decision* (2012) App nos. 46744/07 and others [60]. The UNSG observes that cases of missing persons and enforced disappearances arise because of a 'conduct that may constitute criminal offences and may also, in certain circumstances, amount to war crimes or crimes against humanity. States have an obligation, clearly established in international law, to investigate and prosecute such conduct.' UNSG, 'Report of the Secretary General - Missing Persons' (2012) UN Doc. A/67/267 para 49.

[163] For instance, the IACommHR affirms 'the State is obliged to investigate all situations entailing violations of personal integrity through the commission of torture and cruel, inhuman, and degrading treatments or punishments and that it must do so on an *ex officio* basis [...] and, in addition, it must initiate the corresponding criminal proceedings.' Cf. IACommHR, *Tirso Roman Valenzuela Avila v Guatemala, Case 723/01, Report No 24/04* [31]. The IACtHR also affirms that 'in cases of extrajudicial executions, forced disappearances and other grave human rights violations, the State has the obligation to initiate, *ex officio* and immediately, a genuine, impartial and effective investigation, which is not undertaken as a mere formality predestined to be ineffective (footnotes omitted)'.

the development of a climate of impunity that can generate further violations.[164] The reality shows that not every violation committed during an armed conflict can be effectively investigated.[165] As noted earlier, humanitarian measures aimed at accounting for missing persons do not meet the standards of an effective investigation required under human rights treaties, [166] especially when these measures are solely intended for 'determining whether or not any of the missing persons [...] were dead or alive'.[167]

Despite the judicial convergence concerning the accountability-driven purpose of the duty to investigate (sub-section 3.1), this section will show that human rights adjudicators do not share the same position vis-à-vis the degree of accessibility of investigation proceedings to the victim's family members. Obstacles to the access to information concerning investigative proceedings might depend on external factors to the investigation *per se*; hindrances that prevent families from accessing relevant information might also have an impact on the efforts run by the authorities (sub-section 3.2).[168] Moreover, a blurred overlapping between the accessibility claim and the right to the truth[169] claim

---

IACtHR, *Pueblo Bello Massacre v. Colombia (Merits ...)* (n 66) [143]; *Mapiripán Massacre v. Colombia (Merits ...)* (n 66) [219].

[164] S Sivakumaran, 'International Humanitarian Law' in Sangeeta Shah and others (eds), *International Human Rights Law* (2nd edn, Oxford University Press 2010) 485.

[165] Appointed by the UN Human Rights Council as head of a fact-finding committee with the task of examining the investigations carried out by Palestinians and Israelis in the aftermath of the conflict in Gaza between 2008-2009, Tomuschat stressed that there 'are constraints during armed conflict that do impede investigations. For example, not every death during an armed conflict can be effectively investigated. Similarly, the level of transparency expected of human rights investigations is not always achievable in situations of armed conflict, particularly as questions of national security often arise. The nature of hostilities might obstruct on-site investigations or make prompt medical examinations impossible. The conflict might have led to the destruction of evidence, and witnesses might be hard to locate or be engaged in conflict elsewhere. When the fighting is over, some of these constraints tend to lose their relevance.' C Tomuschat, 'Report of the Committee of Independent Experts in [IHL] and [IHRL] to Monitor and Assess Any Domestic, Legal or Other Proceedings Undertaken by Both the Government of Israel and the Palestinian Side, in the Light of General Assembly Resolution 64/254, Including the Independence, Effectiveness, Genuineness of These Investigations and Their Conformity with International Standards' (UN Human Rights Council 2010) UN Doc. A /HRC/15/50 para 32.

[166] ECtHR, *Cyprus v. Turkey (GC)* (n 45) [135]; *Varnava and Others v. Turkey (GC)* (n 41) [187].

[167] The CMP is not empowered to make findings either on the cause of death or on the issue of responsibility for any deaths so established. Cf. *Cyprus v. Turkey (GC)* (n 45) [27].; ECtHR, *Varnava and Others v. Turkey (GC)* (n 41) [187].

[168] In cases of enforced disappearances perpetrated in the context of a NIAC, the IACtHR has held that 'the States must provide the corresponding authorities with the necessary logistic and scientific resources to collect and process evidence and, in particular, with the authority to access pertinent documentation and information to investigate the facts denounced and to obtain indications or evidence of the whereabouts of the victims.' Cf. IACtHR, *Contreras et al v El Salvador, Judgment - Merits, Reparations and Costs* (2011) Series C no. 232 [145].

[169] In its Grand Chamber Judgment - *Janowiec et al.* case - the ECtHR concluded that there was no lingering uncertainty on the fate of the applicants' relatives. Although not all the bodies had been recovered, their death was publicly acknowledged by Soviet and Russian authorities. Thus, it had become an established historical fact. Cf. ECtHR, *Janowiec and others v. Russia (GC)* (n 41) [186]. The passage of time can have an impact on the implementation of the obligation to carry out an investigation as well as on the realization of the right to truth. In this regard, see, for instance,

arises in certain cases. [170] However, this confusion seems to overlook that family members are not the sole stakeholders.

3.1. The duty to investigate as a conditio sine qua non for the elucidation of facts and responsibilities

States have a general duty to investigate human rights violations in order to clarify what happened and to identify who is responsible;[171] the duty to carry out a criminal investigation is mainly related to the violation of the most fundamental human rights (e.g., the right to life, the prohibition of torture, the prohibition of enforced disappearance). In the human rights case law, an investigation is deemed effective when it is capable of leading to the identification of those responsible; this is different from arguing that the duty to investigate must result into prosecution and punishment of those responsible (sub-section 3.1.1). Furthermore, other requirements must be met in order for the investigation to be considered in line with human rights standards:[172] it must be

---

Alessandra La Vaccara, 'Past Conflicts, Present Uncertainty: Legal Answers to the Quest for Information on Missing Persons and Victims of Enforced Disappearance. Three Case Studies from the European Context' (2018) XXXVII/2017 Polish Yearbook of International Law 35, 58-67.

[170] For instance, in *Tzilivaki* case, the ECtHR noted that some families, who have obtained the remains of their relatives reported missing during the events of 1974 in Cyprus, declined to participate in the late re-identification process of the remains or could not participate as they destroyed the remains as soon as they got them; the need to know was not felt as a priority by all the families. Cf. ECtHR, *Tzilivaki v. Cyprus* (n 79) [35].

[171] In the Inter-American context, the duty to investigate derives from the general obligation of the States Parties to ACHR to respect and ensure the human rights embodied in it (cf. Article 1(1) ACHR) together with the substantive right that should have been protected or ensured. Cf., for instance, IACtHR, *Mapiripán Massacre v. Colombia (Merits ...)* (n 66) [166]. The ECtHR subsumes a duty to investigate under Article 2 (right to life) and Article 3 (prohibition of Torture) ECHR read in conjunction with Article 1 ECHR (cf. *Cyprus v. Turkey (GC)* (n 45) [131] and the case law cited therein; *Janowiec and others v. Russia* (n 137) [152]); the HRCee subsumed this duty under, *inter alia,* Article 7 (prohibition of Torture), 6 (right to life) read in conjunction with Article 2(3) (right to remedy) ICCPR (cf., for instance, *Sharmila Tripathi v. Nepal* (n 17) [7.8]) Such a duty has been also considered by the AfCommHPR, but it is not clear from the case law whether it is a standalone obligation or whether it is a procedural obligation subsumed under the substantive facet of some of the provisions under AfChHPR (Cf. *Commission nationale des droits de l'Homme et des libertés v. Chad* (n 53) [19–22]). Pursuant to the Istanbul Protocol (non-binding document), the purpose of the investigation is to establish the facts on the alleged case of torture with a view to 'identifying those responsible for the incidents and facilitating their prosecution, or for use in the context of other procedures designed to obtain redress for victims'. UN OHCHR, 'Manual on the Effective Investigation and Documentation of torture and Other Cruel, Inhuman or Degrading Treatment or Punishment ("Istanbul Protocol")' (2004) UN Doc. HR/P/PT/8/Rev.1, paras 77-84.

[172] The human rights case law converges with regard to the requirements for an effective investigation. Under the ICCPR system, derived from the right to an effective remedy under Article 2 (3), the duty to investigate is considered fulfilled when the State conducts a prompt, thorough, impartial, and independent investigation in order to determine the factual circumstances and to identify those responsible. Cf. HRCee, 'General Comment No. 31' (n 106) para 10. In the ECHR system, in the context of Article 2, an investigation is deemed effective when 'it is capable of leading to a determination of whether the force used was or was not justified in the circumstances and to the identification and punishment of those responsible.' Any deficiency in the investigation, which undermines its capability of establishing the circumstances of the case or the person responsible, is liable to fall foul of the required standard of effectiveness. Cf. ECtHR, *Aslakhanova and others v*

independent; there must be a sufficient public scrutiny; it must be accessible to the victim's family; should violations be committed by private persons, a due diligence duty arising from the positive obligations to ensure and protect human rights requires State authorities to abide by the duty to investigate in conformity with the same requirements as for a violation committed by State agents.[173]

The contextual setting can affect the capacity of State authorities to carry out an investigation and to meet these requirements (sub-section 3.1.2). Thus, the way this duty is framed by the human rights bodies reduces/expands the investigations' purpose accordingly. The duty to investigate is framed as a procedural obligation subsumed under the substantive limb of human rights provisions and, in most cases, articulated through the lenses of the positive obligations doctrine (see *supra* sub-section 2.1). Investigations into human rights violations may also fulfill an important preventive function in light of the direct link that exists between investigations of past violations and the need to prevent future violations. As such, investigations can be regarded as measures of protection;[174] furthermore, the duty to investigate constitutes a remedial measure (sub-section 3.1.3). Yet the purpose of and the criteria to be met by the investigation do not change on the basis of its nature.

Russia, Judgment (2012) App nos. 2944/06 and others [121]. However, 'the lack of conclusions of any given investigation does not, by itself, mean that it was ineffective', cf. ECtHR, *Mikheyev v Russia, Judgment* (2006) App no. 77617/01 [107]. The following are the requirements that the ECtHR lists as key to comply with the duty to investigate: i) independence, i.e., 'the persons responsible for and carrying out the investigation' must be 'independent from those implicated in the events'; ii) '[a] requirement of promptness and reasonable expedition is implicit' in the context of a violation of the right to life' (however, in historical cases, such a requirement might no longer be relevant, cf. ECtHR, *Gürtekin et al v Cyprus, Ayse Akay et al v Cyprus and Ayse Eray et al v Cyprus, Decision* (2014) App nos 60441/13, 68206/13, 68667/13 [21]); iii) the degree of public scrutiny required may well vary from case to case and is regarded as 'essential in maintaining public confidence in the authorities' adherence to the rule of law'; iv) accessibility to the family, i.e., the victim's next of kin must be involved in the procedure to the extent necessary to safeguard his or her legitimate interests. Cf. ECtHR, *Al-Skeini and others v The UK, Judgment (GC)* (2011) App no. 55721/07 [166–167]. Pursuant to the Minnesota Protocol (non-binding document), an investigation shall be prompt, transparent, and carried out effectively, thoroughly, and with independence. See UN OHCHR, 'The Minnesota Protocol on the Investigation of Potentially Unlawful Death' (2016), UN Doc. HR/PUB/17/4 (UN OHCHR 2017), paras. 20, 22-33.

[173] States have a duty of due diligence, should the violations be committed by private persons; this entails that the requirements above hold valid for those violations that are not attributable to the State, but that the State has the duty to prevent. Cf. ECtHR, *Cyprus v. Turkey (GC)* (n 45) [131]; *Velásquez-Rodríguez v. Honduras (Merits)* (n 70) [177]; HRCee, 'General Comment No. 31' (n 106) para 8. More specifically, a violation of Article 3 ECHR at the detriment of the family members is not limited to cases where State authorities have been found responsible for the disappearance, but also arises in the case of disappearances perpetrated by non-state armed groups. Cf. ECtHR, *Açış v. Turkey* (n 155) [36, 51–54]. Krähenmann underlines that 'the doctrine of positive obligations is instrumental to hold the State accountable for human rights abuses committed by both rebel forces and paramilitary groups'. Krähenmann, 'Positive Obligations in Human Rights Law during Armed Conflicts' (n 131) 177. See also UN OHCHR, 'The Minnesota Protocol' (n 172), para 15.

[174] Amichai Cohen and Yuval Shany, 'Beyond the Grave Breaches Regime: The Duty to Investigate Alleged Violations of International Law Governing Armed Conflicts' (2011) 14 Yearbook of International Humanitarian Law 37, 48–49.

3.1.1. The duty to investigate as an obligation of result?
The standalone assessment of the IACtHR

In the inter-American system, individuals have a right to an investigation in light of the joint reading of Articles 8 (right to a fair trial) [175] and 25 (right to judicial protection) with Article 1(1) ACHR (obligation to respect rights).[176] Since the undertaking of an investigation is key to find and punish those responsible, the need of the victims and of their families to know what happened is met with the fulfillment of the obligation to carry out an investigation.[177] Such obligation does not depend upon the 'the initiative of the victim or his family or upon their offer of proof, without an effective search for the truth by the government'.[178]

Although 'States must prevent, investigate and punish any violation of the rights recognized by the Convention',[179] there might be cases where those individually responsible cannot be legally punished or where the normal course of event is on hold[180] (e.g., armed conflicts, post-conflict settings). In these situations, 'the State is obligated to use the means at its disposal to inform the relatives of the fate of the victims and, if they have been killed, the location of their remains.'[181] Thus, the context and the circumstances on the ground do not affect the obligations of the State; neither these justify a defective conduct, mainly in cases of grave human rights violations.

As a matter of fact, the duty to investigate 'continues as long as there is uncertainty about the fate of the person who has disappeared' and must be conducted not as a mere formality preordained to be ineffective.[182] In recent case

---

[175] In this respect, the IACtHR has clarified that 'the right to fair trial should guarantee, within reasonable time, the right of the alleged victims or their relatives to have adopted all measures necessary to know the truth about the facts and to punish those responsible.' IACtHR, *Ituango Massacres v. Colombia (PO, Merits...)* (n 66) [289].

[176] Burgorgue-Larsen and Torres (n 61) 707; Anja Seibert-Fohr, *Prosecuting Serious Human Rights Violations* (Oxford University Press 2009) 68.

[177] Burgorgue-Larsen and Torres (n 61) 707; Seibert-Fohr (n 176) 68.

[178] IACtHR, *Velásquez-Rodríguez v. Honduras (Merits)* (n 70) [177]. Similarities on this point can be found in the case law of other human rights adjudicators: cf. HRCee, *Jit Man Basnet and Top Bahadur Basnet v. Nepal* (n 20) [8.8]; ECtHR, *Isayeva v Russia, Judgment* (2005) App no. 57950/00 [210].

[179] Cf. IACtHR, *Velásquez-Rodríguez v. Honduras (Merits)* (n 70) [166, 176].

[180] IACtHR, *Durand and Ugarte v Peru, Judgment - Merits* (2000) Series C no. 68 [143]. The State is obliged to organize its apparatus in a way that guarantee the rights under ACHR; thus, forced disappearance presumes disregard of this obligation which contributes to the conditions of impunity in which this type of act may be repeated; hence, the importance of the State adopting all necessary measures to avoid such facts, and to investigate and punish those responsible. IACtHR, *Heliodoro Portugal v. Panama (PO, Merits...)* (n 61) [116]. The Court considered the duty to investigate a *jus cogens* rule in the context of enforced disappearance, cf. IACtHR, *Goiburú et al. v. Paraguay (Merits ...)* (n 61) [84]. Nonetheless, in the *Diario Militar* case, while the Court highlights the *jus cogens* character of the prohibition of enforced disappearance, it simply acknowledged that, as a consequence, the duty to investigate 'becomes particularly strong and important.' cf. IACtHR, *Diario Militar Case (Merits ...)* (n 68) [232].

[181] Cf. IACtHR, *Velásquez-Rodríguez v. Honduras (Merits)* (n 70) [177, 181]; *Lucio Parada Cea et al v El Salvador, Case 10048* (1999) Report No.1/99 [150].

[182] Cf. IACtHR, *Velásquez-Rodríguez v. Honduras (Merits)* (n 70) [177, 181]; *Lucio Parada Cea et al. v. El Salvador* (n 181) [150].

law, the IACtHR has narrowed down the scope *ratione materiae* of the triad – prevent/investigate/punish – to the 'grave violations of human rights',[183] i.e., those violations that entail irreparable attacks on human life[184] (e.g., extrajudicial executions, forced disappearance, and other grave human rights violations).[185]

The Court makes it explicit that the international protection of human rights should not be confused with criminal justice and that the aim of IHRL is not to punish those responsible[186] but to protect the victims. Nevertheless, the foregoing shows a tendency towards criminalization of the assessment of human rights violations.[187] The expected result must be the punishment: if the State apparatus acts in such a way that human rights violations go unpunished and the victim's full enjoyment of human rights is not restored as soon as possible, 'the State has failed to comply with its duty to ensure the free and full exercise of those rights to the persons within its jurisdiction.'[188]

Thus, victims are creditors of the obligation to prosecute and to punish the perpetrators of human rights violations.[189] The duty to investigate is embedded in the triad prevent/investigate/punish, which recasts the right to truth and justice as a right to see those responsible punished;[190] in this sense, the duty to investigate is conceived as a stepping-stone in the fight against impunity[191] as well as a remedial tool against the violation of the right to know the truth.[192] Domestic

---

[183] IACtHR, *The Rochela Massacre v Colombia, Judgment - Merits, Reparations, and Costs* (2007) Series C no. 163 [193].

[184] IACtHR, *Heliodoro Portugal v. Panama (PO, Merits...)* (n 61) [243–247].

[185] Cf. ibid [115].

[186] IACtHR, *Velásquez-Rodríguez v. Honduras (Merits)* (n 70) [134].

[187] For an in-depth critical assessment of such a trend, see F Mégret and JPS Calderón, 'The Move towards a Victim-Centred Concept of Criminal Law and The "criminalization" of Inter-American Human Rights Law' in Yves Haeck, Oswaldo Ruiz-Chiriboga and Clara Burbano-Herrera (eds), *The Inter-American Court of Human Rights: Theory and Practice, Present and Future* (Intersentia 2015).

[188] IACtHR, *Velásquez-Rodríguez v. Honduras (Merits)* (n 70) [176]. However, in the same case the Court underlines that the duty to investigate is an obligation of means and not of result, see ibid [177].

[189] Mégret and Calderón (n 187) 432.

[190] Mégret and Calderón criticize this approach, for the obligation to resort to punishment is inextricably related the rights of victims of human rights violations - right to access to justice, right to a reparation, and right to fair trial – and sets the stage for the exercise of criminal repression as an obligation of the State, but also as a right of the victims. See ibid 422, 424, 425. The IACtHR explicitly states that '[t]he next of kin of the victims also have the right, and the State has the obligation to ensure that the facts are investigated effectively by the State authorities, that criminal proceedings are filed against those responsible for the unlawful facts, and that, if applicable, pertinent sanctions are imposed on the latter, and the damage suffered by the said next of kin is repaired.' IACtHR, *Heliodoro Portugal v. Panama (PO, Merits...)* (n 61) [146].

[191] In the Court's words, impunity means 'the overall lack of investigation, tracing, capture, prosecution and conviction of those responsible for violations of the rights protected by the American Convention', cf. IACtHR, *Maritza Urrutia v Guatemala, Judgment - Merits, Reparations and Costs* (2003) Series C No. 103 [126].

[192] Burgorgue-Larsen and Torres (n 61) 707–709; IACtHR, *Goiburú et al. v. Paraguay (Merits ...)* (n 61) [164]; *Ituango Massacres v. Colombia (PO, Merits...)* (n 66); *Bámaca-Velásquez v Guatemala, Judgment - Reparations and Costs* (2002) Series C No. 91 [74] (where the Court said 'the State "has the obligation to combat [impunity] through all legal means at its disposal because [it] fosters chronic recidivism of human rights violations and total defenselessness of the victims and their next of kin".

judiciary bodies have been reminded by the IACtHR that 'their function is not merely exhausted by enabling due process [...], but they must also ensure, within a reasonable time, the right to the victim or his/her next of kin to learn the truth about what happened and for those responsible to be punished'.[193] Although another common denominator to the human rights adjudicators is to affirm that the obligation to investigate is not an obligation of result,[194] the foregoing seems to prove the contrary as far as the inter-American context is concerned.

3.1.2. The duty to investigate as an obligation of means and its conflict/post-conflict contextualization

Unlike the IACtHR, the ECtHR shows more deference towards the domestic systems, as it proceeds on an *ad hoc* basis in the examination of the procedural obligation to carry out an investigation by considering such an obligation in the context where it must be implemented. The investigation into alleged human rights violations is a key component in the framework for the protection of human rights; accordingly, the Court has declared that

> an adequate response by the authorities in investigating allegations of serious human rights violations [...] may generally be regarded as essential in maintaining public confidence in their adherence to the rule of law and in preventing any appearance of collusion in or tolerance of unlawful acts.[195]

There is almost no difference[196] between the procedural obligation to carry out an investigation subsumed under Article 2 ECHR (right to life) and that under Article 3 ECHR (prohibition of torture) read in conjunction with Article 1 ECHR (obligation to respect human rights).[197]

A State that does not punish human rights violations would, further, not be complying with its duty to guarantee free and full exercise of the rights of persons under its jurisdiction' [footnotes omitted].)

[193] IACtHR, *Bulacio v Argentina, Judgment - Merits, Reparations, and Costs* (2003) Series C no. 100 [114].

[194] The ECtHR stresses that 'this 'is not an obligation of result, but of means'. Cf. ECtHR, *Mikheyev v. Russia* (n 172) [107]; *Al-Skeini and others v. The UK (GC)* (n 172) [166]. The IACtHR underlines that '[t]he duty to investigate [...] is not breached merely because the investigation does not produce a satisfactory result. Nevertheless, it must be undertaken in a serious manner and not as a mere formality preordained to be ineffective.' Cf. IACtHR, *Velásquez-Rodríguez v. Honduras (Merits)* (n 70) [177].

[195] ECtHR, *El-Masri v The Former Yougoslav Republic of Macedonia, Judgment (GC)* (2012) App no 39630/09 [192].

[196] *Contra:* ECtHR, *Janowiec and others v. Russia* (n 137) [152].

[197] In the context of Article 2 ECHR (right to life), the duty to investigate does not arise only when individuals are killed as a result of the use of force by State agents, but also when there exists an arguable claim according to which an individual who was last seen in the custody of agents of the State, subsequently disappeared in a context considered life-threatening. ECHR, *Cyprus v. Turkey (GC)* (n 45) [131–132 and case law cited therein]. In the Court's words 'this investigation, as with that under Article 2, should be capable of leading to the *identification and punishment of those responsible.*' [emphasis added]. Cf. ECtHR, *Assenov and others v. Bulgaria* (n 138) [102]. Mowbray underlines that these duties have the common aim of 'seeking to reinforce, at the national level, practical respect an implementation of the most fundamental substantive rights guaranteed by the Convention [...]. The investigation duties [...] encompass institutional elements (e.g. the requirement for investigators to be organizationally independent from those State agents allegedly involved in the killing or torture under investigation) and procedural obligations (e.g., investigators must utilize appropriate forensic science test to establish the causes and circumstances of a killing). Alastair R

In the context of Article 3 ECHR, the duty to carry out an investigation possesses an inherent duality: if read in light of the suffering of the families it has a 'more general humanitarian nature, for it enjoins the authorities to react to the plight of the relatives of the dead or disappeared individual in a humane and compassionate way';[198] if read in the context of what the direct victim suffered – e.g., ill-treatment by State agents – an effective official investigation into this allegation is required, i.e., an investigation that should be capable of leading to the identification and punishment of those responsible.[199] Should the former be resolved, the latter would remain in force. Indeed, the discovery of the body or the likelihood that the person who disappeared in life-threatening circumstances is already dead merely shed light upon one aspect of the fate of the missing person.[200] Thus, a fresh obligation to carry out an investigation arises when newly-discovered evidence comes to light, e.g., the discovery of bodies of persons reported missing in the context of an armed conflict bearing signs of violence and buried in circumstances highly suggestive of extra-judicial execution.[201]

The ECtHR's emphasis is more on the conduct of the investigation than the outcome.[202] In those cases where the families claimed that the duty to investigate had been disregarded due to the fact that the investigations ended without prosecution, the ECtHR has pointed out that

– there is no requirement on the authorities to launch a prosecution irrespective of the evidence which is available;

– the procedural obligation under Article 2 necessarily requires that there should be a judicial review of investigative decisions as such (e.g., when the decision to discontinue the investigation concerned insufficient evidence to justify prosecution);

Mowbray, 'Duties of Investigation under the European Convention on Human Rights' (2002) 51 International and Comparative Law Quarterly 437, 447–448.

[198] Cf. ECtHR, *Janowiec and others v. Russia* (n 137) [152].

[199] Cf. ECtHR, *El-Masri v. The Former Yougoslav Republic of Macedonia (GC)* (n 195) [182].

[200] Cf. ECtHR, *Aslakhanova and others v. Russia* (n 172) [230]; *Varnava and Others v. Turkey (GC)* (n 41) [145].

[201] Cf. ECtHR, *Gürtekin et al. v. Cyprus and other applications* (n 172) [21]; *Emin (Mustafa) et al v Cyprus, Decision* (2014) App no. 4176/14 [11]; *Cakicisoy et al v Cyprus, Decision* (2014) App no. 5523/12 [40]; *Kayıplar et al v Cyprus, Decision* (2015) App no. 42153/14 [11]. In *Palić v Bosnia and Herzegovina* the Court held that the procedural obligation under Article 2 does not come to an end with the discovery of the body; whether the investigation made it possible to establish the identity of the persons responsible for the disappearance and death of the victim and whether those persons were eventually brought to justice are key factors to assess the compliance of the State with Article 2. Cf. ECtHR, *Palić v. Bosnia and Herzegovina* (n 3) [64]; *Varnava and Others v. Turkey (GC)* (n 41) [145].

[202] Seibert-Fohr (n 176) 115–116. The ECtHR has recognized that the inadequate character of the investigation carried out by the prosecuting authorities can impact on the right to the truth regarding the relevant circumstances of a serious violation of human rights. Nevertheless, the Court has limited itself to declare that, in the context of the specific case of *El Masri*, the prosecuting authorities 'should have endeavored to undertake an adequate investigation in order to prevent any appearance of impunity' vis-à-vis certain acts. The focus on the adequate character of the investigation shows that the ECtHR puts more emphasis on the conduct of the authorities than the result of the investigation. Cf. ECtHR, *El-Masri v. The Former Yougoslav Republic of Macedonia (GC)* (n 195) [191–192].

– where it is in place, such a review may be considered a further safeguard of accountability and transparency;

– in any case, it is not for the Court to micro-manage the functioning of – and procedures applied in – criminal investigative and justice systems in Contracting States which may well vary in their approach and policies; no one model can be imposed.[203]

Consistently with the foregoing and similarly to the IACtHR, the Court acknowledges that in case of (forced) disappearances

characterized by an ongoing situation of uncertainty and unaccountability in which there is a lack of information or even a deliberate a concealment and obfuscation of what has occurred, [...] the procedural obligation will, potentially, persist as long as the fate of the person is unaccounted for; the ongoing failure to provide the requisite investigation will be regarded as a continuing violation. [...].[204]

Prosecution and punishment must be contextualized; in this regard, the Court stresses that

in *the normal course of events*, a criminal trial, with an adversarial procedure before an independent and impartial judge, must be regarded as furnishing the strongest safeguards of an effective procedure for the finding of facts and the attribution of criminal responsibility (emphasis added). [205]

The expectations of families who have lived with uncertainty for years may not coincide with what 'the normal course of events' will give as a result. In the Court's words, 'there is no right [...] to obtain a prosecution or conviction [...] and the fact that an investigation ends without concrete, or with only limited, results is not indicative of any failings as such. The obligation is of means only, not result [...]'.[206] A similar approach has been adopted by the HRCee.[207] The 'normal course of events', therefore, requires a domestic legal system that is capable of dealing effectively with human rights and IHL violations.

An armed conflict and its aftermath are contexts that deeply impact this capability, as recognized by the ECtHR. For instance, in an armed conflict, the duty to carry out an investigation must be read in light of the 'general principles

---

[203] ECtHR, *Gürtekin et al. v. Cyprus and other applications* (n 172) [28]. The case at issue was about the allegation of mass unlawful killings of Greek Turkish by Greek Cypriots in 1963-1964, who were considered missing until the UN CMP exhumed their bodies. Cf. also ECtHR, *Emin (Mustafa) et al. v. Cyprus* (n 201) [17].

[204] ECtHR, *Aslakhanova and others v. Russia* (n 172) [122].

[205] ECtHR, *Gürtekin et al. v. Cyprus and other applications* (n 172) [20]; *Cakicisoy et al. v Cyprus, Decision* (n 201) [39]; *Kayıplar et al v. Cyprus* (n 201) [10].

[206] Ibid. See also ECtHR, *Isayeva, Yusupova and Bazayeva v Russia, Judgment* (2005) App nos. 57950/00, 57948/00, and 57949/00 [211].

[207] The Committee, however, denotes that the duty to prosecute and punish does not have a corresponding individual right to require the State party to criminally prosecute another person. Cf. HRCee, *Messaouda Grioua née Atamna and Mohamed Grioua v Algeria, Comm no 1327/2004* (2007) UN Doc. CCPR/C/90/D/1327/2004 [9]. See also HRCee, *HC M A [name deleted] v The Netherlands, Comm No 213/1986* (1989) UN Doc. Supp. No. 40 (A/44/40) at 267 [11.6]; *José Vicente and Amado Villafañe Chaparro, Luis Napoleón Torres Crespo, Angel María Torres Arroyo and Antonio Hugues Chaparro Torres v Colombia, Comm No 612/1995* (1997) UN Doc. CCPR/C/60/D/612/1995 [8.8].

of international law' which include IHL rules: consequently, the Court has reframed this duty as an

> obligation to protect the lives of those not, or no longer, engaged in hostilities. [...] [W]here combatants have died, or succumbed to wounds, the need for accountability would necessitate proper disposal of remains and require the authorities to collect and provide information about the identity and fate of those concerned, or permit bodies such as the ICRC to do so.[208]

However, in the excerpt above, the Court mixes up accountability-driven and humanitarian courses of action: for instance, the action of the ICRC is not motivated by the need for accountability, as this would imply that this body might contribute to gathering information for accountability purposes, e.g., as evidence in future prosecution of alleged violations; indeed, its action is uniquely humanitarian.[209]

The difficulties and obstacles that State authorities encounter in post-conflict environments can legitimate a certain delay in complying with the obligation to carry out an investigation. The Court has made this point clear in cases revolving around persons reported missing in the context of the conflict in Bosnia-Herzegovina: in the post-conflict time-span taken into account by the Court – ten years following the war – several factors played a role and had an impact on the capacity of the country to face the allegations of violations committed during the conflict, i.e., the unbearable number of people killed/missing/displaced; a post-conflict overhaul of internal structure and political system; the creation of new institutions and the restructuring of the existing ones.[210] Therefore, pursuant to the Court's evaluation, the domestic legal system 'should have become capable of dealing effectively with disappearances and other serious violations of [IHL] by 2005, following comprehensive vetting of the appointment of police and judiciary and the establishment of the War Crimes Sections within the Court of Bosnia and Herzegovina [...]'.[211]

In light of the foregoing, it can be affirmed that the whole RoL system is altered in a post-conflict setting, where the capability of the State of complying with the procedural obligation to carry out an investigation into the disappearance of persons could not be the same as in peacetime. However, the "narrower" scope of the duty to carry out an investigation outlined in the context of armed conflict situations constitutes a minimum that continues to be valid and

---

[208] ECtHR, *Varnava and Others v. Turkey (GC)* (n 41) [185]. The Court exclusively refers to IAC; indeed, Chapter II shows that IHL treaties applicable in this context set down the terms for a more sophisticated system of handling of information. Nevertheless, this reasoning can be extended to NIAC, in light of the considerations put forward in the same Chapter. Along the same lines, see UN OHCHR, Minnesota Protocol (n 172), paras. 14, 20.

[209] On the humanitarian approach of the ICRC, see sub-section 2.2.1 of Chapter V.

[210] ECtHR, *Palić v Bosnia and Herzegovina* (n 3) [70]. *NB* The Republika Sprska was found responsible for the violation, *inter alia*, of Article 2 ECHR by the HRChBH.

[211] Indeed, the Court considers 'post-2005' the period of reference to assess whether an effective domestic criminal investigation was undertaken (the authorities eventually identified the mortal remains of the applicant's relative and carried out an independent and effective criminal investigation into his disappearance and death after 2005, no violation of Article 2 was found). ibid.

must be complied with in post-conflict settings (at least until the full restoration of the domestic legal system).

The HRCee has undertaken an approach that can be deemed "at mid-way" between the victim-centrism of the IACtHR and the context-based one of the ECtHR. In the Committee's words,

> States parties should take specific and effective measures to prevent the disappearance of individuals and establish effective facilities and procedures to investigate thoroughly, by an appropriate and impartial body, cases of missing and disappeared persons in circumstances which may involve a violation of the right to life.'[212]

Furthermore, the Committee has also underlined that

> a failure by a State party to investigate allegations of violations and a failure by a State party to bring to justice perpetrators of certain violations (notably, torture and similar cruel, inhuman and degrading treatment, summary and arbitrary killings and enforced disappearances) could in and of itself give rise to a separate breach of the Covenant.[213]

From the foregoing, an investigation is required in order to shed light upon the alleged violations and to enable the victim to pursue other remedies.[214]

3.1.3. The duty to investigate as a form of reparation

In the case law of the human rights adjudicators, the duty to investigate is also embedded in the reparation scheme:[215] the investigation into a case of

---

[212] HRCee, 'General Comment 6 - Article 6' (1994) UN Doc HRI/GEN/1/Rev.1 at 6 (Sixteenth session, 1982) para 4; *Basilio Laureano Atachahua v Peru, Comm No 540/1993* (1996) UN Doc. CCPR/C/56/D/540/1993 [8.3].

[213] Cf. HRCee, 'General Comment No. 31' (n 106) para 15. Derived from the right to an effective remedy under Article 2 (3) ICCPR, the duty to investigate is considered fulfilled when the State conducts a prompt, thorough, impartial, and independent investigation in order to determine the factual circumstances and to identify those responsible. Cf. HRCee, ibid [10]; *Boucherf v. Algeria* (n 15) [9.9, 11].

[214] Seibert-Fohr (n 176) 35.

[215] The HRCee underlines that it 'considers the State party duty-bound not only to conduct thorough investigations into alleged violations of human rights, particularly enforced disappearances and violations of the right to life, but also to prosecute, try and punish the culprits. Thus, the State party is, therefore, also under an obligation to prosecute, try and punish those held responsible for such violations. The State party is further required to take measures to prevent similar violations in the future.' Cf. HRCee, *Messaouda Grioua and Mohamed Grioua v. Algeria* (n 207) [9]. These duties can be grounded either in Article 2 (3) ICCPR taken together with a substantive right or in Article 2 (3)(a) ICCPR alone; as stressed by David, the first line of reasoning is used by the HRCee when it addresses those duties as part of the procedural dimension of the right to an effective remedy in conjunction with, for instance, the right to life or the prohibition of torture. The second line of reasoning implies that Article 2(3)(a) alone would authorize the HRCee to request investigation, prosecution, and punishment as a means of reparation (which is the case mentioned above). See David (n 20) 267. The IACtHR clarifies the criteria that the State must observe in the implementation of the Court's decision concerning the obligation to investigate as a form of reparation. The duty to investigate forms part of the reparation scheme and, as such, is judicially developed under Article 63 (1) ACHR. See, for instance, IACtHR, *Diario Militar Case (Merits ...)* (n 68) [326–336]. The Court has considered that the obligation to investigate is a measure of reparation, given the need to remedy the violation of the right to know the truth in the specific case at issue. See IACtHR, *Gomes-Lund et al (Guerrilha do Araguaia) v Brazil, Judgment - Preliminary Objections, Merits, Reparations, and Costs* (2010) Series C No. 219 [201]. The degree of detail of the criteria is in line with the purpose

enforced disappearance is deemed as the only measure that can bring relief and satisfaction to the victims, its aim being that of bringing perpetrators to justice.[216] As a form of reparation, the duty to investigate is often accompanied by the duty to prosecute and to punish or by a more general duty to bring those responsible to justice.[217] The common denominator among the human rights adjudicators resides in the fact that no real difference exists between the purpose of the duty to investigate subsumed under the procedural limb of substantive rights, and that of the remedial duty to investigate. Nonetheless, the ECtHR has pointed out that

> where the relatives of a person have an arguable claim that the latter has disappeared at the hands of the authorities, the notion of an effective remedy for the purposes of Article 13 entails, in addition to the payment of compensation where appropriate, a thorough and effective investigation capable of leading to the identification and punishment of those responsible and including effective access for the relatives to the investigatory procedure.[218]

---

that the Court has in mind, i.e., 'reparation through reconstruction' of the democratic system in the context of the fight against impunity: differently from the ECtHR that bans the micro-management of the criminal investigative systems of the Contracting Parties to the ECHR, the IACtHR chooses a different approach. Laurence Burgorgue-Larsen and Amaya Úbeda de Torres, '"War" in the Jurisprudence of the Inter- American Court of Human Rights' (2011) 33 Human Rights Quarterly 148, 234. As for the ECtHR, there is no difference between the duty to investigate subsumed under, *inter alia*, Article 2 and the duty to investigate under Article 13 ECHR (right to a remedy) – a procedural provision – in terms of purpose. As Akandji-Kombe explains, the purpose of this provision is 'to enable the domestic system to play its part to the full by obliging States to make provision for the necessary remedies to redress situations at variance with the Convention.' Akandji-Kombe (n 131) 59. In the African system, the African Commission has often limited itself to declaratory judgments. See, for instance, AfCommHPR, *Commission nationale des droits de l'Homme et des libertés v. Chad* (n 53). It has also set down streamlined lists of recommendations with an inherent remedial purpose. The duty to investigate has been part of the list of recommendations in case of human rights violations as well as in cases of gross and systematic violations of the African Charter; the duty to investigate goes along with the duty to identify and bring those responsible to justice. AfCommHPR, *Zimbabwe Human Rights NGO Forum v Zimbabwe* (2006) Comm no. 245/02 [final recommendations]; *Malawi African Association et al. v. Mauritania* (n 55) [final recommendations].

[216] Manfred Nowak, *U.N. Covenant on Civil and Political Rights: CCPR Commentary* (2nd rev ed, NP Engel 2005) 72 (and case law cited therein). The substantive facet (see *supra* sub-section 1.3) of the remedial scheme of the HRCee under Article 2(3) ICCPR includes the duty to ensure 'a thorough and diligent investigation' into the violations found by the Committee.

[217] See, among others, HRCee, *Bautista v Colombia, Comm No 563/1993* (1995) UN Doc. CCPR/C/55/D/563/1993 [8.6]; Seibert-Fohr (n 176) 13. In the AfCommHPR case law, the IACtHR's triad – duty to prevent/investigate/punish – is referred to and is at the basis of its view according to which 'States must prevent, investigate and punish acts which impair any of the rights recognized under international human rights law'. The African Commission has made often reference to the fight against impunity arguments developed by the IACtHR in *Velasquez Rodriguez* Case. See, for instance, AfCommHPR, *Zimbabwe Human Rights NGO Forum v. Zimbabwe* (n 215) [144–146]. The practice on remedies of the Commission is, however, inconsistent, for remedial measures differ from case to case regardless of the fact that identical violations are found. See Shelton (n 110) 237. Under-developed is the case law of the AfCtHPR.

[218] The Court has examined the issue in the context of Article 5 ECHR (right to liberty and security) and has added that 'seen in these terms, the requirements of Article 13 are broader than a Contracting State's obligation under Article 5 to conduct an effective investigation into the disappearance of a person who has been shown to be under their control and for whose welfare they are accordingly responsible.' Cf. ECtHR, *Kurt v. Turkey* (n 29) [140].

The Court has also emphasized that the duty to investigate under Article 13 ECHR is stricter than the duty subsumed under substantive provisions of ECHR (e.g., Article 2)[219] and that the former is 'broader' than the latter.[220] However, no further explanation has been provided on such dissimilarity.[221]

3.1.4. Concluding observations

The duty to search for persons reported as missing during the conflict regardless of which party he/she stood for and the duty to inform the families of the results of the efforts to account for their missing relatives are humanitarian in nature. The duty to investigate human rights violations, including enforced disappearances, is accountability-driven. These considerations confirm the complementarity of the two duties: the former is intended for providing a direct answer to the family's requests for information; the latter is intended for identifying those responsible for the criminal conduct and for bringing them to justice.[222] The diversity of purposes is reflected in the different temporal dimensions proper to these duties. Indeed, while the former is influenced by and structured according to the IHL rules on the matter, the latter must be implemented from the moment a right is violated until enough evidence is gathered that can lead to find those responsible and bring them to justice.

On this point, as noted in other sub-sections, the approaches of the ECtHR and of the IACtHR differ; while, for the former, the duty to investigate does not presuppose a result and must always be carried out in case of an alleged violation of fundamental human rights, for the latter, prosecution and punishment are the

---

[219] ECtHR, *Yaşa v Turkey, Judgment* (1998) App no. 22495/93 [115]. *Contra*: Mowbray assesses the case law concerning Article 2 that shows how the duty to investigate under such a provision has stringent requirements. Mowbray, *The Development of Positive Obligations under the European Convention on Human Rights by the European Court of Human Rights* (n 131) 7–42.

[220] Cf. ECtHR, *Kurt v. Turkey* (n 29) [140]; *Kaya v Turkey, Judgment* (1998) App no. 158/1996/777/978 [107].

[221] The fact that the scope of the duty under Article 13 is broader due to the accessibility to the family is incorrect, as accessibility to family is one of the criteria that the Court has laid down with regard to the duty to investigate under Article 2 ECHR. Mowbray considers that the Court has been opaque in defining the strictness of article 13's duty to investigate. See Mowbray, *The Development of Positive Obligations under the European Convention on Human Rights by the European Court of Human Rights* (n 131) 205–206. In Akandji-Kombe's view the implications of the two kinds of provision must be regarded as virtually identical. See Akandji-Kombe (n 131) 61.

[222] Apart from the case law mentioned in this sub-section, it is important to mention what the Principles on the Effective Prevention and Investigation of Extra-Legal, Arbitrary and Summary Executions affirm on the purpose of an investigation: '[t]he purpose of the investigation shall be to determine the cause, manner and time of death, the person responsible, and any pattern or practice which may have brought about that death.' Cf. UN ECOSOC, 'Principles on the Effective Prevention and Investigation of Extra-Legal, Arbitrary and Summary Executions, Res. 1989/65 (Annex)' (1989) UN ESCOR Supp. (No 1) at 52, UN Doc. E/1989/89 para 9. Similarly, pursuant to the Principles on the Effective Investigation and Documentation of Torture an effective investigation has multiple purposes, i.e., clarify the facts and establishment of individual and State responsibility for victims and family; identification of measures to prevent recurrence; and facilitation of prosecution and/or as appropriate disciplinary sanctions for those indicated by the investigation as being responsible. Cf. Principles on the Effective Investigation and Documentation of Torture, UNGA, 'Principles on the Effective Investigation and Documentation of Torture and Other Cruel, Inhuman or Degrading Treatment or Punishment, Res. 55/89 Adopted on 4 December 2000' (1999) UN Doc. A/54/426 para 1 (a-c).

expected results. The risk of the latter's approach is, however, to create expectations for the families that might not have a concrete follow-up at the domestic level. The ECtHR is the sole judicial body that contemplates the impact that the circumstances on the ground – conflict/post-conflict situation – can have on the capacity of State authorities to carry out an effective investigation. Based on the Court's understanding, should requests for information on missing persons be forwarded to State authorities in similar circumstances, the State must ensure the proper disposal of remains, collect and provide information about the identity and fate of those concerned, or permit bodies such as the ICRC to do so. In other words, the State must account for the missing; hence, this set of actions represents a protective minimum that cannot be waived or put on hold due to obstacles determined by the circumstances on the ground. Yet the restoration of the normal course of action corresponds to the restoration of a full-fledged duty to carry out an investigation vis-à-vis alleged violations of human rights.

3.2. Degrees of accessibility of the investigation: Implications for the families' quest for information

The role of the family in investigative proceedings depends on how the criminal investigative system is framed at the domestic level. Ideally, the family and the legal representative(s) shall be informed of and have access to any hearing and all pieces of information relevant to the investigation and shall be entitled to present other evidence.[223] Accessibility of domestic investigations is one of the requirements that the HRCee, the IACtHR, and the ECtHR have identified in order for the State to comply with its duty to investigate human rights violations. This requirement is key when the violation concerns an irreparable harm to the physical integrity of the person affected. The human rights judicial bodies have a different position on accessibility, ranging from the most open-ended and favorable to families of the victims (sub-section 3.2.1) to the most protective vis-à-vis the domestic criminal investigative system (sub-section 3.2.2).

3.2.1. Full-fledged accessibility as a consequence of the right to truth in the inter-American system

In the Inter-American context, the duty to investigate has been linked to the right to truth, the former being a medium for the realization of the latter.[224] This

---

[223] UN ECOSOC (n 222) para 16.

[224] IACtHR, *Bámaca-Velásquez v. Guatemala (Merits)* (n 56) [201] (where the Court said that 'the right to truth was subsumed in the right of the victim or his next of kin to obtain clarification of the facts relating to the violations and the corresponding responsibilities from the competent State organs, through the investigation and prosecution established in Article 8 and 25 [ACHR]'). See also IACtHR, *The Disappeared from the Palace of Justice case (P.O., Merits ...)* (n 75) [509, 511]; *19 Tradesmen v Colombia, Judgment - Merits, Reparations and Costs* (2004) Series C No. 109 [176] (referring to the remedial facet of the duty to investigate); *Anzualdo-Castro v. Peru (P.O., Merits, ...)* (n 61) [119]. In the case of enforced disappearances, the duty to account for the fate and the whereabouts of the persons juxtaposes with the duty to carry out a criminal investigation in order to gather information which is necessary to identify those who are responsible. This juxtaposition is due to the 'specific connotations' proper to the phenomenon of enforced disappearance (e.g., continuing character of the crime; denial of the deprivation of liberty of the person concerned and of the

link requires that the entire investigative process be accessible to the family. Full accessibility, therefore, means 'full access and capacity to act at all stages and in all instances of these investigations and proceedings so that [the next of kin] may assert their interests'.[225] The purpose is to guarantee 'access to justice, knowledge of the truth about what happened, and [to obtain] fair reparation'.[226]

As a direct consequence of the right to know the truth – i.e., the final purpose to be reached at the end of the investigative proceedings – the next of kin of the victim 'must be informed of all that occurred' with regard to the human rights violations.[227] The Court alternates two formulas that are not exactly identical at the procedural and substantive level: on the one hand, the granting of full access and legal standing to the victims' relatives at all stages of the investigation and prosecution of those responsible without any limit;[228] on the other, the granting of full access and legal standing 'in accordance with domestic law and the provision of the [ACHR]'.[229] The latter formula seems to take into account that full access needs to be balanced with other stakeholders' interests, e.g., those of the defendant. However, the Court has not explicitly recognized the need for a similar balance in the specific context outlined above.

3.2.2. Accessibility as a safeguard of a legitimate interest of the family members under the ICCPR and the ECHR systems

The HRCee has delineated two facets of the duty to investigate, i.e. the procedural facet from the joint reading of Article 2(3) with the substantive provision concerned; the substantive facet grounded on Article 2(3)(a) read alone as a form of reparation.[230] In relation to both facets of this duty, the HRCee has specified that the investigation must be accessible to the family.[231] In the words of the Committee, accessibility means that the family must be provided with 'a

---

consequential disappearance; uncertainty on the fate of the person who disappeared). In this way the investigation becomes a means for realizing 'the right of the victim's next of kin to know his or her fate and, as appropriate, where the victim's remains [...] represent a reasonable expectation that the State must satisfy using all the means at its disposal.' IACtHR, *Río Negro Massacres v Guatemala, Judgment - Preliminary Objection, Merits, Reparations and Costs* (2012) Series C No. 250 [224].

[225] IACtHR, *Valle-Jaramillo et al. v. Colombia (Merits ...)* (n 63) [233]; *Diario Militar Case (Merits ...)* (n 68) [328]; *Massacres of El Mozote and Nearby Places v El Salvador, Judgment – Merits, Reparations and Costs* (2012) Series C No. 252 [319 (g)].

[226] IACtHR, *Valle-Jaramillo et al. v. Colombia (Merits ...)* (n 63) [233]; *Diario Militar Case (Merits ...)* (n 68) [328]; *Massacres of El Mozote and Nearby Places v. El Salvador (Merits...)* (n 225) [319 (g)].

[227] IACtHR, *Gelman v. Uruguay (Merits...)* (n 70) [243].

[228] IACtHR, *Massacres of El Mozote and Nearby Places v. El Salvador (Merits...)* (n 225) [319 (g)].

[229] IACtHR, *Diario Militar Case (Merits ...)* (n 68) [328].

[230] David (n 20) 267. A more general duty to investigate has been inferred from Article 4 (2), Optional Protocol to the ICCPR (OP-ICCPR), 999 UNTS 171 (16 December 1966), cf. HRCee, *Boucherf v. Algeria* (n 15) [9.4] (where the Committee said 'it is implicit in [Article 4 (2)], of the [OP] that the State party has the duty to investigate in good faith all allegations of violations of the Covenant made against it and its representatives and to furnish to the Committee the information available to it').

[231] In the context of enforced disappearances, 'information on the investigation [...] must be made promptly accessible to the families.' HRCee, *Emina Kožljak and Sinan Kožljak v. Bosnia and Herzgovina* (n 115) [9.5]; *Fatima Rizvanović and Ruvejda Rizvanović v. Bosnia and Herzegovina* (n 19) [9.5].

timely opportunity to contribute their knowledge to the investigation and that information regarding progress of the investigation must be made promptly accessible to the families'.[232] Moreover, family members must also be informed about the results of the investigation.[233] Differently from the IACtHR's approach there is no such a reference to 'a full access' to the investigation; nevertheless, a participative and inclusive approach, must be adopted in the investigative system, in order for the family members to be kept abreast of the investigation proceedings.

The requirement of accessibility is neatly outlined in the ECtHR's case law: families of victims of serious violations of fundamental human rights have a 'right to know the truth about the circumstances surrounding events involving [such violations], which implies the right to an effective judicial investigation and a possible right to compensation.'[234] However, this has nothing to do with i) a right to obtain prosecution,[235] or ii) with full access to investigation proceedings and files.[236] While the Court unequivocally points out that in order for an investigation to be adequately carried out, accessibility to the family must be ensured[237] as well as sufficient public scrutiny, the involvement of the next of kin is solely justified 'to the extent necessary to safeguard his or her legitimate interests.'[238]

---

[232] For instance, HRCee, *Emina Kožljak and Sinan Kožljak v. Bosnia and Herzgovina* (n 115) [9.6]; *Nevzeta Durić and Nedzad Durić v. Bosnia and Herzegovina* (n 19) [9.6].

[233] HRCee, *Jit Man Basnet and Top Bahadur Basnet v. Nepal* (n 20) [10]; *Shanta Sedhai v Nepal, Comm no1865/2009* (2013) UN Doc. CCPR/C/108/D/1865/2009 [10].

[234] ECtHR, *Association '21 December 1989' et al v Romania, Judgment* (2011) App nos. 33810/07 and 18817/08 [144].

[235] Confronted with cases on persons previously reported missing and whose bodies – eventually found – showed clear signs of human rights violations, the ECtHR has noted that the applicants' principal complaint (i.e., that the investigations have ended without prosecutions) was not admissible *per se*. 'Article 2 cannot be interpreted so as to impose a requirement on the authorities to launch a prosecution irrespective of the evidence, which is available. A prosecution, particularly on such a serious charge as involvement in mass unlawful killings, should never be embarked upon lightly as the impact on a defendant who comes under the weight of the criminal justice system is considerable, being held up to public obloquy, with all the attendant repercussions on reputation, private, family and professional life. Given the presumption of innocence enshrined in Article 6 § 2 of the Convention, it can never be assumed that a particular person is so tainted with suspicion that the standard of evidence to be applied is an irrelevance. Rumor and gossip are a dangerous basis on which to base any steps that can potentially devastate a person's life.' ECtHR, *Gürtekin et al. v. Cyprus and other applications* (n 172) [27]. Along the same lines, cf. ECtHR, *Emin (Mustafa) et al. v. Cyprus* (n 201) [16].

[236] The Court has confirmed this reading in successive case law. Cf. ECtHR, *Lejla Fazlić and others v. Bosnia and Herzegovina* (n 42) [38] (the case concerned persons who went missing in Prijedor area during the Balkan conflict in the early 1990s).

[237] Other requirements are effectiveness, sufficient public scrutiny, and independence. Cf. ECtHR, *Gürtekin et al. v. Cyprus and other applications* (n 172) [22]. See *supra* n 172 for an explanation of the requirements.

[238] Cf. ECtHR, *Al-Skeini and others v. The UK (GC)* (n 172) [167]. The Court underlines that there must be a sufficient element of public scrutiny of the investigation or its results to secure accountability in practice as well as in theory. The degree of public scrutiny may well vary from case to case. In all cases, however, the victim's next-of-kin must be involved in the procedure to the extent necessary to safeguard his or her legitimate interests. ECtHR, *Isayeva, Yusupova and Bazayeva v. Russia* (n 206) [213].

For instance, ensuring accessibility should be a means for guaranteeing to family members of the disappeared/deceased victim the opportunity to apply for judicial review of a decision not to prosecute after the end of the investigation. This, in turn, can imply a requirement for the prosecutor to give adequate reasons for such a decision or, in other words, a requirement to inform the family of the reasons why their expectations concerning prosecution and punishment are not met.[239] In the Court's words

> this aspect of the procedural obligation does not require applicants to have access to police files, or copies of all documents during an ongoing inquiry, or for them to be consulted or informed about every step [...]. It cannot be automatically required that the families be provided with the names of the potential suspects against whom insufficient evidence has been gathered for prosecution. This would lead to the risk that the families and others would assume that the individuals were in fact guilty and to potentially unpleasant repercussions.[240] [...] Nor [...] is there any obligation for the victims' relatives to be treated as parties to the investigation as such.[241]

Different is the case for suspended or adjourned investigations: indeed, the ECtHR has deemed problematic the fact that, in Chechnya, families of disappeared could not have access to files related to such investigations. In the Court's words, in order to amend the situation, domestic authorities might set 'a rule that victims would have access to the case files where the investigation has been suspended for failure to identify the suspects, with the possibility of exception for specific documents classified confidential or secret'.[242]

3.2.3. Concluding observations

A participative and inclusive approach to the investigative proceedings at the domestic level takes account of the needs of the family to actively contribute to

---

[239] Cf., *mutatis mutandis*, ECtHR, *Hugh Jordan v The UK, Judgment* (2001) App No. 24746/94 [123–124]. See also Silvia Borelli, 'Domestic Investigation and Prosecution of Atrocities Committed during Military Operations: The Impact of Judgments of the European Court of Human Rights' (2013) 46 Israel Law Review 369, 374.

[240] ECtHR, *Gürtekin et al. v. Cyprus and other applications* (n 172) [29]. *Mutatis mutandis*, the Grand Chamber has clarified that '[t]he disclosure or publication of police reports and investigative materials may involve sensitive issues with possible prejudicial effects for private individuals or other investigations. It cannot therefore be regarded as an automatic requirement under [Article 2] that a deceased victim's surviving next of kin be granted access to the investigation as it goes along. The requisite access of the public or the victim's relatives may be provided for in other stages of the available procedures [...]. The Court does not consider that [Article 2] imposes a duty on the investigating authorities to satisfy every request for a particular investigative measure made by a relative in the course of the investigation.' Cf. ECtHR, *Ramsahai and others v The Netherlands, Judgment (GC)* (2007) App no. 52391/99 [347–348].

[241] ECtHR, *Cakicisoy et al. v Cyprus, Decision* (n 201) [45]; *Kayıplar et al v. Cyprus* (n 201) [13] (both cases are about the killing and disappearance of 84 Turkish-Cypriots committed by Greek-Cypriots in 1974; the families' main complaint revolved around the ineffectiveness of the investigations into the events and on the failure of the authorities in keeping them abreast of the developments of the investigations). *Contra:* The Court has found that the authorities' unjustified denial to the applicant of access to the documents of criminal investigation files was an additional element contributing to the applicant's suffering; such documents might have cast light on the fate of her relatives, either directly or through the proceeding in the ECtHR. cf. ECtHR, *Imakayeva v Russia, Judgment* (2007) App no. 7615/02 [165].

[242] ECtHR, *Aslakhanova and others v. Russia* (n 172) [236 (in fine)].

the elucidation of the fate and whereabouts of their missing relatives; at the same time, this approach allows them to keep track of the investigative activities. The risk to link the duty to investigate with the right to the truth[243] lies in the fact that family members might claim that they should have full access to all the investigative files at all the stages of the investigation. This possibility runs the risk of generating premature conclusions with regard to facts and persons allegedly associated with the facts; it can also have prejudicial effects for private individuals and other investigations at the domestic level.

Moreover, full access might be subjected to exemptions in cases concerning military operations[244] and Special Forces' operations.[245] Where gross human rights violations and international crimes have been committed, the pendulum swings towards disclosure of information to, at least, the judicial officers who are gathering the information as part of the prosecutorial investigation.[246] The IACtHR's position is neat with regard to this point:

---

[243] In this respect, the IACtHR acknowledges that TJ mechanisms, such as a Truth Commission, are not a substitute for the State's obligation to establish the truth through judicial proceedings; to this end, and despite the establishment of a Truth Commission, the State has an obligation to launch a criminal investigation to determine the corresponding criminal responsibilities. IACtHR, *Contreras et al v. El Salvador (Merits...)* (n 168) [135]; *Zambrano Vélez et al v Ecuador, Judgment - Merits, Reparations, and Costs* (2007) Series C no. 166 [128]; *Gomes-Lund et al. v. Brazil (PO, Merits..)* (n 215) [297]; *Ibsen Cárdenas and Ibsen Peña, Judgment - Merits, Reparation, and Costs* (2010) Series C No. 217 [158] (stating that 'the "historical truth" documented in special reports, or tasks, activities and recommendations issued by special commissions' cannot replace the State obligation to establish the truth and investigate).

[244] The Mexican *Instituto General de Acceso a la Informacion Publica* (responsible for implementing and enforcing the Federal Law of Transparency and Access to Public Government Information) has held that the Secretariat of National Defense must elaborate a public version of the documents sought by the Petitioner which contains a description of the country's overall defense strategy – public information – but which leaves out strategic and logistical data; the disclosure would naturally affect military operations and endanger national security. Instituto General de Acceso a la Informacion Publica, *Resolución n 1034/05, Folio de la solicitud n 0000700037605* (Instituto General de Acceso a la Información Publica (México) 34–35.

[245] The UK Upper Tribunal - Administrative Appeals Chambers (UKUT - AAC) has upheld the government's assertions regarding secrecy of information concerning Special Forces implicated in the requests for the policy on capture and statistics concerning Iraqi operations. Where all the information concerned the UK Special Forces, the government could respond by neither confirming nor denying the existence of information responsive to the request. *UK All Party Parliamentary Group on Extraordinary Rendition v Ministry of Defense* (2011) UKUT 153 AAC [23, 87, 101]; cf. Freedom of Information Act 2000 (UK), s1 (access to information held by public authorities) and s23 (information supplied by, or relating to, bodies dealing with security matters). From a more general stance of access to public information, the German Federal Act on Access to Information lists among the issues on which the entitlement to access to information shall not apply to military and other security-critical interests of the Federal Armed Forces, cf. Section 3 (1) (b), Federal Act Governing Access to Information held by the Federal Government (Freedom of Information Act) of 5 September 2005 (Federal Law Gazette [BGBl.] Part I, p. 2722), last amended by Article 2 (6) of the Act of 7 August 2013 (Federal Law Gazette I, p. 3154).

[246] The Guatemalan Constitutional Court upheld an appellate decision recognizing the authority of a trial court judge to order the Ministry of National Defense to release four military operational plans to the prosecutor in the genocide trial of José Efraín Ríos Montt (No. 2290-2007). The Court stated that the public authority must release such military operational plans because they do not constitute State secrets and, as a consequence, are not protected from disclosure under the exemption in Article 30 of the Constitution (NB Article 30 states that all the acts of administration are public except when

the authorities in charge of the investigation must have full access to the documentation in the State's possession, to places of detention, and to military archives containing useful information for determining the whereabouts of the missing; to this end, the State must adopt appropriate measures to ensure "judicial officers" (*operadores de justicia*) and the society, public technical and systematized access to archives containing useful and relevant information to the investigation in cases characterized by violations of human rights committed during the armed conflict; such measures should be supported with adequate budgetary allocations; the State must justify the refusal to provide information, demonstrating that it has taken all available measures to prove that the requested information does not exist.[247]

This position is partly echoed by the ECtHR that has addressed the issue in the context of the military operations in Chechnya:

the investigative authority[248] would have to identify the leading agencies and commanding officers of special operations aimed at identifying and capturing suspected illegal insurgents in given areas and at given times, and the procedure for recording and reporting such operations. [...] One aspect of those general inquiries should be to resolve the problem of access to records of the passage of service vehicles through security roadblocks, including during curfew hours, which appears to be a recurrent feature of many such abductions. Closely connected to the above is the unhindered access of the investigators to the relevant data of the military and security agencies. It is difficult to see how the investigative group, or groups, put in charge of those crimes [abductions of persons allegedly affiliated to terrorist groups] could be effective without having unrestricted access to all relevant data, including information about commanding officers and staff taking part in those operations, and thus without having the possibility to identify and question those who had ordered or performed the deeds which are the subject matter of the investigation.[249]

4. THE LIMITED SCOPE OF POST-CONFLICT LAWFUL DEPARTURES
FROM THE RIGHT OF FAMILIES TO KNOW THE FATE OF THEIR RELATIVES

The right of families to information on the fate of their relatives[250] and the duty of State authorities to inform them and to actively respond to their requests for information are intertwined with one of the fundamental human rights, i.e., the right to be treated humanely. While limitations (also named 'clawback clauses'[251]) are unviable against the right to be treated humanely, as this is

---

military or diplomatic matters relating to national security or information supplied by individuals under the pledge of confidence are involved). Corte de Constitucionalidad de Guatemala. *Apelación de Sentencia en Amparo (in relation to the case Ríos Montt c. Ministerio de la Defensa Nacional)*, Expediente 2290-2008 (2008), considerando II.

[247] IACtHR, *Contreras et al v. El Salvador (Merits...)* (n 168) [171]; *Rochac Hernández and others v. El Salvador (Merits...)* (n 72) [208–209].

[248] In the present case, the investigative authority was the Investigative Committee of the Prosecutor's Office. ECtHR, *Aslakhanova and others v. Russia* (n 172) [184].

[249] Ibid [233–234].

[250] The case law shows that requests for information revolve around whether the person is alive, the whereabouts of his/her remains, the facts surrounding the disappearance, the circumstances that determined the death of the person.

[251] In this book, the term 'clawback clauses' refers to a 'limitation' or 'restriction' clause in a human rights treaty. Scholars have suggested the following definitions: '[a] limitation/restriction clause is a

absolute, these mechanisms allow State authorities to break free of obligations that would ordinarily constrain their actions[252] in the context of the right to respect for private and family life as well as the right to seek, impart, and receive information. Based on the survey of the law in Chapter II and the considerations on the interplay between IHL and IHRL in Chapter III, this section intends to delve deep into the human rights case law in order to set down the terms that allow State authorities to limit the families' quest for information on their missing relatives in a lawful manner.

In the assessment of the lawfulness of the State's interference with the human rights, the adjudicators have taken into account the object and purpose of human rights treaties (i.e., protect individuals on an objective basis) and have sought to interpret and apply this typology of restriction in a manner that renders the treaties' guarantees 'practical and effective'.[253] Thus, the interpretation given to limitations is a key determinant of the utility of rights in practice.[254] As noted in Section 4 of Chapter II, limitations can interfere with the enjoyment of certain human rights (e.g., Article 8 ECHR); in order to be considered lawful under human rights treaties, these measures *i)* must be provided by law; *ii)* must aim at protecting one or more of the collective needs that are listed in the limitation clause; and *iii)* must be necessary in order to protect such need(s).

Interferences with the right to private and family life that have a direct impact on access to information may take different forms: for instance, interferences have materialized under the form of prohibition for the family members to have the human remains of their relative back, the withholding of the information on the whereabouts of the human remains of the relative (sub-section 4.1), and the restriction of detention visits/correspondence on the basis of multiple legitimate purposes (sub-section 4.2). The focus of this section is put on these typologies of interferences; these are interconnected with the subject matter and have taken place, *inter alia*, in contexts affected by armed conflicts as well as other scenarios – including post-conflict situations – characterized by terrorist activities and frequent military operations. In most of the cases, the lawfulness of the measure has been decided on the basis of whether it was necessary for the achievement of a certain purpose.[255]

"clawback" from the substantive right'. H Victor Condé, *A Handbook of International Human Rights Terminology* (University of Nebraska Press 1999) 19. Higgins defines it as a clause that 'permits, in normal circumstances, breach of an obligation for a specified number of public reasons'. Rosalyn Higgins, 'Derogations under Human Rights Treaties' (1977) 48 British Yearbook of International Law 281, 281.

[252] Philip Alston and Ryan Goodman, *International Human Rights* (Oxford University Press 2012) 394.

[253] Cf. ECtHR, *Maskhadova and others v Russia* (n 158) [222]; *Sabanchiyeva and others v Russia* (n 158) [132]; *Kushtova and others v. Russia* (n 158) [38]; *Abdulayeva v. Russia* (n 158) [33]; *Zalov and Khakulova v Russia* (n 158) [81]; *Arkhestov and others v. Russia* (n 158) [87].

[254] Robin CA White and Clare Ovey, *Jacobs, White and Ovey: The European Convention on Human Rights* (4th edn, Oxford University Press 2010) 219.

[255] Doswald-Beck (n 143) 76.

4.1. Forbidding the disclosure of the whereabouts of the relative's human remains

The right of families to know the fate and whereabouts of their missing relatives includes the right to know the whereabouts of the human remains of their relatives. The question of whether the decision to forbid the disclosure of the whereabouts of the relative's human remains is lawful in specific circumstances has emerged in the human rights case law. Specifically, the ECtHR has assessed whether the decision of State authorities to bury the bodies in unspecified locations and not to return them to the families infringed upon the human rights of the family members of those killed by military forces as part of military operations against terrorist activities.[256] The right to respect for private and family life as well as interferences in the enjoyment of this right in the context of counter-terrorism operations in the separatist Russian provinces were at stake.

It is worth noting that the ruling of the Russian Constitutional Court concerning a complaint on the subject matter stressed that

the interest in fighting terrorism, in preventing terrorism in general and specific terms and in providing redress for the effects of terrorist acts [...] may, in a given historical context, justify the establishment of a particular legal regime, such as that provided for by section 14(1) of the Federal Act, governing the burial of persons who escape prosecution in connection with terrorist activity on account of their death following the interception of a terrorist act.

The burial of those who have taken part in a terrorist act, in close proximity to the graves of the victims of their acts, and the observance of rites of burial and remembrance with the paying of respects, as a symbolic act of worship, serve as a means of propaganda for terrorist ideas and also cause offence to relatives of the victims of the acts in question, creating the preconditions for increasing inter-ethnic and religious tension. [...]

In the conditions which have arisen in the Russian Federation as a result of the commission of a series of terrorist acts [...], the return of the body to the relatives ... may create a threat to social order and peace and to the rights and legal interests of other persons and their security [...]. (emphasis added)[257]

The ECtHR found that these measures[258] constituted interference on the right to respect for private and family life of the applicants under Article 8 ECHR.[259]

---

[256] Chechnya had been engaged in waging an armed conflict against Russia; the first Chechen conflict ended with the defeat of Russian forces in 1996; the second one - between 1999 and 2000 - triggered by Chechen incursions in Dagestan ended with the reversal of 1996 conflict conclusion. See Stuart D Goldman, 'Russia - CRS Report for Congress' (Congressional Research Service - The Library of Congress 2006) 6–7 <http://fpc.state.gov/documents/organization/66504.pdf> accessed 1 May 2015. In 2009, Putin declared concluded the counterterrorism operation that followed the conflict. Tanya Lokshina, 'Ending Chechnya's Counterterrorism Operation - or Not' (*Human Rights Watch*, 27 April 2009) <https://www.hrw.org/news/2009/04/27/ending-chechnyas-counterterrorism-operation-or-not> accessed 8 November 2016.
[257] See Judgment no. 8-P of the Constitutional Court quoted in ECtHR, *Sabanchiyeva and others v Russia* (n 158) [33]; *Maskhadova and others v Russia* (n 158) [125].
[258] ECtHR, *Sabanchiyeva and others v Russia* (n 158) [122]; *Maskhadova and others v Russia* (n 158) [212]. This constituted an exception to the general rule in Russia where the relatives of a

The Court considered fulfilled the requirements of the legal basis[260] and of the legitimate aim[261] in all cases revolving around the same typology of interference by Russian authorities in the enjoyment of the right to respect for private and family life. The Court agreed that such interference 'could be considered as having been taken in the interests of public safety, for the prevention of disorder, and for the protection of the rights and freedoms of others'.[262] Nevertheless, the restrictive measures fell short of the third requirement, i.e., 'necessary in a democratic society', despite the margin of appreciation of State authorities: the above-mentioned interference was too 'severe', as 'it involved a ban on the disclosure of the location of the grave, thus permanently cutting the links between the applicants and the location of the deceased's remains'; in addition to that, it was not proportionate to the legitimate aim.[263]

Although State authorities enjoy a margin of appreciation – which in cases of national security or public safety is wider than in other occasions[264] – they should 'first rule out the possibility of having recourse to an alternative measure' in order to comply with the proportionality requirement.[265] Thus, the adoption of

---

deceased person who are willing to organize that person's interment generally 'enjoy a statutory guarantee of having the person's body returned promptly to them for burial after the establishment of the cause of death [...]' (see sections 3 to 8 of the Interment and Burial Act quoted in the case law). Cf. ECtHR, *Sabanchiyeva and others v Russia* (n 158) [65, 121]; *Maskhadova and others v Russia* (n 158) [210].

[259] For a synoptic overview of the parameters that make lawful the interference into the human rights, see section 4 in Chapter II.

[260] The measure in question was taken in accordance with the relevant provisions of the Suppression of Terrorism Act, the Interment and Burial Act, and Decree no. 164 of 20 March 2003, which provided that '[the body of a] terrorist who died as a result of interception of a terrorist act' would not be handed over for burial and that the place of burial would not be disclosed. ECtHR, *Sabanchiyeva and others v Russia* (n 158) [125]; *Maskhadova and others v Russia* (n 158) [214]; *Kushtova and others v. Russia* (n 158) [31]; *Arkhestov and others v. Russia* (n 158) [80].

[261] The legitimate aim of these restrictions is laid down in the Constitutional Court judgment cited above (see n 257).

[262] Cf. ECtHR, *Sabanchiyeva and others v Russia* (n 158) [129]; *Maskhadova and others v Russia* (n 158) [219]; *Arkhestov and others v. Russia* (n 158) [84]; *Zalov and Khakulova v Russia* (n 158) [78]; *Abdulayeva v. Russia* (n 158) [30]; *Kushtova and others v. Russia* (n 158) [35].

[263] Cf. ECtHR, *Sabanchiyeva and others v Russia* (n 158) [146]; *Maskhadova and others v Russia* (n 158) [237]; *Kushtova and others v. Russia* (n 158) [52]; *Abdulayeva v. Russia* (n 158) [47]; *Zalov and Khakulova v Russia* (n 158) [95]; *Arkhestov and others v. Russia* (n 158) [101].

[264] Clare Ovey and Robin White, *Jacobs and White: The European Convention on Human Rights* (4 edition, Oxford University Press 2006) 237. It is fundamental that in the search for the balance between individual rights/social needs the State authorities evaluate the 'individual circumstances of each of the deceased and those of their family member', for the disregard of such a balance oversteps any 'acceptable margin of appreciation in this regard'. In *Sabanchiyeva*, for instance, 95 terrorists were killed; after the recovery and identification of their bodies, the authorities proceeded with the cremation. See ECtHR, *Sabanchiyeva and others v Russia* (n 158) [27, 146].

[265] The Court suggested that depending on the exact location where the ceremonies and the burial were to take place, the authorities could be reasonably expected to intervene in order to avoid possible unlawful actions by people supporting/opposing the deceased; in organizing such intervention the authorities were entitled to act so as to minimize (e.g., deciding the time/location of burial; regulating the burial procedure) the informational and psychological impact of the terrorist act on the population and on the relatives of the victims of terrorism. ECtHR, *Sabanchiyeva and others v Russia* (n 158) [141–142, 145]; *Maskhadova and others v Russia* (n 158) [231–233, 236]; *Kushtova*

an 'individualized approach', i.e., the identification of an alternative manner that 'would cause less damage to the fundamental right at issue whilst fulfilling the same aim', is required.[266] This approach is in line with the object and purpose of the ECHR that calls for 'its provisions to be interpreted and applied in a manner that renders its guarantees practical and effective'.[267] Should the foregoing elements be disregarded, the restrictive measure would turn into a punitive measure for the applicants, who are thus required to bear the burden of the actions of their beloved ones.[268]

The Court's pronouncements have also delineated the contours under the ECHR of the right of families to know and the duty to inform in the context of counter-terrorism operations (including those occurring during the transition from armed conflict to peace).[269] According to the Court, there is no lingering uncertainty affecting the applicants where these are offered the possibility of participating in the identification process of their relatives' bodies, shortly after the security operations.[270] Absent in the applicants' complaints, the impact of uncertainty on the applicants themselves due to restrictive measures following the identification process has remained unaddressed.

The case law of other adjudicators substantiates a certain level of skepticism vis-à-vis the ECtHR's approach: the deprivation of the possibility of knowing the location of the burial site and the prohibition of visiting it can generate mental suffering for the families concerned. For instance, in different contextual settings, the HRCee has recalled that

> the secrecy surrounding the date of execution and the place of burial, as well as the refusal to hand over the body for burial, have the effect of intimidating or punishing families by intentionally leaving them in a state of uncertainty and mental distress.[271]

---

and others v. Russia (n 158) [47–49, 51]; Abdulayeva v. Russia (n 158) [42–44, 46]; Zalov and Khakulova v Russia (n 158) [90–92, 94]; Arkhestov and others v. Russia (n 158) [96–98, 100].

[266] ECtHR, Maskhadova and others v Russia (n 158) [236].

[267] ibid [222]; Sabanchiyeva and others v Russia (n 158) [132]; Kushtova and others v. Russia (n 158) [38]; Abdulayeva v. Russia (n 158) [33]; Zalov and Khakulova v Russia (n 158) [81]; Arkhestov and others v. Russia (n 158) [87].

[268] ECtHR, Sabanchiyeva and others v Russia (n 158) [145]; Maskhadova and others v Russia (n 158) [236]; Kushtova and others v. Russia (n 158) [51]; Abdulayeva v. Russia (n 158) [46]; Zalov and Khakulova v Russia (n 158) [94]; Arkhestov and others v. Russia (n 158) [100].

[269] Some authors identify this phase as 'margins of conflict'. See Antoine Buyse (ed), Margins of Conflict. The ECHR and Transitions to and From Armed Conflict (Intersentia 2010).

[270] ECtHR, Sabanchiyeva and others v Russia (n 158) [110]; Arkhestov and others v. Russia (n 158) [55 ff].

[271] The applicants' relatives were sentenced to death because of a variety of offences ranging from kidnapping to murder. HRCee, Aliboeva v Tajikistan, Comm no 985/2001 (2006) UN Doc CCPR/C/85/D/985/2001 [6.7]; Lyashkevich v Belarus, Comm no 887/1999 (2003) UN Doc CCPR/C/77/D/887/1999 [9.2]; Validzhon Khalilov v Tajikistan, Comm no 973/2001 (2005) UN Doc CCPR/C/83/D/973/2001 [7.7]; Nazriev v Tajikistan, Shukurova (on behalf of Nazriev and Nazriev) v Tajikistan, Comm no 1044/2002 (2006) UN Doc CCPR/C/86/D/1044/2002 [8.7]; Darmon Sultanova v Uzbekistan, Comm no 915/2000 (2006) UN Doc CCPR/C/86/D/915/2000 [7.10]. Although in most of the these cases State authorities have not submitted their considerations, in a case against Belarus, the State authorities emphasized that '[h]aving considered the nature of the crimes [i.e., murder] committed by Mr. Bondarenko [i.e., the applicant's son], the great danger they represented to the public, and his motives and methods, as well as previous information that reflected negatively on the

Despite the claims by State authorities that the individuals sentenced to death were a great danger to the public, the Committee has struck the balance between individual and society's needs in a different manner compared to the ECtHR. According to the HRCee, the failure of the authorities to notify the authors (often the wife or the mother) of the scheduled date for the execution of their relatives and their subsequent persistent failure to notify them of the location of their beloved ones' graves amounted to inhuman treatment against the authors and were in violation of article 7 ICCPR.[272]

No similar cases feature in the case law of the IACtHR and of the AfCommHPR. With regard to the former, the disclosure of the whereabouts of human remains to the family members is conceived as an obligation of the State in the framework of Article 5 ACHR and as part of the reparation scheme (specifically in cases of enforced disappearance).[273] The Court's approach is *pro homine,* as it makes it clear that 'the next of kin of the victims and society as a whole must be informed of everything that has happened' in connection with grave human rights violations.[274] Based on this assertion, the IACommHR and its Special Rapporteur on Freedom of Expression have highlighted that

> [i]t is true that in some cases there is national security information that should remain reserved. However, there are at least three strong arguments according to which the State can, in no case, maintain the secrecy of information on serious human rights violations – especially that related to the forced disappearance of persons – and prevent access to such information by the authorities in charge of investigating said violations, or even by the victims and their relatives.[275]

The arguments are the following:

---

accused's personality, the court came to the conclusion that Mr. Bondarenko constituted a particular menace to society and imposed the death penalty.' See HRCee, *Natalia Schedko (on behalf of Bondarenko) v Belarus, Comm no 886/1999* (1999) UN Doc CCPR/C/77/D/886/1999 [4.4].

[272] HRCee, *Aliboeva v. Tajikistan* (n 271) [6.7]; *Lyashkevich v. Belarus* (n 271) [9.2]; *Validzhon Khalilov v Tajikistan* (n 271) [7.7]; *Shukurova v Tajikistan* (n 271) [8.7]; *Sultanova v. Uzbekistan* (n 271) [7.10]; *Natalia Schedko v Belarus* (n 271) [10.2].

[273] The IACommHR has recommended establishing a mechanism that, to the extent possible, enables complete identification of the disappeared victims and the return of the mortal remains of those victims to their families. Cf. IACommHR, *'Santa Barbara' Campesino Community v Peru, Case 10932* (2011) Report No 77/11 [262 pt 2] (a case focused on forced disappearance of children within the framework of an internal armed conflict). *Mutatis mutandis,* see also IACtHR, *Moiwana Village v Suriname, Judgment - Preliminary Objections, Merits, Reparations and Costs* (2005) Series C No 145 208 (the case concerned the indigenous community of Moiwana where, among the reparations measures, the Court ordered the State to recover the remains of the Moiwana community members killed; if found, to deliver them as soon as possible thereafter to the surviving community members; to conclude, within a reasonable timeframe, the analysis of the human remains found at the grave site in 1993 and communicate the results of said analysis to the representatives of the victims).

[274] Cf. IACtHR, *19 Tradesmen v. Colombia (Merits...)* (n 224) [261]; *Carpio Nicolle et al v Guatemala, Judgment – Merits, Reparations and Costs* (2004) Series C No 117 [128]; *Myrna Mack Chang v Guatemala, Judgment - Merits, Reparations and Costs* (2003) Series C No 101 [274]; *Gomes-Lund et al. v. Brazil (PO, Merits..)* (n 215) [200].

[275] IACommHR, 'Annual Report of the [IACommHR] 2010: Report of the Office of the Special Rapporteur for Freedom of Expression Dr. Catalina Botero' (2011) Doc No OEA/Ser.L/V/II Doc. 5 284.

– 'a State agency may never refuse to provide state-held information that might help establish the facts surrounding such violations to the authorities investigating human rights violations';

– 'denying the relatives of victims of forced disappearance information about the fate of their loved ones contributes to subjecting them to cruel, inhuman or degrading treatment, and therefore is absolutely prohibited under international law. In fact, if the information contained in state records contributes to overcoming such extreme suffering, the government has the obligation to turn it over';

– 'under any circumstance, but especially in processes of transition to democracy, the argument that it is necessary to maintain confidentiality with respect to past atrocities in order to protect present "national security" is inadmissible'.[276]

While Article 13 ACHR (right to freedom of expression, which includes the freedom to seek, impart, and receive information of any kind) can be restricted, the same is not true for the right to have access to information on serious human rights violations; such an extensive reading of the provision is at the benefit of multiple information-seekers, including the relatives.

Although the present analysis is focused on the human rights judicial bodies assessments, it is noteworthy to illustrate the position of a domestic court with regard to the subject matter of this sub-section. The Supreme Court of Israel was confronted to a similar complaint to that brought before the ECtHR. The family members of those killed in the Israel Defense Forces' (IDF) operation named *Operation Defensive Wall*[277] asked the Court that IDF be ordered to allow families to bring their dead, including those ascertained to be terrorists, to a quick and honorable burial. Indeed, IDF were proceeding in recovering the bodies and burying them in locations not chosen by the families. While considering the importance of the security situation on the ground, the Supreme Court held that

> the respondents [the MoD and IDF] were responsible, under international law, for the location, identification, and burial of the bodies. [...] No differentiation will be made between bodies, and no differentiation will be made between the bodies of civilians and the bodies of armed terrorists. [...] The location, identification, and burial of bodies are important humanitarian acts. They are a direct consequence of the principle of respect for the dead – respect for all dead. [...] Needless to say, all of the above is subject to the security situation in the field, and to the judgment of the Military Commander. Indeed, it is usually possible to agree on humanitarian issues. [...][278]

---

[276] ibid 284–288.

[277] The case revolved around the recovery of bodies of 38 Palestinians in the aftermath of an Israel Defense Forces (IDF) operation against the terrorist infrastructure in the areas of the Palestinian Authority ("Operation Defensive Wall").

[278] Israel - High Court of Justice. *Barake and Others v Minister of Defence and Others* (2002) HCJ no 3114/02 [8–12].

At the crossroad between IHL and IHRL, such pronouncement identifies the core nature of the locations, identification, and burial of bodies, i.e., these are humanitarian acts; such a nature does not change in post-conflict environments and is inextricably connected with the right of families to know.

4.2. Preventing families from accessing information on their relatives in case of detention

The disregard of IHL and IHRL guarantees concerning people in detention can reflect a situation of violation of the rights of those held in custody; moreover, uncertainty about their fate directly affects the rights of their family members. This sub-section serves the purpose of examining the legality of limitations to the right of the families to information on their relatives when detained. Yet it is beyond the scope of this sub-section to examine all the guarantees proper to detention situations.

The mutual enjoyment by members of a family of each other's company constitutes a fundamental element of family life.[279] By nature, detention represents a form of restriction of the right to respect for private and family life of both the detainee and of the family members.[280] As Chapter II shows, even in time of armed conflicts, communication rights bestowed upon dispersed family members should not be limited or restricted; nonetheless, in detention cases, the right of the inmate/person held in captivity to correspond with his family can be subjected to restrictions both in IAC and in NIAC.

In post-conflict situations,

– detention – related to the conflict – that started during the conflict could continue (NIAC);

– captivity of protected persons should come to an end (continuation of this situation should be limited in time) (IAC);[281]

– detention cases could follow the end of an armed conflict for acts committed during the conflict (post-IAC/post-NIAC).

---

[279] ECtHR, *El-Masri v. The Former Yougoslav Republic of Macedonia (GC)* (n 195) [248]. See, *mutatis mutandis*, ECtHR, *Olsson v Sweden, Judgment (no 1)* (1988) App no 10465/83 [59]. Protection of family life (Article 17) is underogable and cannot be restricted under the ACHR; the right of every person to be protected from any arbitrary interference against his family is part of the right to the protection of family. See IACtHR, *Rochac Hernández and others v. El Salvador (Merits...)* (n 72) [105, 108].

[280] Detention has been defined as 'the act of [...] confining a person to a certain place, whether or not in continuation of arrest, and under restraints which prevent him from living with his family or carrying out his normal occupational or social activities'. UN Commission on Human Rights, 'Study of the Right of Everyone to Be Free from Arbitrary Arrest, Detention and Exile' (1961) UN Doc E/CN.4/813 para 19. The same study emphasizes that 'arrest...requires separation from family'. ibid para 70. See also Nowak (n 216) 301–302.

[281] Civilian internees and POW are not allowed to receive family visits; nonetheless, they shall be enabled to receive family correspondence. Restrictions can apply pursuant to Articles 71 (correspondence) and 76 (censorship) GC III; 107 (correspondence) and 115 (censorship) GC IV.

The parameters that determine the lawfulness of the measures that might affect the external communication rights are set out under IHRL, even in those cases that represent a continuation of a situation started during an armed conflict. As underlined in sub-section 2.3.2.2 of Chapter III, these parameters are not as carefully circumscribed under IHL as they are under IHRL.[282] Though limitations are admissible under both branches, it is commonly accepted that these cannot fully and permanently deprive the detainee of all contacts with the outside world (including those with the family).[283]

Under IHRL, State authorities have a general obligation to facilitate the contact between the prisoner and his or her family since the inception of the detention period, notwithstanding the restrictions of personal liberty implicit in the condition of the prisoner.[284] Pursuant to IHL treaties, this is also true in case of continuation

---

[282] Doswald-Beck (n 143) 448.

[283] The HRCee made reference to 'prompt and regular access, ...under appropriate supervision when the legitimate purpose of the detention so requires, to family members' as one of the safeguards that are essential for the prevention of torture and necessary for the protection of persons in any form of detention against arbitrary detention and infringement of personal security. Cf. HRCee, 'General Comment No 35' (n 160) para 58. The right of a relative or other appropriate third person to be notified of the detention is included as one of the preventive measures in the African Commission's resolution on torture and other ill-treatment. Cf. AfCommHPR, Association for the Prevention of Torture, and UN OHCHR, 'Resolution on Guidelines and Measures for the Prohibition and Prevention of Torture, Cruel, Inhuman or Degrading Treatment or Punishment In Africa ("The Robben Island Guidelines"), 2nd Ed' (2008) para 20 (a). The IACommHR's Principles and Best Practices on the Protection of Persons Deprived of Liberty narrow down the limitations' scope to the correspondence rights, as they state '[p]ersons deprived of liberty shall have the right to receive and dispatch correspondence, subject to such limitations as are consistent with international law; and to maintain direct and personal contact through regular visits with members of their family, legal representatives, especially their parents, sons and daughters, and their respective partners'. Cf. IACommHR, 'Principles and Best Practices on the Protection of Persons Deprived of Liberty in the Americas, Approved by the Commission during Its 131st Regular Period of Sessions' (2008) Principle XVIII. See also the IACommHR, 'Report on the Human Rights of Persons Deprived of Liberty in the Americas' (2011) Doc no OEA/Ser.L/V/II. para 577. Pursuant to the European Prison Rules, despite the restrictions, 'an acceptable minimum level of contact' shall always be allowed. Cf. Rule 24(2), CoE – Committee of Ministers, 'Recommendation Rec(2006)2 of the Committee of Ministers to Member States on the European Prison Rules, Adopted by the Committee of Ministers at the 952nd Meeting of the Ministers' Deputies' (2006).

[284] HRCee, *Miguel Angel Estrella v Uruguay, Comm no 74/1980* (1983) UN Doc Supp. No. 40 (A/38/40) at 150 [9.2]; IACommHR, *Ms X v Argentina, Case 10506* (1996) Report No. 38/96, Doc no OEA/Ser.L/V/II.95 Doc. 7 rev. at 50 [98]; *Oscar Elías Biscet et al v Cuba, Case no 12476* (2006) Report no 67/06 [237]. ECtHR, *Messina v Italy, Judgment (no 2)* (2000) App no 25498/94 [61]. The ECtHR has recently noted that 'international-law instruments and the practice of international courts and tribunals ... invariably recognize as a minimum standard for all prisoners, without drawing any distinction between life-sentence and other types of prisoners, the right to an "acceptable" or "reasonably good" level of contact with their families'. ECtHR, *Khoroshenko v Russia, Judgment (GC)* (2015) App no 41418/04 [143]. See also the UN Standards on the Minimum Rules for the Treatment of Prisoners emphasize that '[e]very prisoner shall have the right to inform at once his family of his imprisonment or his transfer to another institution; [...][s]pecial attention shall be paid to the maintenance and improvement of [social] relations between a prisoner and his family as are desirable in the best interests of both.' Cf. UN ECOSOC, 'Standard Minimum Rules for the Treatment of Prisoners, Adopted by the First UN Congress on the Prevention of Crime and the Treatment of Offenders on 30 August 1955, Res. 663 C (XXIV), July 31, 1957 and Res. 2076 (LXII), May 13, 1977' UN Doc A/CONF/611, annex I paras 44(3), 79. The UN Principles on Detention as

of captivity of protected persons until their final repatriation (IAC):[285] the minimum correspondence – in case of limitations by the Detaining Power – is of four cards/month and two letters/month.[286] Similarly, in NIAC, the possibility of sending/receiving cards for those 'persons deprived of their liberty for reasons related to the armed conflict' as well as for those 'deprived of their liberty or whose liberty is restricted after the conflict for the same reasons' holds valid 'until the end of such deprivation or restriction of liberty'.[287] To a certain extent, the IHL treaties enshrine guarantees that are in line with IHRL treaties as far as correspondence is concerned. It is submitted that IHL provisions can be a valid legal basis for similar restrictions in post-conflict;[288] nonetheless, such restrictions must meet the requirements proper to the limitation regime under IHRL.

Although depicted as a legal right of the detainee,[289] correspondence is the bare minimum for preserving family links as well as the mental health of both the detainee and of his/her family members. Correspondence and visiting rights are, therefore, fundamental guarantees for ensuring the respect of the personal (both physical and mental) integrity of the inmate[290] and, as a corollary, the right

---

well as the European Committee for the Prevention on Torture (European CPT) affirm that the right to have the fact of his/her detention notified to a relative or another third party should in principle be guaranteed from the very outset of police custody. See UNGA, 'Body of Principles for the Protection of All Persons under Any Form of Detention or Imprisonment' (1988) UN Doc A/RES/43/173 Principle 16(1), Principle 19; European CPT, '12th General Report on the CPT's Activities Covering the Period 1 January to 31 December 2001' (2002) CPT/Inf (2002) 15 para 43. Along the same lines, see UN OHCHR, Istanbul Protocol (n 171), para. 10 (e).

[285] Cf. Article 5, GC III; Article 6, GC IV.

[286] Cf. Article 71, GC III; Article 107, GC IV. With regard to POW, pursuant to Article 71, GC III, '[f]urther limitations may be imposed only if the Protecting Power is satisfied that it would be in the interests of the prisoners of war concerned to do so owing to difficulties of translation caused by the Detaining Power's inability to find sufficiently qualified linguists to carry out the necessary censorship. If limitations must be placed on the correspondence addressed to prisoners of war, they may be ordered only by the Power on which the prisoners depend, possibly at the request of the Detaining Power.' In general, limitations are due to transport-related difficulties or censorship. With regard to civilian internees, Article 107, GC IV states that '[i]f limitations must be placed on the correspondence addressed to internees, they may be ordered only by the Power to which such internees owe allegiance, possibly at the request of the Detaining Power.' In relation to the latter, such limitations should not seriously affect the forwarding of family news to the internees. Jean S Pictet (ed), The Geneva Conventions of 12 August 1949: Commentary, vol IV (ICRC 1958) 449–450.

[287] Cf. Article 2(2) AP II read in conjunction with Article 5 AP II. Limitations can be justified for reasons related to paralysis of postal services or censorship. Yves Sandoz and others, Commentary on the Additional Protocols: Of 8 June 1977 to the Geneva Conventions of 12 August 1949 (Martinus Nijhoff Publishers 1987) para 4585, 1390.

[288] In the case law, adjudicators have never excluded the possibility that the word 'law' be interpreted as international law; an international treaty could constitute a valid legal basis for similar interferences.

[289] Sandoz and others (n 287) para 4585, 1390.

[290] The restriction of the possibility of having contact and maintaining the relationship with the family can constitute a threat to the humanity of the detainee himself. European CPT, '25th General Report of the CPT - 1 January-31 December 2015' (2016) CPT/Inf (2016) 10, 35. Abels underlines that contacts with the outside world help detainees to maintain 'their morale and even their mental sanity'. See Denis Abels, Prisoners of the International Community: The Legal Position of Persons Detained at International Criminal Tribunals (Springer Science & Business Media 2012) 526.

to the protection of the family for all affected parties.[291] Thus, in light of the peculiar situation of the detainees, any limitation must be clearly defined, limited in time, and accompanied by appropriate safeguards.[292] No discretion should be left to prison authorities in limiting correspondence and visiting rights, as any restriction should be 'clearly described by law'.[293]

Article 20 ICPPED outlines some of the reasons that might justify the limitation of the right of family members to be informed about the detained relative, which is provided for under the same convention. A similar situation seems to be improbable under general human rights treaties; the HRCee's General Comment no. 35 (Article 9 ICCPR – freedom from arbitrary arrest or detention) declares that

> [d]etainees should be held only in facilities officially acknowledged as places of detention. A centralized official register should be kept of the names and places of detention, and times of arrival and departure, as well as of the names of persons responsible for their detention, and made readily available and accessible to those concerned, including relatives. Prompt and regular access should be given to independent medical personnel and lawyers and, under appropriate supervision when the legitimate purpose of the detention so requires, to family members [footnotes omitted][294]

In their comments to the draft version of the excerpt above (consultation exercise launched by the HRCee in 2013-2014), States have emphasized that

– 'there are situations where an individual can be taken to a safe place that is not officially acknowledged as a place of detention and required to stay there';[295]

---

[291] From Article 17 ICCPR read in conjunction with Article 10 (1) ICCPR, the HRCee has inferred a general right of prisoners to regular visits by family members at regular intervals. Cf. HRCee, *Miguel Angel Estrella v Uruguay, Comm no 74/1980* (n 284) [9.2]; Nowak (n 216) para 302. See also IACommHR, *Ms. X v. Argentina* (n 284) [99]. Along the same lines, see AfCommHPR, *Interights, ASADHO and Madam O. Disu v. DRC* (n 97).

[292] The UN Principles on Detention boldly affirm that 'communication of the detained or imprisoned person with the outside world, and in particular his family or counsel, shall not be denied for more than a matter of days'. See UNGA (n 284) Principle 15. The European CPT has affirmed that exceptions are allowed if necessary to the protection of the legitimate interests of the police investigation. Among the appropriate safeguards to be put in place are to record in writing with the reasons therefor any delay in notification of custody and to require the approval of a senior police officer unconnected with the case or a prosecutor. See European CPT (n 284) para 43. See also IACommHR, *Oscar Elías Biscet et al v Cuba, Case no 12.476* (n 284) [237].

[293] UN Committee on the Rights of the Child, 'General Comment No 10 - Children's Rights in Juvenile Justice' (2007) UN Doc CRC/C/GC/10 para 87. The ECtHR has noted with concern 'the existence of rules granting a discretionary power in relation to correspondence and prison visits' and has emphasized that 'such rules are arbitrary and incompatible with the appropriate and effective safeguards against abuses which any prison system in a democratic society must put in place'. See *Ilaşcu and others v Moldova and Russia, Judgment (GC)* (2004) App no 48787 [439]. In terms of strict control of the visits, the Court has stressed that it finds it 'unacceptable in principle that a prison guard [be] present during family visits'. Cf. ECtHR, *Mozer v Moldova and Russia, Judgment (GC)* (2016) App no 11138/10 [195].

[294] HRCee, 'General Comment No 35' (n 160) para 58.

[295] The UK has provided this example: 'where there is an urgent need to take an individual to a place of safety that is not necessarily acknowledged as a place of deprivation of liberty in order for their longer term health needs to be assessed'. See Government of the United Kingdom of Great Britain and Northern Ireland, 'Observations by the Government of the United Kingdom of Great Britain and

– 'there may be situations where releasing such information could pose security risks to the detainees and the authorities running the detention facilities';[296]

– 'some detainees may not wish their records to be disclosed to other persons, even to their relatives'.[297]

The tiny line that runs between *incommunicado* detention, i.e., when 'the person is not permitted any contact with the outside world',[298] and secret detention is worrisome.[299] A person is kept in secret detention

> if State authorities acting in their official capacity, or persons acting under the orders thereof, with the authorization, consent, support or acquiescence of the State, or in any other situation where the action or omission of the detaining person is attributable to the State, deprive persons of their liberty; where the person is not permitted any contact with the outside world ("incommunicado detention"); and when the detaining or otherwise competent authority denies, refuses to confirm or deny or actively conceals the fact that the person is deprived of his/her liberty hidden from the outside world, including, for example family, independent lawyers or non-governmental organizations, or refuses to provide or actively conceals information about the fate or whereabouts of the detainee.[300]

From the perspective of situations started during an armed conflict and continuing after the end of the conflict, *incommunicado* captivity (of POW and

---

Northern Ireland on Draft General Comment 35 on Article 9 of the ICCPR - Liberty and Security of Person' (2014) para 25.

[296] ibid, para 26. Instead of the current wording the UK proposed the following 'and made readily available and accessible to those concerned, including relatives, except where the transmission of the information would adversely affect the privacy or safety of the person detained or the State agents supervising their detention, hinder a criminal investigation, or for other equivalent reasons where they are necessary and in accordance with the law, and in conformity with applicable international law.'

[297] Japan, 'Japan's Comments on the Draft General Comment No.35 on Article 9 of the ICCPR' (2014) para 2.

[298] UN Human Rights Council, 'Joint Study on Global Practices in Relation to Secret Detention in the Context of Countering Terrorism' (2010) UN Doc A/HRC/13/42 para 8; Nigel Rodley and Matt Pollard, *The Treatment of Prisoners under International Law* (Oxford University Press 2009) 460.

[299] The IACtHR has stated that: '[p]rolonged isolation and being held incommunicado constitute, in themselves, forms of cruel and inhuman treatment, harmful to the mental and moral integrity of the person and to the right of all detainees of respect for the inherent dignity of the human being' (violation of Article 5 ACHR). Cf. IACtHR, *Fairén-Garbi and Solís-Corrales v Honduras, Judgment – Merits* (1989) Series C No. 6 [149]. The UN Working Group on Arbitrary Detention (WGAD) does not leave any doubt on the unlawfulness of *incommunicado* detention, since this 'constitutes the most heinous violation of the norm protecting the right to liberty of human being under customary international law. The arbitrariness is inherent in these forms of deprivation of liberty as the individual is left outside the cloak of any legal protection'. UN WGAD, 'Report of the Working Group on Arbitrary Detention' (UN Human Rights Council 2012) UN Doc A/HRC/22/44 para 60. The UN study on secret detentions in the context of countering terrorism has emphasized that 'secret detainees are typically deprived of their right to a fair trial when State authorities do not intend to charge or try them. [...] At the same time, secret detention amounts to an enforced disappearance. Every instance of secret detention is by definition incommunicado detention.' Cf. UN Human Rights Council (n 298) 2 and paras 27-28.

[300] UN Human Rights Council (n 298) para 8.

civilian internees) and *incommunicado* detention of those apprehended in the context of a NIAC are not options contemplated by the existing IHL treaties.[301]

Where the families are unlimitedly prevented from visiting their beloved ones and their requests for information repeatedly denied, it is likely that their next of kin has been subjected to serious violations of his/her human rights (including prohibition of enforced disappearance; prohibition of torture and inhuman and degrading treatment; arbitrary deprivation of life).[302] Moreover, the anguish and distress generated by uncertainty on his/her fate and whereabouts constitute cruel, inhumane and degrading treatment of the family members.[303] Despite the fact that *incommunicado* detention may be legally enforced,[304] under IHRL,

---

[301] Only in those cases where absolute military necessity so requires, a *sui generis* form of *incommunicado* detention is permitted in occupied territory when 'an individual protected person is detained as a spy or saboteur' or 'under definite suspicion of activity hostile to the security of the Occupying Power'. Cf. Article 5(2) GC IV. Pursuant to Article 45(3) AP I, the forfeiture of communication rights is admissible only in those cases of detention concerning spies. The Detaining Power is, in any case, obliged to 'to notify the arrest to its official Information Bureau for transmission to the official Information Bureau of the country of which the person concerned is a national'; the Protecting Power (or the ICRC) must be notified in case of proceedings instituted against the person concerned. Pictet (n 286) 57–58. Cf. Articles 71 and 74 GC IV.

[302] See, among others, HRCee, *AMH El Hojouj Jum'a et al v Libya*, *Comm no 1958/2010* (2014) UN Doc CCPR/C/111/D/1958/2010 [6.3]. The Committee has recognized 'the degree of suffering involved in being held indefinitely without contact with the outside world' and, in this respect, it has recalled its General Comment no 20 (1992), in which it recommends that 'States parties make provision against incommunicado detention.' HRCee, *Jit Man Basnet and Top Bahadur Basnet v. Nepal* (n 20) [8.3]; *Ram Kumar Bhandari v Nepal* (n 20) [8.5]; *Fatima Mehalli v Algeria, Comm no 1900/2009* (2014) UN Doc CCPR/C/110/D/1900/2009 [7.4]; *Aïcha Dehimi and Noura Ayache v Algeria, Comm no 2086/2011* (2014) CCPR/C/112/D/2086/2011 [8.4].

[303] HRCee, *A.M.H. El Hojouj Jum'a et al. v Libya* (n 302) [6.3]; *Jit Man Basnet and Top Bahadur Basnet v. Nepal* (n 20) [8.4]; *Ram Kumar Bhandari v Nepal* (n 20) [8.6]; *Fatima Mehalli v Algeria* (n 302) [7.5]; *Aïcha Dehimi and Noura Ayache v Algeria* (n 302) [8.6]. See also IACtHR, *Tibi v Ecuador, Judgment - Preliminary Objections, Merits, Reparations and Costs* (2004) Series C no 114 [160]; UN Human Rights Council (n 298) Summary.

[304] A *sui generis incommunicado* detention is permissible under IHL (see *supra* n 301). The IACtHR has pointed out that '*[i]ncommunicado* detention is an exceptional measure the purpose of which is to prevent any interference with the investigation of the facts. Such isolation must be limited to the period of time expressly established by law. Even in that case, the State is obliged to ensure that the detainee enjoys the minimum and non-derogable guarantees established in the Convention'; in *Suárez-Rosero* Case the fact of keeping an inmate *incommunicado* for a month, while the Ecuadorian Constitution set down the limit up to 24 hours, represented a violation of Article 7 (2) ACHR. IACtHR, *Suárez-Rosero v Ecuador, Judgment - Merits* (1997) Series C no 35 [51]. The HRCee has specified that keeping a person *incommunicado* for 15 days amounts to a violation of Article 10 ICCPR. HRCee, *Lucía Arzuaga Gilboa v Uruguay, Comm No 147/1983* (1990) UN Doc CCPR/C/OP/2 at 176 (1990) [14]. *Incommunicado* detention that prevents prompt presentation before a judge inherently violates Article 9(3) ICCPR. Depending on its duration and other facts, *incommunicado* detention may also violate other rights under the Covenant, including articles 6, 7, 10 and 14. Prolonged *incommunicado* detention violates Articles 9 and 7 ICCPR. HRCee, 'General Comment No 35' (n 160) para 35. Prolonged was considered detaining *incommunicado* a person for a month and 24 days and subsequently for more than a year (cf. HRCee, *Tahar Mohamed Aboufaied v Libya, Comm no 1782/2008* (2012) UN Doc CCPR/C/104/D/1782/2008 [7.2]) or for three years in a row (cf. HRCee, *El Megreisi v The Libyan Arab Jamahiriya, Comm No 440/1990* (1994) UN Doc CCPR/C/50/D/440/1990 [5.4]). Zayas examines the legality of indefinite detention against a number of criteria, including the sheer length of the detention, the time-lapse before being brought before a

family members cannot be left without news or solely be informed about the fact that their next of kin is safe, 'without disclosure of the location or nature of the person's detention'.[305]

The *incommunicado* detention would amount to secret detention – prohibited under international law – [306] in the case where the ICRC 'is granted access by the authorities, but is not permitted to register the case, or, if it is allowed to register the case, is not permitted by the State to, or does not, for whatever reason, notify the next of kin of the detainee on his or her whereabouts'.[307] As noted in the case law,[308] detention visits of the ICRC cannot be considered as an absolute guarantee that the detainee will be treated in accordance with IHRL standards.

In light of ECtHR's pronouncements,[309] limitations of the correspondence and visiting rights amount to an interference into, *inter alia*, the right to respect for private and family life of both the detainee[310] and of his/her family.[311] The non-compliance/disregard/or irresponsiveness of State authorities with regard to the parameters that make restrictions lawful 'must be considered particularly serious when it concerns relations between detainees and their closest relatives'.[312] Indeed, Article 8 ECHR enshrines 'the right to establish and develop relationships with other human beings and the outside world'[313] and, in this respect, the right to be protected from any arbitrary interference by the public authorities.[314]

---

judge, the possibility of having access to counsel and to one's family. See Alfred de Zayas, 'Human Rights and Indefinite Detention' (2005) 87 International Review of the Red Cross 15, 16–17.

[305] UN Human Rights Council (n 298) para 31.

[306] Cf. Article 17 (1) ICPPED. Secret detention violates the right to liberty and security of the person and the prohibition of arbitrary arrest or detention, the prohibition of enforced disappearance; it can also be perpetrated in violation of the right to a fair trial, the prohibition of torture, inhuman and degrading treatment. See UN Human Rights Council (n 298), paras 18, 24, 28, 31.

[307] See ibid para. 11. Although the UN study on secret detention in countering terrorism does seem to refer to situations of conflicts, the ICRC carries out detention visits in post-conflict settings (among many others see Sri Lanka and Kosovo) as well. Therefore, the point highlighted above holds valid in the context of the present study. See ICRC, 'Sri Lanka' (*International Committee of the Red Cross*, 24 July 2014) <https://www.icrc.org/en/where-we-work/asia-pacific/sri-lanka> accessed 4 November 2016; UN OCHA, 'Kosovo Humanitarian Update' (2001) Issue no 36 <http://www.unhcr.org/3c3ab52f4.pdf> accessed 2 March 2014.

[308] In a deportation case (from Italy to Tunisia), the ECtHR noted that ICRC visits in Tunisian prisons could not exclude the risk of violation of Article 3 ECHR at the detriment of the inmates. Cf. ECtHR, *Saadi v Italy, Judgment (GC)* (2008) App no 37201/06 [146].

[309] Abels delineates the evolution of this position: prior to *Golder v the UK Case* the Court and the Commission applied the so-called 'inherent limitations doctrine' according to which the deprivation of liberty automatically entails the loss of other rights; '[a]s a consequence, prisoners were excluded from the protections guaranteed under the ECHR.' In *Golder,* this doctrine was rejected, as the Court assessed the limitation of correspondence rights under Article 8(2) ECHR. See Abels (n 290) 522. See also ECtHR, *Golder v The UK, Judgment* (1975) App no 4451/70 [41 ff].

[310] See, among many others, ECtHR, *Messina v Italy (no 2)* (n 284) [61–62]; *Mozer v Moldova and Russia (GC)* (n 293) [190-192].

[311] ECtHR, *Ivanţoc and Others v Moldova and Russia, Judgment* (2011) App no 23687/05 [142].

[312] ibid.

[313] ECtHR, *Al Nashiri v Poland, Judgment* (2015) App no 28761/11 [538].

[314] ibid.

In the sphere of family visits, the ECtHR has put forward the following clarifications:

– in the majority of the States Parties to the ECHR a generally accepted minimum regarding the frequency of visits is not less than once a month regardless of the typology of prisoner;[315] this sort of consensus directly impacts on the breadth of the margin of appreciation and, in particular, 'the relative importance of the interest at stake' or 'how best to protect it'.[316]

– With regard to this last point, States enjoy a narrower margin of appreciation in the assessment of the permissible limits of the interference with private and family life, as they are under an obligation to prevent the breakdown of family ties (even in the case of life-sentence prisoners);[317]

– in light of the condition of the prisoner, 'severe measures limiting Convention rights must not be resorted to lightly, i.e., the principle of proportionality needs a 'sufficient link' between the applications of these restrictions and the circumstances of the individual concerned;[318]

– in this respect, 'Article 8 [...] requires the States to take into account the interests of the convict and his or her relatives and family members'.[319]

The IACtHR has found that the 'anguish caused by not knowing the whereabouts of the [next-of-kin] immediately after his detention' and 'the feeling of powerlessness and insecurity due to negligence of the State authorities' amounted to a violation of the right of the family members concerned to humane treatment.[320] More generally, the Court has adopted a restrictive approach towards the limitation of the visiting rights and/or the correspondence of the inmates with their families.[321]

---

[315] This assertion derives from the study that the ECtHR has conducted in the context of the *Khoroshenko* Case, where the practice of the States Parties to the ECHR has been reviewed with regard to visiting rights scheme, how this is articulated on the basis of the typology of prisoners (life-sentence prisoners, long-term prisoners, other prisoners), the supervisory restrictions in place. ECtHR, *Khoroshenko v Russia (GC)* (n 284) [81–84].

[316] ibid [120 to be read in conjunction with paras 81-84 and 135-136].

[317] ibid [136]. Nonetheless, the Court has also noted that the State has a wide margin of appreciation in relation to the penal policies. Cf. ibid [132, 134].

[318] ECtHR, *Trosin v Ukraine. Judgment* (2012) App no 39758/05 [41–44]; *Khoroshenko v Russia (GC)* (n 284) [141].

[319] ECtHR, *Khoroshenko v Russia (GC)* (n 284) [142]. *In casu*, the combination of various long-lasting and severe restrictions on the ability of the applicant - a life-sentenced prisoner - to receive prison visits and the failure of the impugned regime on prison visits to give due consideration to the principle of proportionality and to the need for rehabilitation and reintegration of life-sentence prisoners led the Court to conclude that 'the measure in question [i.e., low frequency of authorized visits, solely on account of the gravity of a prisoner's sentence] did not strike a fair balance between the applicant's right to the protection of private and family life, on the one hand, and the aims referred to by the respondent Government on the other [i.e., in the Government's written submission 'to reform the offender'; in the Russian Constitutional Court's Ruling, 'the restoration of justice, reform of the offender and the prevention of new crimes'], and that the respondent State has overstepped its margin of appreciation in this regard'. ibid [137, 146, 148].

[320] Cf. IACtHR, *Tibi v Ecuador (PO, Merits...)* (n 303) [160].

[321] The IACtHR has considered that a 'restrictive visiting schedule' (i.e., highly restrictive regime of visits - even from the children; possibility of seeing his/her relatives only once a month without

CONCLUSIONS

This Chapter demonstrates that, under IHRL, families have a right to be informed on their relatives' fate and whereabouts when these are reported missing; the context – an armed conflict – entails that the State must undertake actions required not only under IHRL, but also under IHL. Uncertainty on a relative's fate and whereabouts can generate unbearable suffering for the family members. The human rights adjudicators have diverse views with regard to the triggering factor of a human right violation at the detriment of family members; however, convergence emerges in recognizing that the disregard by State authorities of the requests of family members for information about their missing relatives or a passive attitude vis-à-vis obstacles placed in the way of their efforts to find information violates their right to be treated humanely.

Under IHRL, State authorities must account for those reported missing and inform the families. State authorities also have a duty to carry out an investigation into alleged violations of human rights; the obligation has an *ex officio* character in relation to enforced disappearances and other serious human rights violations. The ECtHR is the sole adjudicator[322] that neatly pinpoints the distinction between these duties, which resides both in the substance of action and in the nature: the duty to account for missing persons is substantive in nature and aims at responding to the human need of families to know; the duty to investigate is subsumed under the procedural limb of substantive provisions – e.g., the prohibition of torture and inhuman treatment – and aims at the identification and punishment of those responsible. The compliance with the former cannot waive the latter,[323] even in those circumstances, such as armed conflict or post-conflict situations, where the carrying out of an investigation could be difficult. In such circumstances the latter must be 'interpreted in so far as possible in light of the general principles of international law, including the rules of [IHL]'; in other words, State authorities must ensure the proper disposal of remains, collect and provide information about the identity and fate of those concerned, or permit bodies such as the ICRC to do so.[324] Such a protective minimum would not displace the full-fledged duty to carry out an investigation that must be implemented as soon as the normal course of action is restored.

In light of the simultaneous application of IHL and IHRL rules during and after the conflict, this Chapter confirms the considerations outlined in Chapter III: the examination above has shown the legal contours of the duty of former

physical contact) is among those factors that constitute forms of cruel, inhuman or degrading treatment (Article 5(2) ACHR) against the inmate. IACtHR, *Cantoral-Benavides v Peru, Judgment - Merits* (2000) Series C no 69 [64, 89]; *Loayza-Tamayo v Peru, Judgment - Merits* (1997) Series C no 33 [46, 58].

[322] The IACtHR depicts the duty to investigate as inherent in the right to know the truth of the families and of the society. The HRCee's approach does not differ from the IACtHR, although the duty to investigate is not embedded in the framework of the right to truth.

[323] ECtHR, *Cyprus v Turkey* case and *Varnava and others v Turkey* case.

[324] ECtHR, *Varnava and Others v. Turkey (GC)* (n 41) [185].

parties to the conflict to cooperate in accounting for the missing; such duty is intertwined with the duty to account for missing persons and with the right to humane treatment. Under IHRL, the refusal of State authorities to cooperate with the former party(-ies) to the conflict in accounting for the missing would result into a violation of their obligation to exercise due diligence. In other words, lack of cooperation would infringe the human rights of those who live with uncertainty, i.e., family members.

In the context of the efforts undertaken in order to account for a missing person, family members shall ideally have access to the information collected by State authorities; they shall also be involved in the undertaking of these efforts. However, the right to be informed finds some limits when the issue of accessibility of criminal investigative proceedings arises. Affirming that family members and their legal representative(s) shall have full access to any hearings and information gathered in the course of a criminal investigation does not take into consideration the constraints proper to each domestic investigative criminal system. Although a participative and inclusive approach towards the families in the investigative proceedings is advisable (i.e., an investigation must be accessible), providing full access to investigative files at any time of the investigation can have counter-productive effects on the search for the so-called truth – e.g., the information might still need to be verified – and on justice as such. At a minimum, full access to information must be granted upon the *operadores de justicia*.[325]

The Chapter also shows that IHRL and IHL treaties do not exclude the possibility for State authorities to interfere with a set of rights in a lawful manner. In the post-conflict phase, State authorities might have to face the difficult endeavor to find a balance between the individual rights and the social needs generated by the situation on the ground (e.g., counter-terrorism operations aimed at downsizing the capacity of the armed groups previously at war against their government or continuation of detention of persons apprehended during the conflict). From the examination above, it emerges that where similar restrictions are implemented, these should not be aimed at generating uncertainty or worsening the emotional condition of the families concerned. As a matter of fact, uncertainty is not only a source of anguish and suffering for the families affected, but also a factor indicative of possible violations at the detriment of their relatives.

---

[325] IACtHR, *Contreras et al v. El Salvador (Merits...)* (n 168) [170].

CHAPTER V.

ACCOUNTING FOR MISSING PERSONS IN PEACE PROCESSES: WHOSE DUTY?

The contextual setting – e.g., an armed conflict, the phase of transition from conflict to peace – could affect the capacity of State authorities to comply with their human rights obligations. In post-conflict environments, temporary assistance or transitional exercise of governance function can help address such an enforcement gap generated by a weak[1] State apparatus.[2] Both options are indicative of a broader engagement by the international community to help State authorities to restore their institutional capacity and reach an enduring peace. In this respect, the traditional understanding of the international legal architecture shaped by a dispute-settlement conception of international law when applied to the issues related to the transition from war to peace is too narrow;

---

[1] In the transitional phase, the State apparatus might lack the technical and institutional capacity to fully implement its human rights and (residual) humanitarian law obligations. This emerges, for instance, from a cable of UNMIK Office of Missing Persons and Forensics sent to the UNSG on a request for funding concerning the activities of international expertise in the forensics field due to the lack of local capacity to carry out certain highly technical but crucial activities in relation to missing persons. US Department of State - Bureau of Democracy, Human Rights, and Labor, 'Kosovo Missing Persons: OMPF Requests USG Funding for Technical Staff' (2006) 06PRISTINA1091_a <https://wikileaks.org/plusd/cables/06PRISTINA1091_a.html> accessed 12 January 2017.

[2] Carsten Stahn, *The Law and Practice of International Territorial Administration: Versailles to Iraq and Beyond* (Cambridge University Press 2008) 31. For some authors, this can be read in the framework of the collective international responsibility to protect against mass atrocities which 'sovereign Governments have proved powerless or unwilling to prevent'; this responsibility entails actions under the aegis of the UNSC which range from prevention, response to violence, to 'rebuilding shattered societies'. UNSG, 'A More Secure World: Our Shared Responsibility. Report of the Secretary-General's High-Level Panel on Threats, Challenges, and Change' (2004) paras 201–203. See also JK Kleffner, 'Introduction: From Here to There ... and the Law in the Middle' in Carsten Stahn and Jann K Kleffner (eds), *Jus Post Bellum: Towards a Law of Transition From Conflict to Peace* (Springer Verlag 2008) 2–3. Lewandowski, for instance, argues that responsibility to protect and *just post bellum* when executing the rules provided by the law of occupation constitute the only effective methods used by international community to assist post-conflict States in human rights capacity building. See Tomasz Lewandowski, 'Law of Occupation, Jus Post Bellum and Responsibility to Protect: Separate or Complementary Tools for Restoring Human Rights Order After Mass Atrocities?' (2013) 1 Social Transformations in Contemporary Society 120, 120. Österdahl and van Zadel believe that it is time for a shift in thinking about peacebuilding, especially since a well-regulated post-conflict phase is essential for the well-being of the people of a State, something international law is designated to protect. See Inger Österdahl and Esther van Zadel, 'What Will Jus Post Bellum Mean? Of New Wine and Old Bottles' (2009) 14 Journal of Conflict and Security Law 175, 190. *Contra:* this view is too narrow, as it shifts the responsibility focus from the State to the international community. Such a shift is, indeed, based on the idea of the failure of domestic jurisdiction and of domestic incapacity; it indirectly promotes the concept of a neocolonialist form of tutelage. C Stahn, 'R2P and Jus Post Bellum Towards a Polycentric Approach' in Carsten Stahn, Jennifer S Easterday and Jens Iverson (eds), *Jus Post Bellum: Mapping the normative Foundations* (Oxford University Press 2014) 109.

indeed, it does not take into account the 'progressively international society',[3] where the State is no longer the sole and main actor.

Against this backdrop, this Chapter aims at studying what role international law plays in the attempts of the international community to articulate humanitarian and accountability-driven responses to the quest for information on missing persons. Policy and legal aspects of the involvement of the international community in post-conflict scenarios will be part of the analysis: the aim is to answer the question of whether there is room for an internationally coordinated effort to address the issue of missing persons, which balances humanitarian and accountability-based courses of action in compliance with the applicable legal framework.

To this end, the Chapter will proceed in two steps: first, it will examine normative and institutional approaches to the issue of missing persons in actual transitional contexts by narrowing the focus down to those contexts featuring an international component (section 1). Second, it will study the intersection between international attempts of systematization of a global approach to the missing and *ad hoc* international initiatives: the purpose will be to unveil the actual (and potential) implications of both for the realization of the right of families to know the fate of their relatives (section 2). Examples of transitional contexts will be part of this examination in order to assess the 'normative conduct' of international actors, i.e., 'the conduct which is regarded by each actor...as being obligatory';[4] such conduct is behind actual decisions, measures, and approaches undertaken in post-conflict settings. Specifically, the contexts of the former Yugoslavia, including Kosovo, and of Cyprus will be considered as examples, in light of the unprecedented involvement of international actors vis-à-vis the issue of the missing since WWII.

1. THE IMPORTANCE OF THE ISSUE OF MISSING PERSONS
IN PEACE PROCESSES

The issue of missing persons cannot be treated as a secondary issue in peacebuilding processes. In order for this issue to be considered a priority in post-conflict settings, it must be embedded within the peace framework that sanctions the termination of the conflict (sub-section 1.1). Furthermore, in the restoration of the RoL – which is one of the components of post-conflict

---

[3] Stahn refers to the theoretical framework that relates to the international administration of territory and in particular considers the traditional approach laid down by Grotius in *De Jure Belli ac Pacis* which started with the word "controversiae" (disputes). Stahn, *The Law and Practice of International Territorial Administration* (n 2) 33–34. More generally, according to Higgins, the role of law is to 'provide an operational system for securing values that we all desire....it is not as commonly supposed, only about resolving disputes'. Rosalyn Higgins, *Problems and Process: International Law and How We Use It* (Oxford University Press 1995) 1.

[4] Based on this book's methodological premises (see "Introduction"), international law is conceived as a system of normative conduct, i.e., 'the conduct which is regarded by each actor, and by the group as a whole as being obligatory, and for which violation carries a price'. Higgins (n 3) 1.

peacebuilding[5] – the need of families for information on missing persons cannot be disregarded and must be addressed by the actors operating in the context concerned. International actors involved in post-conflict peacebuilding are not exempted from abiding by the relevant international rules on missing persons in the context in which they operate (sub-section 1.2). For instance, where international actors maintain the direct administration of the territory,[6] the international legal framework on the handling of and access to information on missing persons coupled with the domestic legal framework is the reference for actions and measures centered on this issue.[7] Even in those cases where the international actors have not such a mandate, they are not *legibus solutus* and

---

[5] The UNSG defines rule of law as follows: 'a principle of governance in which all persons, institutions and entities, public and private, including the State itself, are accountable to laws that are publicly promulgated, equally enforced and independently adjudicated, and which are consistent with international human rights norms and standards. It requires, as well, measures to ensure adherence to the principles of supremacy of law, equality before the law, accountability to the law, fairness in the application of the law, separation of powers, participation in decision-making, legal certainty, avoidance of arbitrariness and procedural and legal transparency.' UNSG, 'Report on the Rule of Law and Transitional Justice in Conflict and Post-Conflict Societies' (2004) UN Doc S/2004/616 para 6. Gowlland-Debbas and Pergantis develop an in-depth study of the substantive and conceptual aspects concerning the rule of law in the context of post-conflict peacebuilding. In their analysis, rule of law is defined as 'a principle of governance upholding the supremacy of the law adopted through an established procedure, accountability of public authority under the law, equality of all before the law, and access to an impartial and autonomous system of justice. It is ideologically linked to constitutionalism, democracy, and human rights. Rule of law projects in a peacebuilding context focus on elimination of arbitrariness; institutional reform, including the administration of justice; and accountability.' V Gowlland-Debbas and V Pergantis, 'Rule of Law' in Vincent Chetail (ed), *Post-conflict Peacebuilding: a Lexicon* (Oxford University Press 2009) 320.
[6] See the example of the UN Mission in Kosovo (UNMIK), sub-section 1.2.4.2 in the present Chapter.
[7] One author suggests that '[t]he UN's role in the creation of human rights law, the recognition of these obligations as forming international standards, and the regular application of these standards provide strong support for the use of international human rights standards as the basis for UN obligations in interim administrations'. Elizabeth Abraham, 'The Sins of the Savior: Holding the United Nations Accountable to International Human Rights Standards for Executive Order Detentions on Its Mission in Kosovo Comment' (2002) 52 American University Law Review 1291, 1321. Along the same line, other scholars point out that 'acts of international organizations carried out in the exercise of governmental powers (as, for instance, in the context of complex peace-building operations) may constitute acts of a dual nature (concept of functional duality). They might be international in nature, to the extent that they form part of the international organizations legal order, and domestic in character, in so far as they are part of the host country's internal legal system.' M Tondini, 'Putting an End to Human Rights Violations by Proxy: Accountability of International Organizations and Member States in the Framework of Jus Post Bellum' in Carsten Stahn and Jann K Kleffner (eds), *Jus Post Bellum: Towards a Law of Transition From Conflict to Peace* (Springer Verlag 2008) 195 (and references therein with regard to the concept of functional duality). *Contra:* although fascinating, this perspective has been refuted by UNMIK in its first report to the UN HRCee in 2006: '[i]t must be remembered throughout that the situation of Kosovo under interim administration by UNMIK is *sui generis*. Accordingly, it has been the consistent position of UNMIK that treaties and agreements, to which the State Union of Serbia and Montenegro is a party, are not automatically binding on UNMIK [including human rights treaties]. UNMIK, 'Report Submitted by the United Nations Interim Administration Mission in Kosovo to the Human Rights Committee on the Human Rights Situation in Kosovo Since June 1999' (2006) UN Doc CCPR/C/ UNK/1 paras 123-124.

must abide by international human rights law.[8] The motives for these considerations are laid down in the following sub-sections.

1.1. Towards peace

The definition of the status of peace agreements under international law[9] (sub-section 1.1.1) is a key step in the identification of their role in the current debate on the existence of a post-conflict international legal framework (sub-section 1.1.2). Indeed, an understanding of their role will shed light upon the function of such documents in the regulation of the conduct of multiple actors vis-à-vis the pending consequences of the conflict, including the issue of the missing (sub-section 1.1.3).

1.1.1. Peace agreements under international law

The current hybridity of peace agreements in terms of content and negotiators (i.e., domestic/international; State/non-state actors involved) has not facilitated the scholars' examination of such documents through the prism of the international law rules on treaties.[10] The status that these agreements have under international law is still debated:[11] when peace agreements have the form of a treaty, i.e., an 'international agreement concluded between States in written form', they are governed by international law;[12] when these agreements are signed with non-state actors, [13] they no longer fit such definition. However, pursuant to Article 3 VCLT

---

[8] See Andrew Clapham, *Human Rights Obligations of Non-State Actors* (Oxford University Press 2006) 109–135 (focusing on the UN obligations under IHLR, when operating in armed conflict and post-conflict contexts, e.g., with UNMIK). See sub-section 3.1 in Chapter II and sub-section 1.2.3 in the present Chapter.

[9] A detailed examination of the issue has been developed by Bell. See Christine Bell, *On the Law of Peace: Peace Agreements and the Lex Pacificatoria* (Oxford University Press 2008).

[10] See ibid 9-10.

[11] Christine Bell, 'Peace Agreements: Their Nature and Legal Status' (2006) 100 The American Journal of International Law 373, 379; Christine Bell, *Peace Agreements and Human Rights* (Oxford University Press 2003) 304–305; JS Easterday, 'Peace Agreements as a Framework for Jus Post Bellum' in Carsten Stahn, Jennifer S Easterday and Jens Iverson (eds), *Jus Post Bellum: Mapping the normative Foundations* (Oxford University Press 2014); A Klafkowski, 'Les Formes de Cessation de L'état de Guerre En Droit International', *Collected Courses of The Hague Academy of International Law*, vols 217–286 (Sijthoff 1979) 243 (arguing that a peace treaty, when in the form of an international treaty, shall be examined and interpreted in light of the international rules on treaties).

[12] Pursuant to Article 2 (1) (a) VCLT, '"treaty" means an international agreement concluded between States in written form and governed by international law, whether embodied in a single instrument or in two or more related instruments and whatever its particular designation'.

[13] Today's Article 2 (1) (g) VCLT defining the term 'party' was framed differently under the 1962's version: '"[p]arty" means a State or other subject of international law, possessing international personality and having capacity to enter into treaties under the rules set out in Article 3 below, which has executed acts by which it has definitively given its consent to be bound by a treaty in force'. Such definition was changed and today reads as follows: '"party" means a State which has consented to be bound by the treaty and for which the treaty is in force'. Cf. ILC, *Yearbook of the International Law Commission - 1962. Documents of the Fourteenth Session Including the Report of the Commission to the General Assembly*, vol II (United Nations 1964) 31.

[t]he fact that the present Convention does not apply to international agreements concluded between states and other subjects of international law or between such other subjects of international law, or to international agreements not in written form, shall not affect: (a) the legal force of such agreements; (b) the application to them of any of the rules set forth in the present Convention to which they would be subject under international law independently of the Convention; (c) the application of the Convention to the relations of states as between themselves under international agreements to which other subjects of international law are also parties.

In other words, 'agreements between State and non-state parties that are subjects of international law, or indeed between such non-state parties alone, can be legally binding international agreements'.[14]

As posited in the introduction to this book, international law is not just rules, but a dynamic decision-making process. In the framework of this dynamic process there are a variety of participants (e.g., individuals, States, international organizations, multinational corporations, and non-governmental groups).[15] These participants make 'claims across state line, with the object of maximizing various values. Determinations will be made on those claims by various authoritative decision-makers,'[16] e.g., foreign office legal advisers, judicial bodies, including international courts. Should peace agreements fall short of the elements set down under the international rules on treaties, they are in any case one of the instruments through which the parties to the conflict express their

---

[14] Bell, 'Peace Agreements' (n 11) 380. Bell, however, has also admitted the difficulty with classifying all peace agreements as legal documents due to the involvement of both domestic and international actors, States and groups who have a status short of statehood. See Bell, *Peace Agreements and Human Rights* (n 11) 304.

[15] On international organizations, the ICJ has stated that '[i]n order to delineate the field of activity or the area of competence of an international organization one must refer to the relevant rules of the organization and, in the first place, to its constitution. [...] [T]he constituent instruments of international organizations are also treaties of a particular type; their object is to create new subjects of law endowed with a certain autonomy, to which the parties entrust the task of realizing common goals.' See ICJ, *Legality of the Use by a State of Nuclear Weapons in Armed Conflict, Advisory Opinion (WHO request)* (1996) ICJ Reports 1996, p 66 [19]. On individuals, see the position of the ICJ in relation to the Vienna Convention on Consular Relations' Article 36 (while the US argued that such provisions created State's rights, the Court acknowledged that the provision established individual rights). ICJ, *LaGrand Case (Germany v United States of America), Judgment* (2001) ICJ Reports 2001, p 466 [76–77]. On the legal status of agreements to which one or more non-state armed actors are party, the International Commission of Inquiry on Darfur noted that the SLM/A and the JEM 'possess under customary international law the power to enter into binding international agreements (*jus contrahendi*), and have entered into various internationally binding agreements with the Government'. International Commission of Inquiry on Darfur, 'Report of the International Commission of Inquiry on Darfur to the Secretary-General Pursuant to Security Council Resolution 1564 (2004) of 18 September 2004' (2005) UN Doc S/2005/60 para 174. Along the same lines, see Sandesh Sivakumaran, *The Law of Non-International Armed Conflict* (Oxford University Press 2012) 109 (addressing the issue of the normative status of *ad hoc* commitments of armed groups and of bilateral agreements to which armed groups are parties). *Contra*: the Special Court for Sierra Leone held that the Lomé Agreement between the Government of Sierra Leone and the Revolutionary United Front was not a treaty because it was signed by the government and an armed group. Special Court for Sierra Leone. *Prosecutor against Morris Kallon and Brima Bazzy Kamara, Decision on Challenge to Jurisdiction: Lomé Accord Amnesty* (2004) Case no SCSL-2004-15-PT, Case no SCSL-2004-16-PT [45–50].

[16] Higgins (n 3) 50.

claims 'with the object of maximizing various values'.[17] As such, they directly impact on international law and are part of it. The following sub-sections will examine the implications that peace agreements have for the realization of the right of families to know the fate of their relatives as part of the post-conflict legal framework.

1.1.2. Peace agreements within the discussion of a post-conflict international legal framework

Peace agreements are a central piece in the transition from conflict to peace. In order to achieve a sustainable peace, when a peace agreement is negotiated, the terms of negotiation cannot be left to the discretion of the negotiators in their entirety. One of the main scholars – Christine Bell – who has examined the status of peace agreements under international law, underlines the need to re-conceive how international law applies and what it demands vis-à-vis peace agreements and their implementation.[18] She stresses that a new account of the dynamic relationship between law and practice vis-à-vis peace settlements can be boiled down to what she names 'lex pacificatoria', i.e., 'a set of programmatic standards that provide guidance and, at times, goes further in creating a normative expectation as to how dilemmas of peace settlements can be resolved concomitantly with requirements of international law'.[19] She considers that this notion is the most suitable one to capture the dynamic relationship of international law with peace agreements and their implementation. In this sense, she also argues that it is neither possible nor desirable to put the foregoing reasoning in *jus post bellum* terms.[20]

The premises of this book are not in line with what Bell claims. In her view, the conceptualization of this new *lex* looks at 'the law as part of a broader domestic and international negotiation over the end point of transition and the democratic legitimacy of the polity that results'.[21] On the parameters that this new *lex* lays down, she stresses that the final aim of *lex pacificatoria* is

> not to regulate negotiations outcomes, but rather to set out such broad normative parameters that support the idea that negotiated outcomes should be both capable of implementation and accord with some sense of justice, while leaving room for the contestation over what concepts such as "accountability", "justice", and even "peace" require'.[22]

---

[17] ibid.

[18] C Bell, 'Of Jus Post Bellum and Lex Pacificatoria What's in a Name?' in Carsten Stahn, Jennifer S Easterday and Jens Iverson (eds), *Jus Post Bellum: Mapping the normative Foundations* (Oxford University Press 2014) 192.

[19] ibid.

[20] ibid 181.

[21] Under this perspective, the problems and ambiguity of the law in such phase directly derives from the challenges and counter-challenges that emerge between domestic actors and between domestic and international actors. ibid 205.

[22] ibid.

Undoubtedly, the phase that follows the termination of a conflict requires a certain degree of flexibility[23] against the context affected by the conflict, since the regular institutional, legislative, diplomatic, economic, and judicial capacity of State authorities might be *in statu nascendi.*

This, however, cannot lead to ignore that negotiations *per se* are already regulated by existing international rules on treaty law; pursuant to the VCLT – which is considered customary – 'a treaty does not create either obligations or rights for a third State without its consent'.[24] In the purview of this study, this means that when States negotiate a peace treaty 'a fair hearing of the interests of all parties to the conflict at the negotiating table' is required.[25] No room for deal is present when consent is lacking.[26] This is in line with recent practice concerning peace settlement processes: in order to reach a sustainable peace, the victors cannot be allowed to impose rights and/or obligations upon the vanquished.[27] The practice tends towards the application of the same reasoning to those cases where the negotiating parties are State and non-state actors.[28]

Apart from the normative framework within which the peace settlement process[29] should be understood, international law also plays a role within the peace agreements. As stated above, the traditional form of peace agreements is that of treaties between the belligerents (=States), which regulate the disputes underlying the war, the legal consequences of the war and its termination, and future and peaceful relations. Nevertheless, this typology of treaties seems to have fallen in *desuetude,* as most of post-Cold-War's conflicts are of a non-

---

[23] For instance, the ECtHR considered that over ten years the institutional setting of Bosnia and Herzegovina overcome severe difficulties due to the armed conflict, which affected the capacity of Bosnia to abide by the duty to investigate under Article 2 ECHR according to the standards set down in the ECtHR's case law. Cf. ECtHR, *Palić v Bosnia and Herzegovina, Judgment* (2011) App no. 4704/04 (ECtHR) [70].

[24] Cf. Article 34 VCLT.

[25] Carsten Stahn, '"Jus Ad bellum", "Jus in bello"..."Jus Post Bellum"? Rethinking the Conception of the Law of Armed Forces' (2006) 17 European Journal of International Law 921, 938.

[26] Stahn points out that agreements' negotiations cannot be left entirely at the discretion of the negotiators, since a *do ut des* approach may drive their actions. See C Stahn, 'The Future of Jus Post Bellum' in Carsten Stahn and Jann K Kleffner (eds), *Jus Post Bellum: Towards a Law of Transition From Conflict to Peace* (Springer Verlag 2008) 236.

[27] As example of this old-fashioned and detrimental manner to reach peace, Stahn mentions the Treaty of Versailles; recent practice shows an opposite trend: for instance, the Dayton Agreements and the Ethiopia/Eritrea agreement demonstrate that the State that has struck the attack and has used the force against the other(s) should be present at the negotiation table. Stahn, '"Jus Ad bellum", "Jus in bello"..."Jus Post Bellum"?' (n 25) 938.

[28] A recent example is represented by the Colombian situation where all the parties - State and non-state actors - have been invited to participate in the peace process. See Maria José Guembe and Helena Olea, 'No Justice, No Peace: Discussion of a Legal Framework Regarding the Demobilization of Non-State Armed Groups in Colombia' in Naomi Roht-Arriaza (ed), *Transitional justice in the twenty-first century: beyond truth versus justice* (Cambridge University Press 2006); BBC Mundo, 'El Gobierno de Colombia Y Las FARC Llegaron a Un Acuerdo Para Buscar a Los Desaparecidos' (*BBC Mundo,* 18 October 2015) <http://www.bbc.com/mundo/noticias/2015/10/151017_colombia_farc_desaparecidos _acuerdo_ilm> accessed 12 September 2016.

[29] Peace process is *per se* indefinite and has no legally-based semantic contours; indeed, Bell describes it as 'a value judgment attached to efforts to resolve a conflict at a particular time'. Bell, *Peace Agreements and Human Rights* (n 11) 16.

international character.[30] Thus, agreements sanctioning the termination of the conflict can have multiple forms,[31] can be accompanied by other instruments or can even be replaced by alternative instruments and initiatives, e.g., the UNSC Resolutions as well as the involvement of the UNSC in the definition of peace settlements' terms.[32]

1.1.3. The issue of the missing in recent peace agreements

The obligation to cooperate of all the (former) parties to the conflict in their efforts to trace the missing emerges from the international legal framework applicable in both conflict and post-conflict settings (see Chapter II, III and IV). The review of a set of recent peace agreements will demonstrate that the duty to cooperate is a quintessential pillar of an effective post-conflict strategy[33] that aims at addressing, *inter alia,* the issue of the missing (sub-section 1.1.3.1). It will also cast light upon the impact that the international legal framework has on the integration of this issue within peace agreements and vice-versa (sub-section 1.1.3.2).

1.1.3.1. The duty to cooperate: the pillar of a post-conflict strategy to address the issue of the missing

The amplitude of the issue of the missing in WWII did not result in its inclusion in the 1947 Paris Peace Treaties; in most cases, bilateral arrangements were concluded between the parties to the conflict in the aftermath of WWII or following the settlements of pending tensions.[34] Nevertheless, two measures

---

[30] See Randall Lesaffer, 'Peace Treaties - International Law (Oxford Bibliographies)' (2015) <http://www.oxfordbibliographies.com/view/document/obo-9780199796953/obo-9780199796953-0120.xml> accessed 19 January 2017.

[31] For instance, Bell argues that a possible classification could be the following: pre-negotiation agreements; framework or substantive agreements; implementation agreements. Nevertheless agreements rarely fit neatly a category. Bell, *Peace Agreements and Human Rights* (n 11) 20–31.

[32] C Stahn, 'Jus Post Bellum: Mapping the Discipline(s)' in Carsten Stahn and Jann K Kleffner (eds), *Jus Post Bellum: Towards a Law of Transition From Conflict to Peace* (Springer Verlag 2008) 106; SC Neff, 'Conflict Termination and Peace-Making in the Law of Nations: A Historical Perspective' in Carsten Stahn and Jann K Kleffner (eds), *Jus Post Bellum: Towards a Law of Transition From Conflict to Peace* (Springer Verlag 2008) 88 (quoting *inter alia* the example of the Kuwait crisis); see also Lesaffer (n 30).

[33] In the *Congo v Uganda* case the ICJ boldly declared that 'it is incumbent on all those involved in the conflict to support the peace process in the DRC and other peace processes in the Great Lakes area, in order to ensure respect for human rights in the region.' More generally, this holds valid for all the contexts where a peace process is ongoing, particularly when atrocities were committed during the conflict. Cf. ICJ, *Case concerning Armed Activities on the Territory of the Congo (Democratic Republic of the Congo v Uganda), Merits, Judgment* (2005) ICJ Reports 2005, p.168 [221].

[34] Signed on October 18, 1959, the Joint Communiqué by USSR and Italy recorded an understanding that no Italian POW remained in the USSR; it also sanctioned an agreement on continued effective contacts between the Red Cross Societies of the two States concerning data on missing persons in order to settle finally the status of surviving family and kin. Cf. Joint Communiqué by USSR and Italy concerning negotiations on the question of Italian POW and persons missing in the USSR during WWII, signed October 18, 1959 in Moscow in George Ginsburgs, *Soviet Citizenship Law*, vol 1 (A W Sijthoff 1968) 66. Due to the worsening of their relations in the aftermath of WWII, only recently - 2009 - the USA and the Russian Federation were able to exchange diplomatic notes establishing a non-binding framework for the US-Russia Joint Commission on POW and Missing in

resulted from the peace process; these cast light upon the international dimension that the issue of the missing had at that time as well as upon the duty to cooperate to address the issue: first, the establishment of an international tracing service; second, the adoption of an *ad hoc* convention on the issue. With regard to the former, the International Tracing Service (ITS) was the result of the measures adopted during and in the aftermath of the conflict[35] and sanctioned by the peace settlements that followed.[36] The Service was intended for

the purpose of tracing missing persons and collecting, classifying, preserving and rendering accessible to Governments and interested individuals the documents relating to Germans and non-Germans who were interned in National-socialist concentration or labor camps or to non-Germans who were displaced as a result of Second World War.[37]

The signatory parties to the Bonn agreement,[38] which established an international commission to supervise the ITS, expressed their desire 'to maintain the international collaboration existing in this field to enable cooperation of other interested States, the Western European Union, and other interested organizations, and to provide for the protection of the archives and

---

Action to resume its activities (the Commission was originally established in 1992); the Commission would serve as a forum through which both nations seek to determine the fates of their missing servicemen from WWII, the Korean War, the Vietnam war, and the Cold War. See Elizabeth R Wilcox, *Digest of United States Practice in International Law, 2009* (Oxford University Press - USA 2011) 696. The USSR and Japan did not conclude a peace agreement following WWII; in 1956 the two countries agreed on a declaration that put an end to the status of war between the two countries, which included the following provision: '[w]ith regard to those Japanese whose fate is unknown, the USSR, at the request of Japan, will continue its efforts to discover what has happened to them.' Cf. 'Joint Declaration by the USSR and Japan' (19 October 1956) pt 5 <http://www.ioc.u-tokyo.ac.jp/~worldjpn/documents/texts/docs/19561019.D1E.html> accessed 12 July 2016.
[35] During and in the aftermath of WWII, the duplication of tracing services was conducive to the establishment of a centralized tracing service. Jenny Edkins, *Missing: Persons and Politics* (Cornell University Press 2011) 58–59.
[36] Set up as early as 1943 under the form of a central tracing office within the Headquarters of the Allied forces of the British Red Cross in London, the ITS was transferred to Bad Arolsen in 1946 under the coordination of initially UNRRA and, then the International Refugee Organization. Eventually, pursuant to the Bonn Accord, the ITS was put under the control of an international commission in 1955. On the request of the then German Chancellor Konrad Adenauer, the ICRC agreed to assume the leadership of the ITS. See Kenneth Waltzer, 'Opening the Red Cross International Tracing Service Archive' (2008) 26 The John Marshall Journal of Information Technology and Privacy Law 161, 161–164; International Tracing Service - ITS, 'History' (2 August 2016) <https://www.its-arolsen.org/en/about-its/history/> accessed 20 January 2017.
[37] See Preamble, Agreement constituting an International Commission for the International Tracing Service (Bonn Agreement), Bonn, June 6, 1955. There has never been a final peace treaty between allied forces and Germany. Under the Settlement Agreement between the Federal Republic Germany and the allied forces (i.e., the only agreement struck to regulate matters relating to reparations and compensation), the Government of the Federal Republic undertook to assure the continuance of the operations carried out by the ITS. Cf. Article 1 (d), Chapter 7, Convention on the Settlement of Matters Arising out of the War and the Occupation as amended by Schedule IV to the Protocol on the termination of the occupation regime in the Federal Republic of Germany, Paris 23 October 1954.
[38] The parties to the Bonn Agreement were Belgium, France, the Federal Republic of Germany, Greece, Israel, Italy, Luxembourg, the Netherlands, the UK and the USA. The Bonn Agreement was replaced by the Berlin Agreement from 9 December 2011.

documents'.[39] Conceived as a transitional measure,[40] the indeterminate duration of the issue of missing persons led to extend its mandate, which is still operational to date.[41]

As for the *ad hoc* convention, measures to tackle the legal status of those reported as missing during WWII or during the post-conflict years were discussed by States members of the then newly established UN.[42] Their efforts led to the adoption of the Convention on the declaration of death of missing persons – an instrument of private international law – aimed at managing the pending legal situations of thousands of families who were waiting for answers as well as the pending status of those unaccounted for. At that time, some countries did not have a system of declaration of death at all; a large number of countries had a legislation, which was not tailored to cope with the international dimension of the issue of missing persons (many were not citizens of the country where they disappeared; families where dispersed; survivors searching for information settled all over the world).[43] As a matter of fact, such situations of uncertainty engendered 'difficulties of a legal nature' placing 'a great number of human beings in a precarious position':[44] thus, the Convention[45] established a set of rules to be applied in the States parties, including the obligation of every State to permit applications to be filed in tribunals specifically mentioned in the treaty.[46] Although the Convention had a limited temporal[47] scope and uniquely

---

[39] Cf. preamble, Bonn Agreement.

[40] The ITS would have been re-assessed every five years. Cf. Article 10 Bonn Agreement.

[41] It is only in 2008 that public access to its archives was granted to the public (see sub-section 1.4 in Chapter I for the policy and legal factors that hampered access of families to information held by the ITS).

[42] UNGA, 'Resolution 369 (IV) "Draft Convention on the Declaration of Death of Missing Persons"' (1949) UN Doc A/1251 paras 1, 3.

[43] Nehemiah Robinson, *United Nations Convention on the Declaration of Death of Missing Persons: A Commentary* (Institute of Jewish Affairs - World Jewish Congress 1951) 3–4.

[44] Cf. Preamble, Convention on the declaration of death of missing persons (Convention on the Declaration of Death), Lake Success, New York, 6 April 1950, 119 UNTS 99.

[45] The Convention also provided for the establishment of an International Bureau for Declarations of Death: set up in the framework of the UN, this Bureau had the task to create a link between applications which were or could be filed in various States concerning the same missing person so as to avoid unnecessary duplication or the issuance of declarations for persons still alive. Cf. Article 8, Convention on the Declaration of Death. According to the UN legal counsel, the Bureau could be considered part of the UN in light of its link to the organization (expenses included in the budget of the UN and its staff appointed by the UNSG). See UN, *UN Juridical Yearbook - Part II Legal Activities of the United Nations and Related Intergovernmental Organizations (Chapter VI - Selected Legal Opinions of the Secretariat of the United Nations and Related Inter-Governmental Organizations)* (United Nations 1969) 207–208. See also Robinson (n 43) 6.

[46] These included the tribunal of the last domicile, residence or nationality of the missing person, of the location of his property, of the place of his death, of the place of residence of the applicant (should the applicant be a close relative). Cf. Article 2 (1) – (2), Convention on the Declaration of Death.

[47] The Convention was not intended to produce its effects for more than five years, since its adoption; for this reason, it was supposed to cease to have effect on 23 January 1957. However, its duration was extended as a result of the adoption of the Protocols of 16 January 1957 and 15 January 1967, and remained in force until 24 January 1972.

covered people who went missing during WWII,[48] it still stands as the first and unique international attempt specifically aimed at addressing the pragmatic consequences of uncertainty about missing persons in a post-conflict setting through the adoption of a treaty.[49]

Apart from post-WWII initiatives, in other contexts the issue of missing persons has been integrated within peace settlements adopted at the conclusion of NIAC/IAC. As noted in Chapter I (section 2), the Vietnamese armed conflict has been a key event with an impact on the following development of the international legal framework concerning the missing and their families. Indeed, the magnitude of the issue of missing in action on both sides led to include the following provision in the peace settlement that put an end to the US-Vietnam conflict (Paris Agreement):

> [t]he parties shall help each other to get information about those military personnel and foreign civilians of the parties missing in action, to determine the location and take care of the graves of the dead so as to facilitate the exhumation and repatriation of the remains, and to take any such other measures as may be required to get information about those still considered missing in action.[50]

The long-term efforts of the States involved in accounting for the missing in Vietnam are reflected in constant and still active commitment of both parties.[51] The Paris Agreement was preliminary to other peace settlements in the region. Indeed, immediately after the Paris Agreement, the Vientiane Ceasefire Agreement put an end to the NIAC between the Laotian government and the communist group Pathet Lao and laid down the terms for the restoration of peace. Although at that time the international legal framework concerning the missing was inexistent for NIAC and IAC, the agreement boldly stated that '[f]ollowing the completion of the repatriation of captured personnel, each side will have the responsibility to provide the other side with information on those reported missing during the war in Laos.'[52]

---

[48] Article 1 defined the scope *ratione personae* of the Convention on the Declaration of Death as follows: '1. The present Convention provides for declarations of death of persons whose last residence was in Europe, Asia or Africa who have disappeared in the years 1939-1945, under circumstances affording reasonable ground to infer that they have died in consequence of events of war or of racial, religious, political or national persecution. [...] 2. Contracting States may, by notification 10 the Secretary-General of the United Nations, extend its application to persons having disappeared subsequently to 1945 under similar circumstances. [...]'

[49] The first recital of the Preamble made reference to 'the disappearance of persons whose death cannot be established with certainty.' Cf. first recital, Preamble, Convention on the Declaration of Death.

[50] Chapter III, Article 8 (b), Democratic Republic of Vietnam/USA, '(Paris) Agreement on Ending the War and Restoring Peace in Vietnam' (1973) text reproduced in "The Vietnam War and International Law, Volume 4: The Concluding Phase" by Richard Falk (Princeton University Press: 2015).

[51] An example is represented by the 1992 agreement between the USA and Vietnam with regard to the access to the military archives held by Vietnam. See sub-section 1.4 in Chapter I.

[52] Cf. Article 5, Laotian Government/Pathet Lao, 'Vientiane Ceasefire Agreement' (1973) <http://peacemaker.un.org/lao-ceasefire73> accessed 12 July 2016.

Among the most recent peace agreements that address the issue of the missing are the Dayton Agreements,[53] a sophisticated legal instrument that put an end to one of the most violent conflicts since the end of WWII. The Agreements reflected the post-Cold War shift in the peacemaking processes with the direct involvement of various entities. Concluded by the Republic of Bosnia and Herzegovina, the Federal Republic of Yugoslavia, and the Republic of Croatia, the General Framework obliged them to 'fully respect and promote fulfillment of the commitments' made in the Annexes to the General Framework.[54] The Annexes saw the direct involvement of two other entities, which were not parties to the General Framework Agreement, but were actively engaged in the armed conflict, i.e., the Republika Sprska and the Federation of Bosnia and Herzegovina. The obligation set down in the General Framework Agreements to 'fully respect and promote fulfillment of the commitments' in the Annexes thereof entailed that the content to be respected included the Annexes; these were an integral part of the Peace Agreement and, as such, international treaties.[55]

Pursuant to Annex 7, '[t]he Parties shall provide information through the tracing mechanisms of the ICRC on all persons unaccounted for' and 'shall also cooperate fully with the ICRC in its efforts to determine the identities, whereabouts and fate of the unaccounted for'.[56] In the Dayton Agreements, the issue of the missing was treated as a purely humanitarian issue to be solved by means of the ICRC's good offices; accountability-related aspects of the issue or the human rights-oriented efforts, such as the Special Process for Missing Persons in the Territory of the Former Yugoslavia (see *infra*, sub-sect 2.1.1), which were ongoing at the time of negotiations, remained unnoticed.[57]

The Dayton agreements featured the active presence of non-participating States that signed them under the heading 'witnessed by'.[58] Pursuant to the

---

[53] See General Framework Agreement for Peace in Bosnia and Herzegovina and the Annexes thereto (also known as "Dayton Agreements") initialed in Dayton, Ohio, November 21, 1995 and signed in Paris, December 14, 1995. The expression "Dayton Agreements" refers to the whole General Framework Agreements for Peace in Bosnia and Herzegovina, twelve Annexes and the Agreement on Initialing the General Framework, which sets out the terms for conclusion and entry into force of the General Framework and Annexes.

[54] Cf. Articles II-VIII, General Framework, Dayton Agreements.

[55] Cf. ECtHR, *Jeličić v Bosnia and Herzegovina, Decision* (2005) App no 41183/02; *Sejdić and Finci v Bosnia and Herzegovina, Judgment (GC)* (2009) Apps no 27996/06 and 34836/06 [30]. The Annexes are international treaties, despite the fact that some of them (e.g., Annex 4 on the Constitution of Bosnia and Herzegovina, Annex 6 on the Agreement on Human Rights, and Annex 7 on the Agreement on Refugees and Displaced Persons) were signed or approved by Bosnia and Herzegovina and the above-mentioned entities.

[56] Cf. Article V, Annex 7 'Agreement on Refugees and Displaced Persons', Dayton Agreements.

[57] M Nowak, 'Disappearances in Bosnia-Herzegovina' in Michael O'Flaherty (ed), *Post-war protection of human rights in Bosnia and Herzegovina* (Martinus Nijhoff Publishers 1998) 110.

[58] These were USA, France, Germany, the UK, the EU and Russia. Hoffmeister stresses that from a legal point of view a witness is no more than 'any other non-participating State. His "testimony" has no legal effect for the adoption of the text'. See F Hoffmeister, 'Article 9 - Adoption of the Text' in Oliver Dörr and Kirsten Schmalenbach (eds), *Vienna Convention on the Law of Treaties: A Commentary* (Springer Science & Business Media 2011) 140. Another aspect that made the Dayton Agreements peculiar is the modalities of expressing consent: consent to be bound can be expressed in a varied of manners – signature, exchange of instruments constituting a treaty, ratification,

VCLT the legal effect of this testimony is inexistent; however, this element combined with the sanctions' mechanism set out in the UNSC Resolution 1022[59] and other tools – e.g., the apparatus for the civilian implementation led by the High Representative for Bosnia and Herzegovina – should have played the role of international guarantees vis-à-vis the entirety of the commitments taken by the parties under the Peace Agreement.[60] The analysis in Chapter VI of the contribution of the Human Rights Chamber for Bosnia and Herzegovina (HRChBH)[61] – established pursuant to Annex 6 of the Dayton Agreements – will shed light upon the inaction of the international community vis-à-vis the failure of the Bosnia and Herzegovina's entities to cooperate with the recommendations on the missing.

Other agreements have maintained the focus on the primary responsibility of the parties involved in the conflict to account for the missing, the ICRC being the vehicle to transmit information. For instance, with the Agreement for the normalization of their Relations, Serbia and Croatia expressed their commitment to speed up forthwith 'the process of solving the questions of missing persons' and to 'exchange all available information about these persons'.[62]

As for the agreements concluded at the end of a NIAC, the Implementing Guidelines on the Humanitarian, Rehabilitation and Development Aspects of the Government of the Republic of Philippines (GRP) and Moro Islamic Liberation Front (MILF) – integral part of the Tripoli Agreement of Peace – affirm that

[i]n conformity with [IHL], each Party shall provide information, through the tracing mechanism of the ICRC, to families of all persons who are unaccounted for. The GRP and the MILF will cooperate fully in determining the identity, whereabouts, and fate of those missing persons.

The Parties shall cooperate in the investigation and prosecution of serious violations of international humanitarian laws and human rights as well as of this agreement.[63]

---

acceptance, approval or accession. The VCLT leaves the possibility to the parties of agreeing on 'other means' of expressing consent. F Hoffmeister, 'Article 11 - Means of Expressing Consent to Be Bound by a Treaty' in Oliver Dörr and Kirsten Schmalenbach (eds), *Vienna Convention on the Law of Treaties: A Commentary* (Springer Science & Business Media 2011) 157. In the case of the Dayton Agreements the initialing of the General Framework - initialing can be preparatory or may be elevated to signature - was considered as another means of expressing consent, although the same treaty requested a further step, i.e. the entry into force upon final signature of the Dayton Agreements in Paris.

[59] The UNSC's Resolution 1022 stated that the suspension of sanctions shall terminate if the Federal Republic of Yugoslavia or the Bosnian Serb authorities fail significantly to meet their obligations under the Peace Agreement. Cf. UNSC, 'Resolution 1022 on Suspension of Measures Imposed by or Reaffirmed in Security Council Resolutions Related to the Situation in the Former Yugoslavia' (1995) UN Doc S/RES/1022 para 3.

[60] Paola Gaeta, 'The Dayton Agreements and International Law (Symposium: The Dayton Agreements: A Breakthrough for Peace and Justice?)' (1996) 7 European Journal of International Law 147, 162.

[61] See sub-section 1.1.3.1 in Chapter VI.

[62] Cf. Article 6, Agreement on the Normalization of Relations, between Croatia and Federal Republic of Yugoslavia, August 23, 1996.

[63] Cf. Article IV (4-5), Government of the Republic of Philippines (GRP)/Moro Islamic Liberation Front (MILF), 'Implementing Guidelines on the Humanitarian, Rehabilitation, and Development

Pursuant to these guidelines, State and non-state parties are tasked to account for the missing and to inform their families on an equal footing. In a similar vein, a protocol between the Russian Federation and Chechnya signed in 1996 laid down the framework for the establishment of a Joint Working Group mandated to locate persons reported as missing since 1994; the Working Group was also mandated to facilitate the release of forcibly detained persons in the course of the armed conflict.[64] Moreover, the parties to the Protocol agreed upon making arrangements for the 'issuance of orders by both sides calling for the cessation of the practice of detaining persons in a manner not provided for by law', recognized the 'abductions of persons with a view to their subsequent sale or use in exchanges as a criminal offense', and declared to prosecute any persons committing such offenses.[65] The parties also declared to undertake 'a joint effort … to locate burial sites, to exhume the remains of the dead, and hand over such remains to their relatives'.[66]

An example of peace agreement settling a conflict between two non-state armed groups is the 2000 Townsville Peace Agreement signed by the Malaita Eagle Force (MEF) and the Isatabu Freedom Movement (IFM), two militant groups active in the Salomon Islands.[67] The agreement was specifically aimed at restoring peace and ethnic harmony in Solomon Islands after "the tensions"[68] erupted in the late 1990s; among other measures, the Agreement required that 'within ninety days from the date of [its] execution […] both the IFM and MEF shall locate, identify, and allow remains of any persons known to be killed during the course of the crisis to be retrieved by their relatives'.[69] Moreover, although the tensions concerned two non-state groups, the agreement enshrined a sort of remedial system by stating that 'custom means of reconciliation and compensation may be agreed to between concerned persons and communities in connection with killing of persons during the course of the crisis'.[70] The involvement of international actors has been crucial in this setting; the same agreement set up an indigenous Peace Monitoring Council supported by an

---

Aspects of the GRP-MILF Tripoli Agreement on Peace of 2001' (2002) <http://www.c-r.org/downloads/06s_3Key%20texts_2003_ENG.pdf> accessed 12 July 2016.

[64] Russian Federation/Chechen Republic of Ichkeriya, 'Protocol of the Meeting of the Working Groups, Formed under the Negotiations Commissions, to Locate Missing Persons and to Free Forcibly Detained Persons' (1996) <http://peacemaker.un.org/russia-agreementmissingpeople96> accessed 12 July 2016.

[65] Cf. pts. 5, 9, 10, 12, ibid.

[66] Cf. pt. 12, ibid.

[67] The Malaita Group defended the Malaitian diaspora that fled due to the actions of the Isatabu group; the Isatabu Group is a nationalist militant group fighting for federal government system. For more details on this conflict, see Kieren McGovern and Bernarnd Choulai, 'UNDP Human Development Report - Case Study of Solomon Islands Peace and Conflict-Related Development Analysis' (UNDP 2005) 2005/33.

[68] "Tensions" was the official manner to define the conflict that erupted in 1998. See ibid 2.

[69] Cf. Part III Sect 1 (a), Malaita Eagle Force/Isatabu Freedom Movement (Solomon Islands), 'Townsville Peace Agreement' (2000) UN Doc S/2000/1088 <http://peacemaker.un.org/solomonislands-townsville-agreement2000> accessed 12 July 2016.

[70] Cf. Part III Sect 1 (b), ibid.

International Peace Monitoring Team that comprised 50 armed police and civilians from Australia, New Zealand, and Pacific Island Countries.[71]

Although ceasefire agreements *per se* are not final peace agreements, they can prepare the ground for a more substantial peace agreement.[72] For instance, the 1992 Moscow Agreement between Russia and Georgia set down, as the basis of the peace settlement, a ceasefire to take effect as of 5 September 1992; it also defined the terms for the implementation of a series of steps in this direction, e.g., accounting for missing persons.[73] Another example is the Ceasefire Code of Conduct agreed between the Government of Nepal and Nepal Communist Party-Maoist (CPN-M), which laid down 25 points for the achievement of a peace settlement; among these points was the immediate publicizing of the whereabouts of those who had been disappeared.[74] Indeed, the Comprehensive Peace Agreement between Nepal and CPN-M not only confirmed the 25-point ceasefire, but also reiterated the commitment to make public the name, caste, and address of the people 'disappeared' or killed during war and 'to inform the family about it' within 60 days since the signature of the agreement.[75] In addition to this measure, 'both sides agree[d] to set up a High-level Truth and Reconciliation Commission through mutual agreement in order to investigate truth about people seriously violating human rights and involved in crimes against humanity'.[76]

---

[71] Cf. Part 5, Sect 2; Part 6 Sect. 1 ff., ibid.

[72] See C Bell, 'Ceasefire' in Rüdiger Wolfrum (ed), *Max Planck Yearbook of United Nations Law Online* (2009) para 14 <http://opil.ouplaw.com/view/10.1093/law:epil/9780199231690/law-9780199231690-e263?prd=EPIL> accessed 12 July 2016.

[73] Cf. Article 5, Russian Federation/Georgia, 'Moscow Agreement between Russia and Georgia (Annex to the Letter Date 8 September 1992 from the Chargé d'Affaires A.I. of the Permanent Mission of the Russian Federation to the United Nations Addressed to the President of the Security Council)' (1992) UN Doc S/24523. Nevertheless, the ceasefire was never fully implemented and collapsed in October when the fighting resumed in Abkhazia; in July 1993 another ceasefire agreement put an end to the hostilities and laid the ground for the UNOMIG, *inter alia*, tasked to monitor the respect of the ceasefire. This new agreement did not specifically mention the issue of the missing. See, in this respect, UNOMIG, 'Georgia - UN Observer Mission in Georgia (UNOMIG) - Background' (*Georgia - UNOMIG*) <http://www.un.org/en/peacekeeping/missions/past/unomig/background.html> accessed 12 July 2016.

[74] Cf. pt. 17, Government of Nepal/CPN-Maoist, 'Ceasefire Code of Conduct Agreed between the Government of Nepal and the CPN-Maoist - (Unofficial Translation)' (Uppsala University website 2006) <http://www.ucdp.uu.se/downloads/fullpeace/Nep%2020060525.pdf> accessed 12 July 2016.

[75] Cf. para 5.2.3, Government of Nepal/CPN-Maoist, 'Comprehensive Peace Agreement between the Government of Nepal and the CPN-Maoist' (2006) <http://peacemaker.un.org/nepal-comprehensiveagreement2006> accessed 12 July 2016.

[76] Cf. para 5.2.5, ibid. For years, these parts of the Agreement have not been addressed by the Government; in 2014 the Nepalese Supreme Court ordered the Government to amend the existing legislation and to issue ordinances aimed at finally establishing a truth and reconciliation commission, as *per* the Peace Agreement, as well as a separate commission mandated to investigate enforced disappearances. See *Madhav Kumar Basnet et al, v the Government of Nepal et al* (2014) 69-NaN-57. The Commission of Investigation on enforced Disappearances started its work in 2016. For more details see ICTJ, 'Ten Years After Peace, Is Nepal Finally Serious About Finding Its Disappeared?' (29 August 2016) <https://www.ictj.org/news/nepal-disappeared-search> accessed 7 September 2018.

1.1.3.2. The impact of international law on peace agreements…and vice versa: Implications for the issue of the missing

In order for the issue of missing persons to become a prominent factor in the post-conflict international agenda, peace agreements should enshrine this issue and provide for the establishment of specific mechanisms intended for the clarification of the fate of the missing.[77] For instance, the International Commission on Missing Persons (ICMP, see *infra* sub-sect. 3.2.2) has noted that among the factors that have permitted to account for the majority of the 40,000 missing persons in the former Yugoslavia is the support for the inclusion of the issue of missing persons in international peace agreements and treaties.[78] The impact on the ground of the inclusion of the issue of the missing in recent peace agreement is undoubted. For instance, the handling of information on the missing is present in the form of transmission and exchange of information, since the focus is placed on the immediate aftermath of the conflict in most of the treaties; the regulation of how information will be handled and preserved, however, is ignored or is part of separate agreements that are concluded long after the end of the conflict.

Apart from the impact of peace agreements *per se* on the issue of missing persons, important is to shed light on two other aspects: i.e., the impact of international law on peace agreements with regard to the issue of missing persons as well as the impact of peace agreements on international law, particularly in relation to the issue of the missing.

In general, international law does not remain exogenous to these agreements; indeed, peace agreements *per se* are part of international law understood as a decision-making process. In this sense, international law can be of guidance in the design and in the definition of the content of peace agreements.[79] For instance, the obligation to respect and ensure respect for IHL can be present in multiple forms in peace agreements and cease-fires in order for the parties to the conflict − State and non-state actors − to improve their compliance with IHL (including IHL rules that continue to have effects despite the end of the conflict and IHL rules that must be implemented prior to the outbreak of any other conflict).[80] International law can also be present in the phase of implementation (see *infra* the examples of Bosnia and Kosovo, sub-sect. 2.1.3.1 and 2.1.3.2) where *ad hoc* bodies can be established to adjudicate on the compliance with human rights law.[81]

---

[77] For instance, the ICRC tries to promote the inclusion of measures concerning missing persons and their families in settlements, such as cease-fire and peace agreements, and in new government policies. ICRC, 'The Missing. ICRC Progress Report' (ICRC 2006) 13 <goo.gl/og1Gf1> accessed 12 June 2016.

[78] ICMP, 'Missing Persons and the Work of the ICMP' (2014) ICMP.DG.677.2.doc, 3 <https://www.icmp.int/wp-content/uploads/2014/08/icmp-dg-677-2-doc-roundtable-meeting-sussex.pdf> accessed 1 July 2016.

[79] The international community, including international organizations, plays a role in order to ensure that the agreements enshrine provisions concerning human rights and even IHL; Bell provides the example of the Unites States pushing for the embedment of a human rights framework in the Dayton Agreements. Bell, *Peace Agreements and Human Rights* (n 11) 313.

[80] See Chapter II for a detailed examination of these rules. See also sub-section 1.1.3 in the present Chapter for a set of examples of peace agreements enshrining these rules.

[81] Bell, *Peace Agreements and Human Rights* (n 11) 313.

At the same time, peace agreements impact on international law;[82] as sub-sect. 1.1.3.1 shows, in the case of missing persons, peace agreements require the involvement of all the (former) parties to the conflict – including non-state actors – as well as of other actors during the post-conflict phase. This finding confirms that the issue of missing persons in not just a one party's business; indeed, a duty of all the former parties to the conflict to cooperate between each other and/or with the actor tasked to account for the missing emerges as the quintessential pillar of the post-conflict legal framework. Furthermore, peace agreements can influence and ignite the evolution of legal standards, as it has been the case for the Vietnam War-related peace settlements.

The foregoing shows that in the peace agreements there exists a trend that keeps humanitarian and accountability considerations concerning the issue of missing persons separate.[83] The design of institutional mechanisms or remedial tools within the peace agreements, which responds to and balances both sets of considerations, is present at an embryonic stage in a few examples (e.g., the 2000 Townsville Agreement, Implementing Guidelines on the Humanitarian, Rehabilitation and Development Aspects of the GRP and MILF). Moreover, where the conflict has transnational consequences – for instance, it generates internal and cross-border displacement of persons – the issue of the missing is often addressed along with the issue of refugees and displaced persons (e.g., the establishment of ITS; the Convention on the Declaration of Death of Missing Persons; Annex 7, Dayton Agreements).

1.2. Building peace without disregarding the issue of missing persons

Post-conflict efforts and operations[84] are intended not only for ending violence, but also for fostering the process towards a 'positive peace'[85] (sub-

---

[82] Bell dedicate a full section of her book on this shaping process, mainly focusing on the self-determination, the participation of the civic society, ethnic balance, and restorative justice. See ibid 314-317.

[83] In addition to the cases illustrated in this chapter, further examples of agreements concluded in the context of peace processes and addressing the issue of missing persons from a humanitarian perspective include the Memorandum of Understanding between the Georgian and Abkhaz sides, Geneva, December 1, 1993 (cf. para 3 stating that '[u]rgent measures will be taken to find those missing, for which purpose the parties will give each other the appropriate lists. In addition, measures will be taken for the reburial of the dead'); the Protocol on cooperation between the FRY Government Commission for Humanitarian Issues and Missing Persons and the Republic of Croatia Government Commission for Detained and Missing Persons, Zagreb, 17 April 1996; the Framework Agreement on the Collection and Centralized Management of Ante–Mortem Data on Missing Persons in Relation to the Nagorno Karabakh Conflict between the Commission for Prisoners of War, Hostages, and Missing Persons of the Republic of Armenia and the ICRC, October 3, 2008.

[84] Although not abundant, the examples include *interim* territorial administrations, peacekeeping operations, and other typologies of efforts implicating a direct involvement of the Organization in accounting for missing persons.

[85] Kleffner (n 2) 2. Since the adoption of the UN Charter, the maintenance of international peace and security has emerged as a unifying pillar of the international community. This idea was based on the wishful thought that States would 'practice tolerance and live together in peace with one another as good neighbors.' Cf. Preamble, Charter of the United Nations, 24 October 1945, 1 UNTS XVI (hereinafter UN Charter).

section 1.2.1). A peace, which is sustainable for all, cannot exist, should the issue of the missing remain pending; therefore, it is submitted that efforts to build an enduring peace must incorporate it. In this chapter, the focus will mainly be on the UN approach to building a sustainable peace (sub-section 1.2.2): this is the only international organization that can act on behalf of all the States of the world in order to 'establish conditions under which justice and respect for the obligations arising from treaties and other sources of international law can be maintained'.[86]

The underlying assumption of the present sub-section is that, in post-conflict, international actors operate within the boundaries of international law; depending on their mandate, they can temporarily substitute the domestic authorities in discharging their main functions. In light of this consideration, it will be demonstrated that the UN has an obligation to account for missing persons in the context of peace operations (sub-section 1.2.3). The active engagement of the UN as a pivotal actor in the process towards an enduring peace would presuppose the operationalization of this duty in terms of a UN institutionalized approach to the issue of the missing; yet, selected examples from the UN practice show that this is not the case (sub-section 1.2.4).

1.2.1. The conceptual origins of the efforts to build a sustainable peace

The conceptual contours of peacebuilding are inextricably linked with the work developed in the 1970's by the philosopher Johan Galtung who introduced the concept of positive peace.[87] In his argumentation, he considered the possibility of two ideal worlds, i.e., the General Complete War (GCW) and the General Complete Peace (GCP). To get closer to the latter, which is opposite to the Hobbesian world where *bellum omnium contra omnes*, he identified two strands of policies: i.e., those aimed at realizing the absence of violence/war, i.e., negative peace; those aimed at implementing integration among human beings, i.e., positive peace. While the former was characterized by no cooperation and individualism, the latter entailed integrated efforts to transform the potential of violence into mechanisms of conflict resolution.[88]

According to Galtung, creating peace consists in 'reducing violence (cure) and avoiding violence (prevention). And violence means harming and/or hunting.'[89] Therefore, there is someone that is harmed as result of violence (i.e., the receiver of violence). Violence, however, can also have a sender, i.e., someone 'who intends these consequences of violence' (considered as 'direct

---

[86] Cf. Preamble, UN Charter.

[87] The first notion was introduced in the editorial to the first volume of the Journal of Peace Research. See Johan Galtung, 'An Editorial' (1964) 1 Journal of Peace Research 1.

[88] ibid 1–2. Galtung identified three different notions of peace, i.e., peace as stability and equilibrium (covering the law and order sector); peace as absence of organized collective violence (i.e., negative peace); peace as all other good things in the world community (i.e., positive peace). Johan Galtung, 'Theories of Peace: A Synthetic Approach to Peace Thinking' (1967) UNESCO/International Peace Research Association (IPRA) 12.

[89] Johan Galtung, *Peace by Peaceful Means: Peace and Conflict, Development and Civilization* (SAGE 1996) 2.

violence'); with no sender, violence was 'indirect or structural', i.e., generated from the social structure (e.g., between humans, between societies, between regions in the world).[90] In Galtung's thoughts, exploitation and repression are among the major forms of outer structural violence. Behind direct and structural violence, Galtung identified 'cultural violence', i.e., the violence that is enshrined 'in the symbols, in religion and ideology, in language and art, in science and law, in media and education' and that plays the role of legitimizing the other two forms of violence.[91]

In light of these notions of peace and violence, Galtung proposed three approaches to peace: i.e., peace-keeping, i.e., reestablish the *status quo ante* and maintain absence of direct violence; peace-making also known as the conflict-resolution approach, i.e., get rid of the source of tension and engage in compromise (through, for instance, negotiation, mediation, and arbitration); peace-building, i.e., the approach focused on the root causes of the conflict and based on the hypothesis that peace has a different structure from that achieved through peacekeeping or *ad hoc* peacemaking.[92] Accordingly, the mechanisms on which peace is based should be built into the structure and 'be present there as a reservoir for the system itself to draw upon [...]. [S]tructures must be found that remove causes of wars and offer alternatives to war in situations where wars might occur.'[93]

This conceptualization of building peace has evolved since then,[94] but its core, i.e., addressing the root causes of the conflict, has remained an essential part of today's concept. The UN's notion of peacebuilding has built in the Galtung's one and, over the years,[95] has embraced a diversified range of factors

---

[90] ibid.

[91] ibid.

[92] Johan Galtung, 'Three Approaches to Peace: Peacekeeping, Peacemaking, and Peacebuilding' in Johan Galtung (ed), *Essays in Peace Research: War, Peace, Defense*, vol 2 (Christian Ejlers 1975) 283, 293, 297.

[93] ibid 298.

[94] For instance, a leading scholar in this field has framed the definition of peacebuilding as follows: peacebuilding 'is understood as a comprehensive concept that encompasses, generates, and sustains the full array of processes, approaches, and stages needed to transform conflict toward more sustainable, peaceful relationships. The term thus involves a wide range of activities that both precede and follow formal peace accords. Metaphorically, peace is seen not merely as a stage in time or a condition. It is a dynamic social construct.' John Paul Lederach, *Building Peace: Sustainable Reconciliation in Divided Societies* (United States Institute of Peace Press 1997) 20.

[95] The UNSG Boutros Boutros-Ghali's *An Agenda for Peace* framed the concept for the first time: peacebuilding was defined as 'an action to identify and support structures which will tend to strengthen and solidify peace in order to avoid a relapse into conflict.' It was connected to the concepts of 'preventive diplomacy' (i.e., action to prevent disputes from arising between parties), peacemaking (i.e., action to bring hostile parties to agreement), and peace-keeping (deployment of a UN presence in the field to extend the possibility of preventing conflict and making peace). UNSG, 'An Agenda for Peace' (1992) UN Doc A/47/277 paras 20–21. The concept has been expanded with the *Supplement to An Agenda for Peace*, which admitted that 'the implementation of post-conflict peace-building can [...] be complicated. It requires integrated action and delicate dealings between the [UN] and the parties to the conflict in respect of which peace-building activities are to be undertaken'. UNSG, 'Supplement to An Agenda for Peace: Position Paper of the Secretary General on the Occasion of the Fiftieth Anniversary of the United Nations' (1995) UN Doc A/50/60-S/1995/1 para 48. Another cornerstone in the development of a definition is the "Brahimi Report" which

and issues, including the one concerning missing persons. The recent framing of the definition by the UNSG's Policy Committee reads as follows

> [p]eacebuilding involves a range of measures targeted to reduce the risk of lapsing or relapsing into conflict by strengthening national capacities at all levels for conflict management, and to lay the foundations for sustainable peace and development. Peacebuilding strategies must be coherent and tailored to specific needs of the country concerned, based on national ownership, and should comprise a carefully prioritized, sequenced, and therefore relatively narrow set of activities aimed at achieving the above objectives.[96]

Against this backdrop, the UN Advisory Committee of the Human Rights Council has boldly stated that

> the issue of missing persons [...] seriously hampers efforts to achieve peace and reconciliation in areas affected by armed conflicts. On the other hand, efforts to solve the issue of the missing can contribute to solving the conflicts and reducing hostility, mistrust and intolerance.[97]

In this respect, the UNSC has directly addressed the issue of the missing in its resolutions concerning the shift from armed conflict to peace in specific contexts where it acted under Chapter VII of the UN Charter, i.e., with the precise objective of restoring international peace and security. For instance, in framing the terms of the ceasefire after the Iraqi forces had been expelled from Kuwait in 1991, the Council demanded Iraq (under Saddam Hussein) to cooperate with the ICRC in order to search for the Kuwaiti and third-country nationals reported as missing on or after 2 August 1990.[98] The same request was forwarded to the occupying powers after the 2003 intervention in Iraq.[99] These requests served as legal basis for the setting of the Tripartite Commission: this body, still operational to date, works under the auspices of the ICRC (acting as third party) and puts together the Coalition's members and Iraq in order to jointly[100] settle matters of humanitarian concerns, including the elucidation of the

---

defines peacebuilding as the 'activities undertaken on the far side of conflict to reassemble the foundations of peace and provide the tools for building on those foundations something that is more than just the absence of war.' UN High-level Panel on United Nations Peace Operations, 'Report of the Panel on United Nations Peace Operations (Brahimi Report)' (2000) UN Doc A/55/305-S/2000/809 para 13. In its *UN Peacekeeping Operations: Principles and Guidelines*, the UN Department of Peacekeeping operations has reproduced the definition outlined by the UNSG Policy Committee. UNDPKO, 'United Nations Peacekeeping Operations Principles and Guidelines' (2008) 18. For a review of the different definitions of peacebuilding existing at the international and regional level, see among others, V Chetail, 'Introduction: Post-Conflict Peacebuilding - Ambiguity and Identity' in Vincent Chetail (ed), *Post-conflict Peacebuilding: a Lexicon* (Oxford University Press 2009) 4-7.

[96] UN Peacebuilding Support Office, 'Peacebuilding & the United Nations' <http://www.un.org/en/peacebuilding/pbso/pbun.shtml> accessed 24 January 2017.

[97] UN Human Rights Council, 'Report of the Human Rights Council Advisory Committee on Best Practices on the Issue of Missing Persons' (2011) UN Doc A/HRC/16/70 para 14.

[98] Cf. UNSC, 'Resolution 686 (Iraq)' (1991) UN Doc S/RES/686 2 (c); UNSC, 'Resolution 687 (Iraq)' (1991) UN Doc S/RES/687 para 30.

[99] UNSC, 'Resolution 1483 (Iraq)' (2003) UN Doc S/RES/1483 para 6.

[100] The Coalition's members are the UK, USA, France, Saudi Arabia, and Kuwait. Iraq has started being more engaged after the fall of Saddam Hussein. In a report of the UNSG to the UNSC on this matter, the UNSG welcomed the strong bilateral relations between Iraq and Kuwait and, *inter alia,*

fate of persons missing in connection with the 1990-1991 Gulf War.[101] Both the UNSG and the UNGA have stressed the need to address the issue of missing persons in the context of peacebuilding processes, on the basis of transparency, accountability and public involvement and participation.[102]

Thus, reaching a sustainable peace does not solely mean stopping the conflict, but restoring links among communities and people affected by the conflict or, by using Galtung's words, implementing (and restoring) integration among human beings.

1.2.2. General remarks on the UN approach to peacebuilding

The report of the UNSG's High Level Panel on Peace Operations ("HIPPO") clarifies the typology of contribution that is expected by the UN in the framework of operations and efforts aimed at reaching a sustainable peace. The report points out that

> [p]eace processes do not end with a ceasefire, a peace agreement or an election. Such events constitute merely a phase, rather than the conclusion, of a peace process. ... Central to sustaining peace and avoiding a relapse into conflict is the need to maintain and strengthen political momentum, to address underlying causes of the conflict, to deepen and broaden peace processes through inclusion and to advance reconciliation and healing. Peacebuilding is not State-building; those are distinct but interlinked efforts. The challenge for peace operations is to help sustain peace while a long-term, often generational effort to strengthen State institutions gets under way.[103]

Embedded in the above excerpt is the notion of 'peacebuilding', which is a vague term in need of further clarification. The lack of a single definition of 'peacebuilding' entails that actions and measures connected to it can be found across the spectrum of UN peace operations and efforts ranging from UN peacekeeping operations to political missions, and transitional administrations. As the UN illustrates in an online page dedicated to its approach to peacebuilding,[104] peacebuilding efforts are performed across the range of operations aimed at keeping peace and moving forward towards a sustainable peace.[105]

---

commended both Iraq and Kuwait for guaranteeing access of the Tripartite Commission to their respective archives. Cf. UNSG, 'Tenth Report of the Secretary-General pursuant to Paragraph 4 of UNSC Resolution 2107 (2013)' (2016) UN Doc S/2016/372 paras 16, 18.

[101] UNSG, 'Report of the Secretary-General - Missing Persons' (2016) UN Doc A/71/299 para 25.

[102] UNGA, 'Resolution 63/183 - Missing Persons' (2009) UN Doc. A/RES/63/183 para 11; UNSG, 'Report of the Secretary-General - Missing Persons' (2010) UN Doc A/65/285 para 60.

[103] UNSG/UNGA, 'Report of the High-Level Independent Panel on Peace Operations (HIPPO) on Uniting Our Strengths for Peace: Politics, Partnership and People' (2015) UN Doc A/70/95, S/2015/446 paras 131–132.

[104] UN Peacebuilding Support Office (n 96).

[105] Fetherston examines various UN peacekeeping operations, including the UNFICYP, and stresses the multiple tasks of this operation ranging from ensuring the respect of the parties for the ceasefire to restoration of the law and order, return to normal conditions by means, for instance, of the restoration of the economic activities (e.g., escorts for essential civilian movements; harvest arrangements including escort during harvest; arbitration of land and water disputes; normalization of public services such as electricity and social insurance benefits; cooperation with NGOs in assisting refugees). In doing so, the peacekeeping mission engaged in peacebuilding activities. Fetherston also provides other examples (e.g., Congo) in order to demonstrate that peacekeeping and peacebuilding

In addition to multiple definitions provided by other international, regional, and national organizations and bodies, at the UN level, peacebuilding is defined in a variety of manners. [106] The concept of peacebuilding was introduced by the then UNSG Boutros Boutros Ghali in the *Agenda for Peace;* with the term post-conflict peacebuilding he referred to the efforts 'to identify and support structures which will tend to strengthen and solidify peace in order to avoid a relapse into conflict' (e.g., 'rebuilding the institutions and infrastructures of nations torn by civil war and strife; and building bonds of peaceful mutual benefit among nations formerly at war').[107] In this definitional framework, in order to be successful, peacekeeping and peacemaking operations must carry out part of these efforts, e.g., repatriating refugees, advisory and training support for security personnel, monitoring elections, advancing efforts to protect human rights, reforming or strengthening governmental institutions.[108] Once peacemaking and peacekeeping operations have achieved their objectives, 'only sustained, cooperative work to deal with underlying economic, social, cultural and humanitarian problems can place an achieved peace on a durable foundation.'[109]

The subsequent adjustments[110] of the concept have emphasized the need for integrated action in a post-conflict environment where the situation might require the presence of a multifunctional peacekeeping operation; the multi-functionality depends on the performance of a variety of responsibility in the economic, social, humanitarian and human rights fields (normally entrusted to a range of UN agencies, programs, and funds).[111] The transfer of responsibilities from the operation to the domestic system will be possible only when the operation succeeds in restoring normal conditions.

The HIPPO's report adds further emphasis on the role that peace operations can play towards the achievement of a sustainable peace by means of *inter alia* the protection and promotion of human rights. Thus, the relevance of the conceptual aspects of post-conflict peacebuilding is based on the need to cast

---

are not 'mutually exclusive enterprises'. See AB Fetherston, *Towards a Theory of United Nations Peacekeeping* (Springer 1994) 51–54.

[106] Chetail (n 95) 4–7.

[107] UNSG, 'An Agenda for Peace' (n 95) paras 15, 21.

[108] ibid 55.

[109] ibid 57.

[110] There has been a constant evolution of the notion "peacebuilding" with a view to making it more coherent at the UN level: for instance, apart from the Brahimi Report's definition (see *supra* n 95) in 2007, the UNSG's Policy Committee agreed on the following conceptual basis in order to influence the UN conceptual approach: '[p]eacebuilding involves a range of measures targeted to reduce the risk of lapsing or relapsing into conflict by strengthening national capacities at all levels for conflict management, and to lay the foundations for sustainable peace and development. Peacebuilding strategies must be coherent and tailored to specific needs of the country concerned, based on national ownership, and should comprise a carefully prioritized, sequenced, and therefore relatively narrow set of activities aimed at achieving the above objectives'. See UN Peacebuilding Support Office (n 96).

[111] UNSG, 'Supplement to An Agenda for Peace: Position Paper of the Secretary General on the Occasion of the Fiftieth Anniversary of the United Nations' (n 95) paras 47–48, 53.

light upon the role that typical peacebuilding actors[112] play when confronted with the issue of missing persons in the territory where they operate.

1.2.3. The UN obligation to account for missing persons in the context of peace operations

In countries involved in a transition process from an armed conflict to peace, the capacity of State authorities to comply with their obligations vis-à-vis the missing and their families can be negatively affected by various factors (e.g., an unbearable number of missing people, the need for a post-conflict overhaul of internal structure and political system, the need for new judicial institutions and/or for restructuring the existing ones).[113] In similar situations the UN has supplemented – and even substituted – the State in taking on its primary responsibility to account for the missing (e.g., by restoring family links, visiting detainees and informing the families about their conditions, establishing mechanisms that have taken on the humanitarian task of clarifying the whereabouts of those reported as missing, see *infra* sub-section 1.2.3). Generally speaking, the normative foundation for the UN's work is the UN Charter itself, which serves as a 'constitutional framework'[114] for the Organization; the UNSC's resolutions are the basis of the operations and initiatives mentioned above and must be read in light of the boundaries of the UN Charter.

The Charter says nothing about the limits and the international law-based obligations of the Council; however, it specifies that the Council has a 'primary responsibility for the maintenance of international peace and security' which should be discharged 'in accordance with the Purpose and Principles of the [UN].[115] These include

> to maintain international peace and security, and to that end: to take effective collective measures for the prevention and removal of threats to the peace, and for the suppression of acts of aggression or other breaches of the peace, and to bring about by peaceful means, and *in conformity with the principles of justice and international law*, adjustment or settlement of international disputes or situations which might lead to a breach of the peace.[116]

Pursuant to the UN Charter, it seems that only 'the adjustment or settlement of international disputes or situations...' must take place in accordance with 'the principles of justice and international law' (i.e., treaties, customary law, general principles; a connection with natural law is not excluded).[117] The same consideration does not apply to the collective measures for the prevention and

---

[112] The UN Peacebuilding Support Office lists the following among the actors that carry out peacebuilding activities: humanitarian actors, UN peacekeeping operations, territorial administration. See UN Peacebuilding Support Office (n 96).

[113] ECtHR, *Palić v. Bosnia and Herzegovina* (n 23) [70].

[114] ICTY, *Prosecutor v Duško Tadić aka 'Dule', Decision on the Defence Motion for Interlocutory Appeal on Jurisdiction* (1995) Case no. IT-94-1-A [28].

[115] Cf. Article 24 (1) and (2), UN Charter.

[116] Cf. Article 1 (1) UN Charter.

[117] R Wolfrum, 'Article 1' in Bruno Simma and others (eds), *The Charter of the United Nations - A Commentary* (3rd ed, Oxford University Press 2002) 113–114.

removal of threats or other breaches of peace,[118] i.e., when the UNSC acts under Chapter VII.[119] At the San Francisco Conference, the proposal for a different formulation where the maintenance of peace and security shall be carried out in conformity with the principles of justice and international law did not receive the necessary support.[120]

Against this backdrop, some have expressed doubts about whether the Council can take measures which are not in conformity with international law when acting under Chapter VII and, more generally, whether the Council is bound by international law.[121] It is submitted that the Council's measures and decisions are 'subjected to certain constitutional limitations', i.e., those laid down in the Charter; 'however broad [the Council's] powers may be, those powers cannot...go beyond the limits of the jurisdiction of the [UN] at large [...]. [N]either the text nor the spirit of the Charter conceives of the Security Council as *legibus solutus* (unbound by law).'[122] Accordingly, any action or decision of the UN in general, and of the UNSC in particular, cannot be taken in contravention of *jus cogens* norms, [123] which include core human rights norms[124]

---

[118] The Dumbarton Oaks text, which prepared the ground for today's UN Charter, did not mention the reference to the principles of justice and international law; indeed, this was added at the San Francisco Conference. Supported by several States (Chile, Netherlands, Ecuador, Greece, Iran), the proposal is attributable to China, the UK, USA, and the Soviet Union. – cf. for Chile: Doc 2, G/7 (i), *UN Conference on International Organization (UNCIO) Documents*, vol III (1945) 284; for Netherlands: Doc 2, G/7 (j), ibid 311; for Ecuador: Doc 2, G/7 (p), ibid 398, 420; for Greece: Doc 2, G/14 (i), ibid 531; for Iran: Doc 2, G/14 (m) ibid 554; for UK, China, USA, Soviet Union: Doc 2, G/29, ibid 622.

[119] See Wolfrum (n 117) 113; R Wolfrum, 'Article 1' in Bruno Simma and others (eds), *The Charter of the United Nations: A Commentary* (Oxford University Press 1994) 52.

[120] See *UN Conference on International Organization (UNCIO) Documents*, vol IV (1945) 34, 318.

[121] Zwanenburg affirms that Article 24 read in conjunction with Article 1(1) of the UN Charter may be interpreted as allowing the Council to derogate from the principles of international law; this would be confirmed by Article 103 of the UN Charter providing that 'in the event of a conflict between the obligations of the Members of the [UN] under the [UN] Charter and their obligations under any other international agreement, their obligations under the [UN] Charter shall prevail'. See MC Zwanenburg, *Accountability Of Peace Support Operations* (Martinus Nijhoff Publishers 2005) 141–142. See also Gabriël H Oosthuizen, 'Playing the Devil's Advocate: The United Nations Security Council Is Unbound by Law' (1999) 12 Leiden Journal of International Law 549. The 'obligations ...under the [UN] Charter' cover the obligations stemming directly from the Charter, the obligations under secondary norms derived from the Charter (e.g., binding decisions of the UNSC and binding decisions made by other UN organs). This interpretation of Article 103's expression 'Obligations ...' was endorsed at the time of the *travaux préparatoires* (see *UN Conference on International Organization (UNCIO) Documents*, vol XIII (1945) 685 ff) and has been more recently supported by the ICJ. Cf. in this regard, ICJ, *Lockerbie Case, provisional measures*, paras 39, 126, para 42 in A Paulus and J Leiß, 'Article 103' in Bruno Simma and others (eds), *The Charter of the United Nations - A Commentary* (3rd edn, Oxford University Press 2002) 2123–2124.

[122] ICTY, *Prosecutor v. Duško Tadić, Decision on the Defence Motion ...* (n 114) [28].

[123] As pointed out by Judge Lauterpacht, 'the concept of *jus cogens* operates as a concept superior to both customary international law and treaty. The relief which Article 103 of the Charter may give to the Security Council in case of conflict between one of its decisions and an operative treaty obligation cannot - as a matter of simple hierarchy of norms - extend to a conflict between a Security Council resolution and *jus cogens*. Indeed, one only has to state the opposite proposition thus - that a Security Council resolution may even require participation in genocide - for its unacceptability to be apparent.' Separate Opinion of Judge ad hoc Lauterpacht, *Application of the Convention on the*

such as the prohibition of torture[125] or the prohibition of enforced disappearance.[126]

Another element that cannot be overlooked is the connection between Article 24 (Functions and Powers of the UNSC) and the whole Article 1 (Purposes) of the UN Charter.[127] Pursuant to Article 1(3), one of the purposes of the UN is to achieve international cooperation

> in solving international problems of an economic, social, cultural, or humanitarian character, and in promoting and encouraging respect for human rights and for fundamental freedoms for all without distinction as to race, sex, language, or religion.

The *travaux préparatoires* suggest that Article 1(3) is binding upon the organization as a whole, since no mention of any exemption for the Council is reported.[128]

Prevention and Punishment of the Crime of Genocide (Bosnia and Herzegovina v Serbia and Montenegro), Request for the Indication of Provisional Measures (1993) ICJ Reports 4 [100]. One of the main commentaries to the UN Charter affirms that it is widely accepted in international doctrine that conflicts between Charter Law (i.e., the Charter itself and the Charter-based secondary law, including the UNSC's decisions) and *jus cogens* result in the nullity of the Charter Law in question. See Paulus and Leiß (n 121) 2119. Conforti adopts a different perspective, arguing that 'the discretionary power of the Security Council has no other limitations' than the UN Charter itself; 'no other limit exists as far as the determination of a threat to the peace, a breach of the peace or an act of aggression is concerned'. Different is the question of whether measures under Articles 41-42 (Chapter VII) must comply with general international law. In the analysis of UNSC's resolutions *ex* Article 42, Conforti notes that there is a clear 'trend towards the duty of the UNSC to comply with international law when a peacekeeping operation is set up; this duty is parallel to the Council's duty with regard to those measures not involving the use of force'. Benedetto Conforti, *The Law and Practice of the United Nations* (Martinus Nijhoff Publishers 2005) 178, 200.

[124] Cf. Separate Opinion of Judge ad hoc Lauterpacht, *ICJ. Genocide Case* (n 123) [100, 102]. See also ICJ, *Case concerning Barcelona Traction Light and Power Co, Ltd (Belgium v Spain), Judgment* (1970) ICJ Reports 1970, 3 [34]. In its Report of 1966 in relation to the Draft VCLT, the ILC mentioned by way of illustration examples of peremptory norms: e.g., unlawful use of force contrary to Article 2 (4) of the UN Charter, the performance of criminal acts under international law, and the commission of acts such as the trade in slaves, piracy, or genocide, or acts which constitute crimes under international law more generally or violations of human rights norms. Cf. ILC, *Yearbook of the International Law Commission - 1966. Documents of the Fourteenth Session Including the Report of the Commission to the General Assembly*, vol II (United Nations 1966) para 3, 248.

[125] The ICTY has recognized that the prohibition of torture, which is enshrined as an absolute right in many human rights treaties is a peremptory norm. Cf. ICTY, *Prosecutor v Anto Furundžija, Trial Judgment* (1998) Case no. IT-95-17/1-T [144].

[126] Among other cases, IACtHR, *Gudiel Álvarez et al ('Diario Militar') v Guatemala, Judgment - Merits, Reparations, and Costs* (2012) Series C no. 253 [232]; *Goiburú et al v Paraguay, Judgment - Merits, Reparations and Costs* (2006) Series C No. 153 [84].

[127] In this sense, Separate Opinion of Judge ad hoc Lauterpacht, *ICJ. Genocide Case* (n 123) [101].

[128] The final version of Article 1 (3) approved in San Francisco is very different from the Dumbarton Oaks text; indeed, a suggestion was made to draft or to include an already drafted bill of rights of nations and individuals. However, it was decided that the task mentioned in the provision would be left to the Organization. See Wolfrum (n 119) 53. Moreover, Article 55 (c) of the UN Charter builds on Article 1 (3), as it states that '[w]ith a view to the creation of conditions of stability and well-being which are necessary for peaceful and friendly relations among nations [...] the [UN] shall promote [...] universal respect for, and observance of, human rights and fundamental freedoms for all without distinction as to race, sex, language, or religion.' In other words, the UN and the UN system are entrusted with the task to promote universal respect for human rights. See PT Stoll, 'Article 55 (a) and (B)' in Bruno Simma and others (eds), *The Charter of the United Nations - A Commentary* (3rd

Scholars[129] concur to say that the UNSC is bound to respect, at least, the core human rights norms.[130] Moreover, Article 1(3) sheds light on the expected engagement of the UN – including the UNSC – in addressing problems of a humanitarian character: the obligation to account for missing persons is at the crossroad between IHL and IHRL; as such, it cannot be disregarded when the UN operates in post-conflict settings to achieve the purposes mentioned under Article 1 of the UN Charter.[131]

Moreover, the ICJ has clarified that the UN is a 'subject of international law' which is, as such, 'bound by any obligations incumbent upon [it] under general rules of international law', under its constitution (i.e., the UN Charter), and under international agreements to which it is party.[132] Therefore, general international law, i.e., customary international law – including those IHRL and IHL rules that have become customary – and general principles of law, cannot be disregarded by the UN when it discharges its functions during and after an armed conflict. The question that remains pending is which customary rule applies to the UN and if among those rules is the obligation to account for missing persons and to inform their families.

It is accepted that among the IHL rules that have become customary is the obligation to account for missing persons and to inform their families (see Chapters II and IV). This obligation must primarily be implemented by the

---

edn, Oxford University Press 2002) 1541. Indeed, the political and judicial organs of the UN have consistently interpreted Article 55 (c) of the UN Charter as addressed to the UN. See E Riedel and JM Arend, 'Article 55 (c)' in Bruno Simma and others (eds), *The Charter of the United Nations - A Commentary* (3rd edn, Oxford University Press 2002) 1573.

[129] TD Gill, 'Legal and Some Political Limitations on the Power of the UN Security Council to Exercise Its Enforcement Powers under Chapter VII of the Charter' (1995) 26 Netherlands Yearbook of International Law 33, 77–79; Erika de Wet, *The Chapter VII Powers of the United Nations Security Council* (Hart Publishing 2004) 370–371.

[130] de Wet (n 129) 370; Gill (n 129) 79; UN Commission on Human Rights, 'The Adverse Consequences of Economic Sanctions on the Enjoyment of Human Rights. Working Paper Prepared by Mr. Marc Bossuyt' (2000) UN Doc E/CN.4/Sub.2/2000/33 para 26.

[131] The UNGA Resolution 3220 on the assistance and co-operation in accounting for the missing in armed conflicts makes the connection between the obligation to account for missing persons and Article 1(3) UN Charter explicit. See UNGA, 'Resolution on the Assistance and Cooperation in Accounting for Persons Who Are Missing or Dead in Armed' (1974) UN Doc A/RES/3220 (XXIX) Preamble.

[132] The ICJ also stated that the UN holds international personality and has the capacity to bear international rights and duties. Cf. ICJ, *Reparation for Injuries Suffered in the Service of the United Nations, Advisory Opinion* (1949) ICJ Reports 1949, p 174 [179–180]; *Interpretation of the Agreement of 25 March 1951 between the WHO and Egypt, Advisory opinion* (1980) ICJ Reports 1980, p 73 [37]. See also in this respect the European Court of Justice (ECJ) that has held the EU is bound by customary international law. See among others ECJ, *Anklagemyndigheden v Poulsen and Diva Navigation Corp, Judgment* (1992) 286/90, 9. The duty to cooperate with the ICTY bears upon States and international organizations. Cf. ICTY, *Prosecutor v Simić et al, Decision on Motion for judicial Assistance to be provided by SFOR and others* (2000) Case no IT-95-9 [46]. Scholars generally support the view expressed by the ICJ in the *WHO Advisory Opinion*. See among many others, Clapham (n 8) 65; Malcolm N Shaw, *International Law* (6th edn, Cambridge University Press 2008) 1999–2000; Moshe Hirsch, *The Responsibility of International Organizations Toward Third Parties: Some Basic Principles* (Martinus Nijhoff Publishers 1995) 17; A Reinisch, 'The Changing International Legal Framework for Dealing with Non-State Actors' in Philip Alston (ed), *Non-state actors and human rights* (Oxford University Press 2005) 46.

parties to the conflict; this, however, does not exclude the UN when involved in peace enforcement operations. In addition to that, the effects of this obligation persist in the aftermath of an armed conflict for as long as all the possible efforts are undertaken in order to elucidate the fate and whereabouts of persons reported as missing. This means that, in those cases where the UN exercises temporary territorial administration, the organization will take on the task entrusted to the former parties to the conflict to account for missing persons. In addition to that, AP I concisely states that in the implementation of [section III 'Missing and Dead Persons'], the activities of [...] international humanitarian organizations [...] shall be prompted mainly by the right of families to know the fate of their relatives'. In this respect, the ICRC Commentary makes it clear that the reference to 'humanitarian organizations' should be understood in a broad sense; this is 'not a matter of conferring powers, but of reminding those working in this area of a line of conduct which, it is hoped, will always be respected'.[133] In other words, the underpinning principle of the obligation to account for missing persons – i.e., the right of families to know – is the driver of the actions meant to address the issue of missing persons, including the UN's involvement.

A series of guidance documents issued by the UN confirm that IHL and IHRL standards will be at the basis of the work of peace operations.[134] Furthermore, in an effort to build the operational contours of peace-building activities, the UNSG's inter-departmental Task Force has issued *An Inventory of Post-Conflict Peace-Building Activities* that affirms the following

> enhancing respect for human rights, in all its aspects, should be a cornerstone of peacebuilding efforts. Faithful observance of the rules of [IHL] during and immediately after violent conflicts could also advance the goal of peace and stability.[135]

---

[133] Yves Sandoz and others, *Commentary on the Additional Protocols: Of 8 June 1977 to the Geneva Conventions of 12 August 1949* (Martinus Nijhoff Publishers 1987) para 1210, 345.

[134] Specifically, the *Code of Conduct for Blue Helmets* affirms that peacekeepers must 'respect and regard the human rights of all'. Cf. Rule 5, UNDPKO, 'Ten Rules: Code Of Personal Conduct For Blue Helmets' (1998) <https://cdu.unlb.org/UNStandardsofConduct/TenRulesCodeofPersonalConductFor BlueHelmets.aspx> accessed 12 July 2016; Bell, 'Ceasefire' (n 72). In another guidance document by the DPKO it is affirmed that *UN peacekeepers* 'will comply with the Guidelines on [IHL] for Forces Undertaking [UN] Peacekeeping Operations and the applicable portions of the Universal Declaration of Human Rights as the fundamental basis of [their] standards'. UNDPKO Training Unit, 'We Are United Nations Peacekeepers' <http://www.un.org/en/peacekeeping/documents/un_in.pdf> accessed 12 July 2016. In addition to these documents, the Brahimi Report notes that 'whenever the UN efforts in post-conflict coincide with the restoration of the rule of law and the fight against impunity, the UN Charter together with IHL, IHRL, International Criminal Law and International Refugee Law constitute the foundation of its work.' (footnotes omitted) in UNSG, 'Report on RoL and TJ' (n 5) para 9. Along the same lines, the Brahimi Report re-asserts '[t]he essential importance of the [UN] system adhering to and promoting international human rights instruments and standards and [IHL] in all aspects of its peace and security activities'. See UN High-level Panel on United Nations Peace Operations (n 95) para 6.

[135] See UNSG - Task Force on Post-conflict Peacebuilding, 'An Inventory of Post-Conflict Peace-Building Activities' (1995) 35.

Among the activities listed in the inventory is the tracing of those reported as disappeared.[136] Furthermore, the UNSG's bulletin on the 'Observance by UN of IHL' unequivocally asserts that in situations of armed conflict (both IAC and NIAC), in enforcement actions, or in peacekeeping operations the UN 'shall respect the right of the families to know about the fate of their sick, wounded, and deceased relatives. To this end, the peace operation shall facilitate the work of the ICRC Central Tracing Agency'.[137]

The UNSG has remarked elsewhere that the Bulletin, which is binding upon all members of UN peace operations, represents a 'formal recognition of the applicability of [IHL] to [UN] peace operations.'[138] Indeed, this document re-states rules the majority of which forms part of customary international law and constitutes 'the lowest common denominator by which all national contingents would otherwise be bound.'[139] Thus, it is submitted that *durante bello* and in the post-conflict phase, the actions undertaken by the UN peace operations in relation to the missing persons must be prompted by the right of families to know the fate of their relatives. Moreover, the UN has an obligation to account for missing persons whenever its post-conflict role entails the protection and promotion of human rights as well as the taking on of functions that make it a temporary substitute of the State.

1.2.4. Operationalization of the duty to account for missing persons through the prism of selected examples

The lack of an institutionalized approach to the issues of missing persons and of their families has revealed its downsides when UN peace operations have dealt with them on an *ad hoc* basis,[140] by developing the approach *in itinere*.[141]

---

[136] See ibid.

[137] UNSG, 'Secretary-General's Bulletin - Observance by United Nations Forces of International Humanitarian Law' (1999) UN Doc ST/SGB/1999/13 para 11, 9.8.

[138] UNSG, 'Road Map towards the Implementation of the United Nations Millennium Declaration' (2001) UN Doc A/56/326 para 19. Nevertheless, the Bulletin cannot be considered a unilateral act of the UN capable of binding the organization to undertake a certain conduct. Klein affirms that unilateral acts of international institutions, including the UN, may be seen as the expression of the collective will of the organization; these acts reflect the 'legal autonomy of international organizations vis-à-vis the Member States.' See Pierre Klein, 'International Organizations or Institutions, Decision-Making Process', Max Planck Encyclopedia of Public International Law (Online) (2007) <http://opil.ouplaw.com/view/10.1093/law:epil/9780199231690/law-9780199231690-e1709> accessed 25 December 2017. Indeed, the Bulletin is not a unilateral act, but an internal UN document, more specifically an administrative issuance by the UNSG; it is a subsidiary instrument that elaborates the Staff Rules issued by the UNSG as the highest administrative authority of the organization. See Zwanenburg (n 121) 174.

[139] D Shraga, 'The Applicability of the Laws of Armed Conflict to Peacekeeping Operations' in Rain Liivoja and Tim McCormack (eds), *Routledge Handbook of the Law of Armed Conflict* (Routledge 2016) 422; Katarina Grenfell, 'Perspective on the Applicability and Application of International Humanitarian Law: The UN Context' (2013) 95 International Review of the Red Cross 645, 648–649.

[140] From a general perspective on the UN's use of enforcement action to protect human rights, Bianchi harshly criticizes the UNSC and its attitude to adopt *ad hoc* solutions that fall short of any discernible principle of general application; this, inevitably, determines the absence of an institutionalized framework and the lack of consistent patterns of normative standards and policies, which make it difficult to exercise any form of scrutiny over the conduct of international actors. See

Although most of the UN efforts in this field have intermingled with RoL measures in the context of multidimensional peace operations, the humanitarian and RoL/accountability-driven dimensions of the issue of the missing have not immediately been recognized and addressed. The HIPPO's report remarks that

[j]ustice, the rule of law and human rights are mutually reinforcing elements of the work of [UN] peace operations and [UN] country teams, and need to be addressed in an integrated way. Too often, the [UN] has approached justice and the rule of law on the one hand, and human rights on the other, as separate areas of operation. That has sometimes led to programmes aimed at developing capacity for the rule of law without paying due attention to human rights, which are a key component to institutional reform. Efforts are also needed to examine the chain of institutions that must work together effectively, including courts, prosecutors and police. [...]

[UN] peace operations should work to ensure that the rule of law operates in a manner that protects human rights. That includes addressing impunity through supporting appropriate mechanisms of transitional justice in situations where past violations have not been resolved and will be an obstacle to lasting peace.[142]

Nevertheless, as emphasized by the UNSG, '[n]ot all peace operations are mandated to address transitional justice and rule of law activities'.[143] This consideration does not apply to the two examples addressed below, which help understand the implications of the UN involvement for the issue of the missing: i.e.,

– the UN Approach to missing persons in Cyprus after the inter-communal violence erupted in 1964 and after the Greek Junta failed *coup* and reactive occupation by Turkey in 1974 (sub-section 1.2.4.1);

– the UN approach in Kosovo in the context of the UN territorial administration following the NATO intervention in response to the violations committed by Serbian forces in Kosovo in 1999 (sub-section 1.2.4.2).

When the tracing of missing persons and the transmission of information to their families take place in the aftermath of a conflict, these activities are inextricably part of the strategy aimed at restoring a long-lasting and sustainable peace. These examples are particularly meaningful due to the institutional design in which the solutions and measures adopted vis-à-vis the cases of the missing were undertaken: the former is the first example in the history of the UN of a traditional peacekeeping mission entrusted with humanitarian functions

---

Andrea Bianchi, 'Ad Hocism and the Rule of Law' (2002) 13 European Journal of International Law 263, 269–270.

[141] This is reflected in posthumous regulation of access to information, while it should have been taken care of since the beginning of the UN involvement. It is also reflected in the perception of support of one side and not of all sides affected by the problem of missing persons and in the lack of clarity on how to handle information on missing persons that revealed international law's violations.

[142] UNSG/UNGA (n 103) paras 157–158.

[143] The UNSG mentions those operations that deal with such matters (e.g., transitional administrations in Kosovo - UN Interim Administration Mission in Kosovo - and Timor-Leste - UN Transitional Administration in East Timor/UN Mission of Support in East Timor; the UN Observer Mission in El Salvador and the UN Verification Mission in Guatemala). UNSG, 'Report on RoL and TJ' (n 5) para 11.

(including the handling of cases of missing persons); the latter is one of the – supposed temporary – UN territorial administrations, which turned to be a long-term presence with direct implications on the humanitarian and accountability-related aspects of the issue of the missing in Kosovo. The sub-sections below will cast light upon the consequences of *impromptu ad hoc* solutions adopted in both scenarios against missing persons and their families' quest for information.

1.2.4.1. The duty to account for the missing as part of the humanitarian functions of peace-keeping operations: The UNFICYP case

The Cyprus situation is one of the oldest conflicts in today's UNSC agenda, which has led to the adoption of more than one hundred UNSC Resolutions.[144] The issue of missing persons in Cyprus dates back to the inter-communal violence that followed the decision of President Makarios to amend the Constitution in 1963; Turkish Cypriot leaders strongly rejected such decision, as they perceived it as an attempt to increase the power of the Greek Cypriots.[145] The UN started being involved in the peace process since 1964;[146] the issue of the missing became part of the UN Peacekeeping Force in Cyprus (UNFICYP)'s activities since then. The UNFICYP was established in 1964 in response to the situation in the island, which was likely to threaten the international peace and security.[147] The peacekeeping force was mandated to preserve international peace and security, 'to use its best efforts to prevent recurrence of fighting and, as necessary, to contribute to the maintenance and restoration of law and order and a return to normal conditions'.[148] In order to exercise these functions the UN force equipped itself with a civilian police (CIVPOL) unit tasked, *inter alia*, to investigate incidents where Greek and Turkish Cypriots were involved with the opposite community, including searches for persons reported as missing.[149]

---

[144] The Turkish occupation of territory in the north of the Republic of Cyprus is still ongoing at the time of writing. With regard to the activity of the UNSC on Cyprus, see Security Council Report, 'Special Research Report No 3. Cyprus: New Hope after 45 Years on the Security Council Agenda' <http://www.securitycouncilreport.org/special-research-report/lookup-c-glKWLeMTIsG-b-4474149.php?print=true> accessed 12 July 2016.

[145] An historical account of the events preceding the establishment of the UNFICYP is provided in "The Blue helmets". See UN, *The Blue Helmets - A Review of United Nations Peace-Keeping* (UN Department of Public Information 1996) 149, 151, 159–163. See also Iosif Kovras, *Truth Recovery and Transitional Justice: Deferring Human Rights Issues* (Routledge 2014) 43–47; Y Papadakis, N Peristianis and G Welz, 'Introduction: Modernity, History, and Conflict in Divided Cyprus. An Overview' in Yannis Papadakis, Nicos Peristianis and Gisela Welz (eds), *Divided Cyprus. Modernity, History, and an Island in Conflict* (Indiana University Press 2006) 2–4.

[146] Three phases can be detected in the involvement of the UN in the island: the maintenance of the truce between 1964-1974; the crisis of 1974; and the frozen conflict since 1974. See UN, *The Blue Helmets* (n 145) 154, 161, 164; Security Council Report (n 144).

[147] Cf. Preamble, UNSC, 'Resolution 186 (the Cyprus Question)' (1964) UN Doc S/RES/186. Although Chapter VII is not mentioned in the Resolution, in Higgins' opinion, the constitutional basis of the UN force is to be found in Article 40, Chapter VII of the UN Charter due to the existence of a threat to peace. See Rosalyn Higgins, *United Nations Peacekeeping, 1946-1967: Documents and Commentary*, vol 4 (Oxford University Press 1980) 144.

[148] Cf. operative para 5, UNSC, 'Resolution 186 (the Cyprus Question)' (n 147).

[149] The UNSG explained in his report to the UNSC that the experience had already shown that 'the fulfillment of the task of UNFICYP requires an element of police liaison personnel'. The police personnel were provided by various UN members (including Austria, Denmark; Australia; and New

This task resembled that of a normal police unit;[150] indeed, no mention of the humanitarian dimension of the issue was present, nor reference to the collaboration of this unit with the ICRC.

Pursuant to the UNFICYP's regulations enacted at the beginning of its mandate, the force 'shall observe and respect the principles and spirit of the general international conventions applicable to the conduct of military personnel'[151] (e.g., the GCs).[152] In the summer of 1974, the military junta in Greece supported a *coup d'état* in the island, followed by the Turkish intervention to protect the Turkish Cypriots. The UNFICYP's mandate did not allow a direct reaction of the force to these events which generated a humanitarian crisis: a third of the country's population became internally displaced (between 165,000 and 200,000 Greek Cypriots fled to the South of the island, and between 45,000 and 65,000 Turkish Cypriots fled to the North).[153] About 2,000 persons were reported as missing due to the 1964 and 1974 crises;[154] the island remained separated along the ceasefire lines.

Against this backdrop, the UNSC expanded the mandate of the UNFICYP, which, *inter alia,* included humanitarian functions.[155] Thus, the UNFICYP was

---

Zealand). See UNSG, 'Report on the Organization and Operation of the UN Peacekeeping Force in Cyprus (to the UNSC)' (1964) UN Doc S/5679 paras 4–5.

[150] The 2003 UN Handbook on UN multidimensional peacekeeping operations sheds light on the tasks of the military component of UN peacekeeping operations, which include the support to humanitarian activities, considered - in general terms - 'a civilian task'. This Handbook retrospectively makes it clear that, in the context of multidimensional operations, the CIVPOL unit might bear the main responsibility vis-à-vis the issue of missing persons. UNDPKO - Peacekeeping Best Practices Unit, 'Handbook on United Nations Multidimensional Peacekeeping Operations' (2003) 64 <http://www.un.org/en/peacekeeping/resources/policy.shtml> accessed 12 December 2016. According to the 2003 handbook 'a growing number of UN peacekeeping operations have become multidimensional, composed of a range of components including military, civilian police, political, civil affairs, rule of law, human rights, humanitarian, reconstruction, public information and gender.' ibid 1. Indeed, the first civilian police deployment took place in the context of the UN Operation in the Congo (ONUC) from 1960-1964 and the UNFICYP in 1964. Recent involvement in addressing the issue of missing persons of the CIVPOL unit embedded in the UN peacekeeping operations is reported in the context of UN Protection Force - UNPROFOR, the peacekeeping operation that operated in early 1990s in Bosnia and Herzegovina. Before the restructuring of the operation in 1995 the CIVPOL unit reported to the UN Civil Affairs on missing persons and on cases where families had been separated during the war. See T Tanke Holm, 'CIVPOL Operations in Eastern Slavonia, 1992-98' in Tor Tanke Holm and Espen Barth Eide (eds), *Peacebuilding and Police Reform* (Frank Cass 2000) 142.

[151] Cf. Article 40, UNFICYP Regulations, 25 April 1964, 555 UNTS 132.

[152] 'Exchange of Letters (with Annexes) Constituting an Agreement Concerning the Service with the [UNFICYP] of the National Contingent Provided by the Government of Canada (Doc No 8107)' (1966) 555 UNTS 120 para 11, 126.

[153] See Anneke Smit, *The Property Rights of Refugees and Internally Displaced Persons: Beyond Restitution* (Routledge 2012) 51; Norwegian Refugee Council, 'Profile of Internal Displacement: Cyprus - Compilation of the Information Available in the Global IDP Database of the Norwegian Refugee Council' (2005) 4, 35 <http://www.internal-displacement.org/assets/library/Europe/Cyprus/pdf/Cyprus-April-2005-2.pdf> accessed 12 July 2016.

[154] CMP (Cyprus), 'Facts and Figures' (31 December 2016) <http://www.cmp-cyprus.org/content/facts-and-figures> accessed 12 January 2017; ICMP, 'Cyprus' (28 September 2016) <https://www.icmp.int/where-we-work/europe/cyprus/> accessed 12 January 2017.

[155] Security Council Report (n 144).

the first traditional peacekeeping operation to be formally authorized by the UNSC to carry out humanitarian functions in the whole territory and 'in regard to all sections of the population of Cyprus'.[156] The activities carried out by the UN force encompassed *ad hoc* measures to save lives, minimize suffering, and restore essential civilian activities. It has been argued that it was in this capacity that UNFICYP engaged directly in peace-building activities.[157]

In the aftermath of 1974 events, the CIVPOL unit played an active role in contributing to the humanitarian work of the ICRC.[158] Since 1974, as reported by the UNSG, responsibilities of the CIVPOL had covered, 'in co-operation with ICRC, inquiries into cases of missing persons.'[159] Moreover, a special UNFICYP's missing persons bureau was established with the specific task to '[assist] in the collection and exchange of information on missing persons, in close consultation with ICRC.'[160] While at the beginning of its work the Bureau was the only UN-based institutional effort devoted to the issue of the missing, with the passage of time it became clear that a direct involvement of the two sides was needed, through the intermediary of an *ad hoc* body exclusively tasked to search for missing persons on behalf of the two sides. In parallel to the activities carried out on the ground, a series of diplomatic efforts, strongly advocated for by the UN General Assembly, were undertaken by the UNSG towards this direction.[161] As of 1977, the UNSG noted that 'UNCIVPOL continues to maintain a Missing Persons Bureau'[162] and reported the various

---

[156] Cf. operative para 4, UNSC, 'Resolution 359 (Cyprus)' (1974) S/RES/359. For instance, the UNFICYP carried out visits in prisons and refugee camps to help restore family links in collaboration with the ICRC and the UN High Commissioner for Refugees (UNHCR). Every effort was undertaken in order to protect the civilian population; however, it became evident that a more systematic and larger scale operation was needed. Accordingly, in August 1974, the UNSG designated the UNHCR as coordinator of UN Humanitarian assistance for Cyprus. UNSG, 'Report of the Secretary-General pursuant to UNSC Resolution 361 (1974)' (1974) UN Doc/11488 para 2; UN, *The Blue Helmets* (n 145) 163; UNSG, 'Report by the Secretary General on the UN Operation in Cyprus' (1974) UN DOC S/11568 paras 45, 49, 54.

[157] Katarina Månsson, 'The Forgotten Agenda: Human Rights Protection and Promotion in Cold War Peacekeeping' (2005) 10 Journal of Conflict and Security Law 379, 390.

[158] These functions were legally based on the initial mandate of UNFICYP, which included a 'law and order' component. UNSC, 'Resolution 186 (the Cyprus Question)' (n 147).

[159] UNSG, 'Report of the Secretary-General on the United Nations Operation in Cyprus (for the Period 10 June 1975 to 8 December 1975)' (1975) UN Doc S/11900 para 28.

[160] ibid 32; UNSG, 'Report of the Secretary-General on the United Nations Operation in Cyprus (for the Period 9 December 1975 to 5 June 1976)' (1976) UN Doc S/12093 para 33; UNSG, 'Report of the Secretary-General on the United Nations Operation in Cyprus (for the Period 6 June 1976 to 6 December 1976)' (1976) UN Doc S/12253 para 45. The Unit directly collaborated with the ICRC CTA by taking part to search operations to locate the missing. UNSG, 'Report by the Secretary General on the UN Operation in Cyprus' (n 156) paras 45, 49, 54.

[161] On 16 December 1977, the UNGA requested the establishment of an investigatory body with the participation of the Red Cross. In December 1978 it urged the establishment of the body under the chairmanship of a representative of the UNSG. UNGA, 'Resolution 32/128 - Missing Persons in Cyprus' (1977) UN Doc A/RES/32/128 para 1; UNGA, 'Resolution 33/172 - Missing Persons in Cyprus' (1978) UN Doc A/RES/33/172 para 1.

[162] UNSG, 'Report of the Secretary-General on the United Nations Operation in Cyprus (for the Period 7 December 1976 to 7 June 1977)' (1977) UN Doc S/12342 para 32; UNSG, 'Report of the Secretary-General on the United Nations Operation in Cyprus (for the Period 8 June 1977 to 30

steps that were being undertaken by the two sides to find a solution to the issue under his good offices. Indeed, this bureau was a temporary solution to a compelling problem, i.e., the increasing number of inquiries that were addressed not only to the ICRC, but also to the UNFICYP. The work of the missing persons Bureau was no longer reported by the UNSG after the agreement of all sides on the establishment of this new *ad hoc* body in 1981(see *infra* sub-sect. 4.1.2).[163] No institutional connection between the new Committee on Missing Persons (CMP) and the UNFICYP existed.

The humanitarian facet[164] of the mandate of the UNFICYP[165] and the actions undertaken vis-à-vis the requests for information of the families of those reported unaccounted for were consistent with the obligations that the parties to the conflict had under IHL (e.g., the obligation to allow family members to send

---

November 1977)' (1977) UN Doc S/12463 para 39 (mentioning the work of the UNSG towards a new machinery concerning the missing persons-the future CMP-and the then ongoing talks on it with all sides); UNSG, 'Report of the Secretary-General on the United Nations Operation in Cyprus (for the Period 1 December 1977 to 31 May 1978)' (1978) UN Doc S/12723 para 36 (updating on the steps towards the establishment of the CMP including the UNGA Resolution A/32/128); UNSG, 'Report of the Secretary-General on the United Nations Operation in Cyprus (for the Period 1 June 1978 to 30 November 1978)' (1978) UN Doc S/12946 paras 41–43 (highlighting the tensions vis-à-vis the process to establish the CMP and underlining the need to maintain the Bureau); UNSG, 'Report of the Secretary-General on the United Nations Operation in Cyprus (for the Period 1 December 1978 to 31 May 1979)' (1979) UN Doc S/13369 para 38; UNSG, 'Report of the Secretary-General on the United Nations Operation in Cyprus (for the Period 1 June to 30 November 1979)' (1979) UN Doc S/13672 para 36; UNSG, 'Report of the Secretary-General on the United Nations Operation in Cyprus (for the Period 1 December 1979 to 31 May 1980)' (1980) UN Doc S/13972 para 30; UNSG, 'Report of the Secretary-General on the United Nations Operation in Cyprus (for the Period 1 June to 30 November 1980)' (1980) UN Doc S/14275 para 30; UNSG, 'Report of the Secretary General on the UN Operation in Cyprus (For the Period 1 December 1980 to 27 May 1981)' (1981) UN Doc S/14490 para 35.

[163] In his 1980 Report, the UNSG pointed out that he had continued his 'efforts with a view to arriving at a solution of the problem of setting up an investigatory body for the tracing of and accounting for missing persons of both communities in Cyprus'. See UNSG, 'Report of the Secretary-General on the United Nations Operation in Cyprus (for the Period 1 June to 30 November 1980)' (1980) UN Doc S/14275 paras 30–31. In his 1981 report covering the second part of the year (May – November), the UNSG reframed the activities of the UNCIVPOL as follows: 'UNCIVPOL contributes to the maintenance of law and order in the area between the cease-fire lines and to the protection of the civilian population, particularly in areas where inter-communal problems exist. It assists in the control of the movement of civilians in the area between the lines; escorts persons transferring from the north to the south and vice versa, inquires into complaints of criminal activity having inter-communal implications, and, in the north, distributes social welfare payments to Greek Cypriots in their habitations and monitors their welfare, as well as the welfare of Turkish Cypriots living in the south.' UNSG, 'Report of the Secretary-General on the United Nations Operation in Cyprus (for the Period 28 May 1981 to 30 November 1981)' (1981) UN Doc S/14778 para 38.

[164] UNFICYP 'discharges certain humanitarian functions for the Greek Cypriots living in the northern part of the island [...]. UNFICYP periodically visits Turkish Cypriots living in the southern part of the island and helps them maintain contact with their relatives in the north. [UN] civilian police maintain close cooperation and liaison with the Cyprus police and the Turkish Cypriot police on matters having inter-communal aspects. Together with the line units they contribute to law and order in the buffer zone and assist in investigations and in the force's humanitarian activities.' UNFICYP, 'Operations since 1974' <https://unficyp.unmissions.org/operations-1974> accessed 12 January 2017.

[165] One author has argued that similar humanitarian activities demonstrate the human rights facet of the work of peacekeepers. Månsson (n 157) 385.

messages to their next of kin or the obligation of the parties to the conflict to enable those in detention to preserve their external relations with the family members). While the Bureau of the missing had sought to address the queries posed by the families in various part of the island until the establishment of the CMP, its work came to an end with the CMP. The transfer of mandate, however, did not produce the effects expected, since the CMP remained inactive for decades (see *infra* sub-sect 2.1.2).

1.2.4.2. The duty to account for the missing in the context of the protection and promotion of human rights and the restoration of the RoL: The UNMIK case

More than 4,000 persons were reported unaccounted for[166] as a result of the operations undertaken by Serbia against Kosovo between 1998 and 1999, which triggered the NATO non-authorized intervention. The UNSC assumed the responsibility for post-conflict reconstruction by means of one of the most complex mandates ever designed (which is residually operating at the time of writing). Chapter VII-based Resolution 1244 established

> an international civil presence in Kosovo in order to provide an interim administration for Kosovo under which the people of Kosovo can enjoy substantial autonomy within the Federal Republic of Yugoslavia, and which will provide transitional administration while establishing and overseeing the development of provisional democratic self-governing institutions to ensure conditions for a peaceful and normal life for all inhabitants of Kosovo.[167]

As a sort of 'default mechanism' of the international community to address the enforcement gap generated by the failure of Serbia in its role as a domestic governing institution in Kosovo and as an executive agent of international obligations, this solution entailed the transitional exercise of governance functions by the UN.[168]

The connection between the *in bello* and *post bellum* phases in Kosovo is reflected in the trifold mandate of the UN Interim Administration Mission in Kosovo (UNMIK), i.e., a status resolution mandate to solve the dispute over the future status of Kosovo;[169] a State-building mandate;[170] and a legitimizing mandate to reduce the gap between the illegality and the legitimacy of the Kosovo intervention by NATO.[171] In the purview of this mandate, UNMIK was

[166] ICMP, 'The Situation in Kosovo: A Stock-Taking' (2010) Doc no ICMP.DG.264.4.doc 4 <http://www.ic-mp.org/wp-content/uploads/2007/11/icmp-dg-264-4-doc-general.pdf> accessed 12 January 2016. The figure is dramatically higher according to the UN; pursuant to a UN press release a total of 5,206 people were reported missing after the conflict in Kosovo. UN News Service, 'UN News - Over Half Kosovo's Missing Accounted For, Mostly through Body Identification – UN' (*UN News Service Section,* 6 December 2006) <http://www.un.org/apps/news/story.asp?NewsID =20863&Cr=kosovo&Cr1=missing#.WI_YJ7GZOu4> accessed 31 January 2017.
[167] UNSC, 'Resolution 1244 (Kosovo)' (1999) UN Doc S/RES/1244 para 10.
[168] On the institutional design of the international administration of territory, see Stahn, *The Law and Practice of International Territorial Administration* (n 2) 31.
[169] UNSC, 'Resolution 1244' (n 167) para 11 (a).
[170] ibid 11 (b-c).
[171] Stahn, *The Law and Practice of International Territorial Administration* (n 2) 310.

in charge of the protection and promotion of human rights.[172] Although UNMIK could control and regulate each and every aspect of public life, this competence was not based on solid experience stemming from previous UN missions; Resolution 1244 allowed UNMIK to tackle every aspect of the *res publica* and to re-frame the legislation accordingly. And yet UNMIK and, principally, the UN lacked the resources to assess the impact of provisional legislation and institutional tools and their compatibility with international human rights standards.[173]

Multiple actors became involved in the issue of missing persons (e.g., UNMIK, ICTY, ICRC, ICMP, local authorities) without a coordinated approach. The role of UNMIK was peculiar, as it basically ruled Kosovo at least in the initial years of its mandate:[174] from a legal point of view this meant that it was the actor that had the primary responsibility for accounting for the missing and informing their families. This seemed to be confirmed by the Regulations enacted by UNMIK since its inception: for instance, UNMIK clarified that 'in exercising their functions, all persons undertaking public duties or holding public office in Kosovo shall observe internationally recognized human rights standards' which included, *inter alia,* the UDHR, the ICCPR, the ECHR, and the CAT.[175] As Chapter IV shows, the duty to account for missing persons is a substantive obligation in the ECHR context.

Despite the foregoing, the UNSG, who had full executive and legislative authority with regard to UNMIK, [176] interpreted that part of the mandate concerning protection and promotion of human rights in a softer manner; the words 'obliged', 'shall', or 'obligations' were carefully avoided:

> [in] assuming its responsibilities, UNMIK *will be guided by* internationally recognized standards of human rights as the basis for the exercise of its authority in Kosovo. UNMIK will embed a culture of human rights in all areas of activity, and

---

[172] UNSC, 'Resolution 1244' (n 167) para 11 (j). The mandate has evolved; today's priorities remain to promote security, stability, and respect for human rights in Kosovo and the region. Cf. UNSG, 'Report of the Secretary-General on UNMIK' (2016) UN Doc S/2016/901 para 2.

[173] Stahn, *The Law and Practice of International Territorial Administration* (n 2) 327.

[174] Only in 2001, UNMIK enacted the Constitutional Framework for Provisional Self-government in Kosovo through UNMIK Regulation 2001/9. Indeed, this was part of the State-building mandate that UNMIK was granted.

[175] UNMIK, 'UNMIK Regulation No 1999/1 on the Authority of the Interim Administration in Kosovo' (1999) UN Doc UNMIK/REG/1999/1 Section 2; UNMIK, 'UNMIK Regulation No 1999/24 on the Applicable Law in Kosovo' (1999) UN Doc UNMIK/REG/1999/24 Section 1, para 1.3. That UNMIK is obliged to respect and protect human rights has been confirmed by the UNMIK Human Rights Advisory Panel (HRAP). Cf. HRAP, *Snežana Zdravković against UNMIK (opinion, final)* (2013) Case no 46/08 [26]. See also HRCee, 'Concluding Observations of the Human Rights Committee: Kosovo (Serbia)' (2006) UN Doc CCPR/C/UNK/CO/1 para 5.

[176] Pursuant to Article 98 UN Charter, the UNSG performs the functions that are 'entrusted' to him by the UNGA or the UNSC; the provision does not subject this delegation of powers to any condition. Pursuant to Resolution 1244, the UNSG was authorized to establish the international civil presence in Kosovo; accordingly, he had to appoint a Special Representative mandated to control the implementation of the international civil presence and to coordinate closely with the international security presence so as to ensure that both presences operate towards the same goals and in a mutually supportive manner. UNSC, 'Resolution 1244' (n 167) paras 6, 10. On this point, see also Conforti (n 123) 211.

will adopt *human rights policies* in respect of its administrative functions. (emphases added)[177]

Since the beginning of the mission, the UNSG has deemed the issue of missing persons a sensitive and important "human rights issue" that the people of Kosovo needed to handle.[178] Thus, the question that arose was what State or other entity was responsible under international law for the protection of human rights in Kosovo. Before addressing it, important is to briefly examine the operative steps undertaken by UNMIK vis-à-vis the missing and their families.

At the very outset of its work, UNMIK established a focal point within its institution-building component exclusively dedicated to the problems concerning missing persons; this focal point acted in collaboration with the ICRC and ICMP.[179] A Missing persons Unit was established within the UNMIK police with the specific mandate to carry out investigation into the possible location of missing persons and/or their gravesites.[180] This Unit worked together with the Criminal Investigation Unit (then transformed into a War Crimes Investigation Unit), since it was essentially in charge of the criminal aspects of the missing persons cases in Kosovo.[181] Another UNMIK body was created in 2000 – the Victim Recovery and Identification Commission – with the composite task of recovering, identifying, and disposing the mortal remains as well as of collecting related data and providing social and legal support to the families of missing persons.[182] In terms of cooperation with other bodies that at that time were operating in Kosovo, this Commission, chaired by UNMIK, would have directed its systematic efforts towards exhuming graves that the ICTY declined to handle.[183] This multitude of components tasked to deal with the missing persons cases was streamlined in 2002 when UNMIK created the Office of Missing Persons and Forensics (OMPF) as a division within its Department of Justice with a purely humanitarian mandate. Such body had 'overall supervisory and coordination responsibility for the Missing Persons Unit dealing with the historically missing persons'.[184]

Since the establishment of the OMPF, two problems characterized the way the issue of missing persons was handled: on the one hand, the presence of a diversified range of actors directly or indirectly involved in dealing with the issue in Kosovo and in Serbia without any form of coordination at various level (e.g., a coordinated and transparent exchange of information);[185] on the other, the

---

[177] UNSG, 'Report of the Secretary-General on UNMIK' (1999) UN Doc S/1999/779 para 42.
[178] UNSG, 'Report of the Secretary-General on UNMIK' (1999) UN Doc S/1999/987 para 37.
[179] ibid.
[180] HRAP, *Snežana Zdravković (opinion, final)* (n 175) [26].
[181] ibid [37].
[182] UNSG, 'Report of the Secretary-General on UNMIK' (2000) UN Doc S/2000/538 para 54.
[183] UNSG, 'Report of the Secretary-General on the UNMIK' (2000) UN Doc S/2000/177 para 65.
[184] UNMIK, 'UNMIK Pillar 1, Police and Justice, Presentation Paper' (2003) Fourth Quarter 22.
[185] Particularly difficult resulted the exchange of information and the collaboration among the Serbian Authorities, the OMPF, and the ICMP. CoE (Committee on Migration, Refugees and Population; Rapporteur: Mr Mevlüt Çavusoglu), 'Persons Unaccounted for as a Result of Armed Conflicts or Internal Violence in the Balkans' (2004) Doc 10251 para 39.

disregard of the accountability facet of the issue of missing persons, particularly with regard to those cases that amounted to enforced disappearances.

As for the former, paradoxically, in order to address the consequences generated by the array of actors dealing with the missing, a multiplicity of coordination mechanisms with often parallel or overlapping structures had been set up.[186] As for the latter, the CoE's Venice Commission addressed, *inter alia,* the questions of what entity/State was responsible for protecting human rights in Kosovo and of whether the ECtHR could have jurisdiction vis-à-vis Kosovo cases. While a neat answer on the first question was not provided, the Commission concluded that the options to extend the jurisdiction of the ECtHR to Kosovo were unviable in terms of providing a speedy and effective impact on the human rights situation in Kosovo.[187] Furthermore, in the Commission's view, actions by UNMIK, the Kosovo Force (KFOR) – the NATO-led peacekeeping force in charge of the security and military aspects – and the Provisional Institutions of Self-Government (PISG) in Kosovo were all main sources of potential human rights violations; as such, they needed a specific *interim* review mechanism, which should be additional to a Human Rights Court for Kosovo.[188]

The position of the HRCee on the question of what entity/State was responsible is more clear-cut than the Venice Commission's; in light of its general comment No 26 (1977) on continuity of obligations, the Committee has boldly stated that

the rights guaranteed under the [ICCPR] belong to the people living in the territory of a State party, and that once the people are accorded the protection of the rights under the Covenant, such protection devolves with territory and continues to belong to them, notwithstanding changes in the administration of that territory. The protection and

---

[186] Among these are: a Joint Implementation Commission (JIC) between the representatives of the Yugoslav Army and Serbian Police and their counterparts from KFOR and UNMIK Police created in 1999 after the signing of the Kumanovo Military Technical Agreement; the JIC had a missing persons sub-commission mandated to deal with the issue of the missing but not with the exhumations and identifications in Serbia proper; a Contact Group (CG) - a Serbia/UNMIK forum of co-operation on missing persons and detainees - was set up in early summer 2001, later incorporated in the Serbian Coordination Centre for Kosovo and Metohija (CCKM). A Kidnapped and Missing Persons Subcommittee has been established within the Joint Committee for Police Co-operation created in May 2002 between UNMIK and the CCKM; essentially humanitarian, it is mandated to carry out continuous efforts to account for the missing in Kosovo. A Working Group, chaired by the ICRC, was also created in 2004 following the first direct talks between Belgrade and Pristina. The mandate of the Working group was and still is humanitarian, although it can deal with the legal and administrative needs of the families of the missing. ibid paras 42–46. See also ICRC, 'Kosovo: Meeting of Working Group on Missing Persons Held in Belgrade (News No. 05/23)' (*ReliefWeb,* 2005) <http://reliefweb.int/report/serbia/kosovo-meeting-working-group-missing-persons-held-belgrade> accessed 31 January 2017.
[187] The basic obstacle was represented by the fact that the ECHR is open to signature by member States of CoE (cf. Article 59 ECHR). In addition to that, the length of the process that might end up with an extension of the jurisdiction would likely exceed the length of the *interim* administration. European Commission for Democracy through law (Venice Commission), 'Opinion on Human Rights in Kosovo: Possible Establishment of Review Mechanisms, Adopted at the 60th Plenary Session' (2004) CDL-AD (2004)033, Opinion no 280/2004 paras 149–152; for a summary of possible lengthy options, see para 153.
[188] ibid paras 158-159-157.

promotion of human rights is one of the main responsibilities conferred on UNMIK under [UNSC] resolution 1244 (1999). [...] As part of the applicable law in Kosovo [...] the Covenant is binding on the PISG. It follows that UNMIK, as well as PISG, or any future administration in Kosovo, are bound to respect and to ensure to all individuals within the territory of Kosovo and subject to their jurisdiction the rights recognized in the Covenant.[189]

With the passage of time the changes in the administration do not affect the obligation to carry out an investigation on the disappearance, should the disappearance continue. In cases where the body of the person is recovered and shows signs of alleged human rights violations, the obligation to carry out an investigation "revives". Indeed, the conduct of the authorities vis-à-vis the families is another potential source of human rights violations. Chapter VI will explore the role of the review mechanism − eventually created in Kosovo in 2004 − as a form of TJ tool addressing the actions of UNMIK; suffice it here to say that the Venice Commission's proposal of a Human Rights Court for Kosovo did not turn into reality.

The disregard of the accountability facet of the issue of the missing has provoked sharp criticism against UNMIK and,[190] more generally, against the international community. For instance, despite the positive humanitarian impact of the OMPF work,[191] the HRCee noted with concern that 'low priority [had] been given to investigations of disappearances and abductions by the Missing Persons Unit of the UNMIK police and, since 2003, by the Central Criminal Investigative Unit'; the Committee also noted that 'in closed cases of disappearances and abductions perpetrators were rarely, if ever, prosecuted and brought to justice'.[192] In its responses to the Committee, UNMIK pointed out that the OMPF was provided with international staff members with investigating and law enforcement expertise in order to 'correct the lack of results with respect to bringing perpetrators to justice'.[193] UNMIK also stressed the purely humanitarian character of the OMPF's mandate and the lack of authority similar to that of police officers. Since the HRCee recommended UNMIK to ensure that families have access to information on their beloved ones, UNMIK highlighted that limitations were possible in relation to information held in the context of

---

[189] HRCee (n 175) para 4; HRCee, 'General Comment No 26: Continuity of Obligations' (1997) UN Doc CCPR/C/21/Rev.1/Add.8/Rev.1 para 4.
[190] Among the international NGOs, Amnesty International voiced its concerns over the failure of the authorities to open investigations that will lead to bringing the perpetrators to justice. See Amnesty International, 'Serbia and Montenegro (Kosovo): The Legacy of Past Human Rights Abuse' (2004) AI Index: EUR 70/009/2004 7. Similar criticism has been expressed by the WGEID that voiced its concern over reliable information indicating the lack of a proper investigation by UNMIK into cases of enforced disappearances and missing persons. WGEID, 'Report of the WGEID. Addendum: Mission to Serbia, Including Kosovo' (2015) UN Doc A/HRC/30/38/Add.1 para 69.
[191] The ICMP sheds light upon the dual mandate of the OMPF, i.e., clarifying the fate of the missing and providing a medical legal system to Kosovo in line with the European standards. See ICMP, 'The Situation in Kosovo: A Stock-Taking' (n 166) 4.
[192] HRCee (n 175) para 13.
[193] UNMIK/HRCee, 'Comments by the United Nations Interim Administration Mission in Kosovo (UNMIK) on the Concluding Observations of the Human Rights Committee (CCPR/C/UNK/CO/1)' (2008) UN Doc CCPR/C/UNK/CO/1/Add.1 para 12.

criminal proceedings (investigations or trial).[194] It should be recalled that international human rights adjudicators have considered such kinds of restrictions contrary to human rights standards when cases of enforced disappearances are at stake (see sub-sect 3.2 in Chapter IV).

In 2008 the mandate of UNMIK was significantly modified, since the EU, through the European Union RoL Mission in Kosovo (EULEX Kosovo), was asked by the UNSC to operate in relation to the RoL in Kosovo.[195] Thus, EULEX inherited 'a huge number of reports of missing persons submitted to UNMIK, some of which were not well documented and lacked initial investigation'.[196] Accordingly, the OMPF was transferred to EULEX along with the War Crimes Investigation Unit.[197] Instead of streamlining the handling of information on missing persons, this further passage has had the reversed effect reflected in the different definitional approach to the issue of missing persons adopted by EULEX.[198] As emphasized by the WGEID, 'the failures by UNMIK in the early years cannot serve to absolve the current responsibility of EULEX prosecutors and investigators' vis-à-vis cases of enforced disappearances and other grave human rights violations committed in the context of the war.[199] Despite the constant collaboration between the local judicial system and the

---

[194] Pursuant to the Provisional Criminal Procedure Code of Kosovo – adopted by UNMIK Regulation, 'if a missing person has been reported or classified as a criminal offence and criminal proceedings (investigation or trial) are ongoing, [...] the injured party shall be entitled to access case files including records or physical evidence under certain circumstances and within certain limitations'. UNMIK/HRCee, 'Further Information Received from the United Nations Interim Administration Mission in Kosovo (UNMIK) on the Implementation of the Concluding Observations of the Human Rights Committee (CCPR/C/UNK/CO/1)' (2009) UN Doc CCPR/C/UNK/CO/1/Add.2 para 5; UNMIK, 'UNMIK Regulation No 2003/26 - Provisional Criminal Procedure Code of Kosovo' (2003) UN Doc UNMIK/REG/2003/26, cf. Article 143.

[195] UNSC, 'Statement by the President of the Security Council' (2008) UN Doc S/PRST/2008/44. This development followed the proclamation of independence by Kosovo on 17 February 2008 and the adoption of the Constitution of Kosovo on 15 June 2008. Since 10 September 2012, UNMIK has concluded the work of supervision of Kosovo's independence process. See UNMIK, 'UNMIK Background' <http://www.un.org/en/peacekeeping/missions/unmik/background.shtml> accessed 12 January 2017.

[196] WGEID, 'Report of the WGEID. Addendum: Mission to Serbia, Including Kosovo' (n 190) para 71. EULEX concluded its work in June 2018; the end of its mandate entails that hundreds of war crimes files as well as files on missing persons are being handed over to local prosecutors at the time of writing. See Balkan Insight, 'Kosovo Faces Judicial Dilemmas as EU Law Mission Ends' (13 April 2018), http://www.balkaninsight.com/en/article/kosovo-faces-judicial-dilemmas-as-eu-law-mission-ends-04-12-2018 accessed 12 June 2018.

[197] UNMIK/HRCee, 'Further Information Received from the United Nations Interim Administration Mission in Kosovo (UNMIK) on the Implementation of the Concluding Observations of the Human Rights Committee (CCPR/C/UNK/CO/1)' (2009) UN Doc CCPR/C/UNK/CO/1/Add.3 para 3.

[198] Since the beginning of their work in Kosovo, the ICRC as well as the ICMP have implicitly shared the same definitional basis as to 'missing person'. The ICTY's investigative efforts were concerned more broadly with potential victims of war crimes; EULEX addressed not only persons reported as missing, but also cases of war-related deaths more generally. Some of the latter may be included among the unidentified remains in the custody of EULEX, but they may not be represented on either the WG list, or in the ICMP database. It is important to further consider that some remains under the custody of EULEX may not even be of the appropriate time period, but predate the conflict. ICMP, 'The Situation in Kosovo: A Stock-Taking' (n 166) 10.

[199] WGEID, 'Report of the WGEID. Addendum: Mission to Serbia, Including Kosovo' (n 190) para 70.

international counterpart through EULEX, the judicial system in Kosovo has been deemed weak and inefficient due to, *inter alia,* the lack of sufficient support by the international community and a widespread corruption.[200]

The UN involvement in Kosovo demonstrates that a fragmented approach to the issue of the missing is not just unpractical, but also legally unsuitable. The neat separation of humanitarian– and RoL-related aspects has resulted in the lack of answers to those who have suffered the most, i.e., the families. The foregoing examination also shows that the UN has adopted a top-down approach[201] with a pervasive presence and multiple units/bureau/centers concerning the missing persons; and yet, 'international actors can neither hope to resolve the missing persons' problem comprehensively through continuing casework alone, nor can they continuously substitute for domestic responsibility.'[202]

2. POST-CONFLICT RESPONSES PROMPTED BY THE RIGHT OF FAMILIES TO KNOW: BETWEEN AD-HOCISM AND SYSTEMATIZATION

Pursuant to article 32 AP I, the activities of, *inter alia,* 'international humanitarian organizations' shall be prompted by the right of families to know the fate of their relatives; from the analysis of the legal framework in Chapter II it emerges that 'international humanitarian organizations' operating in NIAC and post-NIAC must be prompted by the same right.

Neither the GCs nor the AP I provide more details to facilitate the identification of these bodies.[203] Used elsewhere in the treaties,[204] a similar

---

[200] ibid para 73. It is not by chance that EULEX's mandate supposed to end in 2016 has been extended until 2018. See Council of the EU, 'EULEX Kosovo: Mandate Extended, Budget Approved' (14 June 2016) <http://www.consilium.europa.eu/en/press/press-releases/2016/06/14-eulex-kosovo-budget/> accessed 12 January 2017.

[201] Stahn, *The Law and Practice of International Territorial Administration* (n 2) 327–329.

[202] ICMP, 'The Situation in Kosovo: A Stock-Taking' (n 166) 16. At the same time, 'a greater demonstration of political will to address the issue is required' by the national authorities in Kosovo and Serbia. According to ICMP, such demonstration would include a set of measures to be undertaken by both sides, ranging from legislation-related measures to measures focused on securing the rights of families of missing persons and on the enhancement of technical capacities (including data systems and identification procedures). See ICMP, ' Missing Persons from the Kosovo Conflict and its Aftermath: A Stocktaking' (2017) 40-42 https://www.icmp.int/?resources=missing-persons-from-the-kosovo-conflict-and-its-aftermath-a-stocktaking-2017 accessed 12 July 2018.

[203] Article 32 of AP I includes this specific expression; the first draft of Section III included a vague expression, i.e., 'international organizations'. The degree of precision did not improve in the current version: are the 'international humanitarian organizations' inter-governmental or non-governmental? Shall they have an exclusively humanitarian mandate? The ICRC commentary clarifies that the provision is not limited to inter-governmental organizations: the ICRC and its CTA are therefore included among 'international humanitarian organizations'. ICRC, 'Official Records of the Diplomatic Conference on the Reaffirmation and Development of International Humanitarian Law Applicable in Armed Conflicts, Vol XI' (1974) (CDDH/II/SR.35), para 13, 365; Sandoz and others (n 133) para 1209, 345.

[204] Article 9 AP I (Field of Application of Part II) refers to the 'permanent and medical units and transports' which are made available to a Party to the conflict by, *inter alia,* 'an impartial international humanitarian organization'. Cf. Article 9, para. 2 (c), AP I.

wording adds an interesting detail, i.e., the organization for being humanitarian cannot have a political or commercial character[205] and must be impartial.[206] More generally, the ICRC Commentary notes that the expression should not be limited to intergovernmental organizations, covering the ICRC, its CTA as well as other NGOs.[207] The case of *ad hoc* international humanitarian bodies designed to address the issue of missing persons in post-conflict scenarios, therefore, falls within this framework; the same is true for those bodies that have a hybrid mandate, i.e., which admits a direct involvement in the elucidation of the facts in the pursuance of accountability-driven courses of action.

This section aims at demonstrating that a shared and comprehensive agenda, which integrates the tenets of the international legal framework on missing persons, can be conducive to the realization of the right of families to know the fate of their relatives. To this end, past and ongoing attempts aimed at the formulation of normative and policy responses globally and *ad hoc* will be examined. Although prompted by the right of families to know the fate of their relatives, past *ad hoc* international initiatives have paid lip-service to the families, due to diverse reasons, including the overlap of mandates, legal and substantive confusion about the definitional contours of the issue of the missing, and the disregard of how to balance the responses to the humanitarian and accountability-related needs of the families (sub-section 2.1). At the same time, ongoing global attempts to systematize the approach to the missing can run the risk of fragmenting the international legal and policy-based response, should these attempts be driven by mutually exclusive – and not mutually reinforcing – objectives (sub-section 2.2).

2.1. Ad hoc international responses to the issue of the missing

Resulted by negotiations or diplomatic consultations, *ad hoc* responses – bodies/initiatives created for tackling the issue of the missing in a specific region/country – have proved to be only partially meaningful. This result is due

---

[205] Ibid. In order to cast light on the above expression, Article 125 GC III, on *Relief societies and other organizations*, is a helpful tool: specifically, it mentions 'religious organizations, relief societies, [and] any other organization assisting prisoners of war'. National Red Cross and Red Crescent Societies are part of 'relief societies'. The innovative element in the Convention is the reference to 'religious organizations': the spiritual assistance is part of the relief activities. Moreover, the open-ended character of the expression 'any other organizations [...]' aims to address the activities of those bodies whose main purpose is not the assistance to POW but which during a conflict could include such assistance among their task. The humanitarian character of this type of bodies could be temporary. See Jean S Pictet (ed), *The Geneva Conventions of 12 August 1949: Commentary*, vol III (ICRC 1960) 595.

[206] In the view of the ICJ, '[a]n essential feature of truly humanitarian aid is that it is given "without discrimination" of any kind.' This means that in order for humanitarian assistance to be considered as such and not as an intervention in the internal affairs of a State, 'not only must it be limited to the purposes allowed in the practice of the Red Cross, namely "to prevent and alleviate human suffering" and "to protect life and health and to ensure respect for the human being"; it must also, and above all, be given without discrimination to all in need[...]'. See ICJ, *Case concerning Military and Paramilitary Activities in and against Nicaragua (Nicaragua v United States of America), Merits, Judgment* (1986) ICJ Reports 1986, p.14 paras 243, 125.

[207] Sandoz and others (n 133) para 1210, 345.

to the underestimation of a series of factors, e.g., the underestimation of what the realization of the right to know entails in terms of support from the parties to the conflict or from the international community (e.g., professional expertise and financial resources) and of what its realization means in terms of coordinated efforts that realistically aim at providing answers to those affected. The examples of the Special Process for the issue of missing persons in the territory of the Former Yugoslavia (sub-section 2.1.1) and of the Cyprus Committee on Missing Persons (sub-section 2.1.2) illustrate the downsides that derive from the implications of this underestimation for the realization of the right to know.

2.1.1 (Un)successful humanitarian initiatives under the aegis of the UN human rights system: Lessons to be learnt from the Former Yugoslavia

The then UN Commission on Human Rights did not remain indifferent vis-à-vis thousands of cases of persons reported missing to the WGEID in the context of the conflict in the Balkans in the early 1990s. The mandate of the WGEID,[208] the first UN human rights thematic mechanism,[209] was – and still is – purely humanitarian, i.e., it aims at assisting the relatives of the disappeared and ascertaining the fate and whereabouts of their missing family members.[210] As early as 1981, in its first report, the WGEID included the right to know among 'the human rights of the members of the family of a missing or disappeared person',[211] and made reference to Article 32 AP I in order to authoritatively substantiate the presence of this right in the human rights domain.[212] Nevertheless, at the time of the conflict in the Balkans, cases of

---

[208] UN Commission on Human Rights, 'Resolution on the Question of Missing and Disappeared Persons, Human Rights Resolution 20 (XXXVI)' (1980) UN Doc E/CN.4/RES/1980. The situations in Chile and in Argentina cast light upon the gravity and width of the practice of enforced disappearance, and as a sort of reaction, the UN Commission on Human Rights established the WGEID. Federico Andreu-Guzmán, 'Le Groupe de Travail Sur Les Disparitions Forcées Des Nations Unies' (2002) 84 International Review of the Red Cross 803, 803.

[209] It belongs to the so-called Special Procedures with a thematic mandate of the former UN Commission on Human Rights. It is composed of five members, each one of them coming from a different region (i.e., Eastern Europe; Western Europe and others; Latin America and Caribbean; Asia; Africa), who are independent experts, i.e., their appointment is incompatible with being an active official of any government. Santiago Corcuera, 'L'expérience Du Groupe de Travail Sur Les Disparitions Forcées' in Emmanuel Decaux and Olivier De Frouville (eds), La Convention pour la Protection de Toutes les Personnes Contre les Disparitions Forcées (Bruylant 2009) 21–22.

[210] WGEID, 'Report of the WGEID - Annex II "Revised Methods of Work of the Working Group on Enforced or Involuntary Disappearances"' (2011) UN Doc A/HRC/19/58 para 2. In other words, the WGEID acts as a channel of communication between families of disappeared persons and the governments concerned, with a view to ensuring that sufficiently documented and clearly identified individual cases are investigated and that the whereabouts of the disappeared persons are clarified. In fact, in carrying out its mandate, the WGEID shall seek and receive information from governments, intergovernmental organizations, and humanitarian organizations on missing and disappeared persons. WGEID, 'Civil and Political Rights, Including Questions of Disappearances and Summary Executions. Report of the WGEID' (1998) UN Doc E/CN.4/1999/62 para 2.

[211] WGEID, 'Questions of Human Rights of All Persons Subjected to Any Form of Detention or Imprisonment, in Particular: Questions of Missing and Disappeared Persons - Report of the WGEID' (1981) UN Doc E/CN.4/1435 para 187.

[212] ibid. In its subsequent Report, the WGEID put forward that '[t]here can be no doubt that the families of the disappeared are anxiously hoping that the Group will be able to obtain information for

disappearance arising in IAC were excluded from its mandate, unless it was expressly directed to address them by the UN Commission on Human Rights.[213]

Since these cases fell outside the mandate of the WGEID, the UN Commission on Human Rights expressly requested the Special Rapporteur on the situation of human rights in the former Yugoslavia, in consultation with the WGEID and the ICRC, 'to develop proposals for a mechanism to address the subject of disappearances in the former Yugoslavia'.[214] In light of this request, the Special Rapporteur articulated a proposal with five pillars: i.e.,

– action by the UN on missing persons in the former Yugoslavia (the "special process") should meet minimum standards of effectiveness;

– it must take a pragmatic approach;

– it should take the predicament of the relatives of missing persons as its point of departure and formulate a sensible response to it;

– undue friction with ongoing efforts to trace missing persons should be avoided;

– operating costs are to be realistic.[215]

The WGEID emphasized the humanitarian and non-accusatory nature of the work of the proposed mechanism; it also clarified that the nature of the conflict should be regarded as irrelevant for admissibility of cases by this mechanism.[216] Furthermore, the scope *ratione personae* of the mandate should have been as broad as possible and include all 'missing persons' in the conflict, thereby stretching the target group of the work of the WGEID.[217] On the methods of

---

them on that which they have been unable themselves to discover; the fate or present whereabouts of the disappeared. [...] Unquestionably, their right to know can be neither denied nor ignored.' WGEID, 'Questions of Human Rights of All Persons Subjected to Any Form of Detention or Imprisonment, in Particular: Questions of Missing and Disappeared Persons - Report of the WGEID' (1981) UN Doc E/CN .4/1492 para 5.

[213] Already in 1984, the WGEID had to reply to requests of its involvement in cases concerning disappearances in the Iran/Iraq War, South Atlantic War in 1982, and in Southern Lebanon. At the same time, the WGEID emphasized the role played by the ICRC in these cases. WGEID, 'Question of the Human Rights of All Persons Subjected to Any Form of Detention or Imprisonment, in Particular: Question of Enforced or Involuntary Disappearance - Report of the WGEID' (1983) UN Doc E/CN.4/1984/21 paras 20–21. It was in 2011 that the "Methods of Work" of the WGEID were amended so that the mechanism could handle all cases of enforced disappearance regardless of the type of conflict. Cf. WGEID, 'Report of the WGEID - Annex II Revised Methods of Work of the WGEID' (2012) UN Doc A/HRC/19/58/Rev.1 para 4.

[214] UN Commission on Human Rights, 'Resolution on the "Situation of Human Rights in the Territory of the Former Yugoslavia"' (1993) UN Doc E/CN.4/RES/1993/7 para 33.

[215] WGEID, 'Report on the Visit to Former Yugoslavia by a Member of the WGEID at the Request of the Special Rapporteur on the Situation of Human Rights in the Former Yugoslavia (4-13 August 1993)' (1993) UN Doc E/CN.4/1994/26/Add.1 para 113.

[216] ibid para 114.

[217] Pursuant to the proposal, the process should have dealt with all cases of missing persons, regardless of whether the victim is a civilian (non-combatant) or a combatant and regardless of whether the perpetrators are in effect connected to the Government or not. In other words, the target group would be wider than the one covered by the WGEID and by the Declaration on the Protection of All Persons from Enforced Disappearance. For conceptual clarity, using the wider term "missing

work of the process, the WGEID advised that 'a case should not be considered clarified until it has been established where the missing person is, either alive or dead;' nevertheless, 'the special process should not involve consultations or negotiations on the exchange of information.'[218] The Special Process was set up by the Commission in 1994[219] in line with the proposal above;[220] as an exception to the general *modus operandi* of the WGEID, it was entrusted to one expert of the WGEID with a joint mandate shared with the Special Rapporteur on the situation of human rights in the former Yugoslavia.

The brief outline of the establishment of the Special Process embeds the seeds that led the Commission to fail in its attempts to address the urgent humanitarian issue of the missing. First of all, the connection of the mandate with that of the Special Rapporteur was one of the factors that did not facilitate the carrying out of the tasks of the Special Process. Indeed, the former's mandate had an explicit accusatory nature,[221] which became an excuse used by the authorities of the Federal Republic of Yugoslavia to avoid collaborating with both.[222] Despite the fact that since 1995 the Special Process' work was no longer associated with the Special Rapporteur's activities,[223] the authorities of the Federal Republic of Yugoslavia did not change their attitude vis-à-vis the Special Process (e.g., no access to the territory was accorded, no information was

---

persons" would set the target group apart from the more circumscribed group of "disappeared persons". ibid.

[218] ibid para 115.

[219] UN Commission on Human Rights, 'Resolution on the "Situation of Human Rights in the Territory of the Former Yugoslavia: Violations of Human Rights in Bosnia and Herzegovina, Croatia and the Federal Republic of Yugoslavia (Serbia and Montenegro)"' (1994) UN Doc E/CN.4/RES/1994/72 para 24.

[220] The Special Process' mandate was extended with Resolution 1995/35 and Resolution 1996/71 of the UN Commission on Human Rights.

[221] Pursuant to Resolution 1992/S-1/1 of the Commission on Human Rights, the Rapporteur was asked to 'gather and compile systematically information on possible violations of human rights in the territory of the former Yugoslavia, including those which may constitute war crimes, and to make this information available to the [UNSG]; such information could be of possible future use in prosecuting violators of [IHL]'. Cf. UN Commission on Human Rights, 'The Situation of Human Rights in the Territory of the Former Yugoslavia (Resolution Adopted by the Commission at Its First Special Session)' (1992) UN Doc E/CN.4/1992/S-1/1 para 16.

[222] Mr. Nowak, the expert who was in charge of carrying out the tasks assigned to the Special Process, also reported an explicit resistance of the authorities against Mr. Mazowiecki, i.e., the Special Rapporteur; certainly, Mr. Mazowiecki played a key role in leading a campaign aimed at exposing the conduct of the Federal Republic of Yugoslavia's authorities, e.g., ethnic cleansing in Bosnia and Herzegovina in combination with other acts, including scorched earth policy. See M Nowak, 'Lessons for the International Human Rights Regime from the Yugoslav Experience', *1997 the Protection of Human Rights in Europe - Collected courses of the Academy of European Law*, vol VIII Book 2 (Kluwer Law International 2000) 157–158; Bertrand G Ramcharan, *Human Rights and U.N. Peace Operations: Yugoslavia* (Martinus Nijhoff Publishers 2011) 46–48.

[223] Resolution 1995/35 3 March 1995, para 4. Cf. WGEID, 'Special Process on Missing Persons in the Territory of the Former Yugoslavia Report Submitted by Mr. Manfred Nowak, Member of the WGEID, pursuant to Paragraph 24 of Commission Resolution 1994/72 (First Report)' (1995) UN Doc E/CN.4/1995/37 para 15.

provided).[224] Thus, between 1995 and 1996, the expert shifted his focus on Bosnia and Herzegovina due to the continuing non-cooperative conduct of the Federal Republic of Yugoslavia.[225]

Another factor detrimental to the work of the Special Process was the overlap of its mandate with that of the ICRC,[226] which was better equipped and experienced than the expert to deal with the issue of the missing.[227] Thus, the extraordinary nature, 'both in qualitative and quantitative terms' of the issue of the missing brought about a significant reduction of the ambitious tasks of the expert. For instance, he decided to spend the last part of his mandate in facilitating the excavation of mass graves and exhumations of mortal remains, in raising funds for the launch of a more comprehensive forensic program, and in searching for a more significant support of the international community.[228]

The ambiguity of the mandate of the Special Process was problematic; the requests of the Expert to make it less ambiguous remained unheard.[229] The need to correct the ambiguity was even more evident in light of a multitude of international and domestic bodies, agencies, and *ad hoc* initiatives directly or indirectly working on the issue of the missing in the former Yugoslavia.[230] The overall lack of support from the international community, denounced by the expert in charge of the Special Process' mandate,[231] contributed to the failure of the Commission on Human Rights' involvement into the issue of the missing. The Commission itself expressed a lukewarm response to the Expert's proposal to establish a high-level multilateral commission on missing persons and to carry

---

[224] WGEID, 'Special Process on Missing Persons in the Territory of the Former Yugoslavia. Report Submitted by Mr. Manfred Nowak, Expert Member of the WGEID, Responsible for the Special Process, pursuant to Paragraph 4 of Commission Resolution 1995/35 (Second Report)' (1996) E/CN.4/1996/36 para 12.

[225] WGEID, 'Special Process on Missing Persons in the Territory of the Former Yugoslavia - Report Submitted to Mr. Manfred Nowak, Expert Member of the WGEID, Responsible for the Special Process, pursuant to Commission Resolution 1996/71 (Third Report)' (1997) E/CN.4/1997/55 para 6.

[226] Nowak (n 222) 158.

[227] Nowak stresses that his investigations revealed that the majority of missing persons were civilian victims of ethnic cleansing operations and could be regarded as enforced disappearances in the sense of the 1992 UN Declaration. However, impossible was to distinguish the various types of disappearances; thus, in 1995 the ICRC began to systematically collect tracing requests in relation to all missing persons in Bosnia and Herzegovina. The UN, with its very limited field personnel, was not equipped to undertake a similar effort. ibid.

[228] WGEID, 'Special Process on Missing Persons in the Territory of the Former Yugoslavia (Third Report)' (n 225) paras 7–10, 34.

[229] ibid para 34.

[230] These included the Office of the High Representative (OHR), the Multinational military implementation Force (IFOR), the International Police Task Force, the United Nations Transitional Administration for Eastern Slavonia, Baranja and Western Sirmium (UNTAES), the UNHCR, the ICTY, Physicians for Human Rights, the ICMP, the Association for the Promotion of the Ludwig Boltzmann Institute of Human Rights (BIM), the Finnish Expert Team, the ICRC (chair of the Working Group on Missing Persons), the Expert Group on Exhumations and Missing Persons. For a detailed list of all actors involved and an overview of their involvement in dealing with the issue of missing persons, Cf. ibid paras 18–48.

[231] Jeroen Gutter, *Thematic Procedures of the United Nations Commission on Human Rights and International Law: In Search of a Sense of Community* (Intersentia 2006) 155.

out exhumations in order to clarify the fate of missing persons; this was combined with an overall lack of political and financial support by the Commission.[232]

Furthermore, while the creation of the Special Process occurred during the conflict, its work was partly carried out in the peace-making phase: the absence of any reference to the Special Process in the Dayton Agreements and the exclusive mention of the ICRC as the leading actor in the tracing operations undermined even more the international standing of the Special Process vis-à-vis the former Parties to the conflict. These did not have any obligation, but to cooperate with the ICRC.[233]

Political more than legal were the reasons behind the UN's failure of an *ad hoc* humanitarian response by means of its human rights tools; indeed, the Expert in charge of the Special Process, Manfred Nowak, resigned on 26 March 1997 'because of lack of support by the international community for his efforts to clarify cases of disappearance by all available means, including exhumation of mortal remains'.[234] Following this decision, the confusion that characterized the approach of the Commission persisted, as it requested the Special Rapporteur on the situation of human rights in the former Yugoslavia, whose mandate was not humanitarian, to act on behalf of the UN in dealing with the issue of the missing.[235] Accordingly, the WGEID would no longer report to the Commission on any case of disappearance occurred until the date of the peace agreement – 14 December 1995 – and concerning Croatia and Bosnia and Herzegovina,[236] thereby indirectly depriving of any meaning the work carried out by the Special Process.

Confusion of humanitarian and accusatory mandates and the lack of a full support of the parties to the conflict led to a failure[237] of the efforts of UN Commission on Human Rights 'to effectively address the some 25.000 missing

---

[232] Nowak (n 57) 111; Nowak (n 222) 162.

[233] Cf. Article V, Annex 7, Dayton Agreements; see also WGEID, 'Special Process on Missing Persons in the Territory of the Former Yugoslavia (Third Report)' (n 225) para 35.

[234] WGEID, 'Report of the WGEID' (1998) UN Doc E/CN.4/1998/43 para 21.

[235] UN Commission on Human Rights, 'Resolution on the "Situation of Human Rights in Bosnia and Herzegovina, the Republic of Croatia and the Federal Republic of Yugoslavia (Serbia and Montenegro)"' (1997) UN Doc E/CN.4/RES/1997/57 para 41 (d).

[236] WGEID, 'Report of the WGEID' (n 234) para 22.

[237] The Expert who led the work of the Special Process thoroughly analyzed the main reasons that led to this result. In his words, 'one might conclude that the efforts of the UN Commission on Human Rights to effectively address the problem of some 25, 000 missing persons in the former Yugoslavia were by and large a failure. The Commission paid lip-service to the families of the missing by creating the so-called "special process", but it failed to give a precise definition to this mandate or to clearly distinguish it from that of the ICRC. Furthermore, the Commission did not respond effectively to the Expert's proposals to establish a high-level multilateral commission on missing persons and to carry out exhumations in order to clarify the fate of missing persons, nor did it provide the expert with the necessary political and financial support. The special process was successful only insofar as the Expert's reports and public activities managed to keep the issue on the political agenda of the international community and to exert some pressure on the various authorities in the former Yugoslavia to disclose relevant information. The reasons for the international community's failure to respond effectively to the problem of disappearances are purely political.' Nowak (n 222) 162.

persons in the former Yugoslavia'.[238] Although this might look as a minor incident along the process towards peace in the Former Yugoslavia, it denoted the lack of an institutionalized approach to the issue of missing persons at the UN level. Such an approach is far from being designed by the UN, despite recent talks on the issue at the UNSC level.[239]

2.1.2. The Committee on Missing Persons in Cyprus: The realization of the right to know in "slow-motion"

The application of the term "post-conflict" to the situation in Cyprus is incorrect, as the Turkish occupation is continuing and the tensions between the Greek Cypriots and the Turkish Cypriots are still unsolved.[240] Nevertheless, the peace process is ongoing since the mid-1970s; thus, the efforts to move realistically towards peace have been manifold and include the design of a more structured solution for the problem of the missing. The issue of missing persons in Cyprus has been characterized by major differences in the manners that the two communities – Turkish Cypriots and Greek Cypriots – regarded it.[241] Only in 1981, after a series of inter-communal consultations, the CMP was established under the auspices of the UN and with the consent of all parties.

The Committee, which is still functioning to date, has three Members: i.e., two appointed respectively by the Greek Cypriot and Turkish Cypriot communities and a third international Member selected by the ICRC and

---

[238] ibid.

[239] In the early 2016, the UK hosted an "Arria-formula meeting", i.e., a very informal, confidential gathering enabling the UNSC members to have a frank and private exchange of views, focused on missing persons. See 'Arria-Formula Meeting on Missing Persons' (*What's in Blue - Insights on the work of the UN Security Council*, 26 January 2016) <http://www.whatsinblue.org/2016/01/arria-formula-meeting-on-missing-persons.php> accessed 20 April 2017.

[240] Recent talks between the Greek Cypriots' leader - Nicos Anastasiades - and the Turkish Cypriots' leader - Mustafa Akinci - have been unsuccessful due to the existence of narrow differences on the territorial aspect of a possible deal. See Annyssa Bellal, *The War Report. Armed Conflicts in 2016* (The Geneva Academy of International Humanitarian Law and Human Rights 2017) 45–46. Tensions concerning oil and gas exploration off the east Mediterranean Island may lead to a stalemate; indeed, at the time of writing Turkey is opposing a unilateral Greek Cypriot search for hydrocarbons, since this would infringe upon the rights of Turkish Cypriots to the island's mineral wealth. Michele Kambas, 'Cyprus Leaders to Resume Peace Talks on April 11: UN' *Reuters - World News* (4 April 2017) <http://www.reuters.com/article/us-cyprus-conflict-talks-idUSKBN1761W3> accessed 30 April 2017; Menelaos Hadjicostis, 'UN Envoy: Cyprus Peace Talks at Risk from Possible "Crisis"' *Fox News - World* (11 May 2017) <http://www.foxnews.com/world/2017/05/11/un-envoy-cyprus-peace-talks-at-risk-from-possible-crisis.html> accessed 14 May 2017.

[241] Cassia points out that whereas Turkish Cypriots regarded their missing persons as disappeared/dead/lost, Greek Cypriots regarded their missing as having suffered an unknown fate, as living prisoners at best or, at worst, as concealed bodies requiring proper and suitable burials. PS Cassia, 'Recognition and Emotion. Exhumations of Missing Persons in Cyprus' in Yannis Papadakis, Nicos Peristianis and Gisela Welz (eds), *Divided Cyprus. Modernity, History, and an Island in Conflict* (Indiana University Press 2006) 195. Kovras highlights that until 2003 in the Republic of Cyprus (Greek part) the definition of missing persons enshrined in the legislation solely mentioned the Greek Cypriots; in 2003 a change in the policy approach to the issue determined that the definition encompassed "'any citizen of the Republic" instead of mentioning Greek Cypriots'. Kovras (n 145) 51.

appointed by the UNSG.[242] Pursuant to its mandate, 'the Committee will not attempt to attribute responsibility for the deaths of any missing persons or make findings as to the cause of such deaths'.[243] Thus, it is a purely humanitarian body that aims to recover, identify, and return to their families, the remains of those who went missing (502 Turkish Cypriots and 1,493 Greek Cypriots) during the inter-communal fighting of 1963 to 1964 and the events of 1974.[244] The humanitarian mandate has not facilitated the functioning of the Committee; inoperative over more than two decades, the Committee resumed its work in August 2004 after the resumption of negotiations between the two sides.

Among the scholars who have tried to understand the reasons why this stalemate lasted more than two decades, Cassia highlights that while "missing persons" was and still is a "humanitarian issue" in Cyprus, 'the way it has been dealt with is both an indication that humanitarian issues are easily "politicized" and politicizable'.[245] Cassia considers the following factors the main motives of the lack of exhumations for so many years: i) absence of trust due to the hostile interethnic relations; ii) the consensus-based CMP's system of decision rendered the international member a mere mediator and deprived him/her of independent means to exert pressure; iii) confidentiality as a working principle turned to be a 'euphemism for secrecy'; iv) despite the rejection of any accountability-based task, the likelihood of being held responsible prevented many from supporting the work of the CMP by means of their testimonies.[246]

Kovras explains that the passage of time, although not causally determinant, changed the normative context of decision-making at the executive level of all major actors involved.[247] For instance, Turkey's initial un-collaborative approach changed as a result of external factors, i.e., the improvement in the field of human rights was one of the factors that would be considered in the Turkey's process of accession to the EU;[248] intensification of the abidance by Turkey with the ECtHR's pronouncements occurred following the attribution to Turkey of the status of "candidate" for accession to the EU in 1999. With regard to Cypriot authorities, a decision of the Republic of Cyprus' Attorney General for the implementation of exhumations with the objective of identifying and returning the remains to the families without further legal proceedings contributed to increasing the support from the Turkish side to the resumption of the activities of

---

[242] CMP (Cyprus), 'Terms of Reference and Mandate of the CMP' (1981) pt 1 <http://www.cmp-cyprus.org/content/terms-reference-and-mandate> accessed 12 July 2016.

[243] ibid pt 11.

[244] CMP (Cyprus), 'About the CMP' (1981) <http://www.cmp-cyprus.org/content/about-cmp-0> accessed 12 July 2016.

[245] Paul Sant Cassia, '"Waiting for Ulysses": The Committee for Missing Persons' in Oliver P Richmond and James Ker-Lindsay (eds), *The Work of the UN in Cyprus* (Palgrave Macmillan UK 2001) 193.

[246] ibid 220–222.

[247] Kovras (n 145) 108, 115–118.

[248] See EU Commission, *Regular Report on Turkey's Progress towards Accession,* 13 November 2001, 30; *Regular Report on Turkey's Progress towards Accession,* 9 October 2002, 43; *Regular Report on Turkey's Progress towards Accession,* 10 October 2004, 51 in ibid 118.

the CMP.[249] This has transformed the CMP from an inactive body into a potential game-changer fostering reconciliation between the two sides. Since the resumption of its work in 2004, the Committee has decided 'to place emphasis on local participation and ownership' in the framework of the CMP proposed project focused on the exhumation, identification, and return of remains of missing persons; the aim is that of strengthening the project's positive impact on the broader reconciliation process.[250]

From a legal perspective, under the ECHR, the CMP's humanitarian mandate did not (and does not) waive the obligation of the State − Cyprus on the one hand and Turkey on the other − to carry out investigations into human rights violations. Indeed, the CMP is not 'a procedure of international investigation or settlement'[251] and cannot attribute responsibility for the deaths of any missing persons or make findings as to their cause.[252] The ECtHR has pointed out that '[a]lthough the CMP's procedures are undoubtedly useful for the humanitarian purpose for which they were established, they are not of themselves sufficient to meet the standard of an effective investigation [...]'.[253] The Court also clarifies that the cooperation of the State with a similar body does not *per se* discharge the State of its procedural obligation to carry out an investigation,[254] but the State 'may take the benefit of the work done by the CMP in this respect'.[255] The identification of the bodies represents a preliminary step towards the attribution of responsibility; indeed, 'the bodies having been identified, it falls to the authorities to uncover [...] the facts surrounding the death and the identities of any persons involved in unlawful acts in that regard.'[256]

2.2. Towards a global approach to missing persons?

Multiple are the international mechanisms that deal with missing persons-related issues from a global perspective;[257] nevertheless, only do the ICRC and

---

[249] ibid 108, 115–118, 121.

[250] Cf. UNSG, 'Report of the Secretary-General on the United Nations Operation in Cyprus' (2006) UN Doc S/2006/315 paras 28–29.

[251] ECommHR, *Varnava and Others v Turkey, Decision* (1998) App nos. 16064/90 and others 14.

[252] Pursuant to the Committee's Rules of Procedure, the Committee's investigation 'will be conducted in the sole interest of the families concerned and must therefore convince them'. Cf. ibid.

[253] ECtHR, *Cyprus v Turkey, Judgment (GC)* (2001) App no. 25781/94 [27, 135, 149]. Moreover, the CAT was not and is still not 'empowered to grant redress to the relatives of the missing persons'. CAT, 'Concluding Observations on the Fourth Report of Cyprus' (2014) UN Doc CAT/C/CYP/CO/4 para 21.

[254] CAT (n 253) para 21.

[255] Cf. ECtHR, *Emin (Mustafa) et al v Cyprus and six other applications, Decision* (2012) App no 59623/08 et al [32]. Nevertheless, the CAT has recognized that as a result of the identification of remains carried out by the CMP the Republic of Cyprus' Attorney General opened some criminal investigations. Nevertheless, the CAT has highlighted the shortcomings of the domestic system, as some relatives of missing persons had not been given the opportunity to challenge the acts or omissions of the investigating authorities in court. CAT (n 253) para 21.

[256] ECtHR, *Emin et al (Decision, 2012)* (n 255) [32].

[257] These include UNICEF and its work concerning missing children; the WGEID and its work on enforced disappearances; the CED and its work on enforced disappearances under ICPPED; various NGOs specialized in forensic investigations/medicine, including PHR, EAAF. Marco Sassòli and Jean-François Rioux, 'Study of Existing Mechanisms to Clarify the Fate of Missing People (Report

the ICMP address them in a substantively comprehensive manner. The former exists since the 19th century and pursues the broader mission to protect the lives and dignity of victims of armed conflict (including the missing and their families); the latter[258] has been globally active since 2004 and has become an international organization in 2014.[259]

The ICRC has played and continues to play an important role in supporting the efforts to account for persons reported as missing in armed conflict and situations of internal violence and in assisting with the transmission of information between the parties to the conflict and to the families.[260] Its work is purely humanitarian, i.e., the ICRC does not seek to establish the responsibility for the disappearance of individuals.

The ICMP is the only international organization whose work is exclusively focused on the issue of missing persons.[261] The organization has a strong RoL approach which requires States to take responsibility for missing persons cases.[262] Its purpose is to secure the cooperation of governments and other authorities in locating persons missing as a result of armed conflicts, human rights abuses, natural and man-made disasters and other involuntary reasons and to assist them in doing so.[263] This is the framework that is at the basis of the dual aim of the ICMP in post-conflict settings, i.e., ascertain the fate of the missing and promote peace, security, and reconciliation.[264]

Between 2002 and 2003 the ICRC carried out a study on the mechanisms to deal with persons unaccounted for: the findings of the experts who developed

---

and Recommendations) in the Framework of "The Missing: Action to Resolve the Problem of People Unaccounted for as a Result of Armed Conflict or Internal Violence and to Assist Their Families" (The Missing Project)' (2003) ICRC/TheMissing/01.2003/EN/9 12–15.

[258] The ICMP was established in 1996 at the G-7 Summit in Lyon at the initiative of the then US president Clinton and as part of the peace-building framework in the Former Yugoslavia. ICMP, 'Bosnia i Herzegovina. Missing Persons from the Armed Conflicts of the 1990s: A Stocktaking' (2014) 34.

[259] This means that the Commission will have full international legal personality. Cf. Article 1, Agreement on the Status and Functions of the International Commission on Missing Persons (hereinafter ICMP Framework Agreement), Brussels, 15 December 2014. Belgium, Luxembourg, the Netherlands, Sweden and the UK signed the Agreement on the Status and Functions of the ICMP, to establish the Commission as an international organization, with its headquarters in The Hague. The Agreement was subsequently also signed by Chile, Cyprus, El Salvador and Serbia. UNSG, 'Report of the Secretary-General - Missing Persons' (n 101) para 6.

[260] Article 33 AP I also refers to the Protecting Powers. The system was put in place during the Franco-Prussian war. See Eric David, *Principes de droit des conflits armés* (III, Bruylant 2002) 572–573. Although last applied during WWII (with the neutral States - Sweden and Switzerland - acting as protecting powers), 'the system persists mainly as 'law on the books'. See Frits Kalshoven and Liesbeth Zegveld, *Constraints on the Waging of War: An Introduction to International Humanitarian Law* (Cambridge University Press 2011) 69–70. Their role in the transmission of information is barely reported, for this activity has been carried out by the CTA.

[261] ICMP, 'About US' (2014) <https://www.icmp.int/about-us/> accessed 12 July 2016.

[262] ICMP, 'Conference Report', *The Missing: an Agenda for the Future (29 October – 1 November 2013), The Hague* 32.

[263] Cf. Article II, ICMP Framework Agreement.

[264] ICMP, 'Conference Report' (n 262) 34.

it showed that a worldwide system for missing persons did not exist at the time. The premise of their study was that

> an international system on the missing 'must be based on implicit or explicit rules. [...] The basic rule for every system working in the area under study is that disappearances must be avoided and that families are entitled to know what has happened to their loved ones. This rule brings with it some other paramount principles. [i.e., under IHRL, enforced disappearances are a grave violation of human rights, which it is especially important to prevent; in IHL, disappearances are considered to be an affront to the dignity of the individual; under international criminal law, the practice of instigating forced disappearances on a large scale is a crime against humanity].

> It is generally desirable that a system be underpinned by a central legal document specifying its aims and the respective roles of its components. In the case of the missing, it is possible to envisage the establishment of ... *international systems* based on incomplete treaties [...]. [I]deally, it would be preferable to adopt a central international document to provide guidelines for the establishment of national, regional and international systems.[265]

A uniform system reflecting the description above is still absent to date. The ICRC's (sub-section 2.2.1) and ICMP's (sub-section 2.2.2) perspectives shape two different courses of action. The sub-sections below aim at examining whether these two organizations can trigger the development of such a system. The analysis of their approach to the issue aims at shedding light upon whether, in the future, this system will build in humanitarian and accountability-based considerations, whether a single set of considerations will prevail, or whether two sets of considerations will drive two parallel systems which will be framed in mutually reinforcing/exclusive terms.

2.2.1. The ICRC's humanitarian approach to the missing and their families

Traditionally associated with armed conflicts and internal violence, since the 2003 ICRC-organized Conference dedicated to the issue of the missing, the scope of the ICRC action also includes those 'reported missing as a result of [...] any other situation that might require action by a neutral and independent body'[266] (e.g., natural disasters, migration or other humanitarian crises).[267] The ICRC, therefore, advocates for a broader interpretation of the terminology, as the families of all missing persons suffer regardless of the circumstances of the disappearance.[268]

Against this backdrop, the ICRC pursues a strictly humanitarian approach to the issue of the missing, i.e., the focus is on the needs of the families of the missing (including legal, administrative, socio-economic and psychological/psychosocial

---

[265] Sassòli and Rioux (n 257) 27–28.
[266] ICRC/IPU, *Missing Persons: A Handbook for Parliamentarians* (Inter-Parliamentary Union; ICRC 2009) 9.
[267] ICRC, *Living with Absence. Helping the Families of the Missing.* (ICRC 2014) 4; Andreas Wigger (ICRC), 'Building Local Capacity to Account for Missing Persons and Responding to the Needs of Their Relatives and Others' (The missing: an agenda for the future, The Hague, 30 October 2013) 2.
[268] Wigger (ICRC) (n 267) 2.

issues of the families) and on their right to know.[269] Accordingly, 'obtaining information from families of missing may prove to be easier if the purpose is only to clarify the fate of their missing relatives, because using such information simultaneously for criminal justice purposes may cause fears.'[270]

This approach is not accompanied by general operational guidelines, which would help understand how this tension between humanitarian-led and accountability-based courses of actions can reconcile. This gap, which has been acknowledged by the ICRC itself,[271] is still present to date.[272] The organization has contributed to addressing other gaps, e.g., the lack of uniformity or guidance on forensic investigations for humanitarian purposes, the lack of national legislation design guidelines on the issue of missing persons.[273] In addition to that, the ICRC has also strived to develop internal general operational guidelines.[274] And yet among the policy documents – i.e., documents that ensure that the ICRC is consistent over time, predictable and credible in its work – publicly accessible in its website, none is exclusively dedicated to persons unaccounted for in armed conflicts.[275]

The publicly accessible policy documents shed light upon i) the actions that the ICRC carries out in order to benefit separated family members, missing persons, and their families under its Protection Policy framework; ii) how the ICRC has tried to settle the dilemma concerning the handling of information arising when persons are missing as a result of grave breaches and other serious violations of IHL.[276]

---

[269] ibid 3.

[270] ICMP, 'Conference Report' (n 262) 28.

[271] Marco Sassòli and Marie-Louise Tougas, 'The ICRC and the Missing' (2002) 84 International Review of the Red Cross 727, 748; Sassòli and Rioux (n 257) 27–28; ICRC, 'Mechanisms to Solve Issues on People Unaccounted for (Final Report and Outcome) in the Framework of "The Missing: Action to Resolve the Problem of People Unaccounted for as a Result of Armed Conflict or Internal Violence and to Assist Their Families" (Hereinafter, 'The Missing Project)' (2002) ICRC/TheMissing/12.2002/EN/6 100.

[272] One of the reasons behind this *lacuna* might be the fact that in the ICRC's perspective the beneficiaries of protection activities (i.e., persons deprived of their liberty; the civilian population and other affected persons not in detention; separated family members or persons listed as missing) cannot be rigidly categorized; 'affected persons may benefit from both generic (on behalf of all three categories) and specific (on behalf of some but not all categories) protection activities.' See ICRC, 'ICRC Protection Policy. Institutional Policy' (2008) 90 International Review of the Red Cross 751, 765.

[273] ICRC, 'Operational Best Practices Regarding the Management of Human Remains and Information on the Dead by Non-Specialists in the Framework of 'The Missing Project'' (ICRC 2004); ICRC - Advisory Service on IHL, 'Guiding Principles: "Model Law on the Missing: Principles for Legislating the Situation of Persons Missing as a Result of Armed Conflict or Internal Violence. Measures to Prevent Persons from Going Missing and to Protect the Rights and Interests of the Missing and Their Families."' (2009).

[274] ICRC, 'Mechanisms to Solve Issues on People Unaccounted for (The Missing Project)' (n 271) 100.

[275] ibid.

[276] Originally drafted in 1981, Doctrine 15 ('Action by the ICRC in the Event of Violations of International Humanitarian Law or of Other Fundamental Rules Protecting Persons in Situations of Violence') spells out the ICRC's strategy for addressing IHL violations. Such strategy consists of four main steps: at the outbreak of an IAC, the ICRC reminds warring parties of their core obligations under IHL by means of an aide-mémoire (in NIAC, such document will be sent to the government and insurgent forces as well); then, the ICRC gathers information (in NIAC the ICRC must be invited by the government to operate) on the situation of victims, submits a detailed report to

As for the former, the work of the ICRC in the post-conflict phase is based on IHL, which does not stop applying in period of transition, i.e., 'a period of indeterminate duration which constitutes the prolongation of an armed conflict or situation of internal strife, in which armed confrontation has ended or at least entered a period of remission'.[277] It is in this indeterminate phase that missing persons and their families are among those who still benefit from the protection conferred by IHL and, consequently, from the services of the ICRC.

The organization is responsible, *inter alia,* for ensuring compliance with the IHL rules conferring protection (e.g., the obligation to clarify the fate of people whose disappearance has been notified by the adverse party).[278] Indeed, the ICRC underlines that 'its engagement [...] will last as long as is required by the situation of those it seeks to protect'.[279] The missing, their families, and separated family members are among the beneficiaries of ICRC's protection activities, the other being persons deprived of their liberty and the civilian population and other affected persons not in detention. 'Affected persons may benefit from both generic (in behalf of all three categories) and specific (in behalf of some but not all categories) protection activities'; therefore, the beneficiaries cannot rigidly be categorized.[280]

The traditional "protection activities[281]" that cover the issue of missing persons[282] are the visits to detained persons,[283] the protection of civilians affected by the conflict,[284] the restoration of family links[285] and the processing of tracing requests.[286] These activities[287] can take a number of different forms which can be

---

the States or armed groups, either during or after the conflict, and seeks to foster dialogue between the warring parties; as a third step, should the ICRC believe that the dialogue is not improving, it might consider to interact with other actors who may have influence on the parties (so-called 'mobilization efforts'); should the steps taken prove unsuccessful, the ICRC will abandon confidentiality and issue a public statement of censure (so-called 'public criticism'). In Steven R Ratner, 'Behind the Flag of Dunant: Secrecy and the Compliance Mission of the International Committee of the Red Cross' in Andrea Bianchi and Anne Peters (eds), *Transparency in International Law* (Cambridge University Press 2013) 301–302. See also ICRC, 'Action by the ICRC in the Event of Violations of IHL or of Other Fundamental Rules Protecting Persons in Situations of Violence' (2005) 87 International Review of the Red Cross 393.

[277] Marion Harroff-Tavel, 'Do Wars Ever End? The Work of the International Committee of the Red Cross When the Guns Fall Silent' (2003) 85 International Review of the Red Cross 465, 476. This article is among the policy-related documents of the ICRC; indeed, at the time it was written, its author was Deputy Director for International Law and Cooperation within the Movement at the ICRC.

[278] ibid 476–478. See, more generally, François Bugnion, *The International Committee of the Red Cross and the Protection of War Victims* (Macmillan Education 2003).

[279] ICRC, 'ICRC Protection Policy. Institutional Policy' (n 272) 762.

[280] ibid 765.

[281] ibid 765, 774.

[282] Sassòli and Tougas (n 271) 733–736.

[283] In IACs, cf. Articles 124 and 126, GC III; Articles 76, 142, and 143, GC IV. In NIACs, cf. common Article 3, GC I-IV (parties are encouraged to accept an ICRC offer to make such visits).

[284] Cf. Articles 10, 14, 59, 109, GC IV.

[285] Cf. Article 140, GC IV; Article 123, GC III; Article 78 (3) and Article 81, AP I.

[286] The CTA is devoted to managing the transmission of tracing requests. Cf. Article 4 (1) (e), ICRC Statutes. More broadly, this body acts as an intermediary between the parties to the conflict, and specifically, between the national Information Bureaux for the transmission of information on people

boiled down to five broad categories: provision of tracing services, establishment of mechanisms, adoption of legislation, development of forensic capacity and assessment of, and response to, the needs of the families of the missing.[288] The ICRC adapts such activities 'to the context and to the period of time that has elapsed since the persons concerned were reported missing. Some of these activities necessitate close collaboration with the authorities concerned and with all parties to the conflict.'[289]

For instance, the ICRC encourages the establishment of context-specific mechanisms by the parties concerned in order to meet the needs of the families and centralize the information on the missing at the domestic level; it also helps build their technical capacity in relation to forensic sciences by supporting local authorities and forensic practitioners (e.g., with specialized training) so that its forensic services reflect the local needs.[290] Therefore, by reuniting the members of separated families and by helping to ascertain the fate of the missing, the ICRC 'alleviates the suffering in which may lie the seeds of future conflicts;' hence, these activities help foster peace.[291]

With regard to the second policy approach, according to the ICRC Strategy vis-à-vis violations of IHL, confidentiality is a key factor for obtaining the best possible access to the victims of armed conflicts and other situations of violence. The aim of confidential representations with parties to the conflict is to convince those responsible for unlawful conduct to change their behavior and uphold their obligations.[292] Thus, 'the principle of confidentiality, on which the ICRC relies, refers to its practice not to disclose to third parties information that comes to the knowledge of its personnel in the performance of their functions.'[293] This means that confidentiality is applicable not only before judicial bodies but also towards

---

protected by IHL. Cf. Article 16, GC I; Article 19, GC II; Article 122, GC III; Articles 136, 137, 138, and 139, GC IV.

[287] Pursuant to its policy, 'the ICRC: determines its course of action after analyzing needs and estimating the length of its engagement; it also examines the causes of ruptures in contact and communication (e.g. displacement, restricted access to means of communication and family contact, absence of records of people who have been executed or who have died in detention); acts within a precise methodological framework and employs rigorous working procedures that demand the following: speed in processing cases (which requires the assistance of the Movement's Family News Network, reliability in data management and transmission, protection of personal data, which varies according to the situation and the amount of time that has passed; carries out, in addition to [restoration of family links - RFL], activities that aim to prevent the severance of family ties and to respond to the specific material and psychological needs of persons who are directly affected, as well as to the needs of their families'. ICRC, 'ICRC Protection Policy. Institutional Policy' (n 272) 773.

[288] ibid; ICRC, 'Presentation by the ICRC to the Committee on Juridical and Political Affairs' (Meeting of the Committee on Juridical and Political Affairs of the Permanent Council of the Organization of American States (Doc no OEA/Ser.G CP/CAJP/INF. 218/14), 5 March 2014) 1; Wigger (ICRC) (n 267) 3.

[289] ICRC, 'ICRC Protection Policy. Institutional Policy' (n 272) 773.

[290] Wigger (ICRC) (n 267) 3–4.

[291] Harroff-Tavel (n 277) 491.

[292] ICRC, 'Action by the ICRC in the Event of Violations of IHL or of Other Fundamental Rules Protecting Persons in Situations of Violence' (n 276) 395.

[293] ICTY, *Prosecutor v Simić et al, Decision on the Prosecution Motion under Rule 73 for a Ruling Concerning the Testimony of a Witness* (1999) Case no IT-95-9 [55].

other actors, individuals, and institutions. For instance, warring parties are likely to deny or restrict access of the ICRC, in particular to prisons and detention facilities, if they believe that an ICRC delegate may be collecting evidence for subsequent use in future criminal proceedings.[294] The same can occur in post-conflict situations where the ICRC can play the role of mediator in relation, *inter alia*, to the tracing of the missing and the transmission of information between the former warring parties.[295]

'Naming and shaming'[296] is not part of the working method of this organization, where confidentiality is paramount.[297] Indeed, the ICRC holds a privileged exemption from providing evidence in criminal proceedings[298] and 'a right under customary international law to non-disclosure of the information'.[299]

---

[294] Stéphane Jeannet, 'Recognition of the ICRC's Long-Standing Rule of Confidentiality' (2000) 82 International Review of the Red Cross 403.

[295] The ICRC contributed to establishing *ad hoc* bodies aimed at ascertaining the fate of the missing: see, for instance, the role of the ICRC in connection with the Tripartite Commission for Kuwait/Iraq (Cf. UNSC, 'Resolution 686 (Iraq)' (n 98) para 2 (c); UNSC, 'Resolution 687 (Iraq)' (n 98) paras 30–31); the establishment of the tripartite committee which was set up by a memorandum of understanding signed by Iran, Iraq and the ICRC in 2008 with regard to the issue of people missing in connection with the 1980-1988 Iran-Iraq War [see ICRC, 'Iran/Iraq: Efforts Continue to Clarify Fate of Missing from 1980-1988 War - ICRC (News Release 13/84)' (6 May 2013) </eng/resources/documents/news-release/2013/05-06-iran-iraq-missings.htm> accessed 8 February 2017]; the Working Group on missing persons in Kosovo, chaired by the ICRC, with the full agreement of the parties, where the ICRC insisted on obtaining a commitment from the authorities that they would deal with the issue of missing persons in earnest (Cf. ICRC, 'The Missing. ICRC Progress Report' (n 77) 13).

[296] Sivakumaran (n 15) 471; Ratner (n 276) 297.

[297] In order to have access to persons in need, it is important both to be neutral and to be perceived as neutral, i.e., as an actor who does not take side in the conflict. Neutrality is one of the seven Fundamental Principles of the International Red Cross and Red Crescent Movement on which the operational work of the ICRC is based, the other being, i.e., humanity, impartiality, independence, universality, unity, and voluntary service. Cf. Statutes of the International Red Cross and Red Crescent Movement, Article 4, para. 1 (a).

[298] The sources laying down the legal basis of this exemption are: the ICC Rules of Procedure and Evidence (Rule 73, paras 4-6) that uniquely confers this privilege upon the ICRC; headquarters agreements that provide for testimonial privileges in domestic proceedings; the Special Tribunal for Lebanon Rules of Procedure and Evidence (Rule 164); and the decision of the ICTY Trial Chamber in the case *Prosecutor v. Simić et al.* (1999).

[299] ICTY, *Prosecutor v. Simić et al.* (n 293) [74]. In his separate opinion on the Trial Chamber's decision of 1999, Judge Hunt questioned the customary nature of the absolute character of the ICRC's protection against disclosure: '[...] [h]as the acceptance by States to which the ICRC refers been that its protection should be treated as absolute by everyone, including the international criminal courts, or merely by the States themselves will support the absolute nature of the ICRC protection so far as they are able to give effects to it for example, by entering into agreements to provide an immunity in their own national courts? It is only if the former is the case that there would be a customary international law which binds [the ICTY]. [...] It is an enormous step to assume that the States had contemplated at the time of the Geneva Conventions the existence of a similar immunity in international criminal courts (created for the first time almost a half of a century later) [...]'. ICTY, *Prosecutor v Simić et al, Separate Opinion of Judge David Hunt on Prosecutors motion for a Ruling concerning the Testimony of a Witness* (1999) Case no IT-95-9 [22–23]. And yet the ICTY deemed as unique the ICRC's role in light of its function of protecting and assisting victims of armed conflicts coupled with rights solely granted to it (i.e., the right to be the substitute for a protecting power, the right to visit places of detention of POW and to interview prisoners, and the right of initiative in NIAC). ICTY, *Prosecutor v. Simić et al.* (n 293) [72]. Furthermore, in light of the GCs

311

The mutually beneficial collaboration with TJ mechanisms is, therefore, grounded on the foregoing approach (see sub-sect 2.2 in Chapter VI).

The policy guidelines outlining how the ICRC deals with the issue of the missing shed light on what it means to have a humanitarian approach that has a global reach[300] and that is prompted by the right of families to know the fate of their relatives. The foregoing analysis pinpoints the elements that characterize the terms of action of the ICRC when acting as humanitarian facilitator[301] upon direct request by the UN. In this capacity the ICRC has played a coordinating role vis-à-vis the efforts of the (former) parties to the conflict[302] and/or the international actors working on the issue of missing persons a specific context.[303]

2.2.2. The ICMP's global RoL approach to (all) missing persons

The ICMP's work started in the former Yugoslavia, as a 'blue-ribbon commission' established at a political summit 'to facilitate "high level moral and political interchange with those most directly involved in the resolution of difficult humanitarian issues associated with determining the fate of missing persons"'.[304] From a context-specific commission of experts, the ICMP evolved under several respects between 2003 and 2004: first, it expanded the geographical scope of its mandate and started working at the global level; second, it broadened its scope *ratione personae* by responding to cases of persons reported as missing in a variety of situations, including manmade and natural disasters, human rights violations, migration, armed conflicts, human trafficking, organized crime.[305]

The normative and conceptual baseline of the ICMP is represented by the international law-based distinction between missing persons and enforced disappearances. In the ICMP's perspective, this legal distinction defines the competencies of the different actors in missing persons scenarios: for instance,

---

IV and APs I and II, the Parties to these treaties have accepted the fundamental principles on which the ICRC operates (impartiality, neutrality and confidentiality); the have also accepted that 'confidentiality is necessary for the effective performance by the ICRC of its functions. [notes omitted].' ibid [72].

[300] The ICRC pursues the response to the problem of the missing in some 50 contexts across the globe. See Wigger (ICRC) (n 267) 3; ICRC, 'Presentation by the ICRC to the Committee on Juridical and Political Affairs' (n 288) 1.

[301] Harroff-Tavel (n 277) 472.

[302] For instance, this is the case for the CMP in Cyprus, the Tripartite Commission for Kuwait/Iraq; the Tripartite Committee for Iran/Iraq.

[303] For instance, this is the case for the Working Group on Missing Persons in Kosovo. In 2003, the Group was set up as part of the dialogue between the authorities of Pristina and Belgrade; since then, it has held its session under the auspices of the UN and has been chaired by the ICRC. Various observers have joined the work of the Working Group, including the ICMP, various diplomatic missions, and representatives of the families of Kosovo-Albanian and Kosovo-Serb. This is also the case of the Working Group on Missing Persons in Bosnia and Herzegovina. Established in 1996 following the Dayton Agreements, the Working Group saw the participation of the UN expert on missing persons, of the representatives of the Federal Republic of Yugoslavia, the Republic of Croatia, and the Governments of the Contact Group, association of families – all attending as observers. See Nowak (n 57) 112; ICRC, 'The Missing. ICRC Progress Report' (n 77) 13.

[304] ICMP, 'Bosnia i Herzegovina. A Stocktaking' (n 258) 34.

[305] ICMP, 'ICMP Framework Agreement: An Overview' <https://www.icmp.int/news/icmp-framework-agreement-an-overview/> accessed 2 July 2016.

'[m]issing persons as a consequence of disasters […] are seen primarily as a responsibility of the police, whereas following armed conflict the issue has for a long time been regarded as the competency of parties to such conflicts'.[306] If contextualized in armed conflict settings, this distinction, engenders 'dichotomies between conflict-related humanitarian approaches and RoL-based responses by police, prosecutors and courts.'[307]

According to the ICMP, as a result of the establishment of the ICTY in 1993 and of its mandate in 1996, the RoL approach took precedence in the former Yugoslavia.[308] Although the humanitarian support was deemed important, the RoL/accountability-based processes provided a more 'unified and inclusive response linking support for families with efforts to locate and identify the missing and, in turn, with the overall process of rebuilding a war-torn society'.[309] However, as shown in previous sections, the total lack of attempts to reconcile the humanitarian facet of the issue of the missing with the RoL/accountability facet has resulted in discrepancies of policies with direct negative implications for the families of those affected or for the process aimed at ascertaining the fate of the missing.

The shift undertaken in the early 2000s has allowed the ICMP to pave the way for becoming a potential catalyzer of global action concerning all the missing persons, i.e., persons reported missing following a variety of causes including, but not limited to, armed conflicts. This holistic approach is reflected in the Framework Agreement signed in 2014 that transformed the ICMP in an international organization. The main working pillars of the "new" ICMP revolves around technical capacity-building[310] vis-à-vis the governments in addressing the issue of missing persons as well as promotion of the cooperation of governments and others in relation to missing persons-related aspects, i.e., institutional capacity-building,[311] encouragement of public involvement,[312] and the response to the need for justice.

---

[306] ICMP, 'Bosnia I Herzegovina. A Stocktaking' (n 258) 21.

[307] ibid.

[308] Knut Vollebaek, 'Speech by ICMP Commissioner' (Peace Research Institute Oslo - Roundtable event, 11 June 2014) <https://www.icmp.int/wp-content/uploads/2014/08/icmp-dg-846-3-doc-speech-by-commissioner-vollebaek-roundtable-oslo-12th-june-2014.pdf> accessed 12 June 2016.

[309] ICMP, 'Bosnia I Herzegovina. A Stocktaking' (n 258) 21.

[310] The technical assistance program is a global tool available to governments and others engaged in addressing the issue of persons reported missing in armed conflicts, natural disasters, human rights violations, organized violence and other causes. This tool consists of three main mechanisms, i.e., a standing capacity to conduct high-throughput DNA identifications; forensic archeology and anthropological division; and a custom-designed identification data management system.

[311] The range of activities concerning this aspect in the context of armed conflicts includes the development of: a State structure willing to deal with past atrocities in a non-discriminatory manner; purpose-specific legislation focused on the provision of rights and protections for the families; specialized war crimes and human rights capacity; the use of forensic evidence in criminal trials; reliable information sharing mechanisms between authorities and families and the public; the active engagement of families of the missing and society at large. Apart from the Libyan Identification Center and the Law on the Protection of Mass Graves in Iraq, the other pragmatic examples of these activities are geographically located in the Balkans (e.g., the Missing Persons Institute of Bosnia and Herzegovina; The Kosovo Commission on Missing Persons; The Law on Missing Persons in Bosnia

Thus, the rights of victims of gross violations of human rights to truth and justice prompt the ICMP's action, i.e., assistance to justice institutions, including the international and domestic criminal justice system by providing expert evidence and other specialized forensic capacity.[313] The new phase of the work of the ICMP as global action catalyzer started with the 2016 Memorandum of Understanding (MoU) with the Office of the Prosecutor (OTP) of the ICC[314] sanctioning the beginning of a mutually beneficial relationship. The underpinning principle of the MoU is that States bear the primary responsibility to account for missing persons and to prosecute the most serious crimes under international law. Within this framework, the OTP and the ICMP share the efforts to assist victims of the most serious crimes and to contribute to reinforcing the RoL at the national and international level.[315] To this end, the sharing of information between the two institutions is the core of the MoU: pursuant to Article 5, the OTP can request the ICMP to provide information in its 'custody, possession or control which was disclosed to it in confidence by a State or an intergovernmental, international or non-governmental organization or an individual'.[316] To this end, 'the ICMP shall seek the consent of the originator [...] or, *where appropriate, will inform the OTP that it may seek the consent of the originator* [...] [emphasis added]'.[317] More generally, while the principle of confidentiality covers the work of the ICRC vis-à-vis the work of the ICC – the sharing of information being an exception,[318] the mutual exchange of documents and information is at the basis of the relationship between the ICC's OTP and the ICMP. Thus, the international agenda of the ICMP can complement, but not substitute, a humanitarian course of action.

---

and Herzegovina; and Central Records of Missing Persons in Bosnia and Herzegovina). See ICMP, 'Institutional Development' (18 June 2014) <https://www.icmp.int/what-we-do/institutional-development/> accessed 12 July 2016.

[312] The range of activities concerning this aspect in the context of armed conflicts includes: the promotion of active participation of civil society and families of the missing through training and grant making programs aimed at empowering family members and others. No examples of such activities are provided in the ICMP's website. See ICMP, 'Public Involvement' (18 June 2014) <https://www.icmp.int/what-we-do/public-involvement-civil-society-initiatives/> accessed 12 July 2016.

[313] ICMP, 'Assistance to Justice' (18 June 2014) <https://www.icmp.int/what-we-do/assistance-to-justice/> accessed 12 July 2016.

[314] Memorandum of Understanding between the ICMP and the Office of the Prosecutor of the ICC, signed in The Hague, 7 July 2016 (hereinafter ICC/ICMP MoU).

[315] ICC, 'ICC Office of the Prosecutor and the International Commission on Missing Persons Sign Memorandum of Understanding (ICC-CPI-20160707-PR1230)' (7 July 2016) <http://www.icc-cpi.int/Pages/item.aspx?name=PR1230> accessed 9 February 2017.

[316] Article 5, ICC/ICMP MoU.

[317] Article 5, ICC/ICMP MoU. The provision does not make use of a mandatory language (although 'shall' results to be stronger than 'may') in relation to the consent of the originator.

[318] Pursuant to Rule 73 of the ICC Rules of Procedure and Evidence, information/documentation/evidence held by the ICRC is regarded as privileged and as such not subject to disclosure unless the ICRC has waived such privilege and/or such information is contained in public statement. Moreover, if the information is considered of great importance for a case, the ICC and the ICRC will hold consultation to resolve the problem. Cf. Rule 73 (4-6), ICC, 'Rules of Procedure and Evidence, Official Records of the Assembly of States Parties to the Rome Statute of the International Criminal Court, First Session, Part II.A' (2002) ICC-ASP/1/3 and Corr.1.

The ICMP has not denied the existing difference in carrying out its activities compared to others' work (including the ICRC);[319] in light of the relatively recent shift from a local to a global reach of its services, it is too early to be conclusive with regard to whether the recent agreements with other international organizations[320] would result in a network of stakeholders willing to assist each other in the work concerning the missing or in an international systematized approach founded on common standards, principles, and rules relating to the missing. Organizations like the ICMP can therefore contribute to restoring the capacity of the State to abide by its obligations under international law, including, for instance, the obligation to carry out an investigation into human rights violations.

Conclusions

This Chapter's main argument is that the international measures aimed at accounting for missing persons in the context of peace processes must be prompted by the right of families to know the fate of relatives, i.e., the core of the legal framework concerning the quest for information of the families of missing persons. However, depending on the peace-making process and its outcome, the issue of the missing has/has not a prominent place in the efforts aimed at "constructing" peace.

Peace agreements form an integral part of the international legal framework and, as such, set down the guidelines and principles that regulate the relationship between the former parties to the conflict, the interaction of these with other external actors (e.g., the ICRC, the UN), and the terms under which new entities must be set up in order to address the consequences of the conflict. The secondary place or the absence of the issue of missing persons in these documents has a direct impact on how the issue is addressed on the ground.

Moreover, those UNSC resolutions, which set up peace operations in the context of a conflict situation or in a post-conflict context, outline the terms of action, principles, and guidelines that serve the purpose of delimiting the mandate of these operations and their relationship with domestic authorities, former parties to the conflict, and external actors. Whenever peace operations are exposed to the issue of missing persons the organization must act consistently with the obligation to respect the right of families to know the fate of their

---

[319] ICMP, 'Bosnia i Herzegovina. A Stocktaking' (n 258) 21.
[320] Apart from the ICC/ICMP Agreement, prior to 2014 (when the ICMP became an international organization), the ICMP signed a Cooperation Agreement with the International Organization for Migration (IOM) centered on cooperation (i.e., consultation and coordination) between the two organizations in relation to matters of common interest (i.e., missing persons as a result of migration, displacement or human trafficking; DNA testing in the framework of family reunification; research). Cf. ICMP/IOM, 'Cooperation Agreement between the ICMP and the International Organization for Migration – IOM' (2013). Moreover, it also signed a Cooperation Agreement with INTERPOL focused on cooperation (i.e., mutual consultation, exchange of information, and technical cooperation) between the two organizations in the field of disaster victim identification. ICMP/INTERPOL, 'Co-Operation Agreement between the ICMP and the International Criminal Police Organization – INTERPOL' (2007).

relatives. Nevertheless, in those situations where the UN is involved in the restoration of the RoL of the country and/or is temporarily managing the *res publica,* the organization has the obligation to account for missing persons and to inform their families. The 2003 UN Handbook on UN multidimensional peacekeeping operations does not touch on the issue of missing persons or that of their families, although other vulnerable categories are part of the handbook (e.g., IDPs and refugees).[321] This confirms the lack of an institutionalized approach to this issue at the UN level, despite the recurring involvement of UN peace operations in dealing with missing persons.[322]

The Chapter posits that a shared and comprehensive agenda, which integrates the tenets of the international legal framework on missing persons, can be conducive to the realization of the right of families to know the fate of their relatives. Past and ongoing international attempts aimed at the formulation of normative and policy responses globally and *ad hoc* have been reviewed in order to understand whether a similar global program is *in statu nascendi.*

Attempts to realize the right of families to know the fate of their relatives have been part of the UN human rights and humanitarian *ad hoc* measures aimed at handling the issue of missing persons in conflict/post-conflict situations. The example of the UN Special Process for the missing in the Former Yugoslavia is

---

[321] UNDPKO - Peacekeeping Best Practices Unit (n 150) 169 ff.

[322] For instance, in the context of the post-Iraq/Kuwait conflict, it is reported that Iraqi officials had received assistance from the UN Iraq-Kuwait Observation Mission (UNIKOM) in locating and accessing gravesites of Iraqi soldiers within the demilitarized zone. The Mission, established in 1991 following the forced withdrawal of Iraqi forces from Kuwait, was mandated to monitor the demilitarized zone along the Iraq-Kuwait border, to deter border violations, and to report on any hostile action. UN Department of Public Information, *The Yearbook of the United Nations,* vol 54 (United Nations 2000) 296. In its efforts to prevent the escalation of tensions in the zone of conflict and to facilitate dialogue between Georgia and Abkhazia, the UN Observer Mission in Georgia (UNOMIG, 1993-2009) monitored the subsequent commitments undertaken after the ceasefire with regard to an effective cooperation on missing persons between the two parties. UNOMIG's mandate was focused on the verification of compliance with the ceasefire agreement between the Government of Georgia and the Abkhaz authorities in Georgia. See UNSG, 'Report of the Secretary-General on the Situation in Abkhazia, Georgia' (2008) UN Doc S/2008/38 paras 4–5; UNOMIG (n 73). In 1996 the UNSC established UNTAES, a peacekeeping operation with both military and civilian components, as provided for in the peace settlement - the 1995 Basic Agreement - between Croatia and the local Croatian Serb authorities. The Basic Agreement - which delineated the scope of action of UNTAES - did not mention the issue of missing persons; however, UNTAES was particularly active vis-à-vis this issue in the broader framework of the commitment of both parties to reconciliation. Specifically, UNTAES 'sought to defuse the politically sensitive issue of missing persons in the region by facilitating the efforts of a tripartite (Croats, Serbs, UNTAES) missing persons commission.' Its role also consisted in providing organizational and investigative oversight and security, acting 'as a buffer between the parties during these often emotional activities', and in providing 'objective information to an often exploitative and inflammatory press'. It also succeeded in mediating between the parties and in reaching an agreement for the inclusion of Serbs into the regional Croatian missing persons sub-commission. Cf. UNSG, 'Report of the Secretary-General on the UN Transitional Administration for Eastern Slavonia, Baranja and Western Sirmium' (1997) UN Doc S/1997/767 para 21. See also UNSC, 'Resolution 1037' (1996) UN Doc S/RES/1037 paras 1–2; UNGA/UNSC, 'Letter Dated 15 November 1995 from the Permanent Representative of Croatia to the UN Addressed to the UNSG. Annex - Basic Agreement on the Region of Eastern Slavonia, Baranja, and Western Sirmium' (1995) UN Doc A/50/757-S/1995/951.

indicative of the fact that the design of the mandate of an *ad hoc* measure is not sufficient to address the issue; indeed, the involvement of the parties (or former parties) to the conflict and the support of the international community are essential factors for the success of the measure. The CMP, established under the auspices of the UN, enabled the parties to agree on a common path to be followed with regard to the issue of missing persons in the context of the process towards peace in Cyprus. However, the definition of the issue of missing persons as a purely humanitarian issue[323] has shown its limitations in both examples. More generally, in contexts where ethnic claims clash against each other, multiple considerations – including accountability claims, political agendas, cultural and definitional discrepancies in the approach to the issue – must be seen through the prism of different sets of norms that coexist and regulate the conduct of different actors. The partial failure of the operational *ad-hocism* is imputable to the absence of a globally harmonized operational and normative system focused on the duty to account for missing persons; the secondary place left to missing persons in the context of peace agreements and UNSC resolutions is a direct consequence of this absence.

Tensions still exist in the framing of a global approach to (all) missing persons as the examination of the *modus operandi* of the ICRC and ICMP shows. It has been argued that normative and operational harmonization vis-à-vis the issue of missing persons depends on semantic and terminological uniformity.[324] However, terminological uniformity can be ambiguous where cases of enforced disappearances are present. Indeed, IHRL rules concerning enforced disappearance and IHL rules concerning missing persons maintain their distinct features; yet as Chapter III has demonstrated, these rules are complementary and can simultaneously apply. At the operational level, whenever a compartmentalized – i.e., purely humanitarian or purely accountability/RoL-driven – understanding of the issue of missing persons prevails, unsatisfactory responses are provided to the families. Thus, operational complementarity should reflect the normative complementarity between the rules concerning the missing. From an operational perspective, complementarity can be translated in terms of sequencing of actions to be undertaken in light of a coordinated implementation of humanitarian– and accountability-based approaches to the issue of missing persons.[325]

---

[323] See, for instance, UNSC, 'Resolution 1568 (Cyprus)' (2004) UN Doc S/RES/1568 Preamble; UNSC, 'Resolution 1548 (Cyprus)' (2004) UN Doc S/RES/1548 Preamble; UNSG, 'Report of the Secretary-General on the United Nations Operation in Cyprus' (2004) UN Doc S/2004/427 para 13.

[324] Professor Sarkin, the only scholar advocating for this approach, argues that at the international level the present definition of missing persons is too narrow, as it includes people missing as a result of armed conflict; thus, he contends that the definition ought to be holistic so as to facilitate a global understanding of its scope, thereby facilitating the establishment of a global response to it (at the normative and institutional level). See J Sarkin, 'The Need to Deal with All Missing Persons Including Those Missing as a Result of Armed Conflict, Disasters, Migration, Human Trafficking, and Human Rights Violations (Including Enforced Disappearances) in International and Domestic Law and Processes' (2015) 8 Inter-American and European Human Rights Journal (IAEHR) 112.

[325] As Chapter VI will show, that the RoL approach is the one to be followed whenever the issue of missing arises in conflict/post-conflict settings appears to be unrealistic. For instance, in Bosnia and Herzegovina the "RoL approach" started functioning with the progressive restoration of the justice system put in place after the adoption of the Dayton Agreements.

CHAPTER VI.

THE FAMILIES' QUEST FOR INFORMATION
ON THEIR MISSING RELATIVES:
THE (POTENTIAL) CONTRIBUTION OF "JUSTICE IN TRANSITION"

The attainment of peace is not the result of a fixed strategy or procedure that must be followed after an armed conflict, but 'encompasses a wide range of policy options, some of which could be combined'.[1] Despite the innumerable variety of combinations, '[i]f peace is not intended to be a brief interlude between conflicts, then, in order to avoid future conflict, it must encompass what justice is intended to accomplish: prevent, deter, punish, and rehabilitate.'[2] Thus, there is not a unique combination of accountability-driven mechanisms, since a range of mechanisms can be viable as well as multiple combinations of these.[3] In transition periods[4] the combination of mechanisms is, therefore, chosen to achieve a multifaceted outcome which embraces justice, 'wherever possible, reconciliation, and ultimately, peace.'[5]

Against this backdrop, peace processes should not solely be treated as political ones, but also as a legal phenomenon.[6] The present Chapter intends to look at the issue of missing persons through the prism of an essential component of these processes, i.e., "justice in transition". The aim will be to answer the question of whether "justice in transition" can be one of the pillars of a global system meant to address uncertainty about the fate of missing persons in the transition process from an armed conflict to peace. To this end, the Chapter will

---

[1] M Cherif Bassiouni, 'Searching for Peace and Achieving Justice: The Need for Accountability' (1996) 59 Law and Contemporary Problems 9, 13.

[2] ibid.

[3] ibid 23; AM La Rosa and X Philippe, 'Transitional Justice' in Vincent Chetail (ed), *Post-conflict Peacebuilding: a Lexicon* (Oxford University Press 2009) 371 ff; Carsten Stahn, 'The Geometry of Transitional Justice: Choices of Institutional Design' (2005) 18 Leiden Journal of International Law 425, 428 ff.

[4] By transition La Rosa and Philippe mean a change from one state to another. La Rosa and Philippe (n 3) 369. Transition is also defined as 'a period of indeterminate duration which constitutes the prolongation of an armed conflict or situation of internal strife, in which armed confrontation has ended or at least entered a period of remission. Skirmishes may still take place, but a process of stabilization, at times temporary, has been set in motion'. See Marion Harroff-Tavel, 'Do Wars Ever End? The Work of the International Committee of the Red Cross When the Guns Fall Silent' (2003) 85 International Review of the Red Cross 465, 466.
do wars ever end, 466

[5] Bassiouni, 'Searching for Peace and Achieving Justice' (n 1) 23.

[6] See C Stahn, 'Jus Post Bellum: Mapping the Discipline(s)' in Carsten Stahn and Jann K Kleffner (eds), *Jus Post Bellum: Towards a Law of Transition From Conflict to Peace* (Springer Verlag 2008) 101.

unveil the operational tenets of "justice in transition" bodies when mandated to deal with/incidentally confronted with the issue of missing persons.

By building in the premises laid down in Chapter I, the present Chapter will investigate the mandate of selected examples of TJ bodies that have operated in post-conflict settings, how their *modus operandi* has integrated/addressed the issue of missing persons, and what implications the foregoing has had on the families' quest for information (section 1). The temporary character of these bodies is one of the reasons why the Chapter will broaden the scope of the analysis and examine the work of international justice bodies, i.e., permanent judicial and quasi-judicial bodies (section 2). With regard to the latter, this Chapter will show that their work can positively impact on the design of the domestic approach to the issue of the missing; at the same time, it will demonstrate that their work can have a positive effect on the efforts for the achievement of an enduring peace, particularly when it enables the families to be an active part of the process aimed at establishing what happened.

1. PEACE OR JUSTICE? A FALSE DILEMMA

The dilemma peace or justice dates back to the ancient times;[7] for the sake of peace, justice was put aside or restrained. The work of the International Military Tribunals of Nuremberg and Tokyo in the aftermath of WWII determined a shift[8] towards holding perpetrators accountable for international crimes;[9] in more recent times, the creation of the *ad hoc* tribunals (ICTY/ICTR) and of hybrid courts shows the international community's commitment to end impunity with and contribute to the achievement of a sustainable peace.[10]

---

[7] In 404 BC, after the defeat of the Athenian tyrants, General Thrasybulus forbade the punishment of political acts committed against the tyrants in order to foster oblivion; in the 17th century, Grotius' *De jure belli ac pacis* held that in the aftermath of a war it was not fitting to follow up former wrongs in peace (Ch XX, para XVII); indeed, from the 1648 Westphalia Peace Treaty on until 19th century, peace treaties provided for amnesty clauses. See Seibert-Fohr A., 'Transitional Justice in Post-Conflict Situations' in Rüdiger Wolfrum and Frauke Lachenmann (eds), *The Law of Armed Conflict and the Use of Force. The Max Plank Encyclopedia of Public International Law*, vol 2 (Oxford University Press 2017) 1225 <http://www.mpepil.com>.

[8] The shift, which started, after WWII is also enshrined in the UN Charter: pursuant to its preamble, 'the peoples of the UN' are 'determined [...] to save succeeding generations from the scourge of war, which twice in our lifetime has brought untold sorrow to mankind'. Cf. Preamble, UN Charter. The drafters intended to stress that the creation of the UN was a response to the two world wars, but also that it was the intention of the member States of the UN to suppress the war. Indeed, all delegates accepted the wording above at the San Francisco Conference. The peoples of the UN are also determined 'to establish conditions under which justice and respect for the obligations arising from treaties and other sources of international law can be maintained'. The term 'justice' means something different from 'treaties and other sources...' and, in this sense, there seems to be a direct reference to 'natural law'. R Wolfrum, 'Preamble' in Bruno Simma and others (eds), *The Charter of the United Nations - A Commentary* (3rd edn, Oxford University Press 2002) 103–104.

[9] Seibert-Fohr A. (n 7) 1226.

[10] States have further confirmed this commitment with the adoption of the Rome Statute and the establishment of the ICC. ibid.

As noted in Chapter I, the process from war towards peace is not aimed at bringing back the *status quo ante*. Thus, responding to the need for justice against the wrongdoings committed by all parties during the conflict sets aside the idea that the victors go unpunished. The issue of missing persons is not exogenous to debate on peace and/or justice for two reasons: i) establishing the fate of those reported as missing is one of the means for the achievement of peace and reconciliation;[11] ii) most of the times, persons are reported as missing in the context of IHRL and/or IHL violations committed during the conflict,[12] which cannot remain unpunished.

Goldstone notes that '[t]he merit in securing justice...is that it provides a procedure for exposing the truth'; such exposure allows that public and official acknowledgment is brought to the victims.[13] However, he also acknowledges that 'one must not expect too much from justice', as it represents 'one aspect of a many-faceted approach needed to secure enduring peace in a transitional society'.[14] The practice shows that efforts to account for missing persons are part of humanitarian[15] and accountability-driven[16] courses of action that characterize the peace process.

It is self-evident that no one can argue that peace 'is... preferable to a state of violence. But the attainment of peace is not necessarily to the exclusion of justice, because justice is frequently necessary to attain peace.'[17] The reason for this consideration resides in the fact that '"justice" is often conceived of as an ideal of accountability and fairness in the protection and vindication of rights and the prevention and punishment of wrongs.'[18] Accordingly, peace and justice are not mutually exclusive objectives, but 'rather mutually reinforcing imperatives'; as such they require careful integration and sensible sequencing of activities. Approaches focusing only on one or another institution, or ignoring civil society

---

[11] See the South African Promotion of National Unity and Reconciliation Act No. 34 of 1995, s 3(1)(c). See also UNSG, 'Report of the Secretary General - Missing Persons' (2014) UN Doc A/69/293 para 71; ICMP, 'Conference Report', *The Missing: an Agenda for the Future (29 October – 1 November 2013), The Hague* 7–8.

[12] Monique Crettol and Anne-Marie La Rosa, 'The Missing and Transitional Justice: The Right to Know and the Fight against Impunity' (2006) 88 International Review of the Red Cross 355, 356.

[13] Richard J Goldstone, 'Justice as a Tool for Peace-Making: Truth Commissions and International Criminal Tribunals' (1995) 28 New York University Journal of International Law and Politics 485, 486, 489.

[14] ibid 486.

[15] See Colombia/FARC-EP, Acuerdo Final para la Terminación del Conflicto y la Construcción de una Paz estable y duradera, Bogotá, November 24, 2016 (hereinafter Acuerdo Final), at 141.

[16] Cf. ibid; FARC-EP International, 'Joint Communiqué No 62 on Missing Persons' (*FARC-EP International*) <https://farc-epeace.org/index.php/communiques/joint-communiques/item/879-joint-communique-62-on-missing-persons> accessed 7 September 2018. Interestingly, the Colombian Peace Agreement stresses that for the purpose of structuring the 'Special Unit for the Search of Persons deemed as Disappeared within the context and due to the armed conflict' both the ICMP and ICRC will provide recommendations and suggestions, thereby underlining the complementarity of the accountability-driven and humanitarian approaches. See Colombia/FARC-EP, Acuerdo Final para la Terminación del Conflicto (n 15), 142.

[17] Bassiouni, 'Searching for Peace and Achieving Justice' (n 1) 12.

[18] UNSG, 'Report on the Rule of Law and Transitional Justice in Conflict and Post-Conflict Societies' (2004) UN Doc S/2004/616 para 7.

or victims, will not be effective'.[19] In this respect, UN-endorsed peace agreements 'can never promise amnesties for genocide, war crimes, crimes against humanity or gross violations of human rights'.[20]

The motto 'there is no peace without justice' finds its normative grounds in IHRL and IHL. IHRL adjudicatory bodies do not leave room to those who would advocate for amnesties vis-à-vis serious violations of IHRL: amnesty laws covering forced disappearance, genocide, torture, and crimes against humanity have been deemed in violation of human rights treaties.[21] Furthermore, IHL provides for a duty to prosecute grave breaches of both GCs and AP I.[22] Article 6 (5) AP II is one of the few provisions that explicitly refer to the post-conflict phase ('at the end of hostilities'); specifically, it does so in relation to the opportunity for the authorities in power 'to grant the broadest possible amnesty to persons who have participated in the armed conflict'. Interpreting this provision as the legal basis for amnestying violations of IHL and IHRL in post-NIAC settings[23] does not reflect the intention of the parties to AP II.[24] Neither does it reflect the ICRC's interpretation which sees the provision as 'the equivalent in the law of [NIAC] of what is known in the law of [IAC] as "combatant immunity"',[25] i.e., a sort of protection for having taken part to the hostilities against the government, but not for having perpetrated any IHL or IHRL violation.

This premise serves the purpose of introducing TJ bodies and the impact of their work on the issue of the missing as a key component of the process towards an enduring peace. This section will first illustrate selected examples where the TJ bodies' work has directly/incidentally impacted on the issue of missing persons (sub-section 1.1); then, it will reflect upon the divergences that can arise between the need of families to know the fate of their relatives and the efforts to establish the (judicial) truth through the prism of the ICTY's example (sub-section 1.2). Finally, it will clarify whether the response to the individual need

---

[19] The UN approach proposes the triad 'justice, peace, and democracy'. See ibid Executive Summary; UNSG, 'Report of the Secretary-General on Enhancing Mediation and Its Support Activities' (2009) UN Doc S/2009/189 paras 35–36.

[20] UNSG, 'Report of the Secretary-General on Enhancing Mediation' (n 19) para 36. Pursuant to the UNSC Resolution 827, the establishment of the ICTY would contribute to putting an end to IHL violations, bringing to justice the persons who are responsible for them, and restoring and maintaining peace. UNSC, 'Resolution 827 (ICTY)' (1993) UN Doc S/RES/827 Preamble.

[21] See among others IACtHR, *Barrios Altos v Peru, Judgment - Merits* (2001) Series C no. 75 [41].

[22] Cf. Article 49 GC I, Article 50 GC II, Article 129 GC III, Article 146 GC IV, Article 75 (7) AP I.

[23] See El Salvador, Supreme Court Of Justice Decision on the Amnesty Law, Proceedings no. 10-93 (May 20, 1993) in Neil J Kritz, *Transitional Justice: How Emerging Democracies Reckon with Former Regimes*, vol III (United States Institute of Peace Press 1995) 549–555.

[24] 'The *travaux préparatoires* of [article] 6(5) indicate that this provision aims at encouraging amnesty, i.e., a sort of release at the end of hostilities, for those detained or punished for the mere fact of having participated in hostilities. It does not aim at an amnesty for those having violated [IHL]'. See Letter from Dr Toni Pfanner (Head of the Legal Division, ICRC Headquarters, Geneva) to the ICTY Prosecutor of 24 November 1995 and to the Department of Law at the University of California of 15 April 1997 in Douglass Cassel, 'Lessons from the Americas: Guidelines for International Response to Amnesties for Atrocities' (1996) 59 Law and Contemporary Problems 197, 218.

[25] ibid.

for information on a relative's fate is diametrically opposed to the realization of the collective right to truth (sub-section 1.3).

1.1. The issue of the missing through the prism of international/ internationalized Transitional Justice

The proliferation of international justice mechanisms in post-conflict environments has generated a scholarly debate about the reasons behind this increasing trend. In her seminal work on the genealogy of TJ, Teitel provides a two-pronged explanation of this trend, arguing that the current phase of TJ features a resurgence of international justice after WWII.[26] TJ is becoming the paradigm of the RoL and, as such, is the norm and not the exception due to the contemporary conditions of persistent conflict that are the basis for the normalization of the 'law of violence'.[27] Stahn, instead, attributes this trend to a move towards institutionalism in international law more generally;[28] a system of entities (e.g., national, international, mixed entities) is seen as the tool to overcome the challenges posed by the transition from conflict to peace.

The normalization of the 'law of violence' excludes the very possibility of moving from conflict to peace, since the former is the norm; this contradicts the conceptual explanations and pragmatic examples considered in this book. The international facet of justice in transition reflects the intention of the international community to react to mass atrocities by means of, *inter alia,* temporary judicial tools.[29] In this sense, international/internationalized approaches are considered more viable in contexts where ethnic conflicts or group-oriented oppression continue to divide a society 'where there is no clear break in regime and where the justice system lacks capacity, legitimacy or independence'.[30] Stahn considers that this 'multilateralist approach' to TJ can be of help in transition, 'provided that both the timing of involvement and the distinct mandates of the different players are sufficiently well defined in advance and co-ordinated in practice'.[31] Other scholars are less optimistic in relation to the positive impact that the international component can have: while assistance from the international community appears to be necessary 'in the absence of domestic willingness or capacity', the transitional process should be locally designed, owned, and implemented; this is in line with the emphasis that the traditional view of TJ puts on the human rights framework.[32]

---

[26] Ruti G Teitel, 'Transitional Justice Genealogy' (2003) 16 Harvard Human Rights Journal 69, 70-73.

[27] Ruti G Teitel, 'Transitional Justice Genealogy' (2003) 16 Harvard Human Rights Journal 69, 70-73.

[28] Stahn (n 3) 427 and citations thereof.

[29] Sirleaf argues that the transnational nature of armed conflicts requires a transnational/regional response to the violations committed. Matiangai Sirleaf, 'Regional Approaches to Transitional Justice? Examining the Special Court for Sierra Leone and the Truth and Reconciliation Commission for Liberia' (2009) 21 Florida Journal of International Law 209, 229.

[30] Stahn (n 3) 429.

[31] ibid 427; UNSG, 'Report on RoL and TJ' (n 18) para 26.

[32] The authors conclude their reasoning by arguing that *jus post bellum* would likely have greater appeal and resonance vis-à-vis TJ if its principal subject was the state and not foreign governments or multilateral institutions. Mark Freeman and Drazan Djukić, 'Jus Post Bellum and Transitional

However, the same scholars admit that TJ 'is insufficient in and of itself to ensure a successful peacebuilding process'.[33]

Against this backdrop, this section intends to focus on post-conflict TJ mechanisms that have been established under the auspices of the UN/other International Organizations and/or which have an international/mixed composition. By looking at the timing of their action, recommendations, and decisions as well as at their mandate, the section will shed light on the extent to which these bodies have recognized and furthered the quest of families for information on their missing relatives. It will also analyze the contribution – if any – that they have concretely provided in terms of capacity building for the national authorities expected to implement their recommendations. Among the international TJ mechanisms that will be at the center of the analysis are the *ad hoc* tribunals (sub-section 1.1.1), truth and reconciliation commissions (sub-section 1.1.2), and hybrid criminal/non-criminal justice mechanisms (sub-section 1.1.3).[34] This extensive approach[35] to TJ derives from the idea that all these bodies have tried to be drivers of change in the contexts where they operated; a holistic conception of justice in transition[36] is, therefore, the underlying conceptual premise behind this section.

1.1.1. The ad hoc tribunals and the clash of humanitarian/accountability-driven needs

The two *ad hoc* tribunals – the ICTY and the ICTR – were the expression of a reactive response of the international community to the atrocities committed in the Balkans and in Rwanda in the 1990s. In the purview of their mandate, accounting for missing persons was not specifically contemplated; however, the expectations of the families vis-à-vis the work carried out by the prosecutors to

---

Justice' in Carsten Stahn and Jann K Kleffner (eds), *Jus Post Bellum: Towards a Law of Transition From Conflict to Peace* (Springer Verlag 2008) 226–227.

[33] ibid 227.

[34] This categorization is inspired from Carst Stahn's seminal study on the Geometry of Transitional Justice.

[35] Roht-Arriaza argues that the TJ can be broadly and narrowly approached; in her view, a broad conception of TJ requires an examination of anything that a society devises 'to deal with a legacy of conflict [...], from changes in criminal codes to those in high school textbooks, from creation of memorials [...] to police and court reform'; conversely, a narrow approach consists in considering a few methods and techniques revolving around truth and justice, i.e., 'criminal investigations, truth commissions, vetting or cleansing of security forces, and, to some extent, formal reparation programs'. N Roth-Arriaza, 'The New Landscape of Transitional Justice' in Naomi Roht-Arriaza and Javier Mariezcurrena (eds), *Transitional justice in the twenty-first century: beyond truth versus justice* (Cambridge University Press 2006) 2.

[36] P Hazan, 'The Changing Nature of the Debate on Peace vs. Justice' in Jonathan Sisson (ed), *Dealing with the Past in Post-Conflict Societies: Ten Years after the Peace Accords in Guatemala and Bosnia – Herzegovina* (Swisspeace 2007) 11; M Urban Walker, 'Post-Conflict Truth Telling: Exploring Extended Territory' in Larry May and Andrew Forcehimes (eds), *Morality, Jus Post Bellum, and International Law* (Cambridge University Press 2012) 11–12 (the author underlines that the current trend is an overlap between post-conflict measures such as criminal trials for individuals responsible for war crimes or crimes against humanity, economic reconstruction, local reforms of, *inter alia*, political and military institutions with the 'standard menu of [TJ] devices for re-creating stable and just domestic political order'). Cf. UNSG, 'Report on RoL and TJ' (n 18) para 26.

gather the evidence and bring the accused to trial were different: for them, the investigations might also have served the purpose of identifying all the victims. However, these investigations contained 'a primary mandate of judicial investigation for the purposes of accountability'.[37] It was only in 2003, with the ICRC's Missing Initiative,[38] that the concept of international forensic investigations for purely humanitarian purposes became part of the international response. Indeed, discrepancies in the responses to humanitarian-based needs and evidentiary needs have emerged in the course of action of both tribunals, although the ICTY was the most exposed to it. Sub-section 2.2 is entirely dedicated to exploring this issue in light of the ICTY practice.

1.1.2. Truth Commissions and the limited scope of "truth"

Truth and reconciliation commissions are entities that are set up to investigate a pattern of abuses occurred during past dictatorial regimes or conflicts. Officially authorized or empowered by the State, they have a temporary mandate, which requires them to conclude their work with a public report where they make recommendations for redress and future prevention.[39] To this end, these bodies play the role of 'commissions of inquiry whose primary function is investigation' (and not adjudication); in this sense, they are concerned not only with unveiling the facts of individual cases, but also and foremost with providing an account of the 'broad causes and consequences of the violations that occurred'.[40] Although focused on – and most of the time operative in – the country where the violations occurred, some of these bodies have resulted from UN/other organizations-moderated peace negotiations and/or have had a mixed composition (staff and members) in order to give a perception of neutrality.

Their 'primary function'[41] allows the Commissions to perform other key tasks that contribute to the establishment of the truth; for instance, a Truth and Reconciliation Commission can be mandated to

discover, clarify, and formally acknowledge past abuses; to address the needs of victims; to "counter impunity" and advance individual accountability; to outline

---

[37] SM Drawdy and C Katzmarzyk, 'The Missing Files: The Experience of the International Committee of the Red Cross' in Derek Congram (ed), *Missing Persons: Multidisciplinary Perspectives on the Disappeared* (Canadian Scholars' Press 2016) 62.

[38] ICRC, 'The Missing: Action to Resolve the Problem of People Unaccounted for as a Result of Armed Conflict or Internal Violence and to Assist Their Families. Conference Acts' (ICRC 2003) TheMissing/Conf/03.2003/EN/90.

[39] This definition is a paraphrase of Hayner's; in light of the different forms that these bodies can assume, the author – who is the first to embark on this definitional endeavor - admits that there is still no single and broadly accepted definition of what a Truth and Reconciliation Commission is. Priscilla B Hayner, *Unspeakable Truths: Transitional Justice and the Challenge of Truth Commissions* (2nd edition, Routledge 2010) 10–11. The definition outlined in the text also builds in the definition provided by Freeman who adds further aspects to Hayner's definition, such as the fact that Truth Commissions are *ad hoc*, autonomous, and victim-centered bodies. Mark Freeman, *Truth Commissions and Procedural Fairness* (Cambridge University Press 2006) 16–18.

[40] Freeman (n 39) 14–15.

[41] ibid 14.

institutional responsibility and recommend reforms; and to promote reconciliation and reduce conflict over the past.[42]

Truth and reconciliation commissions are considered beneficial to the establishment of the facts surrounding heinous crimes perpetrated on a massive or systemic scale; therefore, they contribute to ensuring the right of the people to know the truth.[43] Nevertheless, the human rights adjudicators have clarified that 'the "historical truth" included in the reports of the above-mentioned Commissions is no substitute for the duty of the State to reach the truth through judicial proceedings.'[44] Thus, these bodies can be easily distinguishable from courts and administrative tribunals, whose primary function is adjudication.[45]

Among the Commissions that have been established at the end of a NIAC after a lengthy UN-moderated peace process is the Historical Clarification Commission in Guatemala: mixed in its composition,[46] the Commission was established in accordance with the UN-brokered peace deal that put an end to the 36-year armed conflict (1960-1996) in Guatemala. Its mandate revolved around two main pillars: i.e., clarify human rights violations and acts of violence committed during the conflict and provide recommendations to encourage peace and preserve the memory of the victims.[47] Pursuant to the Commission report, persons went missing in Guatemala as a result of the perpetration of enforced disappearances: the Commission found that 6,159 persons had been subjected to enforced disappearance out of 42,275 victims.[48] Mandate-based and context-

---

[42] Hayner (n 39) 20. As the *Joinet* Principles point out the establishment of an extrajudicial Commission of Inquiry is among the guarantees to give effect to the right to know the truth. UN Commission on Human Rights, 'Revised Final Report Prepared by Mr. Joinet pursuant to Sub-Commission Decision 1996/119 - Annexes I and II, Set of Principles for the Protection and Promotion of Human Rights through Action to Combat Impunity (Joinet's Principles)' (1997) UN Doc E/CN.4/Sub.2/1997/20/Rev.1 Principle 5.

[43] UN Commission on Human Rights, 'Promotion and Protection of Human Rights: Impunity. Add.1 "Updated Set of Principles for the Protection and Promotion of Human Rights through Action to Combat Impunity (Orentlicher Principles)"' (2005) UN Doc E/CN.4/2005/102/Add.1 Principle 5.

[44] In this sense, 'Articles 1(1), 8 and 25 of the [ACHR] protect truth as a whole, and hence, [the] State must carry out a judicial investigation of the facts related to [the direct victim]'s death, attribute responsibilities, and punish all those who turn out to be participants.' Cf. IACtHR, *Almonacid Arellano v Chile, Judgment - Preliminary objections, merits, reparations and costs* (2006) Series C No 154 [150]; *La Cantuta v Peru, Judgment - Merits, Reparations and Costs* (2006) Series C no 162 [224].

[45] Freeman (n 39) 14.

[46] The Commission was composed of three members; one of them, the chair of the Commission, was an international member directly appointed by the UNSG. The staff of the Commission was mixed as well, although for security reason and to make it perceived as neutral, none of the field office directors or heads of departments were nationals. See Hayner (n 39) 33.

[47] Cf. Purposes, paras I and III and Operation, para III in 'Agreement on the Establishment of the Commission to Clarify Past Human Rights Violations and Acts of Violence That Have Caused the Guatemalan Population to Suffer, Signed in Oslo' (1994) <https://www.usip.org/sites/default/files/file/resources/collections/commissions/Guatemala-Charter.pdf> accessed 12 January 2018. These terms of reference were strongly opposed by civil society and victims' groups in Guatemala.

[48] The 91% of disappearance were attributable to the State forces and related paramilitary groups. See Guatemala Commission for Historical Clarification, 'Memory of Silence. Report of the Commission for Historical Clarification: Conclusions and Recommendations' (1998) 17, 20.

based obstacles characterized the work of the Commission: i) the Commission could not elucidate the fate or whereabouts of those who disappeared, as this was not part of its mandate; ii) it could not name those responsible, and, consequently, iii) it could not attribute responsibility to any individual in its work/recommendations/report; iv) neither could these documents have any judicial aim or effect. Nevertheless, the Commission concluded that '[t]he majority of human rights violations occurred with the knowledge or by order of the highest authorities of the State'.[49]

In the National Reparation Program, outlined at the end of the report, the Commission acknowledged that, given the extent of the crime of enforced disappearance and of the problems generated by it, it was vital to rectify these problems 'so that the suffering and complications occasioned by the disappearance are not prolonged'.[50] The Commission recommended that the Government and the judiciary initiate investigations regarding all known forced disappearances;[51] it also recommended 'that the Guatemalan Army and the former Guatemalan National Revolutionary Unity provide whatever information they may have in relation to the disappearances of people that occurred during the period of internal armed confrontation'.[52]

The Commission's investigative work turned to be particularly problematic, as the State authorities did not collaborate with the disclosure of the documents requested;[53] in addition to that, after the release of the Report, the authorities declared that the majority of the recommendations put forward were already addressed in the peace agreement.[54] The search for those who had been disappeared during the conflict as well as prosecution of those responsible for

---

[49] ibid 38.

[50] ibid 52.

[51] The Commission recommended that 'all available legal and material resources should be utilized to clarify the whereabouts of the disappeared and, in the case of death, to deliver the remains to the relatives'. ibid.

[52] In this respect, the Commission referred to the services of the ICRC, requesting it to lending its advice and technical support to the Guatemala State in the implementation of these recommendations. ibid.

[53] The IACtHR stresses that 'the appearance of the *Diario Militar* in 1999 and the Historical Archive of the National Police in 2005, both by unofficial channels [...], revealed that the State had withheld information from the [Historical Clarification Commission] with regard to the facts of the instant case'. Cf. IACtHR, *Gudiel Álvarez et al ('Diario Militar') v Guatemala, Judgment - Merits, Reparations, and Costs* (2012) Series C no. 253 [295, 300]. Nevertheless, the Commission could count on the declassification from the US government of relevant files, including detailed information for building a database outlining the structure and personnel of the armed forces in Guatemala over the years of the conflict. Hayner (n 39) 33.

[54] The original text is in Spanish: 'el Gobierno [...] reitera que en todo lo relativo al proceso de paz se guía por la letra y el espíritu de los acuerdos respectivos, y celebra que la mayor parte de las recomendaciones de la Comisión signifiquen el cumplimiento de dichos acuerdos'. See Guatemala, 'Posición Inicial del Gobierno de La República Ante El Informe y Las Recomendaciones de La Comisión de Esclarecimiento Histórico' (16 March 1999) para 3 <http://pudl.princeton.edu/sheetreader.php?obj=c247ds93x> accessed 12 July 2016.

this crime remained dead letter for years.[55] Only recently the need for accountability against the crime of enforced disappearance has been taken into serious consideration in the context of domestic trials against those who have perpetrated them.[56] The current situation features a lack of an integrated response propped by the State[57] vis-à-vis the most essential need of the families, i.e., to know the fate and whereabouts of their relatives. This need has been partly tackled by the work of non-governmental bodies that have carried out exhumations and identification procedures;[58] governmental bodies with a mandate focused on specific categories of persons subjected to enforced disappearance have also been created.[59] Yet, at the time of writing, the National Congress in Guatemala has not approved Bill no 3590 presented in 2007 on the establishment of the national commission for the search for the disappeared persons in the armed conflict.[60]

---

[55] Yet, in 2003, the IACommHR reported that 'as regards prosecution and punishment of persons responsible for past violations of human rights, the Commission observes with profound concern that the worrisome impunity for violations perpetrated during the armed conflict remains unchanged. According to the information collected during the visit, 99 % of cases of forced disappearance, torture, massacres, extrajudicial executions and acts of genocide committed during the armed conflict remain unpunished'. See IACommHR, 'Justice and Social Inclusion: The Challenges of Democracy in Guatemala' (2003) OEA/Ser.L/V/II.118 Doc. 5 rev. 1 para 23.

[56] In this respect, Felipe Cusanero (2009), a former military officer, has been convicted in a Guatemala Court with regard to his responsibility for the disappearance of six peasant farmers and sentenced to 150 years in prison; this was the first case of its genre in Guatemala. ICMP, 'Accountability for the Missing and Disappeared in Guatemala' (24 May 2016) <https://www.icmp.int/news/accountability-for-the-missing-and-disappeared-in-guatemala/> accessed 29 December 2016.

[57] The Guatemalan Forensic Anthropology Foundation has worked since early 1990s in order to take on the requests for information of the families; the Foundation is a non-governmental organization. ibid. In 2006 a temporary Executive Branch commission was created, as a consultative and advisory body, in order to locate people who disappeared during the internal armed conflict. However, the main outcome of its work has been a draft national plan to locate people who disappeared during the internal armed conflict covering the period 2006-2015. See L Corzo, 'Commissions to Resolve the Phenomenon of Missing Persons: Case Studies. Guatemala Case Study' in María Teresa Dutli and Noreen Majeed (eds), *Report of the Second Universal Meeting of National Committees on International Humanitarian Law - Geneva, 19–21 March 2007. Legal Measures and Mechanisms to Prevent Disappearances, to Establish the Fate of Missing Persons, and to Assist Their Families* (ICRC 2007) 151.

[58] In this respect, the WGEID has expressed 'its concern at the lack of coordination in the realization of various programmes and activities between non-governmental organizations and State actors because of lack of mutual trust and consensus among them'. See WGEID, 'Report of the WGEID: Addendum. Mission to Guatemala' (2007) UN Doc A/HRC/4/41/Add.1 para 88.

[59] In 2001 a Commission was mandated to trace children who disappeared during the armed conflict; this was institutionalized in 2003. The work of the Commission has contributed to reuniting 131 families. See Corzo (n 57) 153.

[60] Cf. Congreso de la Republica - Guatemala, 'Iniciativa Que Dispone Aprobar Ley de La Comisión de Búsqueda de Personas, Victimas de La Desaparición Forzada Y Otras Formas de Desaparición (Ley N 3590)' (2007). See also HRCee, 'Concluding Observations of the Human Rights Committee on Guatemala' (2012) UN Doc CCPR/C/GTM/CO/3 para 21 (regretting that no national commission of inquiry has yet been established, as set down in draft act no 3590 and that there is no single registry of disappeared persons); ICRC, 'Guatemala: ICRC Calls for Creation of a National Search Committee (News Release 10/23)' (22 February 2010) <https://www.icrc.org/eng/resources/documents/news-release/2010/guatemala-news-220210.htm> accessed 29 December 2017; Agencia

Another similar example of a body with an internationally framed mandate (but a national composition) is that of the Commission for the Truth and Reconciliation in East Timor: established by the Regulation of the UN Transitional Administration in East Timor, the Commission's mandate revolved around two pillars, i.e., the inquiry and the establishment of the truth regarding human rights violations committed in the context of the armed conflicts in Timor-Leste between 1974 and 1999;[61] the formulation of recommendations concerning reforms and initiatives designed to prevent the recurrence of human rights violations and to respond to the needs of victims.[62]

In light of the enforced disappearances perpetrated in the period under investigation, the Timorese Commission recommended that

families be assisted to locate and to re-bury the remains of relatives and loved ones who perished during the conflict and that, where resources permit, exhumation according to appropriate standards is carried out to allow for identification and establishment of the cause of death.

A public register of the disappeared be established and, in collaboration with the Government of Indonesia, a systematic inquiry is undertaken to establish the whereabouts and fate of those on the list.[63]

These and other recommendations led to the establishment of a bilateral Commission on Truth and Friendship (Timor Leste/Indonesia), instead of pursuing judicial processes concerning the violations committed by the Indonesian military and police as well as the civilian government and militia groups. The commission on truth and friendship had a general mandate revolving around one main objective, i.e., the establishment of 'the conclusive truth in regard to the events prior to and immediately after the popular consultation in 1999, with a view to further promoting reconciliation and friendship, and ensuring the non-recurrence of similar events'.[64]

EFE, 'Exigen Al Congreso de Guatemala Aprobar La Ley Para La Búsqueda de Desaparecidos de Guerra' (8 December 2016) <http://www.efe.com/efe/america/sociedad/exigen-al-congreso-de-guatemala-aprobar-la-ley-para-busqueda-desaparecidos-guerra/20000013-3119610> accessed 29 December 2017.

[61] There are three main phases of the conflict in Timor: an internal phase that characterized the process towards independence from Portugal between 1974-1976; an international phase that followed the independence in 1975 with the invasion from Indonesia and the occupation of the Timor Leste for more than two decades; and a third phase concerning the scorched earth campaign initiated by anti-independence Timorese militias - organized and supported by the Indonesian military in response to the UN-supervised popular referendum for the independence from Indonesia. See Commission for Reception, Truth, and Reconciliation Timor-Leste (CAVR), 'Chega! The Report of the Commission for Reception, Truth, and Reconciliation Timor-Leste. Executive Summary' (2005) 11–14; CIA, 'East & Southeast Asia: Timor-Leste' (*The World Factbook*) <http://teacherlink.ed.usu.edu/tlresources/reference/factbook/geos/tt.html> accessed 12 July 2016.

[62] Commission for Reception, Truth, and Reconciliation Timor-Leste (CAVR) (n 61) 19–20. Although the Commission had full powers of subpoena and the power to search and seize information from any location in the country, it admitted that the excellent cooperation to all activities of the Commission by all levels of the society did not require the activation of these powers. ibid 5.

[63] Commission for Reception, Truth, and Reconciliation Timor-Leste (CAVR) (n 61) 161–162.

[64] Commission of Truth and Friendship (CTF) - Indonesia-Timor-Leste, 'Final Report' (2008) i.

Similarly to the predecessor, the 2008 final report of the bilateral Commission concluded that gross human rights violations were committed by both sides directly or indirectly (through material support, planning, encouragement, etc.) in the form of crimes against humanity (including enforced disappearances).[65] Among the short-term and urgent recommendations, the Commission reiterated the predecessor's recommendation, i.e., that 'the governments of Indonesia and Timor-Leste work together to acquire information about the fate of disappeared people and cooperate to gather data and provide information to their families'.[66] In this regard a commission for disappeared persons should be established and, *inter alia,* be tasked to 'identify the whereabouts of all Timor Leste children who were separated from their parents and to notify their families.'[67] To date, no such a body has been established, despite the additional recommendations that have been forwarded by other international bodies (e.g., the UN WGEID).[68]

Other commissions[69] explicitly mandated to address the issue of the missing have provided a more concrete contribution that goes beyond the mere recommendation to search for missing persons. National in their composition, these commissions have published lists of those reported missing and developed partnerships with other organizations (national and international)[70] for the implementation of their work.

The case of the Truth and Reconciliation Commission in Peru is *sui generis,* since its mandate was as general as the ones examined above.[71] In the course of

---

[65] ibid 277.

[66] ibid 297.

[67] ibid.

[68] See WGEID, 'Report of the WGEID: Addendum. Follow-up Report to the Recommendations Made by the WGEID - Missions to Mexico and Timor Leste' (2015) UN Doc A/HRC/30/38/Add.4 200.

[69] For instance, the Peru's Truth and Reconciliation Commission, the Morocco's Equity and Reconciliation Commission, and the South Africa's Commission of Truth and Reconciliation. Only the Peruvian one has operated in a post-conflict context; while the Morocco's Equity and Reconciliation Commission work revolved around the violations occurred in the post-independence phase under the regime of King Hassan II, the work of the South Africa's one mainly concerned gross human rights violations committed in the country during the apartheid regime (1960- 1994).

[70] This is the case of the Peruvian Commission that in partnership with the ICRC, the *Defensoría del Pueblo,* and the *Coordinadora Nacional de Derechos Humanos* launched the initiative on the disappeared persons (disappearance between1980-2000). Similarly, the South Africa's Commission of Truth and Reconciliation was mandated to, *inter alia,* establish and make known 'the fate or whereabouts of victims'. Cf. Article 3 (1) (c), 'Promotion of National Unity and Reconciliation Act' (President of South Africa 1995) Act 95-34.

[71] The mandate consisted in providing a contribution to the justice system's clarification of the crimes and violations of human rights committed by terrorist organizations or some State agents (considered a NIAC by the Commission), in seeking to determine the whereabouts and situation of the victims, in identifying, to the extent possible, presumptive responsibilities, and in drawing up 'proposals for reparation and dignification of the victims and their family members'. The Truth and Reconciliation Commission (Comisión de la Verdad y Reconciliación) in Peru was established by decree No. 065-2001-PCM (2001); its mandate consisted in, *inter alia,* contributing to 'the justice system's clarification of the crimes and violations of human rights committed by terrorist organizations or some State agents, seeking to determine the whereabouts and situation of the victims and identifying, to the extent possible, presumptive responsibilities'; and in drawing up 'proposals for reparation and

its work, the Commission undertook humanitarian and accountability-driven efforts.[72] Moreover, pursuant to its general mandate, in collaboration with the ICRC, the *Defensoría del Pueblo*, and the *Coordinadora Nacional de Derechos Humanos*, the Commission undertook the humanitarian commitment to promote a joint initiative on missing persons in order to search for information concerning those reported as unaccounted for as a result of the political violence[73] occurred in the country between 1980 and 2000.[74] The purpose of publishing the list of the missing was to share the data with family members and others, 'in the hope of contributing towards clarifying the current location of the persons included in the list.' The assessment of the information carried out in collaboration with the above-mentioned entities was meant to provide answers 'to the family members of those persons included in the list.'[75] These lists and actions have not waived the State obligations: indeed, the Commission pointed out that, after a NIAC, it is a State responsibility to draw up a list of those unaccounted for as a result of the violence during such a conflict.[76] Despite these significant steps and progress, international human rights bodies and procedures have noted that Peru shall assume full responsibility and play a leading role in ensuring that 'these initiatives become part of a comprehensive, consistent, and continuous State policy carried out in cooperation and collaboration with the victims and their relatives.'[77]

---

dignification of the victims and their family members'. The acts covered by its mandate included murders and abduction as well as enforced disappearances. Cf. Article 2 (b), (c), Article 3 (a), (b), 'Supreme Decree No 065-2001-PCM' (President of the Republic of Peru 2001)
<http://www.cverdad.org.pe/lacomision/cnormas/normas01.php> accessed 29 December 2016.

[72] A similar case is that of the Moroccan Equity and Reconciliation Commission, which however operated in relation to the violations that characterized the regime of Hassan II in the country. Specifically, the Commission was mandated to investigate forced disappearances and arbitrary detention between Morocco's independence in 1956 and 1999 as well as to determine the responsibility of the state organisms or any other party. Cf. Article 9 (2), (3) Kingdom of Morocco, 'Dahir (Royal Decree) No 1.04.42 Approving Statutes of the Equity and Reconciliation Commission' (2004) <https://www.usip.org/publications/2004/12/truth-commission-morocco> accessed 12 January 2016.

[73] In its general conclusion, the Commission specifically refers to 'the internal armed conflict experienced by Peru between 1980 and 2000' as the 'most intense, extensive, and prolonged episode of violence in the entire history of the Republic'. See Truth and Reconciliation Commission (Peru), 'General Conclusions - Final Report' (2003) para 1 <http://www.cverdad.org.pe/ingles/ifinal/conclusiones.php> accessed 29 December 2016.

[74] The provisional list counted 7,613 cases among which 2,144 were documented and confirmed. Truth and Reconciliation Commission (Peru), 'Annex 5 "Iniciativa Sobre Personas Desaparecidas Conformada Por La CVR, La Defensoría Del Pueblo, La Coordinadora Nacional de Derechos Humanos, Y El CICR" - Final Report' (2003) <http://www.cverdad.org.pe/ingles/ifinal/index.php> accessed 29 December 2016.

[75] See Truth and Reconciliation Commission (Peru), 'Missing Persons - Do You Know Anything about Them? - Initiative on Missing Persons' (*Truth and Reconciliation*)
<http://www.cverdad.org.pe/ingles/desaparecidos/desaparecidos.php> accessed 29 December 2016. Furthermore, the commission recommended some cases for prosecution. Although slowly implemented, this recommendation did not remain dead letter. See Hayner (n 39) 38–39.

[76] Truth and Reconciliation Commission (Peru), 'Annex 5' (n 74).

[77] WGEID, 'Report of the WGEID on Its Mission to Peru' (2016) UN Doc A/HRC/33/51/Add.3 para 72.

1.1.3. Hybrid criminal and non-criminal justice in post-conflict settings

The expression 'hybrid justice' covers those bodies that have a mixed (international and domestic) composition and apply international and domestic law; they can be integrated in the domestic judicial system or operating as independent institutions outside the traditional realm of domestic jurisdiction.[78] This typology of TJ mechanism reflects the intention of the international community to enable the national system to operate according to and consistently with international law standards as part of a broader strategy aimed at building a sustainable peace. The international community's role in the formation and *modus operandi* of these bodies and their decisions have directly impacted (and continue to impact) on the process concerning the elucidation of the fate of the missing in the contexts where they operated.

The examples examined in this sub-section are different in nature, mandate, and subject matter jurisdiction: the first example – the HRChBH – operated as part of the domestic system, but under international guidance and had jurisdiction over violations of the ECHR (sub-section 1.1.3.1 *(a)*); the second example – the Special War Crimes Chamber in the State Court of Bosnia and Herzegovina – must be understood as the result of the international presence in Bosnia along with the completion strategy of the ICTY (sub-section 1.1.3.1 *(b)*); and the third example – the UNMIK Human Rights Advisory Panel (HRAP) – is a *sui generis* form of hybrid justice, since it could only issue non-binding opinions, but had the overarching purpose of putting under the international law radar the actions of UNMIK authorities (sub-section 1.1.3.2).

1.1.3.1. Post-conflict justice in Bosnia and Herzegovina

a. The Human Rights Chamber for Bosnia and Herzegovina

In the aftermath of the conflict in the Former Yugoslavia, the justice system of Bosnia and Herzegovina was unable to provide an adequate response to the human rights violations committed in the aftermath of the conflict or still continuing immediately after the termination of the conflict.[79] Established in 1995 by the Dayton Agreements (see Chapter V, sub-section 1.1.3), the HRChBH[80] had a hybrid composition, i.e., fourteen members, eight of which were internationals appointed by the Committee of Ministers of the CoE. As remarked by the ECtHR, 'the appointment of the foreign members to the Chamber was motivated by a desire [...] to reinforce its appearance of

---

[78] Stahn differentiates between hybrid courts, i.e., bodies that have a separate international legal identity of their own, and internationalized domestic courts, i.e., those that do not present such a feature. See Stahn (n 3) 437.

[79] Pursuant to its mandate, the Chamber could receive applications on matters which were within the responsibility of one of the Parties to Annex 6 and which occurred or continued after the entry into force of the Dayton Agreements (i.e., 14 December 1995).

[80] Bosnia and Herzegovina, Croatia, and Yugoslavia concluded the Dayton Agreements under the supervision of the Contact Group composed of the EU, Germany, France, Russia, the UK, and the US. The Chamber is established under Annex 6, Article II of the Dayton Agreements. Pursuant to Annex 6, the Chamber was one of the branches of the Commission on Human Rights for Bosnia Herzegovina, the other being the Office of the Ombudsman.

impartiality and to bring to the Chamber knowledge and experience of the [ECHR] and its case law'.[81] The Chamber *per se* was a 'transitional measure, pending Bosnia and Herzegovina's accession to the [CoE]'; despite its hybrid nature, it 'constituted a part, albeit a particular part, of the legal system of Bosnia and Herzegovina'.[82] The fact that international organizations (e.g., OSCE) supervised the execution of the Chamber's decisions was justified by the post-war context of the establishment of the Chamber and did not alter its essentially domestic character.

Its time-bounded mandate (1996-2003) covered the following: the 'alleged or apparent violations of human rights as provided in the [ECHR] and the Protocols thereto' and 'alleged or apparent discrimination on any ground...arising in the enjoyment of any of the rights and freedoms provided for in the international agreements listed' in the Appendix to Annex 6 to the General Framework (e.g., the four GCs I-IV; the APs I-II; the ICCPR; the CAT).[83] The Dayton agreements also established the Constitution of Bosnia and Herzegovina, which recognized the ECHR as directly applicable in the country with priority over all domestic laws.[84]

The decisions of the Chamber were final and binding upon all governmental powers of a respondent Party (i.e., the Federation of Bosnia and Herzegovina; the Republika Srpska; the State of Bosnia and Herzegovina).[85] Even though the case law of the Strasbourg Court[86] served as a baseline for the Chamber's reasoning in its judgments,[87] the Chamber showed a certain degree of intellectual independence in assessing the complaints.[88]

The Chamber adopted a less formalistic approach than that of the ECtHR vis-à-vis the issue of missing persons. The case that incorporates the Chamber's innovative approach to the claims of the missing persons' families is that of *Ferida Selimović et al* also known as *'Srebrenica Cases'*.[89] The case consisted of

---

[81] Cf. ECtHR, Jeličić v Bosnia and Herzegovina, Decision (2005) App no 41183/02 pt A.

[82] ibid. The Court had to decide whether the Chamber constituted a "domestic" rather than "international" body pursuant to Article 35(2) ECHR in order to avoid plurality of international proceedings relating to the same case; moreover, it had to decide whether the Chamber was a 'domestic remedy' pursuant to Article 35 (1) ECHR).

[83] Cf. Article II, para. 2 (a) and (b), Annex 6 and the Appendix of Annex 6, Dayton Agreements. The Appendix's list of "human rights agreements" mentions sixteen agreements in total and includes the IHL treaties. Indeed, although the Chamber was requested to address human rights violations, IHL rules and the parties to the conflict' compliance with such rules were not exogenous to its assessment.

[84] Cf. Article II (2), Annex 4, Dayton Agreements.

[85] Cf. Article XI (3), Annex 6, Dayton Agreements.

[86] J David Yeager, 'The Human Rights Chamber for Bosnia and Herzegovina - A Case Study in Transitional Justice' (2004) 14 International Legal Perspectives 44, 46.

[87] Other bodies' case law was also taken into considerations (e.g., that of the IACtHR and of the HRCee). Tilman Blumenstock, 'Legal Protection of the Missing and Their Relatives: The Example of Bosnia and Herzegovina' (2006) 19 Leiden Journal of International Law 773, 782.

[88] This is notable in light of the transitional context where it operated, i.e., from war to a sustainable peace, 'from a communist system to a market democracy, and from a dysfunctional and confusing judicial system to a coherent system based on the rule of law'. Yeager (n 86) 53.

[89] Among other relevant cases are the *Palić* case and the *Unković* Case: in the former, the Chamber dealt with the facts occurred in the Žepa enclave in July 1995, where Colonel Palić (Army of Bosnia and Herzegovina), who was involved in the negotiations with the Bosnian Serb Army about the

forty-nine applications filed by the families of men who were among the almost 8,000 Bosniaks allegedly killed in the mass execution perpetrated by the Army of the Serb Republic in Srebrenica from 10 to 19 July 1995. Due to its limited competence *ratione temporis,*[90] the HRChBH considered the case only under the angle of the rights of family members to be informed about the fate and whereabouts of their missing loved ones.

This represented a landmark case in the case law of the Chamber under three respects. First of all, the Chamber set out the definitional contours of the issue of the missing within the boundaries of the ECHR. On the admissibility, the respondent Party argued that applications were incompatible *ratione materiae* with the Dayton Agreements, for

> there is a critical distinction between the terms 'disappeared persons' and 'missing persons'. In order to be 'disappeared persons' protected by the [UN] Declaration on the Protection of Persons from Enforced Disappearance, the Republika Srpska contends that the persons must be arrested, detained or abducted against their will. However, in these cases, the presumed victims of the Srebrenica events 'decided to go into the woods' and then 'went missing without a trace'. Therefore, they are only 'unaccounted for persons' or 'missing persons'; they are not 'disappeared persons' within the meaning of the mentioned UN Declaration.[91]

The Chamber rejected the respondent's argument on two grounds: 1) the family members' claims under Articles 3 and 8 of the ECHR were not based upon the UN Declaration on the Protection of All Persons from Enforced Disappearance, and as a corollary the Chamber did not touch on the distinction between 'enforced

---

peaceful evacuation of civilians, was forcibly taken away by armed Serb soldiers (despite the presence of UN soldiers); in the latter, the Chamber addressed the suffering of Đordo Unković who lost contact with his daughter (Vlasta Golubović) and her family in the summer of 1992 and did not receive any information on their fate from the authorities, nor from anyone else for seven years. In the former the complaint revolved around the alleged violation of article 3 ECHR and Article 8 ECHR; while for article 3, the Chamber reiterated the ECtHR's reasoning in *Kurt v Turkey* and found a violation of the provision at the detriment of the applicant, for Article 8 the Chamber drew up a line between the right to respect for family life and the right of families to know the fate of their relatives. Thus, the Chamber set up the conditions under which an applicant can raise an issue under Article 8 (i.e., the applicant must show that the respondent party is in possession of the body of the victim and unreasonably refuses to hand it over to the applicant; the applicant must substantiate that the respondent party is arbitrarily withholding the victim's body from him/her or withholding from him/her information on its whereabouts); both conditions being present, the Chamber found a violation of Article 8 at the detriment of the applicant. Cf. HRChBH, *Avdo and Esma Palić v The Republika Srpska, Decision on Admissibility and Merits* (2001) Case no. CH/99/3196 [36, 78–80, 82]. With regard to the *Unković* case, the Chamber reiterated the ECtHR's reasoning in *Çakici v. Turkey* and applied the criteria thereof to find a violation under Article 3 ECHR at the detriment of the next of kin of the missing person; indeed, it did not find a violation of Article 3 at the detriment of Mr. *Unković,* as the actions of the respondent party toward the applicant did not reach the level of severity required to be considered 'inhuman or degrading treatment'. Cf. HRChBH, *Unković v The Federation of Bosnia and Herzegovina, Decision on Review* (2002) Case No. C/99/2150 [72, 114–115, 119].

[90] The events, which occurred prior to the entry into force of the Dayton Agreements, fell outside the temporal jurisdiction of the Chamber.

[91] HRChBH, *Ferida Selimović et al v The Republika Srpska ('Srebrenica Cases'), Decision on Admissibility and Merits* (2003) Case nos. CH/01/8365 et al. [140]. The submission of the respondent Party did not match the description of facts developed by the ICTY Trial Chamber in the *Prosecutor v. Radislav Kristić* Case (2001), which was reproduced in the judgment. ibid 15 ff.

disappearance' and 'missing persons'; 2) the family members' claim under the two provisions of the ECHR did not require missing persons to be victims of enforced disappearance. Therefore, the Chamber found that the *Srebrenica* cases 'insofar as they allege claims by family members seeking to know the fate and whereabouts of their loved ones who have been missing from Srebrenica since 10-19 July 1995' are compatible *ratione materiae* with the Agreement.[92]

Secondly, the Chamber acknowledged the continuous effects of IHL provisions in post-conflict situations and the role that these can play in relation to human rights standards.[93] On the merits, the Chamber affirmed that AP I

> *reinforces*, in the context of the aftermath of an armed conflict, the positive obligation arising under Article 8 of the [ECHR] for the Republika Srpska *to search for and to share all relevant information with the families about their relatives* who have been reported missing from Srebrenica since July 1995 [emphases added].[94]

The reference to AP I – in particular to Articles 32-33 – as a hermeneutical tool allowed the Chamber to extrapolate the positive obligations of the respondent party under Article 8 ECHR. Two contextual factors appeared to be crucial: i.e., the catastrophic impact of the Srebrenica events on the lives of the surviving family members of missing persons and the exceptionally high level of trauma caused by the lack of information concerning the fate of their loved ones. Based on these two factors and on the conduct of the respondent, the Chamber found that 'the respondent party's failure to take any action aimed at making the requested information available to the families' of missing persons was particularly 'egregious'; indeed, it constituted a breach of its positive obligations under Article 8, i.e., the right to respect for private and family life.[95]

Third, the Chamber laid down the path to remedy the above-mentioned violations by ordering that the respondent i) release all information in its possession with respect to the fate and whereabouts of missing persons, ii) conduct a thorough, meaningful and detailed investigation into the events with a view to informing the applicants and the public about the Serb Republic's role in the facts occurred in Srebrenica, and iii) disseminate, as a 'form of reparation for social damage',[96] the information contained in the judgment as widely as possible.

---

[92] HRChBH, *Srebrenica Cases* (n 91) [164].

[93] That information concerning the fate and whereabouts of a family member falls within the ambit of 'the right to respect for his private and family life, protected by Article 8' of the ECHR was already recognized in the *Unković* Case. In this case, although the Chamber acknowledged that there was a long delay (more than seven years) and many procedural obstacles before the relevant information was made known to the applicant, there was no violation of Article 8, for the respondent Party fulfilled its positive obligations under Article 8 with the disclosure of such information. This conclusion was in sharp contrast with the conditions set down by the Chamber with regard to the failure of the fulfillment of the positive obligations under Article 8, i.e., the refusal of disclosing the information to the family member upon his request must be arbitrary and without any justification. The fact that this happened for seven years was considered a minor aspect compared to the eventual disclosure. HRChBH, *Unković (2002)* (n 89) [126–127].

[94] HRChBH, *Srebrenica Cases* (n 91) [175].

[95] ibid 179–181.

[96] ibid 212–213.

Before coming to closure, the Chamber made an assessment of the level of implementation of its orders: while the Chamber found that both the Federation and the Republika Srpska had an uneven record with respect to implementation, sustained pressure from the international community helped raise the rate of compliance.[97] Nonetheless, the Chamber admitted that some orders seemed to be 'particularly difficult for the respondent Parties and often take years to implement', e.g., those which require investigations into disappearances.[98] In the same report the Chamber expressed its concern over the weaknesses of the Bosnian Constitutional Court, which would play the role of successor of the HRChBH with regard to the human rights violations.[99] More vocal was the concern expressed by Amnesty International; the NGO stated that 'the proposal to disband [the HRChBH] and transfer its caseload to the Constitutional Court would be a serious blow to human rights protection in that country'.[100]

The HRChBH's mandate expired at the end of 2003. Pursuant to the 2003 agreement concluded on the basis of Article XIV of Annex 6 to the Dayton Agreements, its caseload was transferred to the Human Rights Commission operating from 1 January 2004 to 31 December 2004 within the Constitutional Court of Bosnia and Herzegovina. Thus, cases alleging violations of human rights were to be heard by the Constitutional Court of Bosnia and Herzegovina itself.[101] Since then, the Constitutional Court has been assessing cases concerning human rights violations at the detriment of the families of the missing. Recent cases show that the transitional measure – the Chamber – served its purpose of domesticating human rights standards and transferring the knowledge and experience of the ECtHR and its case law. In two recent landmark cases concerning forty-eight applications on missing persons the Constitutional Court has found a violation of the prohibition of inhuman treatment (Article II/3 (b), Constitution of Bosnia and Herzegovina and Article 3 ECHR) as well as of the right to respect for private and family life (Article II/3 (f), Constitution of Bosnia and Herzegovina and Article 8 ECHR) at the detriment of the family members of the missing.[102] Indeed, despite the passage of many years since the cessation of

---

[97] In this respect, the Chamber also noted that '[a]lthough few orders have been directed against the State of Bosnia and Herzegovina, they are virtually ignored'. HRChBH, 'Annual Report 2002' (2002) 6 <http://www.hrc.ba/ENGLISH/annual_report/2002/annual_report.htm> accessed 12 January 2016.
[98] ibid.
[99] It had not been functioning at all since May 2002 due to the failure to appoint two of the new members; when finally constituted, it would already have had its own backlog of cases to deal with. ibid.
[100] Amnesty International, 'Bosnia-Herzegovina: Abolition of Human Rights Chamber Leaves Citizens Unprotected' (2003) EUR 63/015/2003.
[101] See HRW, 'A Chance for Justice? War Crime Prosecutions in Bosnia's Serb Republic' (2006) Vol 18, no 3(D) 13 <https://www.hrw.org/reports/2006/bosnia0306/bosnia0306web.pdf> accessed 12 July 2017. See also Human Rights Commission within the Constitutional Court of Bosnia Herzegovina's Website http://www.hrc.ba accessed 23 July 2016)
[102] Constitutional Court of BiH, *Milena Kusmuk and others, Decision on Merits* (2012) Dec no AP-3783/09 [46]; *RS and others, Decision on Merits* (2013) Dec no AP-2101/11 [30]; *Bosiljka Milanović, Decision on Merits* (2008) Dec no AP-2980/06 [26]. See also TRIAL, 'BiH: Constitutional Court Delivers Landmark Judgment – TRIAL International' (2013) <https://trialinternational.org/latest-post/bih-constitutional-court-delivers-landmark-judgment/> accessed 13 January 2018.

the war, the competent authorities did not provide the applicants with information on their relatives who went missing during the war. The Court also underlined that the applicants did not receive information on the investigative procedures from the authorities and had to collect information on their relatives by themselves.[103] The role played by the Chamber in the transitional phase has been deemed exemplary; its case law has been considered 'guidance for future decision-makers in Bosnia Herzegovina.'[104] Certainly, the current international presence in the bench of the Constitutional Court[105] still plays a role in terms of access to knowledge and know-how relating to international legal standards.

b. The Special War Crimes Chamber in the State Court of Bosnia and Herzegovina

As part of the restoration of the RoL system in the Balkans, in 2003 the Office of the High Representative in Bosnia and Herzegovina[106] and ICTY representatives proposed the establishment of a special chamber to try serious violations of IHL in the State Court of Bosnia and Herzegovina.[107] The chamber is an integral part of the domestic judiciary, namely the State Court of Bosnia and Herzegovina. In Stahn's words, a close correlation exists between 'previous international involvement in the crisis and the design of the framework of post-conflict justice'; in the Bosnian case, the Special Chamber was 'largely the result of the long-term engagement of the High Representative in the post-conflict phase and the completion strategy of the ICTY'.[108]

Indeed, the Special War Crimes Chamber in the State Court of Bosnia and Herzegovina, established in 2005, was mandated to try the cases of lower – to mid-level perpetrators indicted by the ICTY and referred to the Bosnian Court under Rule 11 *bis* of the ICTY rules of procedure and evidence.[109] The Chamber also acquired jurisdiction over all the cases of war crimes, which were at that time before local courts (i.e., cantonal courts from the Federation and district courts from the Republika Srpska, as well as the district court of Brčko District).

---

[103] Constitutional Court of BiH, *Milena Kusmuk and others* (n 102) [46]; *R.S. and others* (n 102) [30].

[104] Yeager (n 86) 53.

[105] Three out of nine judges are appointed by the President of the ECtHR and cannot be nationals of Bosnia and Herzegovina or of any neighboring country. See Constitutional Court of Bosnia Herzegovina, 'Organization' (*Constitutional Court*) <http://www.ccbh.ba/o-sudu/?title=ustrojstvo &lang=en> accessed 12 December 2016. Cf. Article VI.1.a, Annex 4, Dayton Agreements.

[106] The Office of the High Representative is an *ad hoc* international institution responsible for overseeing implementation of civilian aspects of the Dayton agreements ending the war in Bosnia and Herzegovina. Its status is regulated under Annex 10 of the Dayton Agreements.

[107] The Steering Board of the Peace Implementation Council endorsed the proposal in June 2003. The proposal was presented to the Security Council. See UNSC (Press Release), 'Security Council Briefed on Establishment of War Crimes Chamber Within State Court of Bosnia and Herzegovina' (2003) SC/7888. See, more generally, Amnesty International, 'Bosnia-Herzegovina: Shelving Justice – War Crimes Prosecution in Paralysis' (2003) AI Index: EUR 63/018/200.

[108] Stahn (n 3) 447.

[109] Cf. Article 2, Law on the Transfer of Cases from the ICTY to the Prosecutor's Office of Bosnia and Herzegovina and the Use of Evidence Collected by the ICTY in Proceedings Before the Courts in Bosnia and Herzegovina, Official Gazette of Bosnia and Herzegovina, 61/04; Rule 11 *bis*, ICTY, 'Rules of Procedure and Evidence of the ICTY' (2005) IT/32/Rev. 36.

Although the presence of the international judges was deemed an important asset in the functioning of the Chamber, this came to an end in 2012.[110] The consequences of the disregard of the issue of missing persons both in the mandate and in the daily work[111] of this body have generated concerns with regard to how the families' quest for information has been treated and addressed. Specifically, 'it was alleged that the contact between the families and prosecutors were poor or non− existent, and that it was difficult to get information about their cases. Some families [believed] that their cases had not been taken up at all [...].'[112] Against this backdrop, the WGEID has recommended that the

> justice system in Bosnia and Herzegovina should give more attention to the victims. [...] Offices of the prosecutors and courts at all levels should have consistent rules in dealing with the public in general and with families of the disappeared in particular. In particular, families of victims should be more regularly given information on the process of investigation, the results of those investigations and whether trials might be forthcoming. [...] [S]pecial personnel [shall] be appointed to meet with families and inform them, on a regular basis, of progress made in their cases.[113]

Despite the international presence, the potential contribution that trials concerning international crimes could have in unveiling relevant information on the fate of missing persons was and continues to be disregarded.[114] Indeed, the minor importance that the issue of missing persons received during and after the international presence in the judicial system emerges from the reactions of the Prosecutor's office of Brčko District of Bosnia and Herzegovina to the recommendations of the WGEID:[115]

> [the] Prosecution has established an outreach system through strategic documents (the 2011-2014 Strategic Plan and the 2011-2015 Public Relations Strategy), the Rulebook on Internal Structure and Operations and other by-laws. In this sense, an officer is designated for public relations, who is in charge of regular proactive reporting on matters of public concern, singling out the importance of war crimes cases. Further,

---

[110] The positive effects of the international presence were particularly evident with regard to the perception of impartiality in the delivering of justice and the integration of international standards in the domestic legal framework. Cf. WGEID, 'Report of the WGEID. Addendum: Follow-up Report to the Recommendations Made by the Working Group - Missions to Argentina and Bosnia and Herzegovina' (2014) UN Doc A/HRC/27/49/Add.2 81.

[111] The WGEID reported that '[t]he procedure criminal codes at all levels were amended, shifting the approach from civil law to common law, with the abolishment of investigative judges and the creation of an independent prosecutor and the introduction of the guilty plea. This new procedure was questioned because of the use of plea bargaining, which might be used to obtain evidence − for instance to locate mass graves − but also to reduce drastically the sentence incurred. Plea bargaining should be used cautiously in cases of serious crimes, in particular enforced disappearances. The conditions under the plea should include, when appropriate, the obligation to cooperate in uncovering the truth about the fate and whereabouts of disappeared persons, and in particular through the discovery of mass graves.' Cf. WGEID, 'Report of the WGEID. Addendum: Mission to Bosnia and Herzegovina' (2010) UN Doc A/HRC/16/48/Add.1 para 62.

[112] Cf. ibid para 63.

[113] Cf. ibid para 64.

[114] HRW (n 101) 12.

[115] WGEID, 'Report of the WGEID. Addendum: Follow-up Report to the Recommendations Made by the Working Group - Missions to Argentina and Bosnia and Herzegovina' (n 110) Recommendation 90 (b), 83-84.

the officer also acts upon requests for access to information that may be submitted by any interested person.[116]

Thus, no specific consideration has been made in relation to the families of missing persons. This is confirmed by the approach to the WGEID's recommendation on the appointment of special personnel to deal with the families and inform them on a regular basis on the investigation.[117] The Prosecutor's Office stated that

[t]he Instruction on Communication of the Prosecutor's Office with Clients determines procedures of obtaining direct information on a daily basis about the case from the acting prosecutor by parties concerned, including families of missing victims. In the event case of dissatisfaction with the information received from the acting prosecutor party has the right to be heard and listened to by the Chief Prosecutor.[118]

It is noteworthy to mention that, immediately after the termination of the international presence in the State Court of Bosnia and Herzegovina in 2012, the Court amended the Rulebook on Public Access to Information Under the Court's Control and Community Outreach by favoring an anonimization policy in relation to its verdicts and indictments.[119] Thus, the Court not only allowed the defendants' name to be replaced with their initials, but also shielded the perpetrators of international crimes through the limitation of access of victims to relevant information, including the outcome of a trial.[120] The 2014 version of the Rulebook seems to be consistent with international standards, although it states that '[v]erdicts/decisions of interest to the public shall include verdicts/decisions in cases of war crimes...'; these verdicts/decisions should not disclose personal information, including criminal conviction.[121]

---

[116] ibid 83–84.

[117] ibid 90 (c).

[118] ibid 83–84. The other actors solicited by the WGEID (e.g. High Judicial and Prosecutorial Council of BiH; Court of BiH/Office of the President of the Court; Ministry of Justice of Republika Srpska) provided no answer on the recommendations above.

[119] A copy of this document is not available online; nonetheless, in light of the assessment provided by secondary sources – TRIAL's considerations on the WGEID's recommendations to BiH – it is possible to underline that Articles 41 to 46 of the amended rulebook set forth the "anonymization of Court decisions and other documents distributed to the public", i.e., certain data (e.g., names and surnames of those accused, suspected of, or convicted for war crimes, their representatives, the places where the crime has happened, as well as the names of private companies, institutions and the like) would be substituted or removed from Court's decisions and other forms of information. See TRIAL et al., 'Follow-Up Report on the Implementation by Bosnia and Herzegovina of the Recommendations Issued by the WGEID' (2014) 28–29.

[120] University of Cambridge, 'Retribution and Restoration: Bosnia on Trial' (*University of Cambridge*, 15 February 2013) <http://www.cam.ac.uk/research/news/retribution-and-restoration-bosnia-on-trial> accessed 10 January 2018.

[121] Cf. Article 25 (5) (c), The Court of Bosnia Herzegovina, 'Rulebook on Public Access to Information Under the Court's Control and Community Outreach' (2014) <http://www.sudbih.gov.ba/stranica/24/pregled?slug=pristup-informacijama> accessed 12 July 2016.

1.1.3.2. The Human Rights Advisory Panel and the definition of the post-conflict human rights obligations of UNMIK

The HRAP was a *sui generis* body that was established by UNMIK in order to examine 'complaints of alleged human rights violations committed by or attributable to [UNMIK]' and to make 'recommendations to the Special Representative of the Secretary-General [SRSG] in Kosovo when appropriate'.[122] At the beginning of their operations in Kosovo, UNMIK and KFOR set up their 'internal claims offices', mandated to deal with financial and other type of claims. However, such internal bodies did not provide any opportunity to 'individuals to be heard or represented by legal counsel in their proceedings and all decisions [were] taken by a panel of UNMIK staff members'.[123]

As noted by the Venice Commission – the advisory body of the CoE -

UNMIK and KFOR carry out tasks, which are certainly more similar to those of a State administration [than to] those of an international organization proper. It is unconceivable and incompatible with the principles of democracy, the rule of law and respect for human rights that they could act as State authorities and be exempted from any independent legal review.[124]

Based on these considerations, the Commission advised to establish

a provisional Human Rights Court for Kosovo to deal with complaints about violations of the ECHR and its Protocols by UNMIK, the Provisional Institutions of Self-Government and possibly NATO (including NATO member States), also stipulating that this court should base its procedures and case law on those of the [ECtHR].[125]

Following these recommendations and discussions between UNMIK and the CoE, UNMIK Regulation 2006/12 established a Human Rights Panel; this body had jurisdiction over complaints relating to alleged violations of human rights as set forth in the main human rights treaties,[126] including the ECHR.

The Panel had the task to address the effective lack of jurisdiction of the ECtHR over Kosovo.[127] The temporal scope of its jurisdiction was limited to the period running from '23 April 2005 or arising from facts which occurred prior to this date where these facts give rise to a continuing violation of human rights.'[128]

---

[122] See HRAP 'About HRAP' <http://www.unmikonline.org/hrap/Eng/Pages/default.aspx> accessed 12 July 2016.
[123] Ombudsperson Institution in Kosovo, 'Third Annual Report 2002-2003 Addressed to the SRSG of the UN' (2003) 4–5.
[124] European Commission for Democracy through law (Venice Commission), 'Opinion on Human Rights in Kosovo: Possible Establishment of Review Mechanisms, Adopted at the 60th Plenary Session' (2004) CDL-AD (2004)033, Opinion no 280/2004 para 91.
[125] ibid 104.
[126] These included the UDHR, ICCPR, ECHR, CAT, CRC. Cf. UNMIK, 'Regulation No 2006/12 on the Establishment of the Human Rights Advisory Panel' (2006) UN Doc UNMIK/REG/2006/12 Section 1, para 1.2.
[127] UNMIK - Press Office, 'Press Release - UNMIK Establishes the Human Rights Advisory Panel' (2006) UNMIK/PR/1525.
[128] UNMIK (n 126) Section 2.

The mandate of the Panel was advisory in nature, as the '[SRSG] shall have exclusive authority and discretion to decide whether to act on [its] findings'.[129]

Despite its mandate's limitations, the role of the Panel cannot be underestimated as to the methodology[130] of its work with regard to the issue of the missing; furthermore, the scope *ratione materiae* of the mandate allowed the Panel to shed light upon post-conflict international law obligations of international organizations when vested with peacebuilding and RoL functions.

Specifically, the Panel noted that 'the appropriate importance attached to the issue of missing persons in Kosovo meant that UNMIK had to take into account both the humanitarian and criminal dimensions of the situation'.[131] Since UNMIK undertook an obligation to observe internationally recognized human rights standards in exercising its functions,[132] the Panel considered that, despite its *interim* character and related difficulties, 'under no circumstances could these elements be taken as a justification for diminishing standards of respect for human rights, which were duly incorporated into UNMIK's mandate'.[133] The Panel made it clear that both in situations of armed conflict or generalized violence as well as in post-conflict situations the duty to investigate, subsumed under human rights standards (e.g., Article 2 ECHR), holds valid.[134]

A clear tension existed between the Panel and those in charge of reminding the UN of the existing human rights standards and obligations: indeed, the Panel noted that

> the SRSG does not contest that UNMIK had a duty to investigate [alleged violation under] ECHR Article 2. However, according to the SRSG, the "unique circumstances" pertaining to the Kosovo context, shall be taken into account when

---

[129] ibid Sect 17, para 17.3.

[130] For instance, the Panel amended its Rules of Procedure on 21 November 2009 by adding new restrictions on disclosure of evidence. Although disclosure remained the general rule, the Panel deemed it important to have the possibility of authorizing that certain evidence will not be disclosed to the other party in the proceedings in order to 'safeguard an important public interest or to preserve the fundamental rights of the complainant or of any other person concerned'. Cf. Rule 39 *bis* (1), HRAP, 'Rules of Procedure' (2008). Such rule was a response to difficulties encountered in certain cases concerning missing persons, where the matter was still under police investigation. See HRAP, 'Annual Report 2009' (2009) para 47 <http://www.unmikonline.org/hrap/Eng/Documents/annual_report 2009.pdf> accessed 10 July 2016.

[131] HRAP, *Snežana Zdravković against UNMIK (opinion, final)* (2013) Case no 46/08 [114]; *SC against UNMIK (opinion, final)* (2012) Case no 02/09 [92]; *JD against UNMIK (opinion, final)* (2013) Case no 44/09 [66]; *BA against UNMIK (opinion, final)* (2013) Case no 52/09 [69]; *Živorad Ogarević against UNMIK (opinion, final)* (2013) Case no 77/09 [72]; *Milko Milenković against UNMIK (opinion, final)* (2014) Case no 127/09 [89]; *ZI against UNMIK (opinion, final)* (2013) Case no 145/09 [80]; *Zufe Miladinović against UNMIK (opinion, final)* (2013) Case no 86/09 [71]; *RP against UNMIK (opinion, final)* (2014) Case no 120/09 and 121/09 [86]; *GR against UNMIK (opinion, final)* (2013) Case no 12/09 [81].

[132] UNMIK, 'UNMIK Regulation No 1999/1 on the Authority of the Interim Administration in Kosovo' (1999) UN Doc UNMIK/REG/1999/1. See also *Jočić against UNMIK* (opinion, final) (2013) Case no 34/09 (HRAP) [80].

[133] HRAP, *Milogorić against UNMIK (opinion, final)* (2010) Case no 38/08 [44]; *Beriša and other against UNMIK (opinion, final)* (2011) Case no 27/08 [25]; *Snežana Zdravković (opinion, final)* (n 131) [110].

[134] HRAP, *Snežana Zdravković (opinion, final)* (n 131) [111].

assessing whether this investigation is in compliance with Article 2 of the ECHR. [...] In substance, the SRSG argues that it is not possible to apply to UNMIK the same standards applicable to a State in a normal situation.[135]

Despite this, the Panel declared that

the importance attached to the criminal investigations and the difficulties in Kosovo that limited the abilities of investigating authorities to conduct such investigations, as described by the SRSG, made it crucial that UNMIK establish from the outset an environment conducive to the performance of meaningful investigations. This would involve putting in place a system that would include such elements as the allocation of overall responsibility for the supervision and monitoring of progress in investigations, provision for the regular review of the status of investigations, and a process for the proper handover of cases between different officers or units of UNMIK Police.[136]

The Panel clarified another important point concerning the duty to investigate in relation to disappearances occurred at the beginning or even prior to the operations of UNMIK: the disappearance of any person in the territory of Kosovo at or around the time of the conflict gave rise to a 'rebuttable presumption' that the person disappeared in life-threatening circumstances; in other words, UNMIK was obliged to conduct an investigation into that person's disappearance under Article 2 of the ECHR.[137] During its work the Panel also recognized that, pursuant to UNSC Resolution 1244 (1999), UNMIK had the primary responsibility to effectively investigate and prosecute the disappearance and killing of any individual and that its failure to do so 'constituted a further serious violation of the human rights of the victims and their next-of-kin, in particular the right to have the truth of the matter determined.'[138]

Overall, the Panel found in a number of cases that UNMIK violated its procedural obligation to carry out an investigation under Article 2 ECHR[139] due to a set of issues categorized as follows: issues related to the investigation

---

[135] ibid [108].

[136] ibid [114].

[137] HRAP, *BA (Opinion, final)* (n 131) [19]. In this case UNMIK argued that since the victim's death was caused by blunt trauma and that he was 80 years old when he went missing, it was possible that he had fallen and thus his death could have been accidental. According to UNMIK, these elements, combined with the fact that his disappearance was not reported to authorities when it occurred, led to the conclusion that there was very little basis upon which UNMIK could have opened an investigation. ibid [18].

[138] This duty had to be discharged in the period in which UNMIK was in charge of the RoL sector, i.e., from 1999 to 2008. HRAP, *SC (opinion, final)* (n 131) [111]; *JD (Opinion, final)* (n 131) [91]; *BA (Opinion, final)* (n 131) [94].

[139] The HRCee reached a similar conclusion in its 2006 report addressed to UNMIK; the Committee expressed its concern over the low priority that had been given to investigations of disappearances and abductions by the Missing Persons Unit of the UNMIK Police and, since 2003, by the Central Criminal Investigative Unit. Furthermore, the Committee noted that in closed cases of disappearances and abductions perpetrators were rarely, if ever, prosecuted and brought to justice. Cf. HRCee, 'Concluding Observations of the Human Rights Committee: Kosovo (Serbia)' (2006) UN Doc CCPR/C/UNK/CO/1 para 13. The same concern was voiced by the WGEID; the Working Group noted that 'cases of enforced disappearances and missing persons were not properly investigated by UNMIK during its full-range administration in Kosovo' and that the HRAP reached the same conclusion. Cf. WGEID, 'Report of the WGEID. Addendum: Mission to Serbia, Including Kosovo' (2015) UN Doc A/HRC/30/38/Add.1 para 69.

process itself (e.g., important delays in initial actions or lack of protection of witnesses from threats or intimidation); structural issues (e.g., flaws in the coordination and cooperation between UNMIK and the ICTY, or absence of proper prosecutorial review); and policy issues (e.g., inaction of the authorities because such investigations were not considered a priority).[140]

The approach to the obligation of UNMIK to inform the next of kin about any new developments of its investigative activities partly reflected the ECtHR's approach (see sub-section 2.1 in Chapter IV). In this regard, and differently from the assessment concerning the duty to investigate subsumed under Article 2 ECHR, the Panel proceeded on a case-by-case basis and examined the attitude and reactions of UNMIK vis-à-vis the family member concerned. For instance, the Panel found that the complainant 'suffered severe distress and anguish for a prolonged and continuing period of time on account of the way the authorities of UNMIK have dealt with their complaints' (e.g. no contact with complainant, UNMIK's failure to submit a complete investigative file or to provide another plausible explanation for the absence of a sustained regular contact with the complainant, or information about the criminal investigation into the disappearance).[141]

In this respect, echoing *Janowiec et al v Russia* (2012), the Panel pointed out that

the obligation under Article 3 of the ECHR differs from the procedural obligation on the authorities under Article 2. Whereas the latter requires the authorities to take specific legal action capable of leading to identification and punishment of those responsible, the former is more general and humanitarian and relates to their reaction to the plight of the relatives of those who have disappeared or died.[142]

The HRAP's final report grimly recognized that in

an overwhelming majority of cases [...] the families of missing or murdered victims were either provided with no information about the state and progress of investigation, or the amount of this information was insufficient to safeguard their legitimate interests.[143]

In those cases in which the Panel has found that UNMIK violated its obligation to investigate the reported disappearance and to inform the families, it recommended UNMIK: to take all possible steps in order to ensure that the criminal investigation into the disappearance and killing of the complainants is continued in compliance with Article 2 ECHR and that the perpetrators are

[140] HRAP, 'The Human Rights Advisory Panel. History and Legacy: Kosovo 2007-2016. Final Report' (2016) para 33. For a detailed analysis of each issue, see ibid paras 175–177.
[141] HRAP, *Živorad Ogarević (Opinion, final)* (n 131) [107–109]; *Nebojša Petković against UNMIK (opinion, final)* (2013) Case no 125/09 (HRAP) [122–125].
[142] HRAP, *Nebojša Petković (Opinion, final)* (n 141) [107]; *Zufe Miladinović (Opinion, final)* (n 131) [93]; *GR (opinion, final)* (n 131) [103]; *Jočić (opinion, final)* (n 132) [103].
[143] HRAP, 'The HRAP. History and Legacy' (n 140) para 175. From out of the total of 248 missing persons cases declared admissible, in 178 cases the Panel considered that the allegations also included issues under Article 3 of the ECHR. Out of those 178 cases, in 163 the Panel found that UNMIK had not acted in conformity with the substantive requirement of Article 3. See ibid 182.

brought to justice;[144] to acknowledge publicly responsibility for its failure in conducting such investigation; to make a public apology; to take appropriate steps towards payments of adequate compensation as well as towards the realization of a comprehensive reparation program; and to take appropriate steps at the UN level as a guarantee of non-repetition.[145]

Despite the SRSG's reassurance of implementation of the above-mentioned recommendations, there was a clear lack of concrete follow-up.[146] For instance, in relation to compensation and guarantees of non-repetition, the SRSG put the attention on the fact that UNMIK did not continue to have control over the institutions; he also noted that UNMIK did no longer perform police functions, including police investigations.[147] Although the Panel highlighted international law standards binding upon the UN, the SRSG even recalled the fact that 'the principals organs of the [UN] have adopted numerous resolutions and decisions which reflect the importance of promoting and protecting human rights, including by the [UN].'[148] Whether this declaration was a form of wounded pride

---

[144] The WGEID made a similar recommendation in its country-visit report, where it stated that 'the failures by UNMIK should be properly addressed and the victims of those failures should be effectively compensated by the [UN]'. Cf. WGEID (n 139) paras 69, 141.

[145] Cf. HRAP, *Živorad Ogarević (Opinion, final)* (n 131) [final recommendations]; *Nebojša Petković (Opinion, final)* (n 141) [final recommendations]; *Milko Milenković (Opinion, final)* (n 131) [final recommendations]; *Zufe Miladinović (Opinion, final)* (n 131) [final recommendations]; *GR (opinion, final)* (n 131) [final recommendations]; *Z.I. (Opinion, final)* (n 131) [final recommendations]; *RP (Opinion, final)* (n 131) [final recommendations]; *Jočić (opinion, final)* (n 132) [final recommendations].

[146] The SRSG highlighted that UNMIK 'will [...] continue to urge EULEX and other competent authorities to continue to take all possible steps in order to ensure that the criminal investigation into the disappearance and killing of the Complainants family members is continued and that the perpetrators are brought to justice'. See among others *SC against UNMIK* (SRSG's response to the Panel's Recommendations) (2013) Case no 02/09; *JD against UNMIK* (SRSG's response to the Panel's Recommendations) (2013) Case no 44/09; *BA against UNMIK* (SRSG's response to the Panel's Recommendations) (2013) Case no 52/09; *Živorad Ogarević against UNMIK* (SRSG's response to the Panel's Recommendations) (2013) Case no 77/09; *Nebojša Petković against UNMIK* (SRSG's response to the Panel's Recommendations) (2013) Case no 125/09; *RP against UNMIK* (SRSG's response to the Panel's Recommendations) (2014) Case no 120/09 and 121/09; *Zufe Miladinović against UNMIK* (SRSG's response to the Panel's Recommendations) (2013) Case no 86/09. Moreover, the SRSG regretted that there was a lack of an effective investigation into the disappearances See *SC (SRSG's response to the Panel's Recommendations); JD (SRSG's response to the Panel's Recommendations); BA (SRSG's response to the Panel's Recommendations); Živorad Ogarević (SRSG's response to the Panel's Recommendations); Nebojša Petković (SRSG's response to the Panel's Recommendations); RP (SRSG's response to the Panel's Recommendations); Zufe Miladinović (SRSG's response to the Panel's Recommendations); Jočić against UNMIK (SRSG's response to the Panel's Recommendations)* (2013) Case no 34/09.

[147] Cf. *SC (SRSG's response to the Panel's Recommendations)* (n 146); *JD (SRSG's response to the Panel's Recommendations)* (n 146); *BA (SRSG's response to the Panel's Recommendations)* (n 146); *Živorad Ogarević (SRSG's response to the Panel's Recommendations)* (n 146); *Nebojša Petković (SRSG's response to the Panel's Recommendations)* (n 146); *RP (SRSG's response to the Panel's Recommendations)* (n 146); *Zufe Miladinović (SRSG's response to the Panel's Recommendations)* (n 146); *Jočić (SRSG's response to the Panel's Recommendations)* (n 146).

[148] Cf. *SC (SRSG's response to the Panel's Recommendations)* (n 146); *JD (SRSG's response to the Panel's Recommendations)* (n 146); *BA (SRSG's response to the Panel's Recommendations)* (n 146); *Živorad Ogarević (SRSG's response to the Panel's Recommendations)* (n 146); *Nebojša Petković (SRSG's response to the Panel's Recommendations)* (n 146); *RP (SRSG's response to the Panel's*

or a futile reminder of the abundance of UN declaratory documents is unknown; however, the rather rhetorical character of the SRSG's statements deprived his assurance of any meaningful contribution from the UN towards the victims.[149]

The final report of the Panel sadly admitted the total failure with regard to all the recommendations highlighted above; these were fully ignored by UNMIK, which eventually did not take any action. The Panel also admitted that no investigation was re-opened under EULEX; the new entity transferred the cases to local bodies, disregarding the need for anonymity that most of the missing persons cases required.[150]

Le bilan final of the Panel must serve as a *memento* for future experiences. Specifically, the following aspects must be kept in mind: 'the continued lack of investigation of [missing persons] cases reflects the fact that the establishment of the Panel came too late to be able to influence UNMIK's action with respect to law enforcement'; a clear disconnection between the SRSG's role and the Panel resulted in an underestimation of the Panel's recommendations (e.g., public apology in the form of a single letter for all the cases posted on the website) or in a 'diplomatic' rejection of the same (e.g., the complete disregard of the request for compensation); [151] the difficult relationship between the Panel and UNMIK and the lack of clear procedures concerning the transmission of investigative files hampered the work of the former.[152] The Panel also proposed a sort of road map for a future body intended for reaching its same objective: this body should be able to deliver binding and not advisory decisions; the UN headquarters – and not the peace mission – should establish this body since the outset of the mission and should include it into the mandate of the mission; the UN shall consider how to comply with such body's recommendations in order to avoid raising false expectations in the victims.[153]

1.2. Discrepancies between the families' need to know and the judicial efforts to establish the truth: The case of the ICTY

As Judge Schomburg (ICTY) once said, 'there is no peace without justice; there is no justice without truth, meaning the entire truth and nothing but the truth'.[154] The traditional view confers upon victims of international crimes the

---

Recommendations) (n 146); *Zufe Miladinović (SRSG's response to the Panel's Recommendations)* (n 146); *Jočić (SRSG's response to the Panel's Recommendations)* (n 146).

[149] Interestingly, some of the cases presented six and not five recommendations; the sixth - focused on the implementation of recommendation and the request for information on further developments of the case - was never mentioned in the SRSG's response.

[150] HRAP, 'The HRAP. History and Legacy' (n 140) para 243.

[151] The SRSG usually used the following formula to reject the compensatory measures and guarantees of non-repetition: 'had UNMIK continued to have control over these institutions today, UNMIK would have been in a position to refer the Panel's recommendation to those institutions for appropriate action. I am prepared to discuss the possibility of setting up a mechanism to deal with such matters with the relevant authorities at the appropriate juncture'. ibid paras 245–254.

[152] ibid para 274.

[153] ibid paras 280–282.

[154] ICTY, *Dissenting Opinion of Judge Schomburg - Prosecutor v Miroslav Deronjić* (2004) Case no IT-02-61-S [15].

right to obtain justice and, as a corollary, to the establishment of the truth. As Zappalà observes, the judicial truth, i.e., the truth that the judge will try to establish, is different from 'the truth with capital T, but it is still the only justification that today's society can use to impose a penalty on an individual'.[155] From a TJ perspective, truth, justice, reparations, and guarantees of non-recurrence must be part of a comprehensive strategy that aims at paving the way towards reconciliation[156] after the perpetration of heinous crimes in the context of an armed conflict. Thus, a judicial body that operates in a transitional setting has a duty to establish the truth towards the victims, but also towards the accused. The establishment of the judicial truth with regard to international crimes should serve the individual and collective need to know what happened and who did it;[157] however, in the case of the families of missing persons, the most urgent need is to know where the missing relative is, whether he/she is alive, whether the exhumed body is that of the relative who is missing. The question of whether the steps to establish the "judicial truth" coincide with those to meet the right of families to know the fate of their relatives must be addressed in order to cast light upon the consequences of discrepancies between these processes.

The present sub-section examines the example of the ICTY; the aim is twofold, i.e., identify the challenges emerging from the co-presence of the need of families for information on their relatives and the evidentiary needs of the Office of the Prosecutor – OTP (sub-section 1.2.1); assess the cooperation between the ICTY's Prosecutor and humanitarian bodies and cast light upon operational synergies between accountability-driven and humanitarian approaches to the issue of missing persons (sub-section 1.2.2). The Tribunal started working during the armed conflict in the Balkans in 1993 and continued afterwards; this timeline makes this body absolutely peculiar among other international criminal judicial or semi-judicial bodies, usually established in the aftermath of the conflict.

1.2.1. Information as a prosecutorial and families' need

During the twenty years of work, the issue of the missing and the need of their families for information have emerged in the work of the Tribunal under several angles. At the inception of its work in 1993, the ICTY[158] did not integrate humanitarian considerations in relation to the suffering of the families of missing

---

[155] Salvatore Zappalà, 'The Rights of Victims v. the Rights of the Accused' (2010) 8 Journal of International Criminal Justice 137, 145.

[156] Human Rights Council, 'Report of the Special Rapporteur on the Promotion of Truth, Justice, Reparation and Guarantees of Non-Recurrence - Prosecutorial Prioritization Strategies in the Aftermath of Gross Human Rights Violations and Serious Violations of IHL' (2014) UN Doc A/HRC/27/56 paras 18–19. The ICTY's Statute is based on Chapter VII of the UN Charter, which makes the Tribunal a measure to maintain or restore international peace and security.

[157] UN Commission on Human Rights, 'Orentlicher Principles' (n 43) Principle 2.

[158] After the brutal conflict that broke up in the Former Yugoslavia in the early 1990s, the UNSC passed Resolution 827, which formally established the ICTY. The Resolution contained the Statute of the ICTY, which determined the Tribunal's jurisdiction and organization structure, as well as the criminal procedure in general terms. The ICTY has been the first international war crimes tribunal since the Nuremberg and Tokyo Tribunals.

persons into its prosecutorial approach.[159] Investigative activities, including exhumations of mass graves, inevitably led to the discovery of hundreds of bodies or scattered human remains of victims along with information concerning the criminal events, the site (burial site, crime scene, ...), and the statistical data relevant to the investigation.[160] The confusion of roles between forensic experts – external to the ICTY – and investigators[161] and the lack of clarity in the forensic teams' mandate brought about some troubling consequences.[162]

First, the localization of gravesites and the exhumations of human remains were considered by the relatives an opportunity to finally know whether their relatives were still alive. However, under the lead of the ICTY's Chief of Prosecutions, the forensic teams had the mission to find patterns in the methodology used by perpetrators, to compare size/numbers of groups, to highlight the rare against the common, to understand whether there had been attempts to cover the traces.[163]

Second, the identification of the individuals was not, *per se,* part of their work; neither was it part of the tasks carried out by the teams of investigators. Indeed, the OTP was tasked to investigate international crimes, which, by nature, differed from ordinary crimes, as the former were large-scale events occurred across wide areas of the Balkans.[164] In case of evidence (e.g., the discovery of mass graves) pointing towards the crime of genocide, the investigations that followed needed to ascertain 'the categorical identification of the dead', i.e., the victims' ethnicity, religion, or race and the cause of death. In other words, the personal identification of each single body found in the mass graves was not

---

[159] The organization of the ICTY files has been set down without having in mind the possibility that the bulk of information therein might be used for humanitarian purposes; indeed, from a mere organizational perspective, the structure of the information system of the ICTY reflects the prosecutorial needs and disregard the families' needs. See, in this respect, L Milner, 'The ICTY Legacy in Finding Missing Persons' in Richard H Steinberg (ed), *Assessing the Legacy of the ICTY* (Martinus Nijhoff Publishers 2011) 123.

[160] Mark Skinner and Jon Sterenberg, 'Turf Wars: Authority and Responsibility for the Investigation of Mass Graves' (2005) 151 Forensic Science International 221, 225–231.

[161] ICTY, 'Investigations' <http://www.icty.org/en/about/office-of-the-prosecutor/investigations> accessed 12 January 2017.

[162] "Investigators" is a general terminology that, in the case of the ICTY, included investigators, lawyers, and analysts or research officers of the Office of the Prosecutor – OTP. From the forensic experts' viewpoint, the situation under the ICTY was particularly confused. There was a lack of clarity with regard to the accountability for investigations and related results (e.g., exhumations were performed through liaison with the Argentine Forensic Anthropology Team - EAAF, Physicians for Human Rights – PHR; and the ICMP by mixed teams of pathologists, anthropologists, archaeologists and scene of crime officers); a lack of training in relation to international investigation was also reported. See Skinner and Sterenberg (n 160) 222; Eric Stover and Rachel Shigekane, 'The Missing in the Aftermath of War: When Do the Needs of Victims' Families and International War Crimes Tribunals Clash?' (2002) 84 International Review of the Red Cross 845, 864. Similar concerns aroused for the ICTR that commissioned a series of mass grave exhumations that were conducted by PHR; the PHR's exercise encountered criticism as being culturally inappropriate and lacking scientific rigor. See ICMP, 'Rwanda' (7 August 2014) <https://www.icmp.int/the-missing/where-are-the-missing/rwanda/> accessed 12 January 2016.

[163] Stover and Shigekane (n 162) 845; Skinner and Sterenberg (n 160) 229.

[164] See ICTY, 'Investigations' (n 161).

necessary; therefore, it was outsourced to local forensic experts who, only then, would have carried out individual identification procedures.[165]

A case that epitomizes this way of proceeding relates to the investigations for the collection of evidence concerning the Srebrenica events: based on the results of the examinations carried out by the forensic teams over more than 500 bodies and disarticulated human remains, the OTP decided that the establishment of the victims' ethnicity and cause and manner of death would be enough to build the case of genocide against the main perpetrators; in other words, no personal identification was performed.[166] In the immediate aftermath of the investigation, the decision of the OTP was to hand over the exhumed bodies to local authorities which did not have the expertise to carry out the identification procedures and, consequently, placed them in a tunnel near Tuzla.[167] A strong reaction of the families followed the lack of answers to their requests for information: indeed, in February 1996 women demonstrated by the hundreds in front of relief organizations and government buildings; some of them sacked the local offices of the ICRC in order to draw attention to the plight of more than 8,000 men missing after the Bosnian Serbs stormed the enclave.[168] When, in 2001, the ICTY ended its field investigations there was a legacy of more than 6,000 unidentified exhumed remains.[169]

Third, the ICTY as well as the Prosecutor did not have any obligation to carry out investigative activities with the purpose of accounting for those reported as missing. Neither did they have any obligation to develop and provide a comprehensive historical record of the events; they could not and 'should not be expected to document the fate' of all those who were reported missing.[170] Certainly, the Prosecutor's main responsibility was to carry out investigations – including forensic investigations, in relation to alleged crimes that fell under the

---

[165] Stover and Shigekane (n 162) 846–847. Similarly, in case of evidence pointing towards crimes against humanity there is no need to carry out individual identification; the only need is to prove that the victims were civilians and whether the manner in which they were killed was similar in the different areas where such crimes were allegedly perpetrated. A case that exemplifies such situation is that of the investigations carried out in relation to the alleged crimes against humanity perpetrated by Milosevic in Kosovo. See ibid 857.

[166] Stover and Shigekane (n 162) 853 ff.

[167] The situation remained unchanged in Kosovo where the OTP deployed more than 300 forensic experts from 14 countries; despite one of the largest international forensic investigation for war crimes, there was no need to identify each single victim, since the aim was to 'corroborate witness testimonies and documentary evidence by identifying some of the victims of mass killings, determining how they had died, and demonstrating that the systematic and widespread nature of the killings suggested they had been planned in high places.' ibid 857–858.

[168] Kit R Roane, 'The Bosnia Accord in Tuzla: Women Demand News of Srebrenica's Men' *The New York Times* (3 February 1996) <http://www.nytimes.com/1996/02/03/world/the-bosnia-accord-in-tuzla-women-demand-news-of-srebrenica-s-men.html> accessed 2 February 2017.

[169] ICMP, 'Bosnia i Herzegovina. Missing Persons from the Armed Conflicts of the 1990s: A Stocktaking' (2014) 49.

[170] Amnesty International, 'Bosnia-Herzegovina: "To Bury My Brothers" Bones"' (1996) EUR 63/015/1996 15.

mandate of the ICTY.[171] In this sense, the investigative activities were limited to those areas or sites where it was believed that significant evidence could be obtained to support indictments (or gather evidence to support future indictments).

The foregoing demonstrates that there was no systematic approach[172] to the issue of the missing as such, since this issue was incidental to the work of the Prosecutor and, more generally, of the Tribunal.[173] These factors show that there have been pragmatic constraints characterizing the approach of the ICTY to the issue of the missing; and yet it must be recognized that the Tribunal, and more generally, criminal proceedings carried out at the international and domestic level are not designed to address the issue of persons reported missing as a result of an armed conflict from a humanitarian perspective. The scope of their action remains limited to the determination of the guilt or innocence of the accused and, as a corollary, investigations respond to the goal of the prosecution.[174]

A comprehensive peacebuilding strategy cannot disregard the issue of the missing. In the case of the ICTY, which as part of its mandate aims at contributing to the restoration and maintenance of peace,[175] the lack of any form of inclusiveness of the families in the design and implementation of prosecutorial strategies and the absence of any form of institutionalized victim participation turned into a clash of needs in several occasions.[176] Should a similar body be

---

[171] Cf. Article 16 (1), Statute of the ICTY, adopted 25 May 1993 by UNSC Resolution 827 (last amendment 7 July 2009 by UNSC Resolution 1877) (hereinafter, ICTY Statute). It is important to mention that in the Prosecutor's perspective, evidence gathered as a result of exhumations was the most powerful proof of particular events. ICTY, 'Fourth Annual Report of the International Tribunal for the Prosecution of Persons Responsible for Serious Violations of [IHL] Committed in the Territory of the Former Yugoslavia Since 1991' (1997) UN Doc A/52/375-S/1997/729 para 64.

[172] Positive reconciliation followed investigative activities of the OTP in those places where the State infrastructure was not as affected by the conflict as it was in Bosnia. For instance, Stover and Shigekane provide the example of Ovcara where forensic efforts satisfied both the legal and evidentiary needs of an international criminal tribunal and the humanitarian needs of families; the contribution of the Croatian authorities is considered key. See Stover and Shigekane (n 162) 851. A positive example from a different scenario was the approach to forensic investigations adopted by the Argentine Forensic Anthropology Team (EAAF): as a pioneer for development of modern forensic techniques in the 1980s, EAAF has undertaken the identification of the individuals in the context of investigative and forensic tasks aimed at gathering evidence for criminal trials (e.g., in Argentina, in Guatemala); in line with human rights and humanitarian law standards, this has contributed to realizing the right of families to know the fate of their missing relatives. EAAF's work is, indeed, grounded in the understanding that the identification of the remains is a source of solace to families suffering from the disappearance of the loved ones. Argentine Forensic Anthropology Team - EAAF, '2007-2009 Triannual Report' (2009) 3 <http://www.eaaf.org/eaaf_reports/2007-2009/AR09_Covers-p15.pdf> accessed 12 January 2017.

[173] ICTY, 'Fourth Annual Report - ICTY' (n 171) para 64.

[174] Crettol and La Rosa (n 12) 359.

[175] UNSC (n 20) Preamble; E Tabeau and OTP - ICTY, 'ICRC Lists of Missing Persons as Part of the OTP Information System on Victims of IHL Violations Committed in the 1990s Conflict in the Former Yugoslavia' in Maria Teresa Dutli and Noreen Majeed (eds), *Report of the Second Universal Meeting of National Committees on International Humanitarian Law - Geneva, 19–21 March 2007. Legal Measures and Mechanisms to Prevent Disappearances, to Establish the Fate of Missing Persons, and to Assist Their Families* (ICRC 2007) 162.

[176] In his report on prosecutorial strategies, Pablo de Greiff has noted that '[v]ictim participation in the design of prosecutorial strategies at international and hybrid courts has proven crucial in

established again in the future, the foregoing considerations cannot be overlooked. This means that international prosecutorial strategies should not disregard the implications that investigative activities have on the families of the missing, since these implications may hinder the overall process towards a sustainable peace.

1.2.2. The relevance of information on the missing for humanitarian and accountability purposes

TJ bodies are an invaluable source of information that can be conducive to a successful process aimed at accounting for missing persons. The ICTY represents one of such invaluable sources of information; indeed, the ICRC has gained access to information gathered by the ICTY which was not in use for trial purposes or which concerned closed cases.[177] However, as ICRC staff members have remarked in multiple occasions, the examination of this information has been, and still is, time-consuming due to the organization of files according to prosecutorial needs and due to the total disregard of other possible usages, including identification purposes.[178]

From an accountability perspective, the lists of missing persons – notably those of the ICRC and of Physicians for Human Rights (PHR)[179] – and the information contained therein[180] have been one of the sources[181] that the ICTY

---

identifying the array of possible violations. The Special Rapporteur highlights the dearth of institutionalized mechanisms for victim participation at the domestic level'; he has also pointed out that '[v]ictim participation implies recognition of victims as rights holders'. Human Rights Council, 'Prosecutorial Prioritization Strategies' (n 156) paras 115–116.

[177] Crettol and La Rosa (n 12) 359.

[178] AM La Rosa, 'The Right to Know and the Fight against Impunity' in María Teresa Dutli and Noreen Majeed (eds), *Report of the Second Universal Meeting of National Committees on International Humanitarian Law - Geneva, 19–21 March 2007. Legal Measures and Mechanisms to Prevent Disappearances, to Establish the Fate of Missing Persons, and to Assist Their Families* (ICRC 2007) 157; Milner (n 159) 123.

[179] At the same time, the ICTY has used information and data provided by the ICMP as result of its identification work in order to develop statistical data on the missing and the dead from the Balkans, notably the areas related to Srebrenica. See Held Brunborg and others, 'Missing and Dead from Srebrenica: The 2005 Report and List' (2005) Expert Report for the Case of Vujadin Popovic et al. (IT-05-88) 1 <http://www.icty.org/x/file/About/OTP/War_Demographics/en/popovic_srebrenica_050916.pdf> accessed 12 January 2016.

[180] As far as the ICRC's lists of missing persons are concerned, these include, *inter alia*, surname, first name, father's name, sex, date and place of birth, and date and place of disappearance; each list of persons was organized according to five main components, i.e., 'still missing with information about the body not yet available'; 'still missing with information about the body already available'; ICRC closed cases (confirmed death); alive persons (cases no longer valid as part of the missing persons list); and administrative exclusions. Cf. Tabeau and OTP - ICTY (n 175) 164–165.

[181] The information sources also include witness' and survivors' statements, known public and/or classified documents (camp records, police files, military records....), list of the killed compiled by international and/or State commissions, results deriving from additional name searches in existing databases, exhumation, forensic, medical, autopsy reports, and records of identification of the exhumed persons. These sources together with the list of missing persons have helped draw up the list of victims that can be annexed to the indictments. See, ibid 166–167. For instance, the ICMP has provided DNA reports to the ICTY in numerous trials. This has required the consent of those who have provided DNA reference samples. See ICMP, 'Bosnia i Herzegovina. A Stocktaking' (n 169) 121.

has used in the course of its work. As reported by the OTP,[182] these lists could be potentially relevant to all phases of the criminal proceedings:

– in the investigation phase, the names reported in those lists could provide the OTP with an initial idea about potential victims. If used with other sources, the lists could show crime patterns; they could also be cross-referenced with related sources on victims covering the same incidents in order to confirm how many of the missing were also reported dead and in what circumstances. It is not excluded that some names might be among the survivors, which has often entailed an examination of sources on post-conflict survivors.

– In the indictment phase, the names of the missing could be included among those of the victims, depending on the results of the investigations.[183]

– At the trial stage, the Prosecutors can represent the missing in the lists as the actual victims of the incidents in question, if the records are reliable to proceed in this sense; the lists can also be a reference source for victim names that are mentioned in testimonies, documents, or by the defense (this might also occur at the appeal stage).

From the foregoing points, it can be inferred that the use of the lists of missing persons for prosecutorial purposes has contributed to bringing perpetrators to justice[184] and, at the same time, to clarifying the fate of the missing. Nevertheless, the courses of actions undertaken by the ICRC and the OTP have always pursued different objectives, i.e., elucidating the fate and informing the families for the former and gathering evidence of crimes for the latter. And yet the collaboration between the two has been mutually beneficial to the pursuance of such objectives.

Accountability and humanitarian courses of action are intertwined and can be carried out by multiple actors in the same context. This was the case of Kosovo, where the collaboration between the ICTY and other actors did not work as well as expected.[185] As shown in Chapter V, a panoply of international and local organizations were dealing with the missing and their families' claims in the

---

[182] The bullet points listed above are a summary of the presentation given by Ewa Tabeau, Demographer of the OTP on behalf of the Investigations Division of the OTP – ICTY during the 2nd Universal Meeting of National Committees on IHL organized by the ICRC. See Tabeau and OTP - ICTY (n 175) 168.

[183] The list of victims is indeed developed on the bases of multiple sources which include the list of missing persons; such lists can be annexed to the indictments and be, therefore, accessible to the public, but the practice in this regard is not consistent. See ICTY, *ICTY Manual on Developed Practices - Prepared in Conjunction with UNICRI as Part of a Project to Preserve the Legacy of the ICTY* (UNICRI 2009) paras 21, 114.

[184] ICRC lists of missing persons, in particular, have been useful in the trials concerning the events of Srebrenica, including the Kristic Trial, the Popovic and others trial, the Milosevic one, and the Blagojevic and others trial.

[185] In 1998, reports emerged that new crimes falling under the ICTY's jurisdiction were being committed in Kosovo. Hoping to contribute to a peaceful solution of the situation in Kosovo, the Prosecutor Louise Arbour made a public statement in March confirming that the Tribunal's jurisdiction covered any serious violations of IHL taking place in Kosovo and that she was empowered to investigate such crimes. See 'About the ICTY - OTP: History' <http://www.icty.org/en/about/office-of-the-prosecutor/history> accessed 12 December 2016.

Kosovar context, including UNMIK. The lack of effective cooperation between the ICTY and UNMIK impacted on the justice sector and, ultimately, on the families of the missing. Instances of collaboration were described by UNMIK in its reports: for instance, in 2000, UNMIK reported that 'the victim recovery identification commission proposed by UNMIK should [...] give a more accurate figure for the truly missing. This Commission, chaired by UNMIK, would make systematic efforts towards exhuming graves that the [ICTY] declines to deal with.'[186] This Commission was supposed to work closely with the ICTY by, *inter alia,* assisting in the identification of remains exhumed by the Tribunal.[187] Nevertheless, one of the main structural problems of this cooperation was the lack of total coordination between the two entities in terms of transmission of information and of exchange of relevant data with regard to the carrying out of investigations into the disappearances. In this respect, the HRAP pointed out that such downside strongly affected the work of UNMIK's investigators.[188] Specifically, in some cases, UNMIK Police did not investigate the disappearance of a person because the ICTY had taken over the investigations, without providing any further documentation to confirm such distribution of tasks to the Panel.[189] Although no fault was found in the actions of UNMIK organs, the Panel could not assess the actions of the ICTY because of its jurisdictional limitations *ratione personae*.[190] Indeed, in his submission to the Panel, the SRSG confirmed that

> the shortfall of forensic standards was the lack of attention paid to the humanitarian agenda of identifying bodies and restituting their remains to their families. In a focused effort to demonstrate that crimes were systematic and widespread, the ICTY and its gratis teams autopsied as many bodies as possible with little or no identification work. [...] [F]urthermore, some of the unidentified bodies exhumed in 1999 by gratis teams were reburied in locations still unknown to OMPF'.[191]

The limitation of the Panel's jurisdiction did not prevent it from emphasizing that, although 'it [did] not dispute the ICTY's overall primacy jurisdiction to investigate any crime within its jurisdiction'[192], 'there should have been a trail of paperwork between UNMIK and the ICTY, indicating the handover of proceedings, but that it was lacking.'[193] Pursuant to the ICTY's Rules of Procedure (cf. Rules 8-10),

---

[186] UNSG, 'Report of the Secretary-General on the UNMIK' (2000) UN Doc S/2000/177 para 65.

[187] UNSG, 'Report of the Secretary-General on UNMIK' (2000) UN Doc S/2000/538 para 54. Along the same lines, UNMIK reported that the 'ICTY [...] provided information to OMPF, including over 85,000 documents which ICTY agreed to hand over upon condition that OMPF assumes exclusive legal custody.' UNMIK/HRCee, 'Comments by the United Nations Interim Administration Mission in Kosovo (UNMIK) on the Concluding Observations of the Human Rights Committee (CCPR/C/UNK/CO/1)' (2008) UN Doc CCPR/C/UNK/CO/1/Add.1 para 13.

[188] HRAP, 'The HRAP. History and Legacy' (n 140) para 176.

[189] ibid para 120; HRAP, *Vitošević and Majmarević against UNMIK (opinion, final)* (2014) Cases no 139/09 et al [72, 88, 98, 127–132].

[190] HRAP, *Remištar against UNMIK (opinion, final)* (2014) Case no 245/09 [117–118]; *Mitrović and Others (opinion, final)* (2014) Cases no 144/09 et al [193–203].

[191] HRAP, *Remištar (opinion, final)* (n 190) [68].

[192] HRAP, *Mitrović and Others (opinion, final)* (n 190) [194].

[193] HRAP, 'The HRAP. History and Legacy' (n 140) para 176. Important is to note that specialized equipment necessary in the course of the forensic investigations carried out as part of the ICTY's

a formal request for information and cooperation or a request for deferral of proceedings must have been presented by the ICTY to national authorities. Thus, the ICTY must have presented such a request to UNMIK, before taking over [a] case, which would have been formally reflected in UNMIK's documentation. This would, *first*, justify the lack of UNMIK's authorities' action with regard to particular investigations, and, *second*, it would enable future tracking and retrieving of the investigative documents and evidence by national authorities, when needed.[194]

Indeed, such defective form of cooperation hampered the possibility of tracking down the chain of custody of the investigative files between the Tribunal and UNMIK (and then EULEX[195]). This downside might still have negative spillover effects in terms of future criminal proceedings and of realization of rights of the interested parties,[196] including the families of those subjected to enforced disappearances.

1.3. Post-conflict TJ: The incidental character of the individual need for information vs the central character of the collective right to truth?

As underlined in Chapters I and V, post-conflict peacebuilding efforts are aimed at establishing a sustainable peace; this means that, at a minimum, such efforts should succeed in the prevention of a new outbreak of conflict and the occurrence/recurrence of IHL and IHRL violations.[197] In this respect, where international TJ mechanisms are established, these are expected to investigate IHL and IHRL violations, circulate their findings, and make it sure that victims have access to remedies.[198] These mechanisms contribute – to various degrees – to shedding light upon what happened and to responding to the collective claim for truth 'about past events concerning the perpetration of heinous crimes and

---

forensic program were transferred to organizations working in the Balkans - UNMIK, ICMP, EUPOL in Bosnia and Herzegovina - in conformity with the ICTY's completion strategy. ICTY, 'Eleventh Annual Report of the International Tribunal for the Prosecution of Persons Responsible for Serious Violations of International Humanitarian Law Committed in the Territory of the Former Yugoslavia since 1991' (2004) UN Doc A/59/215-S/2004/627 para 388.

[194] In *Mitrović and Others*, the Panel noted with concern that in light of UNMIK's submission 'no record of any formal request of such nature was submitted by the ICTY, or even had to be submitted [...]. Thus, it appears that UNMIK's investigative files might have been simply subject of a "seizure" by the ICTY, without any formal request from the latter and without even any trace of such action. [This...] could seriously affect the possibility of tracking the documents and evidence in the case, as well as ensuring that those are the originals.' HRAP, *Mitrović and Others (opinion, final)* (n 190) [197, 199].

[195] ibid [146].

[196] ibid [199].

[197] Cindy Holder, 'Truthfulness in Transition: The Value of Insisting on Experiential Adequacy' in Larry May and Elizabeth Edenberg (eds), *Jus Post Bellum and Transitional Justice* (Cambridge University Press 2013) 244–245 (arguing that *jus post bellum* includes responsibilities to rebuilt); Robert E Williams and Dan Caldwell, 'Jus Post Bellum: Just War Theory and the Principles of Just Peace' (2006) 7 International Studies Perspectives 309, 317–318 (considering the just war perspective and elaborating on the concept of just peace in the framework of *jus post bellum*); Gary J Bass, 'Jus Post Bellum' 32 Philosophy and Public Affairs 384, 386–387.

[198] Holder (n 197) 245.

about the circumstances and reasons that led, through massive or systematic violations, to the perpetration of those crimes'.[199]

Truth, however, is an imprecise term. In the context of criminal proceedings, truth is a judicially made product resulting from the gathering of information that has been verified[200] in order to hold the perpetrators of violations accountable. Truth has a historical dimension, which can lead State authorities to hide facts and information behind the excuse of historically established facts.[201] Moreover, the establishment of the truth has an inherent societal dimension, as the Orentlicher Principles show ('every people has the inalienable right to know the truth…').[202] However, the failure of judicial bodies to consider the individual perspective about the truth risks impacting on the collective assertion of the truth, as 'each victim may not recognize himself/herself in this general approach […].'[203] Balancing the societal dimension proper to the truth discourse with the

---

[199] UN OHCHR, 'Study on the Right to the Truth' (2006) UN Doc E/CN.4/2006/91 paras 14, 59; UN Commission on Human Rights, 'Orentlicher Principles' (n 43) Principle 2.

[200] Zappalà, in this respect admits that, in the context of the criminal procedure, the 'establishment of the truth can only be carried out through a process of information gathering and of verification of the facts; […] [n]aturally, different procedural systems have different methods of pursuing the search for the truth. In merely descriptive terms, in the inquisitorial system there is a confidence that objective truth exists; it is up to a public organ (the judge) to identify it on the basis of contributions coming from various sources, including the victim and the defendant. In accusatorial systems, on the other hand, the truth can emerge only as a result of the confrontation of two parties. In such a system introducing a third party (e.g. the victim or any other actor, such as States, non-governmental organizations and so on) per se modifies the scheme of truth seeking'. Zappalà (n 155) 145 and 153.

[201] For instance, with regard to the Katyń massacre occurred during WWII the ECtHR noted that 'the Court's jurisdiction extends only to the period starting on 5 May 1998, the date of entry into force of the Convention in respect of Russia. [...] As from that date, no lingering uncertainty as to the fate of the Polish prisoners of war could be said to have remained. Even though not all of the bodies have been recovered, their death was publicly acknowledged by the Soviet and Russian authorities and has become an established historical fact. The magnitude of the crime committed in 1940 by the Soviet authorities is a powerful emotional factor; yet from a purely legal point of view, the Court cannot accept it as a compelling reason for departing from its case-law on the status of the family members of "disappeared persons" as victims of a violation of Article 3 and conferring that status on the applicants, for whom the death of their relatives was a certainty.' Cf ECtHR, Janowiec and others v Russia, Judgment (GC) (2013) App nos. 55508/08 and others [186]. For more details on this peculiar situation, see Gabriella Citroni, 'Janowiec and Others v. Russia: A Long History of Justice Delayed Turned into a Permanent Case of Justice Denied' (2013) XXXIII Polish Yearbook of International Law 279; Delphine Debons, Antoine Fleury and Jean-François Pitteloud (eds), Katyn et la Suisse : experts et expertises médicales dans les crises humanitaires 1920-2007 = Katyn and Switzerland : forensic investigators and investigations in humanitarian crises 1920-2007 (Georg Editeur 2009). State authorities cannot waive the realization of the right to truth as well as the implementation of the obligation to carry out an investigation into human rights violations due to the passage of time. See Alessandra La Vaccara, 'Past Conflicts, Present Uncertainty: Legal Answers to the Quest for Information on Missing Persons and Victims of Enforced Disappearance. Three Case Studies from the European Context' (2018) XXXVII/2017 Polish yearbook of international law 35, 58-67.

[202] UN Commission on Human Rights, 'Orentlicher Principles' (n 43) Principle 1.

[203] Théo Boutruche, 'Seeking the Truth About Serious International Human Rights and Humanitarian Law Violations: The Various Facets of a Cardinal Notion of Transitional Justice' in Mariëlle Matthee, Brigit Toebes and Marcel Brus (eds), Armed Conflict and International Law: In Search of the Human Face (T M C Asser Press 2013) 308.

individual dimension[204] of an overarching right to information (right to be informed + right to have access to information) may erode the humanitarian aspect proper to the latter in the context of missing persons-related cases. Although La Rosa and Crettol optimistically affirm that in post-conflict scenarios '[v]ictims' families can intervene at various stages of criminal proceedings and exercise their right to know the fate of relatives',[205] they also recognize that

> there are serious limits to the ability of criminal proceedings to comprehensively address the issue of persons unaccounted for as a result of armed conflict [...]. They are designed to determine the guilt or innocence of the accused, and investigations are tailored to respond to the goals of the prosecution.[206]

Based on this backdrop, one should assume that TJ mechanisms can and shall uphold the quest of families for information on their relatives in different manners: e.g., i) in the context of judicial processes victims' families may be allowed to intervene at various stages; ii) while investigating the death of missing persons, TJ bodies can act in a way that serves the best interests of the families by providing them with answers on what happened; and iii) their work is deemed essential to bring those responsible for human rights and IHL violations to justice.[207] However, as most of the examples above highlight, the responsiveness of these bodies to the individual claims of the families has been incidental in the pursuance of their mandate. The majority of such bodies were not meant to address the 'special dimension'[208] of the right to truth – i.e., the right of families to know the fate of their relatives – and to shed light upon each single individual that has been reported as missing or, more generally, upon the individual impact of the violations committed.[209]

Accounting for missing persons makes part of the means to achieve peace and reconciliation. When this effort is explicitly mentioned in the mandate of a TJ

---

[204] Information in the context of the missing has a quasi-individual dimension; the collective dimension of the family unit informs the perception of information as a right of those who belong to the family of the missing person. As Chapter IV shows, in the human rights case law, the family link is not secondary. Closely related relatives are considered as those who might have suffered the most. Šarčević emphasizes that 'one of the greatest tasks of a war-torn society is to restore and preserve the family as a unit. For this purpose, the family includes not only parents and relatives in a direct line but also less closely related relatives and even neighbors with close emotional ties'. Petar Šarčević, 'War and Disintegration of the Family' (1999) 1 Journal of Law and Family Studies 109, 120.
[205] Crettol and La Rosa (n 12) 358.
[206] Ibid 359.
[207] UN Human Rights Council, 'Report of the Human Rights Council Advisory Committee on Best Practices on the Issue of Missing Persons' (2011) UN Doc A/HRC/16/70 para 47.
[208] The 2006 Study on the Right to Truth by the UN OHCHR explicitly recognizes that 'in cases of [...] missing persons [...] the right to the truth [...] has a special dimension: to know the fate and whereabouts of the victim.' UN OHCHR (n 199) para 59.
[209] For instance, with regard to truth commissions, as noted by Naqvi, there is a further layer of complexity generated by the fact that their non-judicial role leads to ask whether these bodies 'should name names of those found responsible for serious human rights violations'; thus, there is a triangular clash of rights which involves the individual victim's right to truth, the society's right to truth and the alleged perpetrator's due process rights. Yasmin Naqvi, 'The Right to the Truth in International Law: Fact or Fiction?' (2006) 88 International Review of the Red Cross 245, 272.

mechanism,[210] the work of the mechanism can be more effective: indeed, it can shed light upon the overall picture of the violations committed, contribute to elucidating the fate of each single person reported as missing as result of those violations, and create an enabling environment for addressing the issue of the missing.[211]

As Stahn emphasizes, the international practice in relation to the design of TJ mechanisms can serve the purpose of drawing a baseline for the path to be followed at the national level.[212] In post-conflict situations where the issue of missing persons is one of the consequences of the conflict to be addressed, the design of the mandate of these mechanisms should incorporate elements that enable them to contribute to addressing the issue. Most importantly, the follow-up involvement of the State institutions or international actors performing state-related functions is as important as the work of a TJ body: in the families' quest for information on their relatives, this involvement is essential in order for the transition towards a sustainable peace to be possible for all.

The case of the HRChBH is meaningful in this regard: the way it was designed enabled it to transmit its know-how to the national body – a Commission of the Constitutional Court – that took on its functions at the end of its mandate. The support and guide of the international component is not secondary in the assessment of the work of the Chamber: in addition to the international composition of the Chamber, the compliance of the parties to the Chamber's decisions was monitored by multiple international actors, i.e., OSCE and the Office of the High Representative; furthermore, the compliance with the

---

[210] Indeed, '[t]aking into account the prevalent and recognized urgency to address the issue of missing and forcibly disappeared persons in situations of conflict, and the recent advances in forensics, the Special Rapporteur [on the promotion of truth, justice, reparation and guarantees of non-recurrence] urges those responsible for the design of truth-seeking mechanisms to emphasize the importance of this topic.' See UN Human Rights Council, 'Report of the Special Rapporteur on the Promotion of Truth, Justice, Reparation and Guarantees of Non-Recurrence (Advanced Edited Version)' (2017) UN Doc A/HRC/36/50 para 105.

[211] For instance, the South Africa's Truth and Reconciliation Commission (TRC) recommended the establishment of a task team to investigate the nearly 500 cases of missing persons that were reported to the TRC, but remained unsolved. The President endorsed this recommendation in April 2003, upon tabling the TRC's Final Report in Parliament. A Missing Persons Task Team was established in the Priority Crimes Litigation Unit (PCLU) in the National Prosecuting Authority (NPA) in 2004. The Task Team has since been conducting investigations into cases of missing persons who disappeared in political circumstances between 1 March 1960 and 10 May 1994. Cf. Department of Justice and Constitutional Development (South Africa), 'Exhumation Policy: Cases of Missing Persons Reported to the Truth and Reconciliation Commission (TRC)' (2008) Notice 1539 4. The UN Special Rapporteur on the promotion of truth has emphasized that 'while it would not be advisable to create single-issue truth commissions (no truth commission is likely to be able on its own to solve the huge caseload of disappearances resulting from conflict), ensuring that truth commissions do a proper job on the issue of the missing and that they lay the foundation for continued work on it, including sound recommendations on the establishment of an effective national mechanism to resolve outstanding cases, would constitute a significant accomplishment'. In this sense he has urged those responsible 'for the design of truth-seeking mechanisms to emphasize the importance of this topic.' UN Human Rights Council, 'Report of the Special Rapporteur on the Promotion of Truth, Justice, Reparation and Guarantees of Non-Recurrence (Advanced Edited Version)' (2017) UN Doc A/HRC/36/50 paras 80, 105.

[212] Stahn (n 3) 425–426.

Chamber's decisions and the work for a successful transfer of competences to the Constitutional Court were among the commitments made by Bosnia and Herzegovina in the process of accession to the CoE.[213] Lack of compliance would have hindered the possibility of becoming a member. Equally meaningful is the work of the ICTY with regard to the ascertainment of the facts surrounding the war crimes in the former Yugoslavia. The adjustment of its approach to the issue of the missing and the mutually beneficial exchange of information with the ICRC and other bodies involved in the tracing process confirm that accountability-driven and humanitarian bodies carry out complementary, but not mutually exclusive tasks vis-à-vis the issue of the missing.

The examination of these bodies' work shows that the tension between a collective scope of judicial truth and the individual claims for truth was reflective of the audiences to whom they had to respond and of their jurisdictional mandate. While, for instance, the HRChBH's focus on human rights violations required it to tackle the violations vis-à-vis the individual victims/applicants, the ICTY had to address international crimes, which, by definition, have a collective impact.

2. THE ROLE OF INTERNATIONAL JUSTICE
IN FURTHERING THE REQUESTS OF FAMILIES FOR INFORMATION

Permanent international courts, such as human rights courts or the ICC, can play an important role in furthering the requests of families for information on their missing relatives in post-conflict environments. For instance, human rights courts have ordered remedies and reparations in cases of *durante bello* infringements of the human rights of missing persons and of their relatives; the effects of these measures on the design of the post-conflict domestic response to the issue of the missing will be assessed in order to appreciate the significance of their contribution (sub-section 2.1).

The role of the ICC in transitional phases has been the object of scholarly debate, particularly with regard to its contribution to the achievement of peace in specific contexts.[214] However, the ICC is neither an obstacle to nor an instrument of peace.[215] The peculiarity of a post-conflict context entails that the

---

[213] CoE - Parliamentary Assembly, 'Bosnia and Herzegovina's Application for Membership of the Council of Europe' (2002) Opinion 234 (2002) para 15.

[214] See, among others, Kasaija Phillip Apuuli, 'The ICC Arrest Warrants for the Lord's Resistance Army Leaders and Peace Prospects for Northern Uganda' (2006) 4 Journal of International Criminal Justice 179, 184; Adam Branch, 'Uganda's Civil War and the Politics of ICC Intervention' (2007) 21 Ethics & International Affairs 179, 184; Michael Scharf, 'The Amnesty Exception to the Jurisdiction of the International Criminal Court' (1999) 32 Cornell International Law Journal 507, 508.

[215] The correlation between criminal trials and peace is still under-explored at the scholarly level; therefore, there is not a thorough empirical study that can confirm or refute this study's stance on the ICC's impact on peace. See on this aspect, Janine Natalya Clark, 'Peace, Justice and the International Criminal Court Limitations and Possibilities' (2011) 9 Journal of International Criminal Justice 521, 522, 544.

contributions of the ICC to justice and peace can vary in each single case;[216] indeed, various factors (e.g., how the principle of complementarity plays out in the presence of TJ mechanisms) determine different courses of action.[217] Despite the centrality of this debate in the scholarly conversation on peace and justice, this chapter (sub-section 2.2) intends to narrow down the focus on the restorative justice instrument that has been integrated in the Rome Statute, i.e., the participation mechanism. The aim is twofold: examine the contribution of this instrument to the families' quest for information on their missing relatives, when the Court exercises its jurisdiction in a case; explore whether this instrument can generate an attenuation of the above-mentioned tension between the humanitarian need to know and the efforts to establish a judicial truth.

2.1. Human rights adjudicators and their attempts "to adjust" the State conduct in the transition from conflict to peace

Remedying years of uncertainty proves impossible due to the dire consequences that it has on family life and, individually, on family members. Substantively, a remedy[218] should be understood as the relief afforded to the

---

[216] M Cherif Bassiouni, 'The ICC — Quo Vadis?' (2006) 4 Journal of International Criminal Justice 421, 423.

[217] See, in this regard, Drazan Djukić, 'Transitional Justice and the International Criminal Court – in "the Interests of Justice"?' (2007) 89 International Review of the Red Cross 691; Obiora Chinedu Okafor and Uchechukwu Ngwaba, 'The International Criminal Court as a "Transitional Justice" Mechanism in Africa: Some Critical Reflections' (2015) 9 International Journal of Transitional Justice 90; Scharf (n 214); A Seibert-Fohr, 'The Relevance of the Rome Statute of the International Criminal Court for Amnesties and Truth Commissions' in Armin von Bogdandy and Rüdiger Wolfrum (eds), Max Planck Yearbook of United Nations Law, vol 7 (Martinus Nijhoff Publishers 2003).

[218] This book adopts Shelton's definition of remedies, i.e., 'the range of measures that may be taken in response to an actual or threatened violation of human rights. They [...] embrace the substance of relief as well as the procedures through which relief may be obtained.' As Shelton underlines, the term 'reparation' is also used to indicate measures that serve to redress individual harm from human rights violations (e.g., compensation, restitution, satisfaction, and guarantees of non-repetition). The term is also used for indicating monetary compensation. See Dinah Shelton, Remedies in International Human Rights Law (Oxford University Press 2015) 17 ff. The term 'remedy' has a dual facet, substantive and procedural; under the ICCPR, the French version of Article 2(3) on the right to a remedy (recours) solely integrates the procedural facet. E Klein, 'Individual Reparation Claims under the International Covenant on Civil and Political Rights: The Practice of the Human Rights Committee' in Christian Tomuschat and Albrecht Randelzhofer (eds), State responsibility and the individual : reparation in instances of grave violations of human rights (Martinus Nijhoff Publishers 1999) 33. In his commentary to Article 2(3) ICCPR, Nowak stresses that it is important to distinguish between the procedural right to an effective remedy and the substantive right to reparation. See Manfred Nowak, U.N. Covenant on Civil and Political Rights: CCPR Commentary (2nd rev ed, NP Engel 2005) 70. Naldi stresses that remedies may include provision for reparation that in turn may take the forms of restitution, rehabilitation and payment of compensation. See Gino J Naldi, 'Reparations in the Practice of the African Commission on Human and Peoples' Rights' (2001) 14 Leiden Journal of International Law 681, 681. It is also important to stress that the UN Basic Principles on the right to a remedy and reparation embed the above-mentioned dual nature: 'an adequate, effective and prompt remedy for gross violations of [IHRL] or serious violations of [IHL] should include all available and appropriate international processes in which a person may have legal standing and should be without prejudice to any other domestic remedies'; 'an adequate, effective and prompt reparation is intended to promote justice by redressing gross violations of [IHRL] or serious violations of [IHL]'. Cf. UN Commission on Human Rights, 'Basic Principles and Guidelines

successful claimant; in this sense, a remedy can have a variety of aims, that range from *restitutio ad integrum* and full compensation for pecuniary/non-pecuniary losses to deterrence of violations.[219] Therefore, remedies serve to achieve different purposes,[220] i.e., compensatory,[221] retributive,[222] deterrence-related,[223] and restorative purposes;[224] in this sense, they can contribute to filling the *lacunae* generated by the attitude of State authorities vis-à-vis the humanitarian need of families to know the fate and whereabouts of their relatives during and after an armed conflict. The scope and typology of the remedial measures depend upon the nature of the case and, more specifically, on the rights involved: remedies in response to an enforced disappearance are quite complex in nature,[225] as these are intended for reaching most of the purposes outlined above. The same holds valid for remedial measures in cases of persons reported missing due to a violation of IHRL/IHL (but who do not qualify as enforced disappearances).

An analysis of the remedial approach of the human rights adjudicators sheds light upon how State authorities can provide relief to the families from uncertainty-induced suffering; this becomes essential in the process towards a sustainable peace. This approach is not homogeneous in the human rights case law due to the peculiarities of each human right treaty and of the *modus operandi*

---

on the Right to a Remedy and Reparation for Victims of Gross Violations of IHRL and Serious Violations of IHL - Human Rights Resolution 2005/35' (2005) UN Doc E/CN.4/RES/2005/35. Principles VIII and IX, paras. 14-15.

[219] Shelton (n 218) 16.

[220] Shelton highlights the multiple connotations of the purposes pursued through remedies. ibid 19 ff. van Boven highlights that remedies have a dual facet, i.e., retributive and restorative, see Theo van Boven, 'Victim-Oriented Perspectives: Rights and Realities' in Thorsten Bonacker and Christoph Safferling (eds), *Victims of International Crimes: An Interdisciplinary Discourse* (T M C Asser Press 2013) 24.

[221] Compensatory justice is substantiated by measures that rectify the wrong done to the victim; in other words these measures are intended to correct the injustice. Shelton (n 218) 19.

[222] Retribution-led remedies express opprobrium to the wrongdoer; as such these are exemplified by the punishment of the perpetrators. Punishment has the expressive function of annulling the idea that the victim's rights are not sufficiently important to refrain from violating them in the pursuit of another goal. ibid 20–21.

[223] Deterrence *per se* seeks to influence the future behavior of all potential actors, not only of the defendant; direct correlation seems to exist between certainty of consequences and the reduction of offences (not between the severity of punishment and the reduced incidence of wrongdoing). ibid 22.

[224] In terms of process, restorative justice aims to bring together perpetrators and victims; substantively, restorative justice focuses on redress and reintegration of the offender (not on his punishment). ibid 22–26.

[225] The WGEID's general comment to Article 19 of the Declaration on the Protection of All Persons from Enforced Disappearance highlights that, 'in case of enforced disappearance, in addition to the punishment of the perpetrators and the right to monetary compensation, the right to obtain redress for acts of enforced disappearance under article 19 also includes "the means for as complete a rehabilitation as possible". This obligation refers to medical and psychological care and rehabilitation for any form of physical or mental damage as well as to legal and social rehabilitation, guarantees of non-repetition, restoration of personal liberty, family life, citizenship, employment or property, return to one's place of residence and similar forms of restitution, satisfaction and reparation which may remove the consequences of the enforced disappearance.' WGEID, 'Compilation of General Comments on the Declaration on the Protection of All Persons from Enforced Disappearance' para 75 <http://goo.gl/6P0lzl> accessed 12 May 2018.

of judicial and quasi-judicial bodies'.[226] However, by narrowing down the analysis to the case law examined in Chapter IV, three strands of non-monetary remedial measures[227] characterize the approach of these bodies with regard to

---

[226] The ICCPR and its First Optional Protocol do not contain any provision on reparations similar to Article 63 ACHR or Article 41 ECHR; the HRCee is not a tribunal and, as such, cannot issue binding judgments and, in principle, cannot order reparations. M Nowak, 'Eight Reasons Why We Need a World Court of Human Rights' in Gudmundur Alfredsson and et al. (eds), *International Human Rights Monitoring Mechanisms: Essay in Honour of Jakob Th. Möller* (Martinus Nijhoff Publishers 2009) 699; Valeska David, 'The Expanding Right to an Effective Remedy: Common Developments at the Human Rights Committee and the Inter-American Court' (2014) 3 British Journal of American Legal Studies 259, 280. Buergenthal underlines that in light of the absence of a UN Human Rights Court, the Committee 'can and should discharge some of the normative functions such a tribunal would perform, particularly when adopting general comments and rendering decisions on individual communications' T Buergenthal, 'The U.N. Human Rights Committee' in Armin von Bogdandy, Rüdiger Wolfrum and Christiane E Philipp (eds), *Max Planck Yearbook of United Nations Law Online*, vol 5 (Martinus Nijhoff Publishers 2001) 396. Similar considerations can be outlined for the AfCommHPR: the AfChHPR does not establish a Commission's mandate of affording remedies to the victims; likewise, the Rules of procedure of the Commission do not mention such a mandate. Bekker underlines that despite this lack of an express mandate, the Commission has developed its own practice concerning reparations; the main difference with the other bodies seems to be a State-centric point of departure in relation to remedies. See Gina Bekker, 'The African Commission on Human and Peoples' Rights and Remedies for Human Rights Violations' (2013) 13 Human Rights Law Review 499, 503. Naldi stresses that, at the outset, the AfCommHPR has accepted the principle of reparations in its jurisprudence and little by little has developed its system of remedies by recommending measures to the culpable state in order to redress the situation. Naldi underscores that States seem to be given a large measure of discretion as to how best to remedy any violations; he also points out that this might also be a direct consequence of the fact that the AfChHPR is one of the most state-centered IHRL treaties, which is coupled with a traditional reluctance of African States to accept international supervision. See Naldi (n 218) 685, 691–692. As for the AfCtHPR, the Protocol that established the AfCtHPR recognizes this competence to the Court. Cf. Article 27 (1), Protocol on the establishment of the AfCtHPR; cf. also Article 28 (h) (jurisdiction of the Court, including reparations) and Article 45 (compensation), Protocol on the Statute of the AfCtHPR. At the time of writing, the AfCtHPR has developed a timid approach to remedies in cases which are not relevant to the present studies: for instance, in *Tanganyika Law Society* case the Court has asked the respondent State to take constitutional, legislative, and all other necessary measures within a reasonable time to remedy the violations (i.e., violations of the right to freedom of association and of the right to participate in government) found by the Court and to inform the Court of the measures taken. Cf. AfCtHPR, *Tanganyika Law Society and Another v Tanzania* (2013) App no 011/2011 [2–Order 3].

[227] Non-monetary measures include restitution, rehabilitation, satisfaction, guarantees of non-repetition. Cf. Shelton (n 218) 270–280. Article 2(3) ICCPR has been interpreted as the normative source in order for the HRCee to request States Parties to repair the violations found in its views; this position was adopted quite early in its practice, even though the ICCPR did not set down any provision which might have led to think that its mandate could extend to recommending reparations. Cf. HRCee, *Bazzano, Valentini, de Massera v Uruguay*, Comm no 5/197 [1984] UN Doc CCPRCOP1 40 [10 *in fine*] cited in David (n 226) 280. The IACtHR highlights that, under Articles 62 and 63 (1) ACHR, it is competent to decide reparations, cost and expenses. In light of this competence the Court has considered 'non-pecuniary damages', i.e., 'the suffering and affliction caused to the direct victims and their relatives, detriment to values that are very significant for individuals, as well as non-monetary alterations in the conditions of existence of the victim or the victim's family.' Thus, it has ordered both monetary and non-monetary reparations in response to the said damage (under the heading 'other forms of reparation' or 'measures of satisfaction and guarantees of non-repetition'). Cf. IACtHR, *Bámaca-Velásquez v Guatemala, Judgment - Reparations and Costs* (2002) Series C No. 91 [56, 68 ff]. The Court has also stressed that 'it is a principle of international law that any violation of an international obligation that has produced damage entails the obligation to repair it adequately' Cf. IACtHR, *Serrano-Cruz Sisters v El*

uncertainty about persons reported missing and the paramount need of their families to elucidate their fate and whereabouts. The table below (table 4) illustrates measures to remedy the failure of accounting for the missing, measures to remedy the inhuman treatment and the violation of the mental integrity of the family engendered by the lack of information, and measures to remedy the pitfalls of the institutional/legislative setting with an impact on the missing persons cases. Some of the remedial measures can have an important rehabilitative effect, alleviate the suffering, and provide for responses to material needs.[228] These three aspects integrate humanitarian considerations that go beyond the fact of amending a wrongdoing, as they provide the possibility of concretely overcoming uncertainty and restoring the individual capacity to move forward.

Salvador, Judgment - Merits, Reparations and Costs (2005) Series C No. 120 [133]. More generally, the Court has developed its own principles which correspond better to the types of violation committed in Latin America. Laurence Burgorgue-Larsen and Amaya Úbeda de Torres, *The Inter-American Court of Human Rights. Case Law and Commentary* (Oxford University Press 2011) 224. Pursuant to Article 41 ECHR, the ECtHR may award monetary compensation if it considers this to be 'necessary' for both pecuniary and non-pecuniary damages resulting from the violations of the Convention. Cf. ECtHR, *Cyprus v Turkey, Judgment - Just Satisfaction (GC)* (2014) App no. 25781/94; *Varnava and Others v Turkey, Judgment (GC)* (2009) App nos. 16064/90 and others [224]. Conversely, the Court has never ordered non-monetary measures. This narrow interpretation of 'just satisfaction' does not follow the international practice. Shelton (n 218) 280. However, the ECtHR has decided to provide guidance suggesting non-monetary measures to be implemented in order to comply with its judgment findings. Indeed, pursuant to Article 46 (Binding Force and Execution of Judgments) ECHR, States Parties are required to abide by judgments; the way in which they do so is left largely to their own discretion. Schabas stresses that despite the principle of freedom in determining the means of implementation of obligations, there are cases where the nature of the violation leaves no choice to the Court about the measures that must be taken. William A Schabas, *The European Convention on Human Rights: A Commentary* (Oxford University Press 2015) 868. For instance, in *Aslakhanova and others v. Russia* concerning the practice of enforced disappearances in the context of the armed conflict in Chechnya, the ECtHR has noted that the number of cases featuring the same breaches indicates the existence of a pattern of violations favored by the lack of any remedial action. Considering the 'accumulation of breaches' incompatible with the ECHR, the Court has felt compelled to provide some guidance on the measures to be taken as a matter of urgency by Russia with the aim of 'putting an end to the continued suffering of the relatives of the disappeared persons; conducting effective investigations into the cases of abduction unlawful detention and disappearance allegedly committed by servicemen; and ensuring that the families of the victims are awarded adequate redress.' ECtHR, *Aslakhanova and others v Russia, Judgment* (2012) App nos. 2944/06 and others [221]. The ECtHR's traditional practice is different: 'it falls to the Committee of Ministers, acting under Article 46 [ECHR], to address the issue of what – in practical terms – may be required of the respondent State by way of compliance, and when [...]'. ibid [220]. The AfCommHPR has mainly recommended non-monetary measures as well as made use of declaratory judgments; a certain degree of reluctance vis-à-vis monetary compensation is detectable in its case law. Bekker mentions a series of cases where, despite the explicit request of the Applicant for a monetary compensation, either the Commission has held that the quantum of the compensation should be determined under the domestic law (cf. AfCommHPR, *Embga Mekongo Louis v. Cameroon*, Communication no. 59/91, 1995) or it has disregarded the request by, at least, recognizing the violation of the Charter (cf. AfCommHPR, *Huri-Laws v Nigeria*, Communication no. 225/98, 2000). Bekker (n 226) 509.

[228] Shelton (n 218) 20.

Table 4 – Human rights adjudicators' (post-conflict) remedies		
HRCee – Measures to remedy…		
The failure of accounting for missing persons (MP)	**Uncertainty as a cause of inhuman treatment**	**The pitfalls of the institutional/legislative setting**
The State has an obligation to provide the authors with an effective remedy (Art. 2.3, ICCPR), including		
Search Activities/Investigations • Continue efforts to account for MP; • Adopt an inclusive approach in the course of the investigation (e.g., invite the family to contribute with the information they have);[229] • carry out a thorough and effective investigation into the disappearance and fate of the applicant's victim; • provide adequate information resulting from the investigation.[230]	**Accessibility of Information** • ensure that investigations into allegations of ED are accessible to the families of MP.[231] **Mortal remains handling** • hand over the remains to the family members, in the event that the victim is deceased.[232] **Psychological treatment** • ensure that the necessary and adequate psychological rehabilitation and medical treatment is provided to the applicants.[233]	**MP status and implications for the family** • avoid applying the current legal framework in a manner that requires the relatives to obtain certification of the death of the victim in order to obtain social benefits and measures of reparation;[234] • amend the current legal framework so that social benefits/measures of reparations to relatives are not subjected to a municipal court's decision certifying the victim's death.[235]

---

[229] HRCee, *Tija Hero, Ermina Hero, Armin Hero v Bosnia and Herzegovina, Comm no 1966/2010* (2014) UN Doc. CCPR/C/112/D/1966/2010 [11]; *Fatima Rizvanović and Ruvejda Rizvanović v Bosnia and Herzegovina, Comm no 1997/2010* (2014) UN Doc. CCPR/C/110/D/1997/2010 [11]; *Zilkija Selimović et al v Bosnia and Herzegovina, Comm no 2003/2010,* (2014) UN Doc. CCPR/C/111/D/2003/2010 [14]; *Nevzeta Durić and Nedzad Durić v Bosnia and Herzegovina, Comm No 1956/2010* (2014) UN Doc. CCPR/C/111/D/1956/2010 [11]; *Milan Mandić v Bosnia and Herzegovina, Comm no 2064/2011* (2015) UN Doc CCPR/C/115/D/2064/2011 [10]; *Emira Kadirić and Dino Kadirić v Bosnia-Herzegovina, Comm no 2048/2011* (2015) UN Doc. CCPR/C/115/D/2048/2011 [11].

[230] HRCee, *Sarma v Sri Lanka, Comm No 950/2000* [2003] UN Doc CCPRC78D9502000 [11].

[231] See *supra* n 229.

[232] HRCee, *Sharmila Tripathi v Nepal, Comm no 2111/2011* (2008) UN Doc. CCPR/C/112/D/2111/2011 [9].

[233] HRCee, ibid; *Jit Man Basnet and Top Bahadur Basnet v Nepal, Comm no 2051/2011* (2014) UN Doc. CCPR/C/112/D/2051/2011 [10]; *Milan Mandić v. Bosnia and Herzegovina* (n 229) [10]; *Kadirić and Kadirić v. Bosnia and Herzegovina* (n 229) [11].

[234] See HRCee, *supra* n 229.

[235] HRCee, *Fatima Prutina and others v Bosnia and Herzegovina, Comm nos 1917/2009 and others* (2013) UN Doc. CCPR/C/107/D/1917,1918,1925/2009&1953/2010 [11].

ECtHR – Measures to remedy...		
The failure of accounting for MP	**Uncertainty as a cause of inhuman treatment**	**The pitfalls of the institutional/legislative setting**
Measures to be taken, as a matter of urgency, to address the issue of systemic failure to investigate disappearances:		
Data collection and handling • compilation and maintenance of a unified database of all disappearances by the same body; • allocation of adequate resources required to carry out large-scale forensic work on the ground (e.g., exhumation of presumed burial sites); • collection, storage and identification of remains and, where necessary, systematic matching through up-to-date genetic databanks.[236]	**State Responsibility and Reparations** • payment of financial compensation + an unequivocal admission of State responsibility for the relatives' frustrating and painful situation; • possibility of unilateral remedial offers to the relatives in cases concerning persons who have disappeared by unknown perpetrators and where there is *prima facie* evidence supporting allegations that the domestic investigation fell short of what is necessary under the ECHR.[237]	**Tracing body** • establishment of a high-level body in charge of solving disappearances, which would enjoy unrestricted access to all relevant information and would work on the basis of trust and partnership with the relatives of the disappeared.[238]
AfCommHPR – Measures to remedy...		
The failure of accounting for MP	**Uncertainty as a cause of inhuman treatment**	**The pitfalls of the institutional/legislative setting**
	Duty to put an end to the violations The Commission recommends strongly to the Government: to end the inhuman treatment of the family generated by the refusal to inform them about if and where their relative is being held in detention.[239]	**Tracing body** The Commission recommends to the Government: to arrange for the commencement of an independent enquiry in order to clarify the fate of persons considered disappeared and identify the authors of the violations perpetrated at the time of the facts.[240]

---

[236] ECtHR, *Aslakhanova and others v. Russia* (n 227) [220, 223–228].

[237] ibid.

[238] ibid.

[239] AfCommHPR, *Amnesty International et al v Sudan* (1999) Comm nos. 48/90-50/91-52/91-89/93 [final recommendations].

[240] AfCommHPR, *Malawi African Association et al v Mauritania* (2000) Comm nos. 54/91 et al. Final Recommendations. A similar recommendation has been put forward in *Zimbabwe Human Rights NGO Forum* Case where the Commission has recommended the State i) to establish a Commission of Inquiry to investigate the causes of the violence which took place from February – June 2000 (including cases of kidnapping, torture, and massive killing); ii) to bring those responsible to justice and iii) to identify victims of the violence in order to provide them with just and adequate compensation. Cf. AfCommHPR, *Zimbabwe Human Rights NGO Forum v Zimbabwe* (2006) Comm no. 245/02 [final recommendations].

IACtHR – Measures to remedy...		
The failure of accounting for MP	**Uncertainty as a cause of inhuman treatment**	**The pitfalls of the institutional/legislative setting**
Search activities/Investigations The State must • conduct a genuine search, using the appropriate judicial and administrative channels; • conduct the search in a systematic and rigorous manner; • if necessary, request the cooperation of other States.[241] • A National Search Commission will make a positive contribution to the search for and identification of the victims of forced disappearances.[242] **Whereabouts of mortal remains** The State must: • search for and locate the mortal remains of the disappeared; • deliver them without delay to their next of kin, prior genetic parentage evaluation thereof.[243] **Data handling** The State must • establish a genetic information database to safeguard the information of the osseous remains as well as of the next of kin of the persons presumably executed/disappeared during the acts perpetrated during the conflict;	**Psychological treatment** The State must • relieve the bodily and psychological suffering of the relatives through medical and psychological treatment.[246] **Transmission of Information** The State must • inform the next of kin of the measures aimed at searching for the disappeared and, where possible, their presence procured.[247] • establish a strategy for communicating with the next of kin in relation to the search procedures in order to ensure their participation, awareness and presence in keeping with the relevant protocols and guidelines.[248] **Mortal remains handling** Care for the mortal remains of a person is a form of observance of the right to human dignity. In this sense, the State must • provide the necessary conditions to take those remains to the place chosen by his next of kin, at no cost to them.[249]	**National Tracing Commission/Ad hoc body** The State must establish a national tracing commission to determine the whereabouts of the victims;[250] this body should: • adopt the necessary measures to investigate and collect evidence on the whereabouts of disappeared persons in the armed conflict; • facilitate family reunification and the determination of what happened; • have independent and impartial members; • receive the necessary resources (e.g., human, financial, logistic, scientific) to carry its mandate; • include State institutions that have demonstrated interest in resolving this problem. • Moreover: all State's institutions and authorities should cooperate with it by providing information and access to all records that could contain information on the victims' fate; • civil society should be enabled to participate in its work.[251] **Status and Identification Measures** The State must adopt legislative/administrative measures to establish: • expedite procedure for

[241] IACtHR, *Rodríguez Vera et al (the Disappeared from the Palace of Justice) v Colombia, Judgment - Preliminary Objections, Merits, Reparations and Costs* (2014) Series C no. 287 [564]; *Rochac Hernández and others v El Salvador, Judgment - Merits, Reparations and Costs* (2014) Series C No. 285 [197].

[242] IACtHR, *Diario Militar Case (Merits ...)* (n 53) [335].

[243] IACtHR, *La Cantuta v. Peru (Merits ...)* (n 44) [231–232, 238]; *Goiburú et al v Paraguay, Judgment - Merits, Reparations and Costs* (2006) Series C No. 153 [171]; *Diario Militar Case (Merits ...)* (n 53) [333]; *The Disappeared from the Palace of Justice case (P.O., Merits ...)* (n 241) [563–564]; *Rochac Hernández and others v. El Salvador (Merits...)* (n 241) [199]; *Bámaca-Velásquez v. Guatemala (Reparations ...)* (n 227) [74, 81, 82].

• establish mechanisms for cooperating and exchanging information with the different organizations that have collected this type of data in Guatemala, so as not to duplicate efforts in the creation and implementation of the said measure;[244] • incorporate the best practices to achieve such goals.[245]		statements of absence/ presumptions of death due to forced disappearance; • a genetic information system to clarify parentage of missing children + their identification.[252]

The responsiveness of State authorities to the measures in the table above is inconsistent and often merely declaratory. With regard to the HRCee Views, in some cases, in light of a merely declaratory commitment to implement the recommended remedial measures, the HRCee has urged the State parties to take concrete steps. For instance, it has underlined that the duty to investigate and prosecute those responsible is not fulfilled with the establishment of TJ mechanisms.[253] In other cases, the absence of any – even declaratory – commitment from the State has followed the questioning of the individual communication system under the ICCPR-OP in light of domestic constitutional pronouncements against the accession of the country to the Protocol.[254]

The TJ agenda[255] put forward by the ECtHR in *Aslakhanova* and successive Chechen cases has generated an apparently active follow-up by the Russian authorities that have submitted their action plans to the Committee of Ministers

---

[246] IACtHR, *La Cantuta v. Peru (Merits ...)* (n 44) [231–232, 238]; *Valle-Jaramillo et al v Colombia, Judgment - Merits, Reparations and Costs* (2008) Series C No. 192 [238]; *Diario Militar Case (Merits ...)* (n 53) [339]; *The Disappeared from the Palace of Justice case (P.O., Merits ...)* (n 241) [567]; *Serrano-Cruz Sisters v. El Salvador (Merits...)* (n 227) [197–201]; *Rochac Hernández and others v. El Salvador (Merits...)* (n 241) [219].

[247] IACtHR, *Diario Militar Case (Merits ...)* (n 53) [334]; *Rochac Hernández and others v. El Salvador (Merits...)* (n 241) [197].

[248] IACtHR, *The Disappeared from the Palace of Justice case (P.O., Merits ...)* (n 241) [564].

[249] IACtHR, *Bámaca-Velásquez v. Guatemala (Reparations ...)* (n 227) [74, 81–82].

[250] IACtHR, *Serrano-Cruz Sisters v. El Salvador (Merits...)* (n 227) [184]; *The Disappeared from the Palace of Justice case (P.O., Merits ...)* (n 241) [565].

[251] IACtHR, *Serrano-Cruz Sisters v. El Salvador (Merits...)* (n 227) [184–188]; *Rochac Hernández and others v. El Salvador (Merits...)* (n 241) [198].

[244] IACtHR, *Diario Militar Case (Merits ...)* (n 53) [336].

[245] IACtHR, *Rochac Hernández and others v. El Salvador (Merits...)* (n 241) [205].

[252] IACtHR, *Molina-Theissen v Guatemala, Judgment – Reparations and costs* (2004) Series C no 108 [91 (b)].

[253] HRCee, *Concluding observations on the second periodic report of Nepal* (2014) UN Doc CCPR/C/NPL/CO/2 [6].

[254] HRCee, *Concluding observations on the fifth periodic report of Sri Lanka* (2014) CCPR/C/LKA/CO/5 [6].

[255] V Kogan, 'Implementing the Judgments of the European Court of Human Rights from the North Caucasus: A Closing Window for Accountability or a Continuing Process of Transitional Justice?' in N Szablewska and SD Bachmann (eds), *Current issues in Transitional Justice*, vol 4 (Springer 2015) 178.

of the CoE.[256] Although the first of these plans laid down the strategy to execute the measures requested, the measures concerning the institutional design of a high-level body devoted to the issue of the disappearances remained unaddressed.[257] Following explicit requests by the Committee of Ministers to adjust the strategy in accordance with such measures, the Russian authorities have declared that 'the uniform centralized and independent mechanism of search for missing persons has already been established in the Russian Federation, and it functions successfully'.[258] Furthermore, in light of the ECtHR practice and of the Committee's recommendation, 'uniform information databases' have been created and 'the investigation bodies had unimpaired access to them'.[259] Similarly, genetic databases containing thousands of profiles, including those of missing persons, were already in place.[260] Nevertheless, the Committee has repeatedly stressed the need to create 'a high-level body in charge of solving disappearances', which is still not in place to date.[261]

The IACtHR provides an account[262] of the implementation of the reparations ordered in its judgments: from those reports that are available, it can be inferred that where substantive changes are requested, e.g., enactment of legislation or establishment of a new body, there is a high degree of responsiveness from State authorities in terms of explanations of the measures adopted/to be adopted, but lack of concrete measures on the ground. For instance, El Salvador has reported the steps undertaken to establish a National Commission for the Search for Disappeared Children and the difficulties encountered to adopt a legislation, which would sanction its final creation;[263] while declaring its commitment to create a genetic information system, the State has been unable to provide satisfactory explanations of the measures adopted to develop such a system.[264] Where the State (e.g., Peru) has carried out the search for/localization of the mortal remains of the disappeared, has delivered them to the relatives, and has borne the burial costs, the Court has declared that the State fully complied with the measure ordered in its judgments.[265] Unfortunately, the Court has not done it so often in the cases examined: for instance, in one case, Guatemala did not

---

[256] The Committee of Ministers of the CoE is the body that is mandated to monitor the execution of the ECtHR's judgments under Article 46 ECHR.

[257] CoE – Committee of Ministers, 'Communication from the Russian Federation Concerning the Khashiyev and Akayeva Group of Cases against Russian Federation (Application No. 57942/00)' (2013) DH-DD (2013)935, 1–2.

[258] CoE – Committee of Ministers, 'Communication from the Russian Federation Concerning the Khashiyev Group of Cases against Russian Federation (Application No. 57942/00)' (2014) DH-DD (2014)892 2, 6.

[259] ibid.

[260] ibid 7.

[261] CoE – Committee of Ministers, 'Supervision of the Execution of Judgments and Decisions of the ECtHR' (2016) 9th Annual Report of the CoM 2015, 129–130.

[262] This account does not encompass all the judgments in light of the lack of responses/delayed responses from the States or private hearings.

[263] IACtHR, 'Serrano Cruz Sisters v. El Salvador.' (2010) Monitoring Compliance with Judgments Order para 22.

[264] The Court found that these steps were not satisfactory. ibid para 27.

[265] IACtHR, 'La Cantuta v. Peru' (2009) Monitoring Compliance with Judgment. Order para 2 (b).

accept the judgments of the Court in light of procedural factors[266] and of substantive discrepancies between the domestic reparation program and the reparation measures ordered by the Court; this has led Guatemala to disregard the reparations ordered *in toto.*[267] Furthermore, in relation to one of the leading cases on disappearances – *Bamaca Velasquez* – the Court has declared that the measures concerning the location of the mortal remains of the disappeared remains unattended.[268] Based on documents presented during the bi-annual ordinary sessions of the AfCommHPR, it appears that the State authorities concerned have presented no concrete measure in order to respond to the recommendations highlighted in the table above.[269]

The table above unveils a trend towards micro-managing the tracing process, particularly at the Inter-American level: the reference to provide adequate resources to implement such measures is probably correct in principle, but clashes with political and economic constraints on the ground, particularly in post-conflict contexts. As chapter IV shows, the context is secondary in the assessment of the violations committed by the State for the IACtHR; such an approach can, however, run the risk of creating the false expectation of an immediate redress for the victims. More generally, the follow-up procedures show that the remedial measures can, at least, push the State to expound on the measures adopted; unfortunately, as the ECtHR's example above shows, the illustration of measures on paper does not always correspond to the reality on the ground.

2.2. Information via the victims' participation system: The potential contribution of the ICC

Article 68 (3) of the Rome Statute represents an innovative step undertaken in the domain of international criminal justice, since it states that

> [w]here the personal interests of the victims are affected, the Court shall permit their views and concerns to be presented and considered at stages of the proceedings determined to be appropriate by the Court and in a manner which is not prejudicial to or inconsistent with the rights of the accused and a fair and impartial trial. Such views and

---

[266] The State expressed its disagreement with regard to the interpretation by the Court of the declaration relating to the acceptance by the State of the Court's competence; specifically, it questioned the competence *ratione temporis* of the Court. IACtHR, 'Río Negro and Gudiel Álvarez and Others v Guatemala' (2014) Monitoring Compliance with Judgment. Order.

[267] ibid para 2.

[268] IACtHR, 'Bámaca Velásquez v. Guatemala' (2010) Monitoring Compliance with Judgment. Order 28.

[269] In its initial report, Mauritania did not even mention the recommendations of the Commission which were forwarded the year before. Cf. AfCommHPR/Mauritania, 'Mauritania. Initial Report, 1986-2001' (31st Ordinary Session - 2-16 May 2002) <http://www.achpr.org/states/mauritania/reports/1st-1986-2001/> accessed 12 July 2016. There is very little available information at national or regional levels about the follow-up process concerning the decisions of the African Commission. Nevertheless, the States parties' reports submitted in compliance with Article 62 of the AfChHPR are useful sources of information. See Rachel Murray and Elizabeth Mottershaw, 'Mechanisms for the Implementation of Decisions of the African Commission on Human and Peoples' Rights' (2014) 36 Human Rights Quarterly 349, 350.

concerns may be presented by the legal representatives of the victims, where the Court considers it appropriate, in accordance with the Rules of Procedure and Evidence.

This provision was introduced as a response to the lack of provisions of this kind in the Statutes and Rules of Procedure and Evidence of the *ad hoc* Tribunals (i.e. the ICTY and the ICTR).[270] These neglected to protect victims in two respects: first, victims could not take part in a personal capacity in the proceedings; second, victims were not entitled to obtain compensation for the harm suffered.[271]

The so-called ICC 'participation mechanism' or 'system' contributes to implementing the right of victims to justice implicitly recognized by Article 68 (3) and spelled out in the ICC Rules of Procedure and Evidence.[272] The participation to the proceedings is not tantamount to being full parties: in order to participate in ICC proceedings, victims must be able to demonstrate that particular proceedings against a specific accused affect their interests.[273] Against this backdrop, this section will examine the functioning of the mechanism of participation of victims in criminal proceedings[274] before the ICC[275] (sub-section 2.2.1) and the legal implications of such a mechanism for the families of the missing and for the realization of their right to know (sub-section 2.2.2).

2.2.1. Participation of the victims and their right to know

2.2.1.1. On whether the family members of the missing are 'victims' ex Article 68(3) of the Rome Statute

The substantive approach of the Rome Statute to the phenomenon of victimization has been confirmed by the States Parties at the time of the adoption of a definition of victims in the Rules of Procedure and Evidence. This definition is centred more on the notion of harm than on the restrictive nexus between the

---

[270] David Donat-Cattin, 'Article 68 - Protection of Victims and Witnesses and Their Participation in the Proceedings' in Otto Triffterer and Kai Ambos (eds), *Commentary on the Rome Statute of the International Criminal Court: Observers' Notes, Article by Article* (C H Beck 2008) 1277.

[271] C Jorda and J de Hemptinne, 'The Status and Role of the Victim' in Antonio Cassese, Paola Gaeta and John RWD Jones (eds), *The Rome Statute of the International Court: a Commentary*, vol II (Oxford University Press 2002) 1389–1394.

[272] Article 68 (3) reproduces the content of Article 6 (b) of the Declaration of the Basic Principles of Justice for Victims of Crimes and Abuse of Power annexed to Resolution 40/34 of 29 December 1985 of the UNGA. In Donat-Cattin (n 270) 1279. The mechanism was strongly advocated by the representatives of both governments and NGOs in the course of the preparatory negotiations regarding the Rome Statute and the Rules of Procedure and Evidence, and drew its inspiration from the criminal procedure adopted by judicial systems founded on civil law and from various international conventions and declarations for the protection of fundamental human rights. Jorda and de Hemptinne consider the following examples: France, the Netherlands, Germany and Latin America region. Jorda and de Hemptinne (n 271) 1400–1401.

[273] Carla Ferstman, 'International Criminal Law and Victims' Rights' in William Schabas and Nadia Bernaz (eds), *Routledge handbook of international criminal law* (Routledge 2011) 411.

[274] For a detailed analysis on this aspect, see for instance, T Markus Funk, *Victims' Rights and Advocacy at the International Criminal Court* (Oxford University Press 2010); N Tsereteli, 'Victim Participation in ICC Proceedings' in Carsten Stahn and Larissa van den Herik (eds), *Future perspectives on international criminal justice* (TMC Asser press 2010).

[275] The statutes of the Extraordinary Chambers in the Courts of Cambodia and the Special Tribunal for Lebanon, which were adopted after the Rome Statute, include similar provisions.

crime and the person directly targeted by it, as reflected in the ICTY Rules.[276] According to the ICC Rules of Procedure and Evidence, 'victims' means 'natural persons who have suffered harm as a result of the commission of any crime within the jurisdiction of the Court'.[277] The ICC Chambers have broad discretion to consider the victims' application to participate and to determine the nature and scope of such participation during any phase of the proceedings.[278]

The case law shows that a three-tiered test has been developed in order to facilitate the granting of the victim status: i.e., i) the identity of the victim must appear duly established; ii) the events described in the application for participation must constitute a crime(s) within the jurisdiction of the Court with which the suspects are charged; iii) the applicant's harm has to appear to have arisen as a result of the crime(s) charged.[279]

The question that emerges from this test is whether, in cases of crimes involving the disappearance of the direct victim, family members can participate in the proceedings as victims themselves. So far, the Court has not dealt with cases of disappearance (enforced disappearances as crime against humanity or persons reported missing as result of other criminal conducts). Nevertheless, the ICC Chambers have considered whether to extend participation beyond those persons who suffered directly from the crimes, e.g., family members, in a variety of cases (e.g., in cases of deceased victims); the answers that have been formulated are promising. For instance, in the *Bemba* case, it was determined that applications could be made on behalf of deceased persons;[280] in the *Katanga and Ngudjolo* case, while requiring that the relatives of a deceased victim could only apply in their own name and not on behalf of the deceased victim, the Chamber accepted that, in cases where a victim dies after having filed an

---

[276] Donat-Cattin (n 270) 1287. Cf. Rule 2, ICTY, 'Rules of Procedure and Evidence' (2001) IT/32/Rev. 22.

[277] Cf. Rule 85 (a), ICC, 'Rules of Procedure and Evidence' (2000) UN Doc PCNICC/2000/1/Add.1. Such definition is inspired by the definition of victim contained in the Declaration of Basic Principles for Justice for Victims of Crimes and Abuse of Power. See UNGA, 'Declaration of the Basic Principles of Justice for Victims of Crimes and Abuse of Power' (1985) UN Doc A/RES/40/34. The Rules state that '[v]ictims may include organizations or institutions that have sustained direct harm to any of their property, which is dedicated to religion, education, art or science or charitable purposes, and to their historic monuments, hospitals and other places and objects for humanitarian purposes'. Cf. Rule 85 (b), ICC Rules of Procedure and Evidence (2000).

[278] Cf. Rule 85 (b) and Rule 89, ICC Rules of Procedure and Evidence (2000). Thus, the ICC Chamber has to determine how close a connection must be between the victim and the accused, and how relevant a particular issue or phase of the proceedings under consideration by the Chamber must be for the victim, in order for her/his interests to be sufficiently affected.

[279] Initially a four-tiered test was developed, which did not change in substance the understanding of Rule 85 (a) concerning the definition of victim. See *Prosecutor v Francis Kirimi Muthaura, Uhuru Muigai Kenyatta, Mohammed Hussein Ali*, Decision on victims' participation at the confirmation of charges hearing and in the related proceedings (2011) ICC-01/09-02/11 (ICC - Pre-Trial Chamber II) [40]; *Prosecutor v Bosco Ntaganda*, Decision on victims' participation at the confirmation of charges hearing and in the related proceedings (2014) ICC-01/04-02/06 (ICC - Pre-Trial Chamber II) [18].

[280] The Single Judge saw 'no impediment that the rights of the deceased victim [were] exercised by their successors during the proceedings, if these successors are victims recognized as participants in the proceedings'. *Prosecutor v Jean-Pierre Bemba Gombo*, Fourth Decision on victims' participation (2008) ICC-01/05-01/08 (ICC - Pre-Trial Chamber III) [47].

application, a person appointed by the family can continue the action triggered by the victim.[281]

The second tier does not seem to be problematic, as it entails that the victim applicant demonstrates a link with a crime falling within the jurisdiction of the ICC. In light of Rule 85, which delineates who is a victim, 'for the purposes of participation in the trial proceedings, the harm alleged by a victim and the concept of personal interests under article 68 (3) of the Statute must be linked with the charges confirmed against the accused'.[282] The provision enshrined in Article 68 (3) is specifically addressed to individual victims of a given crime; therefore, the 'personal interests' must be found on a case-by-case basis by the relevant Chamber in order to permit the exercise of the victims' right to participate.[283]

The third tier is more challenging. The meaning of the term 'harm' is not spelled out under the Rules of Procedure and Evidence (neither under the Statute). The ICC Appeals Chambers have tried to clarify the contours of this term as follows:

– 'the harm suffered by a natural person is harm to that person, i.e. personal harm' and, as long as it is suffered personally by the victim can take different forms, i.e., material, physical, and psychological harm;

– 'harm suffered by one victim as a result of the commission of a crime within the jurisdiction of the Court can give rise to harm suffered by other victims.' This is the case when a close personal relationship exists between the victims;

– 'the notion of victim necessarily implies the existence of personal harm but does not necessarily imply the existence of direct harm'; therefore, a person can be the direct or indirect victim of a crime within the jurisdiction of the ICC.[284]

Based on these standards, the Appeals Chamber has not hesitated to affirm that 'the recruitment of a child soldier may result in personal suffering of both the child concerned and the parents of that child';[285] similarly, this has occurred vis-à-vis the emotional suffering engendered by family displacement.[286]

By analogy to the foregoing considerations, in a case where a person is missing as a result of a crime falling under the jurisdiction of the Court, the emotional suffering deriving from the absence of the person is undoubted for

---

[281] *Prosecutor v Mathieu Ngudjolo Chui*, Motifs de la deuxième décision relative aux demandes de participation de victimes à la procédure (2009) ICC-01/04-01/07 (ICC - Pre-Trial Chamber III) [30–31, 33].

[282] *Prosecutor v Thomas Lubanga Dyilo Judgment on the appeals of The Prosecutor and The Defence against Trial Chamber I's Decision on Victims' Participation of 18 January 2008* (2008) ICC-01/04-01/06 OA 9 OA 10 (ICC - Appeals Chamber) [58].

[283] Donat-Cattin (n 270) 1286–1287.

[284] ICC, *Lubanga Case. Judgment on the appeals of the Prosecutor and the Defence against Trial Chamber I's Decision on Victims' Participation (2008)* (n 282) [31–32, 38].

[285] ibid [32].

[286] *Situation in Darfur* - Corrigendum to Decision on the Applications for Participation in the Proceedings of Applicants a/0011/06 to a/0015/06 and others (2007) ICC-02/05 (ICC - Pre-Trial Chamber I) [41].

his/her relative. In order to be granted the victim status, the applicant has the obligation to duly establish the kinship between the disappeared and the applicant him/herself[287] as well as the obligation to establish that 'as a result of [the] relationship with the direct victim, the harm suffered by the latter gives rise to [his/her] harm.'[288]

The participation of victims could, however, be limited by virtue of the burden of proof: as underlined by the Appeals Chamber in the *Lubanga* Case,

> the notion of victim necessarily implies the existence of personal harm but does not necessarily imply the existence of direct harm. [...] If the applicant is unable to demonstrate a link between the harm suffered and the particular crimes charged, then even if his or her personal interests are affected by an issue in the trial, it would not be appropriate under article 68 (3) read with rule 85 and 89 (1) of the Rules [of Procedure and Evidence] for his or her views and concerns to be presented.[289]

This limitation could hamper the right to participate and, as a corollary, the other rights subsumed therein. The Chamber has not taken into account the fact that, in certain cases, victims will be unable to prove that their relatives disappeared and that they consequently endured emotional suffering and other damages. The case law of the human rights adjudicators could serve the purpose of interpreting this caveat in a manner which is favourable to (indirect) victims in situations where the direct victim is missing. Wisely, the Trial Chamber, in its Decision on Principles and Procedures on Reparations in the *Lubanga* Case, has underscored that '[s]everal factors are of significance in determining the appropriate standard of proof at this stage, including the difficulty victims may face in obtaining evidence in support of their claim due to the destruction or unavailability of evidence'.[290] The list of data to be provided would, therefore, be weighed against the accessibility of victims to documents, names, and addresses of witnesses.

---

[287] *Prosecutor v Bosco Ntaganda,* Decision on victims' participation in trial proceedings (2015) ICC-01/04-02/06 (ICC - Trial Chamber IV) [48].

[288] *Prosecutor v Laurent Gbagbo,* Second decision on victims' participation at the confirmation of charges hearing and in the related proceedings (2013) ICC-02/11-01/11 (ICC - Pre-Trial Chamber I) [33].

[289] *Prosecutor v Thomas Lubanga Dyilo,* Judgment on the appeals of the Prosecutor and the Victims' Participation of 18 January 2008 (2008) ICC-01/04-01/06 OA 9 OA 10 (ICC - Appeals Chamber) [38, 64]. The issue of the burden of proof is also relevant with regard to reparations: victims can make a request for reparations under Article 75 of the Rome Statute, which, however, does not specify the data to be provided in this request. Rule 94 of the ICC Rules of Procedures and Evidence bridges this gap by providing a detailed list of such data which *inter alia* includes 'a description of the injury, loss or harm'; 'the location and date of the incident and, to the extent possible, the identity of the person or persons the victim believes to be responsible for the injury, loss or harm'; and 'to the extent possible, any relevant supporting documentation, including names and addresses of witnesses'. Victims of any of the crimes enshrined in the Rome Statute would encounter practical and psychological difficulties in gathering such information.

[290] *Prosecutor v Thomas Lubanga Dyilo,* Decision establishing the principles and procedures to be applied to reparations (2012) ICC-01/04-01/06 (ICC - Trial Chamber I) [252].

2.2.1.2. The right to know among the "rights" embedded in the participation system under the Rome Statute

The right of victims to know the truth is one of the fundamental principles of human rights law.[291] Such a right is depicted as multifaceted, for it includes the right to determine what happened, the right to know the whereabouts of the remains (should the person be reported dead), the identification of perpetrators of the crimes. The ICC Statute does not include a list of victims' rights: the reason for this *lacuna* could lie in the fact that 'under no circumstances may the rights of victims prevail over the rights of the defendant, nor may the interest in discovering the truth'.[292] Indeed, in considering the right to know the truth of victims under international criminal law, one cannot ignore the fact that the respect for the human rights of the defendants in international criminal trials contributes to achieving the rightful aspiration of justice, and, as a consequence, cannot be overlooked.[293]

The participation in the proceedings has specific features under the Rome Statute: first, participation does not mean that victims may address the Chamber, for they must submit a participation application in writing to the Registrar, who shall then transmit it to the relevant Chamber; second, should the application be considered well-founded, the Chamber concerned will determine the nature and scope of such participation[294] during every phase of the proceedings.[295]

At the pre-trial level, the Rome Statute confers upon victims a right to 'make representations to the Pre-Trial Chamber' concerning the Prosecutor's decision to proceed with an investigation.[296] At the trial level, the right to participate consists in the possibility of submitting observations to the Court as to the jurisdiction or admissibility.[297] As for the latter, the role of victims can be

---

[291] Basic Principles and Guidelines on the Right to a Remedy (n 218) Principle X; Orentlicher Principles (n 43) Principles 2, 4.

[292] Zappalà (n 155) 164.

[293] Thomas Margueritte, 'International Criminal Law and Human Rights' in William Schabas and Nadia Bernaz (eds), *Routledge handbook of international criminal law* (Routledge 2011) 446.

[294] One common misinterpretation is that victims' interests are represented by the prosecution; therefore, there is no need for independent victim participation. Sub-section 1.2 of the present Chapter on the ICTY shows what consequences this understanding can have in post-conflict situations (e.g., the interests of victims do not always coincide with those of the prosecution). For this reason, victims have their own legal representative. This role is played by persons whose professional features are laid down in Rule 90 (6) of the ICC Rules of Procedures and Evidence (2000). On this aspect, see Mariana Pena and Gaelle Carayon, 'Is the ICC Making the Most of Victim Participation?' (2013) 7 The International Journal of Transitional Justice 1, 8; Funk (n 274) 86–87.

[295] Cf. Rule 89, ICC Rules of Procedure and Evidence (2000).

[296] Cf. Article 15 (3), Rome Statute of the International Criminal Court, July 17, 1998, 2187 UNTS 90 (hereinafter, Rome Statute). For instance, the Prosecutor notified the victims of alleged war crimes and crimes against humanity committed in Georgia during the armed conflict in 2008 that they could send their comments to the Judges of Pre-Trial Chamber I on whether an investigation on such alleged crimes should be opened. See ICC/OTP, 'Public Notice of the ICC Prosecutor to the Victims of Violence Committed in the Context of the August 2008 Armed Conflict in Georgia' (2015) <https://www.icc-cpi.int/iccdocs/otp/Article_15_Application--Notice_to_victims-ENG.pdf> accessed 12 July 2016.

[297] Cf. Article 19 (3), Rome Statute.

crucial: they could provide the Court with relevant information on the functioning of national systems and on the ability and willingness of relevant national authorities to genuinely investigate and prosecute.[298]

The participation in the proceedings entails that victims can present their views and concerns when their interests are affected: in those proceedings where this opportunity has been afforded, their legal representatives have been able, *inter alia,* to examine witnesses, adduce evidence into the records, file submission throughout the proceedings, and file written submissions.[299] Thousands of victims have filed the application to participate in the proceedings,[300] which confirms that one of the main interests of victims of international crimes is not only uncovering the truth, but being active contributors in the process of clarification of what happened. Therefore, the right to know the truth is broader and more comprehensive than the right of families to know the fate and whereabouts of their relatives;[301] the former is understood as 'the determination of the facts, the identification of the responsible persons and the declaration of their responsibility'.[302] At the procedural level, the search for

---

[298] Commentary of the Human Rights Watch to the Preparatory Commission on the International Criminal Court (1999) at 28-29 in Jorda and de Hemptinne (n 271) 1404.

[299] *Prosecutor v Mathieu Ngudjolo Chui,* Judgment Pursuant to Article 74 of the Statute (2012) ICC-01/04-02/12 (ICC | Trial Chamber II) [31]; *Prosecutor v Germain Katanga,* Judgment pursuant to Article 74 of the Statute (2014) ICC-01/04-01/07 (ICC | Trial Chamber II) [27].

[300] For instance, 2,149 victims were authorized to participate in the *Ntaganda* trial. 4,107 victims have been authorized to participate in the proceedings concerning Dominic Ongwen; 130 victims were authorized to participate in the pre-trial stage of the *Mbarushimana* case; 146 persons were authorized to participate in the *Lubanga Dyilo* Case; 725 victims were authorized to participate in proceedings in the *Kenyatta* case; 366 victims were authorized to participate in the proceedings in the *Katanga* Case. See ICC, 'Case Information Sheet - Situation in the DRC: The Prosecutor v. Bosco Ntaganda (ICC-01/04-02/06)' (2017) ICC-PIDS-CIS-DRC-02-011/15_Eng; ICC, 'Case Information Sheet - Situation in Uganda: The Prosecutor v. Dominic Ongwen (ICC-02/04-01/15)' (2017) ICC-PIDS-CIS-UGA-02-012/16_Eng; ICC, 'Case Information Sheet - Situation in the DRC: The Prosecutor v. Callixte Mbarushimana ICC-01/04-01/10' (2012) ICC-PIDS-CIS-DRC-04-003/12_Eng; ICC, 'Case Information Sheet - Situation in the DRC: Thomas Lubanga Dyilo ICC-01/04-01/06' (2016) ICC-PIDS-CIS-DRC-01-015/16_Eng; ICC, 'Case Information Sheet - Situation in the DRC: The Prosecutor v. Germain Katanga ICC-01/04-01/07' (2015) ICC-PIDS-CIS-DRC-03-011/15_Eng; ICC, 'Case Information Sheet - Situation in the Republic of Kenya The Prosecutor v. Uhuru Muigai Kenyatta ICC-01/09-02/11' (2015) ICC-PIDS-CIS-KEN-02-014/15_Eng.

[301] The victims' right to the truth 'can be traced back to articles 32 and 33 of the 1977 Additional Protocol I to the Geneva Conventions, and has subsequently been developed by national and international case law, especially in cases of forced disappearances'. *Prosecutor v Germain Katanga and Mathieu Ngudjolo Chui,* Decision on the Set of Procedural Rights attached to Procedural Status of Victim at the Pre-Trial Stage of the Case (2008) ICC-01/04-01/07 (ICC | Pre-Trial Chamber I) [32 (n 39)].

[302] At the Pre-Trial Stage of the *Katanga and Ngudjolo Chui* Case, the Judge observed that 'when [the right to the truth] is to be satisfied through criminal proceedings, victims have a central interest in that the outcome of such proceedings: (i) bring clarity about what indeed happened; and (ii) close possible gaps between the factual findings resulting from the criminal proceedings and the actual truth. As a result, [...] the issue of the guilt or innocence of persons prosecuted before [the ICC is not only relevant, but also affects the very core interests of those granted the procedural status of victim in any case before the Court insofar as this issue is inherently linked to the satisfaction of their right to the truth. [...] The victims' central interest in the search for the truth can only be satisfied if (i) those responsible for perpetrating the crimes for which they suffered harm are declared guilty; and

truth is the 'hallmark of the inquisitorial model',[303] such as the Romano-Germanic systems: this model provides for the appointment of an investigating judge with the responsibility for collecting all items of evidence that will help establish the truth.[304] Such an inquisitorial model is not enshrined in any of the international criminal tribunals, including the ICC, which reflect an adversarial model. In the latter, the decision on the evidence to be presented rests with the parties (the prosecutor on the one hand, and the defendant on the other), and not with the judge. Thus, Article 68 (3) of the Rome Statute, along with other provisions,[305] provides victims with the possibility of having a say in this context.

In the legal framework and human rights case law concerning enforced disappearance, the right to know the truth is often subsumed under the so-called right to obtain reparation;[306] as a matter of fact, the ICC derives its conclusions on reparations from the said case law by recognizing the right to reparations as 'a well-established and basic human right that is enshrined in universal and regional human rights treaties'.[307] The victims' representatives have frequently added that 'the victims' rights to justice, namely, to "have those who victimized them prosecuted, tried convicted, and subject to a certain punishment," is to be differentiated from the victims' right to reparations. [notes omitted].'[308] Indeed, victims are 'entitled to truth and justice, which implies three consequences: that the perpetrators of the crimes are prosecuted; that the perpetrators of those

---

(ii) those not responsible for such crimes are acquitted, so that the search for those who are criminally liable can continue.' ibid [34–36].

[303] A Eser, 'Procedural Structure and Features of International Criminal Justice: Lessons from the ICTY' in Bert Swart, Alexander Zahar and Göran Sluiter (eds), *The legacy of the International Criminal Tribunal for the Former Yugoslavia* (Oxford University Press 2011) 122.

[304] Jorda and de Hemptinne (n 271) 1412.

[305] Pursuant to Article 15 (3) of the Rome Statute, victims are allowed to make representation to the Pre-Trial Chamber on the Prosecutor's decision to proceed with an investigation; Article 19 (3) of the Rome Statute grants victims permission to submit observations on jurisdiction of the ICC and the admissibility of cases; Article 43 (6) of the Rome Statute empowers the Registrar to set up Victims and Witness Unit within the Registry; Article 53 (1) (c) requires the Prosecutor to consider the interests of victims when deciding whether to initiate an investigation; Article 75 provides for reparations to victims; Article 82 (4) accords to victims the right to appeal reparations orders. For a critical appraisal of the participation system under the Rome Statute, see Funk (n 274) 81–82.

[306] 'The right to reparations' is intertwined with the victims' right to know the truth. Bassiouni points out that the victim's right to truth is encompassed by the right to remedies. Understanding and public disclosure of the truth is important to victims because the truth alleviates the suffering of the surviving victims; it also vindicates the memory or status of the direct victim of the violation and encourages the State to confront its dark past. See M Cherif Bassiouni, 'The International Recognition of Victims' Rights' (2006) 6 Human Rights Law Review 203, 260, 275.

[307] *Prosecutor v Thomas Lubanga Dyilo*, Judgment on the appeals against the 'Decision establishing the principles and procedures to be applied to reparations' of 7 August 2012 (2015) ICC-01/04-01/06 A A 2 A 3 (ICC - Appeals Chamber) [186].

[308] *Prosecutor v Jean-Pierre Bemba Gombo*, Response by the Legal Representative of Victims to the 'Prosecution's Request for Leave to Appeal the Trial Chamber's Oral Ruling Denying Authorisation to Add and Disclose Additional Evidence after 30 November 2009' (2009) ICC-01/05-01/08 (ICC | Pre-Trial Chamber III) [11]; *Prosecutor v Jean-Pierre Bemba Gombo*, Response by the Legal Representative of Victims to the Defence's Challenge on Admissibility of the Case pursuant to articles 17 et 19 (2) (a) of the Rome Statute with 102 Annexes Confidential ex parte OPCV only and same Annexes Public Redacted (2010) ICC-01/05-01/08 (ICC | Pre-Trial Chamber III) [81].

crimes are tried and convicted; that the victims are entitled to reparations. [notes omitted]'[309]

Accordingly, the Court has considered that both direct victims and indirect victims – including the family members of the direct victim and individuals who suffered harm[310] when helping or intervening on behalf of direct victims – should be included in the reparation scheme that is provided for under Article 75 of the Statute. [311] The reparation scheme was introduced in the ICC Statute to allow the judges to decide upon the widest possible range of remedies with regard to victims' rights violations.[312] The Court might award victims reparations on an individualized or collective basis, and with a twofold dimension, i.e., monetary and symbolic,[313] thereby recalling the approach undertaken by the IACtHR.[314]

Before ordering reparations measures, the Court 'may invite and shall take account of representations from or on behalf of' the victims or other interested persons:[315] thus, victims, families' associations, or/and organizations concerned can forward their views on reparations and "participate" in framing the

---

[309] *Prosecutor v Germain Katanga and Mathieu Ngudjolo Chui*, Observations of the Legal Representatives of the Victims Represented by Mr Jean-Louis Gillisen and Mr Joseph Keta on 'The Defence motion for a declaration on unlawful detention and stay of proceedings (ICC-01/04-01/07-125-Conf-Exp)' ICC-01/04-01/07 (ICC | Pre-Trial Chamber I) [13].

[310] Pursuant to the reasoning of the Appeals Chambers, 'there is a distinction to be made between identifying the harms to direct and indirect victims caused by the crimes for which the person was convicted and assessing the extent of that harm for purposes of determining the nature and/or size of reparation awards'. ICC, *Lubanga Case. Judgment on the appeals against the 'Decision establishing the principles ....' of 7 August 2012* (n 307) [181].

[311] ibid [185, 195–196]. On the right to reparations, the Chamber specifically referred to Article 8, UDHR; Article 9(5), ICCPR; Article 6, International Convention on the Elimination of All Forms of Racial Discrimination; Article 14(1), CAT; Article 21(2), AfChHPR; and Article 63(1), ACHR. See ibid [185 (n 372)].

[312] Article 75 of the Rome Statute includes a specific provision on the reparations to, or in respect of, victims including restitution, compensation, and rehabilitation.

[313] 'Reparation' is a broad and flexible concept: for instance, especially in cases of mass or collective victimization, 'reparation' may be better achieved through means other than restitution or monetary compensation; such measures could be qualified as non-pecuniary forms of compensation or means of rehabilitation, insofar as they respond to the need to acknowledge publicly and transparently the causes, effects and remedies of international crimes, as well as to restore the dignity of victims in a societal context. David Donat-Cattin, 'Article 75 - Reparations to Victims' in Otto Triffterer and Kai Ambos (eds), *Commentary on the Rome Statute of the International Criminal Court: Observers' Notes, Article by Article* (C H Beck 2008) 1405.

[314] Article 75 confers upon the Court the competence to establish principles on reparations such as (but not limited to) restitution, compensation, and rehabilitation. Therefore, it might order 'satisfaction measures' by getting inspiration from the measures listed in the UN Basic Principles under the heading 'satisfaction': i.e., '[v]erification of the facts and full and public disclosure of the truth to the extent that such disclosure does not cause further harm or threaten the safety and interests of the victim, the victim's relatives, witnesses, or persons who have intervened to assist the victim or prevent the occurrence of further violations; [and] the search for the whereabouts of the disappeared, for the identities of the children abducted, and for the bodies of those killed, and assistance in the recovery, identification and reburial of the bodies in accordance with the expressed or presumed wish of the victims, or the cultural practices of the families and communities'. Cf. Basic Principles and Guidelines on the Right to a Remedy, Principle IX, para 22.

[315] Cf. Article 75 (3), Rome Statute.

reparation scheme. This is relevant, as long as 'symbolic' reparation measures are concerned; such measures may be better pinpointed if the victims' views on reparations are taken into consideration: against this backdrop, a claim for the right to know the truth would not be unrealistic.[316] In this sense, the subtle divide between the judicial truth and the 'truth with capital 'T''[317] seems to be purely academic: the role of victims in ICC proceedings would probably lead to uncover the 'judicial truth', but could also place them in a position to ask for uncovering a more general truth (e.g., by means of the disclosure of national archives, of the publication of the documents which purport the perpetration of the criminal conduct, ...) at the reparation stage.

Another manner for the victims to have access to relevant information can be inferred from Rule 121 of the ICC Rules of Procedure and Evidence; the Rule provides victims and their representatives with the right to access the record of proceedings prior to the confirmation hearing (subject to restrictions concerning confidentiality and the protection of national security information).

Since the Nuremberg Tribunals, very limited consideration has been given to victims' rights, and namely to their right to know as a tool to enhance the process of clarification of the events characterized by a criminal course of actions. The right to know is not a stand-alone right under the Rome Statute. To a certain extent, it is a *fil rouge* running through the victims' needs before the ICC.[318] As a corollary, this right is inextricably related to the participation of the victims in the ICC proceedings, which emerges as a *sui generis* right enshrined in the Rome Statute.

2.2.2. Looking at the issue of missing persons through the prism of the ICC statute

2.2.2.1. Introductory remarks on enforced disappearances and missing persons

Acts falling under the category of crimes against humanity, such as enforced disappearance,[319] could be perpetrated to the detriment of the civilian population. This could also happen independently from armed conflicts or situations of internal violence; the Rome Statute does not require a specific connection with an armed conflict, for an act to be considered a crime against humanity. In this

---

[316] The example of the IACtHR's case law, referred to several times in the Chamber Decision, confirms this consideration. On this twofold dimension of reparations, see, for instance, IACtHR, *Godínez-Cruz v Honduras, Judgment – Reparations and Costs* (1989) Series C No. 8 [8 ff]; *Neira-Alegría et al v Peru, Judgment - Reparations and Costs* (1995) Series C no. 29 [69]; *Bámaca-Velásquez v. Guatemala (Reparations ...)* (n 227) [76].

[317] Zappalà (n 155) 145. See also sub-section 1.2 in the present Chapter.

[318] These needs include the recognition and validation of the victimization; the creation of a permanent historic record of the criminal activity, as well as of a record of how the conduct affected particular victims; the publication of the truth about the political and social environment which permitted the crimes to take place; an explanation of the victimization; the possibility of taking part in proceedings that will determine the punishment of those responsible for the criminal conduct. Funk (n 274) 80–81.

[319] Despite the focus on enforced disappearance as a crime against humanity, this sub-section will not illustrate the elements of the international crimes under the Rome Statute and, in particular, of the crime against humanity. Indeed, the focus is on the families' quest for information and on the potential implications of the Statute's provisions for the realization of their right to know.

regard, pursuant to the ICPPED, 'the widespread or systematic practice of enforced disappearance constitutes a crime against humanity as defined in applicable international law and shall attract the consequences provided for under such applicable international law'.[320] The provision enshrines an indirect reference to the Rome Statute and to customary international law: Article 7 of the Rome Statute lists 'enforced disappearance' among those acts that fall under the category of 'crimes against humanity', i.e., acts that are 'committed as part of a widespread or systematic attack directed against any civilian population, with knowledge of the attack'.[321] Pursuant to the *chapeau* of Article 7 (1) of the Rome Statute, the victim of the offence of enforced disappearance is not the individual *per se*: the individual is victimized not because of his/her individual attributes, but rather because of his membership of a targeted civilian population (in this case he/she would be a direct victim of the offence).[322]

Furthermore, persons can go missing as result of the commission of other crimes against humanity included in the Rome Statute: for instance, the fate and whereabouts of a person might remain unknown as a result of the deportation or forcible transfer of population[323] (i.e., forced displacement of the persons concerned by expulsion or other coercive acts from the area in which they are lawfully present, without grounds permitted under international law).

One should not ignore the fact that cases of missing persons could also emerge in the context of war crimes: persons could be reported missing as a result of the unlawful deportation or transfer or unlawful confinement,[324] or of

---

[320] Cf. Preamble and Article 5, ICPPED.

[321] Cf. Article 7 (1), Rome Statute.

[322] Kolb, Robert. *Droit International Pénal*, Basel 2008, 96 1 cited in Lisa Ott, *Enforced Disappearance in International Law* (Intersentia 2011) 174. The definition of 'civilian population' brings about problematic issues both in time of armed conflict and in peacetime. Even the search for a definition of civilian population in a situation of armed conflict in the case law of the ICTY is pointless. Nonetheless, with regard to Article 5 of the ICTY Statute (*crimes against humanity*), the Trial Chamber interpreted it broadly: '[i]t would seem that a wide definition of "civilian" and "population" is intended. [...] One fails to see why only civilians and not also combatants should be protected by these rules (in particular by the rule prohibiting persecution), given that these rules may be held to possess a broader humanitarian scope and purpose than those prohibiting war crimes.' ICTY, *Prosecutor v Kupreškić et al, Trial Judgment* (2000) Case no IT-95-16-T [574]. As deGuzman observes, it is hard to establish what types of connections among the victims will satisfy the requirement of a 'population'. MM deGuzman, 'Crimes against Humanity' in William Schabas and Nadia Bernaz (eds), *Routledge handbook of international criminal law* (Routledge 2011) 132. Whilst in armed conflicts one could use IHL rules to define the term 'civilian' and adopt a broad interpretation, with the subsequent inclusion of those not actively engaged in hostilities at the time of the crime, regardless of their formal status, in peacetime it proves difficult to draw the contours of 'civilian population'. In this regard, the ICTR has concluded that all persons are civilian 'except those who have the duty to maintain public order and have legitimate means to exercise force'. ICTR, *The Prosecutor v Clément Kayishema and Obed Ruzindana, Trial Judgment* (1999) ICTR-95-1-T [127]. However, should one accept such an interpretation, the scope of provisions such as the one relating to enforced disappearances would be narrowed. More generally, Cassese underlines that without the protection of IHL, in the absence of an armed conflict, 'military personnel too may become the object of crimes against humanity at the hands of their own authorities'. Antonio Cassese, *International Criminal Law* (2nd edn, Oxford University Press 2008) 122.

[323] Cf. Article 7 (1) (d), Rome Statute.

[324] Cf. Article 8 (2) (a) (vii) (IAC situation); Article 8 (2) (e) (viii) (NIAC situation), Rome Statute.

attacks intentionally directed against the civilian population.[325] In such cases, the fact of being forcibly displaced could leave the loved ones without any information on the persons subjected to the displacement; the attack against the civilians could provoke the death of persons whose fate and whereabouts might remain unknown if their bodies are not recovered from the place of the attack.

2.2.2.2. *Legal and practical considerations on the participation system and its potential effects on the families' quest for information in post-conflict*

The participation of victims in the proceedings is not limited to direct victims; direct and indirect[326] victims can present their views and concerns when their personal interests are affected. In this regard, the role of the participation mechanism is even more important: the international criminal justice system could become more transparent in relation to war crimes victims that, in the past, have been considered 'passive-object of the international criminal proceedings'.[327]

The innovative aspects of this mechanism are the exposure of indirect victims to information concerning the events surrounding the crime, the possibility for them to add further evidence, and the opportunity of being part of the process aimed at establishing what happened. Such exposure is inherent in the victims' "right to participate", which includes the possibility for the victims to have access to the records of proceedings before the confirmation hearing, to submit observations to the Court as to the Court's jurisdiction and the admissibility of cases, and the victims' right to seek and obtain reparations.

The cases of the Court have not addressed neither enforced disappearances as crime against humanity nor the issue of missing persons in other criminal contexts. Nevertheless, cases of enforced disappearance and of persons reported missing following other alleged criminal conducts have emerged from the OTP's preliminary examinations[328] – ongoing at the time of writing – in relation, *inter alia*,[329] to the situations in Ukraine (ongoing armed conflict)[330] and in Colombia

---

[325] Cf. Article 8 (2) (b) (i), (iv), and (v) (IAC situation); Article 8 (2) (e) (i) (NIAC situation), Rome Statute.

[326] As sub-section 2.2.2.1 has tried to demonstrate, this can be the case of family members of persons reported missing as a result of war crimes or crimes against humanity.

[327] Jorda and de Hemptinne (n 271) 1389, 1397.

[328] Preliminary examinations are not tantamount to an investigation of the OTP; the examinations proceed in four phases: Phase 1, i.e., the initial assessment of all information on alleged crimes received under Article 15 of the Rome Statute; Phase 2, i.e., the formal commencement of a preliminary examination focuses on whether the preconditions to the exercise of jurisdiction under Article 12 of the Rome Statute are satisfied and on whether there is a reasonable basis to believe that the alleged crimes fall within the subject matter jurisdiction of the Court; Phase 3, i.e., admissibility of potential cases in terms of complementarity and gravity; Phase 4, i.e., examination of the interests of justice consideration in order to formulate a final recommendation to the Prosecutor on whether there is a reasonable basis to commence an investigation. See ICC/OTP, 'Report on Preliminary Examination Activities 2016' (2016) 4–5 <https://www.icc-cpi.int//Pages/item.aspx?name=161114-otp-rep-PE> accessed 10 January 2017.

[329] Enforced disappearances have been part of the preliminary examinations concerning, for instance, the situation in Guinea-Conakry (phase 3 of preliminary examination; the country has been taking investigative steps, but no trial has taken place to date). See ibid 51, 270, 273. The OTP has concluded that the information available provides a reasonable basis to believe that a set of crimes

(ongoing post-conflict[331] phase).[332] The considerations enhanced in this part of the study would fully apply to the families of those reported missing in both scenarios, should the situations meet the legal criteria – jurisdiction, admissibility, and the interests of justice – under the Rome Statute to warrant an investigation by the OTP. Indeed, the opportunity for the families of the missing in Colombia and Ukraine to participate in the proceedings would contribute to the realization of their right to know.

The victims' right to take part in the proceedings denotes a development towards a restorative international criminal justice system that can positively affect post-conflict environments. Retribution is, of course, an important factor: a sentence of an international tribunal should 'make plain the condemnation of the international community of the behavior in question and show "that the international community was not ready to tolerate serious violations of [IHL] and human rights"'.[333] However, the punishment of perpetrators is just one facet of the issue, the others being the recognition of the victims and of their harm, their

---

against humanity were committed in the national stadium in Conakry on 28 September 2009 and in their immediate aftermath; these included enforced disappearance of persons under article 7(1)(i) of the ICC Statute. ICC/OTP, 'Report on Preliminary Examination Activities 2017' (2017) 37 https://www.icc-cpi.int/itemsDocuments/2017-PE-rep/2017-otp-rep-PE_ENG.pdf accessed 15 March 2018.

[330] The situation of Ukraine has been under preliminary examination since 25 April 2014; at the time of writing, the situation is in the so-called Phase 2 of the preliminary examination. Based on the information received and on available public information, the OTP has developed a preliminary list of alleged crimes: in Crimea (situation of IAC), among other crimes at least 10 people have been reported missing since March 2014 (alleged crime: killing and abduction); in Easter Ukraine (IAC and NIAC, still under consideration) more than 400 people were registered as "missing", though it remained unclear how many of these individuals had been forcibly disappeared (alleged crime: disappearance). ICC/OTP, 'Report on Preliminary Examination Activities 2016' (n 328), 146, 173, 181; ICC/OTP, 'Report on Preliminary Examination Activities 2017' (n 329), 22, 25.

[331] In March 2017, the ICRC specified that, in light of the still existing tensions between the Colombian government and groups that are not affiliated with the FARC, it would avoid referring to this historical moment as "post-conflict" thereby preferring the expression "post-agreement". See ICRC, 'Humanitarian Challenges 2017. Colombia Report: Results and Perspectives' (2017) 10.

[332] The situation in Colombia has been under preliminary examination since June 2004 (the situation is in the so-called Phase 3 of the preliminary examination). Areas that since 2012 – when the OTP received information and reports on this conduct – are of continuing focus include the proceedings relating to killings and enforced disappearances, known as 'false positives' cases (i.e., cases falsely presented as guerilla killed in combat), committed by Colombian soldiers between 2002 and 2010. In particular, the OTP affirmed that in the context of false positives cases 'at a minimum the following acts constituting crimes against humanity have been committed by organs of the State: murder under article 7(1)(a) of the Statute; enforced disappearance under article 7(1)(i) of the Statute'. See ICC/OTP, 'Report on Preliminary Examination Activities 2012' (2012) paras 105–106 <https://www.icc-cpi.int//Pages/item.aspx?name=161114-otp-rep-PE> accessed 10 January 2017. The OTP has noted that internal proceedings against some of these alleged crimes (criminal investigations and prosecutions) are ongoing, but has yet to receive detailed information from the Colombia authorities on the cases reportedly investigated. Based on this consideration, the OTP has updated its analysis of the allegations of false positives killings for the purpose of identifying potential cases. See ICC/OTP, 'Report on Preliminary Examination Activities 2016' (n 328) paras 231-232, 241-244; ICC/OTP, 'Report on Preliminary Examination Activities 2017' (n 329), 31.

[333] ICTY, *Prosecutor v Zlatko Aleksovski, Appeals Chamber Judgment* (2000) Case no IT-95-14/1-A (Appeals Chamber) [185].

participation in the proceedings, and the right to seek and obtain reparation.[334] All these factors taken together can help establish a reconciliation process between individual offenders and victims, thereby contributing to the achievement of a sustainable peace.[335]

CONCLUSIONS

"Justice in transition" can play a significant role in addressing the issue of missing persons and in furthering the quest of their families for information. Peace and justice processes cannot be depicted as two opposite processes with regard to the subject matter and, more generally, with regard to the formulation of efforts to foster reconciliation. This Chapter has examined a variety of mechanisms that can be boiled down to two broad categories: those specifically created during or after an armed conflict and with a mandate that relates to this situation and those that have a permanent and more generally framed mandate. The requests for information of the families of persons reported as missing in armed conflicts have featured – or may feature in the future – in the work of both categories.

With regard to the former, the focus has been mainly on the mandate, on their *modus operandi*, and on the implications of their work for the families' quest for information. As for the Truth Commissions, the main finding is that the inclusion/disregard of the issue of the missing in their mandate directly impact on the concrete actions that these bodies can undertake to contribute to ascertaining the fate and whereabouts of persons reported as missing. The analysis of the hybrid criminal/non-criminal justice, particularly in the context of the Balkans, leads to conclude that the international presence within these bodies can be key under several respects: it can help shape the domestic approach to international law; it can also guide the domestic authorities in the integration process of human rights and IHL standards in the domestic context, thereby contributing to responding to the need of families for justice and for information (e.g., the HRChBH).

---

[334] Pena and Carayon (n 294) 5–6. This trend is reflected in Article 69 (3) of the Rome Statute: 'the Court has the authority to request the submission of all evidence that it considers necessary for *the determination of the truth* [emphasis added]'. In other words, the Court has the additional duty to clarify as much as possible the historical facts of the case (if the facts of the particular crime are sufficiently clear, the Court will not consider other evidence). DK Piragoff, 'Article 69 - Evidence' in Otto Triffterer and Kai Ambos (eds), *Commentary on the Rome Statute of the International Criminal Court: Observers' Notes, Article by Article* (C H Beck 2008) 1321. With regard to reparations, in the Decision on Reparations' Principles and Procedure in the *Lubanga* Case, the Trial Chamber held that '[r]eparations can assist in promoting reconciliation between the convicted person, the victims of the crimes and the affected communities'. Cf. ICC, *Lubanga Case. Decision establishing the principles and procedures to be applied to reparations* (n 290) [179].

[335] Baumgartner underlines that the relatively broad participation scheme under the Rome Statute is today widely recognized as an instrument to promote reconciliation. See Elisabeth Baumgartner, 'Aspects of Victim Participation in the Proceedings of the International Criminal Court' (2008) 90 International Review of the Red Cross 409, 410.

From a more general stance, the majority of the international TJ bodies examined were not meant to address the need of families to know the fate of their relatives; neither were they mandated to account for the missing. The ICTY's *modus operandi* − taken as example − demonstrates that the disregard of the inclusiveness of the families in the design and implementation of prosecutorial strategies and the absence of any form of institutionalized victim participation system can be problematic factors. These can negatively affect the work of the judicial bodies as well as the families' quest for information.[336] Thus, one of the main inferences that emerges from the analysis of its work is that the formulation of prosecutorial strategies of future bodies involved in adjudicating international crimes where persons have been reported missing should take into consideration the impact of the investigative work on the families of missing persons. This would require, for instance, that the management of information gathered for prosecutorial purposes be designed in a manner that does not ignore humanitarian considerations that are intimately related to cases of disappearances.

The example of the ICTY as well as that of the Special War Crimes Chamber in the State Court of Bosnia and Herzegovina serve the purpose of recognizing the limits of criminal "justice in transition": criminal proceedings carried out at the international and domestic level are not designed to address the issue of missing persons from a humanitarian perspective. The scope of their action remains limited to the determination of the guilt or innocence of the accused; as a corollary, investigations respond to the goal of the prosecution. Chapter V has proposed to translate normative complementarity into operational complementarity; the present Chapter shows that the work of international criminal judicial bodies can be operationally complementary to the work of humanitarian organizations − e.g., the ICRC − and vice-versa in ascertaining the fate and whereabouts of the missing and in elucidating the circumstances of a crime. In other words, they pursue complementary objectives and carry out mutually reinforcing − not exclusive − tasks in the case of the missing.[337]

Permanent judicial bodies like the human rights courts and the ICC are not secondary actors in the families' quest for information on missing persons within the broader framework of the efforts to build an enduring peace. The illustrative overview of the remedial measures ordered/recommended by human rights

---

[336] In his report on prosecutorial strategies, Pablo de Greiff has noted that '[v]ictim participation in the design of prosecutorial strategies at international and hybrid courts has proven crucial in identifying the array of possible violations.' He has also pointed out that '[v]ictim participation implies recognition of victims as rights holders'. Human Rights Council, 'Prosecutorial Prioritization Strategies' (n 156) paras 115–116.

[337] The Special Rapporteur on the promotion of truth, justice, reparation and guarantees of non-recurrence has stressed that it is essential that, in the context of TJ processes implemented in post-conflict settings, 'efforts are made to satisfy both humanitarian and judicial aims with regard to missing and disappeared persons. [...] Such an ambition is not feasible in the short run [...]. It is therefore important to be clear about the diversity of the ends to be reconciled.' UN Human Rights Council, 'Report of the Special Rapporteur on the Promotion of Truth, Justice, Reparation and Guarantees of Non-Recurrence (Advanced Edited Version)' (n 210) para 82.

adjudicatory bodies cast light upon the importance of their role in formulating the measures to repair a wrongdoing and to pave the way that might assist the families in moving forward. Their follow-up system (e.g., IACtHR and ECtHR), aimed at checking the responsiveness of State authorities to these measures, is an exercise that can facilitate and guide the steps towards a concrete response to the families and, ultimately, towards a peace which is sustainable for all.

The advances in the international criminal justice area reflect a major attention of the international community vis-à-vis all those directly and indirectly affected by international crimes, including the families of missing persons. The participation mechanism under the Rome Statute constitutes a response to the criticism raised by the lack of inclusiveness of the victims and by the clash of the families' needs against the prosecutorial needs in the work of the *ad hoc* Tribunals.

As Eser observes, a sustainable individual and social healing process can neither get started nor last without satisfying the victims' legitimate interest in establishing the truth.[338] While the judicial truth might not fully satisfy the search for information of the families of those reported as missing, the participatory approach to the family's suffering and the exposure of family members to information concerning the events where their relatives went missing can contribute to realizing their right to know. The participation system under the Rome Statute makes direct and indirect victims of international crimes active actors of international criminal justice. Only time will tell whether the 'victims' transplant' could work in a system focused primarily – but not solely – on criminal repression, and whether the families of those unaccounted for would be enabled to obtain relevant information in that environment.[339]

---

[338] Eser (n 303) 121–122.

[339] Crettol and La Rosa (n 12) 358–359. A similar concern is expressed by Baumgartner who points out that '[s]erious consideration of victims' interests also implies an obligation not to create erroneous hopes and expectations that cannot be fulfilled, will leave victims frustrated, and may place them in an even more difficult situation than they would have been without participating in ICC proceedings.' Baumgartner (n 335) 440.

Conclusions

1. Final Remarks

The objective of this book has been to answer the question of how the existing international legal framework meets two distinct, but intertwined needs emerging during and after an armed conflict, i.e., the need of families to receive information on the fate of their missing relatives and the societal and individual need for accountability for violations and abuses committed during the conflict. To this end, the book has captured the diversity of international rules concerning the situation of persons reported missing in armed conflict situations as well as the complexity of their implementation in the transition phase from an armed conflict to peace. Moreover, it has examined the relationship[1] of these rules in case of sequential or simultaneous application and has defined their interplay with policy tools in post-conflict environments. In light of the findings emerging from this analysis, the book has explored how to build linkages between humanitarian and accountability-driven efforts vis-à-vis post-conflict claims for information on missing persons.

The importance of considering the issue of missing persons in peace processes (including peacebuilding) has been widely recognized.[2] At the UN level, in particular, it has been acknowledged that 'humanitarian efforts to locate, identify and return missing persons, as well as accountability and [TJ] processes, should be mutually reinforcing'.[3] How the linkages between these efforts should be conceived in a legally sound manner has not been subjected to comprehensive legal research. Yet the absence of a common understanding of this key aspect has not prevented calls for an extensive approach to the issue of missing persons beyond the limits of armed conflicts and human rights abuses.[4] Solutions and proposals to address this and other aspects peculiar to the issue of missing persons are still fragmented and unclear from an international law and policy perspective. This study has aimed to contribute to filling these gaps by providing a more effective reading of the international legal framework concerning the subject matter, and by translating such reading into practical terms.

---

[1] C Stahn, 'The Future of Jus Post Bellum' in Carsten Stahn and Jann K Kleffner (eds), *Jus Post Bellum: Towards a Law of Transition From Conflict to Peace* (Springer Verlag 2008) 234; V Chetail, 'Introduction: Post-Conflict Peacebuilding - Ambiguity and Identity' in Vincent Chetail (ed), *Post-conflict Peacebuilding: a Lexicon* (Oxford University Press 2009) 17 ff.
[2] UNGA, 'Resolution on Missing Persons' (2016) UN Doc A/RES/71/201 para 16.
[3] UNSG, 'Report of the Secretary-General - Missing Persons' (2016) UN Doc A/71/299 para 71.
[4] ibid 66.

1.1. Accounting for missing persons: An integral part of the international legal framework applicable in conflict and post-conflict settings

Under IHL the obligation of all parties to account for missing persons runs through the pre-, *durante*, and post− phases of an armed conflict. In light of this consideration, the exact definition of the scope of application *ratione temporis* of IHL is purposeless: should it be possible to define the exact start/end date in an objective manner, this would not affect the duration of the temporally open-ended obligation to account for missing persons.[5] Within the limits of what is concretely possible, the (former) parties to the conflict still bear this obligation in the post-conflict phase.

Although it has been advanced that there exists a customary rule[6] applicable in NIAC and IAC[7] concerning the duty of each party to the conflict to account for missing persons and to provide family members with any information on their fate,[8] the customary nature of this obligation in NIAC does not depend on the fact that the same rule exists in IAC.[9] The present study has pointed out that there is an increasing practice of embedding the core of the rules on missing persons in post-conflict settlements between State authorities and non-state armed groups. The connection of these rules with other customary rules under international law (e.g., the prohibition of inhuman treatment) and with other rules in various bodies of law (e.g., the duty to investigate under IHRL) signals the fact that, if these rules are not customary, they are on their way to becoming customary with regard to the NIAC settings.[10] The existence of a customary rule applicable in NIAC fills the IHL treaty gap with regard to the missing, but does not clarify whether the non-state armed group(s) would be allowed to exchange information and data on an equal footing[11] at the end of the conflict.

---

[5] The human rights case law confirms the foregoing. Cf. ECtHR, *Varnava and Others v Turkey, Judgment (GC)* (2009) App nos. 16064/90 and others [148]. See Chapter IV, sect. 2.

[6] For a critical appraisal, see, among others, V Chetail, 'Droit International Général et Droit International Humanitaire: Retour Aux Sources' in Vincent Chetail (ed), *Permanence et mutations du droit des conflits armés* (Bruylant 2013) 43.

[7] Rule 117, which states that each Party to the conflict bears the aforementioned duties, poses other problematic issues: in a NIAC the expression 'each Party to the conflict' is clearly referring to both the governmental side and the non-State armed group(s); the ICRC CTA could help perform the activities concerning the gathering of information and its transmission to the families (the consent of the State being necessary); yet the extent of this provision is to be weighed against the capabilities of Parties. On this last aspect, see Sandesh Sivakumaran, *The Law of Non-International Armed Conflict* (Oxford University Press 2012) 285.

[8] Cf. Rule 117 'Accounting for Missing Persons', in Jean-Marie Henckaerts and Louise Doswald-Beck, *Customary International Humanitarian Law: Volume 1, Rules* (Cambridge University Press 2005) 421 ff.

[9] Jean d'Aspremont and Jérôme de Hemptinne, *Droit International Humanitaire: Thèmes Choisis* (Pedone 2012) 39; Chetail (n 6) 38.

[10] Sivakumaran (n 7) 285.

[11] The commentary note to Rule 117 solely underlines that 'the obligation to account for missing persons is recognized in numerous agreements between parties to both international and non-international armed conflicts'. See Henckaerts and Doswald-Beck (n 8) 422.

Furthermore, the study has identified *lacunae* with regard to the regulation of access to information on missing persons and the management of information in the phase that follows the general close of military operations. For instance, while during an IAC there exists a duty to keep records on deceased persons[12] and on persons deprived of their liberty,[13] nothing is stated about the management of these records after the termination of the conflict; the duty to record information and data with regard to persons – not falling under the category "protected persons" – who have been deprived of their liberty, solely refers to cases of deprivation of liberty that last 'for more than two weeks as a result of hostilities or occupation'.[14]

IHRL, which is applicable at all times, partly fills these *lacunae*. In terms of individual entitlements, IHRL fills the normative gap left under IHL treaties by means of the recognition of the right of each victim to know the truth about the circumstances of the enforced disappearance, the progress and results of the investigation, and the fate of the disappeared person. Nevertheless, this entitlement is narrowly focused on those cases that fit the definition of 'enforced disappearance' provided for under the ICPPED. Moreover, while the rules concerning the missing under IHL revolve around the relationship between the parties to the conflict, the rules under the ICPPED reflect a vertical[15] understanding of human rights.

1.2. IHL and IHRL rules on the missing: A mutually reinforcing relationship

The interconnectedness between the *pre-, durante,* and *post–* phases of an armed conflict justifies a reformulation of the relationship between IHL and IHRL traditionally framed within the *durante bello* dimension. To this end, the study has unpacked the basic principles of the *corpus juris* for the protection of all human beings in order to identify the common denominators to this framework and pave the way towards the identification of possible synergies. This exercise has proved essential to explain the reason why the recent IHRL advances concerning enforced disappearances – i.e., the adoption of the ICPPED – do not represent a merger of IHL rules on missing persons with the IHRL's.[16] Humanity is *per se* a general principle of international law founded on the idea of respect for human dignity; as such it represents the common denominator to all the

---

[12] Cf. Article 19 GC II; Article 129 GC IV.

[13] Cf. Articles 122, 123, GC III on the establishment of an official Information Bureau for POW as well as of a CTA; Articles 136, 137, and 140 GC IV on the establishment of similar institutions for collecting information and particulars on civilian internees.

[14] Cf. Article 33 AP I.

[15] Henry J Steiner, Philip Alston and Ryan Goodman, *International Human Rights in Context: Law, Politics, Morals* (3 edition, Oxford University Press 2007) 1087; Jean-Marie Henckaerts and Cornelius Wiesener, 'Human Rights Obligations of Non-State Armed Groups: A Possible Contribution from Customary International Law?' in Robert Kolb and Gloria Gaggioli (eds), *Research Handbook on Human Rights and Humanitarian Law* (Edward Elgar Publishing 2013) 150.

[16] Gloria Gaggioli, 'The Prohibition of Enforced Disappearances: A Meaningful Example of a Partial Merger between Human Rights Law and International Humanitarian Law' in Gloria Gaggioli and Robert Kolb (eds), *Research Handbook on Human Rights and Humanitarian Law* (Edward Elgar Publishing 2013) 331.

branches that are aimed at the protection of all human beings, including IHRL and IHL. This principle legally entitles 'any relevant international subject to claim compliance by any other international subject, whether or not non-compliance has damaged the former subject'.[17] Therefore, the principle of humanity is intimately related to the principle of accountability: within the purview of this study, demanding compliance with IHL and IHRL as an entitlement of the whole international community[18] inevitably generates two courses of action, i.e., actions vis-à-vis the requests of families for information on the one hand; and reactions vis-à-vis large-scale infringements of IHL and IHRL as the cause of uncertainty about the fate and whereabouts of people, on the other. Accountability pertains to the legal policy sphere in the broadest sense and, as such, serves the purpose of influencing the institutional design after a period of internal violence or a political change (not solely after an armed conflict).

Based on the foregoing, the rules on missing persons share a common denominator, i.e., the notion of respect for human dignity, which is the core of the principle of humanity. Two strands of intertwined considerations drove their formulation: humanitarian considerations motivated the amendment of the initial draft of AP I, which led to the codification of the right of families to know the fate of their relatives (*a basic human need*); accountability-based considerations are the drivers of the object and purpose of the ICPPED spelled out in its Preamble (i.e., the States parties express their determination 'to prevent enforced disappearances and to combat impunity for the crime of enforced disappearance').

Such considerations make these rules distinct but complementary, i.e., they mutually reinforce each other in the case of simultaneous application. Nevertheless, the 'rhetoric of complementarity'[19] about the fact that IHL and IHRL 'complete and perfect each other'[20] is a mere theoretical assertion that does not help to find practical solutions to actual cases.[21] The main problems of this assertion are its application to the two branches as a whole and not in terms of rules and the lack of fixed criteria that make complementarity a workable concept, *inter alios,* for lawyers, legal advisors, and judges. In this respect, this assertion leaves a

---

[17] Antonio Cassese, *International Law* (Oxford University Press 2005) 64–65. Cassese identifies 'respect for human rights' as a principle of international law that requires States to 'refrain from seriously and repeatedly infringing a basic right [...], and from trampling upon a whole series of rights'. In these terms, the principle of respect for human rights derives 'its most solid guarantee from the UN system'. ibid 59.

[18] Bassiouni emphasizes that as a result of the demands for compliance at the international level (see, for instance, the establishment of the *ad hoc* tribunals), accountability and justice emerge 'as internationally recognized values that are necessary for the maintenance of world order and for the restoration and maintenance of peace.' See MC Bassiouni, 'Accountability for Violations of International Humanitarian Law and Other Serious Violations of Human Rights', in MC Bassiouni (ed), *Post Conflict Justice* (Transnational Publishers 2002) 384.

[19] John Tobin, 'Seeking Clarity in Relation to the Principle of Complementarity: Reflections on the Recent Contributions of Some International Bodies' 8 Melbourne Journal of International Law 356.

[20] JK Kleffner, 'Scope of Application of International Humanitarian Law' in Dieter Fleck and Michael Bothe (eds), *The Handbook of International Humanitarian Law* (Oxford University Press 2008) 73.

[21] M Milanović, 'Norm Conflicts, International Humanitarian Law, and Human Rights Law' in Orna Ben-Naftali (ed), *International Humanitarian Law and International Human Rights Law - Pas de deux* (Oxford University Press 2011) 100.

wide margin of appreciation to those who have to figure out the functioning of the co-application of rules belonging to different regimes, which might be detrimental to legal certainty. Thus, this study has defined and expounded on the criteria to be used in resorting to the complementarity approach in the case of simultaneous application of rules belonging to IHL and IHRL: i.e., the nature of the rights at stake (absolute/limitable; derogable/underogable), the systemic integration principle, and the principle of the most favorable rule. Intertwined with each other, these criteria can be a helpful guidance in other comparable scenarios of normative simultaneousness.

From an application standpoint, the first of these criteria is the typology of right at stake, i.e., derogable/non-derogable, absolute/relative. *In bello* and in its aftermath, the protection offered by IHRL does not cease except for the effects of derogations admitted under a limited number of IHRL treaties.[22] However, the derogation regime seems to be irrelevant in post-conflict scenarios, as it is acknowledged that the end of the conflict would signal 'the resumption of the normal IHRL regime (to the extent that IHL was actually capable of displacing it).'[23] Different is the case of restrictions: in light of the examination of the legal framework, the regulatory framework of the IHL-based restrictions is not as carefully defined as in IHRL,[24] particularly with regard to the restriction of the correspondence and communication rights of persons held in captivity. This scenario has been examined through the prism of the second criterion.

Affirming that IHL and IHRL are complementary means that the provisions belonging to one of these branches should be read and interpreted by taking into account other relevant rules belonging to the other.[25] From the analysis in Chapters III and IV it emerges that the restriction regime under IHRL is much more developed in terms of parameters – almost absent under IHL – that State authorities must meet to interfere lawfully with the rights and guarantees of persons in detention (e.g., communication rights/family visits/external correspondence). Where overlap of restrictions coming from the two branches arises, the regulatory regime of the IHL-based restrictions should be interpreted in

---

[22] For instance, Article 4, ICCPR; Article 15, ECHR; Article 27 ACHR; Article 4, ArChHR.

[23] An assessment of the notifications of derogations from the ICCPR and the ECHR shows that States derogating from these instruments have terminated the effects of the derogations at the end of the conflicts where they were involved. See sub-section 2.3.2.1 in Chapter III.

[24] Louise Doswald-Beck, *Human Rights in Times of Conflict and Terrorism* (Oxford University Press 2011) 448-449.

[25] Various international judicial bodies have made used of this principle. These include, for instance, the ICJ and the WTO Appellate Body. For a review of the international and regional case law where this principle has been used, see d'Aspremont, J and E Tranchez, 'The Quest for a Non-Conflictual Coexistence of International Human Rights Law and Humanitarian Law: Which Role for the Lex Specialis Principle?' in Gloria Gaggioli and Robert Kolb (eds), *Research Handbook on Human Rights and Humanitarian Law* (Edwar Elgar Publishing 2013) 235–238; Campbell McLachlan, 'The Principle of Systemic Integration and Article 31(3)(C) of the Vienna Convention' (2005) 54 The International and Comparative Law Quarterly 279. With regard to its use in relation to the interplay between IHL and IHRL rules, see ECtHR, *Hassan v The UK, Judgment (GC)* (2014) App no 29750/09 [102]; IACommHR, *Inter-State Petition IP-02 Admissibility, Franklin Guillermo Aisalla Molina, Ecuador - Colombia* (2010) Report No 112/10 [121]; AfCommHPR, 'General Comment No. 3 on the African Charter on Human And Peoples' Rights: The Right to Life (Article 4)' (2015) para 13.

light of the restriction regime under IHRL.[26] Interferences have materialized in the form of the restriction of family's detention visits/correspondence; this and other typologies are addressed in detail in Chapter IV. Any justification for these restrictions based on military necessity would not hold valid in post-conflict scenarios; therefore, this cannot be the parameter of reference to delineate the boundaries of the IHL restrictions. Accordingly, the parameters set down under IHRL fill this gap, should the IHL restrictions continue to be applicable in post-conflict situations. Although in the post-conflict phase the State might have to face the difficult endeavor of finding a balance between individual rights and social needs generated by the situation on the ground,[27] restrictions of communication rights and family visits should not be aimed at generating uncertainty or at worsening the emotional condition of the family concerned. As a matter of fact, uncertainty can be the source of anguish and suffering of the families as well as a telling factor related to possible violations to the detriment of their relatives.

Where the provision at stake concerns an absolute – i.e., not limitable – right or guarantee, which is present under both branches with different degrees of protection, the principle of the most-favorable/protective-rule for the individual applies. Specifically, where IHL and IHRL rules regulate the same conduct or provide for the same guarantee with a different degree of protection for the same person, the most-protective-rule clause clarifies and helps understand how the cumulative application of these rules works. The immediate implication of this clause for State authorities is that of serving as a reminder of their obligations under other treaties, if these are more favorable to the protection of the individual concerned.[28] For instance, the investigative character of the measures aimed at implementing the obligation to account for missing persons entails two possible scenarios: on the one hand, efforts to account for missing persons exclusively aim at informing the family about the fate and whereabouts of their relatives; on the other, in case of serious human rights violations, the duty to account for missing persons might intermingle with the duty to carry out a prompt, impartial, thorough, and independent official investigation aimed at identifying those responsible and prosecuting them. These two obligations are not mutually exclusive; yet the duty to account for a missing person is not mandatorily triggered by an alleged violation of IHL or IHRL. In this sense, the duty to account for missing persons constitutes a humanitarian-driven protective baseline to which further layers of protection can be added depending on the circumstances of the case. Simultaneous application of similar rules belonging to different branches of international law can generate interpretative discrepancies; such discrepancies result from the foundational tenets enshrined in the measures aimed at handling uncertainty.

---

[26] The interpretation of IHL in light of IHRL is not unusual. Cf. ICTY, *Prosecutor v Anto Furundžija, Trial Judgment* (1998) Case no. IT-95-17/1-T [143]. See also IACommHR, *Inter-State Petition IP-02 Admissibility, Franklin Guillermo Aisalla Molina, Ecuador - Colombia* (n 25) [121].

[27] For instance, the situation on the ground might be characterized by counter-terrorism operations aimed at downsizing the capacity of the armed groups previously at war against their government or by the continuation of detention of persons apprehended during an armed conflict. See section 4 in Chapter IV.

[28] Ali Sadat-Akhavi, *Methods of Resolving Conflicts Between Treaties* (Martinus Nijhoff Publishers 2003) 231.

Uncertainty regarding a relative's fate and whereabouts can generate unbearable suffering for family members. Although human rights adjudicators have diverse views on the triggering factor of human rights violations against the family members of missing persons, convergence emerges in considering that disregarding requests for information on persons reported as missing and ignoring possible obstacles that prevent the family members from pursuing their quest for information violate their right to be treated humanely. Thus, a duty to inform the family members of the fate of their missing relatives emerges under IHRL both in armed conflict and in post-conflict situations. Despite the absence of a treaty-based provision under IHL applicable in NIAC, this means that under IHRL State authorities bear the aforementioned duties in NIAC/post-NIAC settings. The prohibition of inhuman treatment is embedded in Common Article 3 GC I-IV under the form of an obligation of humane treatment to be implemented by both State and non-state parties to a NIAC vis-à-vis all the persons not or no longer participating in the hostilities. In light of the interconnectedness between conflict/post-conflict phases, this obligation does not stop providing its effects abruptly at the termination of an armed conflict. In addition to that, the customary duty of the parties to the conflict to account for the missing also continues to be applicable in post-conflict contexts and, consequently, requires the direct involvement of the non-state armed group. The simultaneous application of IHL and IHRL rules concerning investigative activities in relation to the missing entails that the duty to account for missing persons is the protective baseline that should be guaranteed regardless of the circumstances on the ground. Thus, all former parties to the conflict must cooperate to account for missing persons and, consequently, comply with their obligation of humane treatment vis-à-vis the family members of the missing.[29]

The duty to cooperate in accounting for the missing as well as in general efforts to restore the situation on the ground do not waive the obligations that State authorities bear under general human rights treaties.[30] Similarly, the establishment of bodies mandated to ascertain the whereabouts of missing persons does not fulfill the requirements for the implementation of the procedural limb of substantive human rights, such as the prohibition of inhuman and degrading treatment.

The diversity of purposes of the duty to account for the missing/the duty to carry out an investigation is reflected in the different temporal dimensions specific to them. The former appears to be structured according to the IHL rules applicable during the conflict and in its aftermath (should the issue of missing persons be pending); the latter must be implemented from the moment a right is violated until enough evidence is gathered in order to bring those responsible to justice. And yet, in the European context, the ECtHR has accepted post-conflict circumstances on

---

[29] See sub-section 2.2 in Chapter IV. Indeed, 'it is incumbent on all those involved in the conflict to support the peace process [...], in order to ensure respect for human rights [...].' ICJ, *Case concerning Armed Activities on the Territory of the Congo (Democratic Republic of the Congo v Uganda), Merits, Judgment* (2005) ICJ Reports 2005, p.168 [221].

[30] Cf. ECtHR, *Cyprus v Turkey, Judgment (GC)* (2001) App no. 25781/94 [174]. For a thorough examination of this aspect, see section 2 in Chapter IV.

the ground as a valid motive to justify delay in the compliance of State authorities with their duty to carry out an investigation into disappearances that have occurred in armed conflict situations (cf *Palic v Bosnia and Herzegovina*).

If one explores the evolution of the judicial reasoning, the ECtHR admits that, due to the circumstances on the ground generated by the armed conflict, State authorities have a duty to carry out an investigation in case of alleged human rights violations resulting in the disappearance of individuals; this duty must be interpreted according to the general principles of international law, including IHL rules.[31] Based on this reasoning, in order to respond both to the need for accountability and to the need for information, State authorities must ensure the proper disposal of remains, collect and provide information about the identity and fate of those concerned, or permit other bodies to do so.[32] Thus, it appears unfounded to affirm that, after the conflict, the circumstances on the ground (e.g., the scarce capability of State authorities of dealing with human rights/IHL violations) can justify any disregard or delay in the implementation of the duty to account for missing persons; the assistance of external bodies represents a viable alternative, should such circumstances affect the capacity of the State to account for the missing.

1.3. Back to the roots? The right of families to know as the harmonizing principle of humanitarian/accountability-driven approaches to the issue of the missing in post-conflict

The only international treaty laying down the right of families to know the fate of their relatives − AP I − frames it as a general principle, i.e., as a driver of measures concerning missing persons and the treatment of the remains of deceased persons. The range of actors supposedly involved in the implementation of such measures is not limited to the Parties to the conflict but include international humanitarian organizations mentioned in the GCs/API as well as the High Contracting Parties. The continuation of the effects of the duty to account for missing persons in a post-conflict situation implies that efforts undertaken in this phase must be prompted by the right of families to know. These efforts include international measures integrated in the context of peace processes, starting from the design of peace settlements.

Peace settlements set down the guidelines and principles that regulate, *inter alia,* the relationship between former parties to the conflict, the interaction of these with other external actors (e.g., the ICRC, the UN, the ICMP), and the terms under which new entities must be set up in order to address the consequences of the conflict. In light of the methodological premise of this study (i.e., international law is a decision-making process and not just rules), peace agreements are part of international law. International law can impact and be

---

[31] The Court exclusively refers to IAC; indeed, Chapter II shows that IHL treaties applicable in this context set down the terms for a more sophisticated system of handling of information. Nevertheless, this reasoning can be extended to NIAC, in light of the considerations put forward in the same Chapter.
[32] Cf. ECtHR, *Varnava and Others v. Turkey (GC)* (n 5) [185].

impacted by these agreements. For instance, it guides the design and definition of their content: the obligation to respect and ensure respect for IHL – which binds all the States of the World – might be the basis of international and national efforts during the whole peace-making process; therefore, the final agreements can integrate it under various forms (e.g., IHL rules that continue to have effects despite the end of the conflict could explicitly be mentioned; similarly, there might be an explicit commitment that IHL-based preventive measures be implemented prior to the outbreak of any other conflict).[33] International law is also the baseline for the establishment of *ad hoc* bodies mandated to adjudicate on the compliance of various actors with human rights law. At the same time, peace agreements impact on international law: indeed, in the case of missing persons, the practice shows that these agreements require the cooperation of all the (former) parties to the conflict – including non-state actors – as well as of other actors in the efforts to account for the missing and in the sharing of information during the post-conflict phase; such practice confirms that, under international law, there is an obligation of the former parties to the conflict to cooperate in accounting for missing persons in the post-conflict phase.

From the examination of a set of relatively recent peace agreements, it emerges that the duty of all the former parties to the conflict to cooperate with each other and/or with the actor mandated to account for the missing is one of the quintessential pillars of the post-conflict legal framework. This finding reveals a pressing need to integrate the issue of missing persons in those documents aimed at laying down the basis for the transition from conflict to peace, since this has a direct impact on how the issue is handled on the ground. The study of a set of peace agreements – the majority dating back to the early 1990s – also reveals that humanitarian and accountability courses of action vis-à-vis the issue of missing persons are designed as two distinct aspects; the lack of any reference to a coordinated formulation of these approaches has resulted in institutional fragmentation and multiplicity of – often diverging – responses to the families.[34]

This study has highlighted the meaningful role that the UN, by means of *multidimensional* peace operations, plays in complementing and even substituting State authorities in the implementation of the duty to account for the missing (e.g., by restoring family links, visiting detainees and informing the families about their conditions, establishing internal humanitarian units mandated to clarify the whereabouts of those reported as missing). Those UNSC resolutions, aimed at establishing peace operations in conflict or in post-conflict situations, outline the terms of action, principles, and guidelines that serve the

---

[33] See Chapter II for a detailed examination of these rules. See also sub-section 1.1.3 in Chapter V for a set of examples of peace agreements enshrining these rules.

[34] See, for instance, the example of UNMIK and the multiple internal units that dealt with the issue of missing persons in Kosovo as well as the example of the Special Process on Missing Persons in the territory of the Former Yugoslavia that had to co-exist with a panoply of international and domestic actors directly or indirectly dealing with the issue of missing persons, in sub-section 1.2.4.2 and sub-section 2.1.1 in Chapter V.

purpose of delimiting the mandate of these operations and their relationship with domestic authorities, former parties to the conflict, and external actors. The role of these operations in the restoration of the RoL and the justice system make them key actors in the protection and promotion of human rights.[35] Although each context transitioning from conflict to peace is unique and, therefore, requires an *ad hoc* answer, *ad hoc* responses must be in line with the general principle that drives the whole legal framework on the missing, i.e., the right of families to know the fate of their relatives. This consideration holds valid in the case where the issue of missing persons is integrated in the range of humanitarian functions of peace operations as well as in the case where the role of the UN is equated to that of a State. Whenever its post-conflict role entails the protection and promotion of human rights and the restoration of the RoL, the UN has an obligation to account for missing persons.[36] A quasi-State role (e.g., the UN's role in Kosovo) generates for the organization the same obligations that State authorities would have, should they be principally responsible for the situation on the ground.

In the context of peace processes, actions that respond to the right of families to know the fate of their relatives cannot substitute those actions that are needed to ascertain responsibility in the case of IHL/IHRL violations and international crimes and vice-versa. In this respect, confusion in the design of the mandate of *ad hoc* bodies might be detrimental to the accomplishment of both sets of actions.[37] Operational attempts to design a global approach to the issue of missing persons are in *statu nascendi* (e.g., the ongoing attempts of the ICRC and of ICMP).

Operational complementarity in post-conflict settings can be translated in terms of sequencing of actions to be undertaken in light of a coordinated implementation of humanitarian and accountability-based approaches to the issue of the missing. As stressed in Chapters V and VI, there is not a perfect combination of mechanisms and supportive tools available to States in the transition phase in order for them to effectively address the pending consequences of an armed conflict. In transition periods the combination of mechanisms should be framed so as to achieve a triadic purpose, i.e., justice, reconciliation, and 'ultimately, peace.'[38] Peace and justice processes cannot be described in opposite terms with regard to the subject matter and, more generally, in the context of the formulation of efforts to foster reconciliation. In this sense, "justice in transition" can play a significant role in addressing the issue of missing persons and in furthering the quest of their families for information. This study has assessed the work of a variety of "justice in

---

[35] UNSG/UNGA, 'Report of the High-Level Independent Panel on Peace Operations (HIPPO) on Uniting Our Strengths for Peace: Politics, Partnership and People' (2015) UN Doc A/70/95, S/2015/446 paras 157–158, 160.

[36] See the example of Kosovo and the work of UNMIK analyzed in Chapter V (sub-section 1.2.4.2).

[37] This is substantiated by the exploration of the examples of the different mechanisms integrated within UNMIK; the Special Process on Missing Persons in the Territory of the Former Yugoslavia; and the narrowly focused mandate of the CMP in Cyprus. See sub-sections 2.1.1 and 2.1.2 in Chapter V.

[38] M Cherif Bassiouni, 'Searching for Peace and Achieving Justice: The Need for Accountability' (1996) 59 Law and Contemporary Problems 9, 23.

transition" mechanisms that can be boiled down to two broad categories: those specifically created during or after an armed conflict and with a mandate that relates to this situation and those that have a permanent and more generally framed mandate. The requests for information of the families of persons reported missing in armed conflicts have featured – or may feature in the future – in the work of both categories.

Ad hoc forms of justice in transition can be framed in a variety of manners (truth commissions, hybrid criminal and non-criminal justice mechanisms, *ad hoc* international tribunals). [39] The exploration of the mandates and of the impact of the *modus operandi* of those TJ bodies integrating an international component reveals that the international presence within these bodies is key under several angles. For instance, the international presence can be a source of know-how in shaping the approach to the integration of certain human rights and IHL standards in the domestic context (e.g., the HRChBH). Nevertheless, justice in transition does not respond to the right of family members to know the fate and whereabouts of their missing relatives, but to a collective and individual need for justice and truth.

The analysis of the example of the ICTY, a fully international *ad hoc* form of justice in transition, puts forward a set of considerations that shall be kept in mind in light of the role that the ICC – a fully international permanent mechanism – might play in the transition phase:[40] *i)* the work of international criminal judicial bodies can be operationally complementary to the work of humanitarian organizations – e.g., the ICRC – and vice-versa; *ii)* operational complementarity is not only feasible, but also advisable, since this may contribute to ascertaining the fate and whereabouts of the missing and to elucidating the circumstances of a crime (e.g., the example of the exchange of lists of missing persons between the ICRC and the ICTY is telling); *iii)* such complementarity should be reflected in the design and the implementation of prosecutorial strategies, which should not ignore the value that an inclusive approach vis-à-vis the families of the victims can have to the work of the judicial body and for the families' quest for information; *iv)* more generally, criminal proceedings carried out at the international and domestic levels are not designed to address the issue of persons unaccounted for as a result of an armed conflict from a humanitarian perspective; the limits of their contribution with regard to the humanitarian facet of the issue must be acknowledged. This last point confirms the need for operational complementarity among bodies and actors driven by different sets of principled considerations and objectives.

---

[39] With regard to the design of TJ bodies in contexts where the issue of the missing arises, the Special Rapporteur on the promotion of truth, justice, reparation, and guarantees of non-recurrence has underlined 'the prevalent and recognized urgency to address the issue of missing and forcibly disappeared persons in situations of conflict' and has urged 'those responsible for the design of truth-seeking mechanisms to emphasize the importance of this topic.' See UN Human Rights Council, 'Report of the Special Rapporteur on the Promotion of Truth, Justice, Reparation and Guarantees of Non-Recurrence (Advanced Edited Version)' (2017) UN Doc A/HRC/36/50 para 105.

[40] For a thorough exploration of the work of the ICTY and its impact on the missing, see sub-section 1.2 in Chapter VI.

Advances in the international criminal justice area reflect the major attention of the international community vis-à-vis all those directly and indirectly affected by international crimes, including families of missing persons. The participation mechanism under the Rome Statute constitutes a response to criticism raised regarding the lack of inclusiveness of victims and by the clash of the families' needs against the prosecutorial needs in the work of, *inter alia,* the *ad hoc* Tribunals. The innovative aspects of this mechanism are the exposure of indirect victims – e.g., family members of the direct victim – to information concerning the events surrounding the crime, the possibility for them to add further evidence, and the opportunity of being part of the process aimed at establishing what happened.[41] Specifically, by means of participation in the proceedings, family members can gain access to the records of proceedings before the confirmation hearings and submit observations to the Court as to the Court's jurisdiction and the admissibility of cases. Thus, the punishment of perpetrators is just one facet of international criminal justice; the participation mechanism makes international criminal justice partly restorative by recognizing the role of the victims and their harm, by enabling family members to be exposed to relevant information before the end of proceedings, and by providing them with the opportunity to furnish information. These features transform direct and indirect victims into active actors vis-à-vis the disclosure of the circumstances.[42] All these factors taken together can help foster the reconciliation process between individual offenders and victims, thereby contributing to the achievement of a sustainable peace.[43]

As a matter of fact, while the judicial truth might not fully satisfy the search for information of the families of those reported as missing, the participatory approach to the families' suffering and the exposure of family members to information concerning the events where their relatives went missing can contribute to realizing their right to know.

---

[41] Although the issue of missing persons has not arisen in any of the contexts where the ICC has already expressed its pronouncements, cases of enforced disappearance and of persons reported missing following other alleged criminal conducts have emerged from the ongoing OTP's preliminary examinations in relation to, *inter alia,* the situations in Ukraine (ongoing armed conflict) and in Colombia (initial steps towards peace). What has been said so far fully applies to the families of those reported missing in such scenarios, should the situations meet the legal criteria - jurisdiction, admissibility, and the interests of justice - under the Rome Statute to warrant an investigation by the OTP. ICC/OTP, 'Report on Preliminary Examination Activities 2016' (2016) paras 51, 146, 173, 181, 231–232, 242–244, 270, 273 <https://www.icc-cpi.int//Pages/item.aspx?name=161114-otp-rep-PE> accessed 10 January 2017. See sub-section 2.2.2.2 in Chapter VI.

[42] Mariana Pena and Gaelle Carayon, 'Is the ICC Making the Most of Victim Participation?' (2013) 7 The International Journal of Transitional Justice 1, 5–6. This trend is reflected in Article 69 (3) of the Rome Statute. See DK Piragoff, 'Article 69 - Evidence' in Otto Triffterer and Kai Ambos (eds), *Commentary on the Rome Statute of the International Criminal Court: Observers' Notes, Article by Article* (C H Beck 2008) 1321.

[43] Baumgartner underlines that the relatively broad participation scheme under the Rome Statute is today widely recognized as an instrument to promote reconciliation. See Elisabeth Baumgartner, 'Aspects of Victim Participation in the Proceedings of the International Criminal Court' (2008) 90 International Review of the Red Cross 409, 410.

2. AVENUES FOR FURTHER RESEARCH

The illustration of avenues for further research is determined by the complexity of the subject matter, which has led to mention in passing multiple legal questions connected to it; these could not adequately be addressed in the remit of a single manuscript. Nevertheless, they deserve further research that would serve the purpose of filling existing gaps in legal scholarship, but also – and foremost – of tackling the issue of missing persons in a more effective and comprehensive manner.

First of all, this study has stated that full compliance with IHL provisions during an armed conflict would reduce the number of missing persons. In light of the empirical turn in the international legal scholarship, an empirical study would provide valuable contributions to the subject matter by helping close the gap 'between abstract theory, empirical research, and the world of practice'.[44] Among the possible contributions, this empirical study might lead to the confirmation/refutation of the correlation between respect for IHL and mitigation of the number of missing persons; depending on the methods used (for instance a combination of qualitative and quantitative methods), an explanation of the correlation/absence of correlation; a new understanding of how and under which conditions IHL rules work; and the development of further avenues of reflections for ongoing or future normative projects aimed at addressing the global dimension of the issue of missing persons.

Second, the examination of the developments under international law and policy vis-à-vis the issue of missing persons has revealed a direct link between the issue of missing persons and the issue of displaced persons. For instance, this link has emerged in relation to the only international treaty ever adopted to handle the international dimension that the issue of missing persons had after the termination of WWII, i.e., the Convention on the Declaration of Death of Missing Persons.[45] Indeed, the displacement of thousands of people accompanied by the heavy death toll of the conflict emphasized the lack of legislative and institutional tools to address concrete consequences related to a global problem of missing persons. For instance, how could a State issue a declaration of death without the identification of the body of the person allegedly dead? Could the circumstances of disappearance and the length of the period of absence be sufficient to presume the death of the person? How could wives, children, and other relatives exercise their property rights, or ask to be adopted, or for a new marriage? These questions concerned millions of people who asked for a declaration of death of those allegedly missing; most of the time these declarations had to be issued abroad where families relocated. Thus, an urgent international problem arose with regard to how to treat the application for a declaration of death of an alien as well as with regard to what legal merit such a

---

[44] Gregory Shaffer and Tom Ginsburg, 'The Empirical Turn in International Legal Scholarship' (2012) 106 American Journal of International Law 1, 1.

[45] For the impact of this treaty, see sub-section 1.4 in Chapter I and sub-section 1.1.3 in Chapter V.

declaration had when issued abroad vis-à-vis the country of nationality or habitual residence.[46] The Convention treated these problems for a short period of time. What is the international legal response to similar issues related to, for instance, the management by European countries of the bodies of migrants who are fleeing, *inter alia,* from conflicts, human rights abuses, and poverty? The International Organization for Migration (IOM) has framed a thematic-specific project named 'Missing Migrants Project'[47] in order to quantify at the global level the phenomenon of dead and missing migrants, trigger political commitment at the national and international level to record and account for them, and to emphasize the need for the development of an improved system of identification. However, a new – more comprehensive – study might further explore these – almost[48] uncharted waters and, in particular, clarify the role of international law in providing legal responses and solutions to the pragmatic consequences of uncertainty in the context of migration (connected or not with armed conflicts).

---

[46] Andrew Friedmann, 'Declarations of Death - A New International Convention Notes and Comment' (1950) 25 St. John's Law Review 18, 27–30.

[47] IOM, 'About' (*Missing Migrant Project*) <https://missingmigrants.iom.int/about> accessed 12 January 2017.

[48] Stephanie Grant has argued that, in relation to migrants' deaths, the problems related to the absence of proper identification procedures make them similar to deaths of persons in armed conflicts (and natural disasters), where the lack of identification entails the likelihood that the person be reported missing. She considers that the principles of IHL and IHRL, which apply in the latter, 'should be developed to create legal and policy frameworks for use in the case of migrants who are missing or who die on EU sea frontiers.' See Stefanie Grant, '"Identity Unknown": Migrant Deaths at Sea' (2011) 38 Forced Migration Review 43; Stefanie Grant, 'Migration and Frontier Deaths: A Right to Identity' in Marie-Bénédicte Dembour and Tobias Kelly (eds), *Are human rights for migrants?: critical reflections on the status of irregular migrants in Europe and the United States* (Routledge 2011); Stephanie Grant, 'Recording and Identifying European Frontier Deaths' (2011) 13 European Journal of Migration and Law 135. From a policy perspective, the ICRC has released its recommendations to policy-makers concerning missing migrants and their families; the organization stresses that 'by implementing these 13 recommendations States will be able to build important humanitarian safeguards to prevent people from going missing and respond to the growing problem of missing migrants and the needs of their families, in line with their international obligations'. See ICRC, 'Missing Migrants and Their Families - The ICRC's Recommendations to Policy-Makers' (2017) Policy Paper 26. At the initiative of the ICMP, in June 2018, Cyprus, Greece, Malta, and Italy undertook a historic effort by asserting their intention to develop a Joint Process to Account for Persons Missing as result of Migration in the Mediterranean Region. This initiative proves that while governments must be the leading actors in addressing the issue of missing persons, including missing migrants, cooperation among them is key. See 'Statement on the issue of Missing Migrants by Representatives of Cyprus, Greece, Italy, and Malta at the Conclusion of their Meeting in Rome on 11 June 2018', 11 June 2018 (Rome, Italy) https://www.icmp.int/?resources=statement-on-the-issue-of-missing-migrants-by-representatives-of-cyprus-greece-italy-and-malta-at-the-conclusion-of-their-meeting-in-rome-on-11-june-2018 accessed 30 July 2018. From the civil society organizations' perspective: co-led by Catriona Jervis and Syd Bolton, "The Last Rights Project" gathered experts and activists from across the world on the island of Lesvos in May 2018 to call upon States to comply with a Declaration of international standards to be applied when dealing with the tragic deaths of migrants known as the Mytilini Declaration. See Last Rights, 'The Mytilini Declaration for the Dignified Treatment of all Missing and Deceased Persons and their Families as a Consequence of Migrant Journeys', 11 May 2018 (Thermi, Mytilini, Lesvos, Greece) http://lastrights.net/home/4592071170 accessed 20 July 2018.

The third avenue, which is partly connected to the preceding one, revolves around the need for further research in relation to how the international legal framework impacts on the domestic legal framework. In the introduction, this study briefly stated that uncertainty has an emotional, but also socio-economic impact on family members. In this respect, the ICPPED states that 'each State Party shall take the appropriate steps with regard to the legal situation of disappeared persons whose fate has not been clarified and that of their relatives, in fields such as social welfare, financial matters, family law and property rights'.[49] The undertaking of these steps will be without prejudice to 'the obligation to continue the investigation until the fate of the disappeared person has been clarified'.[50] Whether the same holds valid in relation to persons reported unaccounted for in armed conflicts and whose disappearance does not present the legal contours of an enforced disappearance[51] should be addressed in a conclusive manner. Moreover, a comparative study on the design of domestic legislation and on the manners of tackling the pragmatic consequences of uncertainty at the domestic level would serve the purpose of identifying legislative/regulatory practices that can prospectively be of guidance to other contexts where family members may be obliged to live with uncertainty.[52]

Finally, the impact that armed conflict-induced uncertainty has on the enjoyment of the economic, social, and cultural rights of family members has remained unexplored in this study. Article 10(1) of the International Covenant on the Economic, Social, and Cultural Rights (ICESCR) affirms that

> [t]he States Parties to the [ICESCR] recognize that the widest possible protection and assistance should be accorded to the family, which is the natural and fundamental group unit of society, particularly for its establishment and while it is responsible for the care and education of dependent children.[53]

The question of whether uncertainty about a person's fate and the irresponsive conduct of States authorities infringe these rights for his/her family members deserves a conclusive answer. Likewise, whether post-conflict difficulties, which characterize the process towards a sustainable peace, are a

---

[49] Cf. Article 24 (6), ICPPED.

[50] Ibid.

[51] The issue has been tackled by Gabriella Citroni who has voiced her concern over the pitfalls of regulating the legal status of a forcibly disappeared person through the declaration of death, thereby arguing that a declaration of absence is the correct way to go. Gabriella Citroni, 'The Pitfalls of Regulating the Legal Status of Disappeared Persons Through Declaration of Death' (2014) 12 Journal of International Criminal Justice 787, 802 ff.

[52] The model law on missing persons formulated by the ICRC is a valuable document at the operational level, but does not elaborate on the intellectual part concerning the first question nor on the comparative part. See ICRC - Advisory Service on IHL, 'Guiding Principles: "Model Law on the Missing: Principles for Legislating the Situation of Persons Missing as a Result of Armed Conflict or Internal Violence. Measures to Prevent Persons from Going Missing and to Protect the Rights and Interests of the Missing and Their Families."' (2009).

[53] Cf. Article 10 (1) ICESCR.

legally viable excuse for inaction of State authorities under the ICESCR is worth further consideration in legal scholarship.[54]

The exploration of these avenues will help define whether there is room to advocate for a comprehensive global normative and operational system aimed at "solving" the issue of missing persons, at mitigating the impact that uncertainty can have on those who survive an armed conflict, a natural disaster, the crossing of a border or of a sea; it will also consolidate the idea that prevention of uncertainty should be the premise, while reaction to it the last resort.

---

[54] One of the rare studies on this topic is a working paper by professor Chinkin on the protection of economic, social and cultural rights in post-conflict contexts: see Christine Chinkin, 'The Protection of Economic, Social and Cultural Rights Post-Conflict'
<http://www2.ohchr.org/english/issues/women/docs/Paper_Protection_ESCR.pdf> accessed 12 March 2017.

TABLE OF TREATIES, LEGISLATION, PEACE AGREEMENTS

Treaties

African [Banjul] Charter on Human and Peoples' Rights, June 27, 1981, OAU Doc. CAB/LEG/67/3 rev. 5, 21 I.L.M. 58 (1982)

African Charter on the Rights and Welfare of the Child, OAU Doc. CAB/LEG/24.9/49 (1990)

Agreement on the Status and Functions of the International Commission on Missing Persons (ICMP Framework Agreement), Brussels (15 December 2014)

American Convention on Human Rights, 1144 UNTS 143 (21 November 21, 1969)

Arab Charter on Human Rights adopted by the League of Arab States (23 May 2004)

Charter of the International Military Tribunal, London (8 August 1945)

Charter of the United Nations, 1 UNTS XVI (24 October 1945)

Convention (I) for the Amelioration of the Condition of the Wounded and Sick in Armed Forces in the Field, Geneva, 75 UNTS 31 (12 August 1949)

Convention (II) for the Amelioration of the Condition of Wounded, Sick and Shipwrecked Members of Armed Forces at Sea, Geneva, 75 UNTS 85 (12 August 1949)

Convention (II) with Respect to the Laws and Customs of War on Land and its annex: Regulations concerning the Laws and Customs of War on Land, The Hague (29 July 1899)

Convention (III) relative to the Treatment of Prisoners of War, Geneva, 75 UNTS 125 (12 August 1949)

Convention (IV) relative to the Protection of Civilian Persons in Time of War, Geneva, 75 UNTS 287 (12 August 1949)

Convention (IV) respecting the Laws and Customs of War on Land and its annex: Regulations concerning the Laws and Customs of War on Land, The Hague (18 October 1907)

Convention (X) for the Adaptation to Maritime Warfare of the Principles of the Geneva Convention, The Hague, 18 October 1907

Convention against Torture and Other Cruel, Inhuman or Degrading Treatment or Punishment, 1465 UNTS 85 (10 December 1984)

Convention for the Amelioration of the Condition of the Wounded and Sick in Armies in the Field, Geneva (6 July 1906)

Convention for the Amelioration of the Condition of the Wounded and Sick in Armies in the Field, Geneva (27 July 1929)

Convention for the Amelioration of the Condition of the Wounded in Armies in the Field, Geneva (22 August 22 1864)

Convention for the Protection of Human Rights and Fundamental Freedoms (ECHR), 213 UNTS 222 (4 November 1950)

Convention on the declaration of death of missing persons, Lake Success, New York, 119 UNTS 99 (6 April 1950)

Convention on the Rights of the Child, 1577 UNTS 3 (2 September 1990)

Convention relating to the Status of Refugees, Geneva, 189 UNTS 137 (28 July 1951)

Convention relative to the Treatment of Prisoners of War, Geneva (27 July 1929)

Inter-American Convention on Forced Disappearance of Persons, 33 ILM 1429 (9 June 1994)

International Convention for the Protection of All Persons from Enforced Disappearance, UNGA Res. 61/177, UN Doc A/RES/61/177, 2716 UNTS 3 (20 December 2006)

International Covenant on Civil and Political Rights, 999 UNTS 171 (16 December 1966)

International Covenant on Economic, Social and Cultural Rights, 993 UNTS 3 (16 December 1966)

Optional Protocol to the ICCPR, 999 UNTS 171 (16 December 1966)

Protocol Additional to the Geneva Conventions of 12 August 1949, and relating to the Protection of Victims of International Armed Conflicts (Protocol I) 1125 UNTS 3 (8 June 1977)

Protocol Additional to the Geneva Conventions of 12 August 1949, and relating to the Protection of Victims of Non-International Armed Conflicts (Protocol II) 1125 UNTS 609 (8 June 1977)

Protocol on the Statute of the African Court of Justice and Human Rights, Sharm el-Sheik (1 July 2008)

Protocol to the African Charter on the Establishment of the African Court on Human and Peoples' Rights, OAU Doc. OAU/LEG/AFCHPR/PROT (III) (25 January 2004)

Rome Statute of the International Criminal Court, 2187 UNTS 90 (17 July 1998)

Statute of the International Court of Justice, 59 Stat. 1055, 33 UNTS 993 (26 June 1945)

Vienna Convention on the Law of Treaties, 1155 UNTS 331 (23 May 1969)

Legislation

Argentina

Decreto 1430/2004 del 19 de octubre de 2004 sobre la creación de la Oficina Nacional de Información, https://www.boletinoficial.gob.ar/#!Portada/Primera/all/20041021 accessed on 20 May 2015

Bosnia and Herzegovina

Law on Missing Persons, PS BiH No 109/04, October 21, 2004 https://www.icmp.int/wp-content/uploads/2014/08/law-on-missing-persons.pdf Accessed 10 April 2016

Law on the Transfer of Cases from the ICTY to the Prosecutor's Office of Bosnia and Herzegovina and the Use of Evidence Collected by the ICTY in Proceedings Before the Courts in Bosnia and Herzegovina, Official Gazette of Bosnia and Herzegovina, 61/04

Egypt

Law No. 2 of 2006 amending some provisions of Act No. 25 of 1929 concerning certain personal status provisions, February 15, 2006, http://goo.gl/PMe8Uw Accessed 20 May 2013.

El Salvador

Decreto núm. 45: créase la Comisión Interinstitucional de Búsqueda de Niños y Niñas Desaparecidos a Consecuencia del Conflicto Armado en El Salvador - Decree No 45 creating the Inter-institutional Commission of search for missing children as a consequence of the armed conflict, October 6, 2004, http://goo.gl/S7vSb4 Accessed 20 May 2013

Germany

Federal Act Governing Access to Information held by the Federal Government (Freedom of Information Act) of 5 September 2005 (Federal Law Gazette [BGBl.] Part I, p. 2722), last amended by Article 2 (6) of the Act of 7 August 2013 (Federal Law Gazette I, p. 3154)

Guatemala

Congreso de la Republica - Guatemala, 'Iniciativa Que Dispone Aprobar Ley de La Comisión de Búsqueda de Personas, Victimas de La Desaparición Forzada Y Otras Formas de Desaparición (Ley N 3590)' (2007)

Presidential Decree No. 264 on the Creation of a Permanent Commission on Missing Persons, May 25, 2006, http://goo.gl/CZM4DG Accessed 23 May 2013

Kosovo

Law No. 04/L–023 on missing persons, Official Gazette of the Republic of Kosova/No. 16, September 14, 2011

Morocco

'Dahir (Royal Decree) No 1.04.42 Approving Statutes of the Equity and Reconciliation Commission' (2004) <https://www.usip.org/publications/2004/12/truth-commission-morocco> accessed 12 January 2016

Peru

'Supreme Decree No 065-2001-PCM' (President of the Republic of Peru 2001) <http://www.cverdad.org.pe/lacomision/cnormas/normas01.php> accessed 29 December 2016

Russian Federation

Russian Federation/State Duma, Federal Law on 'Amendments and additions to the Federal Law "on Burial and undertaking"', Draft no 256538-3 (2002)

Spain

Ley 52/2007 por la que se reconocen y amplían derechos y se establecen medidas en favor de quienes padecieron persecución o violencia durante la guerra civil y la dictadura, 26 December 2007, available at Agencia Estatal Boletín Oficial del Estado, www.boe.es/diario_boe/txt.php?id=BOE-A-2007-22296, accessed 12 October 2015.

Sri Lanka

Sri Lanka/Parliament. Office on Missing Persons (Establishment, Administration and Discharge of Functions) Act No 14, 23 August 2016

South Africa

'Promotion of National Unity and Reconciliation Act' (President of South Africa 1995) Act 95-34

Peace agreements and related documents

'Agreement constituting an International Commission for the International Tracing Service' (Bonn Agreement), Bonn, 6 June 1955

'Agreement on the Establishment of the Commission to Clarify Past Human Rights Violations and Acts of Violence That Have Caused the Guatemalan Population to Suffer, Signed in Oslo' (1994) <https://www.usip.org/sites/default/files/file/resources/collections/commissions/Guatemala-Charter.pdf> accessed 12 January 2018

'Agreement on the Normalization of Relations, between Croatia and Federal Republic of Yugoslavia', August 23, 1996

Colombia/FARC-EP, 'Acuerdo Final para la Terminación del Conflicto y la Construcción de una Paz estable y duradera', Bogotá, November 24, 2016

'Convention on the Settlement of Matters Arising out of the War and the Occupation as amended by Schedule IV to the Protocol on the termination of the occupation regime in the Federal Republic of Germany', Paris, 23 October 1954

Democratic Republic of Vietnam/USA, '(Paris) Agreement on Ending the War and Restoring Peace in Vietnam' (1973) text reproduced in "The Vietnam War and International Law, Volume 4: The Concluding Phase" by Richard Falk (Princeton University Press: 2015)

FARC-EP International, 'Joint Communiqué No 62 on Missing Persons' (*FARC-EP International*) <https://farc-epeace.org/index.php/communiques/joint-communiques/item/879-joint-communique-62-on-missing-persons> accessed 7 September 2018

'Framework Agreement on the Collection and Centralized Management of Ante–Mortem Data on Missing Persons in Relation to the Nagorno Karabakh Conflict between the Commission for Prisoners of War, Hostages, and Missing Persons of the Republic of Armenia and the ICRC', 3 October 2008

'General Framework Agreement for Peace in Bosnia and Herzegovina and the Annexes thereto (also known as "Dayton Agreements")' initialed in Dayton, Ohio, November 21, 1995 and signed in Paris, December 14, 1995.

Government of Nepal/CPN-Maoist, 'Ceasefire Code of Conduct Agreed between the Government of Nepal and the CPN-Maoist - (Unofficial Translation)' (Uppsala University website 2006) <http://www.ucdp.uu.se/downloads/fullpeace/Nep%2020060525.pdf> accessed 12 July 2016

—— , 'Comprehensive Peace Agreement between the Government of Nepal and the CPN-Maoist' (2006) <http://peacemaker.un.org/nepal-comprehensiveagreement2006> accessed

12 July 2016

Government of the Republic of Philippines (GRP)/Moro Islamic Liberation Front (MILF), 'Implementing Guidelines on the Humanitarian, Rehabilitation, and Development Aspects of the GRP-MILF Tripoli Agreement on Peace of 2001' (2002) <http://www.c-r.org/downloads/06s_3Key%20texts_2003_ENG.pdf> accessed 12 July 2016

GRP/National Democratic Front of the Philippines, Comprehensive Agreement on Respect for Human Rights and International Humanitarian Law between the GRP and the National Democratic Front of the Philippines (1998) <http://peacemaker.un.org/philippines-agreement-human-rights98> accessed 17 October 2015

'Joint Declaration by the USSR and Japan' (19 October 1956) <http://www.ioc.u-tokyo.ac.jp/~worldjpn/documents/texts/docs/19561019.D1E.html> accessed 12 July 2016

Laotian Government/Pathet Lao, 'Vientiane Ceasefire Agreement' (1973) <http://peacemaker.un.org/lao-ceasefire73> accessed 12 July 2016

Memorandum of Understanding between the Georgian and Abkhaz sides, Geneva, December 1, 1993.

Malaita Eagle Force/Isatabu Freedom Movement (Solomon Islands), 'Townsville Peace Agreement' (2000) UN Doc S/2000/1088 <http://peacemaker.un.org/solomonislands-townsville-agreement2000> accessed 12 July 2016

'Protocol on cooperation between the FRY Government Commission for Humanitarian Issues and Missing Persons and the Republic of Croatia Government Commission for Detained and Missing Persons', Zagreb, 17 April 1996

'Protocol of the Meeting of the Working Groups, Formed under the Negotiations Commissions, to locate Missing Persons and to Free Forcibly Detained Persons between the Russian Federation and Chechnya', Nazran, 10 June 1996

Russian Federation/Chechen Republic of Ichkeriya, 'Protocol of the Meeting of the Working Groups, Formed under the Negotiations Commissions, to Locate Missing Persons and to Free Forcibly Detained Persons' (1996) <http://peacemaker.un.org/russia-agreementmissingpeople96> accessed 12 July 2016

Russian Federation/Georgia, 'Moscow Agreement between Russia and Georgia (Annex to the Letter Date 8 September 1992 from the Chargé d'Affaires A.I. of the Permanent Mission of the Russian Federation to the United Nations Addressed to the President of the Security Council)' (1992) UN Doc S/24523

UNGA/UNSC, 'Letter Dated 15 November 1995 from the Permanent Representative of Croatia to the UN Addressed to the UNSG. Annex - Basic Agreement on the Region of Eastern Slavonia, Baranja, and Western Sirmium' (1995) UN Doc A/50/757-S/1995/951

TABLE OF CASES

European Court of Human Rights (ECtHR)

Abdulayeva v Russia, Judgment (2014) App no 38552/05

Açış v Turkey, Judgment (2011) App no 7050/05

Akdeniz and others v Turkey, Judgment (2001) App no 23954/94

Aksu v Turkey, Judgment (GC) (2012) App nos 4149/04 and 41029/04

Al Nashiri v Poland, Judgment (2015) App no 28761/11

Al-Skeini and others v The UK, Judgment (GC) (2011) App no 55721/07

Amann v Switzerland, Judgment (GC) (2000) App no 27798/95

Anguelova v Bulgaria, Judgment (2002) App no 38361/97

Antonio Gutiérrez Dorado and Carmen Dorado Ortiz v Spain, Decision (2012) App no 30141/09

Arkhestov and others v Russia, Judgment (2014) App no 22089/07

Aslakhanova and others v Russia, Judgment (2012) App nos 2944/06 and others

Assenov and others v Bulgaria, Judgment (1998) App no 24760/94

Association '21 December 1989' et al v Romania, Judgment (2011) App nos 33810/07 and 18817/08

B v The UK, Judgment (1987) App no 9849/82

Çakici v Turkey, Judgment (GC) (1999) App no 23657/94

> Partly dissenting opinion of Mrs Thomassen joined by Mr Jungwiert and Mr Fischbach annexed to *Çakici v Turkey* (GC) App no. 23657/94

Cakicisoy et al v Cyprus, Decision (2014) App no 5523/12

Charalambous and others v Turkey and other applications, Decision (2012) App nos 46744/07 and others

Çiçek v Turkey, Judgment (2001) App no 25704/94

Cyprus v Turkey, Judgment (GC) (2001) App no 25781/94

Cyprus v Turkey, Judgment - Just Satisfaction (GC) (2014) App no 25781/94

Connors v The UK, Judgment (2004) App no 66746/01

Di Sarno and others v Italy, Judgment (Merits and Just Satisfaction) (2012) App no 30765/08

Dissenting Opinion of Judge Martens - Gül v Switzerland, Judgment (1996) App no 23218/94

Elbika Shabazova v Russia, Decision (2009) App no 402305

Elli Poluhas Dödsbo v Sweden, Judgment (2006) App no 61564/00

El-Masri v The Former Yugoslav Republic of Macedonia, Judgment (GC) (2012) App no 39630/09

Emin (Mustafa) et al v Cyprus, Decision (2014) App no 4176/14

Emin (Mustafa) et al v Cyprus and six other applications, Decision (2012) App no 59623/08 et al

Georgia v Russia (II), Decision (2011) App no 38263/08

Golder v The UK, Judgment (1975) App no 4451/70

Gurgenidze v Georgia, Judgment (2006) App no 71678/01

Gürtekin et al v Cyprus, Ayse Akay et al v Cyprus and Ayse Eray et al v Cyprus, Decision (2014) App nos 60441/13, 68206/13, 68667/13

Hadri-Vionnet v Switzerland, Judgment (2008) App no 55525/00

Hassan v The UK, Judgment (GC) (2014) App no 29750/09

Hugh Jordan v The UK, Judgment (2001) App No. 24746/94

Ilaşcu and others v Moldova and Russia, Judgment (GC) (2004) App no 48787

Imakayeva v Russia, Judgment (2007) App no. 7615/02

İpek v Turkey, Judgment (2004) App no 25760/94

Ireland v The UK, Judgment (1978) App no 5310/71

Isayeva v Russia, Judgment (2005) App no 57950/00

Isayeva, Yusupova and Bazayeva v Russia, Judgment (2005) App nos 57950/00, 57948/00, and 57949/00

Ivanţoc and Others v Moldova and Russia, Judgment (2011) App no 23687/05

Janowiec and others v Russia, Judgment (2012) App nos 55508/08 and others

Janowiec and others v Russia, Judgment (GC) (2013) App nos 55508/08 and others

Jeličić v Bosnia and Herzegovina, Decision (2005) App no 41183/02

K and T v Finland, Judgment (GC) (2001) App no 25702/94

Kaya v Turkey, Judgment (1998) App no 158/1996/777/978

Kayıplar et al v Cyprus, Decision (2015) App no 42153/14

Khoroshenko v Russia, Judgment (GC) (2015) App no 41418/04

Kurt v Turkey, Judgment (1998) App no 24276/94

Kushtova and others v Russia, Judgment (2014) App no 21885/07

Lejla Fazlić and others v Bosnia and Herzegovina, Decision (2014) App no 66758/09

Luluyev and others v Russia, Judgment (2006) App no 69480/01

Maskhadova and others v Russia, Judgment (2013) App no 18071/05

Malone v The UK, Judgment (1984) App no 8691/79

Mamatkulov and Askarov v Turkey, Judgment (GC) (2005) App nos 46827/99 46951/99

Messina v Italy, Judgment (no 2) (2000) App no 25498/94

Mikheyev v Russia, Judgment (2006) App no 77617/01

MM v The UK, Judgment (2012) App no 24029/07

Mozer v Moldova and Russia, Judgment (GC) (2016) App no 11138/10

Olsson v Sweden, Judgment (no 1) (1988) App no 10465/83

Orhan v Turkey, Judgment (2002) App No 2565694

Osmanoğlu v Turkey, Judgment (2008) App no 48804/99

Palić v Bosnia and Herzegovina, Judgment (2011) App no 4704/04

Pannullo and Forte v France, Judgment (2001) App no 37794/97

Paul and Audrey Edwards v The UK, Judgment (2002) App no 46477/99

Ramsahai and others v The Netherlands, Judgment (GC) (2007) App no 52391/99

Saadi v Italy, Judgment (GC) (2008) App no 37201/06

Sabanchiyeva and others v Russia, Judgment (2013) App no 38450/05

S and Marper v the UK, Judgment (GC) (2008) App nos 30562/04 and 30566/04

Sejdić and Finci v Bosnia and Herzegovina, Judgment (GC) (2009) Apps no 27996/06 and 34836/06

Selmouni v France, Judgment (1999) App no 25803/94

Soering v The UK, Judgment (1989) App no 14038/88

Tekdag v Turkey, Judgment (2004) App no 27699/95

Timurtas v Turkey, Judgment (2000) App no 23531/94

Tomasi v France, Judgment (1992) App no 12850/87

Trosin v Ukraine, Judgment (2012) App no 39758/05

Tzilivaki v Cyprus, Decision (2014) App no 23082/07

Varnava and Others v Turkey, Judgment (GC) (2009) App nos 16064/90 and others

X v Germany, Decision (1981) App no. 8741/79

Yaşa v Turkey, Judgment (1998) App no 22495/93

Zalov and Khakulova v Russia, Judgment (2014) App no 7988/09

Znamenskaya v Russia, Judgment (2005) App no 77785/01

Zorica Jovanović v Serbia, Judgment (2013) App no 21794/08

Human Rights Advisory Panel (HRAP) - UNMIK

BA against UNMIK (opinion, final) (2013) Case no 52/09

BA against UNMIK (SRSG's response to the Panel's Recommendations) (2013) Case no 52/09

Beriša and other against UNMIK (opinion, final) (2011) Case no 27/08

GR against UNMIK (opinion, final) (2013) Case no 12/09

JD against UNMIK (opinion, final) (2013) Case no 44/09

JD against UNMIK (SRSG's response to the Panel's Recommendations) (2013) Case no 44/09

Jočić against UNMIK (opinion, final) (2013) Case no 34/09

Jočić against UNMIK (SRSG's response to the Panel's Recommendations) (2013) Case no 34/09

Milko Milenković against UNMIK (opinion, final) (2014) Case no 127/09

Milogorić against UNMIK (opinion, final) (2010) Case no 38/08

Mitrović and Others (opinion, final) (2014) Cases no 144/09 et al

Nebojša Petković against UNMIK (opinion, final) (2013) Case no 125/09

Nebojša Petković against UNMIK (SRSG's response to the Panel's Recommendations) (2013) Case no 125/09

Remištar against UNMIK (opinion, final) (2014) Case no 245/09

RP against UNMIK (opinion, final) (2014) Case no 120/09 and 121/09

RP against UNMIK (SRSG's response to the Panel's Recommendations) (2014) Case no 120/09 and 121/09

SC against UNMIK (opinion, final) (2012) Case no 02/09

SC against UNMIK (SRSG's response to the Panel's Recommendations) (2013) Case no 02/09

Snežana Zdravković against UNMIK (opinion, final) (2013) Case no 46/08

Vitošević and Majmarević against UNMIK (opinion, final) (2014) Cases no 139/09 et al

ZI against UNMIK (opinion, final) (2013) Case no 145/09

Živorad Ogarević against UNMIK (opinion, final) (2013) Case no 77/09

Živorad Ogarević against UNMIK (SRSG's response to the Panel's Recommendations) (2013) Case no 77/09

Zufe Miladinović against UNMIK (opinion, final) (2013) Case no 86/09

Zufe Miladinović against UNMIK (SRSG's response to the Panel's Recommendations) (2013) Case no 86/09

Human Rights Committee (HRCee)

Abubakar Amirov v Russia Federation, Comm no 1447/2006 (2009) UN Doc CCPR/C/95/D/1447/2006

Aïcha Dehimi and Noura Ayache v Algeria, Comm no 2086/2011 (2014) CCPR/C/112/D/2086/2011

Aliboeva v Tajikistan, Comm no 985/2001 (2006) UN Doc CCPR/C/85/D/985/2001

AMH El Hojouj Jum'a et al v Libya, Comm no 1958/2010 (2014) UN Doc CCPR/C/111/D/1958/2010

Basilio Laureano Atachahua v Peru, Comm no 540/1993 (1996) UN Doc CCPR/C/56/D/540/1993

Bautista v Colombia, Comm no 563/1993 (1995) UN Doc CCPR/C/55/D/563/1993

Bazzano, Valentini, de Massera v Uruguay, Comm no 5/1977 (1984) UN Doc CCPR/C/OP/1 at 40

Benaziza v Algeria, Comm no 1588/2007 (2010) UN Doc CCPR/C/99/D/1588/2007

Boucherf v Algeria, Comm no 1196/2003 (2006) UN Doc CCPR/C/86/D/1196/2003

Bousroual v Algeria, Comm no 1085/2002 [2006] UN Doc CCPRC86D10852002

Cifuentes Elgueta v Chile, Comm no 1536/2006 (2009) UN Doc CCPR/C/96/D/1536/2006

> Individual opinion of Committee members Ms Helen Keller and Mr Fabián Salvioli (dissenting) in *Cifuentes Elgueta v Chile,* (2009) UN Doc CCPR/C/96/D/1536/2006

Darmon Sultanova v Uzbekistan, Comm no 915/2000 (2006) UN Doc CCPR/C/86/D/915/2000

Dev Bahadur Maharjan v Nepal, Comm no 1863/2009 [2012] UN Doc CCPRC105D18632009

El Abani v The Libyan Arab Jamahiriya, Comm no 1640/2007 (2010) UN Doc CCPR/C/99/D/1640/2007

El Alwani v The Libyan Arab Jamahiriya, Comm no 1295/2004 (2007) UN Doc CCPR/C/90/D/1295/2004

Elcida Arévalo Perez et al v Colombia, Comm no 181/1984 (1989) UN Doc CCPR/C/37/D/181/1984

El Megreisi v The Libyan Arab Jamahiriya, Comm no 440/1990 (1994) UN Doc CCPR/C/50/D/440/1990

Emina Kožljak and Sinan Kožljak v Bosnia and Herzgovina, Comm no 1970/2010, (2014) UN Doc CCPR/C/112/D/1970/2010

Emira Kadirić and Dino Kadirić v Bosnia and Herzegovina, Comm no 2048/2011 (2015) UN Doc CCPR/C/115/D/2048/2011

Fatima Mehalli v Algeria, Comm no 1900/2009 (2014) UN Doc CCPR/C/110/D/1900/2009

Fatima Prutina and others v Bosnia and Herzegovina, Comm nos 1917/2009 and others (2013) UN Doc CCPR/C/107/D/1917,1918,1925/2009&1953/2010

> Individual opinion of Committee member Fabián Salvioli (partly dissenting) in *Fatima Prutina and others v Bosnia and Herzegovina* (2013) UN Doc CCPR/C/107/D/1917,1918,1925/2009&1953/2010

Fatima Rizvanović and Ruvejda Rizvanović v Bosnia and Herzegovina, Comm no 1997/2010 (2014) UN Doc CCPR/C/110/D/1997/2010

HC M A [name deleted] v The Netherlands, Comm no 213/1986 (1989) UN Doc Supp No 40 (A/44/40) at 267

Jit Man Basnet and Top Bahadur Basnet v Nepal, Comm no 2051/2011 (2014) UN Doc CCPR/C/112/D/2051/2011

José Vicente and Amado Villafañe Chaparro, Luís Napoleón Torres Crespo, Angel María Torres Arroyo and Antonio Hugues Chaparro Torres v Colombia, Comm No 612/1995 (1997) UN Doc CCPR/C/60/D/612/1995

Kimouche et al v Algeria, Comm no 1328/2004 (2007) UN Doc CCPR/C/90/D/1328/2004

Lucía Arzuaga Gilboa v Uruguay, Comm No 147/1983 (1990) UN Doc CCPR/C/OP/2 at 176 (1990)

Lyashkevich v Belarus, Comm no 887/1999 (2003) UN Doc CCPR/C/77/D/887/1999

María del Carmen Almeida de Quinteros et al v Uruguay, Comm no 107/1981 (1983) UN Doc CCPR/C/OP/2 at 138

Messaouda Grioua née Atamna and Mohamed Grioua v Algeria, Comm no 1327/2004 (2007) UN Doc CCPR/C/90/D/1327/2004

Miguel Angel Estrella v Uruguay, Comm no 74/1980 (1983) UN Doc Supp no 40 (A/38/40) at 150

Natalia Schedko (on behalf of Bondarenko) v Belarus, Comm no 886/1999 (1999) UN Doc CCPR/C/77/D/886/1999

Nazriev v Tajikistan, Shukurova (on behalf of Nazriev and Nazriev) v Tajikistan, Comm no 1044/2002 (2006) UN Doc CCPR/C/86/D/1044/2002

Nevzeta Durić and Nedzad Durić v Bosnia and Herzegovina, Comm no 1956/2010 (2014) UN Doc CCPR/C/111/D/1956/2010

Norma Yurich v Chile, Comm no 1078/2002 (2005) UN Doc CCPR/C/85/D/1078/2002

Piandiong et al v the Philippines, Comm no 869/1999, (2000) UN Doc CCPR/C/70/D/869/1999

Ram Kumar Bhandari v Nepal, Comm no 2031/2011 (2014) UN Doc CCPR/C/112/D/2031/2011

Raul Noel Martinez Machado v Uruguay, Communication No 83/1981 (1984) UN Doc Supp no 40 (A/39/40)

Salem Saad Ali Bashasha v The Libyan Arab Jamahiriya, Comm no 1776/2008 (2010) UN Doc CCPR/C/100/D/1776/2008

Sarma v Sri Lanka, Comm no 950/2000 (2003) UN Doc CCPRC78D9502000

Shanta Sedhai v Nepal, Comm no1865/2009 (2013) UN Doc CCPR/C/108/D/1865/2009

Sharmila Tripathi v Nepal, Comm no 2111/2011 (2008) UN Doc CCPR/C/112/D/2111/2011

Tahar Mohamed Aboufaied v Libya, Comm no 1782/2008 (2012) UN Doc CCPR/C/104/D/1782/2008

Tija Hero, Ermina Hero, Armin Hero v Bosnia-Herzegovina, Comm no 1966/2010 (2014) UN Doc CCPR/C/112/D/1966/2010

Validzhon Khalilov v Tajikistan, Comm no 973/2001 (2005) UN Doc CCPR/C/83/D/973/2001

Yubraj Giri v Nepal, Comm no 1761/2008 (2011) UN Doc CCPR/c/101/D/1761/2008

Zarzi v Algeria, Comm No 1780/2008 (2011) UN Doc CCPR/C/101/D/1780/2008

Zilkija Selimović et al v Bosnia and Herzegovina, Comm no 2003/2010, (2014) UN Doc CCPR/C/111/D/2003/2010

Inter-American Commission on Human Rights (IACommHR)

Inter-American Court of Human Rights (IACtHR)

Gómez-Paquiyauri Brothers v Peru, Judgment – Merits, reparations and costs (2004) Series C no 110

Gudiel Álvarez et al ('Diario Militar') v Guatemala, Judgment - Merits, reparations and costs (2012) Series C no 253

Heliodoro Portugal v Panama, Judgment - Preliminary objections, merits, reparations and costs (2008) Series C no 186

Ibsen Cárdenas and Ibsen Peña, Judgment - Merits, reparation, and costs (2010) Series C no 217

Ituango Massacres v Colombia, Judgment - Preliminary objections, merits, reparations and costs (2006) Series C no 148

Loayza-Tamayo v Peru, Judgment - Merits (1997) Series C no 33

La Cantuta v Peru (2009) Monitoring Compliance with Judgment. Order

La Cantuta v Peru, Judgment - Merits, reparations and costs (2006) Series C no 162

Mapiripán Massacre v Colombia, Judgment - Merits, reparations and costs [2005] Series C no 134

Maritza Urrutia v Guatemala, Judgment - Merits, reparations and costs (2003) Series C no 103

Massacres of El Mozote and Nearby Places v El Salvador, Judgment – Merits, reparations and costs (2012) Series C no 252

Moiwana Village v Suriname, Judgment - Preliminary objections, merits, reparations and costs (2005) Series C no 145

Molina-Theissen v Guatemala, Judgment – Reparations and costs (2004) Series C no 108

Miguel Castro-Castro Prison v Peru, Judgment – Merits, reparations and costs (2006) Series C no 160

Myrna Mack Chang v Guatemala - Judgment - Merits, reparations and costs (2003) Series C no 101

Neira-Alegría et al v Peru, Judgment - Reparations and costs (1995) Series C no 29

Pueblo Bello Massacre v Colombia, Judgment - Merits, reparations and costs (2006) Series C no 140

Radilla Pacheco v Mexico, Judgment - Preliminary Objections, Merits, Reparations and Costs (2009) Series C No. 209

Río Negro and Gudiel Álvarez and Others v Guatemala (2014) Monitoring Compliance with Judgment. Order

Río Negro Massacres v Guatemala, Judgment - Preliminary objection, merits, reparations and costs (2012) Series C no 250

Rochac Hernández and others v El Salvador, Judgment - Merits, reparations and costs (2014) Series C no 285

Rodríguez Vera et al (the Disappeared from the Palace of Justice) v Colombia, Judgment - Preliminary objections, merits, reparations and costs (2014) Series C no 287

Serrano Cruz Sisters v. El Salvador (2010) Monitoring Compliance with Judgments Order

Serrano-Cruz Sisters v El Salvador, Judgment - Merits, reparations and costs (2005) Series C no 120

Serrano-Cruz Sisters v El Salvador, Judgment - Preliminary objections (2004) Series C no 118

Suárez-Rosero v Ecuador, Judgment - Merits (1997) Series C no 35

The Rochela Massacre v Colombia, Judgment - Merits, Reparations, and Costs (2007) Series C no. 163

International Court of Justice (ICJ)

International Criminal Court (ICC)

Prosecutor v Bosco Ntaganda, Decision on victims' participation at the confirmation of charges hearing and in the related proceedings (2014) ICC-01/04-02/06 (ICC - Pre-Trial Chamber II)

Prosecutor v Bosco Ntaganda, Decision on victims' participation in trial proceedings (2015) ICC-01/04-02/06 (ICC - Trial Chamber IV)

Prosecutor v Francis Kirimi Muthaura, Uhuru Muigai Kenyatta, Mohammed Hussein Ali, Decision on victims' participation at the confirmation of charges hearing and in the related proceedings (2011) ICC-01/09-02/11 (ICC - Pre-Trial Chamber II)

Prosecutor v Germain Katanga and Mathieu Ngudjolo Chui, Decision on the Set of Procedural Rights attached to Procedural Status of Victim at the Pre-Trial Stage of the Case (2008) ICC-01/04-01/07 (ICC | Pre-Trial Chamber I)

Prosecutor v Germain Katanga and Mathieu Ngudjolo Chui, Observations of the Legal Representatives of the Victims Represented by Mr Jean- Louis Gillisen and Mr Joseph Keta on 'The Defence motion for a declaration on unlawful detention and stay of proceedings (ICC-01/04-01/07-125-Conf-Exp)' ICC-01/04-01/07 (ICC | Pre-Trial Chamber I)

Prosecutor v Germain Katanga, Judgment pursuant to Article 74 of the Statute (2014) ICC-01/04-01/07 (ICC | Trial Chamber II)

Prosecutor v Jean-Pierre Bemba Gombo, Response by the Legal Representative of Victims to the 'Prosecution's Request for Leave to Appeal the Trial Chamber's Oral Ruling Denying Authorisation to Add and Disclose Additional Evidence after 30 November 2009' (2009) ICC-01/05-01/08 (ICC | Pre-Trial Chamber III)

Prosecutor v Jean-Pierre Bemba Gombo, Fourth Decision on victims' participation (2008) ICC-01/05-01/08 (ICC - Pre-Trial Chamber III)

Prosecutor v Jean-Pierre Bemba Gombo, Response by the Legal Representative of Victims to the Defence's Challenge on Admissibility of the Case pursuant to articles 17 et 19 (2) (a) of the Rome Statute with 102 Annexes Confidential ex parte OPCV only and same Annexes Public Redacted (2010) ICC-01/05-01/08 (ICC | Pre-Trial Chamber III)

Prosecutor v Laurent Gbagbo, Second decision on victims' participation at the confirmation of charges hearing and in the related proceedings (2013) ICC-02/11-01/11 (ICC - Pre-Trial Chamber I)

Prosecutor v Mathieu Ngudjolo Chui, Motifs de la deuxième décision relative aux demandes de participation de victimes à la procédure (2009) ICC-01/04-01/07 (ICC - Pre-Trial Chamber III)

Prosecutor v Mathieu Ngudjolo Chui, Judgment Pursuant to Article 74 of the Statute (2012) ICC-01/04-02/12 (ICC | Trial Chamber II)

Prosecutor v Thomas Lubanga Dyilo, Decision establishing the principles and procedures to be applied to reparations (2012) ICC-01/04-01/06 (ICC - Trial Chamber I)

Prosecutor v Thomas Lubanga Dyilo, Judgment on the appeals against the 'Decision establishing the principles and procedures to be applied to reparations' of 7 August 2012 (2015) ICC-01/04-01/06 A A 2 A 3 (ICC - Appeals Chamber)

Prosecutor v Thomas Lubanga Dyilo, Judgment on the appeals of The Prosecutor and The Defence against Trial Chamber I's Decision on Victims' Participation of 18 January 2008 (2008) ICC-01/04-01/06 OA 9 OA 10 (ICC - Appeals Chamber)

Prosecutor v Thomas Lubanga Dyilo, Judgment on the appeals of the Prosecutor and the Victims' Participation of 18 January 2008 (2008) ICC-01/04-01/06 OA 9 OA 10 (ICC - Appeals Chamber)

National Courts

Bosnia and Herzegovina

Constitutional Court of BiH

Bosiljka Milanović, Decision on Merits (2008) Dec no AP-2980/06

Milena Kusmuk and others, Decision on Merits (2012) Dec no AP-3783/09

RS and others, Decision on Merits (2013) Dec no AP-2101/11

HRChHR

Avdo and Esma Palić v The Republika Srpska, Decision on Admissibility and Merits (2001) Case no CH/99/3196

Ferida Selimović et al v The Republika Srpska ('Srebrenica Cases'), Decision on Admissibility and Merits (2003) Case nos CH/01/8365 et al.

Unković v The Federation of Bosnia and Herzegovina, Decision on Review (2002) Case no C/99/2150

Guatemala

Corte de Constitucionalidad de Guatemala. *Apelación de Sentencia en Amparo (in relation to the case Ríos Montt c. Ministerio de la Defensa Nacional)*, Expediente 2290-2008 (2008)

Israel

Anonymous Persons v Minister of Defense (1997) A.D.A. 10/94 (Supreme Court of Israel)

Barake and Others v Minister of Defence and Others (2002) High Court of Justice (HCJ) no 3114/02

Mexico

Instituto General de Acceso a la Información Publica, Resolución n 1034/05, Folio de la solicitud n 0000700037605

Nepal

Madhav Kumar Basnet et al, v the Government of Nepal et al (2014) 69-NaN-57 (Supreme Court of Nepal)

The UK

UK All Party Parliamentary Group on Extraordinary Rendition v Ministry of Defense (2011) UKUT 153 AAC

RELEVANT INTERNATIONAL AND NATIONAL DOCUMENTS

IHL-related instruments

Draft International Convention on the Condition and Protection of Civilians of enemy nationality who are on territory belonging to or occupied by a belligerent, Tokyo (1934)

Instructions for the Government of Armies of the United States in the Field (Lieber Code) (1863)

Project of an International Declaration concerning the Laws and Customs of War. Brussels (1874)

Resolution I, Adoption of the Declaration and Agenda for Humanitarian Action, 28th International Conference of the Red Cross and Red Crescent, Geneva (2003)

Resolution II, Forced or Involuntary Disappearances, 24th International Conference of the Red Cross and Red Crescent, Manila (1981)

Resolution I 'Wearing of identity discs', 24th International Conference of the Red Cross and Red Crescent (Manila, 1981).

Resolution V, The Missing and Dead in Armed Conflicts, 22nd International Conference of the Red Cross and Red Crescent, Teheran (1973)

Resolution VII, Measures to diminish the number of unaccounted for in time of war, 12th International Conference of the Red Cross and Red Crescent, Geneva (1925)

Statutes of the International Committee of the Red Cross, 21 June 1973 (last revision 8 May 2003)

Statutes of the International Red Cross and Red Crescent Movement, adopted by the 25th International Conference of the Red Cross, Geneva, 1986 (amended in 1995 and 2006)

Study on Measures to Diminish the Number of Unaccounted for in Time of War, 13th International Conference of the Red Cross and Red Crescent, The Hague (1928)

The Laws of War on Land, International Law Institute (the Oxford Manual), Oxford (1880)

Reports and documents of international and regional judicial and quasi-judicial bodies

AfCommHPR

AfCommHPR, Association for the Prevention of Torture, and UN OHCHR, 'Resolution on Guidelines and Measures for the Prohibition and Prevention of Torture, Cruel, Inhuman or Degrading Treatment or Punishment In Africa ("The Robben Island Guidelines"), 2nd Ed' (2008)

AfCommHPR/Mauritania, 'Mauritania. Initial Report, 1986-2001' (31st Ordinary Session – 2-16 May 2002 2001) <http://www.achpr.org/states/mauritania/reports/1st-1986-2001/> accessed 12 July 2016

Declaration of Principles on Freedom of Expression in Africa, adopted during its 32nd session, on October 17-23, 2002 (Banjul).

'General Comment No. 3 on the African Charter on Human And Peoples' Rights: The Right to Life (Article 4)' (2015)

Principles and Guidelines on the Right to a Fair Trial and Legal Assistance in Africa, Doc. No. DOC/OS(XXX)247 (29 May 2003).

'Rules of Procedures of the AfCommHPR', approved by the AfCommHPR during its 47th ordinary session held in Banjul (Gambia) from May 12 to 26, 2010

AfCtHPR

'Interim Report of the AfCtHPR Notifying the Executive Council of Non-Compliance by a State, in Accordance with Article 31 of the Protocol' with Regard to Non-Compliance with the Measures Indicated in Relation to Application No. 002/2013 (on Gaddafi's Son)' <http://goo.gl/kbIUfT>

'Rules of Court', replacing the Interim Rules of Procedure of 20 June 2008, following the harmonization of the Interim Rules of the Court and the Commission, July 2009 Arusha, October 2009 Dakar

Committee Against Torture (CAT)

'Concluding Observations on the Fourth Report of Cyprus' (2014) UN Doc CAT/C/CYP/CO/4

'Considerations of Reports Submitted by States Parties under Article 19 of the Convention − Algeria. Concluding Observations of the Committee against Torture.' (2008) UN Doc. CAT/C/DZA/CO/3

Committee on Enforced Disappearances (CED)

'Working Methods'
<http://www.ohchr.org/EN/HRBodies/CED/Pages/WorkingMethods.aspx> accessed 12 March 2015

ECtHR

ECtHR, 'Interim Measure Granted in Inter-State Case Brought by Ukraine against Russia' (Press Release)' (2014) Doc. ECHR 073

——, 'European Court of Human Rights Extends Time Allowed for Russia's Observations on Admissibility of Cases Concerning Crimea and Eastern Ukraine (Press Release)' (2015) Doc. ECHR 122

ECtHR (President of the Court), 'Practice Directions − Rules of Court' (2016) <http://www.echr.coe.int/Documents/PD_interim_measures_ENG.pdf> accessed 2 March 2016

ECtHR (Press Unit), 'Factsheet − Interim Measures' (2016)

HRAP − UNMIK

'Annual Report 2009' (2009)
<http://www.unmikonline.org/hrap/Eng/Documents/annual_report2009.pdf> accessed 10 July 2016

'Rules of Procedure' (2008)

'The Human Rights Advisory Panel. History and Legacy: Kosovo 2007-2016. Final Report' (2016)

HRCee

'Concluding Observations of the Human Rights Committee: Kosovo (Serbia)' (2006) UN Doc CCPR/C/UNK/CO/1

'Concluding Observations of the Human Rights Committee on Guatemala' (2012) UN Doc CCPR/C/GTM/CO/3

'Concluding observations on the fifth periodic report of Sri Lanka' (2014) CCPR/C/LKA/CO/5

'Concluding observations on the second periodic report of Nepal' (2014) UN Doc CCPR/C/NPL/CO/2

'General Comment 6 – Article 6' (1994) UN Doc HRI/GEN/1/Rev.1 at 6 (Sixteenth session, 1982)

'General Comment No. 16: Article 17 (Right to Privacy)' (1988) UN Doc HRI/GEN/1/Rev.1 at 21 (1994)

'General Comment No 20: Article 7 (Prohibition of Torture or Cruel, Inhuman or Degrading Treatment or Punishment)' (1992) UN Doc HRI/GEN/1/Rev.9 (Vol.1) at 182

'General Comment No 26: Continuity of Obligations' (1997) UN Doc CCPR/C/21/Rev.1/Add.8/Rev.1

'General Comment No 29: States of Emergency (Article 4)' (2001) UN Doc CCPR/C/21/Rev.1/Add.11

'General Comment No. 31: The Nature of the General Legal Obligation Imposed on State Parties to the Covenant' (2004) UN Doc. CCPR/C/21/Rev.1/Add.13

'General Comment No. 33: The Obligations of States Parties under the Optional Protocol to the International Covenant on Civil and Political Rights' (2008) UN Doc. CCPR/C/GC/33,

General Comment No. 34: Article 19 (Freedoms of Opinion and Expression)' (2011) UN Doc CCPR/C/GC/34

'General Comment No 35: Article 9 (Liberty and Security of Person)' (2014) UN Doc CCPR/C/GC/35

'Rules of procedure of the Human Rights Committee', UN Doc CCPR/C/3/Rev.10 (2012)

IACommHR

'Annual Report of the [IACommHR] 2010: Report of the Office of the Special Rapporteur for Freedom of Expression Dr. Catalina Botero' (2011) Doc No OEA/Ser.L/V/II Doc. 5

'Justice and Social Inclusion: The Challenges of Democracy in Guatemala' (2003) OEA/Ser.L/V/II.118 Doc. 5 rev. 1

'Precautionary Measures 1999', http://www.cidh.org/medidas/1999.eng.htm accessed 12 July 2015

'Precautionary Measures 2000', http://www.cidh.org/medidas/2000.eng.htm accessed 12 July 2015

'Precautionary Measures 2001', http://www.cidh.org/medidas/2001.eng.htm accessed 23 June 2015

'Principles and Best Practices on the Protection of Persons Deprived of Liberty in the Americas, Approved by the Commission during Its 131st Regular Period of Sessions' (2008)

'Report on the Situation of Human Rights in Peru' (1993) OEA/Ser.L/V/II.3, Doc. 31

IACtHR

Rules of Procedure of the IACtHR approved by the Court of its 49th Regular Session, 16-25 November 2000

'Rules of procedure of the IACtHR', approved by the Court of its LXXXV Regular Period of Sessions, 16-28 November 2009

ICC

'Case Information Sheet – Situation in the DRC: The Prosecutor v. Callixte Mbarushimana ICC-01/04-01/10' (2012) ICC-PIDS-CIS-DRC-04-003/12_Eng

'Case Information Sheet – Situation in the DRC: The Prosecutor v. Germain Katanga ICC-01/04-01/07' (2015) ICC-PIDS-CIS-DRC-03-011/15_Eng

'Case Information Sheet – Situation in the Republic of Kenya The Prosecutor v. Uhuru Muigai Kenyatta ICC-01/09-02/11' (2015) ICC-PIDS-CIS-KEN-02-014/15_Eng

'Case Information Sheet – Situation in the DRC: Thomas Lubanga Dyilo ICC-01/04-01/06' (2016) ICC-PIDS-CIS-DRC-01-015/16_Eng

'Case Information Sheet – Situation in the DRC: The Prosecutor v. Bosco Ntaganda (ICC-01/04-02/06)' (2017) ICC-PIDS-CIS-DRC-02-011/15_Eng

'Case Information Sheet – Situation in Uganda: The Prosecutor v. Dominic Ongwen (ICC-02/04-01/15)' (2017) ICC-PIDS-CIS-UGA-02-012/16_Eng

'Rules of Procedure and Evidence' (2000) UN Doc PCNICC/2000/1/Add.1

'Rules of Procedure and Evidence, Official Records of the Assembly of States Parties to the Rome Statute of the International Criminal Court, First Session, Part II.A' (2002) ICC-ASP/1/3 and Corr.1

ICC/OTP, 'Public Notice of the ICC Prosecutor to the Victims of Violence Committed in the Context of the August 2008 Armed Conflict in Georgia' (2015) <https://www.icc-cpi.int/iccdocs/otp/Article_15_Application--Notice_to_victims-ENG.pdf> accessed 12 July 2016

——, 'Report on Preliminary Examination Activities 2012' (2012) <https://www.icc-cpi.int//Pages/item.aspx?name=161114-otp-rep-PE> accessed 10 January 2017

——, 'Report on Preliminary Examination Activities 2016' (2016) <https://www.icc-cpi.int//Pages/item.aspx?name=161114-otp-rep-PE> accessed 10 January 2017

——, 'Report on Preliminary Examination Activities 2017' (2017) 19-27, 36-39 https://www.icc-cpi.int/itemsDocuments/2017-PE-rep/2017-otp-rep-PE_ENG.pdf accessed 15 March 2018

ICJ

Reuter (Professor) P, 'Oral Argument, Counsel of the Government of Cambodia, Case Concerning the Temple of Preah Vihear (Cambodia v. Thailand), ICJ Reports, Pleadings, Oral Arguments (in French)' (1962) Documents, II

ICTY

Brunborg H and others, 'Missing and Dead from Srebrenica: The 2005 Report and List' (2005) Expert Report for the Case of Vujadin Popović et al. (IT-05-88) <http://www.icty.org/x/file/About/OTP/War_Demographics/en/popovic_srebrenica_0 50916.pdf> accessed 12 January 2016

'Eleventh Annual Report of the International Tribunal for the Prosecution of Persons Responsible for Serious Violations of International Humanitarian Law Committed in the Territory of the Former Yugoslavia since 1991' (2004) UN Doc A/59/215-

S/2004/627

'Fourth Annual Report of the International Tribunal for the Prosecution of Persons Responsible for Serious Violations of [IHL] Committed in the Territory of the Former Yugoslavia Since 1991' (1997) UN Doc A/52/375-S/1997/729

ICTY Manual on Developed Practices – Prepared in Conjunction with UNICRI as Part of a Project to Preserve the Legacy of the ICTY (UNICRI 2009)

'Rules of Procedure and Evidence' (28 December 2001) IT/32/Rev. 22

'Rules of Procedure and Evidence of the ICTY' (2005) IT/32/Rev. 36

Statute of the ICTY, adopted 25 May 1993 by UNSC Resolution 827 (last amendment 7 July 2009 by UNSC Resolution 1877)

Permanent Court of International Justice – PCIJ

PCIJ – Advisory Committee of Jurists, 'Procès-Verbaux of the Proceedings of the Committee, with Annexes' (1920)

Resolutions, reports, and other documents of international and regional organizations

ASEAN

ASEAN Human Rights Declaration, adopted on 18 November 2012, 21st ASEAN Summit and Special Meeting of the ASEAN Intergovernmental Commission on Human Rights.

CoE

Committee of Ministers, 'Communication from the Russian Federation Concerning the Khashiyev and Akayeva Group of Cases against Russian Federation (Application No. 57942/00)' (2013) DH-DD(2013)935

——, 'Communication from the Russian Federation Concerning the Khashiyev Group of Cases against Russian Federation (Application No. 57942/00)' (2014) DH-DD(2014)892

——, 'Recommendation Rec(2006)2 of the Committee of Ministers to Member States on the European Prison Rules, Adopted by the Committee of Ministers at the 952nd Meeting of the Ministers' Deputies' (2006)

——, 'Recommendation No. CM/Rec(2009)12 on "Principles Concerning Missing Persons and the Presumption of Death"' (2009)

——, 'Search for Missing Persons, Recommendation No R (79) 6' (1979)

——, 'Supervision of the Execution of Judgments and Decisions of the ECtHR' (2016) 9th Annual Report of the CoM 2015

—— – European Commission of Human Rights, 'Preparatory Work on Article 10 ECHR' (1956) Doc no DH (56) 15

—— – ECtHR, Dialogue between Judges 2011: 'What Are The Limits to the Evolutive Interpretation of the Convention?' (CoE 2011)

Committee on Migration, Refugees and Population; Rapporteur: Mr Mevlüt Çavusoglu, 'Persons Unaccounted for as a Result of Armed Conflicts or Internal Violence in the Balkans' (2004) Doc 10251

European Commission for Democracy through law (Venice Commission), 'Opinion on Human Rights in Kosovo: Possible Establishment of Review Mechanisms, Adopted at the 60th Plenary Session' (2004) CDL-AD (2004)033, Opinion no 280/2004

Parliamentary Assembly, 'Bosnia and Herzegovina's Application for Membership of the Council of Europe' (2002) Opinion 234 (2002)

European Committee for the Prevention of Torture and Inhuman or Degrading Treatment or Punishment (European CPT)

European CPT, '12th General Report on the CPT's Activities Covering the Period 1 January to 31 December 2001' (2002) CPT/Inf (2002) 15

——, '25th General Report of the CPT – 1 January-31 December 2015' (2016) CPT/Inf (2016) 10

European Union

Council of the European Union, 'EULEX Kosovo: Mandate Extended, Budget Approved' (14 June 2016) <http://www.consilium.europa.eu/en/press/press-releases/2016/06/14-eulex-kosovo-budget/> accessed 12 January 2017

International Commission on Missing Persons (ICMP)

'Bosnia i Herzegovina. Missing Persons from the Armed Conflicts of the 1990s: A Stocktaking' (2014)

'Conference Report', The Missing: an Agenda for the Future (29 October – 1 November 2013), The Hague

Declaration on The Role Of The State In Addressing The Issue Of Persons Missing As A Consequence Of Armed Conflict And Human Rights Abuses', Mostar, 29 August 2014 https://www.icmp.int/wp-content/uploads/2014/08/signed-declaration-2.pdf accessed 12 January 2017.

Knut Vollebaek, 'Speech by ICMP Commissioner' (Peace Research Institute Oslo – Roundtable event, 11 June 2014) <https://www.icmp.int/wp-content/uploads/2014/08/icmp-dg-846-3-doc-speech-by-commissioner-vollebaek-roundtable-oslo-12th-june-2014.pdf> accessed 12 June 2016

'Missing Persons and the Work of the ICMP' (2014) Doc no ICMP.DG.677.2.doc <https://www.icmp.int/wp-content/uploads/2014/08/icmp-dg-677-2-doc-roundtable-meeting-sussex.pdf> accessed 1 July 2016

'Missing Persons from the Kosovo Conflict and its Aftermath: A Stocktaking' (2017) 40-42 https://www.icmp.int/?resources=missing-persons-from-the-kosovo-conflict-and-its-aftermath-a-stocktaking-2017 accessed 12 July 2018.

'The Situation in Kosovo: A Stock-Taking' (2010) Doc no ICMP.DG.264.4.doc <http://www.ic-mp.org/wp-content/uploads/2007/11/icmp-dg-264-4-doc-general.pdf> accessed 12 January 2016

ICMP/INTERPOL, 'Co-Operation Agreement between the ICMP and the International Criminal Police Organization – INTERPOL' (2007)

ICMP/IOM, 'Cooperation Agreement between the ICMP and the International Organization for Migration – IOM' (2013)

Memorandum of Understanding between the ICMP and the Office of the Prosecutor of the ICC, signed in The Hague, 7 July 2016

International Committee of the Red Cross (ICRC)

ICRC, Commentary on the First Geneva Convention: Convention (I) for the Amelioration of the Condition of the Wounded and Sick in Armed Forces in the Field (2nd edn, 2016) <https://www.icrc.org/applic/ihl/ihl.nsf/Treaty.xsp?documentId=4825657B0C7E6BF

0C12563CD002D6B0B&action=openDocument> accessed 20 July 2018

——, 'Families of Missing Persons in Nepal: A Study of Their Needs' (ICRC 2009)

——, 'Final Record of the Diplomatic Conference of Geneva of 1949. Vol. I' (Federal Political Department 1950)

——, 'Final Record of the Diplomatic Conference of Geneva of 1949. Vol. II A' (Federal Political Department 1950)

——, 'Guatemala: ICRC Calls for Creation of a National Search Committee (News Release 10/23)' (22 February 2010) <https://www.icrc.org/eng/resources/documents/news-release/2010/guatemala-news-220210.htm> accessed 29 December 2017

——, *Handbook of the International Red Cross and Red Crescent Movement* (ICRC 2009)

——, 'Humanitarian Challenges 2017. Colombia Report: Results and Perspectives' (2017)

——, *Increasing Respect for International Humanitarian Law in Non-International Armed Conflicts* (ICRC 2008) <https://www.icrc.org/en/publication/0923-increasing-respect-international-humanitarian-law-non-international-armed-conflicts> accessed 12 September 2016

——, 'Iran/Iraq: Efforts Continue to Clarify Fate of Missing from 1980-1988 War – ICRC (News Release 13/84)' (6 May 2013) </eng/resources/documents/news-release/2013/05-06-iran-iraq-missings.htm> accessed 8 February 2017

——, 'Kosovo: Meeting of Working Group on Missing Persons Held in Belgrade (News No. 05/23)' (*ReliefWeb*, 2005) <http://reliefweb.int/report/serbia/kosovo-meeting-working-group-missing-persons-held-belgrade> accessed 31 January 2017

——, 'Living with Uncertainty. Needs of the Families of Missing Persons in Sri Lanka' (2016) <https://www.icrc.org/en/document/sri-lanka-families-missing-persons> accessed 2 August 2016

——, 'Mechanisms to Solve Issues on People Unaccounted for (Final Report and Outcome) in the Framework of "The Missing: Action to Resolve the Problem of People Unaccounted for as a Result of Armed Conflict or Internal Violence and to Assist Their Families" (Hereinafter, "The Missing Project")' (2002) ICRC/TheMissing/12.2002/EN/6

——, 'Member of Armed Forces and Armed Groups: Identification, Family News, Killed in Action, Prevention – Final Report and Outcome, in the Framework of "The Missing Project"' (ICRC 2002)

——, *Minutes from Meetings of the International Prisoner-of-War Agency, 21 August 1914 – 11 November 1918* (Daniel Palmieri ed, ICRC 2014)

——, 'Missing Migrants and Their Families – The ICRC's Recommendations to Policy-Makers' (2017) Policy Paper

——, 'Official Records of the Diplomatic Conference on the Reaffirmation and Development of International Humanitarian Law Applicable in Armed Conflicts, Vol I' (1974)

——, 'Official Records of the Diplomatic Conference on the Reaffirmation and Development of International Humanitarian Law Applicable in Armed Conflicts, Vol III' (1974)

——, 'Official Records of the Diplomatic Conference on the Reaffirmation and Development of International Humanitarian Law Applicable in Armed Conflicts, Vol VII' (1974)

——, 'Official Records of the Diplomatic Conference on the Reaffirmation and

Development of International Humanitarian Law Applicable in Armed Conflicts, Vol XI' (1974)

——, 'Official Records of the Diplomatic Conference on the Reaffirmation and Development of International Humanitarian Law Applicable in Armed Conflicts, Vol XII' (1974)

——, 'Official Records of the Diplomatic Conference on the Reaffirmation and Development of International Humanitarian Law Applicable in Armed Conflicts, Vol XV' (1974)

——, 'Operational Best Practices Regarding the Management of Human Remains and Information on the Dead by Non-Specialists' in the Framework of "The Missing Project" (ICRC 2004)

——, 'Presentation by the ICRC to the Committee on Juridical and Political Affairs' (Meeting of the Committee on Juridical and Political Affairs of the Permanent Council of the Organization of American States (Doc no OEA/Ser.G CP/CAJP/INF. 218/14), 5 March 2014)

——, 'Report: The Missing and Their Families. Summary of the Conclusions Arising from Events Held prior to the International Conference of Governmental and Non – Governmental Experts (Geneva, February 19 -21, 2003). The Missing Project' (ICRC 2003) Doc no TheMissing/Conf/01.2003/EN/10

——, *Restoring Family Links Strategy – Including Legal References* (ICRC 2009) <https://www.icrc.org/eng/assets/files/other/icrc_002_0967.pdf> accessed 12 June 2015

——, 'The Families of People Missing in Connection with the Armed Conflicts That Have Occurred in Lebanon since 1975. An Assessment of Their Needs' (ICRC 2013) <http://www.icrc.org/eng/assets/files/2013/lebanon-missing-06-2013-icrc.pdf> accessed 12 May 2015

——, 'The Missing: Action to Resolve the Problem of People Unaccounted for as a Result of Armed Conflict or Internal Violence and to Assist Their Families. Conference Acts' (ICRC 2003) TheMissing/Conf/03.2003/EN/90

——, 'The Missing. ICRC Progress Report' (ICRC 2006) <goo.gl/og1Gf1> accessed 12 June 2016

——, *The Need to Know: Restoring Links between Dispersed Family Members* (ICRC 2010)

ICRC – Advisory Service on IHL, 'Guiding Principles: "Model Law on the Missing: Principles for Legislating the Situation of Persons Missing as a Result of Armed Conflict or Internal Violence. Measures to Prevent Persons from Going Missing and to Protect the Rights and Interests of the Missing and Their Families."' (2009)

ICRC/IPU, *Missing Persons: A Handbook for Parliamentarians. No. 17* (Inter-Parliamentary Union; ICRC 2009)

Sassòli M and Rioux J-F, 'Study of Existing Mechanisms to Clarify the Fate of Missing Persons", in the Framework of "The Missing Project"' (ICRC 2003)

'Study on Measures to Diminish the Number of Unaccounted for in Time of War – 13th International Conference of the Red Cross and Red Crescent' (1928)

Wigger (ICRC) A, 'Building Local Capacity to Account for Missing Persons and Responding to the Needs of Their Relatives and Others' (The missing: an agenda for the future, The Hague, 30 October 2013)

MERCOSUR

Comunicado conjunto de los Presidentes de los Estados Partes del MERCOSUR y de los Estados asociados, XXVIII Summit of Heads of State held in *Asunción*, Paraguay, 20 June 2005

Organization of American States (OAS)

Declaration of Principles on Freedom of Expression, adopted on October 19, 2000, http://www.oas.org/en/iachr/expression/showarticle.asp?artID=26 accessed 10 January 2015

OAS – General Assembly. 'Resolutions on the Right to the Truth' adopted between 2006-2014:

AG/RES. 2175 (XXXVI-O/06), 2006

AG/RES. 2267 (XXXVII-O/07), 2007

AG/RES. 2406 (XXXVIII-O/08), 2008

AG/RES. 2509 (XXXIX-O/09), 2009

AG/RES. 2595 (XL-O/10), 2010

AG/RES. 2662 (XLI-O/11), 2011

AG/RES. 2725 (XLII-O/12), 2012

AG/RES. 2800 (XLIII-O/12), 2013

AG/RES. 2822 (XLIV-O/14), 2014

Organization of Islamic Cooperation

Cairo Declaration on Human Rights in Islam, adopted on 5 August 1990 by the Nineteenth Islamic Conference of Foreign Ministers of the Organization of Islamic Cooperation, Annex to Resolution no. 49/19-P

United Nations (UN)

Commission on Human Rights

'Basic Principles and Guidelines on the Right to a Remedy and Reparation for Victims of Gross Violations of IHRL and Serious Violations of IHL – Human Rights Resolution 2005/35' (2005) UN Doc E/CN.4/RES/2005/35

'Draft Report of the Inter-Sessional Open-Ended Working Group to Elaborate a Draft Legally Binding Normative Instrument for the Protection of All Persons from Enforced Disappearances (Document Subject to Restricted Distribution)' (2005) UN Doc. E/CN.4/2005/WG.22/CRP.9

'Promotion and Protection of Human Rights: Impunity. Add.1 "Updated Set of Principles for the Protection and Promotion of Human Rights through Action to Combat Impunity (Orentlicher Principles)"' (2005) UN Doc E/CN.4/2005/102/Add.1

'Report of the Independent Expert to Update the Set of Principles to Combat Impunity' (UN Commission on Human Rights 2005) UN Doc E/CN.4/2005/102

'Report of the Inter-Sessional Open-Ended Working Group to Elaborate a Draft Legally Binding Normative Instrument for the Protection of All Persons from Enforced Disappearances' (2003) UN Doc. E/CN.4/2003/71

'Report of the Inter-Sessional Open-Ended Working Group to Elaborate a Draft Legally Binding Normative Instrument for the Protection of All Persons from Enforced Disappearances' (2004) UN Doc E/CN.4/2004/59, Annex 2

'Report of the Inter-Sessional Open-Ended Working Group to Elaborate a Draft Legally Binding Normative Instrument for the Protection of All Persons from Enforced Disappearances' (2005) UN Doc. E/CN.4/2005/66

'Report of the Inter-Sessional Open-Ended Working Group to Elaborate a Draft Legally Binding Normative Instrument for the Protection of All Persons from Enforced Disappearances' (2006) UN Doc. E/CN.4/2006/57, Annex 2

'Report of the Representative of the Secretary-General, Mr. Francis M. Deng, Submitted pursuant to Commission Resolution 1997/39. ⌞SEP⌟Addendum: ⌞SEP⌟Guiding Principles on Internal Displacement' (UN Commission on Human Rights 1998) UN Doc E/CN.4/1998/53/Add.2

'Report of the Special Rapporteur on the Question of Torture' (1995) UN Doc E/CN.4/1995/34

'Report of the UN Commissioner on Human Rights on the Situation of Human Rights in Colombia' (2005) UN Doc E/CN.4/2005/10

'Report Submitted by Mr. Manfred Nowak, Independent Expert Charged with Examining the Existing International Criminal and Human Rights Framework for the Protection of Persons from Enforced or Involuntary Disappearances, pursuant to Paragraph 11 of Commission Resolution 2001/46' (2002) UN Doc E/CN.4/2002/71

'Resolution on Impunity, Res 2004/72' (2004) UN Doc E/CN.4/RES/2004/72

'Resolution on "Protection of the Human Rights of Civilians in Armed Conflicts"' (2005) UN Doc E/CN.4/RES/2005/63

'Resolution on the Question of Missing and Disappeared Persons, Human Rights Resolution 20 (XXXVI)' (1980) UN Doc E/CN.4/RES/1980

'Resolution on the Right to the Truth, Human Rights Resolution 2005/66' (2005) UN Doc E/CN.4/RES/2005/66

'Resolution on the "Situation of Human Rights in the Territory of the Former Yugoslavia"' (1993) UN Doc E/CN.4/RES/1993/7

'Resolution on the "Situation of Human Rights in the Territory of the Former Yugoslavia: Violations of Human Rights in Bosnia and Herzegovina, Croatia and the Federal Republic of Yugoslavia (Serbia and Montenegro)"' (1994) UN Doc E/CN.4/RES/1994/72

'Resolution on the "Situation of Human Rights in Bosnia and Herzegovina, the Republic of Croatia and the Federal Republic of Yugoslavia (Serbia and Montenegro)"' (1997) UN Doc E/CN.4/RES/1997/57

'Resolution on Torture and Other Cruel, Inhuman or Degrading Treatment or Punishment, Human Rights Resolution 2003/32' (2003) UN Doc E/CN.4/RES/2003/32

'Revised Final Report Prepared by Mr. Joinet pursuant to Sub-Commission Decision 1996/119 – Annexes I and II, Set of Principles for the Protection and Promotion of Human Rights through Action to Combat Impunity' (UN Commission on Human Rights 1997) UN Doc E/CN.4/Sub.2/1997/20/Rev.1

Salama I and Hampson F, 'Working Paper on the Relationship between Human Rights Law and International Humanitarian Law' (UN Commission on Human Rights 2005) UN Doc E/CN.4/Sub.2/2005/14

'Study of the Right of Everyone to Be Free from Arbitrary Arrest, Detention and Exile' (1961) UN Doc E/CN.4/813

'The Administration of Justice and the Human Rights of Detainees: Question of Human Rights and States of Emergency' (1995) UN Doc E/CN.4/Sub.2/1995/20

'The Adverse Consequences of Economic Sanctions on the Enjoyment of Human Rights. Working Paper Prepared by Mr. Marc Bossuyt' (2000) UN Doc E/CN.4/Sub.2/2000/33

'The Situation of Human Rights in the Territory of the Former Yugoslavia (Resolution Adopted by the Commission at Its First Special Session)' (1992) UN Doc E/CN.4/1992/S-1/1

Committee on the Rights of the Child

'General Comment No 10 – Children's Rights in Juvenile Justice' (2007) UN Doc CRC/C/GC/10

General Assembly (UNGA)

'Body of Principles for the Protection of All Persons under Any Form of Detention or Imprisonment' (1988) UN Doc A/RES/43/173

'Declaration of the Basic Principles of Justice for Victims of Crimes and Abuse of Power' (1985) UN Doc A/RES/40/34

'Principles on the Effective Investigation and Documentation of Torture and Other Cruel, Inhuman or Degrading Treatment or Punishment, Res. 55/89 Adopted on 4 December 2000' (1999) UN Doc. A/54/426

'Report of the Special Rapporteur on the Promotion and Protection of the Right to Freedom of Opinion and Expression' (2013) UN Doc A/68/362

'Resolution Adopting the Declaration on the Protection of All Persons from Enforced Disappearances, Res 47/133' (1992) UN Doc A/RES/47/133

'Resolution for Human Rights in Armed Conflicts' (1968) Res 2444 (XXIII)

'Resolution for Human Rights in Armed Conflicts' (1970) Res 2674 (XXV)

'Resolution on Human Rights in Chile' (1980) Res 35/188, UN Doc A/RES/35/188 at 203

'Resolution on Protection of Human Rights in Chile' (1979) Res 34/179 (English version), UN Doc A/RES/34/179 at 193

'Resolution on the Assistance and Co-Operation in Accounting for Persons Who Are Missing or Dead in Armed' (1974) UN Doc A/RES/3220 (XXIX)

'Resolution 369 (IV) "Draft Convention on the Declaration of Death of Missing Persons"' (1949) UN Doc A/1251

'Resolution 32/128 – Missing Persons in Cyprus' (1977) UN Doc A/RES/32/128

'Resolution 33/172 – Missing Persons in Cyprus' (1978) UN Doc A/RES/33/172

'Resolution 63/183 – Missing Persons' (2009) UN Doc. A/RES/63/183

'Resolution 61/155 – Missing Persons' (2007) UN Doc. A/RES/61/155

'Resolution 63/183 – Missing Persons' (2009) UN Doc. A/RES/63/183

'Resolution 65/210 – Missing Persons' (2011) UN Doc. A/RES/65/210

'Resolution 67/177 – Missing Persons' (2013) UN Doc. A/RES/67/177

'Resolution 69/184 – Missing Persons' (2015) UN Doc. A/RES/69/184

'Resolution on Missing Persons' (2016) UN Doc A/RES/71/201

'Third Committee Approves Draft Resolution Concerning Convention on Enforced Disappearances' (2006) UN Doc GA/SHC/3872

Universal Declaration of Human Rights, Res. 217A (III), UN Doc. A/RES/217(III) A at 71 (10 December 1948)

Human Rights Council

'2nd Report of the Independent International Commission of Inquiry on the Syrian Arab Republic' (2012) UN Doc A/HRC/19/69

'7th Report of the Independent International Commission of Inquiry on the Syrian Arab Republic' (2012) UN Doc A/HRC/21/50

'Joint Study on Global Practices in Relation to Secret Detention in the Context of Countering Terrorism' (2010) UN Doc A/HRC/13/42

'Progress Report of the Human Rights Council Advisory Committee on Best Practices on the Issue of Missing Persons' (2010) UN Doc A/HRC/14/42

'Report of the Human Rights Council Advisory Committee on Best Practices on the Issue of Missing Persons' (2011) UN Doc A/HRC/16/70

Report of the Special Representative of the Secretary– General on the Issue of Human Rights and Transnational Corporations and Other Business Enterprises, John Ruggie. Guiding Principles on Business and Human Rights: Implementing the United Nations "Protect, Respect and Remedy" Framework' (2011) UN Doc A/HRC/17/31

'Report of the Special Rapporteur on Extra-Judicial, Summary or Arbitrary Executions Concerning the Mission to Sri-Lanka' (2006) UN Doc E/CN.4/2006/53/Add.5

'Report of the Special Rapporteur on the Promotion of Truth, Justice, Reparation and Guarantees of Non-Recurrence (Advanced Edited Version)' (2017) UN Doc A/HRC/36/50

'Report of the Special Rapporteur on the Promotion of Truth, Justice, Reparation and Guarantees of Non-Recurrence – Prosecutorial Prioritization Strategies in the Aftermath of Gross Human Rights Violations and Serious Violations of IHL' (2014) UN Doc A/HRC/27/56

'Resolution 9/11 – Right to the Truth' (2005) UN Doc A/HRC/RES/9/11

'Resolution 12/12 – Right to the Truth' (2009) UN Doc A/HRC/RES/12/12

'Resolution 21/7 – Right to the Truth' (2012) UN Doc A/HRC/RES/21/7

Tomuschat C, 'Report of the Committee of Independent Experts in [IHL] and [IHRL] to Monitor and Assess Any Domestic, Legal or Other Proceedings Undertaken by Both the Government of Israel and the Palestinian Side, in the Light of General Assembly Resolution 64/254, Including the Independence, Effectiveness, Genuineness of These Investigations and Their Conformity with International Standards' (UN Human Rights Council 2010) UN Doc A /HRC/15/50

International Law Commission (ILC)

'ILC's Articles on the Responsibility of States for Internationally Wrongful Acts. Annex to Resolution 56/83 Responsibility of States for Internationally Wrongful Acts.' (2001) UN Doc A/RES/56/83

ILC, 'Report of the International Law Commission, Fifty-Seventh Session, Chapter XI "Fragmentation of International Law: Difficulties Arising From Diversification and Expansion of International Law"' (2005) UN Doc A/60/10

——, 'Titles an Texts of the Draft Articles on the Effects of Armed Conflicts on Treaties Adopted by the Drafting Committee on Second Reading' (2011) UN Doc. A/CN.4/L.777

——, *Yearbook of the International Law Commission – 1962. Documents of the Fourteenth Session Including the Report of the Commission to the General Assembly*, vol II (United Nations 1964)

——, *Yearbook of the International Law Commission – 1966. Documents of the*

Fourteenth Session Including the Report of the Commission to the General Assembly, vol II (United Nations 1966)

Koskenniemi M, 'Report of the Study Group of the International Law Commission on Fragmentation of International Law: Difficulties Arising from the Diversification and Expansion of International Law' (2006) UN Doc. A/CN.4/L.682

Office of High Commissioner for Human Rights (OHCHR)

High Commissioner on Human Rights, 'Statement to the Security Council on Missing Persons' (Security Council open Arria formula meeting 'The Global Challenge of Accounting for Missing Persons from Conflict, Human Rights Abuses, Disasters, Organized Crime, Migration and other Involuntary Causes', 27 January 2016)

OHCHR, 'Manual on Human Rights Monitoring' (United Nations 2011) UN Doc HR/P/PT/7/Rev.1

_____, 'Manual on the Effective Investigation and Documentation of torture and Other Cruel, Inhuman or Degrading Treatment or Punishment ("Istanbul Protocol")' (2004) UN Doc. HR/P/PT/8/Rev.1

_____, 'The Minnesota Protocol on the Investigation of Potentially Unlawful Death' (2016), UN Doc. HR/PUB/17/4 (UN OHCHR 2017)

——, 'Opening Statement – Panel Discussion "Promoting Tolerance, Dispelling Myths, Protecting Rights: An Evidence-Based Conversation on Migration"' (2015) <www.ohchr.org/EN/NewsEvents/Pages/DisplayNews. aspx?NewsID=16889&LangID=E>> accessed 12 June 2016

——, 'Recommended Principles and Guidelines on Human Rights at International Borders' (2014) <www.ohchr.org/Documents/Issues/ Migration/OHCHR_Recommended_Principles_Guidelines.pdf> accessed 12 July 2016

——, 'Study on the Right to the Truth' (2006) UN Doc E/CN.4/2006/91

——, 'Training Manual on Human Rights Monitoring' (United Nations 2001) UN Doc HR/P/PT/7

Secretary-General (UNSG)

'A More Secure World: Our Shared Responsibility. Report of the Secretary-General's High-Level Panel on Threats, Challenges, and Change' (2004)

'An Agenda for Peace' (1992) UN Doc A/47/277

'Report of the Experts on the Question of the Fate of Missing and Disappeared Persons in Chile, Note by the Secretary-General' (1979) UN Doc A/34/583/Add.1

'Report of the Secretary General – Missing Persons' (2009) UN Doc A/HRC/10/28

'Report of the Secretary-General – Missing Persons' (2010) UN Doc A/65/285

'Report of the Secretary General – Missing Persons' (2012) UN Doc. A/67/267

'Report of the Secretary-General – Missing Persons' (2016) UN Doc A/71/299

'Report of the Secretary-General on the Situation in Abkhazia, Georgia' (2008) UN Doc S/2008/38

'Report of the Secretary General on the UN Operation in Cyprus' (1974) UN DOC S/11568

'Report of the Secretary-General on the United Nations Operation in Cyprus (for the Period 10 June 1975 to 8 December 1975)' (1975) UN Doc S/11900

'Report of the Secretary-General on the United Nations Operation in Cyprus (for the Period 9 December 1975 to 5 June 1976)' (1976) UN Doc S/12093

'Report of the Secretary-General on the United Nations Operation in Cyprus (for the Period 6 June 1976 to 6 December 1976)' (1976) UN Doc S/12253

'Report of the Secretary-General on the United Nations Operation in Cyprus (for the Period 7 December 1976 to 7 June 1977)' (1977) UN Doc S/12342

'Report of the Secretary-General on the United Nations Operation in Cyprus (for the Period 8 June 1977 to 30 November 1977)' (1977) UN Doc S/12463

'Report of the Secretary-General on the United Nations Operation in Cyprus (for the Period 1 December 1977 to 31 May 1978)' (1978) UN Doc S/12723

'Report of the Secretary-General on the United Nations Operation in Cyprus (for the Period 1 June 1978 to 30 November 1978)' (1978) UN Doc S/12946

'Report of the Secretary-General on the United Nations Operation in Cyprus (for the Period 1 December 1978 to 31 May 1979)' (1979) UN Doc S/13369

'Report of the Secretary-General on the United Nations Operation in Cyprus (for the Period 1 June to 30 November 1979)' (1979) UN Doc S/13672

'Report of the Secretary-General on the United Nations Operation in Cyprus (for the Period 1 December 1979 to 31 May 1980)' (1980) UN Doc S/13972

'Report of the Secretary-General on the United Nations Operation in Cyprus (for the Period 1 June to 30 November 1980)' (1980) UN Doc S/14275

'Report by the Secretary General on the UN Operation in Cyprus (For the Period 1 December 1980 to 27 May 1981)' (1981) UN Doc S/14490

'Report of the Secretary-General on the United Nations Operation in Cyprus (for the Period 28 May 1981 to 30 November 1981)' (1981) UN Doc S/14778

'Report of the Secretary-General on the United Nations Operation in Cyprus' (2004) UN Doc S/2004/427

'Report of the Secretary-General on the United Nations Operation in Cyprus' (2006) UN Doc S/2006/315

'Report of the Secretary-General on UNMIK' (1999) UN Doc S/1999/779

'Report of the Secretary-General on UNMIK' (1999) UN Doc S/1999/987

'Report of the Secretary-General on the UNMIK' (2000) UN Doc S/2000/177

'Report of the Secretary-General on UNMIK' (2000) UN Doc S/2000/538

'Report of the Secretary-General on UNMIK' (2016) UN Doc S/2016/901

'Report of the Secretary-General on Enhancing Mediation and Its Support Activities' (2009) UN Doc S/2009/189

'Report of the Secretary-General's Panel of Experts on Accountability in Sri Lanka' (2011)

'Report of the Secretary-General pursuant to UNSC Resolution 361 (1974)' (1974) UN Doc/11488

'Report on Peacebuilding in the Immediate Aftermath of Conflict' (2009) UN Doc A/63/881–S/2009/304

'Report on the Organization and Operation of the UN Peacekeeping Force in Cyprus (to the UNSC)' (1964) UN Doc S/5679

'Report on the Rule of Law and Transitional Justice in Conflict and Post-Conflict Societies' (2004) UN Doc S/2004/616

'Road Map towards the Implementation of the United Nations Millennium Declaration' (2001) UN Doc A/56/326

'Secretary-General's Bulletin – Observance by United Nations Forces of International Humanitarian Law' (1999) UN Doc ST/SGB/1999/13

'Supplement to An Agenda for Peace: Position Paper of the Secretary General on the Occasion of the Fiftieth Anniversary of the United Nations' (1995) UN Doc A/50/60-S/1995/1

'Tenth Report of the Secretary-General pursuant to Paragraph 4 of UNSC Resolution 2107 (2013)' (2016) UN Doc S/2016/372

UN High-level Panel on United Nations Peace Operations, 'Report of the Panel on United Nations Peace Operations (Brahimi Report)' (2000) UN Doc A/55/305-S/2000/809

UNSG – Task Force on Post-conflict Peacebuilding, 'An Inventory of Post-Conflict Peace-Building Activities' (1995)

UNSG/UNGA, 'Report of the High-Level Independent Panel on Peace Operations (HIPPO) on Uniting Our Strengths for Peace: Politics, Partnership and People' (2015) UN Doc A/70/95, S/2015/446

Security Council (UNSC)

'Report of the Panel of Experts Established pursuant to Resolution 1591 (2005) Concerning the Sudan Prepared in Accordance with Paragraph 2 of Resolution 1713 (2006)' (2007) S/2007/584

'Resolution 186 (the Cyprus Question)' (1964) UN Doc S/RES/186

'Resolution 237' (1967) UN Doc S/RES/237

'Resolution 359 (Cyprus)' (1974) S/RES/359

'Resolution 686 (Iraq)' (1991) UN Doc S/RES/686

'Resolution 687 (Iraq)' (1991) UN Doc S/RES/687

'Resolution 827 (ICTY)' (1993) UN Doc S/RES/827

'Resolution 1022 on Suspension of Measures Imposed by or Reaffirmed in Security Council Resolutions Related to the Situation in the Former Yugoslavia' (1995) UN Doc S/RES/1022

'Resolution 1037' (1996) UN Doc S/RES/1037

'Resolution 1244 (Kosovo)' (1999) UN Doc S/RES/1244

'Resolution 1483 (Iraq)' (2003) UN Doc S/RES/1483

'Resolution 1548 (Cyprus)' (2004) UN Doc S/RES/1548

'Resolution 1568 (Cyprus)' (2004) UN Doc S/RES/1568

'Resolution 1882' (2009) UN Doc S/RES/1882

'Statement by the President of the Security Council' (2008) UN Doc S/PRST/2008/44

UNSC (Press Release), 'Security Council Briefed on Establishment of War Crimes Chamber Within State Court of Bosnia and Herzegovina' (2003) SC/7888

UN Economic and Social Council

'Principles on the Effective Prevention and Investigation of Extra-Legal, Arbitrary and Summary Executions, Res. 1989/65 (Annex)' (1989) UN ESCOR Supp. (No 1) at 52, UN Doc. E/1989/89

'Siracusa Principles on the Limitation and Derogation Provisions in the ICCPR' (1985) UN Doc E/CN.4/1985/4, Annex

'Standard Minimum Rules for the Treatment of Prisoners, Adopted by the First UN Congress on the Prevention of Crime and the Treatment of Offenders on 30 August

1955, Res. 663 C (XXIV), July 31, 1957 and Res. 2076 (LXII), May 13, 1977' UN Doc A/CONF/611, annex I

1985 UN Standard Minimum Rules for the Administration of Juvenile Justice ("The Beijing Rules"), UN Doc. A/RES/40/33, 29 November 1985

Working Group on Arbitrary Detention (WGAD)

'UN Basic Principles and Guidelines on the Right of Anyone Deprived of Their Liberty to Bring Proceedings before a Court' (2015) UN Doc WGAD/CRP.1/2015

'Report of the WGAD' (UN Human Rights Council 2012) UN Doc A/HRC/22/44

Working Group on Enforced or Involuntary Disappearances (WGEID)

'Civil and Political Rights, Including Questions of Disappearances and Summary Executions. Report of the WGEID' (1998) UN Doc E/CN.4/1999/62

'Compilation of General Comments on the Declaration on the Protection of All Persons from Enforced Disappearance' <http://goo.gl/6P0Izl> accessed 12 May 2018

'Questions of Human Rights of All Persons Subjected to Any Form of Detention or Imprisonment, in Particular: Questions of Missing and Disappeared Persons – Report of the WGEID' (1981) UN Doc E/CN.4/1435

'Questions of Human Rights of All Persons Subjected to Any Form of Detention or Imprisonment, in Particular: Questions of Missing and Disappeared Persons – Report of the WGEID' (1981) UN Doc E/CN .4/1492

'Question of the Human Rights of All Persons Subjected to Any Form of Detention or Imprisonment, in Particular: Question of Enforced or Involuntary Disappearance –
Report of the WGEID' (1983) UN Doc E/CN.4/1984/21

'Report of the WGEID' (1998) UN Doc E/CN.4/1998/43

'Report of the WGEID: Addendum. Follow-up Report to the Recommendations Made by the WGEID – Missions to Mexico and Timor Leste' (2015) UN Doc A/HRC/30/38/Add.4

'Report of the WGEID. Addendum: Follow-up Report to the Recommendations Made by the Working Group – Missions to Argentina and Bosnia and Herzegovina' (2014) UN Doc A/HRC/27/49/Add.2

'Report of the WGEID. Addendum: Mission to Bosnia and Herzegovina' (2010) UN Doc A/HRC/16/48/Add.1

Report of the WGEID: Addendum. Mission to Guatemala' (2007) UN Doc A/HRC/4/41/Add.1

'Report of the WGEID. Addendum: Mission to Serbia, Including Kosovo' (2015) UN Doc A/HRC/30/38/Add.1

'Report of the WGEID – Annex II "Revised Methods of Work of the Working Group on Enforced or Involuntary Disappearances"' (2011) UN Doc A/HRC/19/58

'Report of the WGEID – Annex II Revised Methods of Work of the WGEID' (2012) UN Doc A/HRC/19/58/Rev.1

'Report of the WGEID on Its Mission to Peru' (2016) UN Doc A/HRC/33/51/Add.3

'Report on the Visit to Former Yugoslavia by a Member of the WGEID at the Request of the Special Rapporteur on the Situation of Human Rights in the Former Yugoslavia (4-13 August 1993)' (1993) UN Doc E/CN.4/1994/26/Add.1

'Special Process on Missing Persons in the Territory of the Former Yugoslavia Report Submitted by Mr. Manfred Nowak, Member of the WGEID, pursuant to Paragraph 24 of Commission Resolution 1994/72 (First Report)' (1995) UN Doc E/CN.4/1995/37

'Special Process on Missing Persons in the Territory of the Former Yugoslavia. Report Submitted by Mr. Manfred Nowak, Expert Member of the WGEID, Responsible for the Special Process, pursuant to Paragraph 4 of Commission Resolution 1995/35 (Second Report)' (1996) E/CN.4/1996/36

'Special Process on Missing Persons in the Territory of the Former Yugoslavia – Report Submitted to Mr. Manfred Nowak, Expert Member of the WGEID, Responsible for the Special Process, pursuant to Commission Resolution 1996/71 (Third Report)' (1997) E/CN.4/1997/55

Documents, Regulations, Reports of UN Peace Operations

'Exchange of Letters (with Annexes) Constituting an Agreement Concerning the Service with the [UNFICYP] of the National Contingent Provided by the Government of Canada (Doc No 8107)' (1966) 555 UNTS 120

Ombudsperson Institution in Kosovo, 'Third Annual Report 2002-2003 Addressed to the SRSG of the UN' (2003)

UNFICYP, 'Operations since 1974' <https://unficyp.unmissions.org/operations-1974> accessed 12 January 2017

UNMIK, 'Report Submitted by the United Nations Interim Administration Mission in Kosovo to the Human Rights Committee on the Human Rights Situation in Kosovo Since June 1999' (2006) UN Doc CCPR/C/ UNK/1

——, 'UNMIK Pillar 1, Police and Justice, Presentation Paper' (2003) Fourth Quarter

——, 'UNMIK Regulation No 1999/1 on the Authority of the Interim Administration in Kosovo' (1999) UN Doc UNMIK/REG/1999/1

——, 'UNMIK Regulation No 1999/24 on the Applicable Law in Kosovo' (1999) UN Doc UNMIK/REG/1999/24

——, 'UNMIK Regulation No 2003/26 – Provisional Criminal Procedure Code of Kosovo' (2003) UN Doc UNMIK/REG/2003/26

——, 'Regulation No 2006/12 on the Establishment of the Human Rights Advisory Panel' (2006) UN Doc UNMIK/REG/2006/12

UNMIK/HRCee, 'Comments by the United Nations Interim Administration Mission in Kosovo (UNMIK) on the Concluding Observations of the Human Rights Committee (CCPR/C/UNK/CO/1)' (2008) UN Doc CCPR/C/UNK/CO/1/Add.1

——, 'Further Information Received from the United Nations Interim Administration Mission in Kosovo (UNMIK) on the Implementation of the Concluding Observations of the Human Rights Committee (CCPR/C/UNK/CO/1)' (2009) UN Doc CCPR/C/UNK/CO/1/Add.2

——, 'Further Information Received from the United Nations Interim Administration Mission in Kosovo (UNMIK) on the Implementation of the Concluding Observations of the Human Rights Committee (CCPR/C/UNK/CO/1)' (2009) UN Doc CCPR/C/UNK/CO/1/Add.3

UNMIK – Press Office, 'Press Release – UNMIK Establishes the Human Rights Advisory Panel' (2006) UNMIK/PR/1525

Other UN documents

International Commission of Inquiry on Darfur, 'Report of the International Commission of Inquiry on Darfur to the Secretary-General Pursuant to Security Council Resolution 1564 (2004) of 18 September 2004' (2005) UN Doc S/2005/60

McGovern K and Choulai B, 'UNDP Human Development Report – Case Study of Solomon Islands Peace and Conflict-Related Development Analysis' (UNDP 2005)

2005/33

'Tehran Conference, General Resolution XXIII, "Respect for Human Rights in Armed Conflicts"' (1968) UN Doc A/Conf.32/41

UN Department of Peacekeeping Operations – UNDPKO (Criminal Law and Judicial Advisory Service), *Handbook for Judicial Affairs Officers in UN Peacekeeping Operations,* (2013) <http://www.un.org/en/peacekeeping/publications> accessed 13 October 2015

UNDPKO, 'Ten Rules: Code Of Personal Conduct For Blue Helmets' (1998) <https://cdu.unlb.org/UNStandardsofConduct/TenRulesCodeofPersonalConductForBl ueHelmets.aspx> accessed 12 July 2016

——, 'United Nations Peacekeeping Operations Principles and Guidelines' (2008)

UNDPKO Peacekeeping Best Practices Unit, 'Handbook on United Nations Multidimensional Peacekeeping Operations' (2003) <http://www.un.org/en/ peacekeeping/resources/policy.shtml> accessed 12 December 2016

UNDPKO Training Unit, 'We Are United Nations Peacekeepers' <http://www.un.org/ en/peacekeeping/documents/un_in.pdf> accessed 12 July 2016

UN Department of Public Information, *The Yearbook of the United Nations,* vol 54 (United Nations 2000)

UN OCHA, 'Kosovo Humanitarian Update' (2001) Issue no 36 <http://www.unhcr.org/ 3c3ab52f4.pdf> accessed 2 March 2014

UN Peacebuilding Support Office, 'UN Peacebuilding: An Orientation' (2010) <http://www.un.org/en/peacebuilding/pbso/pdf/peacebuilding_orientation.pdf> accessed 12 July 2016

UN Peacebuilding Support Office, 'Peacebuilding & the United Nations' <http://www.un.org/en/peacebuilding/pbso/pbun.shtml> accessed 24 January 2017

UN, *The Blue Helmets – A Review of United Nations Peace-Keeping* (UN Department of Public Information 1996)

——, *UN Juridical Yearbook – Part II Legal Activities of the United Nations and Related Intergovernmental Organizations (Chapter VI – Selected Legal Opinions of the Secretariat of the United Nations and Related Inter-Governmental Organizations)* (United Nations 1969)

——, *Yearbook of the United Nations,* vol 28 (United Nations 1974)

UN Conference on International Organization (UNCIO) Documents, vol III (1945)

UN Conference on International Organization (UNCIO) Documents, vol IV (1945)

UN Conference on International Organization (UNCIO) Documents, vol XIII (1945)

Documents and Reports of various national bodies

Belgium

Belgium, *Structure et Fonctionnement Du Bureau de Renseignements Sur Les Prisonniers de Guerre, Procédure Spécifique* (Ministère de la Défense 2007)

Bosnia and Herzegovina

Constitutional Court of Bosnia Herzegovina, 'Organization' (*Constitutional Court*) <http://www.ccbh.ba/o-sudu/?title=ustrojstvo&lang=en> accessed 12 December 2016

HRChBH (Bosnia-Herzegovina), 'Annual Report 2002' (2002) <http://www.hrc.ba/ ENGLISH/annual_report/2002/annual_report.htm> accessed 12 January 2016

The Court of Bosnia Herzegovina, 'Rulebook on Public Access to Information Under the Court's Control and Community Outreach' (2014) <http://www.sudbih.gov.ba/stranica/24/pregled?slug=pristup-informacijama> accessed 12 July 2016

Canada

Canada National Defence, *Law of Armed Conflict at the Operational and Tactical Level (Canada Joint Doctrine Manual)* (Office of the Judge Advocate General 2001)

Government of Canada, 'Comments by the Government of Canada – HRCee, Draft General Comment No 35 (Article 9)' (2014)

France

'Circulaire n°126/DEF/EMA/ESMG/JUROPS du 2 février 2010 relative au bureau national de renseignements sur les prisonniers de guerre'

Guatemala

Guatemala Commission for Historical Clarification, 'Memory of Silence. Report of the Commission for Historical Clarification: Conclusions and Recommendations' (1998)

Guatemala, 'Posición Inicial Del Gobierno de La República Ante El Informe Y Las Recomendaciones de La Comisión de Esclarecimiento Histórico' (16 March 1999) <http://pudl.princeton.edu/sheetreader.php?obj=c247ds93x> accessed 12 July 2016

Japan

Japan, 'Japan's Comments on the Draft General Comment No.35 on Article 9 of the ICCPR' (2014)

Mexico

Mexico, *Manual de Derecho Internacional Humanitario Para El Ejercito Y La Fuerza Aérea Mexicanos* (Ministry of National Defence 2009)

Peru

Truth and Reconciliation Commission (Peru), 'Annex 5 "Iniciativa Sobre Personas Desaparecidas Conformada Por La CVR, La Defensoría Del Pueblo, La Coordinadora Nacional de Derechos Humanos, Y El CICR" – Final Report' (2003) <http://www.cverdad.org.pe/ingles/ifinal/index.php> accessed 29 December 2016

——, 'General Conclusions – Final Report' (2003) <http://www.cverdad.org.pe/ingles/ifinal/conclusiones.php> accessed 29 December 2016

——, 'Missing Persons – Do You Know Anything about Them? – Initiative on Missing Persons' (*Truth and Reconciliation*) <http://www.cverdad.org.pe/ingles/desaparecidos/desaparecidos.php> accessed 29 December 2016

South Africa

Department of Justice and Constitutional Development (South Africa), 'Exhumation Policy: Cases of Missing Persons Reported to the Truth and Reconciliation Commission (TRC)' (2008) Notice 1539

The UK

Government of the United Kingdom of Great Britain and Northern Ireland, 'Observations by the Government of the United Kingdom of Great Britain and Northern Ireland on Draft General Comment 35 on Article 9 of the ICCPR – Liberty and Security of Person' (2014)

UK Ministry of Defence, *The Manual of the Law of Armed Conflict* (OUP Oxford 2004)

UK Ministry of Defence, *The Manual of the Law of Armed Conflict* (OUP Oxford 2005)

Timor-Leste

Commission for Reception, Truth, and Reconciliation Timor-Leste (CAVR), 'Chega! The Report of the Commission for Reception, Truth, and Reconciliation Timor-Leste. Executive Summary' (2005)

Commission of Truth and Friendship (CTF) – Indonesia-Timor-Leste, 'Final Report' (2008)

USA

'Note Verbale Dated 20 June 2006 from the Permanent Mission of the United States of America to the UN Office at Geneva Addressed to the Secretariat of the Human Rights Council (Geneva)' (2006) UN Doc A/HRC/1/G/1

Oceans Law and Policy Department (US), *Annotated Supplement to the Commander's Handbook on the Law of Naval Operations* (Center for Naval Warfare Studies, Naval War College 1997)

USA, 'Observations of the United States of America on the HRCee's General Comment 31 (Nature of the General Legal Obligation Imposed on States Parties to the Covenant)' (2007)

——, 'Observations of the United States of America on the HRCee's Draft General Comment 35: Article 9' (2014)

USA Department of Defence. Instruction, No. 1000.1, 16 April 2012, Incorporating Change 1, 9 June 2014

USA Department of State, 'Law of War Conference: US Proposal for a New Article on Missing and Dead (Electronic Telegram Sent to Various US Embassies) – Declassified Document – Released by Wikileaks' (6 March 1974)

—— – Bureau of Democracy, Human Rights, and Labor, 'Kosovo Missing Persons: OMPF Requests USG Funding for Technical Staff' (2006) 06PRISTINA1091_a <https://wikileaks.org/plusd/cables/06PRISTINA1091_a.html> accessed 12 January 2017

Miscellaneous

'Statement on the issue of Missing Migrants by Representatives of Cyprus, Greece, Italy, and Malta at the Conclusion of their Meeting in Rome on 11 June 2018', 11 June 2018 (Rome, Italy) https://www.icmp.int/?resources=statement-on-the-issue-of-missing-migrants-by-representatives-of-cyprus-greece-italy-and-malta-at-the-conclusion-of-their-meeting-in-rome-on-11-june-2018 accessed 30 July 2018.

BIBLIOGRAPHY

MONOGRAPHS

Abels D, Prisoners of the International Community: The Legal Position of Persons Detained at International Criminal Tribunals (Springer Science & Business Media 2012)

Akandji-Kombe J-F, Positive Obligations under the European Convention on Human Rights. A Guide to the Implementation of the European Convention on Human Rights (Council of Europe 2007)

Alston P and Goodman R, International Human Rights (Oxford University Press 2012)

Arai Y, *The Law of Occupation: Continuity and Change of International Humanitarian Law, and Its Interaction With International Human Rights Law* (Martinus Nijhoff Publishers 2009)

Ballin MFHH, *Anticipative Criminal Investigation: Theory and Counterterrorism Practice in the Netherlands and the United States* (Springer Science & Business Media 2012)

Bell C, *On the Law of Peace: Peace Agreements and the Lex Pacificatoria* (Oxford University Press 2008)

——, *Peace Agreements and Human Rights* (Oxford University Press 2003)

Bellal A, *The War Report. Armed Conflicts in 2016* (The Geneva Academy of International Humanitarian Law and Human Rights 2017)

Bettati M, *Droit Humanitaire* (Dalloz 2012)

Bordwell P, *The Law of War Between Belligerents: A History and Commentary* (Callaghan & Company 1908)

Bothe M and others, *New Rules for Victims of Armed Conflicts: Commentary on the Two 1977 Protocols Additional to the Geneva Conventions of 1949* (Second Edition, Martinus Nijhoff Publishers 2013)

——, Partsch KJ and Solf WA, *New Rules for Victims of Armed Conflicts: Commentary on the Two 1977 Protocols Additional to the Geneva Conventions of 1949* (Martinus Nijhoff Publishers 1982)

Bugnion F, *The International Committee of the Red Cross and the Protection of War Victims* (Macmillan Education 2003)

Burbano Herrera C, *Provisional Measures in the Case Law of the Inter-American Court of Human Rights* (Intersentia ; Portland, OR 2010)

Burgorgue-Larsen L, de Torres AU and Greenstein R, *The Inter-American Court of Human Rights: Case Law and Commentary* (Oxford University Press 2011)

Calogeropoulos-Stratis A., *Droit Humanitaire et Droits de L'homme – La Protection de La Personne En Période de Conflit Armé* (UHEI, Sijthoff 1980)

Cançado Trindade AA, *Judge Antônio A. Cançado Trindade. The Construction of a Humanized International Law: A Collection of Individual Opinions (1991-2013)* (Brill-Nijhoff 2014)

Cassese A, *International Law* (Oxford University Press 2005)

——, *International Criminal Law* (2nd edn, Oxford University Press 2008)

Castrén E, *Civil War* (Suomalainen tiedeakatemia 1966)

Cheng B, *General Principles of Law as Applied by International Courts and Tribunals* (Cambridge University Press 1994)

Clapham A, *Human Rights Obligations of Non-State Actors* (Oxford University Press 2006)

Conforti B, *The Law and Practice of the United Nations* (Martinus Nijhoff Publishers 2005)

Congram D (ed), *Missing Persons. Multidisciplinary Perspectives on the Disappeared* (Canadian Scholars' Press 2016)

d'Aspremont J and de Hemptinne J, *Droit International Humanitaire: Thèmes Choisis* (Pedone 2012)

Daillier P, Pellet A and Nguyen Quoc Dinh, *Droit International Public* (7e éd, LGDJ 2009)

David E, *Principes de droit des conflits armés* (III, Bruylant 2002)

——, *Principes de droit des conflits armés* (IV, Bruylant 2008)

Davis J, Seeking Human Rights Justice in Latin America. Truth, Extra-Territorial Courts, and the Process of Justice (Cambridge University Press 2015)

De Brabandere E, *Post-Conflict Administrations in International Law: International Territorial Administration, Transitional Authority, and Foreign Occupation in Theory and Practice* (Martinus Nijhoff Publishers 2009)

Debuf EE, *Captured in War: Lawful Internment in Armed Conflict* (A Pedone 2013)

Delupis ID, *The Law of War* (Cambridge University Press 2000)

Detrick S, *A Commentary on the United Nations Convention on the Rights of the Child* (Martinus Nijhoff Publishers 1999)

de Vattel E, *The Law of Nations: Or, Principles of the Law of Nature Applied to the Conduct and Affairs of Nations and Sovereigns* (GG and J Robinson 1797)

de Wet E, *The Chapter VII Powers of the United Nations Security Council* (Hart Publishing 2004)

Diaz D and McCann VL, *Tracking Humans: A Fundamental Approach to Finding Missing Persons, Insurgents, Guerrillas, and Fugitives from the Law* (Lyons Press 2013)

Dixon M, *Textbook on International Law* (Oxford University Press 2013)

Doswald-Beck L, *Human Rights in Times of Conflict and Terrorism* (Oxford University Press 2011)

Dunant H, *Un souvenir de Solferino* (anastatic reprint), Slatkine 1980)

Đurović G, 'L'Agence centrale de recherches du Comité international de la Croix-rouge : activité du CICR en vue du soulagement des souffrances morales des victimes de guerre' (University of Geneva – Institut Henry Dunant 1981)

Edkins J, *Missing: Persons and Politics* (Cornell University Press 2011)

——, Trauma and the Memory of Politics (Cambridge University Press 2003)

Fetherston AB, *Towards a Theory of United Nations Peacekeeping* (Springer 1994)

Freeman M, *Truth Commissions and Procedural Fairness* (Cambridge University Press 2006)

Funk TM, *Victims' Rights and Advocacy at the International Criminal Court* (Oxford University Press 2010)

Galtung J, *Peace by Peaceful Means: Peace and Conflict, Development and Civilization* (SAGE 1996)

Giacca G, *Economic, Social, and Cultural Rights in Armed Conflict* (Oxford University Press 2014)

Ginsburgs G, *Soviet Citizenship Law*, vol 1 (A W Sijthoff 1968)

—— and Slusser RM, *A Calendar of Soviet Treaties: 1958-1973* (Sijthoff & Noordhoff International Publishers BV 1981)

Gouttes PD, *Commentaire de la Convention de Genève du 27 juillet 1929* (Comité International de la Croix-Rouge 1930)

Grignon J, *L'applicabilité Temporelle Du Droit International Humanitaire* (Schulthess éd romandes 2014)

Guggenheim P and Bindschedler-Robert D, *Traité de Droit International Public: Avec Mention de La Pratique Internationale et Suisse*, vol 1 (Librairie Georg & Cie 1953)

Gutter J, *Thematic Procedures of the United Nations Commission on Human Rights and International Law: In Search of a Sense of Community* (Intersentia 2006)

Harouel-Bureloup V, *Traité de Droit Humanitaire* (Presses Universitaires de France – PUF 2005)

Hart HLA, *The Concept of Law* (2nd with a new Postscript, Oxford University Press 1994)

Hayner PB, *Unspeakable Truths: Transitional Justice and the Challenge of Truth Commissions* (2nd edition, Routledge 2010)

Hazan P, *Judging War, Judging History. Behind Truth and Reconciliation* (Stanford University Press 2010)

Henckaerts J-M and Doswald-Beck L, *Customary International Humanitarian Law: Practice*, vol II (Cambridge University Press 2005)

——, *Customary International Humanitarian Law: Volume 1, Rules* (Cambridge University Press 2005)

Higgins R, *Problems and Process: International Law and How We Use It* (Oxford University Press 1995)

——, *United Nations Peacekeeping, 1946-1967: Documents and Commentary*, vol 4 (Oxford University Press 1980)

Hirsch M, *The Responsibility of International Organizations Toward Third Parties: Some Basic Principles* (Martinus Nijhoff Publishers 1995)

Joseph S and Castan M, International Covenant on Civil and Political Rights: Cases, Materials, and Commentary (3rd ed, Oxford University Press 2013)

Kälin W, *Guiding Principles on Internal Displacement. Annotations* (The American Society of International Law 2008)

—— and Künzli J, *The Law of International Human Rights Protection* (Oxford University Press 2009)

Kalshoven F and Zegveld L, *Constraints on the Waging of War: An Introduction to International Humanitarian Law* (Cambridge University Press 2011)

Klafkowski A, 'Les Formes de Cessation de L'état de Guerre En Droit International', *Collected Courses of The Hague Academy of International Law*, vols 217–286 (Sijthoff 1979)

Klein E, 'Individual Reparation Claims under the International Covenant on Civil and Political Rights: The Practice of the Human Rights Committee' in Christian Tomuschat and Albrecht Randelzhofer (eds), *State responsibility and the individual: reparation in instances of grave violations of human rights* (Martinus Nijhoff Publishers 1999)

Kogan V, 'Implementing the Judgments of the European Court of Human Rights from the North Caucasus: A Closing Window for Accountability or a Continuing Process of Transitional Justice?' in N Szablewska and SD Bachmann (eds), *Current issues in Transitional Justice*, vol 4 (Springer 2015)

Kolb R, *Ius in bello: le droit international des conflits armés; précis* (II, Helbing & Lichtenhahn 2009)

Kouhene ME, *Les Garanties Fondamentales de la Personne en Droit Humanitaire et Droits de l'Homme* (Martinus Nijhoff Publishers 1986)

Koutroulis V, *Le Début et La Fin de L'application Du Droit de L'occupation* (Pedone 2010)

Kovras I, *Truth Recovery and Transitional Justice: Deferring Human Rights Issues* (Routledge 2014)

Krähenmann S, Positive Obligations in Human Rights Treaties (PhD Dissertation No. 949) (Graduate Institute of International and Development Studies 2012)

Kritz NJ, *Transitional Justice: How Emerging Democracies Reckon with Former Regimes*, vol III (United States Institute of Peace Press 1995)

Kyriakou N, 'An Affront to the Conscience of Humanity: Enforced Disappearance in International Human Rights Law (PhD Thesis)' (European University Institute – Department of Law 2012)

Lauterpacht H, *The Development of International Law by the International Court* (Cambridge University Press 1982)

Lederach JP, *Building Peace: Sustainable Reconciliation in Divided Societies* (United States Institute of Peace Press 1997)

Meron T, *The Making of International Criminal Justice: A View from the Bench: Selected Speeches* (Oxford University Press 2011)

Morewitz S and Sturdy Colls C (eds), *Handbook of Missing Persons* (Springer 2016)

Mosse GL, *Fallen Soldiers: Reshaping the Memory of the World Wars* (Oxford University Press 1991)

Mowbray AR, Cases, Materials, and Commentary on the European Convention on Human Rights (3rd ed, Oxford University Press 2012)

——, The Development of Positive Obligations under the European Convention on Human Rights by the European Court of Human Rights (Hart Publishing 2004)

Murray R, *The African Commission on Human and People's Rights and International Law* (Hart Publishing 2000)

Necatigil ZM, *The Cyprus Question and the Turkish Position in International Law* (Oxford University Press 1993)

Nowak M, *U.N. Covenant on Civil and Political Rights: CCPR Commentary* (2nd rev ed, NP Engel 2005)

Oberleitner G, *Human Rights in Armed Conflict: Law, Practice, Policy* (Cambridge University Press 2015)

Oppenheim LFL-, *International Law: A Treatise /Vol 2, Disputes, War and Neutrality* (Hersch Lauterpacht ed, 7th ed, [5th impr], Longmans Green 1963)

Orend B, *War and International Justice: A Kantian Perspective* (Wilfrid Laurier Univ Press 2006)

Ott L, *Enforced Disappearance in International Law* (Intersentia 2011)

Ovey C and White R, Jacobs and White: The European Convention on Human Rights (4 edition, Oxford University Press 2006)

Paenson I, *Manual of the Terminology of the Law of Armed Conflicts and of International Humanitarian Organizations* (Bruylant and Martinus Nijhoff Publishers 1989)

Parlett K, *The Individual in the International Legal System: Continuity and Change in International Law* (Cambridge University Press 2011)

Pauwelyn J, *Conflict of Norms in Public International Law: How WTO Law Relates to Other Rules of International Law* (Cambridge University Press 2003)

Pérez Solla MF, *Enforced Disappearances in International Human Rights* (McFarland & Co, Publishers 2006)

Pictet JS, *Development and Principles of International Humanitarian Law: Course Given in July 1982 at the University of Strasbourg as Part of the Courses Organized by the International Institute of Human Rights* (Martinus Nijhoff Publishers 1985)

——, *Les principes du droit international humanitaire* (Comité international de la Croix-Rouge 1966)

——, *Humanitarian Law and the Protection of War Victims* (Henry Dunant Institute 1975)

—— (ed), *The Geneva Conventions of 12 August 1949: Commentary*, vol I (ICRC 1952)

—— (ed), *The Geneva Conventions of 12 August 1949: Commentary*, vol IV (ICRC 1958)

—— (ed), *The Geneva Conventions of 12 August 1949: Commentary*, vol II (ICRC 1960)

—— (ed), *The Geneva Conventions of 12 August 1949: Commentary*, vol III (ICRC 1960)

Provost R, *International Human Rights and Humanitarian Law* (Cambridge University Press 2004)

Rainey B, Wicks E and Ovey C, *The European Convention on Human Rights* (6 edition, Oxford University Press 2014)

Ramcharan BG, *Human Rights and U.N. Peace Operations: Yugoslavia* (Martinus Nijhoff Publishers 2011)

Rieter ER, *Preventing Irreparable Harm: Provisional Measures in International Human Rights Adjudication* (Intersentia 2010)

Robben A, *Political Violence and Trauma in Argentina* (Univ. of Pennsylvania Press 2005)

Robinson N, *United Nations Convention on the Declaration of Death of Missing Persons: A Commentary* (Institute of Jewish Affairs – World Jewish Congress 1951)

Robins S, *Families of the Missing. A Test for Contemporary Approaches to Transitional Justice* (Routledge 2013)

Rousseau Ch., *Le Droit des conflits armés* (Editions A. Pedone 1983)

Rousseau J-J, *Du contrat social ou principes du droit politique*, vol Livre I (Le Prieur, Libraire 1791)

Sadat-Akhavi A, *Methods of Resolving Conflicts Between Treaties* (Martinus Nijhoff Publishers 2003)

Saint Augustine/Outler, *Confessions and Enchiridion* (Albert Cook ed, Albert Cook tr, SCM Press 1955)

Sandoz Y and others, *Commentary on the Additional Protocols: Of 8 June 1977 to the Geneva Conventions of 12 August 1949* (Martinus Nijhoff Publishers 1987)

Sassòli M, Bouvier AA and Quintin A, *How Does Law Protect in War?: Cases, Documents, and Teaching Materials on Contemporary Practice in International Humanitarian Law. Vol. I – Outline of International Humanitarian Law. III (Online Version)* (ICRC 2011)

——, A, *How Does Law Protect in War?: Cases, Documents, and Teaching Materials on Contemporary Practice in International Humanitarian Law*, vol I-Outline of International Humanitarian Law (III, ICRC 2011)

Schabas WA, *The European Convention on Human Rights: A Commentary* (Oxford University Press 2015)

Schwarzenberger G, *International Law: As Applied by International Courts and Tribunals /. Vol. 2, The Law of Armed Conflict* (Stevens 1968)

——, *The Fundamental Principles of International Law*, vol 87–Collected Courses of the Hague Academy of International Law (Brill | Nijhoff 1955)

Scovazzi T and Citroni G, *The Struggle against Enforced Disappearance and the 2007 United Nations Convention* (Martinus Nijhoff Publishers 2007)

Seibert-Fohr A, Prosecuting Serious Human Rights Violations (Oxford University Press 2009)

Shalev Greene K and Alys L (eds), *Missing Persons. A Handbook of Research* (Routledge 2017)

Shaw MN, *International Law* (6th edn, Cambridge University Press 2008)

Shelton D, Remedies in International Human Rights Law (Oxford University Press 2015)

Sivakumaran S, *The Law of Non-International Armed Conflict* (Oxford University Press 2012)

Smit A, *The Property Rights of Refugees and Internally Displaced Persons: Beyond Restitution* (Routledge 2012)

Smith RKM, *Textbook on International Human Rights* (OUP Oxford 2012)

Solis GD, *The Law of Armed Conflict: International Humanitarian Law in War* (Cambridge University Press 2010)

Stahn C, *The Law and Practice of International Territorial Administration: Versailles to Iraq and Beyond* (Cambridge University Press 2008)

Steiner HJ, Alston P and Goodman R, *International Human Rights in Context: Law, Politics, Morals* (3 edition, Oxford University Press 2007)

Sudre F, Les grands arrêts de la Cour européenne des droits de l'homme (Presses universitaires de France 2003)

Teitel R, *Transitional Justice* (Oxford University Press 2002)

Thucydide (translated by Steven Lattimore), *The Peloponnesian War* (Hackett Publishing 1998)

Thürer D, *International Humanitarian Law: Theory, Practice, Context* (Martinus Nijhoff Publishers 2011)

Tomuschat C, *International Law: Ensuring the Survival of Mankind on the Eve of a New Century: General Course on Public International Law*, vol 281 (1999) (Brill, Nijhoff 2001)

Vermeulen ML, *Enforced Disappearance: Determining State Responsibility under the International Convention for the Protection of All Persons from Enforced Disappearance* (Intersentia 2012)

Villiger ME, Commentary on the 1969 Vienna Convention on the Law of Treaties (Martinus Nijhoff Publishers 2009)

Xenos D, The Positive Obligations of the State under the European Convention of Human Rights (Routledge 2012)

Yildiz K and Breau S, The Kurdish Conflict: International Humanitarian Law and Post-Conflict Mechanisms (Routledge 2010)

Walzer M, *Just and Unjust Wars: A Moral Argument With Historical Illustrations* (3rd edn, Basic Books 2000)

White RCA and Ovey C, *Jacobs, White and Ovey: The European Convention on Human Rights* (Oxford University Press 2010)

Wilcox ER, *Digest of United States Practice in International Law, 2009* (Oxford University Press – USA 2011)

Willemin G, Heacock R and Freymond J (eds), *The International Committee of the Red Cross* (M Nijhoff 1984)

Wittman L, *The Tomb of the Unknown Soldier, Modern Mourning, and the Reinvention of the Mystical Body* (University of Toronto Press 2011)

Zwanenburg MC, *Accountability Of Peace Support Operations* (Martinus Nijhoff Publishers 2005)

Zyberi G, *The Humanitarian Face of the International Court of Justice: Its Contribution to Interpreting and Developing International Human Rights and Humanitarian Law Rules and Principles* (Intersentia 2008)

Zorgbibe C, *La Guerre Civile* (Presses univ de France 1975)

SECTIONS IN BOOKS/ANTHOLOGIES

Abi-Saab G, 'Human Rights and Humanitarian Law in Internal Conflicts' in Daniel Warner (ed), *Human Rights and Humanitarian Law. The quest for Universality*, vol 29 (Martinus Nijhoff Publishers 1997)

——,'The Specificities of Humanitarian Law' in Christophe Swinarski (ed), *Studies and Essays on International Humanitarian Law and Red Cross Principles in Honour of Jean Pictet* (Martinus Nijhoff Publishers 1984)

Aguilar A., 'Procedimiento Que Debe Aplicar La Comisión Interamericana de Derechos Humanos En El Examen de Las Peticiones O Comunicaciones Individuales Sobre Presuntas Violaciones de Derechos Humanos' in Carlos Alberto Dunshee de Abranches and Inter-American Commission on Human Rights (eds), *Derechos humanos en las Américas: homenaje a la memoria de Carlos A. Dunshee de Abranches* (Organización de los Estados Americanos, 1984)

Akande D, 'Classification of Armed Conflicts: Relevant Legal Concepts' in Elizabeth Wilmshurst (ed), *International Law and the Classification of Conflicts* (Oxford University Press 2012)

Akandji-Kombe J-F, 'L'obligation Positive D'enquête Sur Le Terrain de L'article 3 CEDH' in Catherine-Amélie Chassin (ed), La portée de l'article 3 de la Convention européenne des droits de l'homme (Bruylant 2006)

Aldrich G, 'Why the United States of America Should Ratify Additional Protocol I' in Astrid JM Delissen and Gerard J Tanja (eds), *Humanitarian Law of armed conflict. Challenges ahead. Essays in honour of Frits Kalshoven* (Martinus Nijhoff Publ. 1991)

Alleweldt R, 'Preamble to the 1951 Convention' in Andreas Zimmermann, Jonas Dörschner and Felix Machts (eds), *The 1951 Convention Relating to the Status of Refugees and Its 1967 Protocol: A Commentary* (Oxford University Press 2011)

Bartels R, 'From Jus in Bello to Jus Post Bellum: When Do Non-International Armed Conflicts End?' in Carsten Stahn, Jennifer S Easterday and Jens Iverson (eds), *Jus Post Bellum: Mapping the normative Foundations* (Oxford University Press 2014)

Bassiouni MC, 'Accountability for Violations of International Humanitarian Law and Other Serious Violations of Human Rights', in MC Bassiouni (ed), *Post Conflict*

Justice (Transnational Publishers 2002)

Baxter R, 'Humanitarian Law or Humanitarian Politics? The 1974 Diplomatic Conference on Humanitarian Law' in Theodor Meron and others (eds), *Humanizing the Laws of War: Selected Writings of Richard Baxter* (Oxford University Press 2013)

Bell C, 'Post-Conflict Accountability and the Reshaping of Human Rights and Humanitarian Law' in Orna Ben-Naftali (ed), *International Humanitarian Law and International Human Rights Law* (Oxford University Press 2011)

Bell C, 'Of Jus Post Bellum and Lex Pacificatoria What's in a Name?' in Carsten Stahn, Jennifer S Easterday and Jens Iverson (eds), *Jus Post Bellum: Mapping the normative Foundations* (Oxford University Press 2014)

——, 'Post-Conflict Accountability and the Reshaping of Human Rights and Humanitarian Law' in Orna Ben-Naftali (ed), *International Humanitarian Law and International Human Rights Law* (Oxford University Press 2011)

Bostedt F, 'The African Court on Human and Peoples' Rights and the Use of Provisional Measures for the Protection of the Civilian Population in Armed Conflict Situations' in Philipp Ambach and others (eds), *The protection of non-combatants during armed conflict and safeguarding the rights of victims in post-conflict society: essays in honour of the life and work of Joakim Dungel* (Martinus Nijhoff Publishers 2015)

Bothe M, 'The Law of Neutrality' in Dieter Fleck and Michael Bothe (eds), *The Handbook of International Humanitarian Law* (Oxford University Press 2008)

Boutruche T, 'Missing and Dead Persons' in Rudiger Wolfrum (ed), *The Max Planck Encyclopedia of Public International Law – Ozone Layer, international protection*, vol VII (Oxford University Press 2012)

——, 'Seeking the Truth About Serious International Human Rights and Humanitarian Law Violations: The Various Facets of a Cardinal Notion of Transitional Justice' in Mariëlle Matthee, Brigit Toebes and Marcel Brus (eds), *Armed Conflict and International Law: In Search of the Human Face* (T M C Asser Press 2013)

Buergenthal T, 'The U.N. Human Rights Committee' in Armin von Bogdandy, Rüdiger Wolfrum and Christiane E Philipp (eds), Max Planck Yearbook of United Nations Law Online, vol 5 (Martinus Nijhoff Publishers 2001)

Burbano-Herrera C, 'The Inter-American Court of Human Rights and Its Role in Preventing Violations of Human Rights through Provisional Measures' in Yves Haeck, Oswaldo Ruiz-Chiriboga and Clara Burbano-Herrera (eds), *The Inter-American Court of Human Rights: Theory and Practice, Present and Future* (Intersentia 2015

——, Viljoen F and Haeck Y, 'Preventing Human Rights Violations: Recommendations for Enhancing the Effectiveness of Interim Measures Before the Inter-American and African Human Rights Commissions' in Clara Burbano Herrera and others (eds), *The Realisation of Human Rights: When Theory meets Practice – Studies in Honour of Leo Zwaak* (Intersentia 2013)

Burgorgue-Larsen L, 'La Prohibition de La Torture et ses Équivalents dans le Système Interaméricain des Droits de L'homme' in Catherine-Amélie Chassin (dir.), La Portée de l'Article 3 de la Convention Européenne des droits de l'homme (Bruylant 2006)

Buyse A (ed), Margins of Conflict. The ECHR and Transitions to and From Armed Conflict (Intersentia 2010)

Cançado Trindade AA, 'Quelques reflexions sur l'humanité comme sujet du droit international' in Denis Alland and others (dir.), *Unité et diversité du droit international/Unity and Diversity of International Law: Ecrits en l'honneur du Professeur Pierre-Marie Dupuy/Essays in Honour of Professor Pierre-Marie Dupuy*

(Martinus Nijhoff Publishers 2014)

——, 'Some Reflections on the Principle of Humanity in Its Wide Dimension' in Gloria Gaggioli and Robert Kolb (eds), *Research Handbook on Human Rights and Humanitarian Law* (Edward Elgar Publishing 2013)

Cassia P, 'Recognition and Emotion. Exhumations of Missing Persons in Cyprus' in Yannis Papadakis, Nicos Peristianis and Gisela Welz (eds), *Divided Cyprus. Modernity, History, and an Island in Conflict* (Indiana University Press 2006)

Cassia PS, '"Waiting for Ulysses": The Committee for Missing Persons' in Oliver P Richmond and James Ker-Lindsay (eds), *The Work of the UN in Cyprus* (Palgrave Macmillan UK 2001)

Chetail V, 'Armed Conflict and Forced Migration: A Systemic Approach to International Humanitarian Law, Refugee Law and Human Rights Law' in Paola Gaeta and Andrew Clapham (eds) (Oxford University Press 2014)

——, 'Droit International Général et Droit International Humanitaire: Retour Aux Sources' in Vincent Chetail (ed), *Permanence et mutations du droit des conflits armés* (Bruylant 2013)

——, 'Introduction: Post-Conflict Peacebuilding — Ambiguity and Identity' in Vincent Chetail (ed), *Post-conflict Peacebuilding: a Lexicon* (Oxford University Press 2009)

——, 'The Legal Personality of Multinational Corporations, State Responsibility and Due Diligence: The Way Forward' in Vincent Chetail and others (eds), Unité et diversité du droit international/Unity and Diversity of International Law. Essays in Honour of Prof. Pierre-Marie Dupuy (Brill | Nijhoff 2014)

Clapham A, 'The Complex Relationship between the Geneva Conventions and International Human Rights Law' in Andrew Clapham, Paola Gaeta and Marco Sassòli (eds), *The 1949 Geneva Conventions: A Commentary: A Commentary* (Oxford University Press 2015)

——, 'The Concept of International Armed Conflict' in Andrew Clapham, Paola Gaeta and Marco Sassòli (eds), *The 1949 Geneva Conventions: A Commentary: A Commentary* (Oxford University Press 2015)

Combacau J, 'L'écoulement du temps' in Société française pour le droit international. Colloque (ed), *Le droit international et le temps : Colloque de Paris* (APedone 2001)

Conte A, 'Limitations to and Derogations from Covenant Rights' in Alex Conte and Richard Burchill (eds), *Defining Civil and Political Rights: The Jurisprudence of the United Nations Human Rights Committee* (Routledge 2016)

Corcuera S, 'L'expérience Du Groupe de Travail Sur Les Disparitions Forcées' in Emmanuel Decaux and Olivier De Frouville (eds), *La Convention pour la Protection de Toutes les Personnes Contre les Disparitions Forcées* (Bruylant 2009)

Corzo L, 'Commissions to Resolve the Phenomenon of Missing Persons: Case Studies. Guatemala Case Study' in María Teresa Dutli and Noreen Majeed (eds), *Report of the Second Universal Meeting of National Committees on International Humanitarian Law — Geneva, 19–21 March 2007. Legal Measures and Mechanisms to Prevent Disappearances, to Establish the Fate of Missing Persons, and to Assist Their Families* (ICRC 2007)

d'Aspremont, J and Tranchez E, 'The Quest for a Non-Conflictual Coexistence of International Human Rights Law and Humanitarian Law: Which Role for the Lex Specialis Principle?' in Gloria Gaggioli and Robert Kolb (eds), *Research Handbook on Human Rights and Humanitarian Law* (Edwar Elgar Publishing 2013)

Debons D, Fleury A and Pitteloud J-F (eds), *Katyn et la Suisse : experts et expertises médicales dans les crises humanitaires 1920-2007 = Katyn and Switzerland : forensic investigators and investigations in humanitarian crises 1920-2007* (Georg Editeur 2009)

De Brabandere E, 'The Concept of Jus Post Bellum in International Law: A Normative Critique' in Carsten Stahn, Jennifer S Easterday and Jens Iverson (eds), *Jus Post Bellum: Mapping the normative Foundations* (Oxford University Press 2014)

deGuzman MM, 'Crimes against Humanity' in William Schabas and Nadia Bernaz (eds), *Routledge handbook of international criminal law* (Routledge 2011)

De Pauw M, 'The Inter-American Court of Human Rights and the Interpretative Method of External Referencing: Regional Consensus v. Universality' in Yves Haeck, Oswaldo Ruiz-Chiriboga and Clara Burbano-Herrera (eds), The Inter-American Court of Human Rights: Theory and Practice, Present and Future (Intersentia 2015)

Dinstein Y, 'The Initiation, Suspension and Termination of War' in Michael N Schmitt (ed), *International Law Across the Spectrum of Conflict: essays in honour of Professor L.C. Green on the occasion of his eightieth birthday*, vol 75 (Naval War College 2000)

——, 'The Principle of Proportionality' in Kjetil Mujezinović Larsen, Camilla Guldahl Cooper and Gro Nystuen (eds), *Searching for a 'Principle of Humanity' in International Humanitarian Law* (Cambridge University Press 2013)

Donat-Cattin D, 'Article 68 – Protection of Victims and Witnesses and Their Participation in the Proceedings' in Otto Triffterer and Kai Ambos (eds), *Commentary on the Rome Statute of the International Criminal Court: Observers' Notes, Article by Article* (C H Beck 2008)

——, 'Article 75 – Reparations to Victims' in Otto Triffterer and Kai Ambos (eds), *Commentary on the Rome Statute of the International Criminal Court: Observers' Notes, Article by Article* (C H Beck 2008)

Drawdy SM and Katzmarzyk C, 'The Missing Files: The Experience of the International Committee of the Red Cross' in Derek Congram (ed), *Missing Persons: Multidisciplinary Perspectives on the Disappeared* (Canadian Scholars' Press 2016)

Dumont H and Hachez I, 'Les Obligations Positives Déduites du Droit International des Droits de L'homme : Dans Quelles Limites?' in Yves Cartuyvels and et al. (eds), Les droits de l'homme, bouclier ou épée du droit pénal? (Facultés Universitaires Saint-Louis 2007)

Dupuy P-M, 'Evolutionary Interpretation of Treaties: Between Memory and Prophecy' in Enzo Cannizzaro (ed), The Law of Treaties Beyond the Vienna Convention (Oxford University Press 2011)

Easterday J, 'Peace Agreements as a Framework for Jus Post Bellum' in Carsten Stahn, Jennifer S Easterday and Jens Iverson (eds), *Jus Post Bellum: Mapping the normative Foundations* (Oxford University Press 2014)

Elliott HW, 'Identification' in Roy Gutman and David Rieff (eds), *Crimes of war: what the public should know* (W W Norton & Company 1999)

Eser A, 'Procedural Structure and Features of International Criminal Justice: Lessons from the ICTY' in Bert Swart, Alexander Zahar and Göran Sluiter (eds), *The legacy of the International Criminal Tribunal for the Former Yugoslavia* (Oxford University Press 2011)

Ferstman C, 'International Criminal Law and Victims' Rights' in William Schabas and Nadia Bernaz (eds), *Routledge handbook of international criminal law* (Routledge 2011)

Fischer H, 'Protection of Prisoners of War' in Dieter Fleck and Michael Bothe (eds), *The Handbook of International Humanitarian Law* (Oxford University Press 2008)

Freeman M and Djukić D, 'Jus Post Bellum and Transitional Justice' in Carsten Stahn and Jann K Kleffner (eds), *Jus Post Bellum: Towards a Law of Transition From Conflict to Peace* (Springer Verlag 2008)

Gaeta P, 'Are Victims of Serious Violations of International Humanitarian Law Entitled to Compensation?' in Orna Ben-Naftali (ed), *International Humanitarian Law and International Human Rights Law* (Oxford University Press 2011)

Gaggioli G, 'The Prohibition of Enforced Disappearances: A Meaningful Example of a Partial Merger between Human Rights Law and International Humanitarian Law' in Gloria Gaggioli and Robert Kolb (eds), *Research Handbook on Human Rights and Humanitarian Law* (Edward Elgar Publishing 2013)

Gaja G, 'General Principles of Law' in Rudiger Wolfrum (ed), *The Max Planck Encyclopedia of Public International Law*, vol III (Oxford University Press 2007)

Gallen J, 'Jus Post Bellum. An Interpretive Framework' in Carsten Stahn, Jennifer S Easterday and Jens Iverson (eds), *Jus Post Bellum: Mapping the normative Foundations* (Oxford University Press 2014)

Galtung J, 'Three Approaches to Peace: Peacekeeping, Peacemaking, and Peacebuilding' in Johan Galtung (ed), *Essays in Peace Research: War, Peace, Defense*, vol 2 (Christian Ejlers 1975)

Gavshon D, 'The Dead' in Andrew Clapham, Paola Gaeta and Marco Sassòli (eds), *The 1949 Geneva Conventions: A Commentary: A Commentary* (Oxford University Press 2015)

Giuffrida R, 'Subsidiarity Protection in International and European Law' in Pia Acconci and others (eds), *International Law and the Protection of Humanity. Essays in honor of Flavia Lattanzi*, vol 3 (Brill | Nijhoff 2016)

Gowlland-Debbas V and Pergantis V, 'Rule of Law' in Vincent Chetail (ed), *Post-conflict Peacebuilding: a Lexicon* (Oxford University Press 2009)

Graf-Brugère A-L, 'A Lex Favorabilis? Resolving Norm Conflicts between Human Rights Law and Humanitarian Law' in Gloria Gaggioli and Robert Kolb (eds), *Research Handbook on Human Rights and Humanitarian Law* (Edward Elgar Publishing 2013)

Grant S, 'Migration and Frontier Deaths: A Right to Identity' in Marie-Bénédicte Dembour and Tobias Kelly (eds), *Are human rights for migrants ?: critical reflections on the status of irregular migrants in Europe and the United States* (Routledge 2011)

Greenwood CJ, 'Scope of Application of Humanitarian Law' in Dieter Fleck and Michael Bothe (eds), *The Handbook of International Humanitarian Law* (Oxford University Press 2008)

Grossman CM, 'Disappearances' in Rudiger Wolfrum (ed), *The Max Planck Encyclopedia of Public International Law*, vol III (2013)

Guembe MJ and Olea H, 'No Justice, No Peace: Discussion of a Legal Framework Regarding the Demobilization of Non-State Armed Groups in Colombia' in Naomi Roht-Arriaza (ed), *Transitional justice in the twenty-first century: beyond truth versus justice* (Cambridge University Press 2006)

Haeck Y and Burbano-Herrera C, 'The Use of Interim Measures Issued by the European Court of Human Rights in Times of War or Internal Conflict' in Antoine Buyse (ed), *Margins of Conflict: The ECHR and Transitions to and from Armed Conflict* (Intersentia 2011)

Hall CK, 'Enforced Disappearance of Persons' in Otto Triffterer and Kai Ambos (eds), *Commentary on the Rome Statute of the International Criminal Court: Observers' Notes, Article by Article* (C H Beck 2008)

Hampson F, 'Other Areas of Customary Law in Relation to the Study' in Elizabeth Wilmshurst and Susan Breau (eds), *Perspectives on the ICRC study on customary international humanitarian law* (Cambridge University Press 2007)

Hazan P, 'The Changing Nature of the Debate on Peace vs. Justice' in Jonathan Sisson (ed), *Dealing with the Past in Post-Conflict Societies: Ten Years after the Peace Accords in Guatemala and Bosnia – Herzegovina* (Swisspeace 2007)

Henckaerts J-M and Wiesener C, 'Human Rights Obligations of Non-State Armed Groups: A Possible Contribution from Customary International Law?' in Robert Kolb and Gloria Gaggioli (eds), *Research Handbook on Human Rights and Humanitarian Law* (Edward Elgar Publishing 2013)

Hoffmeister F, 'Article 9 – Adoption of the Text' in Oliver Dörr and Kirsten Schmalenbach (eds), *Vienna Convention on the Law of Treaties: A Commentary* (Springer Science & Business Media 2011)

——, 'Article 11 – Means of Expressing Consent to Be Bound by a Treaty' in Oliver Dörr and Kirsten Schmalenbach (eds), *Vienna Convention on the Law of Treaties: A Commentary* (Springer Science & Business Media 2011)

Holder C, 'Truthfulness in Transition: The Value of Insisting on Experiential Adequacy' in Larry May and Elizabeth Edenberg (eds), *Jus Post Bellum and Transitional Justice* (Cambridge University Press 2013)

Hozic A, 'The Origins Of "post-Conflict"' in Keith Brown and Chip Gagnon (eds), *Post-conflict studies: an interdisciplinary approach* (Routledge 2014)

Iguyovwe R, 'The Inter-Play between International Humanitarian Law and International Human Rights Law' in Aldo Zammit Borda (ed), *International Humanitarian Law and the International Red Cross and Red Crescent Movement* (Routledge 2013)

Iverson J, 'Contrasting the Normative and Historical Foundations of Transitional Justice and Jus Post Bellum' in Carsten Stahn, Jennifer S Easterday and Jens Iverson (eds), *Jus Post Bellum: Mapping the normative Foundations* (Oxford University Press 2014)

——, Easterday J and Stahn C, 'Epilogue: Jus Post Bellum – Strategic Analysis and Future Directions' in Carsten Stahn, Jennifer S Easterday and Jens Iverson (eds), *Jus Post Bellum: Mapping the normative Foundations* (Oxford University Press 2014)

Janmyr M, 'Revisiting the Civilian and Humanitarian Character of Refugee Camps' in Jean-François Durieux and David Cantor (eds), *Refuge from Inhumanity: war refugees and international humanitarian law* (Martinus Nijhoff Publishers 2014)

Jorda C and de Hemptinne J, 'The Status and Role of the Victim' in Antonio Cassese, Paola Gaeta and John RWD Jones (eds), *The Rome Statute of the International Court: a Commentary*, vol II (Oxford University Press 2002)

Kleffner JK, 'Human Rights and International Humanitarian Law: General Issues' in Terry D Gill and Dieter Fleck (eds), *The Handbook of the International Law of Military Operations* (Oxford University Press 2011)

——, 'Introduction: From Here to There ... and the Law in the Middle' in Carsten Stahn and Jann K Kleffner (eds), *Jus Post Bellum: Towards a Law of Transition From Conflict to Peace* (Springer Verlag 2008)

——, 'Scope of Application of International Humanitarian Law' in Dieter Fleck and Michael Bothe (eds), *The Handbook of International Humanitarian Law* (Oxford University Press 2008)

——, 'Towards a Functional Conceptualization of the Temporal Scope of Jus Post Bellum' in Carsten Stahn, Jennifer S Easterday and Jens Iverson (eds), *Jus Post Bellum: Mapping the normative Foundations* (Oxford University Press 2014)

Klein P, 'International Organizations or Institutions, Decision-Making Process', *Max Planck Encyclopedia of Public International Law (Online)* (2007) <http://opil.ouplaw.com/view/10.1093/law:epil/9780199231690/law-9780199231690-e1709> accessed 25 January 2017.

Krähenmann S, 'Positive Obligations in Human Rights Law during Armed Conflicts' in Gloria Gaggioli and Robert Kolb (eds) (Edward Elgar Publishing 2013)

La Rosa A-M, 'The Right to Know and the Fight against Impunity' in María Teresa Dutli and Noreen Majeed (eds), *Report of the Second Universal Meeting of National Committees on International Humanitarian Law – Geneva, 19–21 March 2007. Legal Measures and Mechanisms to Prevent Disappearances, to Establish the Fate of Missing Persons, and to Assist Their Families* (ICRC 2007)

—— and Philippe X, 'Transitional Justice' in Vincent Chetail (ed), *Post-conflict Peacebuilding: a Lexicon* (Oxford University Press 2009)

Lesaffer R, 'Peace Treaties – International Law (Oxford Bibliographies)' (2015) <http://www.oxfordbibliographies.com/view/document/obo-9780199796953/obo-9780199796953-0120.xml> accessed 19 January 2017

Margueritte T, 'International Criminal Law and Human Rights' in William Schabas and Nadia Bernaz (eds), *Routledge handbook of international criminal law* (Routledge 2011)

Mathez P, 'L'Agence internationale des prisonniers de guerre (1914 – 1923): un patrimoine exceptionnel' in Sylvie Caucanas and others (eds), *Les prisonniers de guerre dans l'histoire: contacts entre peuples et cultures* (Éditions Privat 2003)

May L, 'Jus Post Bellum, Grotius, and Meionexia' in Carsten Stahn, Jennifer S Easterday and Jens Iverson (eds), *Jus Post Bellum: Mapping the normative Foundations* (Oxford University Press 2014)

—— and Edenberg E, 'Introduction' in Larry May and Elizabeth Edenberg (eds), *Jus Post Bellum and Transitional Justice* (Cambridge University Press 2013)

Mégret F, 'Nature of Obligations' in Sangeeta Shah and others (eds), *International Human Rights Law* (Oxford University Press 2010)

—— and Calderón J-PS, 'The Move towards a Victim-Centred Concept of Criminal Law and The "criminalization" of Inter-American Human Rights Law' in Yves Haeck, Oswaldo Ruiz-Chiriboga and Clara Burbano-Herrera (eds), The Inter-American Court of Human Rights: Theory and Practice, Present and Future (Intersentia 2015)

Meron T, 'Convergence of International Humanitarian Law and Human Rights Law' in Daniel Warner (ed), *Human Rights and Humanitarian Law. The quest for Universality*, vol 29 (Martinus Nijhoff Publishers 1997)

Milanović M, 'Norm Conflicts, International Humanitarian Law, and Human Rights Law' in Orna Ben-Naftali (ed), *International Humanitarian Law and International Human Rights Law – Pas de deux* (Oxford University Press 2011)

Milner L, 'The ICTY Legacy in Finding Missing Persons' in Richard H Steinberg (ed), *Assessing the Legacy of the ICTY* (Martinus Nijhoff Publishers 2011)

Moir L, 'Towards the Unification of International Humanitarian Law?' in Richard Burchill, Nigel D White and Justin Morris (eds), *International Conflict and Security Law* (Cambridge University Press 2005)

Moïse Mbengue M, 'Preamble', *Max Planck Encyclopedia of Public International Law (Online)* (2006) <http://opil.ouplaw.com/view/10.1093/law:epil/9780199231690/law-9780199231690-e1709> accessed 25 January 2017

Montoya Céspedes MN, 'The Inter-American Court of Human Rights' Positive Obligations Doctrine: Between Unidirectional Influence and Judicial Dialogue' in Yves Haeck, Oswaldo Ruiz-Chiriboga and Clara Burbano-Herrera (eds), The Inter-American Court of Human Rights: Theory and Practice, Present and Future (Intersentia 2015)

Mugerva N, 'Subjects of International Law' in Max Sørensen (ed), Manual of Public International Law (MacMillan 1968)

Mujezinović Larsen K, Guldahl Cooper C and Nystuen G, 'Introduction by the Editors: Is There a "Principle of Humanity" in International Humanitarian Law?' in Kjetil Mujezinović Larsen, Camilla Guldahl Cooper and Gro Nystuen (eds), Searching for a 'Principle of Humanity' in International Humanitarian Law (Cambridge University Press 2013)

——, 'Conclusions: Is There a "Principle of Humanity" in International Humanitarian Law?' in Kjetil Mujezinović Larsen, Camilla Guldahl Cooper and Gro Nystuen (eds), Searching for a 'Principle of Humanity' in International Humanitarian Law (Cambridge University Press 2013)

Murphy SD, 'The Relevance of Subsequent Agreement and Subsequent Practice for the Interpretation of Treaties' in Georg Nolte (ed), Treaties and Subsequent Practice (Oxford University Press 2013)

Neff SC, 'Conflict Termination and Peace-Making in the Law of Nations: A Historical Perspective' in Carsten Stahn and Jann K Kleffner (eds), Jus Post Bellum: Towards a Law of Transition From Conflict to Peace (Springer Verlag 2008)

Nowak M, 'Disappearances in Bosnia-Herzegovina' in Michael O'Flaherty (ed), Post-war protection of human rights in Bosnia and Herzegovina (Martinus Nijhoff Publishers 1998)

——, 'Eight Reasons Why We Need a World Court of Human Rights' in Gudmundur Alfredsson and et al. (eds), International Human Rights Monitoring Mechanisms: Essay in Honour of Jakob Th. Möller (Martinus Nijhoff Publishers 2009)

——, 'Lessons for the International Human Rights Regime from the Yugoslav Experience', in 1997 the Protection of Human Rights in Europe – Collected courses of the Academy of European Law, vol VIII Book 2 (Kluwer Law International 2000)

Papadakis Y, Peristianis N and Welz G, 'Introduction: Modernity, History, and Conflict in Divided Cyprus. An Overview' in Yannis Papadakis, Nicos Peristianis and Gisela Welz (eds), Divided Cyprus. Modernity, History, and an Island in Conflict (Indiana University Press 2006)

Partsch KJ, 'Human Rights and Humanitarian Law' in Rudolf Bernhardt (ed), Encyclopedia of Public International Law (North-Holland Publishing Company 1985) 292

Paulus A and Leiß J, 'Article 103' in Bruno Simma and others (eds), The Charter of the United Nations – A Commentary (3rd edn, Oxford University Press 2002)

Petrig A, 'Search for Missing Persons' in Andrew Clapham, Paola Gaeta and Marco Sassòli (eds), The 1949 Geneva Conventions: A Commentary: A Commentary (Oxford University Press 2015)

Peters A, 'Are We Moving towards Constitutionalization of the World Community?' in Antonio Cassese (ed), Realizing Utopia: the Future of International Law (Oxford University Press 2012)

Piragoff DK, 'Article 69 – Evidence' in Otto Triffterer and Kai Ambos (eds), Commentary on the Rome Statute of the International Criminal Court: Observers' Notes, Article by Article (C H Beck 2008)

Ratner SR, 'Behind the Flag of Dunant: Secrecy and the Compliance Mission of the International Committee of the Red Cross' in Andrea Bianchi and Anne Peters (eds), *Transparency in International Law* (Cambridge University Press 2013)

Reinisch A, 'The Changing International Legal Framework for Dealing with Non-State Actors' in Philip Alston (ed), *Non-state actors and human rights* (Oxford University Press 2005)

Riedel E and Arend J-M, 'Article 55 (c)' in Bruno Simma and others (eds), *The Charter of the United Nations – A Commentary* (3rd edn, Oxford University Press 2002)

Robben A, 'The Human Right to Mourning. Social Trauma and Transitional Justice in Post-Conflict Argentina' in Ineke Boerefijn and Ronald Janse (eds), *Human Rights and Conflict: Essays in Honour of Bas De Gaay Fortman* (Intersentia 2012)

Roth-Arriaza N, 'The New Landscape of Transitional Justice' in Naomi Roht-Arriaza and Javier Mariezcurrena (eds), *Transitional justice in the twenty-first century: beyond truth versus justice* (Cambridge University Press 2006)

Salinas Burgos H, 'The Application of International Humanitarian Law as Compared to Human Rights Law in Situations Qualified as Internal Armed Conflict, Internal Disturbances and Tensions, or Public Emergency, with Special Reference to War Crimes and Political Crimes' in Yves Sandoz and Frits Kalshoven (eds), *Implementation of International Humanitarian Law* (Martinus Nijhoff Publishers 1989)

Scobbie I, 'The Approach to Customary International Law in the Study' in Elizabeth Wilmshurst and Susan Breau (eds), *Perspectives on the ICRC study on customary international humanitarian law* (Cambridge University Press 2007)

Scovazzi T, 'Il lato oscuro dei diritti umani: aspetti di diritto internazionale' in Massimo Meccarelli, Carlo Sotis and Paolo Palchetti (eds), *Il lato oscuro dei diritti umani: esigenze emancipatorie e logiche di dominio nella tutela giuridica dell'individuo* (Editorial Dykinson, SL 2014)

Seibert-Fohr A., 'Transitional Justice in Post-Conflict Situations' in Rüdiger Wolfrum and Frauke Lachenmann (eds), *The Law of Armed Conflict and the Use of Force. The Max Plank Encyclopedia of Public International Law*, vol 2 (Oxford University Press 2017) http://www.mpepil.com

Shelton D, 'Jura Novit Curia in International Human Rights Tribunals' in Nerina Boschiero and others (eds), International Courts and the Development of International Law (T M C Asser Press 2013)

—— and Gould A, 'Positive and Negative Obligations' in Dinah Shelton (ed), The Oxford Handbook of International Human Rights Law (Oxford University Press 2013)

Shraga D, 'The Applicability of the Laws of Armed Conflict to Peacekeeping Operations' in Rain Liivoja and Tim McCormack (eds), *Routledge Handbook of the Law of Armed Conflict* (Routledge 2016)

Sivakumaran S, 'International Humanitarian Law' in Sangeeta Shah and others (eds), *International Human Rights Law* (2nd edn, Oxford University Press 2010)

Stahn C, 'Jus Post Bellum: Mapping the Discipline(s)' in Carsten Stahn and Jann K Kleffner (eds), *Jus Post Bellum: Towards a Law of Transition From Conflict to Peace* (Springer Verlag 2008)

——, 'R2P and Jus Post Bellum Towards a Polycentric Approach' in Carsten Stahn, Jennifer S Easterday and Jens Iverson (eds), *Jus Post Bellum: Mapping the normative Foundations* (Oxford University Press 2014)

——, 'The Future of Jus Post Bellum' in Carsten Stahn and Jann K Kleffner (eds), *Jus Post Bellum: Towards a Law of Transition From Conflict to Peace* (Springer Verlag 2008)

Stoll P, 'Article 55 (a) and (B)' in Bruno Simma and others (eds), *The Charter of the United Nations – A Commentary* (3rd edn, Oxford University Press 2002)

Stover, Eric and Shigekane, Rachel, 'Exhumation of Mass Graves: balancing Legal and Humanitarian Needs' in Stover, Eric and Weinstein, Harvey M. (eds), *My neighbor, my enemy. Justice and Community in the aftermath of mass atrocity* (Cambridge University Press 2004)

Sudre F, L'économie Générale de L'article 3 CEDH' in Catherine-Amélie Chassin (dir.), La portée de l'article 3 de la Convention européenne des droits de l'homme (Bruylant 2006)

Tabeau E and OTP – ICTY, 'ICRC Lists of Missing Persons as Part of the OTP Information System on Victims of IHL Violations Committed in the 1990s Conflict in the Former Yugoslavia' in María Teresa Dutli and Noreen Majeed (eds), *Report of the Second Universal Meeting of National Committees on International Humanitarian Law – Geneva, 19–21 March 2007. Legal Measures and Mechanisms to Prevent Disappearances, to Establish the Fate of Missing Persons, and to Assist Their Families* (ICRC 2007)

Tanke Holm T, 'CIVPOL Operations in Eastern Slavonia, 1992-98' in Tor Tanke Holm and Espen Barth Eide (eds), *Peacebuilding and Police Reform* (Frank Cass 2000)

Toman J, 'Missing and Dead Persons' in Rudolf Bernhardt (ed), *Encyclopedia of Public International Law* (North-Holland Publishing Company 1997) 428

Tondini M, 'Putting an End to Human Rights Violations by Proxy: Accountability of International Organizations and Member States in the Framework of Jus Post Bellum' in Carsten Stahn and Jann K Kleffner (eds), *Jus Post Bellum: Towards a Law of Transition From Conflict to Peace* (Springer Verlag 2008)

Tsereteli N, 'Victim Participation in ICC Proceedings' in Carsten Stahn and Larissa van den Herik (eds), *Future perspectives on international criminal justice* (TMC Asser press 2010)

Urban Walker M, 'Post-Conflict Truth Telling: Exploring Extended Territory' in Larry May and Andrew Forcehimes (eds), *Morality, Jus Post Bellum, and International Law* (Cambridge University Press 2012)

——, 'Nunca Más: Truth Commissions, Prevention, and Human Rights Culture' in Larry May and Elizabeth Edenberg (eds), *Jus Post Bellum and Transitional Justice* (Cambridge University Press 2013)

van Boven T, 'Victim-Oriented Perspectives: Rights and Realities' in Thorsten Bonacker and Christoph Safferling (eds), *Victims of International Crimes: An Interdisciplinary Discourse* (T M C Asser Press 2013)

Veuthey M, 'From Solferino to Kosovo: The Contribution of International Humanitarian Law to International Security' in John Carey, William V Dunlap and R John Pritchard (eds), *International Humanitarian Law: Origins, Challenges, Prospects (3 Vols)* (Transnational Publishers 2005)

Wählisch M, 'Conflict Termination from a Human Rights Perspective: State Transitions, Power-Sharing, and the Definition of the "Post"' in Carsten Stahn, Jennifer S Easterday and Jens Iverson (eds), *Jus Post Bellum: Mapping the normative Foundations* (Oxford University Press 2014)

Wilde R, 'Are Human Rights Norms Part of the Jus Post Bellum, and Should They Be?' in Carsten Stahn and Jann K Kleffner (eds), *Jus Post Bellum: Towards a Law of Transition From Conflict to Peace* (Springer Verlag 2008)

Wolfrum R, 'Article 1' in Bruno Simma and others (eds), *The Charter of the United Nations: A Commentary* (Oxford University Press 1994)

——, 'Article 1' in Bruno Simma and others (eds), *The Charter of the United Nations – A Commentary* (3rd edn, Oxford University Press 2002)

——, 'Preamble' in Bruno Simma and others (eds), *The Charter of the United Nations – A Commentary* (3rd edn, Oxford University Press 2002)

JOURNAL ARTICLES AND ACADEMIC PAPERS AND REPORTS

Abraham E, 'The Sins of the Savior: Holding the United Nations Accountable to International Human Rights Standards for Executive Order Detentions on Its Mission in Kosovo Comment' (2002) 52 American University Law Review 1291

Aldrich GH, 'Customary International Humanitarian Law — An Interpretation on Behalf of the International Committee of the Red Cross' (2006) 76 British Yearbook of International Law 503

Ambrus M and Wessel RA, 'Between Pragmatism and Predictability: Temporariness in International Law' (2014) 45 Netherlands Yearbook of International Law 1

Andreu-Guzmán F, 'Le Groupe de Travail Sur Les Disparitions Forcées Des Nations Unies' (2002) 84 International Review of the Red Cross 803

Anderson K, 'How Effective Is the International Convention for the Protection of All Persons from Enforced Disappearance Likely to Be in Holding Individuals Criminally Responsible for Acts of Enforced Disappearance?' (2006) 7 Melbourne Journal of International Law 245

Apuuli KP, 'The ICC Arrest Warrants for the Lord's Resistance Army Leaders and Peace Prospects for Northern Uganda' (2006) 4 Journal of International Criminal Justice 179

Arthur P, 'How "Transitions" Reshaped Human Rights: A Conceptual History of Transitional Justice' (2009) 31 Human Rights Quarterly 321

Avery, Lisa, 'The Right to Identity and the Right to Identify Argentina's Living Disappeared' (2004) 27 Harvard Women's Law Journal 235

Bass GJ, 'Jus Post Bellum' 32 Philosophy and Public Affairs 384

Bassiouni MC, 'A Functional Approach to General Principles of International Law' (1990) 11 Michigan Journal of International Law

——, 'Searching for Peace and Achieving Justice: The Need for Accountability' (1996) 59 Law and Contemporary Problems 9

——, 'The ICC — Quo Vadis?' (2006) 4 Journal of International Criminal Justice 421

Baumgartner E, 'Aspects of Victim Participation in the Proceedings of the International Criminal Court' (2008) 90 International Review of the Red Cross 409

Bekker G, 'The African Commission on Human and Peoples' Rights and Remedies for Human Rights Violations' (2013) 13 Human Rights Law Review 499

Bell C, 'Peace Agreements: Their Nature and Legal Status' (2006) 100 The American Journal of International Law 373

Bellal A, Giacca G and Casey-Maslen S, 'International Law and Armed Non-State Actors in Afghanistan' (2011) 93 International Review of the Red Cross 47

Ben-Naftali O and Gleichgevitch SS, 'Missing in Legal Action: Lebanese Hostages in Israel' (2000) 41 Harvard International Law Journal 185

—— and Shany Y, 'Living in Denial: The Application of Human Rights in the Occupied Territories' (2003) 37 Israel Law Review 17

Benvenisti E, 'Part III. Governing Space in International Law. The Origin of the Concept of Belligerent Occupation' (2008) 26 Law and History Review 621

Benzimra-Hazan J, 'En Marge de L'arrêt Timurtas C. La Turquie (13 Juin 2000) : Vers L'homogénéisation Des Approches Du Phénomène Des Disparitions Forcées de Personnes' (2001) 12 Revue trimestrielle des droits de l'homme 983

Bianchi A, 'Ad Hocism and the Rule of Law' (2002) 13 European Journal of International Law 263

Blondel J-L, 'The Meaning of the Word "humanitarian" in Relation to the Fundamental Principles of the Red Cross and Red Crescent' (1989) 29 International Review of the Red Cross (1961 – 1997) 507

Blumenstock T, 'Legal Protection of the Missing and Their Relatives: The Example of Bosnia and Herzegovina' (2006) 19 Leiden Journal of International Law 773

Boon K, 'Legislative Reform in Post-Conflict Zones: Jus Post Bellum and the Contemporary Occupant's Law-Making Powers' (2005) 50 McGill Law Journal/Revue de Droit de McGill 285

Borelli S, 'Domestic Investigation and Prosecution of Atrocities Committed during Military Operations: The Impact of Judgments of the European Court of Human Rights' (2013) 46 Israel Law Review 369

——,'Positive Obligations of States and the Protection of Human Rights' (2006) 15 Interights Bulletin 101

Boss P, 'Ambiguous Loss: Working with Families of the Missing' (2002) 17 Family Process 14

——, 'Ambiguous Loss in Families of the Missing' (2002) 360 Medicine and Conflict – The Lancet Supplement 39

Branch A, 'Uganda's Civil War and the Politics of ICC Intervention' (2007) 21 Ethics & International Affairs 179

Breau SC and Joyce R, 'The Legal Obligation To Record Civilian Casualties Of Armed Conflict' (Oxford Research Group – Building Bridges for Global Security 2011)

——, RCAC Legal Team Briefing: Obligations to Record Civilian Casualties (ORG 2010)

Brilmayer L and Chepiga G, 'Ownership or Use? Civilian Property Interests in International Humanitarian Law' (2008) 49 Harvard International Law Review 413

Bugnion F, 'Jus Ad Bellum, Jus in Bello and Non-International Armed Conflicts' (2003) 6 Yearbook of International Humanitarian Law 167

Burgorgue-Larsen L and de Torres AÚ, '"War" in the Jurisprudence of the Inter– American Court of Human Rights' (2011) 33 Human Rights Quarterly 148

Cançado Trindade AA, 'The Time Factor in the Application of the Rule of Exhaustion of Local Remedies in International Law' (1978) 61 Rivista di Diritto Internazionale 61 232

Capdevila L and Voldman D, 'Du Numéro Matricule Au Code Génétique: La Manipulation Du Corps Des Tués de La Guerre En Quête D'identité' (2002) 84 International Review of the Red Cross 751

Cassel D, 'Lessons from the Americas: Guidelines for International Response to Amnesties for Atrocities' (1996) 59 Law and Contemporary Problems 197

Cassese A, 'The Martens Clause: Half a Loaf or Simply Pie in the Sky?' (2000) 11 European Journal of International Law 187

Chayes, A, 'Chapter VII½: Is Jus Post Bellum Possible?' (2013) 24 European Journal of International Law 291

Chinkin C, 'The Protection of Economic, Social and Cultural Rights Post-Conflict' <http://www2.ohchr.org/english/issues/women/docs/Paper_Protection_ESCR.pdf> accessed 12 March 2017

Citroni G, 'Janowiec and Others v. Russia: A Long History of Justice Delayed Turned into a Permanent Case of Justice Denied' (2013) XXXIII Polish Yearbook of International Law 279

——, 'The Pitfalls of Regulating the Legal Status of Disappeared Persons Through Declaration of Death' (2014) 12 Journal of International Criminal Justice 787

—— and Bianchi MG, 'The Committee on Enforced Disappearances : Challenges Ahead' (2012) 6 Diritti umani e diritto internazionale 127

Clapham A, 'Human Rights Obligations of Non-State Actors in Conflict Situations' (2006) 88 International Review of the Red Cross 491

Clark JN, 'Peace, Justice and the International Criminal Court Limitations and Possibilities' (2011) 9 Journal of International Criminal Justice 521

Cohen A and Shany Y, 'Beyond the Grave Breaches Regime: The Duty to Investigate Alleged Violations of International Law Governing Armed Conflicts' (2011) 14 Yearbook of International Humanitarian Law 37

Collège d'Europe, 'Le Champ D'application Du Droit International Humanitaire', *Actes du Colloque de Bruges, 13th Bruges Colloquium, 19-19 October 2012* <https://www.icrc.org/fre/resources/documents/news-release/2012/belgium-news-2012-10-18.htm> accessed 12 June 2015

Corten O, 'Le Jus Post Bellum Remet-il En Cause Les Règles Traditionnelles Du Jus Contra Bellum?' (2011) 44 Revue Belge de Droit International / Belgian Review of International Law 38

Coupland R, 'Humanity: What Is It and How Does It Influence International Law?' (2001) 83 International Review of the Red Cross 969

Crettol M and La Rosa A-M, 'The Missing and Transitional Justice: The Right to Know and the Fight against Impunity' (2006) 88 International Review of the Red Cross 355

David V, 'The Expanding Right to an Effective Remedy: Common Developments at the Human Rights Committee and the Inter-American Court' (2014) 3 British Journal of American Legal Studies 259

Dawidowicz M, 'The Effect of the Passage of Time on the Interpretation of Treaties: Some Reflections on Costa Rica v. Nicaragua' (2011) 24 Leiden Journal of International Law 201

De Frouville O, 'La Convention Des NU Pour la Protection de toutes les Personnes contre les Disparitions Forcées: Les Enjeux Juridiques D'une Négociation exemplaire. Première Partie : Les Dispositions Substantielles' (2006) 6 Droits fondamentaux 1

de Greiff P, 'Theorizing Transitional Justice' (2012) 51 Nomos 31

Dennis MJ, 'Application of Human Rights Treaties Extra-Territorially in Times of Armed Conflict and Military Occupation – Agora: ICJ Advisory Opinion on Construction of a Wall in the Occupied Palestinian Territory' (2005) 99 American Journal of International Law 119

de Zayas A, 'Human Rights and Indefinite Detention' (2005) 87 International Review of the Red Cross 15

Dinstein Y, 'The International Law of Inter-State Wars and Human Rights' (1977) 7 Israel Yearbook of Human Rights

Djukić D, 'Transitional Justice and the International Criminal Court – in '"the Interests of Justice"?' (2007) 89 International Review of the Red Cross 691

Doswald-Beck L, 'International Humanitarian Law and the Advisory Opinion of the International Court of Justice on the Legality of the Threat or Use of Nuclear Weapons' (1997) 316 International Review of the Red Cross 35

—— and Vité S, 'International Humanitarian Law and Human Rights Law' (1993) 33 International Review of the Red Cross (1961 – 1997) 94

Draper G i.a.d., 'La Réunion Des Familles En Période de Conflit Armé' (1977) 59 International Review of the Red Cross 65

Droege C, 'The Interplay between International Humanitarian Law and International Human Rights Law in Situations of Armed Conflict' (2007) 40 Israel Law Review 310

Dworkin R, 'The Model of Rules' (1967) 35 University of Chicago Law Review 14

Egeland J, 'Political "Disappearances" – a Challenge for Humanitarian Law' (1982) 51 Nordic Journal of International Law 189

Fargues P, 'Work, Refuge, Transit: An Emerging Pattern of Irregular Immigration South and East of the Mediterranean' (2009) 43 International Migration Review 544

Fassbender B, 'Uncertain Steps into a Post-Cold War World: The Role and Functioning of the UN Security Council after a Decade of Measures against Iraq' (2002) 13 European Journal of International Law 273

Feldman T, 'Indirect Victims, Direct Injury: Recognising Relatives as Victims under the European Human Rights System' [2009] European Human Rights Law Review 50

Finucane B, 'Enforced Disappearance as a Crime Under International Law: A Neglected Origin in the Laws of War' (2010) 35 The Yale Journal of International Law 171

Friedmann A, 'Declarations of Death – A New International Convention Notes and Comment' (1950) 25 St. John's Law Review 18

Gaeta P, 'The Dayton Agreements and International Law (Symposium: The Dayton Agreements: A Breakthrough for Peace and Justice?)' (1996) 7 European Journal of International Law 147

Galtung J, 'An Editorial' (1964) 1 Journal of Peace Research 1

——, 'Theories of Peace: A Synthetic Approach to Peace Thinking' (1967) UNESCO/International Peace Research Association (IPRA)

Garibaldi OM, 'The General Limitations on Human Rights: The Principle of Legality United Nations' (1976) 17 Harvard International Law Journal 503

Gasser H-P, 'International Humanitarian Law and Human Rights Law in Non-International Armed Conflict: Joint Venture or Mutual Exclusion' (2002) 45 German Yearbook of International Law 149

Ghandhi S, 'The Human Rights Committee and Interim Measures of Relief' (2007) 13 The Canterbury law Review 203

Gill TD, 'Legal and Some Political Limitations on the Power of the UN Security Council to Exercise Its Enforcement Powers under Chapter VII of the Charter' (1995) 26 Netherlands Yearbook of International Law 33

Goldman SD, 'Russia – CRS Report for Congress' (Congressional Research Service – The Library of Congress 2006) <http://fpc.state.gov/documents/organization/66504.pdf> accessed 1 May 2015

Goldstone RJ, 'Justice as a Tool for Peace-Making: Truth Commissions and International Criminal Tribunals' (1995) 28 New York University Journal of International Law and Politics 485

Gowlland-Debbas V, 'The Relevance of Paragraph 25 of the ICJ's Advisory Opinion on Nuclear Weapons' (2004) 98 Proceedings of the Annual Meeting (American Society of International Law) 358

Grant S, '"Identity Unknown": Migrant Deaths at Sea' (2011) 38 Forced Migration Review 43

——,'Recording and Identifying European Frontier Deaths' (2011) 13 European Journal of Migration and Law 135

Grenfell K, 'Perspective on the Applicability and Application of International Humanitarian Law: The UN Context' (2013) 95 International Review of the Red Cross 645

Grignon J, 'The Beginning of Application of International Humanitarian Law: A Discussion of a Few Challenges' (2014) 96 International Review of the Red Cross 139

Haimbaugh GDJ, 'Introduction to Panel II: Humanitarian Law: The Lincoln-Lieber Initiative' (1983) 13 Georgia Journal of International and Comparative Law 245

Harroff-Tavel M, 'Do Wars Ever End? The Work of the International Committee of the Red Cross When the Guns Fall Silent' (2003) 85 International Review of the Red Cross 465

Higgins R, 'Derogations under Human Rights Treaties' (1977) 48 British Yearbook of International Law 281

——, 'Policy Considerations and the International Judicial Process' (1968) 17 The International and Comparative Law Quarterly 58

——, 'Time and the Law: International Perspectives on an Old Problem' (1997) 46 International and Comparative Law Quarterly 501

Huttunen L, 'Liminality and Missing Persons: Encountering the Missing in Postwar Bosnia-Herzegovina' (2016) 2 Conflict and Society 201

ICRC, 'Action by the ICRC in the Event of Violations of IHL or of Other Fundamental Rules Protecting Persons in Situations of Violence' (2005) 87 International Review of the Red Cross 393

——, 'ICRC Protection Policy. Institutional Policy' (2008) 90 International Review of the Red Cross 751

Iles K, 'Limiting Socio-Economic Rights: Beyond the Internal Limitations Clauses' (2004) 20 South African Journal on Human Rights 448

Iverson J, 'Transitional Justice, Jus Post Bellum and International Criminal Law: Differentiating the Usages, History and Dynamics' (2013) 7 International Journal of Transitional Justice 413

Jinks D, 'The Temporal Scope of Application of International Humanitarian Law in Contemporary Conflicts' [2003] HPCR Background Paper

Jeannet S, 'Recognition of the ICRC's Long-Standing Rule of Confidentiality' (2000) 82 International Review of the Red Cross 403

Johnston KA, 'Transformations of Conflict Status in Libya' (2012) 17 Journal of Conflict and Security Law 81

Keller H and Chernishova O, 'Disappearance Cases before the European Court of Human Rights and the UN Human Rights Committee: Convergence and Divergences' (2012) 32 Human Rights Law Journal 237

—— and Marti C, 'Interim Relief Compared: Use of Interim Measures by the UN Human Rights Committee and the European Court of Human Rights' (2013) 73 Heidelberg Journal of International Law 325

Lassée I, '"Criminal" and "Humanitarian" Approaches to Investigations into the Fate of Missing Persons: A False Dichotomy (Position Paper)' (South Asian Centre for Legal Studies 2016)

La Vaccara A, 'Past Conflicts, Present Uncertainty: Legal Answers to the Quest for Information on Missing Persons and Victims of Enforced Disappearance. Three Case

Studies from the European Context' (2018) XXXVII/2017 Polish yearbook of international law 35.

Lewandowski T, 'Law of Occupation, Jus Post Bellum and Responsibility to Protect: Separate or Complementary Tools for Restoring Human Rights Order After Mass Atrocities?' (2013) 1 Social Transformations in Contemporary Society 120

Lewkowicz G, 'Jus Post Bellum: Vieille Antienne Ou Nouvelle Branche Du Droit: Sur Le Mythe de l'Origine Venerable Du Just Post Bellum' (2011) 44 Revue Belge de Droit International / Belgian Review of International Law 11

Lindroos A, 'Addressing Norm Conflicts in a Fragmented Legal System: The Doctrine of Lex Specialis' (2005) 74 Nordic Journal of International Law 27

Ludwin King EB, 'A Conflict of Interests: Privacy, Truth, and Compulsory DNA Testing for Argentina's Children of the Disappeared' (2011) 44 Cornell International Law Journal 535

Månsson K, 'The Forgotten Agenda: Human Rights Protection and Promotion in Cold War Peacekeeping' (2005) 10 Journal of Conflict and Security Law 379

Martin S, 'The Missing' (2002) 84 International Review of the Red Cross 723

McCrory S, 'The International Convention for the Protection of All Persons from Enforced Disappearance' (2007) 7 Human Rights Law Review 545

McGoldrick D, 'Human Rights and Humanitarian Law in the UK Courts' (2007) 40 Israel Law Review 527

McLachlan C, 'The Principle of Systemic Integration and Article 31(3)(C) of the Vienna Convention' (2005) 54 The International and Comparative Law Quarterly 279

Melish TJ and Aliverti A, 'Positive Obligations in the Inter-American Human Rights System' (2006) 15 Interights Bulletin 120

Meron T, 'Editorial Comment. The Time Has Come for the United States to Ratify Geneva Protocol I' (1994) 88 American Journal of International Law 678

——, 'The Martens Clause, Principles of Humanity, and Dictates of Public Conscience' (2000) 94 American Journal of International Law

——, 'The Humanization of Humanitarian Law' (2000) 94 American Journal of International Law 239

Meyrowitz H, 'Droit de Guerre et Droits de L'homme' [1972] Revue du Droit Public et de la Science Politique en France et à l'étranger 1059

Milanović M, 'The End of Application of International Humanitarian Law' (2014) 96 International Review of the Red Cross 163

Modirzadeh N, 'The Dark Sides of Convergence: A Pro-Civilian Critique of the Extraterritorial Application of Human Rights Law in Armed Conflict' (2010) Vol. 86 U.S. Naval War College International Law Studies 349

Mowbray AR, 'Duties of Investigation under the European Convention on Human Rights' (2002) 51 International and Comparative Law Quarterly 437

Mulgan R, '"Accountability": An Ever-Expanding Concept?' (2000) 78 Public Administration 555

Murray R and Mottershaw E, 'Mechanisms for the Implementation of Decisions of the African Commission on Human and Peoples' Rights' (2014) 36 Human Rights Quarterly 349

Naqvi Y, 'The Right to the Truth in International Law: Fact or Fiction?' (2006) 88 International Review of the Red Cross 245

Naldi GJ, 'Interim Measures of Protection in the African System for the Protection of Human and Peoples' Rights' (2002) 2 African Human Rights Law Journal 1

——, 'Interim Measures in the UN Human Rights Committee' (2004) 53 International & Comparative Law Quarterly 445

——, 'Limitation of Rights under the African Charter on Human and Peoples' Rights: The Contribution of the African Commission on Human and Peoples' Rights Notes and Comments' (2001) 17 South African Journal on Human Rights 109

——, 'Reparations in the Practice of the African Commission on Human and Peoples' Rights' (2001) 14 Leiden Journal of International Law 681

Nybakken OE, 'Humanitas Romana' (1939) 70 Transactions and Proceedings of the American Philological Association 396

O'Connell ME, 'Saving Lives through a Definition of International Armed Conflict [Armed Conflicts and Parties to Armed Conflicts under IHL: Confronting Legal Categories to Contemporary Realities – 10th Bruges Colloquium 22-23 October 2009]' (2010) 40 Collegium 19

Okafor OC and Ngwaba U, 'The International Criminal Court as a "Transitional Justice" Mechanism in Africa: Some Critical Reflections' (2015) 9 International Journal of Transitional Justice 90

Olinga AD, 'The African Charter on Human and Peoples' Rights and Positive Obligations' (2006) 15 Interights Bulletin 117

Oosthuizen GH, 'Playing the Devil's Advocate: The United Nations Security Council is Unbound by Law' (1999) 12 Leiden Journal of International Law 549

Österdahl I and van Zadel E, 'What Will Jus Post Bellum Mean? Of New Wine and Old Bottles' (2009) 14 Journal of Conflict and Security Law 175

Pasqualucci, Jo M., 'Interim Measures in International Human Rights: Evolution and Harmonization' (2005) 38 Vanderbilt Journal of Transnational Law 1

Paulus A, 'Non International Armed Conflict under Common Article 3 [Armed Conflicts and Parties to Armed Conflicts under IHL: Confronting Legal Categories to Contemporary Realities – 10th Bruges Colloquium 22-23 October 2009]' (2010) 40 Collegium 28

Paust JJ, 'Dr. Francis Lieber and the Lieber Code' (2001) 95 Proceedings of the Annual Meeting (American Society of International Law) 112

Pejic J, 'Terrorist Acts and Groups: A Role for International Law' (2004) 75 British Year Book of International Law 71

Pena M and Carayon G, 'Is the ICC Making the Most of Victim Participation?' (2013) 7 The International Journal of Transitional Justice 1

Petrig A, 'The War Dead and Their Gravesites' (2009) 874 International Review of the Red Cross 341

Petty C, 'Family Tracing and Reunification – Safeguarding Rights and Implementing the Law' (1996) 4 International Journal of Children's Rights 165

Pictet JS, 'The New Geneva Conventions for the Protection of Victims of War' (1951) 45 American Journal of International Law 462

Prud'homme N, 'Lex Specialis: Oversimplifying a More Complex and Multifaceted Relationship' (2007) 40 Israel Law Review 356

Rieter E, 'Provisional Measures: Binding and Persuasive? Enabling Human Rights Adjudicators to Follow up on State Disrespect' (2012) 59 Netherlands International Law Review 165

Rodley N and Pollard M, The Treatment of Prisoners under International Law (Oxford University Press 2009)

Rodríguez-Pinzón D, 'Precautionary Measures of the Inter-American Commission on Human Rights: Legal Status and Importance' (2013) 20 The Human Rights Brief 13

Ruzé R, 'Chronique des Faits Internationaux. La XIIe Conférence internationale de la Croix Rouge à Genève, 7-10 octobre 1925.' (1925) 7 Revue Generale de Droit International Public 471

Salmon E, 'Institutional Approach between IHL and IHRL: Current Trends in the Jurisprudence of the Inter-American Court of Human Rights' (2014) 5 Journal of International Humanitarian Legal Studies 152

Šarčević P, 'War and Disintegration of the Family' (1999) 1 Journal of Law and Family Studies 109

Sarkin J, 'The Need to Deal with All Missing Persons Including Those Missing as a Result of Armed Conflict, Disasters, Migration, Human Trafficking, and Human Rights Violations (Including Enforced Disappearances) in International and Domestic Law and Processes' (2015) 8 Inter-American and European Human Rights Journal (IAEHR) 112

Sassòli M, 'Le Bureau National de Renseignements En Faveur Des Victimes Des Conflits Armés' (1987) 69 International Review of the Red Cross 6

——, 'Les disparus de guerre : Les règles du droit international et les besoins des familles entre espoir et incertitude' (2003) 15 Frontières 38

—— and Tougas M-L, 'The ICRC and the Missing' (2002) 84 International Review of the Red Cross 727

Schabas WA, 'Lex Specialis − Belt and Suspenders − The Parallel Operation of Human Rights Law and the Law of Armed Conflict, and the Conundrum of Jus Ad Bellum' (2007) 40 Israel Law Review 592

Scharf M, 'The Amnesty Exception to the Jurisdiction of the International Criminal Court' (1999) 32 Cornell International Law Journal 507

Schindler D, 'Le Comité International de La Croix-Rouge et Les Droits de L'homme' (1979) 61 International Review of the Red Cross 3

Shaffer G and Ginsburg T, 'The Empirical Turn in International Legal Scholarship' (2012) 106 American Journal of International Law 1

Shapiro S, 'The "Hart-Dworkin" Debate: A Short Guide for the Perplexed' (2007) Working Paper no. 77 University of Michigan Law School Public and Legal Theory Working Paper Series <http://www.law.yale.edu/documents/pdf/Faculty/Shapiro_Hart_Dworkin_Debate.pdf> accessed 4 April 2016

Sirleaf M, 'Regional Approaches to Transitional Justice? Examining the Special Court for Sierra Leone and the Truth and Reconciliation Commission for Liberia' (2009) 21 Florida Journal of International Law 209

Skinner M and Sterenberg J, 'Turf Wars: Authority and Responsibility for the Investigation of Mass Graves' (2005) 151 Forensic Science International 221

Stahn C, '"Jus Ad bellum", "Jus in bello"..."Jus Post Bellum"? Rethinking the Conception of the Law of Armed Forces' (2006) 17 European Journal of International Law 921

——, 'The Geometry of Transitional Justice: Choices of Institutional Design' (2005) 18 Leiden Journal of International Law 425

——, Iverson J and Easterday J, 'Special Issue: Jus Post Bellum and Foreign Investment' (2015) 16 The Journal of World Investment & Trade 583

Stephens D, 'Human Rights and Armed Conflict − The Advisory Opinion of the International Court of Justice in the Nuclear Weapons Case' (2001) 4 Yale Human Rights & Development Law Journal 1

xBIBLIOGRAPHY

Stover E and Shigekane R, 'The Missing in the Aftermath of War: When Do the Needs of Victims' Families and International War Crimes Tribunals Clash?' (2002) 84 International Review of the Red Cross 845

Sudre F, 'Les "obligations Positives" dans La Jurisprudence Européenne Des Droits de L'homme' (1995) 6 Revue trimestrielle des droits de l'homme 363

Taxil B, 'À La Confluence Des Droits : La Convention Internationale Pour La Protection de Toutes Les Personnes Contre Les Disparitions Forcées' (2007) 53 Annuaire français de droit international 129

Teitel R, 'Rethinking Jus Post Bellum in an Age of Global Transitional Justice' [2013] European Journal of International Law 335

——, 'Symposium − Human Rights on the Eve of the next Century: Beyond Vienna & Beijing. Human Rights Theory: Human Rights Genealogy.' (1997) 66 Fordham Law Review 301

——, 'Transitional Justice Genealogy' (2003) 16 Harvard Human Rights Journal 69

Tobin J, 'Seeking Clarity in Relation to the Principle of Complementarity: Reflections on the Recent Contributions of Some International Bodies' 8 Melbourne Journal of International Law 356

Turgis N, 'What Is Transitional Justice?' (2010) 1 International Journal of Law, Transitional Justice and Human Rights 9

University of Cambridge, 'Retribution and Restoration: Bosnia on Trial' (*University of Cambridge*, 15 February 2013) <http://www.cam.ac.uk/research/news/retribution-and-restoration-bosnia-on-trial> accessed 10 January 2018

Waltzer K, 'Opening the Red Cross International Tracing Service Archive' (2008) 26 The John Marshall Journal of Information Technology and Privacy Law 161

Williams RE and Caldwell D, 'Jus Post Bellum: Just War Theory and the Principles of Just Peace' (2006) 7 International Studies Perspectives 309

Yeager JD, 'The Human Rights Chamber for Bosnia and Herzegovina − A Case Study in Transitional Justice' (2004) 14 International Legal Perspectives 44

Zappalà S, 'The Rights of Victims v. the Rights of the Accused' (2010) 8 Journal of International Criminal Justice 137

Zegveld L, 'Remedies for Victims of Violations of International Humanitarian Law' (2003) 85 International Review of the Red Cross 497

OTHER SOURCES

Documents, Reports, and Contributions of NGOs, academic institutions, and other entities

Amnesty International, 'Bosnia-Herzegovina: Abolition of Human Rights Chamber Leaves Citizens Unprotected' (2003) EUR 63/015/2003

——, 'Bosnia-Herzegovina: Shelving Justice − War Crimes Prosecution in Paralysis' (2003) AI Index: EUR 63/018/200

——, 'Bosnia-Herzegovina: "To Bury My Brothers" Bones"' (1996) EUR 63/015/1996

——, 'Irregular Migrants in Mexico: Ten Urgent Measures to Save Lives.' (2012)

——, 'Serbia and Montenegro (Kosovo): The Legacy of Past Human Rights Abuse' (2004) AI Index: EUR 70/009/2004

Argentine Forensic Anthropology Team – EAAF, '2007-2009 Triannual Report' (2009) <http://www.eaaf.org/eaaf_reports/2007-2009/AR09_Covers-p15.pdf> accessed 12 January 2017

CMP (Cyprus), 'Figures and Statistics of Missing Persons up to 30 September 2015' <goo.gl/tRJxV8> accessed 12 June 2016

——, 'Terms of Reference and Mandate of the CMP' (1981) <http://www.cmp-cyprus.org/content/terms-reference-and-mandate> accessed 12 July 2016

Global Principles on National Security and the Right to Information (known as the Tshwane Principles)", Tshwane, South Africa (12 June 2013) published by the Open Society Justice Initiative https://goo.gl/I9aCpy accessed 13 June 2015

HRW, 'A Chance for Justice? War Crime Prosecutions in Bosnia's Serb Republic' (2006) Vol 18, no 3(D) <https://www.hrw.org/reports/2006/bosnia0306/bosnia0306web.pdf> accessed 12 July 2017

——, 'Selling Justice Short. Why Accountability Matters for Peace' (2009) 1-56432-508-3

Institut de Droit International (IDI), 'The Application of International Humanitarian Law and Fundamental Human Rights, in Armed Conflicts in Which Non-State Entities Are Parties' (1999) Berlin Session

ILA, 'Final Report: Accountability of International Organisations (Berlin Conference)' (2004)

——, 'Final Report on the Meaning of Armed Conflict in International Law – The Hague Conference' (2010) <http://www.ila-hq.org/en/committees/index.cfm/cid/1022> accessed 12 July 2016

Last Rights, 'The Mytilini Declaration for the Dignified Treatment of all Missing and Deceased Persons and their Families as a Consequence of Migrant Journeys', 11 May 2018 (Thermi, Mytilini, Lesvos, Greece) http://lastrights.net/home/4592071170 accessed 20 July 2018

Lokshina T, 'Ending Chechnya's Counterterrorism Operation – or Not' (Human Rights Watch, 27 April 2009) <https://www.hrw.org/news/2009/04/27/ending-chechnyas-counterterrorism-operation-or-not> accessed 8 November 2016

Norwegian Refugee Council, 'Profile of Internal Displacement: Cyprus – Compilation of the Information Available in the Global IDP Database of the Norwegian Refugee Council' (2005) <http://www.internal-displacement.org/assets/library/Europe/Cyprus/pdf/Cyprus-April-2005-2.pdf> accessed 12 July 2016

PILPG, 'Victim Recognition and Satisfaction of Reparations – Third Party Intervention in Janowiec and Others v. Russia' (2012)

Security Council Report, 'Special Research Report No 3. Cyprus: New Hope after 45 Years on the Security Council Agenda' <http://www.securitycouncilreport.org/special-research-report/lookup-c-glKWLeMTIsG-b-4474149.php?print=true> accessed 12 July 2016

TRIAL, 'BiH: Constitutional Court Delivers Landmark Judgment – TRIAL International' (2013) <https://trialinternational.org/latest-post/bih-constitutional-court-delivers-landmark-judgment/> accessed 13 January 2018

—— et al., 'Follow-Up Report on the Implementation by Bosnia and Herzegovina of the Recommendations Issued by the WGEID' (2014)

Universal Islamic Declaration of Human Rights, adopted by the Islamic Council in Paris on 19 September 1981

Yakinthou C, 'Living with the Shadows of the Past. The Impact of Disappearance on Wives of the Missing in Lebanon' (ICTJ 2015)

Online documents

'About HRAP' <http://www.unmikonline.org/hrap/Eng/Pages/default.aspx> accessed 12 July 2016

'About the ICTY – OTP: History' <http://www.icty.org/en/about/office-of-the-prosecutor/history> accessed 12 December 2016

'Arria-Formula Meeting on Missing Persons' (*What's in Blue – Insights on the work of the UN Security Council*, 26 January 2016) <http://www.whatsinblue.org/2016/01/arria-formula-meeting-on-missing-persons.php> accessed 20 April 2017

CIA, 'East & Southeast Asia: Timor-Leste' (*The World Factbook*) <http://teacherlink.ed.usu.edu/tlresources/reference/factbook/geos/tt.html> accessed 12 July 2016

CMP (Cyprus), 'About the CMP' (1981) <http://www.cmp-cyprus.org/content/about-cmp-0> accessed 12 July 2016

——, 'Facts and Figures' (31 December 2016) <http://www.cmp-cyprus.org/content/facts-and-figures> accessed 12 January 2017

Crawford J, '"Missing Persons Are More Than A Humanitarian Issue"' (*Justiceinfo.net*, 6 July 2016) <http://www.justiceinfo.net/en/component/k2/28188.html> accessed 7 September 2016

Gligorevic T, 'Colombia: Government and FARC to Search Together for the Missing' [2015] *Inserbia Network Foundation* <http://inserbia.info/today/2015/10/colombia-government-and-farc-to-search-together-for-the-missing/#> accessed 7 September 2016

ICC, 'ICC Office of the Prosecutor and the International Commission on Missing Persons Sign Memorandum of Understanding (ICC-CPI-20160707-PR1230)' (7 July 2016) <http://www.icc-cpi.int/Pages/item.aspx?name=PR1230> accessed 9 February 2017

ICMP, 'About US' (2014) <https://www.icmp.int/about-us/> accessed 12 July 2016

——, 'Accountability for the Missing and Disappeared in Guatemala' (24 May 2016) <https://www.icmp.int/news/accountability-for-the-missing-and-disappeared-in-guatemala/> accessed 29 December 2016

——, 'A Cornerstone of Peacebuilding – Addressing the Issue of Missing and Disappeared Persons' (28 January 2016) <http://www.icmp.int/?story=a-cornerstone-of-peacebuilding-addressing-the-issue-of-missing-and-disappeared-persons;> accessed 10 June 2016

——, 'Assistance to Justice' (18 June 2014) <https://www.icmp.int/what-we-do/assistance-to-justice/> accessed 12 July 2016

——, 'Cyprus' (28 September 2016) <https://www.icmp.int/where-we-work/europe/cyprus/> accessed 12 January 2017

——, Framework Agreement: An Overview' <https://www.icmp.int/news/icmp-framework-agreement-an-overview/> accessed 2 July 2016

——, 'Institutional Development' (18 June 2014) <https://www.icmp.int/what-we-do/institutional-development/> accessed 12 July 2016

——, 'Kosovo' <https://www.icmp.int/where-we-work/europe/western-balkans/kosovo/> accessed 12 June 2016

——, 'Public Involvement' (18 June 2014) <https://www.icmp.int/what-we-do/public-involvement-civil-society-initiatives/> accessed 12 July 2016

——, 'Rwanda' (7 August 2014) <https://www.icmp.int/the-missing/where-are-the-missing/rwanda/> accessed 12 January 2016

——, 'The Missing: Who Are the Missing?' <?" http://www.icmp.int/the-missing/who-are-the-missing/> accessed 12 October 2015

——, 'Where Are the Missing? – Kosovo' <http://www.ic-mp.org/the-missing/where-are-the-missing/kosovo/> accessed 12 June 2018

——, 'Where Are the Missing? – Vietnam' <http://www.ic-mp.org/the-missing/where-are-the-missing/vietnam/> accessed 2 July 2015

ICRC, 'Customary IHL – Online Database' <https://www.icrc.org/customary-ihl/eng> accessed 1 July 2016

——, 'Glossary of Restoring Family Links Terms' <http://goo.gl/eQiumM> accessed 20 September 2013

——, 'History of the Central Tracing Agency of the ICRC – ICRC' (2002) <https://www.icrc.org/eng/resources/documents/misc/57jqrj.htm#1> accessed 12 September 2016

——, 'IHL National Implementation Database' <goo.gl/hr5j2C> accessed 10 June 2015

——, 'ICRC Central Tracing Agency: Half a Century of Restoring Family Links' (7 April 2010) <goo.gl/o9wVTw> accessed 3 June 2016

——, 'Iran-Iraq: Still Missing since the 1980-1988 War' (10 October 2014) <https://www.icrc.org/en/document/iran-iraq-still-missing-1980-1988-war> accessed 2 June 2015

——, 'Nepal: Nine Years into the Peace Process, Relatives Still in the Dark about the Fate of Their Missing Members' (3 September 2015) <https://www.icrc.org/en/document/nepal-nine-years-peace-process-relatives-still-dark-about-fate-their-missing-members> accessed 7 September 2016

——, 'Sri Lanka' (ICRC, 24 July 2014) <https://www.icrc.org/en/where-we-work/asia-pacific/sri-lanka> accessed 4 November 2016

——, 'Sri Lanka: Clarifying the Fate of Missing Persons Requires Sustained Commitment' (*International Committee of the Red Cross*, 26 March 2015) <https://www.icrc.org/en/document/clarifying-fate-missing-persons-sri-lanka-requires-sustained-commitment> accessed 12 September 2016

ICTJ, 'Ten Years After Peace, Is Nepal Finally Serious About Finding Its Disappeared?' (29 August 2016) <https://www.ictj.org/news/nepal-disappeared-search> accessed 7 September 2018

——, 'What Is Transitional Justice? | ICTJ' (*International Center for Transitional Justice*, 2011) <https://www.ictj.org/about/transitional-justice> accessed 11 September 2016

ICTY, 'Investigations' <http://www.icty.org/en/about/office-of-the-prosecutor/ investigations> accessed 12 January 2017

International Tracing Service – ITS, 'History' (2 August 2016) <https://www.its-arolsen.org/en/about-its/history/> accessed 20 January 2017

IOM, 'About' (*Missing Migrant Project*) <https://missingmigrants.iom.int/about> accessed 12 January 2017

Oficina del alto Comisionado para La Paz, 'Comunicado Conjunto | Gobierno Y FARC-EP Anunciamos Que Hemos Llegado a Un Acuerdo Final, Integral Y Definitivo' (24 August 2016) <http://www.altocomisionadoparalapaz.gov.co/procesos-y-conversaciones/documentos-y-comunicados-conjuntos/Paginas/Comunicado-Conjunto-No-93-24-de-agosto-de-2016.aspx> accessed 31 August 2016

UNMIK, 'UNMIK Background' <http://www.un.org/en/peacekeeping/missions/unmik/background.shtml> accessed 12 January 2017

UN News Service, 'UN News – Over Half Kosovo's Missing Accounted For, Mostly through Body Identification –UN' (*UN News Service Section*, 6 December 2006)

<http://www.un.org/apps/news/story.asp?NewsID=20863&Cr=kosovo&Cr1=missing #.WI_YJ7GZOu4> accessed 31 January 2017

UNOMIG, 'Georgia – UN Observer Mission in Georgia (UNOMIG) – Background' (*Georgia – UNOMIG*) <http://www.un.org/en/peacekeeping/missions/past/unomig/background.html> accessed 12 July 2016

UN WGEID, 'The Working Group on Enforced or Involuntary Disappearances Concludes Its Official Visit to Pakistan' (2012) <http://goo.gl/p3ZhBe> accessed 12 October 2015

Newspaper articles

Agencia EFE, 'Exigen Al Congreso de Guatemala Aprobar La Ley Para La Búsqueda de Desaparecidos de Guerra' (8 December 2016) <http://www.efe.com/efe/america/sociedad/exigen-al-congreso-de-guatemala-aprobar-la-ley-para-busqueda-desaparecidos-guerra/20000013-3119610> accessed 29 December 2017

Balkan Insight, 'Kosovo Faces Judicial Dilemmas as EU Law Mission Ends' (13 April 2018), http://www.balkaninsight.com/en/article/kosovo-faces-judicial-dilemmas-as-eu-law-mission-ends-04-12-2018 accessed 12 June 2018.

BBC, 'Israel Court Orders Prisoner Access' (*BBC News*, 23 August 2001) <http://news.bbc.co.uk/2/hi/middle_east/1506129.stm> accessed 7 September 2016

BBC Mundo, 'El Gobierno de Colombia Y Las FARC Llegaron a Un Acuerdo Para Buscar a Los Desaparecidos' (*BBC Mundo*, 18 October 2015) <http://www.bbc.com/mundo/noticias/2015/10/151017_colombia_farc_desaparecidos_acuerdo_ilm> accessed 12 September 2016

El Hassan J, 'Families of Disappeared Remain Skeptical' (*The Daily Star (Lebanon)*, 2014) http://www.dailystar.com.lb/News/Lebanon-News/2014/Mar-14/250203-families-of-disappeared-remain-skeptical.ashx

Hadjicostis M, 'UN Envoy: Cyprus Peace Talks at Risk from Possible "Crisis"' *Fox News – World* (11 May 2017) <http://www.foxnews.com/world/2017/05/11/un-envoy-cyprus-peace-talks-at-risk-from-possible-crisis.html> accessed 14 May 2017

Kambas M, 'Cyprus Leaders to Resume Peace Talks on April 11: UN' *Reuters – World News* (4 April 2017) <http://www.reuters.com/article/us-cyprus-conflict-talks-idUSKBN1761W3> accessed 30 April 2017

Partlow J and Miroff N, 'Colombia's Congress Approves Historic Peace Deal with FARC Rebels' *The Washington Post* (30 November 2016) <https://www.washingtonpost.com/world/the_americas/colombian-congress-approves-historic-peace-deal/2016/11/30/9b2fda92-b5a7-11e6-939c-91749443c5e5_story.html> accessed 26 April 2017

Roane KR, 'The Bosnia Accord in Tuzla; Women Demand News of Srebrenica's Men' *The New York Times* (3 February 1996) <http://www.nytimes.com/1996/02/03/world/the-bosnia-accord-in-tuzla-women-demand-news-of-srebrenica-s-men.html> accessed 2 February 2017

'Shadows from the Past' (*The Kathmandu Post*, 3 August 2016) <http://kathmandupost.ekantipur.com/news/2016-08-03/shadows-from-the-past.html> accessed 7 September 2016

Sputnik International, 'Court Upholds Ban on Returning Terrorists' Bodies to Relatives - 1' (28 June 2007) <https://sputniknews.com/russia/20070628/67977135.html> accessed 7 September 2016

The Associated Press, 'Red Cross Collecting Samples to ID Missing From Lebanon War' (*NYTimes.com*, 11 July 2016) <http://mobile.nytimes.com> accessed 18 July 2016

LIST OF TABLES

Achevé d'imprimer par Corlet Numéric, Z.A. Charles Tellier, 14110 Condé-en-Normandie
N° d'Imprimeur : 155561 - Dépôt légal : mars 2019 - *Imprimé en France*